EXAMINING BILLY GRAHAM'S

THEOLOGY OF EVANGELISM

Thomas Paul Johnston, Ph.D.

Wipf and Stock Publishers
Eugene, Oregon

Wipf and Stock Publishers
199 West 8th Avenue, Suite 3
Eugene OR 97401

ISBN: 1-59244-162-9

Chapters 1, 3, 4, and 6 were submitted and approved as a Ph.D. dissertation, "The Work of an Evangelist: The Evangelistic Theology and Methodology of Billy Graham," The Southern Baptist Theological Seminary, December 2001. Chapters 2, "Authority," and 5, "Cooperation," were not part of the approved dissertation due to space limitations. Appendix 1 of the dissertation, Graham's 1952 sermon, "The Work of an Evangelist," was removed to avoid copyright infringement. Editorial changes have also been made to the text.

To Raschelle,

my beloved, for her love and support,

and to my father, Arthur P. Johnston,

for his encouragement and example

TABLE OF CONTENTS

FOREWORD

I am delighted to commend Tom Johnston's book, *Examining Billy Graham's Theology of Evangelism*, on my long-time friend and colleague. Billy Graham and I have served together in the cause of the Gospel for more than forty years. I have prayed for him, prayed with him, and spent long hours discussing evangelistic messages and methods. So, I thoroughly enjoyed Tom's intense cross-examination of my knowledge of God's servant who has been used so mightily and globally in our generation. Beyond this, however, is the personal reading and research that Tom has covered to accomplish his goal. The sources are certainly voluminous and diversified! Nonetheless, he has plodded on and produced a truly significant work. He has my approbation and I congratulate him on earning his Ph.D!

"The work of an evangelist," as the Apostle Paul describes it (2 Tim 4:5), is unique and sacrosanct. The illustrious New Testament scholar, prolific writer and expositor, Professor F. F. Bruce, has stated that: "There is no nobler gift than the gift of an evangelist—a gift I do not possess." (*Christianity Today*, 10 October 1980). Young Timothy, even though manifestly a <u>teacher</u> in gifting, was told to "<u>do the work</u> of an evangelist."

With Billy Graham, however, we have the gift of the evangelist incarnationally exemplified. In his *Word Studies in the New Testament* (321-22), Dr. Marvin R. Vincent characterizes the evangelist as "a traveling minister whose work was not confined to a particular church."

In *The Teaching of the Twelve Apostles* (about 100 AD), it was prescribed that an apostle (evangelist) not remain in one place longer than two days, and that "when he departs he shall take nothing with him except enough bread to last until his next station!"

Dr. Tom Johnston has traced Billy Graham's work around the world, studying his methodology and, especially, his theology. He has given us an understanding of the evangelist's mind, message, and motivation. The book, therefore, will become a helpful guide to those whom God will call as evangelists in years to come.

As an evangelist, myself, I welcome this work and rejoice that, at a time in our culture when the terms "evangelist" and "evangelism" are being denigrated by the world, and even by some sections of the church, we have yet another definitive resource to which preachers can turn for instruction and encouragement. We urgently need "New Testament" evangelists; men who can <u>expound God's word evangelistically</u>. Men who can stand with the Apostle Paul and declare: "I (determine) not to know any . . . except Jesus Christ and Him crucified . . . and my speech and preaching (are) in demonstration of the Spirit and of power" (2 Cor. 2:2, 4). It was the puritan, Thomas Godwin, who observed: "God had only one Son, and He made Him a preacher!" May God raise up anointed evangelists to His eternal glory.

Dr. Stephen F. Olford
Founder and Senior Lecturer of the
Stephen Olford Center for Biblical Preaching
Memphis, Tennessee

ABBREVIATIONS

BFM	*Baptist Faith and Message* (1963 or 2000 will be specified in text)
BGC	Billy Graham Center
BGEA	The Billy Graham Evangelistic Association
BGS	Billy Graham School of Missions, Evangelism, and Church Growth of the Southern Baptist Theological Seminary
CBF	Cooperative Baptist Fellowship
C&MA	Christian and Mission Alliance
FCC	Federal Council of Churches
HOD	Hour of Decision radio broadcast
HOD	*Hour of Decision Sermons*
IMC	International Missionary Council
LCWE	Lausanne Committee for World Evangelization
NAE	National Association of Evangelicals
NCC	National Council of Churches
RCC	Roman Catholic Church
SBC	Southern Baptist Convention
SBTS	Southern Baptist Theological Seminary
SPCK	Society for the Propagation of Christian Knowledge
WCC	World Council of Churches
WEF	World Evangelical Fellowship
WVI	World Vision, International
YFC	Youth for Christ, International

LIST OF TABLES

LIST OF ILLUSTRATIONS

PREFACE

It has been a privilege to delve into the evangelistic theology of the evangelist who has likely preached the Gospel to more people face-to-face than anyone else in the history of the Church. Billy Graham's spiritual impact in the last half of the twentieth century is likely unsurpassed. A study of his theology and practice is thus timely and pertinent.

For the recommendation to research this topic I am indebted to my father, Arthur P. Johnston, who has been on the Board of the Billy Graham Evangelistic Association (BGEA) since 1976. I am also grateful to the spiritual and intellectual legacy that he left me at home, in the classroom, and in his books. My father learned that this topic may open a new area of inquiry from the archivist of the BGEA, Lois Ferm. I am also indebted to Lois for the idea and for her knowledge of the holdings of the Billy Graham Archives in Wheaton, Illinois.

It was a privilege to spend four and a half years in doctoral research at the Billy Graham School of Missions, Evangelism, and Church Growth (BGS) at the Southern Baptist Theological Seminary (SBTS). I am grateful to SBTS's president, Albert Mohler, for his leadership, the BGS dean, Thom Rainer, as well as professors Timothy Beougher and John Mark Terry. I am grateful for the opportunity to found the Southern Evangelistic Teams of the BGS. Weekly involvement in door-to-door evangelism with local churches kept my thoughts focused on the practice of evangelism.

The organization of which I am president, Evangelism Unlimited, has stood behind me during my doctoral studies and to the present. Many people sacrificed financially and wrestled in prayer. Their behind the scenes support allowed and encouraged me to take the time to lead evangelism while also being a doctoral student. Thank you!

David Butler, senior pastor of Springdale Baptist Church, affirmed the Lord's call upon my life as an evangelist and set me apart by ordination. I was privileged to participate in the last several Conference of Southern Baptist Evangelists. I count it a blessing to colabor in the harvest with these men.

It is now my second academic year as assistant professor of evangelism at Midwestern Baptist Theological Seminary. I am particularly grateful to President R. Philip Roberts for his invitation to teach evangelism at this school and for his practical evangelistic leadership of the seminary. I am walking among giants who have taught and teach evangelism in Southern Baptist seminaries since the days of L. R. Scarborough at Southwestern.

A note of thanks is also due those who provided academic assistance in my studies. Margaret Simmons, interlibrary loan assistant at Southern's Boyce library sought out numerous obscure books, pamphlets, and newspaper articles for me. Ferne Weimer, librarian of the Billy Graham Center library in Wheaton, Illinois, provided me a goldmine of material in the early publishings of the *Hour of Decision* sermons. These sermons were the backbone of this study. John Corts, president of the BGEA, and his assistant, Carol Mellott, were also helpful in providing me several *Hour of Decision* sermons that I did not have, as well as information on Graham's crusade sermon series.

A special thanks to Stephen Olford who graciously granted me a telephone interview and wrote the foreword for this manuscript. His kind words are an encouragement to press on. Thanks also to Jim Tedrick of Wipf & Stock Publishers who encouraged me to get endorsements for this work, and who has been patient with me as I have revised and finalized the work for publication.

It has been an honor to study the theology of Billy Graham. He has left large footsteps for those who go behind him. His more than sixty-three years of crusade evangelism ministry have restored honor to a profession misunderstood by the world. I am grateful for the honor and integrity with which he ministered the Gospel.

While I am indebted to many people for their input in my research, any omissions or overstatements are mine. I am especially grateful for the blood of Christ that cleanses from all sin, and for the Gospel of Jesus Christ which is the power of God unto salvation to all who believe.

Thomas Paul Johnston
Kansas City, Missouri
March 2003

CHAPTER 1

CONTEXT

On March 20, 1952, Billy Graham preached a sermon before seven hundred English clergymen in the Assembly Hall of the Church House, Westminster. Buttressed by his sincerity,[1] this sermon paved the way for the London 1954 crusade, his other major crusades in Europe in 1954,[2] and opened a door of opportunity for over forty-five years of worldwide ministry.[3] The title of this important sermon was "The Work of an Evangelist."[4]

"The Work of an Evangelist" was preached two and a half years after the famous 1949 words of newspaper mogul William Randolf Hearst were wired to all his newspapers: "Puff Graham."[5] Graham had been

---

[1]Lee Strobel quoted the elderly Charles Templeton, preaching partner of Billy Graham in 1946: "'Billy is pure gold,' he remarked fondly. 'There's no feigning or fakery in him. He's a first rate human being. Billy is profoundly Christian—he's the genuine goods, as they say. He sincerely believes—unquestionably. He is as wholesome and faithful as anyone can be'" (Lee Strobel, *The Case for Faith* [Grand Rapids: Zondervan, 2000], 16).

[2]In his dissertation (Robert L. Kennedy, "Best Intentions: Contacts Between German Pietists and Anglo-American Evangelicals, 1945-1954" [Ph.D. diss., University of Aberdeen, 1990], 435), Kennedy explained how this sermon was translated into German by Wilhelm Brauer and published in a book titled *Billy Graham: Ein Evangelist der Neuen Welt,* Geleitwort von Karl Heim (Giessen: Brunnen-Verlag, 1954). This introduction opened Graham's crusade ministry in Germany.

[3]Once Graham was accepted in London in 1954, the door opened to the Commonwealth countries, as well as to many other countries of the world. See Billy Graham, *Just As I Am* (New York: Harper Collins, 1997), 238.

[4]Billy Graham, "The Work of an Evangelist," in Frank Colquhoun, ed., *Introducing Billy Graham: The Work of an Evangelist. An Address Given in the Assembly Hall of the Church House, Westminster, on 20th March, 1952* (London: World Evangelical Alliance, 1953, 1961).

[5]Billy Graham, *Just As I Am,* 150. Walter Martin commented on these words, "Accounts of Graham's career have typically portrayed the Hearst endorsement as a complete surprise, unsought and unexpected. The reality was less dramatic" (Walter

preaching for twelve years by that time, as he first spoke at a Baptist church in Bostick, Florida, on Easter Sunday evening, 1937.[6] His first evangelistic meetings were December 30, 1937, to January 2, 1938 (Thursday through Sunday), at Hope Mission in West Tampa, Florida. As his reputation as an evangelist grew, so did his opportunities to preach. By 1944 Billy Graham was asked to preach at four Youth for Christ (YFC) rallies in Indianapolis, Indiana (May 6), Chicago, Illinois (May 27), Miami, Florida (December), and Orlando, Florida (December 16). In 1946, Graham preached at twenty-four YFC rallies, both in the United States and Europe.[7] That same year he also preached an evangelistic rally; he became the first vice president of YFC; Zondervan published his first book, *Calling Youth to Christ*;[8] and Cliff Barrows joined his team. Three years later, when the words of Hearst propelled the name Billy Graham into mainstream media in the United States, Graham had already had a fairly significant ministry of evangelism both in the United States and in Europe for several years.

Yet in 1952, Graham's challenge was to return to Europe, not as a YFC evangelist, but as a citywide evangelist under the auspices of the Billy Graham Evangelistic Association (BGEA). During his 1946 trip to England and Europe, Graham met with pastors on March 19 to introduce himself to his English sponsors. He wrote, "The majority of them [pastors] had some connection with the Plymouth Brethren."[9] By 1952, Graham had a broader audience in the United States, and sought to expand his audience in England. If Graham were able to secure the confidence of the Anglican Church in England, it would open his ministry to the world, since in the early nineteenth century the Queen's navy ruled most of the seas of the world—a time called the *Pax Britannica*. Thus Britain's Commonwealth

---

Martin, *A Prophet with Honor: The Billy Graham Story* [New York: William Morrow and Co., 1991], 117).

[6]Stanley High and William Martin state that Graham's first revival series was at East Palatka Baptist Church in Palatka, Florida, the same church where he was baptized and later ordained as a Southern Baptist (Stanley High, *Billy Graham: The Personal Story of the Man, His Message, and His Mission* [New York: McGraw-Hill, 1956], 81-82; Martin, *A Prophet with Honor,* 76).

[7]"Select Chronology Listing of Events in the History of the Billy Graham Evangelistic Association" [on-line]; accessed 15 June 2000; available from http://www.wheaton.edu/bgc/archives/bgeachro/bgeachron02.htm; Internet; hence-forth referred to as "BGEA Chronology." Days of the week were determined through use of a calendar found on the Internet at "Calendar" [on-line]; accessed 15 June 2000; available from http://earth.com/calendar; Internet.

[8]Billy Graham, *Calling Youth to Christ*, with Introduction by Torrey M. Johnson (Grand Rapids: Zondervan, 1947; London: Marshall, Morgan and Scott, n.d.).

[9]Billy Graham, *Just As I Am*, 116.

provided an entrée to almost every continent of the world. His future worldwide ministry depended upon success in this sermon to seven hundred clergy gathered at the Church House, Westminster, March 20, 1952.

"The Work of an Evangelist"

Billy Graham spoke frankly and candidly to the seven hundred clergy gathered at the Assembly Hall. "The Work of an Evangelist" was a mid-length discourse in which Graham touched on major points of his approach to evangelism. The common thread throughout the sermon was the movement of the Spirit of God through the proclamation of the Word of God—evangelism.

He began by discussing the three perils facing the United States of that day. Graham highlighted the "peril from within" by noting the moral and spiritual decline in the United States. He discussed the "peril from without" by noting the spread of fanatical Communism in the world. Then he appealed to the greatest peril, being "the judgment of the Almighty God."[10] After addressing the peril of God's wrath, Graham turned to the only answer—revival.[11]

In his next point, Graham walked through a brief history of awakenings. He mentioned Jonathan Edwards and George Whitefield. He described the revival at Yale College under President Timothy Dwight. Then he continued by describing the Fulton Street revival in New York City in 1858. He mentioned D. L. Moody and Billy Sunday, tactfully distancing himself from some of the extravagances and sensationalisms that were associated with the latter. He continued his historical overview by explaining the spiritual drought from the 1920s to the 1940s. Yet, in the present day United States, Graham reported that things had changed. Billy Graham reported to the seven hundred English clergy that a new day of evangelism had dawned in the United States.[12]

---

[10]Colquhoun, *Introducing Billy Graham,* 8.

[11]"I can see the picture as I stand before you this moment, of the hand of God in judgement falling upon the Western world unless . . . and there is only one thing that will stop it. That is a turning to God by the people of God—only one thing, and we must face it" (ibid., 9).

[12]"But I am delighted to report to you to-day that all that has changed. There is an entirely new outlook in America at the moment towards evangelism. At this moment every major denomination in the United States is putting nearly all its emphasis on evangelism.

About 80 per cent of our preachers, I believe, and about 80 per cent of our church people, are catching the fire of evangelism. In that 80 per cent it goes all the way from the Pentecostal group to the Episcopal group. All sorts of messages are preached

Graham continued by distinguishing between the use of the word evangelism and revival. He stated that the terms are used interchangeably in some areas. Then he focused on revival. Rather than strategize on revival, Graham emphasized that the important point was to do something about it. He affirmed that true revival is marked by three signs: a fear of God, a sense of personal sin, and obedience to the word of God.

He then turned to evangelism. He began with a definition of evangelism from the Archbishops' Committee on Evangelism in 1918.[13] Graham then proceeded to explain three methods of the practice of evangelism. First he discussed evangelism "through the worship of the Church." After quoting portions of 1 Corinthians 14:24, Graham continued:

> Ladies and gentlemen, suppose your church was so endued with spiritual power that when a sinner came into your church he would fall upon his knees and cry out to be saved? There is evangelism at its best.[14]

Next he discussed evangelism "by consistent Christian living." He continued, "Wouldn't it be great if there was something about the way you walked that would compel men to say, 'I want to be a Christian?'" And lastly he discussed "preaching to crowds as a method of evangelism." For this last item, Graham identified three words used for evangelism in the Bible: to reason, to talk, and to preach.[15] From the context of Paul's preaching until midnight in Acts 20:7, Graham developed the desperate need for "discussion evangelism." The second word was "to talk." From this word Graham emphasized the idea of gossiping Christ. In a paraphrase of Acts 8:25, Graham stated, "They went everywhere gossiping Christ."[16] The

---

and all sorts of methods are used, but at least evangelism has come back into its own, and the new evangelism in America to-day, thanks be unto God, is church-centered, where it ought to be" (ibid., 12).

[13]"To evangelize is so to present Christ Jesus in the power of the Holy Spirit that men shall come to put their trust in God through Him, to accept Him as their Saviour and serve Him as their King in the fellowship of His Church" (ibid., 15). The identical words are found in *The Evangelistic Work of the Church, Being the Report of the Archbishops' Third Committee of Inquiry* (London: Society for the Promoting Christian Knowledge for the National Mission, 1918), 18.

[14]Colquhoun, *Introducing Billy Graham,* 15.

[15]Ibid.

[16]"Now there, to my way of thinking, is the greatest means of evangelism that God has given us. Not mass evangelism—mass evangelism is not God's greatest. The greatest is personal evangelism—the church going out to the highways and by-ways and presenting Christ . . . gossiping the Lord Jesus." (ibid., 16).

third word Graham mentioned was "to preach."[17] From this word, Graham transitioned into discussion of mass evangelism. He began by downplaying the concept of mass evangelism as implying a large group of people. "When you preach to your congregation," he told the seven hundred ministers, "if you've got more than two or three to preach to, that's a mass." He then addressed two dangers to mass evangelism. The first danger was the danger of false emotion.[18] The second danger that Graham addressed as associated with mass evangelism was, "Converts don't last." To this "old criticism," Billy Graham appealed to Jesus' words in the Parable of the Sower. He said that Jesus must have heard the same criticism. He appealed to the seed sown on the road as proof that not all of those that hear will respond positively. Then Graham asked the question, "Did the Lord Jesus tell us that because so much seed-sowing is apparently fruitless that we are not to sow? Never!" Then he challenged the pastors that the same pattern was evident among new converts in their churches.[19]

After addressing the danger of emotionalism and the criticism that converts don't last, Graham addressed his follow-up program. Of Graham's follow-up program, he states, "I do not think—and I say it humbly before God, for we give Him the praise for giving it to us—I do not think it has any parallel possibly in the history of modern evangelism."[20] He then began to explain his follow-up program used in the Washington, DC, crusade (January 13-February 18, 1952) as an example. After explaining that a team of men goes to the city six months before the crusade to train personal workers or counselors, he then stated:

---

[17]"And that carries with it the idea of proclaiming as a herald—preaching to masses, or mass evangelism, if you please. Mass evangelism can be of no effect at all unless it comes down to personal evangelism; and no evangelism can be effective unless it is church-centered, in my opinion" (ibid., 17).

[18]"If you would come to our meetings you would say that there is no emotion whatsoever. You would wonder how anybody made a decision. A man must be convinced intellectually. His emotions must be touched—yes, because emotions have drive and will; but it is the will of man that exerts all feeling in making a decision for Christ. His will must change to the will of God" (ibid., 17-18).

[19]Ibid., 18.

[20]"But let me tell you, you clergymen and ministers and pastors, you face exactly the same problem in your church work as we face in our evangelistic missions. You receive ten people into your church on a Sunday. You are going to do well if three or four of those ten people are faithful in church attendance every Sunday for the next year. In our country, we have great hoards of people who are members of the church, but you see them only on Christmas and Easter. Would you call them faithful church members on which seed has fallen on good ground? I doubt it!" (ibid., 19).

We have learned that it takes about 5 per cent effort to win a man to Christ and 95 per cent to keep him resting in Christ and growing into maturity in Christ and in the church. And so our major effort is to get the man to grow in Christ.[21]

He continued, "We now have thirteen men in follow-up—full time in follow-up—headed up by Dawson Trotman." He explained that the follow-up of an individual after the crusade could take from fifteen minutes up to one or two hours. Then the individual would be sent to the church of his choice. "If he has no preference the card is sent to a committee or ministers appointed by the churches of that city." He explained the detailed attention they gave to follow-up.[22]

Following these words regarding follow-up, Billy Graham addressed another criticism of evangelism—"there is too much excitement." After explaining the need for certain excitement in spiritual matters, Graham continued by stating that he tried to avoid any sensationalism. In this light he discussed the lack of music in his campaigns,[23] as well as the issue of lightness and frivolity in his services.[24]

---

[21]Ibid.

[22]"We can pull out a card and give the whole spiritual case history of each convert from the night he came to make his decision for Christ. If he is not in the church—and thousands are in the church—what happened to him? How many times was he contacted? How many times did ministers visit him? How many times did the church visitor see him? All of these things are there. Where are the converts? We can tell you where they are; and if any one of them fell by the wayside, we can tell you where he is and why he is, and all the rest of it . . . . In Seattle, Washington, we had approximately 9,000 who made decisions for Christ in the campaign there. Now those were the ones who said "Yes" to Christ as personal Saviour. About 30 per cent or 40 per cent of them were already church members. The rest were completely outside the church. Out of those 50 per cent or 60 per cent that were not members of the church, over 40 per cent have already joined some church and are now active in the church" (ibid., 20-21).

[23]"We accept no instruments in our service except the organ and the piano, except that once in a while Cliff Barrows will bring his trombone. Many of our evangelistic services in America have been more or less a programme of all sorts of music, and have become a musical event. We don't have that. We have Beverly Shea to sing, and he and the choir choose songs in which they bring a message to the people, to prepare them spiritually. Cliff Barrows has also cut out all choruses—not because we do not like choruses or because we don't believe in choruses, but because the pendulum has swung so far to this type of business, that we decided to swing it back the other way. And the shock of having none of this is attracting large numbers of people. And so we sing nothing but the old hymns" (ibid., 22).

[24]"In our services I've had many ministers come on the platform and they would whisper to me, "Isn't the meeting dead to-night?" And I would say, "No, I don't see that there is any deadness. It's just heavy with conviction." I want to tell you that the

Next Graham addressed evangelism and the church. He stated that a campaign is not effective unless it is integrated into the church. He then explained the theological parameters of those who can join in his campaigns—they must lift up Christ. By lift up Christ, Graham explained:

> On the Executive Committee or our campaigns we have only men who accept the deity of the Lord Jesus Christ, which includes the Virgin birth, the vicarious atonement and the bodily resurrection.[25]

He added that they had men on his committees who fully accepted "the deity of our blessed Lord and whose heart was in evangelism." Graham explained that they never went to any city unless invited by the church or the Church Federation. Then Graham hinted at the renewal of evangelism to which he alluded earlier in this message:

> By the grace of God, and we give glory to Him, we are increasing in favour with the churches in this type of evangelism. So much is this so that the National Council of Churches, which has been dominated and led largely by liberal elements in our country, for the first time in its history has recently appointed a full-time evangelist to conduct this type of meeting—Charles Templeton, I tell you, unusual things are taking place.[26]

Graham alluded to the fact that a reform was taking place in churches. Ministers, who had not preached the cross of Christ, were preaching this vital truth, and using words like "prayer meeting," "sin," "hell," and "judgment."

Graham then touched on the issue of finances. He stated that when he goes to a city he never handles the finances himself, "We have nothing to do with it." They would advise the committee of pastors, but they would not deal directly with it. Often, related Graham, most of the money for the campaign was raised before he arrived. They did not have an offering unless the committee asked for one, and then they allowed the person appealing for the offering no more than two or three minutes.

He returned, then, to the working of God's Spirit: His moving through people talking about religion, His moving through newspapers

---

quieter and the heavier the atmosphere in our meetings, that's the night I know God is about to do something. Heavy with the power of the Holy Spirit! I want to tell you, when the Holy Spirit is moving, you don't have much time for lightness and joking and frivolity" (ibid).

[25]Ibid., 23.

[26]Ibid., 23.

printing articles and also full sermons he preached, His moving through pastors working together for the cause of Christ, His moving through other evangelists, and in other ways.[27] Graham then described the conversion of Stuart Hamblen, host of a daily radio program in Los Angeles.[28] He told of the conversions of gangster Jim Vaus, golf champion Henry Harper, baseball player Kirby Higbe, and Mayor *pro tem* of Greensboro, South Carolina, Boyd Morris. Graham described that "thousands of dollars have been turned in to the Internal Revenue Department in the State of North Carolina alone by people who have been converted in our meetings and had refused to pay income taxes the week before."[29]

He concluded his sermon to the seven hundred ministers gathered at the Assembly Hall in the Church House, Westminster, with the following challenge:

> Do you believe it can happen in Britain? Is there a need in Britain? That is the first question. There is a need—we grant that. What is the message? It is the Word—the holy Word of God. That is the answer to our problem, There is no other answer. What is the method? You will have to get before God to find out the method. But I want to tell you this as a closing word: unless you have a spiritual awakening in Great Britain, you can say good-bye to the old Britain that you once knew. Communism is a spiritual force and it is moving with all of its dark and evil strength in every direction. The only thing that will stop it will be a spiritual force—the glorious light of the Gospel of Christ.
>
> To-day the Church has its greatest opportunity. There has never been an hour in the history of the world—not in Paul's day, not in Luther's day, not in Wesley's day—when the Church has had a greater opportunity. Do you know why? Because more people in the United States and Great Britain are ready to-day to admit that they

---

[27]"I can see movings of the Spirit of God in our country. There is an awakening taking place, and we give the praise and glory to God. Do you know what happened last year? We had more people attend church in America per capita last year than any other year in American history. Isn't that something? And our Bible Schools, like the great Moody Bible Institute, Bob Jones College, Wheaton College, Baylor University—all of these places are filled to capacity, so that they cannot accommodate all the young people who are wanting to train as missionaries and pastors and evangelists" (ibid., 26-27).

[28]For more information, see John Pollock, *Billy Graham: The Authorized Biography* (New York: McGraw-Hill, 1966), 56.

[29]Colquhoun, *Introducing Billy Graham*, 29-30.

need something—more than at any time in the history of the Church. And that's the first step towards revival.[30]

With these rousing words, Graham left London and began his European tour. This tour in March and April of 1952 was not a preaching tour. Yet it prepared the groundwork for his 1954 preaching tour, and for Graham's future evangelistic endeavors. Through his sermon titled "The Work of an Evangelist" preached at Westminster to seven hundred clergy, God opened the world to the ministry of evangelist Billy Graham.

Introducing Billy Graham

Graham preached "The Work of an Evangelist" at the Church House, Westminster, when he was thirty-three years old. Graham preached regularly at a trailer park in Florida just fifteen years earlier. In 1955 he was to preach before the Queen of England.[31] In this section we will note major milestones in Graham's rise to prominence.

Billy Graham was born and grew into his teens at a farmhouse near Charlotte, North Carolina. His varied denominational background began with a Methodist father and Presbyterian mother. They attended Steele Creek Presbyterian Church outside of Charlotte. His father supported the Christian Businessmen's Association in Charlotte, and his mother was influenced by some Plymouth Brethren neighbors. Graham explained the authors that his mother read:

In addition, she read the writings of noted Bible teachers Arno Gaebelein, Harry A. Ironside of the Moody Memorial Church in Chicago, and Donald Grey Barnhouse, a renowned preacher who pastored Tenth Presbyterian Church in Philadelphia.[32]

While having a varied denominational background, it was both conservative and evangelical Protestant.

Billy Graham was converted to Christ at the age of sixteen under the preaching of Mordecai Ham, a traveling evangelist of the day. Ham had been pastor of First Baptist Church in Oklahoma City prior to his traveling as an evangelist. Following high school, Graham went to Bob

---

[30]Ibid., 30.

[31]High, *Billy Graham*, 69.

[32]Billy Graham, *Just As I Am,* 25. In this case, the childhood of Billy Graham may be equated with the upbringing of Timothy, as described in 2 Tim 3:14-15. Both Timothy's mother and grandmother passed on their faith in God to Timothy.

Jones College for one semester. T. W. Wilson was already at Bob Jones, and Grady Wilson went with Billy Graham. Both became an important part of the Billy Graham team.[33] After one semester Billy transferred to Florida Bible Institute in Temple Terrace, Florida. At Florida Bible Institute he came under the influence of "a former Christian and Missionary Alliance minister from North Carolina, W. T. Watson."[34] Watson, founding president of this college, gave reduced rates in room and board for preachers who would preach in chapel and at his Gospel Tabernacle in St. Petersburg, Florida. In this way Billy Graham heard renowned conservative pastors, missionaries, and evangelists, such as Gipsy Smith, William Evans, E. A. Marshall, W. B. Riley, A. B. Winchester, W. R. Newell, E. R. Neighbor, Theodore Elsner, A. C. Gaebelein, Donald G. Barnhouse, Oswald J. Smith, E. J. Pace, Homer Rodeheaver, and Harry Rimmer.[35] Graham wrote:

> One thing that thrilled me was the diversity of viewpoints we were exposed to in the classroom, a wondrous blend of ecumenical and evangelical thought that was really ahead of its time. Our teachers came from different backgrounds and denominations, exhibiting to us what harmony could be present where Christ and His Word were loved and served.[36]

In this multi-denominational evangelical environment, Billy Graham's ecclesiology took shape.

As a minister of the gospel, Graham felt called to be associated with the Southern Baptist Convention of churches. Graham was earlier baptized by sprinkling in 1919 at Chalmers Memorial Church. Later, being convinced of his need for baptism by immersion, he was baptized by Rev. John R. Minder, dean of Trinity Bible Institute. However, wanting to identify with a local church, he was baptized a third time under the auspices of a Southern Baptist church. Graham found among the Southern Baptists a group that believed in evangelism and the revival ministry to which he felt

---

[33]T.W. and Grady were to become lifetime co-workers with Graham. In his autobiography, Graham included two interesting quotations from Bob Jones, Sr.: "If the Devil is going your way, ride the Devil," and "If a hound dog is barking for Jesus, I'm for the hound dog" (ibid., 40).

[34]Ibid., 43. Later in his autobiography, Graham calls Watson his "old mentor" (ibid., 661).

[35]Ibid., 45-46.

[36]Ibid., 46.

called.[37] Thus, while Billy Graham had many denominational influences in his early life and education, three conclusions may be made as to why Graham became Southern Baptist.[38] First, the Southern Baptist Mordecai Ham was the catalyst for his conversion to Christ. Second, Graham concurred with the Southern Baptist belief in believer's baptism. And third, Graham had noted the clear conviction of Southern Baptists to emphasize proclamational evangelism and their corresponding openness to the role of evangelists and revival preachers in their ecclesiology.

Graham's early preaching ministry was oriented to church revivals and youth rallies (1938-1939). Then in 1940 Graham moved to Chicago to attend Wheaton College. It was in Chicago that he met Torrey Johnson, founder of YFC. While in Chicago he became the main speaker for Torrey's "Songs in the Night," and pastored at the United Gospel Tabernacle in Wheaton,[39] as well as at Western Springs church.[40] Then in 1944 he began speaking at YFC rallies all across the United States. By 1946, Graham's speaking ministry extended into Europe. That year, 84 percent (thirty-one of thirty-seven) of the cities where Graham spoke at YFC rallies were in Europe. In 1947 Graham held YFC rallies in thirteen cities; 69 percent (nine of thirteen) of these were in Europe.[41] The influence and opportunities provided by Torrey Johnson and YFC gave Graham a network of contacts throughout the United States and in Europe.

During his time with YFC, Graham began holding his own evangelistic crusades, inter-church crusades after the style of Mordecai Ham. The evangelistic campaigns began in 1947 with a crusade in Grand

---

[37]Graham wrote, "Early in 1939, Woodrow came to me and said, 'I think you ought to be ordained. That would give you a standing in the Baptist Association and would be of great benefit to you in many ways'" (ibid., 56).

[38]Graham was told "for Southern Baptists to invite preachers from other denominations—especially Presbyterians—into their pulpits was like defying a sacred tradition" (ibid.). It must be noted that Presbyterians and Baptists in the South have shared pulpits since the early nineteenth century. Hence, Basil Manly, Sr., former Pastor of the Baptist Church, Charleston, South Carolina, was accused of compromise when he took the interim pastorate of a Presbyterian church. He responded to this accusation in an insert letter "To the editor of the Wesleyan Journal," *The Columbian Star*, 5 September 1826.

[39]Billy Graham, *Just As I Am,* 66.

[40]Ibid., 79.

[41]Please note Appendix 3, which summarizes the early crusade ministry of Graham, as found in "BGEA Chronology," and all subsequent crusades of Billy Graham as found in Billy Graham's *Just As I Am,* 736-39, with the addition of crusades which took place after the publishing of *Just As I Am* from the "BGEA Chronology."

Rapids, Michigan, and another in Charlotte, North Carolina.[42] Also in 1947, Graham assumed the presidency of the Northwestern Schools in Minneapolis, Minnesota, fulfilling the deathbed wish of its founding President, the fundamentalist W. B. Riley.[43] In 1948 Graham's time was divided between Northwestern College, YFC, and crusade ministry. He spoke at eight YFC rallies, conventions, or banquets, and attended the important YFC World Congress in Beatenburg, Switzerland.[44] Also in 1948, along with his responsibilities as President of the Northwestern Schools, he preached two crusades: seventeen days in Augusta, Georgia and fifteen days in Modesto, California. Three other events attended by Graham in 1948 were a National Association of Evangelicals (NAE) convention, the founding of the World Council of Churches (WCC) in Amsterdam, and the first Inter-Varsity sponsored conference held in Urbana, Illinois. In 1948 Graham also received two honorary doctorates: Doctor of Divinity from King's College, Newcastle, Delaware, and Doctor of Humanities from Bob Jones University, Greenville, South Carolina.[45]

While the ministry of Billy Graham was increasing in opportunity, impact, and stature, 1949 is often seen as the beginning of his crusade ministry because of the Los Angeles crusade. It is important to note, however, that Graham had an evangelistic ministry that began in 1937, and a European ministry that began in 1946. In 1949, prior to the September "Christ for Greater Los Angeles Crusade," while maintaining the demands of the presidency of the Northwestern Schools, Graham spoke at three World Vision conferences, three YFC rallies, and held three crusades: nineteen days in Miami, Florida, twelve days in Baltimore, Maryland, and

---

[42]Billy Graham's *Just As I Am* (736) listed Grand Rapids as Graham's first crusade, whereas the "BGEA chronology" (9) listed Grand Rapids as a "YFC evangelistic campaign." The discrepancy portrays the close relationship between Graham's early crusade ministry and YFC.

[43]See William Vance Trollinger, Jr., "God's Empire: William Bell Riley and Midwestern Fundamentalism" (Ph.D. diss., University of Wisconsin, Madison, 1990), 152.

[44]Among the 400 evangelicals gathered by Torrey Johnson for this event were Billy Graham; Dawson Trotman, founder of the Navigators; Robert Evans, founder of Greater Europe Mission; and Hubert Mitchell (see Betty Lee Skinner, *Daws: The Story of Dawson Trotman, Founder of the Navigators* [Grand Rapids: Zondervan, 1974], 196).

[45]All dates are derived from the "BGEA Chronology." Other sources of dates will be identified only when they disagree with or expand on this chronology.

two weeks in Altoona, Pennsylvania.[46] With this busy schedule, he prepared for the September evangelistic campaign in Los Angeles.

Graham in his autobiography calls the "Christ for Greater Los Angeles Crusade" in 1949 the "watershed" of his ministry. This crusade moved Graham from growing fame in evangelical circles to instant fame as an evangelist in the entire United States. Prior to coming to Los Angeles, Graham placed three conditions on the committee that invited him: broad church support, over triple the budget that was planned, and a larger tent. These conditions were met, and Graham went to Los Angeles with Cliff Barrows, and George Beverly Shea. The crusade began on September 25, 1949, continuing to the first scheduled end of the campaign of October 16, 1949. At that time, Graham and Cliff Barrows went before the Lord to determine if the Campaign should be extended. God gave the answer that night through a phone call, a visit by Graham, and the conversion of Stuart Hamblen. Hamblen came forward in the next meeting. The campaign was extended, and people kept coming forward in each service. Then in the midst of the campaign, Randolph Hearst was said to have sent two words to his editors: "Puff Graham." The 1949 *Los Angeles Examiner* wrote a headline story on Graham. The evening *Los Angeles Herald Express* followed suit. Graham wrote, "The story was picked up by the Hearst papers in New York, Chicago, Detroit, and San Francisco, and then by all their competitors."[47] From that time on, Graham's name became a household name in the United States.[48] The Los Angeles campaign continued until November 20, 1949.

In 1956, just seven years after the 1949 Los Angeles Campaign, Stanley High, the Methodist editor of *Reader's Digest,* remarked on Graham's astounding ministry:

In a relatively short ministry, Billy Graham has probably preached, face to face, to more people than any spokesman for the faith in all history: by the end of 1955, no less than 20,000,000. It is probable,

---

[46]Graham recalled the Altoona crusade of 1949: "But if ever I felt I conducted a Campaign that was a flop, *humanly* speaking, Altoona was it!" (Billy Graham, *Just As I Am,* 134).

[47]Ibid., 149.

[48]William Martin wrote, "The Washington crusade [1952] and his developing relationship with [United States President] Eisenhower enhanced Graham's symbolic importance as an official spokesman for Protestant Christianity" (Martin, *A Prophet with Honor,* 149). "Martin Luther King, Jr., and Billy Graham are certainly the two best known Protestant clerics in America. They and they alone have names which are immediately recognized by virtually the whole public" ("Graham and King as Ghetto Mates," Editorial, *Christian Century,* 10 August 1966, 976-977). This wide recognition is also noted in the honors received by Billy Graham (see Appendix 4).

also, that more people, under his ministry, in his crusades and through his radio and film ministries, have made "decisions for Christ": an estimated 1,000,000.[49]

The 1956 statistics multiplied tenfold by the year 2000:

> Mr. Graham has preached the Gospel to more people in live audiences than any one else in history—over 210 million people in more than 185 countries and territories—through various meetings, including Mission World and Global Mission.[50]

The "Billy Graham statistics" through the end of 1998 accounted for 3,082,686 inquirers from 1947 to 1998.[51] The size and impact of Billy Graham's ministry was certainly statistically astonishing.[52]

Graham's leap from preaching at a trailer park in Florida to becoming a world-renowned evangelist hinged on the crucial years from 1948 to 1954. It was in these years that his methodology was hammered out and that the early team came together. Many of his ministry initiatives have their roots in these years. However, once Graham began his ministry of

---

[49]High, *Billy Graham*, 2.

[50]"Profile, William (Billy) F. Graham" (Minneapolis: Billy Graham Evangelistic Association, August, 1997), 1; Appendix D in Lewis A. Drummond's *The Canvas Cathedral: Billy Graham's Ministry Seen through the History of Evangelism* (Nashville: Thomas Nelson, 2003) contains statistics on attendance and inquirers at Billy Graham crusades from Grand Rapids, MI (1947) to Louisville, KY (2001).

[51]"Billy Graham Crusade Statistics" (Minneapolis: Billy Graham Evangelistic Association, December, 1997), 15. Speaking of his 1957 crusade in New York, Graham stated, "An estimated 96 million people had seen at least one of the meetings from Madison Square Gardens" (Billy Graham, *Just As I Am*, 323). John Pollock's 1979 biography of Billy Graham contained a picture with this caption, "Billy Graham closed his five-day Seoul, Korea, crusade at Yoi-do Plaza on the banks of the Han River before a crowd of more than 1,000,000. This group was the largest single crowd in the history of his ministry (1973)" (John Pollock, *Billy Graham: Evangelist to the World* [San Francisco, CA: Harper and Row, 1979], 212b).

[52]Billy Sunday did not keep statistics of his meetings: "He himself did not keep records of his work. His motto seems to have been 'Forgetting those things which are behind'" (William T. Ellis, *Billy Sunday: The Man and His Message* [Philadelphia: John C. Winston, 1936], 331). On a flyer titled "More than a Million Souls Hit the Sawdust Trail," thirteen Billy Sunday Evangelistic Crusades from Rockford 1904 to New York 1917 accounted for 280,559 professions of faith ("More than a Million Souls Hit the Sawdust Trail," in Basic Church Evangelism, Jack Stanton, ed., Kansas City, MO: Midwestern Baptist Theological Seminary, n.d.)

crusade evangelism, he also had the foresight to keep it moving.[53] We will note how Graham systematically covered major regions in the United States, and then how he "conquered" the world.

Graham's United States Ministry Methodology

Graham systematically brought the gospel to all regions of the United States, and then to open regions of the world much like a general would set out to conquer the world. It was obvious that he needed to go where he was invited, and only those who knew of his ministry would invite him. Also important was who invited him. Graham wanted invitations from those who would provide the broadest base for city-wide and church-wide emphases in his crusades. Thus his early challenge was not only to become known, but also to be supported and invited by the right people.[54]

The "Christ for Greater Los Angeles Crusade" in 1949 gave Graham national prominence in the United States. Yet he still needed to earn the trust of certain denominations and regions. For this reason, Graham systematically visited major cities in North America with one-day rallies. This method was called "tours" and was borrowed from the YFC approach to one-day "rallies" in major cities. The major difference between Graham and YFC was that Graham was seeking broad church support. After

---

[53]As an example, Billy Sunday's ministry as an itinerant evangelist lasted approximately twenty-four years (1996-1920; see William T. Ellis, *Billy Sunday*, vi, and William G. McLoughlin, *Revivals, Awakenings, and Reform* [Chicago: University of Chicago Press, 1978], 149-50). Graham's ministry has more than doubled that length of time. Toward the end of Sunday's ministry his supposed financial indiscretion may have occasioned Sinclair Lewis's *Elmer Gantry* (Berlin: E. Rowolht, 1928; New York: Harcourt, Brace and Company, 1929), a satirical novel portraying an evangelist as a greedy and self-serving individual. Comparative lengths of the itinerant ministries of other evangelists are as follows: Jonathan Edwards, twenty-five years (1734-1758); George Whitefield, thirty-four years (1737-1770); John Wesley, fifty-two years (1739-1791); Charles Finney, six years (1827-1832; "Forced in 1832 to curtail his travels because of medical problems, Finney became a pastor. . ."); D. L. Moody, thirty-four years (1866-1899); R. A. Torrey, ten years (1902-1911); J. Wilbur Chapman, eighteen years (1892-1910) (dates derived from *Concise Dictionary of Christianity in America* [Downers Grove, IL: InterVarsity Press, 1995] and other sources). Of all these evangelists, only John Wesley preached over fifty years. If Graham's first crusade is considered to be in Palatka, Florida, in 1937 (where he was ordained a minister of the gospel), then his evangelistic ministry has lasted over sixty-three years.

[54]One of the criticisms of Graham's Crusade in New York 1957 was that he turned down two earlier invitations from conservative evangelist Jack Wyrtzen in 1951 and 1954, accepting an invitation to preach in New York only when he was sponsored by the Protestant Council of New York (a part of the National Council of Churches).

Graham's reputation was established in an area, he was then able to return with crusades in major cities the following year, seeking the support of key churches in the area. In this way, Graham toured the New England states in 1950, after his campaign in Boston. This solidified the network of relationships already established by the New England Fellowship.[55] That same year he also held crusades in five American cities.[56]

In 1951 Graham held crusades in seven American cities, from Hollywood, California, to Raleigh, North Carolina. He also went on a tour of southern states, which included a rally in St. Petersburg, Florida and visits in five large cities in Texas, culminating in his Fort Worth Crusade. In 1952 Graham also planned a tour of American cities. It was during these early years of the expansion of his ministry in the United States that Graham founded the Billy Graham Evangelistic Association, the "Hour of Decision" weekly radio broadcast aired across the United States over ABC—the American Broadcasting Corporation, and gospel films were produced by what was to become World Wide Pictures. It was not long before Graham initiated his worldwide ministry.

Developing a Vision for the World

Graham's ministry did not stop with the United States. By 1956 Graham had gathered unsurpassed statistics in his worldwide evangelistic preaching. Forty-five years later he had preached in 185 countries. The impact of his worldwide ministry was evident from the delegates of his three international conferences on evangelism. For example, delegates at Amsterdam 2000 numbered 10,732 from 209 countries and territories.[57] These participants from this number of countries surpassed any international gathering for any reason in the known history of the world.

Three precedents spurred Graham in his vision for worldwide ministry: Dwight L. Moody, John R. Mott, and Torrey Johnson. Moody provided the precedent of an American evangelist who was well-received in England, as well as in other European countries. Mott went from overseeing

---

[55]The New England Fellowship, founded in 1929 by J. Elwin Wright, was the incipient organization which became the model for the National Association of Evangelicals founded with Wright's assistance in 1942 (James A. Johnston, "National Association of Evangelicals," unpublished research for Th.M. Thesis, Trinity Evangelical Divinity School, 1992).

[56]In 1950 Graham held crusades in Atlanta, Georgia; Boston, Massachusetts; Minneapolis, Minnesota; Portland, Oregon; and Columbia, South Carolina.

[57]"Amsterdam 2000: For One Simple Purpose," *Decision Magazine,* October 2000, 4.

the Student Volunteer Movement, a North American entity, to founding the Student World Federation in 1905, a worldwide ministry.[58] Mott was the chair of the World Missionary Conference in Edinburgh in 1910, and a major force in the development of the International Missionary Councils, which were formative in the founding of the WCC in 1948.[59] The third influence on Billy Graham regarding a worldwide ministry was Torrey Johnson, founder of YFC.

Torrey Johnson poured his vision into Graham in three ways. First, in 1944 Johnson shared his vision for a world-wide ministry to Billy Graham during a mutual week of vacation in Florida.[60] Second, like a general with his lieutenants, Torrey was pictured in 1946 with Charles Templeton and Billy Graham studying a map as they planned out, and later executed their first European trip with YFC.[61] Third in August 1948 at a YFC World Congress on evangelism at Beatenburg, Switzerland, Graham learned of the world visions of Dawson Trotman, founder of the Navigators, and of Bob Evans, founder of Greater Europe Mission. Each of these events, and the ongoing association with Johnson planted a worldwide vision in the young evangelist. However, Graham desired more than youth ministry. His plan was for inter-church city-wide crusades all across the world. The first step in Graham's worldwide vision was being realized as he preached before 700 members of clergy in Westminster in 1952.

London 1954 and World Anglicans

Billy Graham was introduced to clergy from a variety of denominations when he spoke on March 20, 1952, at the Assembly Hall of the Church House, Westminster. Graham came at the request of the Evangelical Alliance, "since the Archbishop of Canterbury, Geoffrey

---

[58]Lois Ferm mentioned that Graham was "greatly influenced" by Mott and found in Mott "great inspiration" (phone conversation with author, handwritten notes, 19 September 1999).

[59]Latourette describes Mott's leadership positions in relation to Edinburgh 1910: "John R. Mott, who headed the first of the preparatory commissions, who presided at most of the sessions, who became Chairman of the Continuation Committee and of its outgrowth, the International Missionary Council, and who was in many ways the master mind of the gathering, was a spiritual child of the revival movement" (Kenneth Scott Latourette, "Ecumenical Bearings of the Missionary Movement and the International Missionary Council," in Ruth Rouse and Stephen Charles Neill, eds., *A History of the Ecumenical Movement 1517-1948* [London: SPCK, 1954], 356).

[60]High, *Billy Graham,* 140.

[61]Billy Graham, *Just As I Am,* 132h.

Fischer, viewed the prospect of a crusade with courteous caution."[62] Nor was Graham endorsed by the British Council of Churches for a London crusade unless pilot crusades were attempted in countryside towns.[63] Yet those who were present were predominantly Anglican.[64] This was a different group than those he met on March 19, 1946, when he began his European tour sponsored by YFC. Graham described those present at the 1946 meeting, "The majority of them had some connection with the Plymouth Brethren"[65]—and also the [British] Evangelical Alliance.[66] In accordance with his policy of broad-based local church support, the second meeting was important for participation of the Anglican Church in his 1954 crusade, and possibly even more important for his worldwide ministry in the future.[67]

By 1998 there were 51.6 million Anglicans across the world. [68] From a strategic perspective, if Graham were to launch a worldwide ministry, it would prove helpful for him to have the backing of the worldwide body of Anglicans. These Anglicans were located predominantly in Great Britain, Australia, New Zealand, South Africa, India, Canada's United Church, and the United States' Episcopal Church, a representation of four continents of the world. Following the initial reluctance, the support of the Anglican Church was confirmed when "Archbishop Fisher of Canterbury (who had previously declined to give his approval) pronounced the benediction at a final London gathering estimated to number more than

---

[62]Pollock, *Billy Graham,* 111.

[63]Ibid.

[64]Stephen Olford, telephone interview with author, handwritten notes, June 26, 2001.

[65]Billy Graham, *Just as I Am,* 116.

[66]Murray wrote, "The London Crusade [1954] was the more remarkable in view of the fact that at the outset it was backed only by a private body, the Evangelical Alliance, with the denominations (Anglicans and Nonconformists) all standing to one side and declining to endorse it" (Iain Murray, *Evangelicalism Divided: A Record of the Crucial Years of Theological Change* [Edinburgh: Banner of Truth Press, 2000], 34).

[67]"It [Harringay, 1954] did for the evangelist on the world stage what the Los Angeles Crusade of 1949 had done in the USA" (ibid., 33-34).

[68]Peter Brierly and Heather Wraight, *Atlas of World Christianity: A Complete Visual Reference to Christianity Worldwide, Including Growth Trends into the New Millennium* (Nashville: Thomas Nelson Publishers, 1998).

one hundred thousand."[69] The 1954 London crusade opened the door for Graham's future worldwide ministry.

Graham's World Conquest Methodology

Graham became established in the United States in several short years, it was not long before his eyes turned to the rest of the world. Graham's world-wide campaign began in 1946 and 1947 when Torrey Johnson of YFC brought him to war-torn Europe, where Graham ministered primarily in England, but also ventured to major capitals of Northern Europe. In 1952 Graham visited Japan and Korea, publishing the book *I Saw Your Sons at War*.[70] In 1952 Graham also went on a European tour, preaching in key cities, according to his methodology, and making contact with key leaders. It was during this tour that he preached the sermon mentioned above, "The Work of an Evangelist." However, it was the London 1954 crusade that opened the world to him.[71] This crusade marked a pivotal period in Graham's ministry. In the decades following 1954 he conducted from 25 to 50 percent of his ministry outside the United States[72]—with the exception of 1957 when he spent all his time on New York.[73] His overseas tours were often planned in January and February, seeking to advance the gospel into new areas each year. His international ministry will be noted as a series of gospel offensives, as if a general was planning a world conquest by the Word of God.

His first gospel offensive consisted of a two-year focus on Northern Europe. In 1954 he held a three-month crusade in London. He then

---

[69]Murray, *Evangelicalism Divided*, 34.

[70]Billy Graham, *I Saw Your Sons at War: The Korean Diary of Billy Graham* (Minneapolis: Billy Graham Evangelistic Association, 1953).

[71]"If our 1949 meeting in Los Angeles marked a decisive watershed for our ministry in the United States, the London Crusade in 1954 did the same for us internationally. . . . As invitations poured in to hold Crusades on every continent, we knew that our ministry could no longer be limited mainly to the English-speaking world" (Billy Graham, *Just As I Am*, 238).

[72]Graham was able to have a worldwide ministry partly because of his uncanny cultural sensitivity. Sébastien Fath explained that even though Graham was an American revivalist, his partnership with Jacques Blocher, graduate of Northwestern Bible College, provided Graham with credibility among the French (Sébastien Fath, *Une Autre Manière d'Être Chrétien en France: Socio-histoire de l'Implantation Baptiste—1810-1950* [Geneva: Labor et Fides, 2001], 445-48).

[73]See Appendix 3, "Crusades of Billy Graham and Franklin Graham."

spent the next month visiting six major cities in northern Europe.[74] The next year, in 1955, Graham did not plan his habitual January-February preaching tour. Rather he held spring and summer crusades in Glasgow, Scotland; London, England; Paris, France; and Rotterdam, the Netherlands. His preaching tour that year consisted of a June tour of Switzerland, Sweden, Germany, Denmark, and Norway in which he held nine one-day rallies in Scotland and Germany.

Graham's January-March 1956 preaching tour took him to the continent of Asia, where he toured India and the Far East.[75] During this tour Graham held rallies in eight cities of India,[76] in Hong Kong, in Taipei, Formosa, in three Japanese cities, in Seoul, Korea, and in Honolulu, Hawaii. He then held crusades in three cities in the Southern United States: Richmond, Virginia; Oklahoma City, Oklahoma; and Louisville, Kentucky. During his United States ministry he held rallies in Akron, Ohio, St. Louis, Missouri, and Buffalo, New York. His associate, Joe Blinco, also held a crusade in Muskee, Oklahoma, on the heels of Graham's crusade in Oklahoma City.

Graham's third gospel offensive came in January-February 1958 when he held two-day crusades in five cities in the Caribbean and a rally in Costa Rica. Before he preached these crusades, three of his associates prepared the way with crusades from ten days to three weeks.[77] This simultaneous campaign preparatory approach was used fifty years earlier by evangelist and pastor J. Wilbur Chapman (1859-1918).[78] Graham ended the

---

[74]In 1954 books on Graham were also published in Denmark (F. Bredahl Peterson, *Billy Graham Som Han Er: Med en Tal af Billy Graham* [Kobenhaven: J. Frimodts Forlag, 1954]); in the Netherlands (T. B. Van Houten, *Billy Graham: Een Evangelist van Onze Tijd* [Den Haag, J. N. Voorhoeve, 1954]); and in Sweden (Arvid Svärd, *Billy Graham, Tänd av Gud, Sänd av Gud: Några Drag i Bilden av de Moderna Miljonstädernas Apostel* [Stockholm: Westerbergs, 1954]). In 1955 a book on Graham was published in German-speaking Switzerland (Alfred Stucki, *Billy Graham und Charles Fuller: Amerikas grosse Evangelisten* [Basel: H. Majer, 1955]).

[75]Twelve years later, Graham met with Mother Teresa, Prime Minister Indira Gandhi, and the Shah of Iran in November 1972 ("BGEA Chronology").

[76]The India tour followed a propaganda tour of the communists Nikita Khrushchev and Nikolai Bulganin held six weeks earlier (High, *Billy Graham,* 190). High added, "Yet the crowds—Christian and non-Christian—which came to hear Billy Graham equaled, and in some instances greatly surpassed, those that gathered to hear Khrushchev and Bulganin" (ibid.).

[77]Leighton Ford was in Jamaica (two weeks), Joe Blinco in Trinidad (nineteen days), and Grady Wilson in Barbados (ten days).

[78]"Chapman introduced the method of the simultaneous campaign into urban evangelism (one central meeting, with other meetings in various parts of a target

Caribbean tour with two days of rallies in the region's largest city, Mexico City. Graham also held four crusades and seven rallies in the United States in 1958.

Graham targeted a fourth continent of the world in 1959 when he held crusades in Australia and New Zealand.[79] He spent February to May in Australia and New Zealand in his "Southern Cross Crusade." He began his tour with visits to the Australian cities of Carberra, Hobart, and Launceston. Graham continued his Australian ministry holding simultaneous crusades: a four-week crusade in Melbourne, a four-week crusade in Sydney, and three overlapping crusades over a three week span in Perth (eight days), Adelaide (fourteen days), and Brisbane (fifteen days), using the same three associates as in the Caribbean tour. At the end of these crusades, Graham visited the Queen of England.[80] Graham's United States crusades that year were in Wheaton, Illinois, and Indianapolis, Indiana.

Graham's 1960 African tour marked his fifth gospel offensive. Graham's team of evangelists during this tour included Leighton Ford, Joe Blinco, Grady Wilson, Howard Jones, Larry Love, and Roy Gustafson. Together the teams held crusades in nineteen cities in seven countries of Africa, moving from Ghana to Liberia, Nigeria, Southern and Northern Rhodesia, Ruanda-Urundi, and Kenya. Included in his African tour were rallies in Tanganyika, Ethiopia, and Egypt, and a tour of Israel and Jordan.[81]

---

city)" (Reid et al., *Concise Dictionary of Christianity in America* [Downers Grove, IL: Intervarsity Press, 1995], 70-71). It is interesting to note that Graham used the simultaneous campaign approach the year after he spoke at the Baptist General Conference of Texas Conference on Evangelism in 1957. The speaker right after Graham spoke on the topic of "The Simultaneous Crusade" (Frank Weedon, "The Simultaneous Crusade," in C. Wade Freeman, ed., *The Doctrine of Evangelism* [Nashville: Baptist General Convention of Texas, 1957], 39-42).

[79]John Pollock entitled the Sydney crusade of 1959 the "pattern crusade," although the reason he does so is not clear. Perhaps it was the influence of Howard Mowll, archbishop of Sydney, "a strong evangelical leader and a leader in the ecumenical movement, [who] was so trusted by other denominations that virtually the entire Protestant Church community was officially committed to support" (Pollock, *Billy Graham* [1966], 205). Lois Ferm told me that the Australia crusade in 1959 was the closest thing to revival that she had ever experienced (personal interviews by author, Amsterdam, The Netherlands, handwritten notes, 31 July 2000 and 6 August 2000).

[80]Graham began reporting to political leaders following his overseas preaching tours on a regular basis.

[81]While Graham corresponded with the Presidents of the United States regularly beginning in the late 1940s, he now began to report to them after his overseas trips. On March 31, 1960, Graham met with President Eisenhower and Vice-President Nixon on his Africa tour. While some may criticize this possible politicizing of his role as an evangelist, it must be remembered that he spoke on behalf of the missionaries that were on the fields of the world. In his first *Hour of Decision Sermon*, Graham spoke of

In June, Graham held a crusade in Washington, DC, in the United States. Then in August and September 1960, Graham held a series of simultaneous crusades in four cities of Switzerland and in Berlin, West Germany, along with rallies in Essen and Hamburg, West Germany. He then returned to the United States for the "Spanish American Billy Graham Crusade" in New York. This last crusade showed that he was beginning to diversify his crusade approach through segmented marketing. Graham had begun to reach many of his early objectives and was reworking his evangelistic vision.

In 1961 it seems that Graham took a reprieve from his world emphasis to maximize use of the simultaneous campaign method in Florida, which he had previously used in the Caribbean, Australia, and Africa. Graham and his associates peppered the state with crusades, rallies and meetings from January to April. Graham ended the three-month blitz with a crusade in Miami. Also by 1961, during other times of the year, Graham's associates were holding their own meetings across the United States and internationally. Graham's ministry was multiplying.

In 1962 Graham launched a sixth campaign on the last Continent he needed to reach, South America. He spent slightly more than one month touring Venezuela, Columbia, Ecuador, Peru, and Chile. He only held two crusades during this month, one in Mariacibo, Venezuela and one in Barranquilla, Columbia. The tour ended with a rally in Lima, Peru.

After 1962 Graham's crusades were held approximately every twelve to fifteen years in most major cities in the United States. There were only ten cities where Graham held four or five crusades in his fifty years of worldwide ministry. The five United States cities were:

1. Charlotte, North Carolina (Number 92 "C" market city):[82] 1947, 1958, 1972, and 1996

---

the dismissal of General MacArthur and of his replacement: "I cabled David Morken in Formosa to make a survey of Christian reaction to the dismissal of General MacArthur. He reported that all were deeply grieved and all felt that Christianity had suffered a major blow. . . . It is possible that the *policy toward Missions* will not change under General Matthew Ridgway. Let us pray that this will be so" (Billy Graham, "Hate Versus Love," *Hour of Decision Sermons*, no. 1 [Minneapolis: Billy Graham Evangelistic Association, 1950], 1-3; emphasis mine). In this case, his concern was evangelical mission work in the Far East.

[82]Market information (provided to show relative size with respect to other U. S. cities) taken from J. Walter Thompson Co., *Population and Its Distribution* (New York: McGraw-Hill Book Company, 1952), 10-14. Graham visited the eight "A" market cities a total of twenty-four times, or an average of three times per city, and a crusade in an "A" market city in the United States an average of every two years of his ministry.

2.   Los Angeles, California (Number 3 "A" market city): 1949, 1958, 1963, and 1974 (25th Anniversary Celebration)

3.   Minneapolis, Minnesota (Number 13 "B" market city): 1950 and 1961, and 1973 and 1996 (with St. Paul)

4.   New York City, New York (Number 1 "A" market city): 1957, 1960 (Spanish), 1969, 1970, and 1991

5.   Seattle, Washington (Number 20 "B" market city): 1951, 1962, 1965, 1976, and 1991.

The five non-United States cities were:

1.   Berlin, West Germany: 1954, 1960, 1966, 1982 (East Germany), and 1990

2.   London, England: 1954, 1955, 1966, (1967), and 1989

3.   Moscow, Russia: 1982, 1984, 1988, and 1992

4.   Paris, France: 1954 (meeting), 1955, 1963, and 1986

5.   Toronto, Ontario, Canada: 1955, 1967, 1978, and 1995.

Each of these cities merits detailed attention as to the ministry of Billy Graham and his impact on evangelicalism in the region. Research could also done on each of the 271 cities[83] and each of the 185 countries and territories in which he ministered.[84]

---

[83]It is interesting to note that Graham never held a crusade in Salt Lake City, Utah (Number 71 "C" market city according to Thompson, *Population and Its Distribution,* 13). The largest United States cities (according to the 1951 population) where he did not hold crusades were in New England (Worcester and Fall River, Massachusetts; and Fairfield, Connecticut) and Ohio/Pennsylvania (Youngstown, Dayton, Akron, Toledo, and Wheeling, Ohio; and Allentown, Wilkes-Barre, Harrisburg, and Johnstown, Pennsylvania).

[84]Numbering countries and territories presented a challenge with the change in the borders and names of countries. Numbering cities presented an equal challenge when a university is visited in a given city, or when satellite relays are located in a city. The number of cities in the 271 was taken from a hand count of the cities in "Statistics: Alphabetical (city)" (Minneapolis: Billy Graham Evangelistic Association, November 2000).

By 1962 Graham's ministry seems to have attained much of his early vision.[85] He had toured or held crusades on all the continents of the world:

1. 1949-1962, North America

2. 1954-1955, Europe

3. 1956, India and the Far East

4. 1957, North America, New York

5. 1958, Central America (simultaneous crusades)

6. 1959, Australia (simultaneous crusades)

7. 1960, Africa (simultaneous crusades)

8. 1961, North America, Florida (simultaneous crusades)

9. 1962, South America.

In conjunction with his world conquest, by 1962 *Decision* magazine was being published in four English editions: United States, Canada, Australasia, and United Kingdom. French and German would soon be added in 1963, and Spanish in 1964. Mission historian John Mark Terry wrote of the growth of *Decision* magazine, "In 1960 the Evangelistic Association founded *Decision* magazine, and by 1984 it had a circulation of two million."[86] His gospel films were being translated and shown in select countries. Yet three major challenges remained. In hindsight, his final forty years increased his presence in the United States and worldwide while meeting these challenges.

---

[85]John Corts concurred that this was probably accurate (John Corts, personal interview by author, 29 January 2001, Minneapolis, MN: Handwritten notes in author's possession).

[86]John Mark Terry, *Evangelism: A Concise History* (Nashville: Broadman and Holman, 1994), 168.

Three Remaining Challenges

Three challenges remained for the ministry of Billy Graham after 1962. These were the challenge of closed countries, the challenge of closed denominations, and the challenge of passing on his ministry to the next generation. He addressed these challenges in the final forty years of his ministry.

The first challenge was the closed countries of the world, especially communist countries behind the so-called Iron and Bamboo Curtains. Graham was not able to impact the Middle East or the Muslim world as far as crusade ministry.[87] The Iron Curtain loosened for Graham through a 1977 tour of Hungary. He published the book *Billy Graham in Hungary* after this visit.[88] His Hungary tour opened the door for a 1982 tour of Russia, a speaking opportunity in the Moscow Baptist Church on May 9, 1982, and an address at the "World Conference of Religious Workers for Saving the Sacred Gift of Life from Nuclear Catastrophe" on May 11, 1982. Hungary 1977 also opened the door for Graham's tour of six cities in the German Democratic Republic from October 14-25, 1982: Berlin, Dresden, Gorlitz, Stendal, Stralsund, and Wittenberg. Graham then returned to the Soviet Union in 1984 for a visit of four cities, Leningrad, Russia; Tallinn, Estonia; Moscow, Russia; and Novosibirsk, Siberia,[89] and published *Billy Graham in the Soviet Union.*[90] Then on March 10, 1990, Graham preached at the Berlin Wall[91] three months before the official destruction of the wall

---

[87]The exception to this was the one-day rally in Cairo, Egypt, and the tour of Israel—both in March 1960. Graham's associate Akbar Haqq maintained evangelistic efforts in India and the Middle East following Graham's 1956 tour of India and the Far East.

[88]Bob Terrell, *Billy Graham in Hungary* (Minneapolis: World Wide, 1978); Hungarian translation: *Billy Graham Magyarországon: Szeptember 3-10, 1977* (Budapest, Hungary: Magyarországi Szabadegyházak Tanácsa, 1978).

[89]Graham met with writer Aleksandr Isaevich Solzhenitzyn on December 8, 1974.

[90]Bob Terrell, *Billy Graham in the Soviet Union* (Minneapolis: Billy Graham Evangelistic Association, 1985).

[91]Bill Yoder and Wolfgang Polzer, "Graham Preaches at Berlin Wall," *Christianity Today,* 9 April 1990, 59.

on June 13, 1990.[92] Whereas Communism had a potent missionary emphasis in Graham's early ministry,[93] it was now symbolically dismantling.

He broke through the Bamboo Curtain in thirty years of effort, beginning with a tour of the Far-East in 1956 and crusade in Tokyo in 1967. In 1988 Graham was able to visit the People's Republic of China, speaking in Beijing and four other cities. In 1992 and 1994, Graham visited North Korea as a guest of The Great Leader Kim Il Sung.[94] Thus Graham surmounted his first challenge—the Iron Curtain and the Bamboo Curtain.

Graham's second challenge was to increase the reception of his ministry by the World Council of Churches[95] and by three Christian denominations that had not broadly accepted him before: the Lutheran World Federation,[96] the Eastern Orthodox churches, and the Roman

---

[92]"A Concrete Curtain: The Life and Death of the Berlin Wall, 6—What is Left of the Wall" [on-line]; accessed 10 August 2000; available at http://www.wall-berlin.org/gb/trace.htm; Internet.

[93]"Communism is a fanatical religion that has declared war upon the Christian God" (Billy Graham, "Christianism Vs. Communism," *Hour of Decision Sermons*, No. 2 (Minneapolis: Billy Graham Evangelistic Association, 1951), 3. "Christians hold your hat! Communism says, 'Ye must be born again.' I am told that in communist countries a man can be a ne'er-do-well, lazy, lackadaisical; he can be converted to communism and over-night he becomes a fanatic, willing to work, toil, and even die for his new-found religion" (ibid., 7).

[94]Graham begins his autobiography with an introduction entitled "Between Two Presidents: Harry S. Truman, 1950 and Kim Il Sung, 1992" (Billy Graham, *Just As I Am,* xvii). It is clear that he felt that arranging for a crusade in North Korea was a major accomplishment in his life. Also Graham brought messages to President Kim Il Sung from President George Bush, Sr. and Pope John Paul II (ibid*.,* 626).

[95]To this end, Billy Graham wrote "Conversion—a Personal Revolution" (*The Ecumenical Review* 19, no. 3 [1967]: 271-84). Donald McGavran preceded Graham in the reception of his church growth methodology as noted in the written statement resulting from the Consultation convened by the World Council of Churches Department of Missionary Studies at Iberville, Quebec, July 31-August 2, 1963. In *Effective Evangelism*, McGavran wrote of the statement penned by Victor Hayward, "It was an open, well-stated, reasoned description of the church growth movement." He continued, "The Institute of Church Growth and later the School of World Mission at Fuller Theological Seminary found this statement an excellent exposition of the whole church growth position. We published and republished it many times" (Donald A. McGavran, *Effective Evangelism* [Phillipsburg, NJ: Presbyterian and Reformed Publishing, 1988], 74).

[96]While Graham sought the support of Lutheran Bishops through the work of Wilhelm Brauer, by 1963 he did not gain the full support of the Lutheran World Federation (Kennedy, "Best Intentions*,*" 502-06). Among the reasons Robert Kennedy cites were: the theological concern that the Graham methodology "corresponds much more to the mentality of the free churches than to the spirit of the Wittenberg

Catholic Church. This challenge and the concept of cooperation is discussed in Chapter Five.

Graham's third challenge was to pass on his ministry to the next generation. He accomplished this challenge in two ways: through conferences and through empowering his associates. Graham sponsored a number of conferences to train leaders. His world conferences included the 1,262 participants at the World Congress on Evangelism, Berlin 1966,[97] the 2,700 participants at the International Congress on World Evangelization, Lausanne 1974,[98] the 4,000 evangelists at the International Conferences for Itinerant Evangelists, Amsterdam 1983,[99] the 7,000 at Amsterdam 1986,[100] the 4,000 participants at the North American Conference for Itinerant Evangelists, Louisville 1994 (United States delegates primarily), and the 10,732 participants at Amsterdam 2000[101]—an international conference for preaching evangelists, as well as a number of other regional conferences at

---

Reformation" (correspondence of Bishop Otto Dibelius to Wilhelm Brauer, June 28, 1957, Archives of the German Evangelical Alliance, Berlin; quoted by Kennedy, "Best Intentions," 504). Wilhelm Stoll's *The Conversion Theology of Billy Graham in the Light of the Lutheran Confessions* (St. Louis, MO: Concordia Student Journal, 1980) was an example of the negative view of Graham in some Lutheran circles. On the other hand, Timo Pokki's doctoral dissertation, *America's Preacher and His Message: Billy Graham's View of Conversion and Sanctification* (doctoral diss., University of Helsinki, Finland, 1998; Lanham, MD: University Press of America, 1999), showed a warming of Continental Lutherans to the ministry of Billy Graham.

[97]"The numerical goal of delegates was set at 1,262" (Arthur P. Johnston, *The Battle for World Evangelism* [Wheaton, IL: Tyndale House, 1978], 173).

[98]John R. W. Stott wrote that Lausanne 1974 "assembled 2,700 participants from 150 nations and from a whole spectrum of Protestant denominations" (John R. W. Stott *Making Christ Known: Historic Mission Documents from the Lausanne Movement, 1974-1989* [Grand Rapids: Eerdmans, 1996], xi).

[99]Graham wrote of Amsterdam 1983: "For ten days, almost 4,000 active itinerant evangelists from 133 countries—plus some 1,000 staff, press, observers, and people involved in other types of evangelistic ministries—gathered in Amsterdam for an intense schedule of meetings, workshops, informal discussions, and outreach. Over 60 percent of the participants were from non-Western or Third World countries" (Billy Graham, "Foreword," in J. D. Douglas, ed., *The Work of an Evangelist: International Congress for Itinerant Evangelists, Amsterdam, The Netherlands* [Minneapolis: World Wide, 1984], xiii).

[100]"What a marvelous sight it has been to see these banners representing 174 countries of the world" (Billy Graham, "Opening Words," in J. D. Douglas, ed., *The Calling of an Evangelist: The Second International Congress for Itinerant Evangelists, Amsterdam, The Netherlands* [Minneapolis: World Wide, 1987], xiii).

[101]Amsterdam 2000 numbered 10,732 from 209 countries and territories ("Amsterdam 2000: for One Simple Purpose," *Decision Magazine,* October 2000, 4).

various times.[102] This totals 25,694 participants at five major conferences on evangelism.

Graham's associates provided another avenue through which his ministry could also be multiplied into the future. Among the numerous associates were Joe Blinco, Robert Cunville, Leighton Ford, Grady Wilson, Akbar Haqq, Howard Jones, Larry Love, Roy Gustafson, Victor Hamm, Ralph Bell, John Wesley White, Ross Rhoads, Lane Adams, and others. On January 16, 1969, Graham announced that his brother-in-law, Leighton Ford, an associate evangelist since 1955, would share "Hour of Decision" preaching duties. It was felt that Leighton Ford would soon assume Graham's mantle.[103] However, in 1985 Ford announced the founding of Leighton Ford Ministries.[104] Ten years later, on November 8, 1995, Graham announced that the BGEA board elected his son Franklin Vice Chairman of the Board, and that he would become its head when Billy Graham died or was incapacitated.[105] Prior to 1996 and since that time, Franklin Graham has increased the number of crusades that he has held both in the United States and Canada.[106]

---

[102]For example, regional conferences were held in Singapore, 1968, Minneapolis and Bogotá, 1969, and Australia, 1971 in preparation for Lausanne 1974 (Stott, *Making Christ Known*, xiii).

[103]"BGEA Chronology." In 1955 Ford joined the BGEA as an Associate Evangelist. In 1962 the BGEA published Ford's sermon "The Secret Power of Evangelism." In 1966 Graham wrote the foreword for Ford's *The Christian Persuader* (New York: Harper and Row, 1966). Then of the thirty *Hour of Decision Sermons* (*HOD*) published between 1969-1975 (numbers 180 and 210), thirteen were by Leighton Ford (see Appendix 2). During that same period, only twelve Graham sermons were published as *HOD*. The BGEA also published three sermons by long time associate Grady Wilson: 182, 191, and 192 (all within that same time period). The BGEA published three sermons of Roy Gustafson, long time friend and associate: 127, 193, and 241 (one within the above time period). The BGEA also published one sermon of associate Joe Blinco: 170. The BGEA published no other sermons by anyone other than Billy Graham of the 322 *HOD*. For a listing of select English published sermons and *HOD* see Appendix 2.

[104]On August 22, 1985, Leighton Ford announced the forming of his own ministry ("BGEA Chronology," 148), which was formed on June 5, 1986 (ibid., 152).

[105]"BGEA Chronology," 186. See also "The Return and Rise of the Prodigal Son—Franklin Graham was born to be born again—and to inherit the Evangelical kingdom of his father Billy. It was an overwhelming fate for the Grahams' first-born son and he rebelled against it," *Time*, 13 May 1996, 66-76.

[106]For a listing of Franklin Graham's crusades see Appendix 3.

Another way Graham could have passed the torch to the next generation was in the founding of a Christian University.[107] Late in the 1960s, a wealthy businessman offered him "thousands of acres of land in Florida on the Atlantic Ocean, with millions of dollars to back it up."[108] Graham studied the opportunity to found "Graham University: Campus of Nations."[109] However, perhaps due to his prior experience as president of Northwestern Bible College, the plan was never implemented. Rather, the BGEA studied the concept of building the Billy Graham Center from 1970-1973. The building was built from 1977-1980 on the campus of his alma mater, Wheaton College, Wheaton, Illinois, where Graham was a member of the Board of Trustees. Among other things, it houses the Wheaton Graduate School, the Graduate School Library, and the Billy Graham Archives. Later, in 1994, Graham gave his name to the Billy Graham School of Missions, Evangelism, and Church Growth at the Southern Baptist Theological Seminary, Louisville, Kentucky. This school specializes in preparing pastors, missionaries, evangelists, and teachers for evangelistic ministry in the Southern Baptist Convention. Thus, while never founding his own institution, Graham maintained a close relationship with educational institutions throughout his ministry, showing his appreciation for the development of minds for evangelism and Christian ministry.[110]

With this introduction to the life and ministry of Billy Graham, we must now move to the study of his evangelistic theology and methodology. This endeavor necessitates the defining of terms. Whereas Chapter Three of this book will be devoted to defining parameters of

---

[107]This would have allowed Graham to follow in the path of some evangelists and revival preachers that had gone before him. For example, revival preacher Charles Finney founded "Intensely revivalist Oberlin" College (George M. Marsden, *The Soul of America: From Protestant Establishment to Established Nonbelief* [New York: Oxford University Press, 1994], 23). Evangelist Dwight L. Moody founded four schools: the Mount Hermon School for Boys, Northfield Seminary, the Chicago Bible Institute, later known as Moody Bible Institute, and Northfield Bible Training School (Lyle W. Dorsett, *A Passion for Souls: The Life of D. L. Moody* [Chicago: Moody, 1997], 24).

[108]Billy Graham, *A Biblical Standard for Evangelists A Commentary on the Fifteen Affirmations Made by Participants at the International Congress for Itinerant Evangelists in Amsterdam July 1983* (Minneapolis: Billy Graham Evangelistic Association, 1984), 32.

[109]Information on this project is found in Collection Number SC33 at the Billy Graham Center archives in Wheaton, Illinois.

[110]Graham sat on the boards of Wheaton College, Fuller Theological Seminary, and Gordon-Conwell Theological Seminary. His wife, Ruth, sat on the board of Moody Bible Institute.

evangelism, the following section will note three concepts: evangelism, evangelism in theology, and a theology of evangelism.

Defining a Theology of Evangelism

Graham's ministry of evangelism presupposes a system of Christian doctrine and its practical outworking regarding evangelism—a theology of evangelism. The concept of a theology of evangelism is relatively new in ecclesial history.[111] For this reason care must be taken in properly defining the concept, especially as this definition provides the elements of this thesis. Three concepts necessitate investigation to properly define a theology of evangelism: evangelism, evangelism in theology, and a theology of evangelism.

Defining Evangelism

First in defining a theology of evangelism is a look at the word *evangelism*. A definition of evangelism will be derived from four sources: the origin of the word *evangelism* in the English language, a look at the concept of evangelism in the Bible, an overview of the 1918 Archbishop's definition of evangelism, and a brief look at some of Graham's definitions of evangelism.

David Barrett wrote a good review of the English use of the word *evangelize* in his *Evangelize! A Historical Survey of the Concept*. In this book Barrett ascribed the first English use of the word *evangelize* to John Wycliffe. Wycliffe first used *evangelize* as a transliteration of the Latin Vulgate's *evangelizare*.[112] Barrett then noted that the second Wycliffe version, revised posthumously by some of Wycliffe's followers "replaced all of these English words commencing 'evangel-' by, in most cases,

---

[111]The influence of the German university system on American higher education in the mid-nineteenth century led to increasing specialization among faculty members and departments (George M. Marsden, *The Soul of the American University: From Protestant Establishment to Established Nonbelief* [New York: Oxford University Press, 1994], 103-10). This specialization also influenced the field of theology. A theology of evangelism is one of the byproducts of this movement in education.

[112]"In 1348 in England, John Wycliffe completed the first translation of the whole Bible in the English language, using the Latin Vulgate. In the earlier of his two extant versions, Wycliffe translated almost all usages of the Latin *evangelizare* (and hence the Greek *euangelizein*) into the new English word 'euangelisen' (in some orthographies, 'evangelisen')." (David B. Barrett, *Evangelize! A Historical Survey of the Concept* [Birmingham, AL: New Hope, 1987], 22).

30

'prechinge', and sometimes by synonyms like 'schewinge the Lord Jhesu.'"[113] The change from "evangelize" to "preaching" continued through William Tyndale's translation and "has been perpetuated in all subsequent Bible translations up to the present day."[114] Barrett explained the difficulty that the loan word from the Latin and Greek underwent, "Because it [evangelisen] was not current, it could not be used; and because it could not be used, it could never become current."[115] The words *evangelism* and *evangelize* came into greater use during what Kenneth Scott Latourette calls "The Great Century of Missions," (1815-1914). It is in the context of world evangelization that the term *evangelize* gained importance in the English language.

What Barrett omitted from his discussion were the terms used for the concept of evangelize in early Protestant theological writings.[116] For example, Martin Luther (1483-1545) spoke of the "outward Word"[117] which was necessary unto salvation, and he prayed, "that the Gospel be preached properly throughout the world."[118] Richard Baxter (1615-1691) wrote of the "work of conversion" and "personal ministry" in his *The Reformed Pastor.*[119] Increase Mather, president of Harvard (1685-1701), spoke of the

---

[113]Ibid.

[114]Ibid.

[115]Ibid.

[116]It is historically narrow to limit the beginnings of evangelism to the nineteenth and twentieth centuries. For example, the Archbishop's third committee wrote of "revival preachers" during the medieval times, "In mediæval times there was deep in the consciousness of those revival preachers a terror of God the Avenger and the fear of hell" (*The Evangelistic Work of the Church*, 13). In fact, there were many examples of missionaries and preachers of the gospel prior to the nineteenth century.

[117]Martin Luther, "Of Confession," Smalcald Articles, Part 3, Section 8, "Of Confession" [on-line], accessed 11 October 2001, available from http://www.frii.com/~gosplow/ smalcald.html#smc-03h; Internet.

[118]Martin Luther, *Martin Luther's Larger Catechism,* Part 3, "Of Prayer," "The Lord's Prayer," "Second Petition" [on-line]. Accessed 19 October 2001. Available from http://www.iclnet.org/pub/resources/text/wittenberg/ wittenberg-luther.html#sw-lc.

[119]Richard Baxter, *The Reformed Pastor* (Portland, OR: Multnomah, 1982; based on William Orme's edition of 1920, first edition, 1656), 15: "The work of conversion, of repentance from dead works, and faith in Christ, must be taught first and in a frequent and thorough manner." "The work of conversion is the first and most vital part of our ministry. For there are those who are Christian only in name, who have need to be truly 'born again.' . . . The next part of the ministry is the upbuilding of those that are truly converted'" (ibid., 73). Baxter even extolled the benefits of personal ministry [evangelism], "Personal ministry is a vital advantage for the conversion of many souls" (ibid., 106), and encouraged church members in personal witness, "(2) Urge them to step

"work of conversion" and "converting" in 1683.[120] Jonathan Edwards (1703-1758) also used "work of conversion" in his *A Narrative of Surprising Conversions*: "And the work of *conversion* was carried on in a most *astonishing* manner, and increased more and more; souls did as it were come by flocks to Jesus Christ."[121] Thus there is a strong historic tradition for the use of other words for the concept of "evangelize." This fact should allay two misconceptions. First, the fact that our Protestant forebears did not use the word "evangelize" does not mean that they did not practice, speak of, or write of the concept. Second, the use of other words did not imply that they did not admonish the practice nor "do the work of an evangelist."

Barrett reminded his readers that it was not long before the meaning of "evangelize" came to include more than just the proclamation of the gospel. In the early twentieth century "evangelize" began to include the Christianization of the social order, or social improvement.[122] John R. Mott, chair of the important Edinburgh 1910 World Missionary Conference,[123] explained the transition of meaning in his mind when he published *The World's Student Christian Federation: Origin, Achievements, Forecast*. He

---

out and visit their poor, ignorant neighbors. (3) Urge them to go often to the impenitent and scandalous sinners around them, to deal with them in all possible skill and earnestness" (ibid., 136).

[120]"There is already a great death upon religion, little more left than a name to live. . . . Consider we then how much it is dying representing the [very] being of it, by the general failure of the work of conversion, whereby only it is that religion is propagated, continued and upheld in being, among any people. As converting doth cease, so does religion die away; though more insensibly, yet most irrecoverably. . . . How much it is dying, respecting the visible profession and practice of it, partly by the formality of churches, but more by the hypocrisy and apostasy of formal hypocritical professors" (Increase Mather, quoted in Isaac Backus, *A History of New England With Particular Reference to the Denomination of Christians Called Baptists*, vols. 1-3, 2nd ed. with notes [1777, 1784, 1796; Newton, MA: Backus Historical Society, 1871; New York: Arno Press and The New York Times, 1969], 1: 458-59).

[121]*Jonathan Edwards on Revival* (Edinburgh: Banner of Truth, 1999), 13. Other terms used by Edwards to describe evangelism were the "preaching of it [the gospel]" (ibid., 75-76, William Cooper, "Preface," in *The Distinguishing Marks of a Work of the Spirit of God* [1741]), to convince others (ibid., 43), and to warn sinners (ibid., 57). Results of evangelism, according to Edwards, were a "conversion of many souls" (ibid., 8), the "ingathering of souls" (ibid., 17), a person "truly born again" (ibid., 20), and "the revival of religion" (ibid., 148). Edwards described a woman who "longed to have the whole world saved" (ibid., 60). He explained this woman's zeal, "[This same woman] expressed, on her deathbed, an exceeding longing, both for persons in a natural state, that they might be converted, and for the godly, that they might see and know more of God" (ibid., 61).

[122]Barrett, *Evangelize!*, 26-30.

[123]Latourette, "Ecumenical Bearings," 356.

wrote of this emphasis in a section entitled "The Federation and a New Social Order."[124] Mott wrote of "fifteen years," referring back to 1905 as the date when he became aware of the social aspects of the ministry, ten years after the founding of the World Student Christian Federation, and five years before Edinburgh 1910. Thus, in Mott's mind, the addition of a social mandate into the concept of "evangelize" originated in 1905. Mott highlighted that a sermon of Bishop Thoburn that brought a "great change in me."[125] Could this have been the point of change in 1905? While a direct correlation is difficult to prove, Mott's change in response to Bishop Thoburn led him to coin the phrase "The Larger Evangelism."[126] Through Mott's leadership, Edinburgh 1910, the International Missionary Councils, and the World Council of Churches moved participating mission agencies and churches to adopt a broader definition of evangelism, moving away from the pietistic primacy of conversion and "mere proclamation"[127] as in the century before.[128]

---

[124]The Christianizing of the social order and particularly of the industrial system, in all the countries, calls for deeper and more adequate attention from all movements. As the survey of the quarter-century has shown, the Federation has, during the past fifteen years, laid increasing emphasis upon the study of social problems and upon social service as could be performed by undergraduates without neglect of primary university duties" (John R. Mott, *The World's Student Christian Federation: Origin, Achievements, Forecast* [New York: World's Student Christian Federation, 1920], 76).

[125]Thirty-nine years later, Mott wrote of a sermon by Bishop Thoburn of India that seemed to have greatly influenced him in this regard: "The larger desire so essential to evangelism is a product not only of meditation but also of contagion. It is communicated by Christ himself. One of the most helpful sermons I ever heard was by Bishop Thoburn of India on the text, 'The love of Christ constraineth us.' The truth in his message which laid most powerful hold and wrought a great change in me was that love of Christ enables one to love the unlovable. I do not find this in non-Christian faiths or in the areas of unbelief. It is a divine product" (John R. Mott, *The Larger Evangelism: The Sam P. Jones Lectures at Emory University, 1944* [New York: Abingdon-Cokesbury Press, 1944], 8-9).

[126]Mott described larger evangelism as "larger in the sense of larger desire" (ibid., 7). Two of his points were, "The larger evangelism we long to see will result inevitably from larger unity" (ibid., 13), and "The larger evangelism demands a larger message. Nothing short of the integral individual and social gospel will suffice" (ibid., 14).

[127]Gustav Warneck opposed the idea of mere proclamation ("blosse Jundmachung") in his *Outline of a History of Protestant Missions*, 3rd English ed. (New York: Revell, 1904), 406-07, as was David Bosch in *Transforming Mission* (Maryknoll, NY: Orbis, 1991), 411-12.

[128]Arthur P. Johnston writes, "A major theological shift took place among those who became leaders of the IMC" (Arthur P. Johnston, *World Evangelism and the World of God* [Minneapolis: Bethany Fellowship, 1974], 54).

Therefore, by 1905 the term *evangelize* began to include more than the proclamation of the gospel of Jesus Christ. This discussion naturally leads to the question: what does the Bible say about the concept of evangelism? Barrett in his *Evangelize!* included two chapters on the New Testament concept of "evangelize." Chapter three focused on uses of the word ευαγγελιζω, and chapter four dealt with synonyms. Barrett wrote of "42 New Testament Greek words overlapping in meaning around *euangelizo.*"[129] These words were used a total of 2,468 times. To summarize Barrett, he discussed the nine close synonyms, the forty-two synonyms, the "big seven", and the "100 related verbs," the "180 dimensions," the "300 definitions," the "700 near synonyms," and the "2,000 cognates."[130] While Barrett's big seven and nine close synonyms are helpful for the purposes of defining evangelism, the meaning becomes confused due the immensity of his range. This author followed a similar but more limited approach in researching the biblical concept of evangelism.

This author summarized biblical concepts of evangelism in "The Mindset of Eternity: A Biblical Introduction to Evangelism" focusing, however, only on specific evangelistic contexts.[131] I divided the terminology into five categories: persons (nouns), method (verbs), dynamic (dealing with the word of God), result (nouns and verbs), and process (verbs). While the bulk of the verbs fit into the "method" category, the other categories prove important in deriving a biblical definition. Under the methods there were nineteen Greek root words used in the context of evangelism.[132] Ευαγγελω had eight additional cognate forms, and μαρτυρεω had two additional cognate forms. This totaled twenty-nine different verbs used in evangelistic contexts, for a total of 173 uses. The Bible is not without a clear witness as

---

[129]Barrett, *Evangelize!*, 16.

[130]Ibid., 17, 19.

[131]Thomas P. Johnston, "The Mindset of Eternity: A Biblical Introduction to Evangelism," 22nd rev. (Deerfield, IL: Evangelism Unlimited, 1992), 32-36. Contexts for evangelism include those wherein discussion relates to the proclamation of the gospel and its direct results (e.g., saving or winning). Under methods the only passages consulted related verbs used when describing the verbal proclamation of the gospel. The possible accusation of circular reasoning, defining evangelism prior to deciding what verbs are evangelistic, is invalid as it ignores the root meaning of the word ευαγγελιζω, "to proclaim the Good News."

[132]The Greek root words are αγγελλω, ηρυσσω, μαρτυρεω, λαλεω, διδασκω, γνωριζω, κοινονια, νουθετεω, παρακαλεω, πειθω, απολογια, εκτιθημι, παρατιθημι, διαλεγομαι, συμβιβαζω, διακατελεγομαι, επιδεικνυμι, διανοιγω, and βεβαιοω (ibid.).

to what is meant by evangelize. Simply stated, evangelism is the verbal communication of the gospel of Jesus Christ.[133]

Of special interest to this study, however, are the definitions of *evangelize* used and put forth by Billy Graham. First, the primary definition which Graham used in 1952 and in subsequent years to define evangelism was from *The Evangelistic Work of the Church: Being the Report of the Archbishops' Third Committee of Inquiry* (1918).

After 1916's "National Mission of Repentance and Hope," the Archbishop of Canterbury appointed five committees to "bring fresh guidance" to the ministry for Anglican churches after World War One. The Archbishop described their tasks of the committees.[134] The Lord Bishop of Southwark, chair of the committee on evangelistic work, described the mandate given to him in light of the National Mission.[135] The definition of evangelism quoted by Graham in his sermon "The Work of an Evangelist" was found in Part Two of this committee's report.[136] The definition was preceded by five chapters in Part One: (1) Religious Situation, (2) Evangelistic Deficiencies, (3) First Fruits of the National Mission, (4) Message for To-day, and (5) Approach. In these chapters the committee provided further expression of its brief definition. The definition followed the breadth of Edinburgh 1910 in at least two ways. First, under the

---

[133]This author summarized the emphases of "evangelize" in the following definition: "Evangelism is the verbal proclamation of the Gospel of Jesus Christ to the unsaved in the power of the Holy Spirit, to the end of persuading them to repent of their sin, to believe in the work of Jesus Christ on their behalf, and to accept Him as their Savior and Lord, and to nurture them that they might become reproducing members of a local church." (Thomas P. Johnston, "The Mindset of Eternity," 36).

[134]"As we appraised the outcome of the Mission-call five subjects in the life of Church and nation stood out with obvious claim for our rehandling. The character and manner of our teaching: our worship: our evangelistic work: the discovery and removal of hindrances to the Church's efficiency: the bearing of the Gospel message to the industrial problems of to-day" (Randall Cantuar [Archbishop of Canterbury], "Foreword," in *The Evangelistic Work of the Church*, iii).

[135]"To consider and report on the facts and lessons with the experience of the National Mission has brought to light as to the evangelistic work of the Church at home, and the best methods of improving and extending it" (Hubert M. Southwark, "Introduction," in *The Evangelistic Work of the Church*, v).

[136]The definition was as follows: "To evangelize is so to present Christ Jesus in the power of the Holy Spirit that men shall come to put their trust in God through Him, to accept Him as their Saviour and serve Him as their King in the fellowship of His Church" (ibid., 18).

message, the report spoke of a broad view of salvation.[137] The message of the gospel considered was broader than the death, burial, and resurrection of Christ, which was the essence of the gospel as described by the Apostle Paul in 1 Corinthians 15:1-8. Rather than a message of man's sin from which they need safety, the "message for to-day" was described as "the rule of Christ as the hope of the nations."[138] Thus the Archbishops' report had a note of triumphalism in a post-millennial sense, to which mainstream denominations ascribed toward the end of the nineteenth century. This post-millennial triumphalism when combined with evangelism led to a social mandate along with the proclamation of the gospel. Second, the committee brought into evangelism the need for social service, while not making it a part of the evangelistic mandate, *but prior to it*:

> He who applies Christian faith and living to the common relationships of life is the best evangelist. The translation of our creed into action by social service rendered from Christian motives is a true *preparatio evangelica*, and a presentation of the Gospel which ignores the social obligations of Christianity will not receive serious attention from increasing numbers of people to-day.[139]

Thus, the Archbishops' report, although having a good definition of evangelism, included clarifications that blunted the pietistic impact of the power of the Word of God in the gospel proclaimed. These additions may be the reason that Charles Templeton encouraged its use, "with minor changes," as the definition of evangelism for the National Council of

---

[137]"The eternal element in the Christian message is unchanging. Salvation in its widest sense and from all that hinders spiritual life and development must always be at the heart of the Gospel that we preach" (ibid., 11).

[138]"There is a unique opportunity at the present time of offering to the world the rule of Christ as the hope of the nations, and we believe that the presenting of the highest motives of true discipleship—the call to win the world for Christ—is one of the most valuable methods of evangelistic approach to-day" (ibid., 13).

[139]*The Evangelistic Work of the Church*, 17. The use of *preparatio evangelica* reminds this author of Franz Delitzsch's use of *gracia præparans* to described the preparatory work of the Holy Spirit causing the peoples of the islands and the coastlands to await the Good News—"that the messenger to the Gentile world will be welcomed by a consciousness of need already existing in the heathen world itself" (Franz Delitzsch, *Biblical Commentary on the Prophecies of Isaiah*, trans. James Martin [1877; reprint, Grand Rapids: Eerdmans, 1986], 2:177). Delitzsch, however, referred to a supernatural work of the Holy Spirit independent of the need for human mediation as described by the *Archbishop's Committee*.

Churches of Christ, U.S.A.[140] While this definition was helpful when Graham was preaching before a group of Anglican ministers in 1952, Graham's early ministry did not follow the two clarifications of this definition. Rather, Graham's practice was oriented to the biblical definition of evangelism that finds the power of the gospel inherent within the Word of God itself.[141]

The second point of interest regards the definitions of evangelism put forth by Graham himself. In a sermon published in 1947, Graham described witnessing as "God's purpose for you and me after we have been converted is that we be witnesses to his saving grace and power."[142] Fifty years later, in his autobiography, Graham defined evangelism in the context of his ministry as an evangelist:

> An evangelist is a person who has been called and especially equipped by God to declare the Good News to those who have not yet accepted it, with the goal of challenging them to turn to Christ in repentance and faith and to follow Him in obedience to His will.[143]

---

[140]"The Archbishop's Committee of the Church of England framed a definition of evangelism which later became a part of the 'Report of the Archbishop's Commission' (popularly known as 'Towards the Conversion of England') and has, with some minor changes, been adopted as a definition of evangelism by the Madras Foreign Missions Council, the National Council of the Churches of Christ in the U. S. A., the Commission on Evangelism of the Presbyterian Church, U.S.A., and other bodies" (Charles B. Templeton, *Evangelism for Tomorrow* [New York: Harper and Brothers, 1957], 41-42).

[141]Martin Luther shared the absolute necessity for the Word of God in salvation: "And in those things which concern the spoken, outward Word, we must firmly hold that God grants His Spirit or grace to no one, except through or with the preceding outward Word" (Martin Luther, "Of Confession," Smalcald Articles, Part 3, Section 8 [on-line]; accessed 11 October 2001; available from http://www.frii.com/~gosplow/smalcald.html#smc-03h; Internet). The Word of God as the "principal means" of conversion was also shared by Jonathan Edwards in his *The Distinguishing Marks of a Work of the Spirit of God*: "The Scripture speaks of the word as the principal means of carrying on God's work; for the word of God is the principal means, nevertheless, by which other means operate and are made effectual. Even the sacraments have no effect but by the word; and so it is that example becomes effectual; for all that is visible to the eye is unintelligible and vain without the word of God to instruct and guide the mind" (*Jonathan Edwards on Revival*, 99-100).

[142]Billy Graham, "Retreat! Stand! Advance!," in *Calling Youth to Christ: Messages by Billy Graham* (Grand Rapids: Zondervan, 1947), 44.

[143]Billy Graham, *Just As I Am*, xv.

The Later Graham added a distinction regarding the ministry of the evangelist, and also to the definition of evangelize: "The evangelist is not called to do *everything* in the church or in the world that God wants done. On the contrary, the calling of the evangelist is very specific."[144] In his 1953 *Hour of Decision Sermons* (*HOD*), number 22, "Three Minutes to Twelve," Graham described the gospel in this way, "The Good News that I declare to you today is that Christ died for your sins and that he rose again for your justification."[145] Then he continued on the mandate to evangelize:

> It is this Gospel that has been commissioned to the church. It is the sole obligation of the church to carry this Good News throughout the world before we blow ourselves to oblivion.[146]

In his 1959 sermon "The Gospel for the Whole World," Graham stated:

> "Go," said our great Commander. "Go into all the world and preach the Gospel." This word was spoken with a tremendous sense of urgency. We must live for the truth He died for! We must carry out our commission!
>
> "Go" with love and compassion! "Go" with your gifts and offerings! "Go" with your prayers! "Go" denying yourselves and following Him.[147]

Clearly, evangelism for the early Graham was the proclamation of the gospel.

However, it seems that Graham went through a time of testing in the late sixties and early seventies as far as what was entailed in evangelism.[148] In 1967, in his address to the Kansas City School of Evangelism, Graham included six points answering the question "How do we communicate the Gospel of Christ?" His six points were (1) the authoritative proclamation of the gospel, (2) a holy life, (3) by love, (4) a compassionate social concern, (5) demonstration of unity in the spirit, and

---

[144]Ibid.

[145]Billy Graham, "Three Minutes to Twelve," *Hour of Decision Sermons,* no. 22 (Minneapolis: Billy Graham Evangelistic Association, 1953), 5.

[146]Ibid.

[147]Billy Graham, "The Gospel for the Whole World," *Hour of Decision Sermons,* no. 112 (Minneapolis: Billy Graham Evangelistic Association, 1959), 5.

[148]Graham's definition of evangelism will be discussed in greater detail in Chapter Two.

(6) contagious excitement about Christ.[149] He preached an article that he had prepared for the *Ecumenical Review*. The two marks of ecumenical evangelism came through in the sermon: social concern and unity. These two marks were among the points that differentiated Berlin 1966 from Lausanne 1974.

Therefore, when the term evangelism was interpreted historically, biblically, with regards to the *Archbishop's Committee* of 1918, or as used by the Early Billy Graham, it referred to the verbal proclamation of the Gospel of Jesus Christ. We now move on to define a theology of evangelism.

Evangelism in Theology

The development of doctrinal theology began primarily to disavow heresies that surfaced in the Early Church. In this light, theology was shaped in a defensive posture. However, catechistic purposes provided theology a positive posture in explaining the truth. These positive and negative tensions in the theological task pose a challenge to theologians, as well as to pastors and evangelists. However, in the negative or positive structure of theology comes the danger of question framing or begging the question. Begging the question "does not mean a direct assumption of the truth but an indirect assumption reached in a circuitous manner by the appearance of logical reasoning."[150] Thus the danger in any arrangement of the truth is question framing—defining the terms in such a way as to eventuate the outcome.

In looking at theology, the danger of question framing is noted as whole theologies can be written with little or no mention of evangelism, or the proclamation of the gospel.[151] The result to the student of theology is

---

[149]Billy Graham, "Communicating the Gospel," *Lectures: Kansas City School of Evangelism, September 1967* (Kansas City, MO: Billy Graham Evangelistic Association, 1967). Graham stated at the beginning of this message that the material he was presenting was a condensation of material prepared for an article in the *Ecumenical Review* (Billy Graham, "Conversion—a Personal Revolution," *The Ecumenical Review* 19, no. 3 [1967]: 271-84).

[150]Victor A. Ketcham, *The Theory and Practice of Argumentation and Debate* (New York: Macmillan, 1914), 249.

[151]For example, Puritan divine William Ames, in his *The Marrow of Theology*, trans. John D. Eusden (Grand Rapids: Eerdmans, 1997 [orig. pub. 1629]), apparently had nothing to say of the responsibility of the Christian in evangelism, much less of the work of evangelism. This was an unusual omission in light of the fact that his second book dealt with the Christian life. He divided this book into two sections, "religion" and "justice." Interestingly for the history of evangelism in theological studies

that evangelism is non-theological, non-academic, and hence not important. These conclusions are without warrant and actually infer the importance of evangelism and confirm the necessity of its place in theological inquiry. The fallacies involved in leaving evangelism out of theological inquiry are as follows:[152]

1. Fallacies of tautology: evangelism is not a part of theology; thus evangelism is not a part of theology, evangelists do not concern themselves with theology; thus evangelists do not concern themselves with theology, or, evangelism is not academic; thus evangelism is not academic.

2. Fallacies of prevalent proof (or of false historical precedent): theology does not concern itself with evangelism because most theologians do not concern themselves with evangelism; evangelism is not a valid part of theology because most theologians do not concern themselves with evangelism; or, evangelism is not an academic discipline (of the higher type), because evangelism has not historically been considered a part of academic pursuit.

3. Fallacy of false interpolation: Evangelists do not seem to concern themselves with the differentiations of classical theology; therefore evangelists are a-theological.

The presupposition of this dissertation is that evangelism is closely related to theology, and is a legitimate part of theology.

The apparent delegitimizing of the work of conversion in theological education was inherited through some modern divisions of theology. Hence we will briefly note how three theologians fit evangelism into their programs of study. Friedrich Schleiermacher in his *Kurze Darstellung des theologischen Studiums zum Behuf einleitender Vorlesungen* (second edition, 1830) divided the study of theology into three main parts: philosophical theology, historical theology, and practical theology. Under practical theology Schleiermacher included three points: introduction, principles of church service, and principles of church government. Under principles of church service, Schleiermacher had a sub-section entitled pastoral work under which he placed "calling and

---

in the United States, "Both Thomas Hooker and Increase Mather recommended the *Marrow of Theology* as the only book beyond the Bible needed to make a student into a sound theologian" (ibid., back cover).

[152]These fallacies are found described in David Hackett Fischer, *Historians' Fallacies: Toward a Logic of Historical Thought* (New York: Harper and Row, 1970).

conversion." In this section which dealt with pastoral care, after dealing with the catechetics of children, he addressed others outside of the fold of the "evangelical church" in three paragraphs. Since Schleiermacher believed that evangelism was not "naturally grounded" (hence empirically measurable), it did not seem to fit into educational categories.[153] However, being a part of the Christian experience, he placed evangelism (and conversion) as a subset of *process* of Christian education necessitating a prior understanding of "principles of catechetics" (gradual conversion through an extended educational process).[154]

About sixty years after Scheiermacher's second edition of *Kurze Darstellung,* Philip Schaff published his *Theological Propædeutic* (fifth edition 1902). Schaff divided theology into five categories: religion and theology, exegetical theology, historical theology, systematic theology, and practical theology. The thirty-second chapter of thirty-four in practical theology is titled "Evangelistic." In two pages Schaff described "The new branch of theological learning, demanded by the growing zeal in missions."[155]

---

[153]"§296. On similar grounds, those who live within the neighborhood or vicinity of the congregation—as religious strangers, as it were—may also become subjects of similar activity [catechetics]. This requires a theory of how to deal with converts. For the more definitely the principles of catechetics are set forth the easier it will be to derive this theory from them.

§297. However, since this activity is not so naturally grounded certain indications should be drawn up for recognizing whether it is properly motivated. For it is possible to err in both directions here: in hasty self-confidence and in anxious hesitation.

§298. Conditionally, the theory of missions might also be attached here, one which is as good as completely lacking at the present time. It could most easily be attached if it were possible to assume that all efforts of this kind are successful only where a Christian congregation is in existence" (Friedrich Schleiermacher, *Brief Outline on the Study of Theology,* 2nd ed., trans. Terrence N. Tice [Richmond, VA: John Knox Press, 1966; orig. pub. 1830], 102).

[154]Schleiermacher's view of conversion as "quiescent self-consciousness" shaped his view of the work of conversion as a process of informing the self (see Friedrich Schleiermacher, *The Christian Faith,* 2nd ed. [Edinburgh: Clark, 1960], 478-479). He opposed instantaneous conversion: "The idea that every Christian must be able to point to the very time and place of his conversion is accordingly an arbitrary and presumptuous restriction of divine grace, and can only cause confusion" (ibid., 487).

[155]Philip Schaff, *Theological Propædeutic: A General Introduction to the Study of Theology,* 5th ed. (New York: Charles Scribner's Sons, 1902), 517. Perhaps Schaff was perhaps referring to the work of Gustav Warneck, who wrote *An Outline of a History of Protestant Missions from the Reformation to the Present Time,* ed. by George Robson, translated from the 7th German ed. (New York: Revell, 1901), which became foundational in the study of the Protestant mission movement. Schaff then went on to include two other sections on missions: "Epochs of Missions" and "Missionary Literature." While quoting the Great Commission in his section titled "Evangelistic,"

TABLE 1
ERICKSON'S TYPES OF THEOLOGICAL INQUIRY[156]

Broad Area	Four Types of Study	Four Types of Doctrinal Study	Areas of Systematic Theology
Theological studies	Biblical studies	Biblical theology	Scripture
	Historical studies	Historical theology	God
			Man
	Doctrinal studies	Systematic theology	Sin
	Practical studies		Christ
		Philosophical theology	Salvation
			Church
			Last things

     More recently, Millard Erickson divided theological studies as noted in Table 1. In Erickson's table, and from his presupposition, Christian theology finds its derivation from a study of the Bible. Hence at the left hand side of the table, Erickson placed biblical, historical, doctrinal, and practical studies. These studies were combined in various ways to form biblical theology (dealing with a book, author, or genre), historical theology (dealing with a period in history), systematic theology (gathering theological ideas into a system of thought), and philosophical theology (the philosophical paradigms underlying the system of thought). Erickson's right hand column listed eight doctrinal items that are a part of systematic theology. These eight points were considered central in the study of Christian theology, and will be used in this dissertation to define aspects of systematic theology. Evangelism or the work of conversion was considered

---

Schaff never addressed conversion, but rather dealt with missions from a historical and ecclesial point of view, culminating in a post-millenial triumphalism: "The extraordinary progress of missionary zeal and enterprise is phenomenal, and one of the greatest evidences for the vitality of Christianity, and an assurance of its ultimate triumph to the ends of the earth. . ." (Schaff, *Theological Propædeutic,* 522).

    [156]Adapted from Millard Erickson, *Christian Theology* (Grand Rapids: Baker, 1985), 23.

on three pages of his 1,247 pages in a chapter titled "The Role of the Church," and under the heading "The Functions of the Church."[157]

Therefore, the concept of evangelism, so clearly central to the Great Commission, has been buried in the mainstream conceptions of theological education. When the word *theology* is combined with the word *evangelism*, there comes a unique meaning. Theology becomes more narrowly defined by the practice of evangelism. Hence the next section will seek to delineate the meaning of a theology of evangelism.

Defining a Theology of Evangelism

As the usual shape of systematic theology is an ordered sequence of the gospel presentation, some understand a theology of evangelism as a reformulation of systematic theology. The problem with this arrangement can be that unique emphases of evangelism are ignored. In this case the question framing of classical theologians may ignore important aspects of a theology of evangelism.

Because theology of evangelism is a practical study, dealing primarily with the practice of evangelism, it has led some practitioners, for their part, to focus on the humanities. Thus, Ernst Troelsch and his American counterpart, H. Richard Niebuhr, founded the field of church sociology. They viewed the church as a social institution, and began to deconstruct the mission of the church and its practice by viewing it primarily or solely in an anthropological sense. The same happened in the field of a theology of mission(s). Built upon the foundation of Gustav Warneck,[158] a theology of missions digressed into a study of cultural anthropology and/or comparative religions. The concepts of the fatherhood of God, the brotherhood of men, and the Spirit of God at work in all world religions replaced a burning zeal to see souls saved. Harold Lindsell in his *An Evangelical Theology of Missions* sounded the battle cry for evangelical missions over a half a century ago.[159] He denounced the movement of the

---

[157]Millard Erickson spoke of evangelism in his *Systematic Theology* (ibid., 1052-54), as a function of the church. He gave a brief summary of the thrust of the Great Commission in this section. Then he made the point, "It appears that he [Jesus] regarded evangelism as the very reason for their being" (1052). For what Erickson stated was the reason for the church's being, evangelism or the work of conversion, he devoted three pages of text, and he wrote another eight pages on the gospel. Erickson did, however, devote an entire chapter (17 pages) to unity and the ecumenical movement.

[158]Warneck, *An Outline of a History of Protestant Missions.*

[159]Harold Lindsell, *An Evangelical Theology of Missions* (Wheaton, IL: Van Kampen, 1949).

International Missionary Councils and the World Council of Churches away from the Bible and the Great Commission. With all the polemic in the literature on a theology of missions, the evangelist once again needs discernment to define a practical theology of evangelism.

Historically, evangelists, in order to conform their lives to their theology, emphasized the practice of evangelism. Hence comes a third and voluminous source for a theology of evangelism—the many books providing guidelines for the practice of evangelism. While some books have been written on a theology of evangelism,[160] these are few in relation to the vast numbers of books written on areas of systematic theology, or even those written on a theology of the church or of missions. The reason for this seems to be that many evangelists have overruled the need to delineate a clear theology of evangelism, as the Bible was their rulebook for both theology and practice. Thus they have often been accused of ignorance and anti-intellectualism.[161] Evangelists have also been accused of "dumbing-down" the gospel or theology to fit their methods or to unite churches in evangelism. One the other hand, evangelists (and evangelicals) have been seen by others as "dangerous" literal Biblicists.[162] Ours is a foreboding task,

---

[160]There are some notable exceptions to a lack of theologies of evangelism. The following, for example, are arranged chronologically: J. E. Conant, *No Salvation without Substitution* (Grand Rapids: Eerdmans, 1941); Samuel M. Zwemer, *Evangelism Today: Message not Method* (London: Revell, 1944); Henry Cook, *The Theology of Evangelism: The Gospel in the World of To-Day* (Carey Kingsgate Press, 1951); T. A. Kantonen, *The Theology of Evangelism* (Philadelphia: Muhlenberg, 1954); Julian N. Hartt, *Toward a Theology of Evangelism* (New York: Abingdon, 1955); C. E. Autrey, *The Theology of Evangelism* (Nashville: Broadman, 1966); A. Skevington Wood, *Evangelism: Its Theology and Practice* (Grand Rapids: Zondervan, 1966); Ernest D. Pickering, *The Theology of Evangelism* (Clarks Summit, PA: Baptist Bible College Press, 1974); Lewis A. Drummond, *The Word of the Cross: A Contemporary Theology of Evangelism* (Nashville: Broadman, 1992); Timothy Beougher and Alvin Reid, eds., *Evangelism for a Changing World* (Wheaton, IL: Harold Shaw, 1995); and Donald A. Carson, gen. ed., *To Tell the Truth* (Grand Rapids: Zondervan, 2000).

[161]"Tillich and Bultmann early in life revolted decisively against all traditionalistic Christian faith. For them modern man can no longer swallow the superstition of pre-critical dogma. For them it is beyond dispute primitive thinking that has been outmoded by the modern education of 'any schoolboy' anywhere in the world. All transcendence in terms of supernaturalism, the classical Christian stance, is discarded with condescension or with contempt" (Nels Ferré, *The Atonement and Mission,* Essay on Mission, no. 2 [London: London Missionary Society, 1960], 10).

[162]Hence the Pontifical Commission on Biblical Interpretation wrote of the "Fundamentalist Reading": "The fundamentalist reading begins from the principle that the Bible, being the inspired Word of God and exempt from error, must be read and interpreted literally in all of its details. But by 'literal interpretation' it understands a basic, literalistic interpretation, that is to say excluding all effort of comprehension of the

to distill a theology of evangelism from the four above mentioned sources: systematic theology, theology of mission(s), practicum of evangelism, and theology of evangelism.

A theology of evangelism is a cross-section of systematic theology, with its emphasis on the gospel, a theology of mission with its emphasis on the proclamation of the gospel, the practicum of evangelism in its insistence upon certain motives and methods for evangelism, and varying theologies of evangelism each with their emphases. For the purposes of this dissertation, a theology of evangelism will be defined as follows: the study of God's revelation, the Bible, which specifically relates to the mandate of preaching the gospel or evangelism, and is divided into four words: authority, parameters, message, and cooperation. The first and third words parallel two topics in systematic theology. The second and fourth words focus on issues pertaining to evangelism. *Parameters* include an understanding of the Great Commission, the role of social concern, and the place of lifestyle evangelism. *Cooperation* regards the cooperation or separation between Christian churches in the work of evangelism. The following chapters will report on the four words, authority, parameters, message, and cooperation, as they relate to the evangelistic ministry of Billy Graham.

Statement of Problem

The ministry of Billy Graham begs the question: what has driven this man to minister as a Christian evangelist for all these years? What are the theological presuppositions that have buttressed his theology? What is Graham's theology of evangelism? The answer to these questions will be addressed in the following pages of this book. While it will be impossible to delineate every aspect of his theology of evangelism, it is the goal of this author that the broad strokes of Graham's theology will be

---

Bible that considers its historical growth and its development. She [fundamentalist reading] opposes herself thus to the use of the historico-critical method, as with every other scientific method, for the interpretation of Scripture" (Commission Biblique Pontificale, *L'Interprétation de la Bible dans l'Eglise* [Montreal: Fides, 1994], 48; translation mine). The commission continued: "The fundamentalistic approach is dangerous, for she is attractive to persons who are looking for biblical answers to their life problems. She can trick them by offering them pious but illusory interpretations, rather than telling them that the Bible does not necessarily contain an immediate response to each of these problems. Fundamentalism invites, without saying it, a form of intellectual suicide. It places a false sense of security to life, for it unconsciously confuses the human limitations of the biblical message with the substance of the divine message" (ibid., 50; translation mine).

clearly established through his preaching, his writings, and his crusade methodology.

A secondary purpose related to the first is to ascertain changes in the evangelistic theology of Billy Graham. With proper definition of the terms, and proper interaction with the primary sources, it may be possible to note changes in the emphases of Graham on issues relating to a theology of evangelism.

The final goal looks to the future. While research into original sources provides the researcher the solace and joy of learning about the past, its ultimate purpose is application in the present and future (cf. Deut 32:7; 1 Cor 10:11). In this light, the ministry of Billy Graham will be analyzed with an eye to the future of evangelism. Each chapter will provide the raw materials of analysis for marching orders in future action. In this way, the legacy and ministry of Billy Graham will live on to prompt future generations to "Be imitators of me, just as I also am of Christ" (1 Cor 11:1).

Research to Date

Billy Graham's evangelistic theology of evangelism is largely unstudied to date.[163] There has been extensive study on Graham, some of which is relevant to the study of a theology of evangelism. Three doctoral dissertations have studied conversion in Billy Graham's thought: William Dale Apel,[164] Carolo W. Dullea,[165] and more recently Timo Pokki.[166] These three dissertations deal directly with salvation in Billy Graham that parallels our chapter on message. More recently, Howell W. Burkhead studied the

---

[163]For example, Iain Murray commented on the lack of research in Graham's understanding of exclusiveness: "The Steps by which Graham moved away from his former exclusiveness has not been recorded" (*Evangelicalism Divided*, 28). Murray then provided a quick overview on the issue. His comment shows that substantive research on Billy Graham's evangelistic theology remains open to investigation.

[164]William Dale Apel, "The Understanding of Salvation in the Evangelistic Message of Billy Graham: A Historical-Theological Evaluation" (Ph.D. diss., Northwestern University, 1975).

[165]Carolo W. Dullea, S.J., "W. F. 'Billy' Graham's Decision for Christ: A Study in Conversion" (Dissertatione ad Lauream, Rome, Typis Pontificiae Universitatis Gregorianae, 1971).

[166]Pokki, "America's Preacher and His Message."

development of Graham's conception of sin.[167] Sin is important in understanding the atonement, which is the heart of the evangelist's message.

James Guy Newbill wrote a master's thesis entitled "The Theology of Billy Graham, Its Practical Applications, and Its Relative Position in the Contemporary Religious Scene."[168] Newbill's thesis provided insight into the social and theological debates of the 1950s, and dealt with six areas of systematic theology. However, the greatest amount of research on Billy Graham related to his preaching, rhetorical method, and mass persuasion. Some essays and dissertations considered a particular crusade, Graham in the political arena, the public invitation, or Graham's follow-up system.[169]

Other studies of interest in researching the evangelistic theology of Graham include Robert Ferm's unpublished *The Theological Presuppositions of Billy Graham*, written in approximately 1959.[170] David Lockard's book, *The Unheard Billy Graham*,[171] also has a helpful synopsis of Graham's theological and social positions. This volume has proven helpful in understanding sin and salvation in Graham. To these resources may be added the book *Biblical Standard for Evangelists*, officially published under the name of Billy Graham.[172] This volume includes a

---

[167]Howell Walker Burkhead, "The Development of the Concept of Sin in the Preaching of Billy Graham" (Ph.D. diss., Southwestern Baptist Theological Seminary, 1998).

[168]James Guy Newbill's thesis is divided into three sections: "The Theology of Billy Graham: (fifty-three pages); "The Applied Theology of Billy Graham" (fifty-eight pages); and "Billy Graham in the Contemporary Religious Scene" (eleven pages). Under the heading of "The Theology of Billy Graham," Newbill discussed the Bible, the Trinity, Sin, Satan, Salvation, the Future, and the "Fundamentalism" of Billy Graham. Under "the Applied Theology of Billy Graham," Newbill discussed Man and His World, the World and Peace, America, Social Obligations, Marriage, a Christian's Secular Conduct, a Christian's Religious Life, and Personal Christian Characteristics. Under "Billy Graham and the Contemporary Religious Scene," Newbill discussed Popular Religion and the Intellectual Scene—R. Niebuhr (James Guy Newbill, "The Theology of Billy Graham, Its Practical Applications, and Its Relative Position in the Contemporary Religious Scene" [M.A. thesis, University of Washington, 1960], iii).

[169]See the section "Dissertations, Theses, and Doctoral Essays" in the bibliography.

[170]Robert O. Ferm, "The Theological Presuppositions of Billy Graham," unpublished manuscript (Collection No 19, Billy Graham Center Archives, Wheaton College, n.d.).

[171]David Lockard, *The Unheard Billy Graham* (Waco, TX: Word, 1971).

[172]Billy Graham, *A Biblical Standard for Evangelists*. In actuality, the only book that Graham wrote word-for-word was *Peace with God*. All of the other official

discussion of each topic in focus. To these books may be added the two volumes of Lewis A. Drummond on Billy Graham: *The Evangelist: The World-Wide Impact of Billy Graham* (2001)[173] and *The Canvas Cathedral: Billy Graham's Ministry Seen through the History of Evangelism* (2003).[174] These studies were not as helpful to this research as they focused almost uniquely on the theology of the "Later Graham" (1965 and following).[175] Rather than noting the evolution in his thinking, Drummond seemed to frame the question from the point of view of his later theology and practice.[176]

Numerous articles and books have been published on Billy Graham. The *Christian Century* editorial was correct in its assessment of attacks on Billy Graham:

Evangelist Billy Graham was recently criticized from opposite poles. Colin Williams, National Council of Churches' parish and community

---

Graham titles were written by ghostwriters, often compiling material from his recent sermons (William Martin, conversation with author, Louisville, Kentucky, June 24, 2001, handwritten notes in author's possession).

[173]Lewis A. Drummond, *The Evangelist: The World-Wide Impact of Billy Graham* (Nashville: Word, 2001).

[174]Lewis A. Drummond, *The Canvas Cathedral.*

[175]Three points need to be considered in using these books. First is the possibility of question framing. In *The Evangelist*, Drummond began his chapter titled "The Full and True Gospel" by listing the seven points of C. H. Dodd's *kerygma*. The remainder of the chapter then placed the Gospel preaching of Graham into an expansion of Dodd's categories. Among the problems with this methodology is the fact that sin was listed as point fourteen of his fifteen points. In Graham's preaching, however, sin was not a secondary afterthought, it was front and center in many of his sermon introductions. Second, Drummond relied on secondary sources. For example, he relied on David Lockard's *The Unheard Billy Graham* (Waco, TX: Word, 1971), especially in Chapter 6 of *The Evangelist,* "The 'Social Gospel,'" and in Chapter 6 of *Canvas Cathedral*, "Holistic Ministry and Evangelism," which included 10 citations of this resource. For his part, Lockard relied heavily on T. B. Maston in his sociological approach to Graham's preaching. Third, most of Drummond's quotes came from Graham books of the later years that were written and edited by ghostwriters—as the only book penned by Graham was the 1953 *Peace with God*. It would seem that Graham sermons provide a more authoritative source of the authentic Graham.

[176]An example of Drummond's efforts to prove that Graham balanced the social and the spiritual is the chapter in *The Evangelist* called "The 'Social Gospel.'" Drummond wrote of Graham, "In the United States, evangelism became synonymous with fundamentalism, and social action became synonymous with modernism. In his ministry, Billy Graham has *always* sought to repair this split. He sees the divide between the two theological viewpoints as artificial" (Drummond, *The Evangelist*, 82. Emphasis mine). This statement was not "always" true, as is explained in Chapter 3 of this book.

life director, told American Baptist ministers in California that Graham's traditional evangelism is dangerous to the kingdom of God because it "holds to the church in the conservative past." Fundamentalist Bob Jones, Jr., president of Bob Jones University in Greenville, South Carolina, ordered students in his school to stay away from the unsegregated Graham crusade in Greenville, charging that Graham "is doing more harm to the cause of Jesus Christ than any living man." Graham wisely declined comment on these two criticisms, a decision which in this case deserves commendation.[177]

Graham was attacked from both sides. From a more liberal perspective Donald Bloesch found fault and hope in Graham in his eight-page article, "Billy Graham: A Theological Appraisal," published in *Theology and Life*.[178] Bloesch described Graham's concept of conversion as a "dialectic encounter." He faulted Graham's lack of social involvement, and found Graham's belief in the authority of the Bible "too uncritical and naïve." "One can only hope," wrote Bloesch, "that as Graham grows . . . he will rise above those elements in his fundamentalist background that blur the impact of his message."[179] This freedom to criticize Graham on theological grounds was also found in the writings of Nels Ferré, Reinhold Niebuhr, and Martin Marty.[180] From the fundamentalist side, Graham also received open criticism from Bob Jones, Sr. and Jr., John R. Rice, R. T. Ketcham, Charles

---

[177]"A Case of Mistaken Identity," *Christian Century*, 23 March 1966, 358.

[178]Bloesch, "Billy Graham," 136-43.

[179]Ibid., 143. Bloesch ended by stating that "because Christ is exalted in his preaching and also because of his flexibility, we believe that a Reformation Christian can give him [Graham] support—but only with reservations."

[180]Ferré stoutly commented against "pre-critical Christianity" in mission: "The earlier mood was that of traditionalistic faith, an almost pre-critical 'Fundamentalism'. The Bible was taken for granted as a divinely inspired book in such a way that its picture of creation and world history was considered to be literally true. It was a textbook of authority. This naïve dependence on the Bible, however, was torn away for all honest and competent believers by critical modern knowledge" (Ferré, *The Atonement and Mission*, 8). For Niebuhr, see Reinhold Niebuhr, "Billy Graham's Christianity—and the World Crisis" (*Christian and Society* [Spring 1955], 3-4), "Literalism, Individualism, and Billy Graham" (*Christian Century*, 23 May 1956, 641-42), "Proposal to Billy Graham" (*Christian Century*, 8 August 1956, 921-22), and "After Comment, the Deluge" (*Christian Century*, 4 November 1957, 1034-35). For Marty, see Martin E. Marty, "Watergate Year as Watershed Year" (*Christian Century* 26 December 1973, 1272-75). *Christian Century* editorials also regularly attacked Graham. For example, "Graham Wins Friends but Alienates Moslems" (*Christian Century*, 17 February 1960, 180-81) and "Graham and King as Ghetto Mates" (*Christian Century*, 10 August 1966, 976-77).

Woodbridge, J. A. Johnson, David Cohen, A. G. Kerr, Ernest Pickering, Fred Moritz, Wilson Ewin, and Brad Gsell. The issue of separation and Graham's compromising associations with apostate Christian teachers became a defining issue for many fundamentalist antagonists of Graham.[181] Iain Murray and Erroll Hulse also wrote critiques of Graham questioning his theology and practice.[182] They raised concerns about the theological nature of Graham's invitation system and his theological compromise.

The battleground involved in Graham's ministry of evangelism is apparent. The challenge of this dissertation will be to investigate the four words mentioned above in an even-handed way. Because of the polemic nature of the topic, appropriate steps will be taken to research a topic broadly in order to delineate clear conclusions, being aware of the problems of historiography.

Research Methodology

A study of four biographies of evangelist D. L. Moody portrays the challenges of historiography. Henry Northrop in his *Memorial Volume: Life and Labors of Dwight L. Moody the Great Evangelist* emphasized the social aspects of Moody's career.[183] He omitted Moody's conversion experience, as well as his call to the ministry of an evangelist. The next year, William R. Moody wrote *The Life of Dwight L. Moody: The Authorized Version*.[184] William Moody spent an entire chapter on the conversion of his father, approaching the ministry of his father from the standpoint of an evangelist. He noted the central elements of his father's preaching, while not ignoring the philanthropic aspects of his ministry.[185]

---

[181]"The pivotal question was what one thought of Billy Graham" (George Marsden, *Reforming Fundamentalism: Fuller Seminary and the New Evangelicalism* [Grand Rapids: Eerdmans, 1987], 165).

[182]Iain H. Murray, *The Invitation System* (Edinburgh: Banner of Truth, 1967); and *Evangelicalism Divided*; also Erroll Hulse, *Billy Graham: The Pastor's Dilemma* (Hounslow, Middlesex, Great Britain: Maurice Allan, Publishers, 1966, 1969); and *The Great Invitation* (Welwyn: Evangelical Press, 1986).

[183]Henry Northrop, *Memorial Volume: Life and Labors of Dwight L. Moody the Great Evangelist* (Chicago: Providence Publishing, 1899).

[184]William R. Moody, *The Life of Dwight L. Moody: The Authorized Version* (New York: Fleming H. Revell, 1900).

[185]Thomas P. Johnston, "Dwight L. Moody, Three Views: A Historiographic Study" (paper for American Church History, Trinity Evangelical Divinity School, 1985), 5-7.

James F. Findlay wrote *Dwight L. Moody: American Evangelist* in 1969.[186] In his volume, Findlay wrote of an evangelist that stressed the love of God and failed to preach on the wrath of God.[187] More recently Lyle Dorsett wrote *A Passion for Souls: The Life of Dwight L. Moody.*[188] Dorsett included three aspects of the life of Dwight L. Moody: his organizational initiatives, his benevolent work with children, and his warm relationship with Roman Catholics.[189] Four biographies of Dwight L. Moody resulted in four interpretations of his life.

How may this author address the superimposing a predetermined historiography over the theology of Billy Graham? While it is impossible to research and write outside of personal experience and study,[190] this author will seek objectivity by diligently researching and quoting primary source material, the sermons of Billy Graham.[191] As Graham was an evangelist and communicated primarily through his sermons, his sermons will provide the foundational material to examine his evangelistic theology.

Four other avenues provide information on the topic of Billy Graham's evangelistic theology. His books[192] and other writings clarify

---

[186]James F. Findlay, *Dwight L. Moody: American Evangelist* (Grand Rapids: Baker, 1969).

[187]Ibid., 229.

[188]Lyle Dorsett, *A Passion for Souls: The Life of Dwight L. Moody* (Chicago: Moody, 1997).

[189]The flyleaf states that Lyle Dorsett and his wife were the founders and directors of Christ for Children International, "a mission to impoverished children in Mexico" (ibid., dust cover).

[190]David H. Fischer calls the postulation of objectivity the "Baconian Fallacy" (Fischer, *Historians' Fallacies,* 4).

[191]See Appendix 2. A mild disclaimer may be made at this point. John Wesley, Jonathan Edwards, and George Whitefield wrote their own sermons. However, Graham received help from others in the preparation of sermons. While it was his right to include and omit information at his discretion, the use of sermons written by others may decrease the impact of the use of sermons as a theological tool. The repeated use of sermons and the repetition of themes and biblical texts in sermons, however, provided proof of authentic Graham doctrine. For information on his use of the sermons of others, see Billy Graham, *Just As I Am,* 318-19 (he explained that he had run out of sermons in New York 1957); High, *Billy Graham,* 77; Martin, *A Prophet with Honor,* 118; and Pollock, *Billy Graham* (1966), 94.

[192]The only book that was written word for word by Graham was *Peace with God.* All other official Graham books were authored by others and edited and revised by Graham and those he listed as readers in his introductions (William Martin,

points of his theology and practice. Graham's crusade methodology adds insight into his views as to cooperation. Biographies of Graham shed light on the historical context and individual issues with which Graham was dealing. The writings of his associates, associate evangelists, theological advisors, and those who have chaired and/or preached at his conferences and school's of evangelism provide secondary insight into the theological parameters of Graham's theology. All of these will be consulted to derive a clear and succinct theology of evangelism.

The procedure for researching the theology of Billy Graham will be as follows. First, resources dealing with the topic of Billy Graham's evangelistic theology will be gathered. Second, sources will be categorized as to their primary and secondary value. Third, the given subject will be addressed searching for the *sensus plenior,* or the parameters of Graham's theology on the subject, given its historical context, much as one would expect a comparison of texts in the study of a specific doctrine of the Bible.

The possibilities for further research on this topic seem limitless. Each of the 185 countries where he has preached contains its own story. Each has a history of Protestant missionary work, and was approached in a unique way as to cooperating churches and organizations and to those who served as interpreters. As Graham visited countries several times, the cooperating churches and individuals in leadership changed. In certain language groups books of Graham, as well as *Decision Magazine,* were translated and published, providing another area for research and study. Graham's international ministry affords much information for study.[193] Regrettably, this dissertation will not be able to investigate information on each country and language group as to the impact of Billy Graham.

While Graham's international ministry provides multiple sources for further study, his impact on evangelicalism in the United States provides another avenue for further investigation. The conferences he sponsored on the theology and practice of evangelism had an impact on evangelicalism. Also, Graham impacted different regions of the United States. Each region includes denominational and theological emphases. Graham's ministry and impact in these regions is worthy of study. The BGEA could be studied in terms of sociological life-cycle, as the addition of new voices in the leadership of the BGEA may have led to changes that could be studied. There are certainly many interesting points that may be studied in the life and ministry of Billy Graham. This dissertation, however, will limit itself to the study of Graham's evangelistic theology and

---

conversation with author, Louisville, Kentucky, June 24, 2001, handwritten notes in author's possession).

[193]Two significant studies have already emerged, one on Graham's impact in Germany (Kennedy, "Best Intentions"), and another which discusses Graham's impact in Great Britain (Murray, *Evangelicalism Divided*).

methodology, looking primarily at his *Hour of Decision Sermons* and United States ministry.

Thesis Statement

The distinct purpose of this volume is to discern and delineate Billy Graham's theology of evangelism. Its thesis is that he operated with a clear theology of evangelism. Some elements of that theology have remained fairly constant throughout his fifty years of ministry. Other aspects of his theology of evangelism shifted significantly. The goal of this manuscript is to distill Billy Graham's theology and methodology of evangelism, to note any changes that may have occurred, and to make it available to others for their consideration and application.

CHAPTER 2

AUTHORITY

I warn the church tonight that if the church does not have an authoritative answer within the next generation the people will turn away from the church in masses after some new doctrine and some new philosophy.[1]

Billy Graham spoke these words at the Conference on Evangelism of the Baptist General Convention of Texas in 1957. He was convinced that the church needed an authoritative word for the world. Just before Graham spoke at this conference, Robert G. Lee, pastor of Bellevue Baptist Church in Memphis, Tennessee, spoke on "Power for Evangelism." Lee stated:

We find one source from which the river of evangelism flows with revival refreshing. It is God's Book, the Bible, and the use of God's Book. . . . This Word of God is what we use—this Book that is divine in authorship, human in penmanship, infallible in authority, worldwide in its interest, infinite in its scope, universal in interest, personal in application, regenerative in power, inspired in totality, the miracle book of diversity and unity of harmony in infinite complexity.
. . . We must use this Book, but use it as those who believe it to be the inspired, infallible, inerrant Word of God.[2]

Not only is it important to note that R. G. Lee placed the authority of Scripture[3] as the first point of his sermon on "Power for Evangelism," but he also described the use of the Word of God in evangelism—a use which was in keeping with Graham's own style, as we shall see. But perhaps more

---

[1]Billy Graham, "The World Need and Evangelism," Clifford Wade Freeman, ed., *The Doctrine of Evangelism* (Nashville: Baptist General Conference of Texas, 1957), 26-27.

[2]Robert G. Lee, "Power for Evangelism," Clifford Wade Freeman, ed., *The Doctrine of Evangelism,* 8-9.

[3]The Scriptures, Scripture, the Bible, and the Word of God are used synonymously by this author.

important was the early use of the word "inerrant" by this former three-term president of the Southern Baptist Convention. While R. G. Lee's understanding of the need for biblical authority in evangelism was in keeping with the Baptist tradition for centuries, his use of "inerrant" in 1957 foreshadowed a growing debate in the Southern Baptist Convention. Inerrancy was a central issue in the growing chasm between conservatives and moderates of the Southern Baptist Convention, beginning with the 1962 convention in San Francisco.[4] This debate among the Southern Baptists led to the founding of the "Cooperative Baptist Fellowship" (CBF) in 1990,[5] while the agencies of the Southern Baptist Convention were falling under the control of the conservatives, who were committed to biblical inerrancy.[6]

---

[4]Nancy Tatom Ammerman discussed the 1962 inerrancy debate in light of the writings of Midwestern Baptist Theological Seminary's professor Ralph Elliott on the historicity of the creation account in Genesis (Nancy Tatom Ammerman, *Baptist Battles: Social Change and Religious Conflict in the Southern Baptist Convention* [New Brunswick, NJ: Rutgers University Press, 1990], 64). Paige Patterson went back to this same Elliott incident as "one of the earliest tremors" in the Southern Baptist Reformation (Paige Patterson, "Anatomy of a Reformation—The Southern Baptist Convention 1978-1994," 17 November 1994, 1). Forty years earlier, in 1920, five years before the Scope's Trial, William Louis Poteat, President of Wake Forest University, an institution of the North Carolina Baptist Convention of the SBC, defended his view of evolution without ever using the word evolution. Poteat was not deposed from Wake Forest, and the demeaning of the authority of the Bible in sciences with the resulting secularization of many Baptist universities began at that point (James Turnstead Burtchaell, *The Dying of the Light: The Disengagement of Colleges and Universities from Their Christian Churches* [Grand RapidsI: Eerdmans, 1998], 367-368; see also George M. Marsden, *The Soul of the American University: From Protestant Establishment to Established Nonbelief* [New York: Oxford, 1994], 319-330). The central issue has been the Bible's authority in the realm of science.

[5]The Cooperative Baptist Fellowship has as its second [doctrinal] commitment a statement on biblical authority: "Bible Freedom—We believe in the authority of Scripture. We believe the Bible, under the Lordship of Christ, is central to the life of the individual and the church. We affirm the freedom and right of every Christian to interpret and apply scripture under the leadership of the Holy Spirit" ("About CBF [Cooperative Baptist Fellowship]" [on-line]; accessed 3 December 2000; available from http://www.cbfonline.org/about/mission.cfm; Internet).

[6]Patterson wrote, "A third reason for conservative success was the decision to focus on one issue, the reliability of the Bible. . . . The goal was to keep the denomination close to a reliable Bible for the sake of evangelistic and missionary outreach" (Paige Patterson, "Anatomy of a Reformation," 9). Later Patterson looked at the result of the conservative resurgence among the Southern Baptists, "At the end of sixteen years of conservative advance, new executives committed to the inerrancy of Scripture have been installed in nine of the [eighteen] agencies and institutions [of the SBC]" (Patterson, 15). Among the books that made a remarkable impact on the victory of the conservatives were Harold Lindsell's *Battle for the Bible* (Grand Rapids:

Did Graham take sides in this ecclesiastical battle? And if he did, whose side did he take?

Nancy Tatom Ammerman in her helpful history of this controversy, *Baptist Battles: Social Change and Religious Conflict in the Southern Baptist Convention,* noted that Graham (rather it was T. W. Wilson) sent a telegram in which he approved of the nomination of the conservative, Charles Stanley, as president of the Southern Baptist Convention in 1985.[7] This nomination was key to moving the SBC toward the conservative position.[8] However, in 1992, the *Christian Century* ran an editorial that read:

> Graham endorsed the group, the Cooperative Baptist Fellowship, in a greeting made public at the opening session of the fellowship's recent national three-day meeting in Fort Worth, Texas. . . .
>
> "I recognize that there are great men on all sides who have differences of opinion and perhaps differences of interpreting the Bible."[9]

While this information does not offer conclusive insight into the theological

---

Zondervan, 1976) and L. Russ Bush's and Tom J. Nettle's *Baptists and the Bible* (Chicago: Moody, 1980).

[7]Ammerman, *Baptist Battles,* 6, 184. Thom Rainer wrote next to Ammerman's citation, "T. W. Wilson sent it in BG's name" (Thom Rainer, Personal comments, September 19, 2001, Notes written on manuscript). It appears, therefore, that T. W. Wilson, an associate of Graham beginning in 1948, was the originator of the 1985 telegram and not Billy Graham.

[8]Patterson wrote, "Since even two-term trustees on the various boards served no more than ten years, the election each year for ten years of a president committed to the renewal [conservative] agenda, in theory, should redirect the entire system." The electing of a conservative began with the election of Adrian Rogers as president in the 1979 Houston Southern Baptist Convention (Patterson, "The Anatomy of a Reformation," 8). The conservatives who followed Rogers were: Bailey Smith, 1980-1981; James Draper, 1982-1983; Charles Stanley, 1984-1985; Adrian Rogers, 1986-1987; Jerry Vines, 1988-1989; Morris Chapman, 1990-1991; Edwin Young, 1992-1993; Jim Henry, 1994-1995; Tom Ellif, 1996-1997; Paige Patterson, 1998-1999 (Daniel L. Akin, ed., "The Southern Baptist Convention Annual Meeting, June 13-14, 2000" [Louisville, KY: The Southern Baptist Theological Seminary, 2000], 51); James Merritt, 2000-2001 ("A Word from SBC President James Merritt" [on-line]; accessed 3 December 2000; available from http://www.sbc.net/default.asp; Internet); and Jack Graham, 2002-2003 ("SBC President's Page" [on-line]; accessed 19 July 2002; available from http://www.sbc.net/presidentspage/default.asp; Internet).

[9]"Graham on the SBC," *Christian Century* 20 May 20 1992, 536. Because a number of staff in the Graham organization are Southern Baptists, it follows that Graham was aware of this debate.

leanings of Billy Graham on the issue of biblical authority, it shows his penchant to avoid debate in this arena. Yet the recent events in the SBC show that biblical authority is an important issue in ecclesiology, and as we shall see in evangelism also.

Graham himself never used the word "inerrant," but always spoke of the Bible as infallible.[10] The words may seem to have the same meaning etymologically, but in contemporary evangelical theology they sometimes have a different meaning.[11] Graham preached and practiced from an inerrancy point of view, yet he verbally affirmed infallibility.[12] Inerrancy contends the Bible to be without error in all it affirms, historical, scientific, theological, and philosophical.[13] Biblical infallibility, as used by some,

---

[10]Arthur P. Johnston mentioned this to me on several occasions in recent years.

[11]Stephen Davis explained, "It is true that in most contexts of English usage the terms 'infallible' and 'inerrant' are synonymous. Nevertheless I believe that each term has come to have its own disctinctive theological connotation" (Stephen T. Davis, *The Debate about the Bible* [Philadelphia: Westminster, 1972], 16). Woodbridge described the contemporary history of the debate: "Since Vatican II a new definition of biblical infallibility has gained a certain currency among Roman Catholic scholars. It questions the church's traditional commitment to inerrancy. . . . He [Loretz] acknowledges that the early church fathers identified biblical infallibility with biblical inerrancy (that is, the Bible teaches truth in every domain upon which it touches). He suggests, however, that the Fathers were simply mistaken. The Bible does contain 'errors'; nevertheless it gives faithful, or 'infallible,' perspectives on salvation. Within the past two decades or so, evangelical Christians have become uneasy due to their growing awareness that scholars from their own ranks are proposing that the Bible is infallible for faith and practice but that it is susceptible to 'technical mistakes'" (John D. Woodbridge, *Biblical Authority: A Critique of the Rogers/McKim Proposal* [Grand Rapids: Zondervan, 1982], 14). Those who adhere to infallibility place the concept of inerrancy in the Scottish Common Sense Realism of Princetonian scholarship of the late nineteenth century, most notably that of its professor of didactic and polemic theology from 1887-1921, Benjamin B. Warfield (as expressed in his *The Inspiration and Authority of the Bible* [Phillipsburg, NJ: Presbyterian and Reformed, 1948]).

[12]See Appendix 5 for the BGEA's Statement of Faith.

[13]The Peace Committee of the SBC further clarified the Baptist Faith and Message's (BFM, 1963) "Statement on Scripture," notably the phrase, "truth without any mixture of error": "We as a Peace Committee, affirm Biblical authority for all of life and for all fields of knowledge. The Bible is a book of redemption, not a book of science, psychology, sociology or economics. But, where the Bible speaks, the Bible speaks truth in all realms of reality and to all fields of knowledge. The Bible, when properly interpreted, is authoritative to all of life" ("Report of the Southern Baptist Convention Peace Committee", *1987 SBC Convention Bulletin,* 12). Warfield stated it this way when he explained plenary inspiration: "the doctrine that the Bible is inspired not *in part* but *fully,* in all its elements alike,—things discoverable by reason as well as mysteries,

softens this to teach that the Bible is without error in areas of faith and practice, but it may err in scientific, historical, or other areas.[14] In the debate among the Southern Baptists, the conservatives held to inerrancy, the moderates to infallibility. Thus, the topic of this chapter in Graham's theology of evangelism provides some surprising complexities. How central is the issue of biblical authority to Graham? What are Graham's views of biblical authority? How have they changed over the years, if they have? And how does biblical authority relate to his proclamation? These questions will be addressed in this chapter.

The major question of this chapter is the role of biblical authority in Billy Graham's theology of evangelism. First, this chapter will discuss the concept of authority. Second, it will note the "five views of inspiration," within the concept of revelation and reason. Third, it will consider the seven views of biblical authority. Fourth, the chapter will address biblical interpretation. Fifth, the chapter will look at the role of biblical authority on evangelism. Each of these points will be considered in terms of Graham's approach to authority. The thesis of this chapter is that Graham was guided by the use of the Bible in his proclamation of the Gospel, particularly in his early and pace-setting years. We begin by looking at the concept of authority.

The Concept of Authority

Webster's defines authority as "the power or right to give commands, enforce obedience, take action, or make final decisions."[15] In areas of the Christian religion, where is the final authority for decision-making vested? Is it vested in a person, such as the Pope in Roman Catholicism or Charles Darwin for the naturalist? Is it vested in a group of persons or creed, as in a council, congress, conference, or convention? Is it vested in experience, such as in existentialism or in mysticism? Or is the final authority vested in the Bible, the written word of God? While various churches and church members proffer their opinions as to the locus of authority in the church, for the majority of evangelicals, and for Billy

---

matters of history and science as well as faith and practice, words as well as thoughts" (Warfield, *The Inspiration and Authority of the Bible,* 113).

[14]The "Report of the Southern Baptist Convention Peace Committee" reads: "One view holds that when the article says Bible has 'truth without any mixture of error for its matter,' it means *all* areas—historical, scientific, theological and philosophical. The other view holds the 'truth' relates only to matters of faith and practice" ("Report of the Southern Baptist Convention Peace Committee", 11).

[15]David B. Guralnik, editor in chief, *Webster's New World Dictionary,* Second College Edition (New York: Simon and Schuster, 1982), 94.

Graham, the Bible was the final authority.

When viewing the Bible as the final authority, a very real question follows, how can a book of words be the final authority in budgetary matters, in personnel job descriptions, in architectural plans, or in the organization and publicity of an evangelistic crusade? If it is to have this level of authority, the Bible must necessarily be more than a mere compilation of the words of men. Every day printing presses print thousands of compilations of the words of men. Some writings in order to maintain the guise of authority contain abstractions, as in horoscopes. Others must be revised from time to time to remain relevant, such as the Book of Mormon.[16] Similarly, in the case of its councils[17] and encyclicals,[18] the

---

[16]Josh McDowell and Don Stewart include a section of their discussion of Mormonism entitled "Changes in the Book of Mormon" (Josh McDowell and Don Stewart, *Handbook of Today's Religions* [San Bernardino, CA: Here's Life Publishers, 1992], 72-73).

[17]For the "Joint Declaration on the Doctrine of Justification" of the Lutheran World Federation and the Roman Catholic Church to be signed by the Roman Catholics, massive revision of the doctrines and anathemas of the Council of Trent were necessary. For example, of the lifting of the anathemas the statement declared, "In light of this consensus, the corresponding doctrinal condemnations of the sixteenth century do not apply to today's partner" (The Lutheran World Federation and the Roman Catholic Church, "Joint Declaration on the Doctrine of Justification," English Language Edition [Grand Rapids: Eerdmans, 2000], 15). For example, on the matter of Justification by "faith alone," The Council of Trent, Canon 9 on Justification declared: "If anyone says that the sinner is justified by faith alone, meaning that nothing else is required to co-operate in order to obtain the grace of justification, and that it is not in any way necessary that he will be prepared and disposed by the action of his own will, let him be anathema" or Canon 26, "If anyone says that the just ought not for good works done in God to expect and hope for an eternal reward from God through His mercy and the merit of Jesus Christ, if by doing well and by keeping the divine commandment they persevere to the end, let him be anathema" (to this could be added canons 12, 14, 24, 27, 28, 29, 30, and 33)." Or "Concerning the Sacraments," Canon 8, "If anyone says that by the sacraments of the New Law grace is not conferred *ex opere operato,* but that faith alone in the divine promise is sufficient to obtain grace, let him be anathema" (John H. Leith, *Creeds of the Churches: A Reader in Christian Doctrine from the Bible to the Present,* 3rd edition [Atlanta: John Knox, 1982], 421, 423, 426). However, the Roman Catholic president and secretary of "The Pontifical Council for Promoting Christian Unity" signed the Joint Declaration which reads: "Together we confess: By grace alone, in faith in Christ's saving work and not because of any merit on our part, we are accepted by God and receive the Holy Spirit, who renews our hearts while equipping and calling us to good works" ("Joint Declaration," 15).

[18]Of the Anglican orders, Pope Leo XIII wrote in his encyclical *Apostolicae Curae* of September 13, 1896, "So it came about that, since the sacrament of ordination and the true Christian priesthood has been utterly cast out of the Anglican rite, and thus in the consecration of bishops of the said rite no priesthood is conferred, so no

Roman Catholic Church has undergone conceptual revision, even in the area of biblical authority.[19] Other theologians take a more skeptical approach to the authority of words.[20] They distort words by using cultural or contextual arguments that words are true only in their context. Thus change the context, and the words must be understood differently.[21] These revisionist

---

episcopacy can be truly or rightly conferred. . . . With this deep-seated defect of form is joined a defect of intention, which is equally necessary for the performance of a sacrament. . . . so . . . we pronounce and declare that ordinations performed according to the Anglican rite are utterly invalid and altogether void" (Henry Bettenson, ed. *Documents of the Christian Church,* 2nd edition [London: Oxford, 1981], 274-275). Yet the Vatican II, in its "Dogmatic Constitution on the Church" declared of other Christian churches, "The Church recognizes that in many ways she is linked with those who, being baptized, are honored with the name Christian, though they do not profess the faith in its entirety or do not preserve unity with the successor of Peter" ("Vatican Council II, Dogmatic Constitution on the Church, Chapter II, The People of God, Section 15," John Leith, *Creeds of the Churches,* 466).

[19]Leo XIII, *Provenditimus Deus: On the Study of Holy Scripture,* 18 November 1893 (*The Great Encyclical Letters of Pope Leo XIII* [New York: Benzinger Brothers, 1903], 271-302), followed the Council of Trent in its view that the Holy Scriptures were dictated by God, and thus were "without error"—a phrase Leo XIII used several times. Pius XII, however, in his *Divino Afflante Spiritu: On Promoting Biblical Studies,* 30 September 1943 ([on-line], accessed 15 July 2001, available from http://www.ewtn.com/library/ ENCYC/P12DIVIN.HTM; Internet), changed the inerrant view of Leo XIII to a limited inerrancy view, where the Bible may contain error of a scientific nature.

[20]While David J. Hesselgrave is clearly an orthodox evangelical, if his words are exaggerated, the importance of human culture can overwhelm the spiritual message: "Missionaries must come to a greater realization of the importance of culture in communicating Christ. . . . But before they can do so effectively, they must study again—not just the language, but also the audience. They must learn before they can teach, and listen before they can speak. They need to know the message for the world, but also the world in which the message must be communicated" (David J. Hesselgrave, *Communicating Christ Cross-Culturally* [Grand Rapids, MI: Zondervan, 1978], 69). While Hesselgrave's words seem obvious and deductive, they subtly undermine the sufficiency of Scriptures. A good thing (cross-cultural communication) undermines a better thing (the power and sufficiency of God's Word—given the people have a Bible in their language). The God side of the equation (the innate power of the Word, the work of the Holy Spirit, and prayer) is ignored in a quest to adequately communicate to the human side—note Hesselgrave's use of the word "must."

[21]"Postmoderns" take the delusion of words one step farther: "On the contrary, it [postmodernism] affirms that through language we create our world and that there are as many differing worlds as world creating languages" (Stanley J. Grenz, *A Primer on Postmodernism* [Grand Rapids: Eerdmans, 1996], 56). In this case words are not absolute, and thus they can convey no absolute meaning. The result regresses to a Zen Buddhist subjectivism: "It is a mistake for people to seek a thing supposed to be good and right, and to flee from another supposed to be bad and evil. Buddha teaches the

tendencies remove authority from the written Word of God.

The Word of God, the Bible, however, is timeless and unchanging. It is "God-breathed" (2 Tim 3:16) and "the sword of the Spirit" (Heb 4:12). Rather than alter the words to make them applicable to a given context, they must be kept as close to the originals as possible for maximum power. Peter answered Christ, "Lord, to whom shall we go? You have *words* of eternal life" (John 6:68).[22] The power for salvation lay in the very words of Christ, not merely in his ideas or example.[23] Therefore, "The *word* of God is living and active" (Hebrews 4:12).[24] The Holy Spirit adds life into His words and He speaks with relevance and authority to the universal needs of mankind.[25] As to the issue of circular reasoning, "the Bible is true because it says it is true," Jesus addressed this issue in dealing with His relationship to His Father in John 5:31 and following. Other credible witnesses that He brought forward were, John the Baptist, Jesus' works, the Father, and Scripture.

In the debate on authority, as in many areas of Christian theology, the discussion may digress into numerous tangential arguments. For example, prior to understanding biblical authority one may debate the Canon of Scripture, the early Ecumenical Councils, or the study of epistemology. Epistemology precludes the study of assumptions, definitions, or methods, leading to the development of a philosophical theology. These debates, however, will be left for other authors to discuss.

Middle Way transcending these prejudiced concepts, where duality merges into oneness" (*The Teaching of Buddha* [Tokyo, Japan: Bukkyo Dendo Kyo Kai (Buddhist Promoting Foundation), 1966], p. 64); or again in the words of Bodhidharma: "A special tradition outside the scriptures, No dependence on words, A direct pointing at man, Seeing into one's own nature and the attainment of wisdom" (Josh McDowell and Don Stewart, *Handbook of Today's Religions* [San Bernardino, CA: Here's Life Publishers, 1983], 318).

[22]The same is true of the "word" of the Samaritan Woman in testifying about Jesus (John 4:39), as well as the word of Christ (John 4:41). Paul stated in Romans 10:17, "So faith comes from hearing, and hearing by the word of Christ."

[23]This idea is buttressed by Jesus' parable of the wise man that built his house upon the rock (Matt 7:24-27; parallel Luke 6:47-49). The rock in this parable is "these words of mine."

[24]The Greek for living is ζωην, also used of God's word in I Peter 1:23. The Greek for active is ενεργης. In Romans 1:16, Paul also added that the Gospel was δυναμις, "the power of God unto salvation."

[25]Billy Graham, "His Unchanging Word in a Changing World," George Paul Butler, ed., *Best Sermons* (New York: T. Y. Crowell Company, 1955), 296: "But, thanks be to God, in the confusion and change of man-made ways and institutions there is the Rock of Ages upon which we can build. God's unchanging Word has through these years met man's most fundamental need."

Our present question is Billy Graham's view of authority, and how that relates to the Bible.

In an interview with Ben Haden, Graham was asked about the legitimacy of Christian students learning about the beliefs of non-evangelical theologians:

> I think we should be acquainted with these men, to keep up with what's going on. But the basis of all our thinking and discussing should be the scriptures themselves. That is our authority. But unfortunately today you quote Tillich or Niebuhr and it has more authority than the scripture itself in the minds of some students. And this is a great tragedy.[26]

Graham's view was that the Bible was to be "our authority" and the "basis for all our thinking and discussing." He vested the Bible with a place of absolute authority. This statement was not just an isolated comment. He often repeated this theme. For example, in the printed *Hour of Decision* sermon number eleven, entitled "Our Bible," Graham stated:

> Many of the listeners to "The Hour of Decision" and attendants of our evangelistic campaign services have often heard me say, "The Bible teaches," or "The Bible reads," or "The Bible explains," and then follow that phrase with an idea found in the Bible. Anyone listening to my preaching, no matter what the particular subject may be, will soon discover that the Bible is the chief source of our preaching evidence. . . . Does the Bible which we believe to be God's Holy Word have anything to say to us in 1952?[27]

Graham expanded on this concept in an article in *Christianity Today* entitled "Biblical Authority in Evangelism." In this article, Graham stated:

> I use the phrase "The Bible says" because the Word of God is the authoritative basis of our faith. I do not continually distinguish between the authority of God and the authority of the Bible because I

---

[26]Ben Haden, "Dr. Graham, Exactly What Is Evangelism?" *Presbyterian Survey* (March 1962): 14-15.

[27]Billy Graham, "Our Bible," *Hour of Decision Sermons,* no. 11 (Minneapolis: Billy Graham Evangelistic Association, 1951): 4-5.

am confident that He has made His will known authoritatively in the Scriptures.[28]

Graham linked the authority of the Bible with the authority of God Himself.[29] William Martin communicated this concept in his insightful and sometimes cynical biography[30] of Billy Graham: "The cornerstone of Graham's theology, of course, was his unshakable belief that the Bible is God's actual Word."[31] When he preached against immorality, Graham affirmed in immutability of the Bible, "God has not changed. What was wrong 2,000 years ago is still wrong today in God's sight."[32] When he preached on the problem of divorce, Graham looked to the Bible:

> It is high time that our so-called experts on marriage, the family and the home turn to the Bible. We have read newspaper columns and listened to counselors on the radio; psychiatrists have had a land office business. In it all the One who performd [sic] the first marriage in the Garden of Eden, and instituted the union between man and woman has been left out.[33]

---

[28]Billy Graham, "Biblical Authority in Evangelism," *Christianity Today,* 15 October 1956, 7.

[29]Stanley High, in his biography of Billy Graham, highlighted this point: "Since, to him, the Bible has Divine authority he preaches it without equivocation or apology" (High, *Billy Graham,* 41).

[30]William Martin in the writing of his *A Prophet with Honor: The Billy Graham Story* (New York: William Morrow, 1991) was given free access to all the information (which was not otherwise specifically restricted by date) in the Billy Graham archives at the Billy Graham Center in Wheaton, Illinois. No other person to date has had this level of access to BGEA information, all of which carries restrictions. With this in mind, as well as his access to interviews, travel, and support, this writer understands why Iain Murray writes of William Martin's biography of Graham: "Martin's book is currently the primary source on Graham's life, being much fuller than the evangelist's own autobiography. Martin was invited to write by Graham but only took the task when he had the assurance that there would be no conditions. For thoroughness of documentation it far exceeds other biographies of Graham" (Iain Murray, *Evangelicalism Divided,* 29, footnote 2).

[31]William Martin, *A Prophet with Honor,* 156.

[32]Billy Graham, "The Bible and Dr. Kinsey," *Hour of Decision Sermons,* no. 31 (Minneapolis: Billy Graham Evangelistic Association, 1953), 9.

[33]Billy Graham, "The Answer to Broken Homes," *Hour of Decision Sermons,* no. 34 (Minneapolis: Billy Graham Evangelistic Association, 1955), 6.

This quote implied that Graham accepted the first verses of Genesis literally[34]—Although he seemed to avoid speaking against the concept of evolution after his Youth for Christ years.[35] He did regularly speak about God as the creator of man and woman in the Garden of Eden.[36]

Graham believed the Word of God to have unseen spiritual power:

> There is a hidden, unseen power in the Word of God that is a mystery to the unbelieving world. It has been my God-given privilege during these few years to witness this power that is in the Word of God. It is awe-inspiring. What we are witnessing in this twentieth century is another experience of the Word of God becoming vocal among men and women of the world.[37]

---

[34]This same is true for his sermons using the illustration of Noah, e.g. "Program for Peace" (*HOD,* no. 10 (Minneapolis: Billy Graham Evangelistic Association, 1951), 9-10).

[35]In his early ministry he spoke plainly about the dangers of Darwinism: "In his book *The Origin of the Species*, Darwin uses more than eight hundred such expressions as 'we infer' and 'we may well suppose.' . . . Evolutionists deny direct creation as taught in the Bible. They deny a personal, creating God" (discussed in six paragraphs or one page; Billy Graham, "America's Hope," Billy Graham, *Calling Youth to Christ* [Grand Rapids: Zondervan, 1947], 21). In 1959 he mentions the name Charles Darwin in a list with Thomas Huxley and Herbert Spencer in his sermon "Christian Philosophy of Education" (*HOD,* no. 113 [Minneapolis: Billy Graham Evangelistic Association, 1959], 2). Yet through most of his ministry he is strangely silent on this issue, especially in sermons like "Gateway to Truth" (written to university students; *HOD,* no. 159 [Minneapolis: Billy Graham Evangelistic Association, 1962]), and "Is God Then Dead?" (*HOD,* no. 160 [Minneapolis: Billy Graham Evangelistic Association, 1966]). Perhaps Graham felt that attacking Darwin would have sounded too fundamentalistic, thereby limiting his potential audience. According to George Marsden, Graham favored something less than absolute inerrancy when it came to the possibility of "a divinely guided development of the species" (George Marsden, *Reforming Fundamentalism: Fuller Seminary and the New Evangelicalism* [Grand Rapids: Eerdmans, 1987], 158-159).

[36]"It was in this same ancient land that God created man and placed him in the Garden of Eden. He created a full-grown human being. . . . Adam was created full grown with every mental and physical faculty developed—the Word of God says so" (Billy Graham, "Position vs. Penalty," *Hour of Decision Sermons,* no. 5 [Minneapolis: Billy Graham Evangelistic Association, 1951], 3-4).

[37]Billy Graham, "His Unchanging Word in a Changing World" (1955), 294.

Graham saw in the Bible an "awe inspiring" power.[38] And because of his view of the Bible's authority, Graham was often accused of being simplistic and literalistic.[39] In fact, Gustave Weigel called Graham's view of biblical authority "mere reflective reading," "autosuggestion," supposition, and "subjective experience." This Jesuit critic of Graham instead found his authority in the "sure guidance and infallible teachings of Christ's one, true Church."[40] Yet Graham remained unshaken in his views on the self-authenticating authority of the Bible.[41] "The Bible says" remained a hallmark of his Gospel proclamation. From a look at authority, we now adjust our focus to a related topic, the inspiration of the Bible.

Five Views of Inspiration

The "five views of inspiration provide a panorama of the variety of views of biblical inspiration. They are: intuition, illumination, dynamic, verbal, and dictation."[42] Behind these views of inspiration enters a more significant issue, the interrelationship of faith and reason, or the God-man interrelationship in inspiration, which extends to virtually every other God-man interaction in theology. Thus Cardinal Ratzinger and the Pontifical Commission on Biblical Interpretation accused evangelicals, called "Fundamentalists,"[43] of being "incapable of accepting the full truth of the

---

[38]"If any one thinks that the air is beaten by an empty sound when the word of God is preached, he is greatly mistaken; for it is a living thing and full of hidden power, which leaves nothing in man untouched" (John Calvin, *Commentary on the Epistle of Paul the Apostle to the Hebrews* [Edinburgh: Calvin Translation Society, 1853; Grand Rapids: Baker, 1996], 98).

[39]Robert Ferm, research assistant to Billy Graham from 1959-1984, wrote, "Some have insisted that his [Graham's] analysis as well as his solution manifests a certain over-simplification" (Robert Ferm, "The Theological Presuppositions of Billy Graham" [unpublished manuscript, n.d.], 3). Note for instance the words of Donald Bloesch, "Considering now the role of the Bible in Graham's preaching, his approach has rightly been criticized as too uncritical and naïve" (Donald Bloesch, "Billy Graham: A Theological Appraisal," *Theology and Life* [1960]: 142).

[40]Gustave Weigel, S.J., "What to Think of Billy Graham," *America*, 4 May 1957, 163, 164.

[41]William Martin wrote of Graham "during these early years . . . he simply delivered this *kerygma* . . . with little attempt at elaboration or defense" (Martin, *A Prophet with Honor*, 155).

[42]Millard Erickson, *Christian Theology*, 206-07.

[43]The Commission defined fundamentalism by the five points of the Niagara Bible Conference of 1895: "Le terme «fondamentaliste» se rattache directement

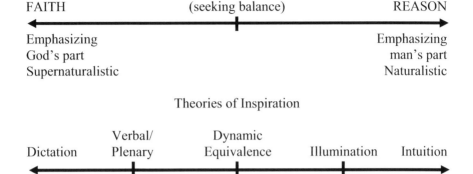

Fig. 1. Faith-Reason Continuum and the Theories of Inspiration.

Incarnation itself." The report continued, "Fundamentalism flees the narrow relationship of the divine and human in its relationship with God."[44] An example of the divine-human interaction is found in cultural anthropology, which speaks of "dynamic equivalence" when the Gospel (God's side or faith) is interrelated to culture (man's side or reason). Charles Arn argues for dynamic equivalence between the Gospel and culture for effective evangelism.[45] Arthur Holmes, who has championed the saying "All truth is

---

au Congrès biblique américain qui s'est tenu à Niagara, dans l'État de New York, en 1895. Les exegetes protestants conservateurs y définir «cinq points de fondamentalisme»: l'inerrance verbale de l'Écriture, la divinité du Christ, sa naissance virginale, la doctrine de l'expiation vicaire et la resurrection corporelle lors de la seconde venue du Christ. . . . Bien que le fondamentalisme ait raison d'insister sur l'inspiration divine de la Bible, l'inerrance de la Parole de Dieu et les autres vérités biblique inclus dans les cinq points fondamentaux, sa façon de presenter ces vérités s'enracine dans une idéologie qui n'est pas biblique, quoi qu'en dissent ses représentants" (Commission biblique pontificale, *L'interprétation de la Bible dans l'Église,* 18-19). Interestingly, Graham calls himself a fundamentalist according to the Niagara 1895 definition: "However, if by fundamentalist you mean a person who accepts the authority of Scriptures, the virgin birth of Christ, the atoning death of Christ, His bodily resurrection, His second coming and personal salvation by grace through faith, then I am a fundamentalist" (High, *Billy Graham,* 56).

[44]Commission biblique pontificale, *L'interprétation de la Bible dans l'Église,* 49, translation mine.

[45]Charles Arn adapted the Great Commission to necessitate cultural accommodation: "The insight is called 'dynamic equivalence.' . . . The concept of 'dynamic equivalence' can be enlarged to identify any communication from one culture to another."(Charles Arn, "A Response to Dr. Rainer: What Is the Key to Effective Evangelism?" *Journal of the American Society for Church Growth,* Vol. 6 [1995]: 75).

God's truth," also corresponds to the need for integration of biblical revelation (faith) and general revelation (reason).[46] Therefore, while the five views of inspiration may at first glance seem to have a narrow application, they provide a stepping stone from which many of the divine-human interactions can be viewed.

The five views of inspiration range from a fully human only approach of inspiration, to a fully God only approach to inspiration (see Figure 1). The middle views take a mediating approach to these extremes. First, "The intuition theory makes inspiration largely a high degree of insight. . . . On this basis, the inspiration of the Scripture writers was essentially no different from that of other great religious and philosophical thinkers, such as Plato, Buddha, and others."[47] Second, the illumination theory acknowledges input from the Holy Spirit in inspiration. However, this illumination does not involve special communication or guidance, but rather an increased sensitivity to perceive the truth. Third, the dynamic theory emphasizes the balance between the divine and human elements in the inspiration of Scripture. This balance is not viewed as one hundred percent/one hundred percent (as in the Incarnation: fully God and fully man), but rather fifty percent/fifty percent. God inspires the concepts, but the choice of words comes from the author. Hence, the dynamic view questions the inspiration of every "jot and tittle" (Matthew 5:18). The fourth view, the verbal theory, maintains that "the influence of the Holy Spirit

---

Repelled [Arn's word] by an emphasis on proclamational or initiative evangelism, Arn rather redefined the Great Commission as nothing more than a restatement of the Great Commandment: "Love is the means of fulfilling the Great Commission" (77). Arn concluded with this manifesto: "The *model* He [Jesus] gave us is love ... the *method* He gave us is love ... the *motive* He gave us is love ... the *message* He gave us is love" (78).

[46]"So we must recognize and respect the value of truth no matter where it is found. We must integrate our understanding of Scripture and theology with what we learn from other sources, relating biblical revelation to general revelation" (Arthur F. Holmes, "Integrating Faith and Learning in a Christian Liberal Arts Institution," David S. Dockery and David P. Gushee, eds., *The Future of Christian Higher Education* [Nashville: Broadman and Holman, 1999], 167). Charles Finney took "all truth is God's truth" one step farther: "True Christian consistency does not consist in stereotyping our opinions and views, and in refusing to make any improvement lest we should be guilty of change, but it consists in holding our minds open to receive the rays of truth from every quarter and in changing our views, and language and practice as often and as fast, as we can obtain further information" (Charles G. Finney, *Lectures on Systematic Theology* (1878; South Gate, CA: Colporter Kemp, 1944), xii.

[47]Erickson, 206. For example, Erasmus, in his *Enchiridion,* wrote, "The divinely inspired Plato wrote of all these things[the primacy of reason over the passions] in his *Timaeus*" (Erasmus of Rotterdam, "*Enchiridion* or The Handbook of the Militant Christian, in *The Essential Erasmus,* John P. Dolan, ed. [New York: New American Library, 1964], 44).

extends beyond the direction of the thoughts to the selection of words used to convey the message."[48] Hence, the verbal theory, similar to plenary inspiration, affirms divine inspiration of every word of Scripture. Lastly, the dictation theory teaches that God dictated every word of Scripture to the authors, thereby circumventing any possibility of human error. These five approaches to inspiration attest to the struggle that has existed in church history to define the doctrine of inspiration, and they portray the variety of methods used to deal with the problem.

An example of the tension is the vacillation of the Roman Catholic Church on the dictation theory (of both Scripture and Tradition), which was approved by the Council of Trent (1546):

> It also perceives that these truths and rules are contained in the written books and in the unwritten traditions, which, received by the Apostles from the mouth of Christ Himself, or from the Apostles themselves, the Holy Ghost dictating, have come down to us, transmitted as it were from hand to hand. Following, then, the examples of the orthodox Fathers, it receives and venerates with a feeling of piety and reverence all the books of the Old and New Testaments, since God is the author of both; also the traditions, whether they relate to faith or morals, as having been dictated either orally by Christ or by the Holy Ghost, and preserved in the Catholic Church in unbroken succession.[49]

Interestingly, the 1994 Pontifical Commission on Biblical Interpretation attacked fundamentalists because they treated the text "as if it were dictated word for word by the Holy Spirit."[50] This contemporary attack portrays the interchange and tension in Christendom between the last three forms of inspiration.[51] It is a struggle between a divine book with divine power given to men through human instruments—dynamic, verbal, or dictation? The struggle continues depending on one's view of the relationship of faith and

---

[48]Ibid., 207.

[49]"The Council of Trent, Fourth Session, Celebrated on the eighth day of April 1546, Decree Concerning the Canonical Scriptures," in John Leith, *Creeds of the Churches,* 402.

[50]"Pour cette raison, il tend à traiter le texte biblique comme s'il avait été dicté mot à mot par l'Esprit et n'arrive pas à reconnaître que la Parole de Dieu a été formulée dans un langage et une phraséologie conditionnés par telle ou telle époque" (Commission Biblical Pontificale, 49, my translation in text).

[51]Davis, who affirms infallibility discounts "any mechanical dictation theory of inspiration" (Davis, 114).

reason.[52] Those who prefer a faith above or prior to reason view often accept the verbal or plenary inspiration of Scripture, leaning toward a dictation theory if necessary to maintain a book that is wholly true. People of faith who place their faith equal to or under the authority of reason often prefer the dynamic view of inspiration or perhaps even the illumination view. The concepts of faith and reason, the inspiration of Scripture, and the authority of Scripture are all interrelated as in an intellectual chain, falling along a faith-reason continuum.

Graham's view of authority has already been noted as falling toward the faith side of the continuum. As to his view on inspiration, Graham wrote:

> If the evangelist is to "preach the Word" (2 Timothy 4:2) with authority and power, he must be convinced of two things.
>
> First, he must be convinced that the Bible, the written Word of God, was prepared under the direction of the Holy Spirit, who preserved the authors from departing from God's revelation in their writing so that they conveyed exactly what God wanted them to record. . . .
>
> Because it is God's inspired Word, the Bible does not contradict itself or teach falsehoods—because God cannot lie.[53]

In Graham's writing, the problem is not with the author or the Bible; the problem is with the recipient of the message. Thus he continued, "With our human limitations we may not always understand every detail of Scripture, but we must never lose sight of the fact that it is God's Word and not man's ideas or opinions."[54] In his *The Holy Spirit*, Graham quoted the Southern Baptist founder of Southwestern Baptist Theological Seminary, B. H. Carroll, to explain his view of plenary inspiration:

> In other words, with reference to the Scriptures, inspiration is plenary, which means full and complete, hence my question is, "Do

---

[52]Interestingly, the interplay between faith and reason was central in Martin Luther's disagreement with the Roman Catholic church. He wrote, "What if the philosophers do not grasp it? The Holy Spirit is greater than Aristotle. . . . Though philosophy cannot grasp it, yet faith can. The authority of the word of God goes beyond the capacity of our mind" (Martin Luther, "Pagan Servitude of the Church," John Dillenberger, ed., *Martin Luther: Selections from His Writings* [Garden City, NY: Doubleday, 1961], 270).

[53]Billy Graham, *A Biblical Standard for Evangelists* (Minneapolis: World Wide Publications, 1984), 18-19.

[54]Ibid., 19.

you believe in the plenary inspiration of the Bible?" If the inspiration is complete, it must be plenary.

My next question is this: "Do you believe in plenary verbal inspiration?"

I do, for the simple reason that the words are mere signs of ideas, and I do not know how to get to the idea except through the words.[55]

Prior to this quote, Graham made a comment using the first person plural to refer to himself: "When we speak of *total* (or *plenary*) *inspiration* of the Bible, we mean that all the Bible, not just some parts of it are inspired."[56] Hence, Graham quoted Carroll because he agreed with him at this point. From the quote of Carroll, we note that the concepts plenary inspiration and verbal inspiration are almost synonymous.[57] Graham confirmed the importance of plenary inspiration in an interview with Stanley Rowland, Jr., religious writer for the *New York Times*, prior to his famous 1957 New York crusade:

"Suppose I take this Bible and say there're parts of it—let's suppose this—that are not inspired of God, that are not authoritative. All right, then I become the judge and I sit up and say, 'Well, this page is no good, I'll rip that one out.'" He tore one hand through the air above his open Bible. "'I can't accept that.' Then I turn over here and I rip another one out. * * * [sic] And after a while I have ten million different kinds of Bibles because one scholar says this and one scholar says that and one scholar says another, until after a while, I have no authority."[58]

Therefore, to Graham, the entire Bible was authoritative and this authority was indispensably necessary for effective Christian preaching.[59]

---

[55]Billy Graham, *The Holy Spirit: Here Is the Power to Change Your Life,* Crusade Edition (New York: Warner Books, 1980), 61. He quoted B. H. Carroll, *Inspiration of the Bible* (New York: Fleming H. Revell, 1930), 54ff.

[56]Ibid., 60.

[57]The concept of plenary inspiration affirms that the entirety of the canon of Scripture is inspired. The concept of verbal inspiration affirms that every word of the Bible is inspired.

[58]Stanley Rowland, Jr. "As Billy Graham Sees His Role," *New York Times*, 21 April 1957, 22-23.

[59]This was the main thrust of his *Christianity Today* article, "Biblical Authority in Evangelism," 7.

Graham, while he accepted verbal inspiration, did not accept the dictation theory for the entire Bible:

> Competent scholars agree that the Holy Spirit did not merely use the biblical writers as secretaries to whom He dictated the Scriptures, although some sincere Christians think He did this. The Bible itself does not state in detail just *how* the Holy Spirit accomplished His purpose in getting the Scripture written. However, we do know that He used living human minds and guided their thoughts according to His divine purposes. Moreover, it has always been clear to me that we cannot have inspired ideas without inspired words.[60]

Thus Graham affirmed verbal or plenary inspiration. A discussion of inspiration leads to a discussion of biblical authority.

Seven Views of Biblical Authority

There are seven views of biblical authority, which correspond somewhat to the five views of inspiration. It is obvious that distinctions in the authority of the Bible are only important to those who have a level of belief in the Bible. In the 1950s to 1970s, the term "inerrancy" became a watchword for evangelical orthodoxy (prior to this time the word "infallible" was sufficient to express absolute authority).[61] Evangelical schools included "inerrancy" in their statements of faith, and the hiring of faculty at these institutions was predicated on a belief in inerrancy.[62] Thus,

---

[60]Graham, *The Holy Spirit,* 60.

[61]This is the approach of Davis, "I regard the Bible as the word of God. . . . But it is also the words of human beings. . . . The Bible is infallible, as I define that term, but not inerrant. That is, there are historical and scientific errors in the Bible, but I have found none on matters of faith and practice" (Stephen T. Davis, *The Debate about the Bible,* 114-15). Davis' approach is not new, Warfield describes a similar approach among nineteenth century rationalists: "In the nineteenth century it has retained a strong hold, especially upon apologetic writers, chiefly in the three forms which affirm respectively that only the *mysteries* of the faith are inspired, i.e. things undiscoverable by unaided reason,—that the Bible is inspired only in *matters of faith and practice,*—and that the Bible is inspired only in its *thoughts or concepts,* not in its words" (Warfield, *The Inspiration and Authority of the Bible,* 112-13).

[62]For example, Iain Murray noted that J. Ramsey Michaels of Gordon-Conwell Seminary was terminated following the authorship of a book which did not conform with the Bible being free from error. Yet he could still say, "The issue is not inerrancy: we agree on that" (Murray, *Evangelicalism Divided,* 191, footnote 4). Trinity

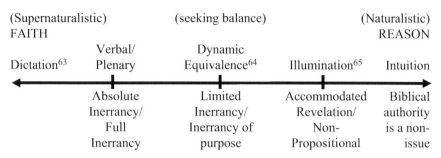

Fig. 2. Seven Views of Biblical Authority. [66]

by the time Millard Erickson began publishing his *Christian Theology* (1983), the term inerrancy had undergone considerable revision.[67] Erickson described four levels of inerrancy and three other levels of biblical authority. They are as follows: absolute inerrancy, full inerrancy, limited inerrancy, inerrancy of purpose, accommodated revelation, non-

---

Evangelical Divinity School has "inerrancy" in their statement of faith, as does Wheaton College. The Evangelical Theological Society requires its members to suscribe in writing on an annual basis to its doctrinal position, which reads: "The Bible alone and the Bible in its entirety, is the Word of God written, and therefore inerrant in the autographs. God is a Trinity, Father, Son, and Holy Spirit, each an uncreated person, one in essence, equal in power and glory" ("doctrinal basis" [on-line]; accessed 15 February 2001; available from http://www.etsjets.org/; Internet).

[63]Dictation was affirmed by the Council of Trent (1546) and by Leo XIII, *Providentissimus Deus*, 18 November 1893.

[64]Position expressed by Pius XII, *Divino Afflante Spiritu,* 30 September 1943.

[65]Position of the Pontifical Commission on Biblical Interpretation (1993).

[66]Terms for inerrancy come from Erickson, *Christian Theology,* 222-24.

[67]Stephen Davis wrote "[Daniel] Fuller is quite prepared to say that the Bible is inerrant, but he does not mean the same thing by this that [Harold] Lindsell does" (Stephen Davis, *The Debate About the Bible,* 38). Erickson defined limited inerrancy as inerrant in faith and practice (Erickson, 222). He refered to inerrancy of purpose to mean that the Bible clearly communicates its purpose, "to bring people into personal fellowship with Christ" (ibid., 223). Both of these were described by Warfield in the prior footnote! These views fall under the category of infallibility as described above. The use of these adjectives or prepositional phrases to the term inerrancy shows that in the late twentieth century inerrancy became a popular belief among evangelicals. Thus, to continue teaching at evangelical institutions and to sign their inerrancy statements of faith, some theologians sensed the need to expand on the meaning of inerrancy.

propositional revelation, and inerrancy is irrelevant. For clarification Figure 2 attempts to place the positions on biblical authority along the faith-reason continuum. The complexity of placing the various views on a figure increases when it is noted that changes are continually taking place. However, the lines of demarcation are fairly clear. The issue of biblical authority lies somewhere between a completely supernatural revelation and seeking a dynamic balance. Once the unique, supernatural authority of the Bible is replaced with some type of dynamic equivalence of inspiration between God and man, an array of intermediate definitions become plausible. The Bible then loses its absolute authority, and one is left with the interpretations of men. This is exactly what Graham wanted to avoid in his interview cited above with *New York Times* religion writer Stanley Rowland, Jr.: "And after a while I have ten million different kinds of Bibles because one scholar says this and one scholar says that and one scholar says another, until after a while, I have no authority."[68] Graham held to plenary inspiration, and he held to verbal inspiration. It naturally follows that he held to full or absolute inerrancy. He admonished evangelists in this way:

> Don't let anything or anyone shake your confidence in the trustworthiness, authority, and power of the Bible. Make it your guide for your life and your ministry, no matter what the future may hold for you.[69]

Then he shared his oft-mentioned testimony:

> At one time in my life I had a struggle believing the Bible as the authoritative Word of God. Some professors and other intellectuals were expressing their own doubts about it and pointing out alleged contradictions in the Bible. . . . Finally, I laid open my Bible on the stump of a tree and prayed, "Oh, Lord, I don't understand everything in this Book, but I accept it by faith as the Word of the living God." . . .
>
> Since that time I have discovered that we need not fear the allegations or arguments of those who would deny the Bible's authority. There is external and internal evidence which shows the absolute trustworthiness of the Bible.[70]

---

[68]Stanley Rowland, Jr. "As Billy Graham Sees His Role," *New York Times,* 21 April 1957, 22-23.

[69]Billy Graham, *A Biblical Standard for Evangelists,* 19.

[70]Ibid., 19-20.

In a 1955 sermon titled "His Unchanging Word in a Changing World," Graham ended with strong words about the Bible's authority, quoting the often-used words of John Locke (1632-1704) with regard to error in the Bible:

> The Bible is more than a book of religion; it is more than a book on the philosophy of religion; it is more than a collection of devotions or of rules for good living. It is all of these, but it is so much more. It is the living Word of the Living God, offering to men who are dead in their trespasses and sins new life through Jesus Christ.
>
> The English philosopher John Locke once said of the Bible: "It has God for its author, salvation for its end and truth without any admixture of error for its matter. It is all pure, all sincere; nothing too much, nothing wanting."[71]

This sounds very much like the language of full inerrancy.[72] Yet, not only does Graham avoid using the term, but the statement of faith of his association did not use inerrancy either. Rather it used the word "infallibility"—which is now often associated with limited inerrancy or inerrancy of purpose.[73] True, since the founding of the BGEA in 1950 the term infallibility has undergone a significant change of meaning. But why has not Billy Graham kept up with the times and changed to use the word "inerrancy"?

The answer might be found in the debate over inerrancy during Billy Graham's years in the ministry. Millard Erickson explained that the

---

[71]Billy Graham, "His Unchanging Word in a Changing World," 298. A similar statement was quoted in "A Word for the Bible" (*The Columbian Star,* 29 April 1826, 1), "Tell them with *Locke,* that profound reasoner, 'The Gospel has God for its author, salvation for its end, and truth, without any mixture of errour, for its matter.'"

[72] Stanley High (who went to great pains to show that Graham was not a rigid fundamental literalist) wrote: "Inside these covers [of the Bible], on these printed pages are guides and signposts to all of man's deepest needs. That is not what I suppose to be true. That is what, in the actual lives of actual people, I have seen to be true. That is why I can open this book in front of you or before an audience and say, 'This is the Word of God'" (High, 40).

[73]The Billy Graham Evangelistic Association believes, "The Bible to be the infallible Word of God, that it is His holy and inspired Word, and that it is of supreme and final authority" (Billy Graham Evangelistic Association, "About Us" [on-line]; accessed 15 February 2001; available from http://www.billygraham.org/about/statementoffaith.asp; Internet). See Appendix 5 for the complete BGEA Statement of Faith. The National Association of Evangelicals (NAE) Statement of Faith also uses "infallible."

concept of inerrancy had gained a polemic tone. When speaking of the view of David Hubbard, he stated:

> Finally, this issue [inerrancy] is harmful to the church. It creates disunity among those who otherwise have a great deal in common. It makes a major issue out of what should be a minor matter at most.[74]

Erickson footnoted a chapter by David Hubbard, "The Current Tensions: Is There a Way Out?" in Jack Rogers' *Biblical Authority*.[75] David Hubbard, president of Fuller Theological Seminary, Pasadena, California (1963-1993;—where Billy Graham was a Board Member since 1958),[76] emphasized the polemic tone of Francis Turretin in the seventeenth century:

> One of the ways in which the seventeenth-century theologians defended the plenary inspiration of Scripture was to insist that if the inspiration of any part of the Bible were in doubt, the inspiration of the whole would be put in question. This "all or nothing" approach to biblical authority has considerable bearing on the present debate. In the Calvinist wing of the church, Francis Turretin took a similar approach. His influence, which reaches to the present evangelical discussion, is sketched in Jack Roger's essay in this volume.[77]

Many scholars of the infallibility persuasion attribute the concept of inerrancy to B. B. Warfield and Scottish Common Sense Realism.[78] It is

---

[74]Millard Erickson, *Christian Theology,* 224.

[75] Jack Rogers, ed. *Biblical Authority* (Waco, TX: Word, 1977).

[76] Iain Murray, *Evangelicalism Divided,* 25, "Ockenga was to become one of its directors while Graham became a Board member at Fuller."

[77]David Hubbard, "The Current Tensions: Is There a Way Out?" in Jack Rogers' *Biblical Authority* (Waco, TX: Word, 1977), 154. Jack Roger's essay was so popular in its historical analysis of the inerrancy issue that he published an entire book on the subject (Jack B. Rogers and Donald K. McKim, *The Authority and Interpretation of the Bible: An Historical Approach* [New York: Harper and Row, 1979]). Three years later, John D. Woodbridge of Trinity Evangelical Divinity School responded with *Biblical Authority: A Critique of the Rogers/McKim Proposal* (Grand Rapids: Zondervan, 1982). In the foreword Kenneth Kantzer wrote, "the battle over the Bible and its authority is worth fighting" (John Woordbridge, *Biblical Authority,* 7). Woodbridge summarizes the main problem with the Rogers/McKim proposal in this way: "They have a penchant for not citing primary evidence that counters their hypothesis and for minimizing the value of scholarly works that countermand their conclusions" (ibid., 24).

[78]Hence Richard J. Mouw wrote of the problem of "doctrinalism": "Certain twentieth century Protestants have placed strong emphasis on the importance of

clear from scholars such as Woodbridge that one can look at any age in Church history and find those who would uphold a concept identical to full inerrancy. It would seem that the doctrine should not be ascribed to man's imagination, but rather to the pages of the Bible itself.[79]

This short contemporary survey of the debate over inerrancy and the polemic nature of the term, along with the introductory material of this chapter on the debate over the Bible among Southern Baptists, show that this issue was a heated debate during the ministry of Billy Graham. The answer to the above question seems to be: Graham has not used the term inerrancy in order to avoid getting embroiled in the debate himself. He was rather happy to have theologians fight that battle. Whether this approach was right is not the issue at hand. As an evangelist, Graham felt that his role was very clearly defined: "The evangelist is not called to do *everything* in the church or in the world that God wants done. On the contrary, the calling of the evangelist is very specific."[80]

Yet there are several problems with this disclaimer. First, as a board member of both Wheaton College and Fuller Theological Seminary, Graham did have an administrative duty. Second, as a member of First Baptist Church, Dallas, Graham had a responsibility to the Southern Baptist Convention during their years of turmoil. Of the latter, Graham may have exerted some influence during the 1985 Convention, as noted above. Yet of the former, it is more difficult to ascertain his position. Marsden pointed out that the 1955 Graham showed appreciation for Bernard Ramm's *The Christian View of Science and Scripture* "in which he [Ramm] challenged the fundamentalist assumption that a high view of biblical inspiration implied that the Bible was a reliable source of scientific data."[81] Further, Graham wrote Harold Lindsell that they should seek a middle of the road position in their founding of *Christianity Today*.[82] Later, at a critical

---

doctrine, and on having the right kinds of doctrinal beliefs. . . . Similarities to the Old Princetonian doctrinalism of Hodge and Warfield can be found in twentieth-century fundamentalism, among other places" (Richard J. Mouw, "The Bible in Twentieth Century Protestantism," Nathan O. Hatch and Mark A. Noll, eds., *The Bible in America: Essays in Cultural History* [New York: Oxford, 1982], 142-43).

[79]See Wayne A. Grudem, "Scripture's Self-Attestation and the Problem of Formulating a Doctrine of Scripture," D. A. Carson and John D. Woodbridge, eds., *Scripture and Truth* (Grand Rapids: Zondervan, 1983), 19-59.

[80]Billy Graham, *Just As I Am* (New York: Harper Collins, 1997), xv.

[81]George Marsden, *Reforming Fundamentalism: Fuller Seminary and the New Evangelicalism,* 158.

[82]"The new periodical, as Graham envisioned it, would 'plant the evangelical flag in the middle of the road, taking a conservative theological position but a definite liberal approach to social problems. It would combine the best in liberalism

juncture in Fuller's choice of a new president in 1963, although Graham favored Harold Ockenga as a resident president, he seemed to be open to the leadership of the limited inerrantist David Hubbard. Hubbard is purported to have lead Fuller more quickly down the path of dynamic equivalence.[83] Nevertheless, Graham's attempts to maintain a spirit of inerrancy are noted by the appointment of Harold Lindsell, author of *Battle for the Bible* (1976), as editor of *Christianity Today* from 1968 to 1978.

Graham seems to have understood his specific role as an evangelist to avoid alienating listeners who could come under the hearing of the Gospel—outside of which there is no salvation. He would cooperate with anyone who would cooperate with him, with the understanding that he would not change the Gospel no matter who was present:

> My own position was that we should be willing to work with all who were willing to work with us. Our message was clear, and if someone with a radically different theological view somehow decided to join with us in a Crusade that proclaimed Christ as the way of salvation, he or she was the one who was compromising personal convictions, not we.[84]

While Graham's message of the Gospel remained unchanged, the illustrations he used in his messages did change.[85] Also, Graham made commitments to avoid critical speech of other religious traditions:

---

and the best in fundamentalism without compromising theologically'" ("Billy Graham to Harold Lindsell," 25 January 1955, quoted in George Marsden, *Reforming Fundamentalism: Fuller Seminary and the New Evangelicalism*, 158).

[83]Iain Murray follows the influences of Edward Carnell, president of Fuller Theological Seminary, David Hubbard, and Daniel Fuller in his *Evangelicalism Divided*, 187-91.

[84]Billy Graham, *Just As I Am*, 303-04. The exception to this statement regards cults or unacceptable churches, proving that the BGEA had an unpublished criteria for cooperation. David P. Bruce explained the existence of such in his D.Min. Research project: "Those who have no church background, who were not brought by church people, and have absolutely no affiliation with a local body of Christ, or who may have listed a cult or unacceptable church, are referred to the Designation Committee made of local pastors from the entire geographical area" (David Phillips Bruce, "A Program to Evaluate the Effectiveness of the Follow-Up Activity of the Spokane, Washington, Billy Graham Crusade" (D.Min. Thesis, The Southern Baptist Theological Seminary, 1986), 58). Bruce never expanded on who was considered a cult or unacceptable church. In all likelihood, they would allow the local sponsors of the church to make the final decisions on this.

[85]William Martin reports that Graham wrote President Truman to encourage his attendance at the January 1952 Washington, DC, crusade: "You may be

Opposition also came from a few in the Roman Catholic and Jewish communities, although I had made it clear I was not going to New York to speak against other traditions or to proselytize people away from them. My goal instead was to preach the Gospel of Jesus Christ as it was presented in the Bible and to call men and women to commit their lives to Him.[86]

Thus Graham's policy of avoiding alienating others to maintain the maximum audience, when applied to use of the term inerrancy, led him to remain aloof of the debate.[87]

While inerrancy was a major issue in the history of Fuller Theological Seminary's change from fundamentalist to neo-evangelical, another issue parallels the issue of biblical authority. The interpretation of the Bible is the practical application of biblical authority, much like evangelism is the practical outflow of belief in the fundamentals of the faith.

Biblical Interpretation

Graham's method of interpretation of the Bible followed the straightforward way that he preached the word. He upheld the plain meaning of the text of Scripture. This approach was confirmed in Robert Ferm's unpublished manuscript, "The Theological Presuppositions of Billy Graham": "Attention must be given to the fact that the Gospel as proclaimed by Billy Graham is a straight-line deduction from the words of Scripture."[88] And this hermeneutic was exactly what the critics called simplistic and literalistic. To them, more complex types of interpretation must be placed on the Scriptures. The Pontifical Commission on Biblical Interpretation attacked the fundamentalist interpretation, as it does not take into account the problems associated with the text of the Bible.[89] Donald Bloesch contended that Graham "seems to be oblivious to the higher criticism of the Bible."[90] Thus Graham, from his early ministry, followed the historic

---

interested to know that I have refused to comment on the Vatican appointment because I didn't want to be put into a position of opposing you" (William Martin, *A Prophet with Honor,* 144). This will be elaborated further in Chapter 5.

[86]Billy Graham, *Just As I Am,* 301.

[87]Robert Evans called this approach the "Tactical Graham" (Robert Evans, telephone interview by author, July 2, 2001).

[88]Ferm, "Theological Presuppositions of Billy Graham," 6.

[89]Commission biblique pontificale, 49.

[90]Bloesch, "Billy Graham: A Theological Appraisal," 142.

Protestant interpretive methodology, which Stephen Neill called "philological, historical, exegetical, and doctrinal,"[91] Bernard Ramm called "Literal, Cultural, and Critical,"[92] and Walter Kaiser called "historical, grammatical, contextual, and critical" or likewise "The Single Meaning of the Text."[93] Similarly, like Martin Luther, Graham sought the plain meaning of the text.[94] However, some theologians did not agree with Graham's emphasis on instantaneous conversion, nor his inside-out approach to solving social problems, so they attacked him as wrongly interpreting Scriptures.

For example, Gustave Weigel faulted Graham's method of interpretation:

> The nearest thing to an argument shooting through all his [Graham's] sermons is his phrase: "The Bible says." This may well be an irrelevant fact rather than an argument. Manifestly Graham knows the *material* expressions of the Bible very well. He uses every book of it in his preachments. He can no doubt tell us what the Bible says; but can he really tell us what the Bible means? That is the question.[95]

---

[91]This method Neill ascribed to the Cambridge Three—Lightfoot, Westcott, and Hort (Stephen Neill and Tom Wright, *The Interpretation of the New Testament: 1861-1986* [Oxford: University Press, 1988], 37). Later he wrote of the impact of Lightfoot as he counteracted the methods of F. C. Baur, "This significance of the work of Lightfoot was at once and generally recognized in England. Bishop A. C. Headlam, no mean authority, affirms that Lightfoot had accomplished exactly what he set out to do; he had brought the study of Christian antiquity back from the realms of theory and fantasy to the sober realities of genuinely critical investigation" (ibid., 60).

[92]Bernard Ramm, *Protestant Biblical Interpretation* (Boston: W. A. Wilde, 1956), 89.

[93]Walter C. Kaiser, *Toward an Exegetical Theology: Biblical Exegesis for Preaching and Teaching* (Grand Rapids: Baker, 1981), 18, 24. To make his point, Kaiser cited the Puritan William Ames, "There is only one meaning for every place in Scripture. Otherwise the meaning of Scripture would be unclear and uncertain, but there would be no meaning at all—for anything which does not mean one thing surely means nothing" (William Ames, *The Marrow of Theology* [Grand Rapids: Baker, 1968], 188). The goal of exegesis to Kaiser is "the author's intended meaning" (Kaiser, *Toward an Exegetical Theology,* 47).

[94]"First, that the word of God does not need to be forced in any way by either men or angels. Rather its plainest meanings are to be preserved; and, unless the context manifestly compels one to do otherwise, the words are not to be understood apart from their proper and literal sense, lest occasion be given to our adversaries to evade Scripture as a whole" (Martin Luther, "Pagan Servitude of the Church," 266).

[95]Gustave Weigel, S.J., "What to Think of Billy Graham," 162.

To Weigel, the Bible had no clear message outside of a Roman Catholic interpretive scheme—the Bible needed the Traditions of the church in order to be rightly interpreted. Because Graham did not interpret according to a chosen set of Roman Catholic Traditions, Weigel did not appreciate his biblical interpretation.

It is interesting to note, however, that Stanley High's biography of Graham painted a Graham who was distancing himself from fundamentalism. In so doing, High noted change in Graham's method of biblical interpretation:

> There has been, too, a considerable change which extreme fundamentalists may regard as a dangerous deviationism in the specifics of Billy Graham's literalism. He is as sure as ever about the reality of Heaven and Hell, for example, but less sure about the literalists' blueprint of them.[96]

Whether this is a change in biblical interpretation or a change in communication strategy, it is unclear. However, as has been noted above with the issues of Darwinism or inerrancy, Graham seems to have avoided topics and language that detracted from his declaring the simple Gospel to his hearers. High's comments do show that there was a shift in the approach of Graham that took place early in his ministry.

Therefore, while Graham's method of biblical interpretation followed along the supernaturalistic lines of his views on biblical authority, his communication of the Bible showed changes in topics that could be potentially divisive. This corresponds with many of the attacks he received from conservatives that his theology had changed.[97] We now turn to one last point under the rubric of biblical authority—the relation of biblical authority to evangelism.

Biblical Authority and the Focus of Evangelism

Paige Patterson in his overview of the conservative resurgence among the Southern Baptists noted the inter-relationship of inerrancy and evangelism:

---

[96]High, *Billy Graham,* 63. Graham's approach to the doctrine of hell is discussed in Chapter 4.

[97]For example, Brad Gsell wrote, "The decade of the '50s saw him [Graham] change into a compromising evangelical, forcing many of his former friends and admirers to diassociate from him" (Brad K. Gsell, *The Legacy of Billy Graham: The Accommodation of Truth to Error in the Evangelical Church* [Charlotte, NC: Fundamental Presbyterian Publications, 1996], v).

We did not, in the final analysis, attempt a reformation movement because we thought it would succeed but because we sincerely believed that we were right about the inerrancy of the Bible and because we didn't want to tell our children and grandchildren that we had no courage to live by our convictions. Above all, the conviction that the continued drift of the Southern Baptist Convention could spell eternal doom for hundreds of thousands of people was the principal compelling motivation.

. . . The goal was to keep the denomination close to a reliable Bible for the sake of evangelistic and missionary outreach.[98]

Arthur P. Johnston agreed with this assessment of Patterson. Johnston noted the setting aside of theological orthodoxy by the International Missionary Councils and the World Council of Churches, and the ensuing shift from evangelism:

The real problem is still the same one that confronted evangelicals in the nineteenth century and the one especially influential in watering down evangelism seventy-five years ago. Are the Scriptures, the Bible, *the* Word of God or not! Are Christians to live under the authority of the Bible or under the authority of a Church or a council of churches? These two questions are linked together.

What a man or a Church thinks about the Bible makes a big difference in what he thinks about the teachings of the Bible: the inspiration and authority of the Bible directly influence how one views the deity of Christ, the sin of man, the death of Christ for sinners, the second coming of Christ, and the teaching of the Scriptures on eternal punishment of the unbelieving, unrepentant sinner.[99]

Billy Graham concurred with the important role of an authoritative Bible in a 1962 interview by Ben Haden:

[Haden] "Do you believe that a person or church is likely to be evangelistic if the Bible is not accepted in full as the inspired word of God?"

[Graham] "Well, that is a difficult question. There are many views of inspiration. Many people will say they believe in the inspiration of the Bible. But when you get down to it, they are in

---

[98]Paige Patterson, "The Anatomy of a Reformation," 5, 9.

[99]Arthur P. Johnston, *World Evangelism and the Word of God*, 251.

disagreement with each other over the method of inspiration and what we mean by inspiration.

"I don't think we want to go into that at this moment. But I think that the person who accepts the scriptures as his authority has a far greater passion for evangelism. He also has far greater possibilities and potential in evangelism, because God uses the Word. Jeremiah said that he used it as a "hammer." It is the quoted Word, I have found, that accomplishes far more than my thoughts about the scriptures, "

[Haden] "You mean actually quoting scripture. . . ?"

[Graham] "Yes, just actually quoting scripture. That has its own impact on the human heart."[100]

The Bible has a supernatural power to transform lives from the inside out. Wolfhart Pannenberg affirmed this inside-out impact when he discussed the relationship of accommodation, theological conservatism, and true social impact:

It has frequently been noted that the mainline and accommodating churches are in decline, while conservative churches continue to grow. Evangelicals and fundamentalists are not embarrassed to challenge the prevailing patterns of thought and behavior associated with secularity. This growth, however, does not come without paying a price. That price includes a loss of openness to the human situation in all of its maddening variety, and a quenching of the unprejudiced search for truth. *That said, the irony is that those churches that are dismissed as irrelevant by more "sophisticated" Christians often turn out to be most relevant to our secular societies.*[101]

"Mainline and accommodating" churches[102] were stated to be *less socially relevant* than "evangelical and fundamentalist" churches—now that was a turn of the tables! Two points characterize each group: mainline and accommodating churches dismiss inerrancy and practice social action; evangelical and fundamental churches affirm inerrancy and practice evangelism. When biblical authority is blunted, the urgent task of world evangelism is extinguished (as churches seek social relevance), with the

---

[100]Ben Haden, "Dr, Graham, Exactly What Is Evangelism?" 14.

[101]Wolfhart Pannenberg, "The Present and Future Church," *First Things,* November 1991, 48-51 (emphasis mine). Pannenberg was Professor of Systematic Theology on the Protestant Theological Faculty at the University of Munich, Germany.

[102]These were the churches from which came Reinhold Niebuhr, Martin Marty, and Donald Bloesch—who accused Graham of social irrelevance.

ensuing result of social irrelevance. Thus, not only is the work of evangelism directly related to biblical authority, biblical authority (full inerrancy) and evangelism are necessary for real impact.

Graham held a practical belief in inerrancy. However, he used the term infallibility to assuage less conservative audiences. His practical belief in the inerrancy of Scripture led Graham to preach the Gospel for over sixty-five years. In the next chapter we will discuss the essence of the message of Billy Graham, and note some of the changes that may have taken place in that message.

CHAPTER 3

PARAMETERS

Today, the world church is not sure what evangelism is, and often the gift of the evangelist is neglected—evangelism is not taught in many of our Bible schools and seminaries. Today we have scores of definitions of what evangelism is, and what an evangelist is. Some think of evangelism simply in terms of getting more people to join the church. Others define evangelism as attempting to change the structures of society.

Unless we believe in a future judgment, or that people are lost without Christ then the cutting edge of evangelism is blunted.[1]

Introduction

Three young evangelists joined Torrey Johnson when he founded Youth for Christ, International (YFC). Bob Pierce, who would later found World Vision International (WVI) and Samaritan's Purse, was one of these young evangelists.[2] Charles Templeton, who would later become the first full-time evangelist hired by the National Council of Churches, was a vice president.[3] Billy Graham, who later founded the Billy Graham Evangelistic Association (BGEA), was the first vice president of YFC, and later its first full-time evangelist.[4] All three of these men were evangelists within the youth movement that was spreading across the United States and around the world.

---

[1]Billy Graham, "The Gift and Calling of the Evangelist," in *The Calling of an Evangelist: Second International Conference for Itinerant Evangelists, Amsterdam, The Netherlands* (Minneapolis: World Wide, 1987), 15-16.

[2]Franklin Graham and Jeannette Lockerbie, *Bob Pierce: This One Thing I Do* (Dallas: Word, 1983), 13, 14, 17.

[3]Charles Templeton, *Farewell to God: My Reasons for Rejecting the Christian Faith* (Toronto: McClelland and Stewart, 1996), 4.

[4]Billy Graham, *Just As I Am* (New York: HarperCollins Publishers, 1997), 92-94.

The three had the common bond of mass evangelism as promoted by Torrey Johnson.[5] Johnson passed on the vision of world evangelization through the fulfillment of the Great Commission in their generation. They were committed to a fundamentalist reading of the Bible as infallible (or, as presently understood, inerrant). They all believed in the power of the gospel and in crusade evangelism. Templeton, Pierce, and Graham all believed in instantaneous conversion. Yet something happened to each of these men to cause each to take significantly different roads.

With the luxury of fifty years of hindsight, it is easy to see that all three of these young evangelists took different roads in their definition of evangelism. Thus, the result of their lives of ministry has ended quite differently. To introduce the important topic of a definition of evangelism, the life and writings of Templeton, Pierce, and Graham will be noted, as well as their different approaches to evangelism. We begin by looking at Charles Templeton.

Charles Templeton

In 1946 Charles Templeton, Billy Graham, and three others joined the founder of YFC, Torrey Johnson, for a two-month evangelistic trip to post-World War II Europe. The six left on March 18, 1946, less than one year after Germany surrendered to the Allied forces—signing a surrender in Rheims on May 7, 1945. The six split up into two teams and made stops in numerous cities in England and western Europe. Templeton was the main speaker for one team and Graham for the other. Templeton recalled, "Billy and I would alternate in the pulpit."[6] Graham called Templeton "my partner in preaching."[7] However, in 1948 Templeton enrolled at Princeton Theological Seminary.[8] Graham stated that "he was undergoing serious theological difficulties, particularly concerning the authority of Scriptures."[9] He shared with Graham the arguments that made

---

[5]For further information on the life and ministry of Torrey Johnson, see Torrey Johnson and Robert Cook, *Reaching Youth for Christ* (Chicago: Moody, 1944), Melvin Gunnard Larson, *Young Man on Fire: The Story of Torrey Johnson and Youth for Christ* (Chicago: Youth for Christ, 1945), and Melvin G. Larson, *Youth for Christ: Twentieth Century Wonder,* introduction by Percy Crawford (Grand Rapids: Zondervan, 1947).

[6]Templeton, *Farewell to God,* 4.

[7]Billy Graham, *Just As I Am,* 135.

[8]Templeton, *Farewell to God,* 6.

[9]Ibid.

him doubt the veracity of Scriptures. Then Templeton was appointed as a full-time evangelist to do "preaching missions" with the National Council of Churches (NCC) following his studies at Princeton.[10] But his theology did not undergird the methodology of crusade evangelism. Templeton wrote, "How does a man who, each night, tells ten to twenty thousand people how to find faith confess that he is struggling with his own?"[11] After several years he resigned from the NCC and became the Director of Evangelism for the Presbyterian Church U.S.A. Then in 1956 he resigned that post and returned to Toronto, entering the field of journalism. He became executive managing editor of the *Toronto Star,* editor-in-chief of *Maclean's* magazine, and director of News and Public Affairs for the CTV television network.

Late in his life, Templeton wrote in *Farewell to God* that he no longer believed in God. He now appealed to rationalism, rather than primitive faith in revealed truth.[12] In addition to rejecting the biblical concept of God, Templeton posited the plurality of gods with the number of followers of world religions as proof that the Bible cannot be exclusive in its claim to have the truth about God. In the remainder of *Farewell to God,* Templeton went on to debunk key Christian doctrines, Bible stories, and beliefs. Prior to his concluding chapter he wrote a section entitled "Giving Up One's Faith in God." In this section he shared his testimony of "a soaring sense of freedom" when he made the decision to irrevocably give up belief in God.[13] His conclusion raised the example of Albert Schweizer who presumably taught "a reverence for all life." It continued with questions that Christians should ponder, which presumably would shake their faith. Then in a final chapter, Templeton ended on a positive note explaining his beliefs, the first of which was the atheistic "there is no supreme being,"[14] and the

---

[10]Ibid., 10.

[11]Ibid., 11.

[12]"But surely as we approach the twenty-first century it is time to have done with primitive speculation and superstition and look at life in rational terms. We are in large measure masters of our fate—subject, of course, to our genetic inheritance, mental illness, accident or disease—and we are all equipped to ponder the eternal questions, explore the unknown, and examine the *mysterium tremendum* secure in the knowledge that in doing so we are not going counter to 'the will of God' and will not bring on ourselves the vengeful wrath of some punctilious deity because we rejected or failed to observe some arcane prohibition" (ibid., 21).

[13] Ibid., 222.

[14]Following the first statement, Templeton shared the following beliefs: "I believe that there is what may best be described as a Life Force, a First Cause, a Primal Energy, and that it is the genesis of all that is, from the simplest atom to the entirety of the expanding universe. I believe that the Life Force is not a 'being.' It does not love nor can it be loved: it simply is. I believe that there is no Father in Heaven who can be

last of which was the humanistic "life is a superlative gift to be celebrated."[15]

In his fascinating interview with Templeton, Lee Strobel recorded his admiration of Jesus: "'He was,' Templeton began, 'the greatest human being that ever lived.'"[16] Following several of Strobel's probing questions, Templeton expanded on his admiration for Jesus.[17] This same Templeton who missed his relationship with Christ, had at one time sought to continue using a revivalistic methodology without adhering to a revivalist theology. The two did not fit together. Templeton, in his honest "Personal Word" introducing *Farewell to God*, demonstrated the dissonance between his theology and practice. This principle applied to Graham implies the inverse: Graham's early theology did buttress his early practice, particularly the area of biblical authority. The doctrine of authority was the fountainhead doctrine that differentiated Graham's theology from Templeton's; everything else followed. Templeton explained a conversation that he felt captured the differences between him and Graham.[18] Templeton did not

---

persuaded by our prayers, but that meditation in the form of prayer can be an instrument of growth" (ibid., 232).

[15]Ibid., 233.

[16]Lee Strobel, *The Case for Faith* (Grand Rapids: Zondervan, 2000), 17.

[17]"[Templeton] '. . . There have been many other wonderful people, but Jesus is Jesus.'
[Strobel] 'And so the world would do well to emulate him?'
[Templeton] 'Oh, my goodness, yes! I have tried—and try is as far as I can go—to act as I have believed he would act. That doesn't mean I could read his mind, because one of the most fascinating things about him was that he often did the opposite thing you'd expect—'
Abruptly, Templeton cut short his thoughts. There was a brief pause, almost as if he was uncertain whether he should continue.
'Uh . . . but . . . no,' he said slowly, 'he's the most . . .' He stopped, then started again. 'In my view,' he declared, 'he is the most important human being who has ever existed.'
That's when Templeton uttered the words I never expected to hear from him. 'And if I may put it this way,' he said as his voice began to crack, '*I . . . miss . . . him!*'
With that, tears flooded his eyes. He turned his head and looked downward, raising his left hand to shield his face from me. His shoulders bobbed as he wept" (ibid., 18).

[18]"In the course of our conversation I said, 'But, Billy, it's simply not possible any longer to believe, for instance, the biblical account of creation. The world wasn't created over a period of days a few thousand years ago; it has evolved over millions of years. It's not a matter of speculation; it's demonstrable fact.'
'I don't accept that,' Billy said. 'And there are reputable scholars who don't.'

have an authoritative conclusion regarding salvation, because he did not have an authoritative Bible on which to base his salvation. Graham had authority to preach because he believed in an authoritative Bible.

Yet flowing from the fountainhead of biblical authority, or lack of it, came Templeton's definition of evangelism. He changed from an individual conversionist to a pluralistic humanist. In 1949 Templeton made his decision to choose a rational reading of the Bible (i.e., higher critical). Yet in 1949 he thought that he could still use revivalist methods—evangelistic crusades, which are buttressed on a belief in instantaneous conversion. His definition of evangelism turned from (1) a conversionist theme, based on God's written words, to (2) apologetic, educating the audience about Christian principles—which he believed to be the most rationally acceptable for life and living—and finally to (3) social transformation. For this "proper balance" Templeton used the 1918 Archbishop's Committee report "with some minor changes" as the definition of evangelism of the National Council of Churches of Christ for the U.S.A.[19] Templeton wrote, "A 'Theology of evangelism' must emerge

---

'Who are these scholars?' I said. 'Men in conservative Christian colleges?'

'Most of them, yes,' he said. 'But that's not the point. I believe the Genesis account of creation because it's in the Bible. I've discovered something in my ministry: when I take the Bible literally, when I proclaim it as the Word of God, my preaching has power. When I stand on the platform and say, "God says," or "the Bible says," the Holy Spirit uses me. There are results. Wiser men than you and I have been arguing questions like this for centuries. I don't have the time or the intellect to examine all sides of each theological dispute, so I've decided, once and for all, to stop questioning and accept the Bible as God's Word.'

'But, Billy,' I protested, 'you can't do that. You don't dare stop thinking about the most important question in life. Do it and you begin to die. It's intellectual suicide.'

'I don't know about anybody else,' he said, 'but I've decided that that's the path for me'" (Templeton, *Farewell to God*, 7-8).

[19]The entire paragraph is included because the Archbishops' Committee is the same definition used by Graham. "Research has unearthed more than fifty specific definitions of evangelism. Many of them are too brief to be comprehensive; others are too lengthy to be useful. The Archbishop's Committee of the Church of England framed a definition of evangelism which later became a part of the 'Report of the Archbishop's Commission' (popularly known as 'Towards the Conversion of England') and has, with some minor changes, been adopted as a definition of evangelism by the Madras Foreign Missions Council, the National Council of the Churches of Christ in the U. S. A., the Commission on Evangelism of the Presbyterian Church, U.S.A., and other bodies. Its gist is as follows: 'Evangelism is so to present Jesus Christ in the power of the Holy Spirit that men shall come to put their trust in God through him, to accept him as their Savior from the guilt and power of sin, to serve him as Lord in the fellowship of the Church and to follow him in the vocations of the common life.' It is evident that this is an excellent statement for it speaks not only of the proclamation of Christ as Savior, but of the

that will hold in balance the flaming heart and the disciplined mind."[20] What was Templeton seeking to balance? He balanced evangelism, "the proclamation of the evangel,"[21] with "anything the Church may do which has as its ultimate end the winning of men and women to Christ and the winning of Christians to a deepened commitment is evangelism."[22] To the former point, Templeton argued that too often methods of evangelism are confused with evangelism. Thus Templeton posited five examples of what evangelism was not: revivalism, religious education, emotionalism, "soul-saving," or lay visitation.[23] He related the latter point to the Church at worship that "bears its witness to the reality of Christian faith." To Templeton, evangelism included "the attempt to end racial segregation, to get better housing, to feed the hungry, to effect healing of sick minds and bodies, to halt injustice, and to work for peace."[24] Once Templeton opened the door to evangelism including more than the simple proclamation of the gospel, evangelism could then include everything the Christian ought to do, thus effectively diluting any clear meaning in the concept. In fact, those who hold to evangelism as mere soul winning[25] according to Templeton "compartmentalize certain emphases."[26]

Once Templeton found the Christian principles to have little

Christian life" (Charles B. Templeton, *Evangelism for Tomorrow* [New York: Harper and Brothers, 1957], 41-42).

[20]Ibid., 37.

[21]Ibid., 42.

[22]Ibid.

[23]"But let us first indicate some of the ways by which the Church has confounded the methods by which evangelism has been done with evangelism itself.

"Evangelism has been confused with *revivalism*—the pattern which evangelism took in the nineteenth century and subsequently.

"Evangelism has been identified with *religious education*—the carrying of Horace Bushnell's *"Christian nurture"* concept to an extreme.

"Evangelism has been identified with *emotionalism*—the frenetic and sometimes weird activity of the snake-handlers, the so-called 'holy rollers' and others.

"Evangelism has been equated with *'soul-saving'*—the over-concern with the salvation of the individual with little sensitivity to the relation of the gospel to social responsibility.

"Evangelism has been identified with *lay visitation*—the revival of the New Testament two-by-two home visitation by laymen" (ibid., 33).

[24]Ibid., 43.

[25]This is reminiscent of Gustav Warneck's antagonism to "blosse Kundmachung," or "mere proclamation" (David B. Barrett, *Evangelize! A Historical Survey of the Concept* [Birmingham, AL: New Hope, 1987], 29).

[26]Templeton, *Evangelism for Tomorrow*, 43.

basis in empirical data, he was left with a deistic First Cause and an evangelism of humanism. He first departed from an authoritative Scripture, and then Templeton added social dimensions to the definition of evangelism. And he finally ended by quitting crusade evangelism as a methodology, the Christian ministry, and belief in the God of the Bible. Another YFC partner in the pulpit with Graham was Bob Pierce.

Bob Pierce

Bob Pierce, partnered with Billy Graham on several occasions. He preached for Graham at the famous 1949 Los Angeles crusade.[27] They traveled together to Korea during the Korean War,[28] leading to the writing of Graham's book, *I Saw Your Sons at War.*[29] Bob Pierce recommended to Graham the production of a movie based on the Portland, Oregon crusade Graham was holding in 1950. This became the incipient start of what would become World-Wide Pictures. Both Pierce and Graham shared a passion for evangelism. In fact, Pierce described himself both as "an evangelistic minister"[30] and as "an old sawdust trail type o'guy."[31] Pierce even spoke on the subject "Commissioned to Communicate" at the Berlin 1966 World Congress on Evangelism![32] Yet what led the BGEA and Bob Pierce's WVI to take such different courses?

Pierce explained his change of heart resulting from an experience on a trip he took to China. He shared the event with Franklin Graham when, early in his ministry, Pierce's view of the mission of the church changed—it was a paradigm shift etched in his mind.[33] Bob Pierce's

---

[27]Billy Graham, "Introduction," in Franklin Graham, *Bob Pierce,* 17; Billy Graham, *Just As I Am,* 155.

[28] Billy Graham, *Just As I Am,* 192-96.

[29]Billy Graham, *I Saw Your Sons at War: The Korean Diary of Billy Graham* (Minneapolis: Billy Graham Evangelistic Association, 1953).

[30]Richard Gehman, *Let My Heart Be Broken . . . with the Things that Break the Heart of God* (New York: McGraw-Hill, 1960), 2. He told Franklin Graham, "All I knew for sure was that I was called to be an evangelist and win souls, and I knew that no one else would hire me to do it" (Franklin Graham, *Bob Pierce,* 51).

[31]Franklin Graham, *Bob Pierce,* 29.

[32]Bob Pierce, "Commissioned to Communicate," in *One Race, One Gospel, One Task,* ed. Carl F. H. Henry and Stanley Mooneyham (Minneapolis: World Wide Publications, 1967), 20-23.

[33]"So for four days, I went out there. The missionary, Tena Hoelkeboer, had heard the simple way in which I taught the university students, and she wanted me to

encounter with the persecution of a young protégé of Dutch missionary Tena Hoelkeboer resulted in a major paradigm shift in his view of evangelism, similar to the impact of Bishop Thoburn's sermon on John R. Mott fifty years earlier.

It is interesting that both Pierce and Mott had clearly etched in their memory the exact time when they changed from an exclusively soul-oriented evangelism to a combination of evangelism and social ministry. It

---

do the same for the children. In the simplest language I knew I told them who Jesus is and how God loves them; that there's not many, but just *one God.* He took the form of an earthly man, Jesus, and gave His life to bear the punishment for any sins they had ever committed. I told them of the wonderful place He has gone to prepare for those who love Him. A place where there will be no tears and where everything is just and pure and good. Then I gave an invitation to any of them who wanted to know this Jesus and to live for Him.

You know, Franklin, I hadn't brains enough, or insight, to know that there was a cultural difference between Youth for Christ in America and the Chinese way up in the interior of China, so I was preaching the same stuff. I never thought through the differences in their cultural background or how incomprehensible my Western Judeo-Christian ideas and concepts would be to this five-thousand-year-old-culture, with little if any knowledge of even the Ten Commandments. I told these kids, 'Go home and tell your folks you're going to be a Christian.'

Well, when I came to the mission school the next morning, Tena met me with a little girl in her arms. The child's back was bleeding from the caning her father had given her when she went home and announced that she was a Christian, and she was going to live for the one true God. And Tena didn't say as Beth had, 'Can you do anything for her?' Oh, no! She just threw that little girl right into my arms and lashed out at me. For one thing, she was Dutch Reformed, and while she was very concerned that her girls hear the gospel, she wasn't one for open invitations or altar calls. And worse, I'd gone ahead and done it as if I were home in the States! And this little kid had not only come forward, but she'd gone home and told her father, who was incensed because that by turning to Christ she had dishonored his ancestors. Tena was breathing fire!

'*You* told this poor little girl to do that,' she stormed, 'Now *you* take care of her. She listened to *you,* she believed what *you* told her, and she obeyed God. Now look at what it's costing her!' She stood there like a general wiping out an ignorant private who had dared to do something without an order.

'And don't you dare think you can walk off this island without doing something for her. Me? I've got six other little kids already sharing my rice bowl. Now here you've given me one more, Bob Pierce. If you think you can preach like you did and teach your message and then walk off and leave this little girl—well, you're *wrong.* Now, tell me, what *are* you going to do about her?' (not 'can you'; she gave me no option, nor did I want one).

I stood there with that child in my arms. Tears were running down her cheeks. She was scared to death, so insecure she was shaking in my arms. She was heavy and my arms were getting tired. I was shaken to the core. I had never had such an experience. Nobody had ever challenged the practicality of what I preached! I had never been held accountable for any *consequences* of my message. Now here I was faced with, 'Is what I say *true?* Is there any responsibility involved?' Believe *me,* you do some thinking at a moment like that" (ibid., 73-74).

would seem in their minds that these events represented a major paradigm shift for them. And so it was—it was a shift from a universal affirmative—the gospel, to a particular affirmative—the gospel and social concern or social ministry.

Billy Graham

Graham, for his part did not include social responsibility directly in his ministry until he added the "World Emergency Fund" to his ministry in 1973 (forty-six years into his crusade ministry). Later, his crusades added a social dimension including food drives, as well as the distribution of clothing and "survival kits." However, the emphasis of Graham remained focused on the preaching of the gospel with an emphasis on instantaneous conversion, individualistic salvation, and the revivalism methodology of crusade evangelism.

This chapter will focus on Graham's definition of evangelism. First, It will begin by noting the importance of small changes, discussing evangelism by way of logic, and noting additions or modifications to the Great Commission. Second, it will study the social gospel movement, and how Graham has responded to it. Third, we will discuss the current trend called lifestyle evangelism, which developed during the ministry of Billy Graham, and note how Graham responded to this new paradigm shift. With these items in focus, we will examine Graham's definition of evangelism, and any changes that may have transpired. We begin a discussion of a definition of evangelism by noting how seemingly small changes in definition produce drastic results.

The Great Commission

At first glance the change in Bob Pierce's definition of evangelism seemed rather insignificant, especially since the change took place without a noticeable change in his doctrinal theology. However, with the luxury of hindsight, the small change of adding a social dimension to a definition of evangelism and the Great Commission did have an incredible methodological and theological impact on Pierce and those he influenced.

World Vision. Fifty years from the founding of WVI, their Internet Homepage listed the organization's mission. The reluctance with which the organization considers the preaching of the gospel is noted by its being imbedded in the sixth commitment: "Witness to Jesus Christ, by life, deed, word, and sign,"—even listed after public awareness.[34] Certainly Bob Pierce's experience with the missionary Tena Hoelkeboer greatly influenced his sense of mission.

By contrast, the Internet Homepage of the BGEA has the following listed as its mission:

> Mission Statement: BGEA exists to support the evangelistic ministry and calling of Billy Graham to take the message of Christ to all we can by every prudent means available to us.[35]

While this statement is concise and lacks some clarity, it is clear that (1) the mission is linked to the ministry of Billy Graham, which is (2) to preach the gospel using a crusade methodology. Its only listed purpose is "to take the message of Christ." Comparing the mission of WVI with that of the BGEA shows a large chasm both in methodology, as well as in theology, as we shall see later.

Joseph Aldrich. Minor changes do not affect only the evangelistic mandate of the church in relation to its social mandate. Recently a change was noted in a methodology called lifestyle evangelism. Joseph Aldrich wrote a book entitled *Lifestyle Evangelism* in 1981, one of several books on this topic written in the late 1970s and early 1980s. The paradigm shift from expectant to lifestyle evangelism was masterfully communicated and widely accepted, with no admonition of theological changes. As will be noted later in this chapter, lifestyle evangelism adds to the *ordo salutis* the necessary *preparatio evangelica* of relationship, effecting numerous theological changes.

---

[34]"World Vision's mission is pursued through integrated, holistic commitment to:

Transformational development that is sustainable and community-based, focused especially on the needs of children.

Emergency Relief that assists people afflicted by conflict or disaster.

Promotion of Justice that seeks to change unjust structures affecting the poor among whom we work.

Strategic Initiatives that serve the church in the fulfillment of its mission.

Public Awareness that leads to informed understanding, giving, involvement and prayer.

Witness to Jesus Christ, by life, deed, word and sign" (World Vision International, "Who Is World Vision?" [on-line]; accessed 2 May 2001; available from http://www.wvi.org/pages/news/who.htm; Internet).

[35]Billy Graham Evangelistic Association, "About Us" [on-line]; accessed 15 February 2001; available from http://www.billygraham.org/about/statementoffaith.asp; Internet.

Square of Opposition

We will now take a brief excursus into the world of logic, to note the importance of small changes as they relate to the Great Commission. Brand Blanshard, the late chairman of the philosophy department at Yale University, explained that the square of opposition relates to any proposition. This square of opposition shows that any proposition may be right all the time, wrong all the time, right some of the time, or wrong some of the time. These are called respectively a universal affirmative, and universal negative, a particular affirmative, and a particular negative. When applied to evangelism, it yields startling results, which may explain the paradigm shifts mentioned above. Although the shifts seemed small for John R. Mott, Bob Pierce, and even Joseph Aldrich, the result meant moving from a universal positive to a particular positive. For example, note Figure 3 as applied to one aspect of the Great Commission. It is clear from Figure 3 that when a person moves from the universal affirmative to the particular affirmative, the sub-contrary is also true. Thus the small shift from "all Christians should evangelize" to "some Christians should evangelize" logically affirms the sub-contrary, "some Christians should not evangelize."

A champion of the universal affirmative was John Wesley. Not only did he teach the universal affirmative, but he lived it as well. In one instance, Wesley told his fellow preachers:

> You have nothing to do but to save souls. Therefore spend and be spent in this work. And go always, not only to those that want you, but to those that want you most. Observe: It is not your business to preach so many times, and to take care of this or that society; but to save as many souls as you can; to bring as many sinners as you possibly can to repentance, and with all your power to build them up in that holiness without which they cannot see the Lord.[36]

The same was true for many evangelical pastors, leaders, and evangelists. For example, J. E. Conant wrote, "'And preach the Gospel,' if it means anything, must certainly mean to witness, or to tell the Good News of salvation through Christ, and this defines the central activity of the Church."[37] W.A. Criswell, Pastor Emeritus of First Baptist Church, Dallas,

---

[36]John Wesley, "Charge to His Preachers," in Robert E. Coleman, *"Nothing to Do but to Save Souls"* (Grand Rapids: Zondervan, 1990), 1.

[37]J. E. Conant, *Every Member Evangelism* (New York: Harper and Brothers, 1922), 6.

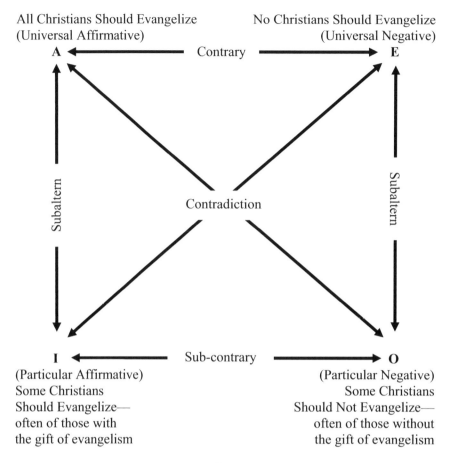

Fig. 3. Logic's Square of Opposition[38] and the Great Commission.

Texas, applied the universal affirmative to the local church.[39] Charles Kelley affirmed the prominence of this universal imperative in the evangelism of Southern Baptists in his analysis *How Did They Do It? The*

---

[38]Figure adapted from Brand Blanshard, "Logic," *Collier's Encyclopedia,* 1961 ed.

[39]"If the pastor is under authority to do the work of an evangelist, then he must do the same thing; namely, he must use his church organization to win the lost. To what better use could they be dedicated? And what a powerful instrument for witnessing the pastor has in the marching members of his many-faceted ministry through the church. The way the church is put together is inherently, intrinsically made for soul-winning, for reaching people. It is the thing that comes naturally" (W. A. Criswell, *Criswell's Guidebook for Pastors* [Nashville: Broadman, 1980], 233).

Story of Southern Baptist Evangelism, in a section titled, "The Moral Imperative to Witness."[40] Similarly, most evangelicals agreed with the universal affirmative, as noted by the name evangelical and the great missionary thrust in the nineteenth century and post-World War II era. Yet we will see that the universal affirmative came under repeated attack among evangelicals.

C. Peter Wagner. If the particular affirmative in Figure 3 is changed to "Only evangelists should evangelize," the result is that all other Christians should not evangelize. C. Peter Wagner wrote of the gift of the evangelist:

> The gift of evangelist is the special ability that God gives to certain members of the Body of Christ to share the gospel with unbelievers in such a way that men and women become Jesus' disciples and responsible members of the Body of Christ.[41]

At the end of his section on the gift of evangelism, Wagner wrote:

> For another thing, every true Christian is a witness for Jesus Christ whether or not they have the gift of evangelist. Furthermore, Christians need to be prepared to share their faith with unbelievers and lead them to Christ whenever the opportunity presents itself.[42]

His use of the equivocal "witness for Jesus Christ" aside, Wagner made

---

[40]"For Southern Baptists there is a stark contrast between the state of those who are lost and the state of those who are saved. To sum up the condition of each with a phrase: the lost are absolutely insecure, and the saved are absolutely secure. That being true, the responsibility of every Christian becomes clear. Each believer must be a witness. Those who know Christ must speak to others about the salvation and new life available through Him.

This responsibility supersedes one's vocational calling. . . .

Bearing witness to others is more than a matter of what one's spiritual gifts are. . . .

The passion which has prompted Southern Baptists to emphasize evangelism and missions is due in part to a sense of moral obligation and responsibility. . . . Those who are secure in Christ must go to the insecure with the news of what Jesus can do. It is a moral and ethical responsibility" (Charles S. Kelley, *How Did They Do It? The Story of Southern Baptist Evangelism* [New Orleans: Insight Press, 1993], 141-43).

[41]C. Peter Wagner, *Your Spiritual Gifts Can Help Your Church Grow* (Ventura, CA: Regal, 1994), 157.

[42]Ibid., 161.

three statements that undermined the universal affirmative that he stated. First, he stated that many Christian circles "tend to overemphasize it [evangelism]".[43] Second he stated, "The gift of the evangelist is probably the most frequently projected of all gifts."[44] Third, he figured that "approximately 5 to 10 percent of its active adult membership have been given the gift of evangelist."[45] Finally, when discussing the gift of the evangelist/evangelism, Wagner stated:

> Whoever uses his or her lack of having a spiritual gift as a cop out from witnessing displeases God. But whoever insists that another person divert valuable spiritual energy that could be used for exercising a spiritual gift into unproductively fulfilling the a Christian role likewise displeases God.[46]

Thus while affirming the above "all Christians should evangelize," Wagner softened the universal affirmative, actually moving to the particular negative in Figure 3.

Christian Schwarz. Christian Schwarz in his *Natural Church Development* debunked the statement "every Christian is an evangelist." He wrote:

> Our research disproves a thesis commonly held in evangelistically active groups: that 'every Christian is an evangelist.' There is a kernel of (empirically demonstrable) truth in this saying. It is indeed the responsibility of every Christian to use his or her own

---

[43]Ibid., 160.

[44]Ibid., 163.

[45]Ibid., 160. The 5 to 10 percent figure was presumably derived from personal observation of those members of D. James Kennedy's church involved in his Evangelism Explosion program. Wagner surmised that since this number were involved in evangelism, they must be the ones who had the gift of evangelism (source: Thom Rainer expanded on his interview of Wagner in a spiritual gifts seminar, as noted in *The Book of Church Growth: History, Theology, Principles* [Nashville: Broadman, 1993], 116 n. 6).

[46]Wagner, *Your Spiritual Gifts,* 168.

specific gifts in fulfilling the Great Commission. This does not, however, make him or her an evangelist.[47]

Based on the observation of Wagner as well as his own sociological research, Schwarz then began to walk around the square of opposition figure to the particular negative:

> We must distinguish between Christians gifted for evangelism and those whom God has otherwise called. If indeed "all Christians are evangelists," then there is no need to discover the 10 percent who really do possess this gift. In this way, the 10 percent with the gift of evangelism would be significantly under-challenged, while the demands on the 90 percent without the gift would be too great. This is a rather frustrating—and very technocratic—model. Our research shows that in churches with a high quality index, the leadership knows who has the gift of evangelism and directs them to a corresponding area of ministry.[48]

Schwarz went on to encourage a "need-oriented" approach to evangelism, rather than "'manipulative methods' where pressure on non-Christians must compensate for the lack of need-orientation."[49] Thus, the methods and examples of the Bible were undermined as pressure tactics, while an ambiguous need-orientation, which is humanistically-acceptable and does not engender persecution, was proclaimed.

Billy Graham. Graham has repeatedly mentioned after someone comes to Christ in a crusade that they should go and tell others.[50] Thus affirming the universal affirmative of the evangelism mandate for Christians. This was stated clearly in sermons throughout his ministry. For example in 1947, Graham preached on witnessing in his sermon "Retreat!

---

[47]Christian Schwarz, *Natural Church Development* (Carol Stream, IL: ChurchSmart Resources, 1998), 34.

[48]Ibid.

[49]Ibid., 35.

[50]For example, after confirming a decision for Christ, the Billy Graham Telephone Worker is encouraged to "point out these follow-up steps," the first of which is as follows: "Take a firm stand for Christ. Tell someone about your decision" (*The Billy Graham Christian Worker's Handbook: A Layman's Guide for Soul Winning and Personal Counseling* [Minneapolis: World Wide, 1984], 8). Telling others was also the first point in follow-up taught by R. A. Torrey in his *How to Work for Christ* (New York: Revell, 1901), 47.

Stand! Advance!":

> God's purpose for you and me after we have been converted is that we be witnesses to his saving grace and power. Are you a daily and constant witness? Are you one of God's minutemen? Are you a commando for Christ? *He expects you to witness at every given opportunity.*[51]

Later Graham preached:

> The greatest testimony to this dark world today would be a band of crucified and risen men and women, dead to sin and alive unto God, bearing in their bodies the marks of the Lord Jesus. When this life of perils and conflict and suffering is over, what marks will you have? . . . Did the whole world know that you belonged to Him— body, soul and spirit? Did you bear His reproach?[52]

In his 1953 *Peace with God,* Graham wrote:

> *The church is for the spreading of the Gospel.* The church is commanded to "Go ye into all the world and preach the gospel" and to baptize those who believe. *The basic and primary mission of the church is to proclaim Christ to the lost.* The need of the world today is sending forth its S.O.S., asking the church to come to its help. The world is being overwhelmed by social, moral, and economic problems. Its people are going down, swept under the waves of crime and shame. The world needs Christ. The mission of the church is to throw the lifeline to the perishing sinners everywhere.[53]

In 1955 Graham preached:

> There are many others that are slothful about witnessing for Christ. How long has it been since you spoke to a soul about Christ? How long has it been since you won another person to a saving knowledge of Jesus Christ? There are scores of people that you contact every day that need the Saviour, and yet not one word has ever

---

[51]Billy Graham, "Retreat! Stand! Advance!" *Calling Youth to Christ* (Grand Rapids: Zondervan, 1947), 44 (emphasis mine).

[52]Billy Graham, "Branded," *Hour of Decision Sermons*, no. 17 (Minneapolis: Billy Graham Evangelistic Association, 1953), 9.

[53]Billy Graham, *Peace with God* (Minneapolis: Grason, 1953, 1984), 185 (emphasis mine).

escaped your lips trying to win them to know Christ. You are guilty of the sin of slothfulness, and others will be lost because you are guilty of this sin.[54]

"The World Need and Evangelism" was published in 1957. Graham told the Conference on Evangelism of the Baptist General Conference of Texas:

> I say this. I that if you are not witnessing for Christ and if you do not have a burning evangelistic fervor within your soul, it could be a sign that you have never repented of sin and have never been born again, because when you are born again of the Holy Spirit, Christ comes to live within you and when Christ lives within you there is that compassion and that fervency and that desire to win others to a knowledge of Jesus Christ.[55]

In 1959 Graham spoke on the need to make every social contact count for Christ:

> Jesus dined with publicans and sinners, but He did not allow the social group to overwhelm Him and conform Him to its ways. *He seized every opportunity to get over a spiritual truth and to lead a soul from death to life.* Our social contacts should not only be pleasant, they should be made opportunities to share our faith and power with those who do not yet know Christ.[56]

Also in 1959 Graham preached a sermon entitled, "The Gospel for the Whole World." In this sermon he reiterated the universal affirmative of the evangelistic mandate:

> The last words of our lord are still binding upon us: "Go ye into all the world and preach the gospel." Where this is being effectively done, light is breaking in upon darkened minds and souls. Where this is being done, literacy is increasing, economic conditions are being

---

[54]Billy Graham, "Slothfulness," in *Freedom from the Seven Deadly Sins* (Grand Rapids: Zondervan, 1955), 94-95.

[55]Billy Graham, "The World Need and Evangelism," in C. Wade Freeman, *The Doctrine of Evangelism* (Nashville: Baptist General Convention of Texas, 1957), 29-30.

[56]Billy Graham, "Nonconformity to the World," *Hour of Decision Sermons,* no. 104 (Minneapolis: Billy Graham Evangelistic Association, 1959), 6 (emphasis mine).

bettered, but greatest of all: human hearts are being released from the power of sin and evil![57]

It is of note that Graham felt the need to include the results of the inside-out change right after he quoted from Mark 16:15. This comment showed the struggle that eventually led Graham to change in his view of the universal affirmative of preaching the gospel as the preeminent responsibility of the church. Graham's message, "Evangelism is Every Christian's Business," was published in 1965. Graham stated:

> In the New Testament, evangelism is a program of proclaiming the good news of the gospel to all peoples and to all nations in every possible way. This program involves the activities of the entire church from the pulpit to every person in the pew. Church members cannot pay a pastor to do their evangelizing for them. *Every individual Christian is called upon to be an evangelist.* The challenge of Christ is a call to clergymen and laymen alike to enter into this program of evangelism.[58]

Even later in his ministry years, Graham still urged young people to give their lives for sacrificial proclamation of the gospel. Examples of this sacrificial proclamation are found in his early addresses to the Urbana youth conventions. In 1976:

> We have the message that can change the world. And we ought not be ashamed of it. Jesus is worthy of our sacrifice. He is worthy of our utmost for his highest. The wonder of it is that we are not alone. God has promised us full resources for the battle.[59]

In 1979:

> Think of the glorious daring of those early apostles. Little wonder that the world called them mad! Paul was satisfied with nothing less than taking the gospel to the whole world including imperial Rome. Magnificent obsessions indeed, everyone of them.

---

[57]Billy Graham, "The Gospel for the Whole World," *Hour of Decision Sermons,* no. 112 (Minneapolis: Billy Graham Evangelistic Association, 1959), 3.

[58]Billy Graham, "Evangelism Is Every Christian's Business," in *Herald of the Evangel,* ed. Edwin T. Dahlberg (St. Louis: Bethany Press, 1965), 72-73 (emphasis mine).

[59]Billy Graham, "Responding to God's Glory," in *Declare His Glory Among the Nations*, ed. David M. Howard (Downers Grove, IL: InterVarsity, 1977), 150.

Who could understand their zeal? The apostles carried the flaming truths of the gospel far and wide. Reckoning nothing of peril and reproach, they surmounted obstacles, overcame difficulties and endured persecution. That was their answer to Christ's command—the magnificent obsession of obeying Christ.[60]

In 1981:

But till then, whatever hour that may be—a thousand years from now, or a hundred years from now or tomorrow—we ought to be about the business of witnessing to the whole world of the gospel of the Lord Jesus Christ.[61]

In 1984:

I'm wondering if there aren't some gamblers for God. C. T. Studd's slogan was, "If Jesus Christ be God and died for me, then no sacrifice can be too great for me to make for him." Jim Elliot went from Wheaton College to become a missionary to the Aucas in Ecuador and was martyred. Before he died, he wrote, "He is no fool who gives what he cannot keep to gain what he cannot lose."

Where are the hard men and women for Jesus? Where are those who will bring all their energies to bear for the sake of Christ? That's the kind of people it's going to take to spread the gospel around the world in these closing years of the twentieth century. In the church today there's a variety of gifts and talents that could change the world if put in the hands of Christ. We have the youth and the health and the energy and the education and the political freedom and the economic opportunity to accomplish God's mission.[62]

To Graham, the clear mandate that every Christian share his faith continued into his late ministry. He continued to encourage youth at Urbana to share Christ and give their lives to Christ. While we will see a slight change in his

---

[60]Billy Graham, "That I Might Believe and Obey," in *Believing and Obeying Jesus Christ: The Urbana 1979 Compendium*, ed. John W. Alexander (Downers Grove, IL: InterVarsity, 1980), 145.

[61]Billy Graham, "Mission Impossible: Your Commitment to Christ," in *Confessing Christ as Lord: The Urbana 81 Compendium*, ed. John W. Alexander (Downers Grove, IL: InterVarsity, 1982), 120.

[62]Billy Graham, "Faithful In Our Commitment to Jesus Christ," in *Faithful Witness: The Urbana 84 Compendium*, ed. James McLeish (Downers Grove, IL: InterVarsity, 1985), 139-40.

message to youth later, Graham's belief in the calling of every Christian to evangelize remained strong. Yet, Graham's unequivocal stand on evangelism as the "basic" or primary purpose for the church shows signs of waning during his ministry years. One place that this was seen was in his disclaimer.

The Disclaimer

In 1965 Graham stated:

Every individual Christian is called upon to be an evangelist. The challenge of Christ is a call to clergymen and laymen alike to enter into this program of evangelism.[63]

This echoed the starting point of Graham. Evangelism was the primary and major task of the church. Yet as Graham's view of evangelism added social emphases, he began to use a disclaimer. Was his view of the church was changing? While this disclaimer seems innocuous on the surface, did it signal a shift in the primacy of evangelism in his approach to evangelism? Graham stated:

In the Bible, an evangelist is a person sent by God to announce the Gospel, the Good News; he or she has a spiritual gift that has never been withdrawn from the Church. Methods differ, but the central truth remains: an evangelist is a person who has been called and especially equipped by God to declare the Good News to those who have not yet accepted it, with the goal of challenging them to turn to Christ in repentance and faith and to follow Him in obedience to His will. The evangelist is not called to do *everything* in the church or in the world that God wants done. On the contrary, the calling of the evangelist is very specific.[64]

In the last sentence, Graham stated that as an evangelist he was not called to do everything in the church or in the world that God wanted done.

In the early part of Graham's ministry, his revivals, evangelistic campaigns, and crusades found a receptive audience among evangelicals. During this time, Graham believed that evangelism was the only mission of the Church, as is noted in the 1947 sermon, "America's Hope," in which

---

[63]Billy Graham, "Evangelism Is Every Christian's Business," 73.

[64]Billy Graham, "Preface," in *Just As I Am* (New York: HarperCollins, 1997), xv.

Graham spoke hard-hitting words for clergy who were not seeking to save souls:

> Is there not now a decay of religion? Less than 5 per cent of the citizenry of our land frequented a place of worship last Sunday night. Is there not something wrong? The President of the Ministerial Association of the greatest churchgoing town in America told me some time ago that 85 per cent of the people in his city never darken the door of a church or attend Sunday school. Is there not something wrong when during the last ten years ten thousand churches have been forced to close their doors? Is there not something wrong when last year seven thousand churches reported not one convert? This means that seven thousand ministers preached for an entire year without reaching one lost soul. Using a low average, suppose that they preached forty Sundays, not including extra meetings, which would mean that these seven thousand ministers preached five hundred and sixty thousand sermons in a year. Think of the labor and the money expended on salaries to make this possible, and yet five hundred and sixty thousand sermons preached by seven thousand ministers in seven thousand churches to thousands of hearers during the last twelve months failed to bring one soul to Christ! There is something radically wrong somewhere. There is either something wrong with these seven thousand ministers, or with their five hundred and sixty thousand sermons, or both!
>
> John Wesley said, "The Church has nothing to do but to save souls; therefore spend and be spent in this work. It is not your business to speak so many times, but to save souls as you can; to bring as many sinners as you possibly can to repentance."
>
> Thousands of these men have denied that the Bible is the Word of God. Thousands of men standing behind the sacred desk today lied when they spoke their ordination vows. They deny the blood atonement; they deny the virgin birth; they deny the bodily resurrection of Christ; they deny the total depravity of man. One segment of the Church has gone into apostasy, another segment has gone into a state of lethargy, indifference, passionless, cold, formal, orthodoxy. Another segment has gone to the extreme of so called "ultra-Fundamentalism" whose object is not to fight the world, the flesh and the devil, but to fight other Christians whose interpretation is not like theirs. Thus the Church has lost its power. Our beautiful sanctuaries have steeples that tower toward the sky, but the millions of

dollars that are being spent every year are making less impact upon the nation today than at any other time in our history.[65]

In 1947 Graham was in the universal affirmative camp on evangelism being the only mission of the church. In 1951 the same emphasis was repeated in a closing illustration on the missionary H. C. Morrison. Graham stated, "H. C. Morrison went to Africa. He went with one purpose—to lead souls to Christ."[66] However, as evangelicalism drifted from a posture of aggressive evangelism,[67] Graham also seems to have drifted from evangelism as being the preeminent mandate of the church. The disclaimer seems to be a bi-product of this shift in thinking. Early in his ministry this disclaimer would have been unnecessary. But as evangelicalism drifted from the universal affirmative (e.g., "Every Member Evangelism"),[68] and as Graham reached out to mainstream Protestant denominations and Roman Catholics, he deemed this distinction necessary.

Early in his ministry Graham felt that the only mission of the church was to save souls (the Universal Affirmative in Figure 4). Many others held this same view: Charles H. Spurgeon,[69] L. R. Scarborough

---

[65]Billy Graham, "America's Hope," in *Calling Youth to Christ* (Grand Rapids: Zondervan, 1947), 22-23.

[66]Billy Graham, "The Home God Honors," in *Revival in Our Time* (Wheaton, IL: Van Kampen, 1950), 103.

[67]David J. Bosch, in his *Transforming Mission: Paradigm Shifts in Theology of Mission* (Maryknoll, NY: Orbis, 1991), blamed premillennialism with a shift "away from social involvement to exclusively *verbal* evangelism" (ibid., 318), thus, not placing the responsibility on the words of the Bible and primitivism, but rather on a theological undercurrent of the mid-nineteenth century. Barrett explained German opposition to the proclamation-oriented American evangelicals, "But the leading German theologian and founder of the science of missions, Gustav Warneck, was a severe critic and the major detractor from 1895 to 1910. In his classic work *Evangelische Missionslehre* (1902) he devoted most of Chapter 32 to combating what he considered to be the naiveté and fallacy of the movement for world evangelization. He was the first, but certainly not the last, to criticize proponents of world evangelization on the specious grounds that they were advocating 'blosse Kundmachung' (mere proclamation) rather than the building-up of Christians and churches" (David Barrett, *Evangelize!*, 29).

[68]J. E. Conant, *Every-Member Evangelism* (New York: Harper and Row), 1922.

[69]"Jesus Christ came not into the world for any of these things, but He came to seek and to save that which was lost; and on the same errand He sent His Church. . . . The business of the Church is salvation. The minister is to use all means to save some; he is no minister of Christ if this be not the one desire of his heart" (Charles H. Spurgeon, "Soul-Saving Our One Business," in *The Soul-Winner* [Grand Rapids: Eerdmans, 1963], 252-53).

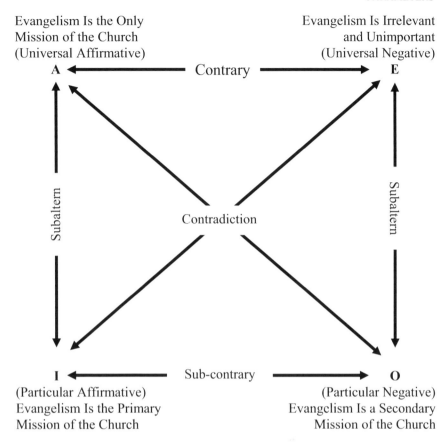

Evangelism Is the Only
Mission of the Church
(Universal Affirmative)
A

Contrary

Evangelism Is Irrelevant
and Unimportant
(Universal Negative)
E

Subaltern

Contradiction

Subaltern

I

Sub-contrary

O

(Particular Affirmative)
Evangelism Is the Primary
Mission of the Church

(Particular Negative)
Evangelism Is a Secondary
Mission of the Church

Fig. 4. Logic's Square of Opposition[70] and the Priority of Evangelism.

(Chair of Fire and President, Southwestern Baptist Theological Seminary),[71]

---

[70]Figure adapted from Brand Blanshard, "Logic."

[71]"The divine obligation of soul-winning rests without exception upon every child of God" (L. R. Scarborough, *With Christ After the Lost* [Nashville: Broadman, 1919, 1952], 2). "The churches which do not constantly seek to win men to a saving knowledge of the truth and enlist them in Christ's service have missed the mark of the divine purpose and requirement. Soul-winning is the main task of every organization claiming to be the church of Christ" (ibid., 62). In another place Scarborough wrote, "It is not wise to say that *soul winning* is the main thing or that *soul building* is the main thing. They are Siamese twins of God's gospel, going hand in hand, and they ought to keep up with each other. . . . And this leads me to say that the main thing in the Kingdom of God is the evangelistic spirit, the martial note and conquest tread" (L. R. Scarborough, *Recruits for World Conquest* [New York: Revell, 1914], 58).

W. B. Riley (founder of Northwestern Bible College),[72] George Truett (Pastor, First Baptist Church, Dallas, Texas),[73] J. E. Conant,[74] C. E. Matthews,[75] Roland Q. Leavell (president of New Orleans Baptist Theological Seminary),[76] L. Nelson Bell (Father-in-law of Graham),[77] W. A. Criswell (Graham's pastor),[78] and Harold Lindsell (former editor of

---

[72]"Other things are important; this thing is absolutely necessary. . . . But the indispensable thing is that the soul be saved" (W. B. Riley, *The Perennial Revival* [Philadelphia: American Baptist Publication Society, 1916], 35). "Every true convert to Christ is a commissioned evangelist. . . . The method of the Wesleyans was in perfect accord with the prescription of the Word; and was equally adapted to the eighteenth, nineteenth, of twentieth century—'All at it: always at it'—every convert to Christ a commissioned Evangelist" (W. B. Riley, *The Crisis of the Church* [New York: Charles C. Cook, 1914], 79, 80).

[73]"What great arguments shall I marshal to get us to do that right now? Shall I talk about duty? Then this is our first duty. And what great word that word duty is! Robert E. Lee was right, that matchless man of the South, when he wrote to his son saying: 'Son, the great word is duty.' Shall I talk about duty? My fellow Christians, your duty and mine, primal, fundamental, preeminent, supreme, tremendously urgent, is that we shall tell these around us that we want them saved" (George W. Truett, *Quest for Souls* [New York: Doran, 1917], 72).

[74]"The main work of the whole Church in the whole world throughout the whole Age is witnessing to the salvation there is in Christ. Anything outside of this forfeits the promised presence and blessing of him who said, 'Lo, I am with you all the days, even unto the consummation of the Age" (Conant, *Every-Member Evangelism*, 29).

[75]"[Without mass or personal evangelism] The church quits majoring on the saving of souls and places chief emphasis on fellowship and social service, leaving the lost in the community to die in their sins" (C. E. Matthews, *The Southern Baptist Program of Evangelism* [Atlanta: Home Mission Board of the Southern Baptist Convention, 1949], 9).

[76]"The Great Commission is the *Magna Charta* of evangelism. It is the marching order of the supreme Commander. It is the proclamation of the King of kings to all his kingdom citizens. It is Christ's imperative for all who name his name" (Roland Q. Leavell, *Evangelism: Christ's Imperative Commission* [Nashville: Broadman, 1951], 3).

[77]L. Nelson Bell, a medical doctor and former missionary compared evangelism with societal improvement: "The Gospel is one thing and the fruits of the Gospel are something else. They are like the roots of a vine and the grapes that grow on it" (L. Nelson Bell, *While Men Slept* [Garden City, NY: Doubleday, 1970], 211).

[78]"But the work that the evangelist does in his itinerant ministry the pastor is to do in his pastoral ministry. If he is faithful in this he is faithful to God. There is no alternative. The pastor is to win souls to Jesus. . . . The main thing has always been and will always be the restoration of the soul, without which all the rest is in vain. . . . To the end that our people might be saved, that our churches might live and grow, that Christ might be glorified and honored, let us give ourselves to the main task for which every

Christianity Today).[79] A strong view of the universal affirmative is still the confessional stance of the Southern Baptist Convention.[80] But presumably when Graham was seeking to appeal to mainline denominations that felt that the major thrust of the church was to be socially-oriented, he may have shifted to the particular affirmative to suit them. Even mainline denominations could be made to acquiesce to the need for and role of the evangelist, especially if the evangelist did not assume that the saving of souls was the only, preeminent, primary, or priority activity of the church— it was one of a number of sound objectives.

Thus, Graham's disclaimer, while seeming commendatory, may indicate a change in Graham's definition of evangelism, as well as his view of the evangelism in the local church. We continue our discussion of parameters by addressing the Great Commission.

The Focus of the Great Commission

The Great Commission has provided a unifying central purpose for conservative Protestant and evangelical churches in past centuries. It drove evangelicals into the nineteenth century as the "Great Century of Missions." Yet in the early part of the twentieth century the Great Commission lost its central spiritual focus. Peter F. Drucker, noted business consultant and writer, discussed this loss of central focus as the reason

---

minister is called and every church exists—evangelism, the hope of the world" (Criswell, *Criswell's Guidebook for Pastors,* 227, 228, 229).

[79]"Let us then encounter the vision of what Christ expected the Church to be. . . . In the hands of the Church is all that she needs to accomplish the task and to proclaim the Evangel unto the uttermost parts of the earth" (Harold Lindsell, *An Evangelical Philosophy of Missions* [Wheaton, IL: Van Kampen, 1949; Grand Rapids: Zondervan, 1970], 233).

[80]Article eleven, "Evangelism and Missions," of the 2000 *Baptist Faith and Message* reads: "It is the duty and privilege of every follower of Christ and of every church of the Lord Jesus Christ to endeavor to make disciples of all nations. . . . It is the duty of every child of God to seek constantly to win the lost to Christ by verbal witness undergirded by a Christian lifestyle, and by other methods in harmony with the gospel of Christ." (Southern Baptist Convention, "SBC Faith and Facts" [on-line]; accessed 15 June 2001; available from http://www.sbc.net/ default.asp; Internet). It must be noted that the *Baptist Faith and Message* also speaks to societal change by regenerate citizens, "Means and methods for the improvement of society . . . can be truly and permanently helpful only when they are rooted in the regeneration of the individual by the saving grace of God in Jesus Christ" (Article XV, "The Christian and Social Order," in *An Exposition from the Faculty of the Southern Baptist Theological Seminary on the Baptist Faith and Message 2000* [Louisville: The Southern Baptist Theological Seminary, 2000], 56).

mainstream Protestant churches are in decline. They were "trying to accomplish too many things at the same time."[81] According to Drucker, the lack of a "single-purpose" (spiritual) versus doing "too many things at the same time" (spiritual and social) led to the demise of mainline Protestant churches. The move from one purpose to multiple purposes in the church necessitated a reinterpretation of the Great Commission.

In the intense debate on the mission of the church, standing central in the discussion is the Great Commission. Figure 4 explains the progress involved in adding to the proclamation of the gospel in the definition of evangelism or in an understanding of the Great Commission. It is another way of showing that if gospel proclamation is not a universal affirmative then it becomes a particular affirmative. The logic chart, noted above, shows that it is impossible to maintain a balance between two contradictory propositions. Yet, additions to the gospel force the church and the Christian into seeking to maintain an impossible balance. If evangelism is truly the preeminent priority of the church, any competing purpose inserted into the Great Commission undermines the preeminence of evangelism. It must be noted that additions to evangelism are often: (1) biblically-mandated; (2) good things; (3) necessary items; and (4) important aspects of the Christian life. However, they do not equal the importance of the Great Commission passages, the examples of evangelism in the Bible, or the thrust of church growth in the Book of Acts. The following eight items are sample additions to the unique priority of evangelism in the local church:

1.   Apologetics[82]

---

[81]"A striking social phenomenon of the last 30 years in the United States, the explosive growth of the new 'mega-churches' (now beginning to be emulated in Europe), rests on these institutions' dedication to a single purpose: the spiritual development of the parishioners. Just as the decline of their predecessors, the liberal Protestant churches of the early years of the 20th century, can largely be traced to their trying to accomplish too many things at the same time, above all, to their trying to be organs of social reform as well as spiritual leaders.

The strength of the modern pluralist organization is that it is a single-purpose institution" (Peter F. Drucker, "The New Pluralism," *Leader to Leader* [Fall 1999]: 22).

[82]For example, Thomas More explained the superiority of apologetics over heated public preaching: "By degrees all the Utopians are coming to forsake their own superstitions and to agree upon this one religion that seems to excel the others in reason. . . . We told them of the name, doctrine, manner of life, and miracles of Christ, and of the wonderful constancy of the many who willingly sacrificed their blood in order to bring so many nations far and wide to Christianity. . . . Whatever the reason, many came over to our religion and were baptized. . . . Those among them that have not yet accepted the

2.   Discipleship[83]

3.   Political involvement or reforming culture[84]

Christian religion do not restrain others from it or abuse the converts to it. While I was there, only one man among the Christians was punished. This newly baptized convert, in spite of all our advice, was preaching in public on the Christian worship more zealously than wisely. He grew so heated that he not only put our worship before all others, but condemned all other rites as profane and loudly denounced their celebrants as wicked and impious men fit for hell fire. After he had been preaching these things for a long time, they seized him. They convicted him not on a charge of disparaging their religion, but of arousing public disorder among the people, and sentenced him to exile" (Thomas More, *Utopia* [1516; Arlington Heights, IL: AHM Publishing, 1949], 70-71).

[83]Robert E. Coleman posited the following argument, "His concern was not with programs to reach the multitudes, but with men who the multitudes would follow. Remarkable as it may seem, Jesus started to gather these men before he ever organized an evangelistic campaign or even preached a sermon in public" (Robert E. Coleman, *The Master Plan of Evangelism* [Old Tappan, NJ: Revell, 1983], 27). However, the preaching of Jesus in Matt 4:17, Mark 1:14-15, and Luke 4:44 preceded His calling of his disciples in Matthew 4:18-22, Mark 1:16-20, and Luke 5:10-11. His lack of considering these passages may render void Coleman's *a priori* statement based on chronology in the discipleship training of Jesus. A look at A. B. Bruce's *The Training of the Twelve,* 4th ed. (1894; Grand Rapids: Kregel, 1971), ix, shows that Bruce, upon whom Coleman relied, did not deal with any of the early preaching passages in his analysis. Coleman's *a priori* led him to state of mass evangelism, "Victory is never won by the multitudes" (Coleman, *The Master Plan,* 36). He shared his views about local church evangelism programs, "we have launched one crash program after another to reach the multitudes . . . . But we have failed. . ." (ibid., 38).

[84]The foreword to Charles Colson's *How Now Shall We Live?* gave away his view of the mission of the church. Colson wrote, "Don't get me wrong. We need prayer, Bible study, worship, fellowship, and witnessing. But if we focus exclusively on these disciplines—and if in the process we ignore our responsibility to redeem the surrounding culture—our Christianity will remain privatized and marginalized" (Charles Colson and Nancy Pearcey, *How Now Shall We Live?* [Wheaton, IL: Tyndale House Publishers, 1999], x). Colson traded belief in the gospel for belief in a Christian worldview or a moral philosophy. He continued later, "It is our contention in this book that the Lord's cultural commission is inseparable from the great commission. That may be a jarring statement for many conservative Christians, who, through much of the twentieth century have shunned the notion of reforming culture, associating that concept with the liberal social gospel. The only task of the church, many fundamentalists and evangelicals believed, is to save as many lost souls as possible from a world literally going to hell. But this explicit denial of a Christian worldview is unbiblical and is the reason we have lost so much of our influence in the world. *Salvation does not consist simply of freedom from sin; salvation also means being restored to the task we were given in the beginning—the job of creating culture*" (295-96; emphasis mine). While agreeing that the Bible has no direct mandate to political involvement, he buttressed his views with knowledge from special revelation and general revelation (296-97) and

4.   Christian education[85]

5.   Church growth[86]

---

through affirming, "all truth is God's truth" (198-99). Thus, due to the cultural mandate superceding theological distinctives, Colson continued, "But if we are to have an impact on culture, the beginning point must be to take our stand united in Christ, making a conscious effort among all true believers to come together across racial, ethnic, and confessional lines. . . .

This is difficult for many evangelicals (as well as Catholics and Orthodox) to accept, and understandably so. . . . Conservative believers are distrustful of ecumenism because of the danger of glossing over those differences.

Focusing on worldview, however, can help build bridges" (303-04). Thus Colson advised unity based on a Christian worldview or moral philosophy, rather than based the gospel and evangelism.

[85]Arthur P. Johnston asserted that the World Missionary Conference in Edinburgh 1910, changed the 'Watchword' of the Student Volunteer Movement from "The Evangelization of the World in This Generation" to the Christianization of the world. He stated, "The majority opinion of the Commission [III] reveals the influence of a new philosophy of Christian education on the mission field" (Arthur P. Johnston, *World Evangelism and the Word of God* [Minneapolis: Bethany Fellowship, 1974], 103).

[86]Originally, Donald McGavran spoke of the fulfilling of the Great Commission through fostering people movements, which characterized rapid growth in the church in India and in other parts of the world. He interpreted the Book of Acts through the lens of people movements in his book *Bridges of God—A Study in a Strategy of Missions* (New York: Friendship Press, 1955). The terminology soon changed to church growth, and the emphasis was placed on research. One strategy seems to have been to blindside liberal churches into believing orthodox truths by showing them that conservative practice would help their churches to grow. Thus the Iberville Statement asked the question, "Is the church growing or not? And if not, why not?" ("The Growth of the Church" *The Ecumenical Review* 16 (October 1963-December 1964): 197). The statement continued, "There are notable exceptions, but in far too many places Christians seem to have lost all expectation that the multitudes can be converted or that churches will significantly increase in size. . . . Its lack of expectancy not only betrays weakness of faith, it is also evidence of a profound misunderstanding of the measure of God's redemptive purpose. For the Church is called into being not merely as a saved community, but as a saving community. . . . It lives as a witness to, and a servant of, God's plan to reconcile, and to sum up, in Christ all things in heaven and on earth. Thus a church without a dynamic missionary purpose belies its own true nature" (ibid., 196). Interestingly, dissociation between evangelism, doctrine, and sociological research has sometimes resulted. Some have emphasized pragmatism seemingly at the expense of biblical truth. For example, Christian Schwarz in his book *Natural Church Development* asked the question: "What should each church and every Christian do to obey the Great Commission in today's world?" With this temporally and culturally couched question he began his "natural" research on church growth. One of his values was the "principle-oriented approach" which approaches theology from a pragmatic sense (Christian Schwarz, *Natural Church Development: A Guide to Eight Essential Qualities of Healthy*

6.   Christian separation[87]

7.   Love[88]

8.   Feeding the hungry and alleviating various social ills.[89]

To this list can be added (1) seeking world peace; (2) speaking in tongues; (3) including power encounters in evangelism; (4) worship; (5) psychological wholeness; and (6) health and wealth. All of these items can be backed up with verses from the Bible. Some of these additions are important, essential, and helpful. However, they do not carry the weight of the proclamation of the gospel as regards the Great Commission. Each one has the potential to shift evangelism from the universal affirmative to a mediating position in the square of opposition. David Bosch in a section entitled "Is Everything Mission?" addressed the issue of the tendency to define mission too broadly:

>   One of the negative results has been the tendency to define mission too broadly—which prompted Neill (1959:81) to formulate

---

Churches. 3rd ed. [Carol Stream, IL: ChurchSmart, 1999], 26). As far as doctrine, Schwarz distanced himself from doctrinal orthodoxy in explaining his "Bipolar paradigm": "Therefore, the biblical concept of faith must be protected from the (monistic) misconception that regards the essence of faith in assenting to a doctrine (*dogmatism*), accepting biblical contents as 'true' (*fundamentalism*), or following a particular moral code (*legalism*)" (Christian Schwarz, *Paradigm Shift in the Church: How Natural Church Development Can Transform Theological Thinking* [Carol Stream: ChurchSmart, 1999], 101).

[87]"Those who espouse the philosophy of New Evangelicalism must confront the scriptural teaching that evangelism and separation are twin strategies which cannot be cut apart. . . . Evangelism and separatism are of equal necessity, inseparable companions." (Fred Moritz, *"Be Ye Holy"—The Call for Christian Separation* [Greenville, SC: Bob Jones University Press, 1994], 65, 66).

[88]Charles Arn responded to Thom Rainer's call for evangelism in church growth with an article encouraging more study of culture and greater "dynamic equivalence." Arn closed with a reinterpretation of the Great Commission based on the Great Commandment: "The *model* He gave us is love . . . the *method* He gave us is love . . . the *motive* He gave us is love . . . the *message* He gave us is love" (Charles Arn, "A Response to Dr. Rainer: What Is the Key to Effective Evangelism?" *Journal of the American Society for Church Growth* 6 [1995]: 78). Arn's emphasis on love coincided with the approach of Horace Bushnell in *The Vicarious Sacrifice Grounded in Principles of Universal Obligation* (Hicksville, NY: Regina Press, 1975).

[89]This was the view developed above by Bob Pierce; it will be discussed in detail later.

his famous adage, "If everything is mission, nothing is mission", and Freytag (1961:94) to refer to "the spectre of panmissionism."[90]

The existence of additions to evangelism cannot be taken lightly.

In order for the weight of these additions to be added to the Great Commission, those who uphold the views often show that they are actually taught either explicitly or implicitly in the Great Commission, or they raise another command to the level of the Great Commission. In the first case, the term μαθετευω in Matthew 28:19 has taken on a variety of meanings, some of which emphasize other than the gospel proclamation for the purpose of bringing people to Christ as the priority. Robert Coleman, for example, places discipleship as prior to evangelism in the ministry of Jesus (see footnote above). John R. W. Stott chose the preposition "as" in John 20:21 to provide him freedom in expanding the evangelistic mandate of the Great Commission. He wrote, "Deliberately, he made his mission the *model* of ours, saying 'as the Father has sent me, *so* I send you.'"[91] Stott then used John 20:21 to link together the Great Commission with the Great Commandment, "To sum up, we are sent into the world, like Jesus, to serve."[92] The number of items that can be added to the Great Commission under the term "serve" are almost endless. In this case the Great Commission suffers from lack of clarity and the mission of the church is diffused in a myriad of directions.[93]

In order to substantiate a broadened or mature view of the Great Commission, it is also common for another biblical command to rival the Great Commission. The commands of choice often used for this purpose are: (1) the "cultural mandate" (Gen 1:28); (2) the "Golden Rule" (Lev 19:18; cf. Matt 22:39; Mark 12:31; Luke 10:27); or (3) the "Great Commandment" (John 13:34). For example, Peter Kuzmič, during the last session of the Theological Task Force at Amsterdam 2000 discussed three points: "[1] Entering the Context; [2] Practicing Compassion; and [3] Exhibiting Credibility." On his second point, Kusmič put forward the "Great Commission (Matt 28) plus Great Compassion (Matt 25)." He stated, "I

---

[90]Bosch, *Transforming Mission,* 511.

[91]John R. W. Stott, *Christian Mission in the Modern World* (Downers Grove, IL: InterVarsity, 1975), 23.

[92]Ibid., 30.

[93]David Bosch approved of this diffusion of mission in his classic *Transforming Mission:* "Instead of trying to formulate one uniform view of mission we should rather attempt to chart the contours of 'a pluriverse of missiology in a universe of mission'" (David Bosch, *Transforming Mission*, 8; Bosch quoted G. M. Soares-Prabhu, S.J., "Missiology or Missiologies?" *Mission Studies* 6 [May 1969]: 87).

started out preaching evangelism." Kusmič explained that he underwent a paradigm change. Moving around the Square of Opposition, he continued, "Proclamation alone can be counter-productive"—as humans are not only ears and soul, and again, "proclamation is second[ary]." Agreeing with the 1918 Archbishop's Committee and Bob Pierce, he concluded that the Christian must earn credibility (*preparatio evangelica*) in order to evangelize: "Because we trust you . . . ; you are credible to us; you became vulnerable for us." He added, "Don't start with literature, show compassion."[94] Kuzmič's use of Matthew 25 for the Great Commandment, which he never explained, provided an example of the desire to rival the clear spiritual mandate of the Great Commission, particularly as found in Mark 16:15: "Go into all the world and preach the gospel to all creation." As shall be noted later, the paradigm shift, which these additions represent, has significant theological ramifications.[95]

In recent years two major issues have led to the demise of evangelism as the universal affirmative in evangelical churches. The first is social responsibility, social duty, or social gospel. The second is lifestyle evangelism, relational evangelism, friendship evangelism, or incarnational evangelism. The reaction, response, and approach of Billy Graham will be noted in relation to these two movements, and then some final conclusions will be made concerning Billy Graham's parameters for evangelism.

Social Responsibility

The social gospel movement of the early Twentieth century was separated from Graham's ministry by years, as well as by theological lines. Yet, Graham, in a fashion that some have noticed,[96] made a striking statement about the social gospel:

There is no doubt that the social gospel has directed its energies toward the release of many of the problems of suffering humanity. I

---

[94]Peter Kuzmič, "Theology of Powers: Socio-Politial Realities as Challenge(s) to World Evangelization," handout for presentation at the Theological Task Force, Amsterdam 2000, August 4, 2000.

[95]Gabriel Fackre used Matthew 25 in a similar way: "According to the twenty-fifth chapter of Matthew that Presence is to be found among the hungry and the hurt" (Gabriel Fackre, *Do and Tell: Engagement Evangelism in the '70s* [Grand Rapids: Eerdmans, 1973], 47).

[96]Karen Jeannine Garvin, "Billy Graham in 1967: A Further Study of Adaptation to Audiences" (Ph.D. diss., University of Minnesota, 1972).

am for it! I believe it is biblical. However, I am convinced that we do not have a personal gospel and a social gospel.

There is one gospel and one gospel only, and that gospel is the dynamic of God to change the individual and, through the individual, society.[97]

This statement was made by Graham in 1967, one year after the Berlin 1966 Congress and seven years before Lausanne 1974. It showed that Graham was somewhat aware of the social gospel, and not against affirming its place as biblically-based. In light of Graham's words and the complexity of evangelism and social concern, this section will provide a brief history of the evangelism and social action debate, and then look at Graham's beliefs on this matter.

At the New York 1900 Ecumenical Missionary Conference, Robert Speer spoke on the topic of "The Supreme and Determining Aim." He stated that it is easy to "confuse the aim of foreign missions with the results of foreign missions."[98] Speer then discussed the difficulty of

---

[97]Billy Graham, "Biblical Conversion," in *Lectures, Kansas City School of Evangelism* (Kansas City, MO: Billy Graham Evangelistic Association, 1967), 10. Graham repeated virtually the same thing in his *Ecumenical Review* article, "There is no doubt that the social gospel has directed its energies toward the release of many of the problems of suffering humanity. I am for it and I believe it is Biblical!" (Billy Graham, "Conversion—A Personal Revolution," 281).

[98]The first two paragraphs are here included to give the context and to carry the weight of Speer's arguments: "It is the aim of foreign missions that is to be defined, and not the aim of the Christian Church in the world, or of the Christian nations of the world. There are many good and Christian things which it is not the duty of the foreign missionary enterprise to do. Some things are to be laid, from the beginning, upon the shoulders of the new Christians; some are to be left to be discharged in due time by the native Christian churches that shall arise, and there are many blessings, political, commercial, and philanthropic, which the Christian nations owe to the heathen world, which are not to be paid through the enterprise of foreign missions. It is the aim of a distinctive, specific movement that we are to consider.

It will help us in defining it to remind ourselves, for one thing, that we must not confuse the aim of foreign missions with the results of foreign missions. There is no force in the world so powerful to accomplish accessory results as the work of missions. Wherever it goes it plants in the hearts of men forces that produce new lives; it plants among communities of men forces that create new social combinations. It is impossible that any human tyranny should live where Jesus Christ is King. All these things the foreign mission movement accomplishes; it does not aim to accomplish them. I read in a missionary paper a little while ago that the foreign mission that was to accomplish results of permanent value must aim at the total reorganization of the whole social fabric. *This is a mischievous doctrine.* We learn nothing from human history, from the experience of the Christian Church, from the example of our Lord and His apostles to justify it. They did not aim directly at such an end. They were content to aim at

separating means from ends in the founding of a school.[99]

In the next phrase, Speer continued defining the aim of foreign missions as evangelization.[100] Speer's views of social gospel in relation to evangelism were clear from his own words. Ministers of the gospel "yield such powerful political and social results because they do not concern themselves with them."[101] L. Nelson Bell, former missionary doctor in China, father-in-law of Billy Graham, and first editor of *Christianity Today*, agreed with Speer on this point.[102] But something happened to divert the Protestant missionary movement from the aims to the results, from the roots to the fruits, and from the universal affirmative of the Great Commission.

The general secretary of the Student Volunteer Movement, chairman of both the (Edinburgh 1910) World Missionary Conference and its Continuation Committee, and founding chairman of the International

---

implanting the life of Christ in the hearts of men, and were willing to leave the consequences to the care of God. It is a dangerous thing to charge ourselves openly before the world with the aim of reorganizing States and reconstructing society. How long could the missions live, in the Turkish Empire or the Native States of India, that openly proclaimed their aim to be the political reformation of the lands to which they went? It is misleading, also, as Dr. Behrends once declared, to confuse the ultimate issues with the immediate aims; and *it is not only misleading, it is fatal*. Some things can only be secured by those who do not seek them. Missions are powerful to transform the face of society, because they ignore the face of society and deal with it at its heart. They yield such powerful political and social results because they do not concern themselves with them" (Robert E. Speer, "The Supreme and Determining Aim," in *Ecumenical Missionary Conference: New York, 1900* [New York: American Tract Society, 1900], 74-75; emphasis mine).

[99]"It is a good and civilizing thing in itself, and by and by we sacrifice for the lesser good the greater aim. Our method rises up into the place of our end and appropriates to its support for its own sake that which the aim had a right to claim should be devoted to it for the aim's sake alone" (ibid., 75).

[100]"Having cleared the ground so far, what is the aim of foreign missions? For one thing, it is a religious aim. We can not state too strongly in an age when the thought of men is full of things, and the body has crept up on the throne of the soul, that our work is not immediately and in itself a philanthropic work, a political work, a secular work of any sort whatsoever; it is a spiritual and a religious work. . . . 'The aim of missions,' to borrow President Washburn's phrase, 'is to make Jesus Christ known to the world.' You can adopt other phraseology, if you please. You can say the aim of missions is the evangelization of the world, or to preach the gospel to the world. And if we understand these terms in their Scriptural sense, they are synonymous with the phrase which I have just quoted" (ibid, 75-76).

[101]Ibid., 75.

[102]"The Gospel is one thing and the fruits of the Gospel are something else. They are like the roots of a vine and the grapes that grow on it" (L. Nelson Bell, *While Men Slept*, 211).

Missionary Council (IMC), Methodist layman John R. Mott, explained his paradigm shift from the universal affirmative under the influence of the preaching of Bishop Thoburn of India in 1905.[103] Mott's 1905 change of heart impacted the evangelistic zeal of most mainline Protestant denominations after 1910. David Barrett, in his *Evangelize! A Survey of the Concept,* noted a parallel change in terminology away from use of the word evangelize between 1910-1912. In a section entitled "1910-1912: Edinburgh and the IRM," Barrett pointed out "The task of evangelism had become broader and the emphasis now was that 'Evangelism involved both verbal witness and a life of discipleship.'"[104] As noted above, at stake was a diminishing of the unique call to preach the gospel. As a result of this change, the China Inland Mission left the IMC in 1916.[105] However, forty-five years later, Bob Pierce, a founder of YFC and founder of WVI and Samaritan's Purse underwent a change similar to Mott through the instrument of missionary Tena Hoelkeboer.[106] Could it be that this change in Bob Pierce likewise has impacted numerous evangelical denominations?

The theological liberalism that snuffed evangelism, eventuating in the Hocking Report of 1932, and the founding of the World Council of Churches (WCC) in 1948, are clear to the conservative evangelical because of the vantage point of years. However, what of the theological foundation of World Vision and other AERDO organizations?[107] The testimony of Bob

---

[103]"The larger desire so essential to evangelism is a product not only of meditation but also of contagion. It is communicated by Christ himself. One of the most helpful sermons I ever heard was by Bishop Thoburn of India on the text, "The love of Christ constraineth us." The truth in his message which laid most powerful hold and wrought a great change in me was that love of Christ enables one to love the unlovable. I do not find this in non-Christian faiths or in the areas of unbelief. It is a divine product" (John R. Mott, *The Larger Evangelism: The Sam P. Jones Lectures at Emory University, 1944* [New York: Abingdon-Cokesbury Press, 1944], 9).

[104]Barrett, *Evangelize!,* 29.

[105]Johnston, *Battle for World Evangelization,* 43.

[106]Franklin Graham, *Bob Pierce,* 73-74.

[107]AERDO stands for The Association of Evangelical Relief and Development Organizations. It was described as follows on its website: "was founded in 1978. It represents a network of 45 of the major evangelical Christian relief and development agencies across North America [including World Vision and Samaritan's Purse]. The Board of Directors is comprised of a representative from each member agency. AERDO is managed by a ten-member Executive Committee, elected from the membership board." Its vision statement was: "AERDO's vision is that all Christian Relief and Development professionals and agencies base their initiatives on biblical principles and work to re-engage the Church in holistic ministry among the poor and needy." Its mission statement reads: "MISSION STATEMENT: AERDO is a professional forum for non-profit Christian agencies and individuals engaged in relief

Pierce as told to Franklin Graham spoke to this issue. The major hallmarks of Pierce's apologetic for evangelical relief and development can be narrowed down to three points:

1. The Christian must earn the right to share the gospel.[108]
2. God's love must be demonstrated before it can be understood.[109]
3. The immediate need must be met before meeting the spiritual need.[110]

These three points were occasioned by the fact that a little girl who indicated her desire to follow Christ was caned by her father. Thus, very real persecution occasioned his paradigm shift. This leads to the question several questions. Is persecution for the sake of Christ to be avoided at all cost? Does persecution indicate a faulty method of evangelism? It would seem from a reading of the Book of Acts and 1 Peter that persecution is a badge of honor for the believer.[111] Paul indicated that it is to be expected (cf. 2 Tim 3:12), and so did Christ (cf. Matt 5:10-12, John 15:18-20). However, what of the three points of Pierce? There are sound reasons to disagree with Pierce's assessment of need-oriented evangelism that combined social responsibility with evangelism:

1. Christ has earned the right for the gospel to be shared with any person by all Christians (or even the rocks will cry out) (cf. Rom 5:8)

2. The Christian bears witness of Christ's goodness not his own goodness (focus upward) (cf. Mark 10:18, Acts 10:38).

3. It is the gospel that converts a darkened heart, not the good deeds either of the proclaimer or the recipient of the message (cf. Rom 1:16-17).

---

and development work. AERDO exists to promote excellence in professional practice; to foster networking, collaboration and information exchange; and to enable its membership to effectively support the Church in serving the poor and needy" (Association of Evangelical Relief and Development Organizations, "About" [on-line]; accessed 2 May 2001; available from http://www.aerdo.org/ about_aerdo.htm; Internet).

[108]Franklin Graham, *Bob Pierce,* 79, 85.

[109]Ibid., 85.

[110]Ibid.

[111]For example: "Beloved, do not be surprised at the fiery ordeal among you, which comes upon you for your testing, as though some strange thing were happening to you; but to the degree that you share the sufferings of Christ, keep on rejoicing; so that also at the revelation of His glory, you also may rejoice with exultation" (1 Pet 4:12-13).

4.　　If people are blind to the gospel (2 Cor 4:3-4), and if they are not open to biblical truth, not even the witnessing of a resurrection from the dead will suffice to open their eyes to spiritual truth (Luke 15:30-31).

5.　　It is the Word of God which is sufficient unto salvation, not the works of men (cf. 1 Thess 2:13).

6.　　The weapons of our warfare are not carnal but spiritual (cf. 2 Cor 10:3). Carnal means do not bring spiritual results; spiritual fruits require spiritual methods.

7.　　Social responsibility undermines the sole responsibility of preaching the gospel (cf. Mark 16:15; 1 Cor 1:17; 2:2).

8.　　Use of social to lead to spiritual may be (a) manipulative, using another's pain as a pretext to share the gospel (cf. 1 Thess 2:3-6); and (b) imposing one's cultural and social standards upon another, leading to cultural imperialism (e.g., what to eat, how to build a home) and inviting cultural antagonism (e.g., our American or Western way is better than your way) (cf. 1 Cor 9:20-21).

These eight points focus on the sufficiency of the gospel and the power of the Word of God. Additional principles can be added to this list, such as (1) human merits that can never attain eternal salvation, whether by the person seeking the salvation or by someone else (cf. Psalm 49:7-8); (2) the uniqueness of the incarnation of Christ; (3) the sufficiency of the cross; and (4) the sole agency of the Holy Spirit in salvation. These biblical concepts are all called to question by a focus on social responsibility as a partner to evangelism. Each of these concepts shakes the very foundation of the gospel message and salvation. Walter Rauschenbusch sought to provide a theological formulation for social ministry in *A Theology for the Social Gospel*. Yet theological consistency led him to reformulate every major doctrine of the Christian faith, including the atonement.

A Theology for Social Ministry

Bob Pierce displayed the same theological weaknesses as the American Baptist theologian Walter Rauschenbusch. Rauschenbusch noted the dissonance between theology and practice with the social gospel. This dissonance led him to reformulate systematic theology to fit practical theology! In his *A Theology for the Social Gospel,* Rauschenbusch used his theological training to frame the major doctrines of the Christian faith to affirm the need for and value of social ministry.

Rauschenbusch began with the *a priori* of social ministry, "We have a social Gospel. We need a systematic theology large enough to match it and vital enough to back it."[112] Methodology was so important to him and his colaborers that it superceded and rendered meaningless the historical methods of biblical interpretation and the corresponding definitions of theology handed down from the past. Thus in his *A Theology for the Social Gospel,* Rauschenbusch sought to develop a completely new theology. To alert his readers to the impact of his "theological readjustment," Rauschenbusch made the disclosure: "Any demand for changes in Christian doctrine is sure to cause a quiver of apprehension and distress."[113] He continued by affirming that the social gospel was more in tune with the needs of mankind, "Doctrinal theology is in less direct contact with the facts than other theological studies."[114] Rauschenbusch then called for change in theology, "Theology needs periodical rejuvenation."[115] Rauschenbusch then went on to readjust every major doctrine of the Christian church to fit his social paradigm.

It is amazing that Rauschenbusch was willing to admit that systematic theology needed adjustment or change in order to fit the practice of social gospel—or the inclusion of social responsibility as equally or more valid to evangelism in the Great Commission. Rauschenbusch proffered a democratic concept of sin, rather than the individualistic conception of theology.[116] This led to a "complete salvation" consisting of "taking his part in the divine organism of mutual service."[117] Rauschenbusch wrote against

---

[112]Walter Rauschenbusch, *A Theology for Social Gospel* (New York: Macmillan, 1917; Nashville: Abingdon, 1978), 1.

[113]Ibid., 10.

[114]Ibid., 11-12.

[115]Ibid., 12.

[116]"Sin is not a private transaction between the sinner and God. Humanity always crowds the audience-room when God holds court. We must democratize the conception of God; then the definition of sin will become more realistic.

We love and serve God when we love and serve our fellows, whom he loves and in whom he lives. We rebel against God and repudiate his will when we set our profit and ambition above the welfare of our fellows and above the Kingdom of God which binds them together.

We rarely sin against God alone" (ibid., 48).

[117]Ibid., 98. The entire sentence read: "Complete salvation, therefore, would consist in an attitude of love in which he would freely co-ordinate his life with the life of his fellows in obedience to the loving impulses of the spirit of God, thus taking his part in a divine organism of mutual service." Later he expanded on this concept, "The saint of the future will need not only a theocentric mysticism which enables him to realize God, but an anthropocentric mysticism which enables him to realize his fellow-men in God" (ibid., 108).

an "individualistic theology."[118] In agreement with Rauschenbusch, Reinhold Niebuhr's chief complaint against Billy Graham and his preaching was an individualistic theology.[119] Niebuhr, along with Nels S. F. Ferré and Donald Blosch, were early critics of Graham for this same reason—his individualistic conception of sin and salvation. Interestingly enough, Ron Sider made similar statements about individualistic sin sixty years after Rauschenbusch.[120]

But in all this, what did Rauschenbusch do with the cross? Did he become Socinian, accepting the cross as an example? Interestingly, creed seemed unimportant to the social gospel, as did the cross, as is the case in social responsibility today:[121]

> The social gospel is believed by trinitarians and unitarians alike, by Catholic Modernists and Kansas Presbyterians of the most cerulean colour. It arouses a fresh and warm loyalty to Christ wherever it goes, though not always a loyalty to the Church. All who believe in it are at one in desiring the spiritual sovereignty of Christ in humanity. Their attitude to the problems of the creeds will usually be determined by other influences.[122]

---

[118]"The individualistic theology was the creation of men with little historical training and historical consciousness, and to that extent the problems they set were the product of uneducated minds. The full greatness of the problem of Jesus strikes us when we see him in his connection with human history" (ibid., 166).

[119]"The irrelevance of his [Billy Graham's] faith is derived from his *wholly individualistic conception of sin* and his perfectionistic ideas of grace" (Reinhold Niebuhr, "Editorial: Billy Graham's Christianity and the World Crisis," *Christianity and Society* 20, no. 2 [Spring 1955]: 3 [emphasis mine]).

[120]"Neglect of the biblical teaching of structural injustice and institutionalized evil is one of the most deadly omissions in evangelicalism today. . . . Christians frequently restrict the scope of ethics to a narrow class of 'personal' sins" (Ron Sider, *Rich Christians in an Age of Hunger* [Downers Grove, IL: InterVarsity, 1977, 1978], 133). Sider continued his attack on individualism: "In the twentieth century, as opposed to the nineteenth, evangelicals have been more concerned with individual sinful acts than with their participation in evil social structures" (ibid.).

[121]Bob Pierce told Franklin Graham, "This was the first time these lepers ever had anybody do anything for them. They were the most radiant bunch, and they all became Christians (but not because of any theology)" (Franklin Graham, *Bob Pierce,* 70). On another occasion Pierce stated, "All too often we simply voice our own orthodoxy amid the rushing traffic of a world jammed with other issues. . . . Our world has little time for theological abstractions" (Bob Pierce, "Commissioned to Communicate," 20, 22).

[122]Rauschenbusch, *A Theology for the Social Gospel,* 148.

The fact that anti-trinitarian Unitarians were said to believe the social gospel did not bode well for the cross or the gospel. In fact, Rauschenbusch wrote very little of the cross, rather his emphasis was on the incarnation.[123] Rauschenbusch finally spoke of the atonement in the last chapter of his book. He noted that every theory of the atonement "used terms and analogies taken from the social life of the age."[124] This belief allowed him to shape the atonement from the social life of his own age, which considered sin in democratic terms, thus the old approaches to the atonement did not meet Rauschenbusch's social criteria:

> These traditional theological explanations of the death of Christ have less authority that we are accustomed to suppose. The fundamental terms and ideas—"satisfaction," "substitution," "imputation," "merit"—are post-biblical ideas, and are alien from the spirit of the gospel.[125]

Hence, Rauschenbusch, in order to remain consistent with his social gospel *a priori,* completely discounted any view of the subsitutionary atonement:

> How did Jesus bear sins which he did not commit? The old theology replied by imputation. But guilt and merit are personal. . . . The solution does not lie in that way.
> Neither is it enough to say that Jesus bore our sins by sympathy. . . .
> How did Jesus bear our sin? The bar to a true understanding of the atonement has been our individualism. The solution of the problem lies in the recognition of solidarity.
> By his human life Jesus bound up backward and forward and sideward with the life of humanity.[126]

Rauschenbusch's "solidaristic interpretation of his death" focused on his coming into humanity (the incarnation), and not on his death. He wrote:

---

[123]"Even if there had been no sin from which mankind had been redeemed, the life of Jesus would have dated an epoch in the evolution of the race by the introduction of a new type and consequently new social standards" (ibid., 152).

[124]Ibid., 243. Rather than the theories coming from the Bible, "social theories . . . lay back of the theories" (244).

[125]Ibid., 242-43.

[126]Ibid., 245.

Theology has made a fundamental mistake in treating the atonement as something distinct, and making the life of Jesus a mere staging for his death, a matter almost negligible in the work of salvation.[127]

The central interpretative motif for Rauschenbusch's socialized gospel was the incarnation of Jesus, the life of Jesus: "The life of Jesus was a life of love and service."[128] The atonement was therefore the Pelagian, Socinian, or the example theory.[129] Similarly, Rauschenbusch thus rejected the subsitutionary atonement and the governmental theory: "This conception is free from the artificial and immoral elements inherent in all forensic and governmental interpretations of the atonement."[130] All that Rauschenbusch had remaining of his Christian theology was the incarnation—Jesus living among men, identifying with their humanity, and showing the way to the new humanity. In a parallel fashion, Ron Sider picked up on Rauschenbusch's emphasis on the incarnation,[131] the concept of Christian community,[132] and a redefinition of the mission of Jesus[133] in his powerful admonition to social responsibility among evangelicals. The only problem was and is that evangelism and social responsibility as missions for the church are theologically antithetical.

It is interesting to note that throughout Rauschenbusch's *A Theology for the Social Gospel,* he quoted Josiah Royce's *Problem of*

---

[127]Ibid., 260.

[128]Ibid., 261. According to Rauschenbusch, "Even on the cross he [Jesus] fought [social sins]. . . . Christian art has misreported him when it makes him suffer with his head down. His head was up and he was in command of the situation" (263).

[129]"Christ was the first to live fully within the consciousness of God and to share his holy and loving will. He drew others into his realization of God so that they too freely loved God and appropriated his will as their own. Thus he set in motion a new beginning of spiritual life within the organized total of the race, and this henceforth pervaded the common life. This was the embryonic beginning of the Kingdom of God within the race. Therewith humanity began to be lifted to a new level of spiritual existence. To God, who sees the end enfolded in the beginning, this initiation of a new humanity was the guarantee of its potential perfection" (ibid., 265).

[130]Ibid., 267.

[131]Sider, *Rich Christians,* 65-69.

[132]Ibid., 95-98, 193-95.

[133]"How did the Incarnate One define his mission?" (ibid., 65).

Christianity (1914).[134] Royce (1855-1916) was an instructor in philosophy at Harvard University for thirty-four years. In his main work, *The World and the Individual* (1908), Royce began his epistemology from the human mind: "For Royce, the Absolute is the mind."[135] Royce then argued against individualism and for the role of society. In defining right and wrong, he maintained that "an act is right so far as, looked at from the point of view of the wider community of which we are members, it can still be approved."[136] With this positive view of community, antagonism to individualism, and dismissing the Scriptures as irrelevant in an understanding knowledge, Royce provided the intellectual foundation upon which Rauschenbusch built his theology of social gospel.

In closing this section, it will suffice to note that in order to substantiate the human element—hence social responsibility—as a part of the mission of the church, major changes were and are necessary in theology. In fact, every major Christian doctrine was changed by Rauschenbusch, even the cross of Christ became irrelevant. The shift from evangelism to social gospel was gradual and took place in the wake of the Great Century of Missions. When a theology was finally published to substantiate the method, major theological alterations were necessary! From this starting point, we will define terms, and then note Graham's response to social responsibility, social action, and social gospel emphasis during his ministry.

Definitions and Current History

In order to define the relationship between evangelism and social action in recent history, the statements of several conferences will be noted, as well as those of key individuals, showing the array of differences on the issue of evangelism and social responsibility.

Three possibilities were posited for the relationship between evangelism and social responsibility at the 1982 Grand Rapids Report on Evangelism and Social Responsibility. The three positions were: social activity as a consequence of evangelism, social activity as a bridge to

---

[134]"Josiah Royce, one of the ablest philosophical thinkers our nation has produced, has given us, in his 'Problem of Christianity,' his mature reflections on the subject of the Christian religion" (Rauschenbusch, *A Theology for the Social Gospel*, 70).

[135]Brand Blanshard, "Royce, Josiah," *Collier's Encyclopedia*, 1961 ed.

[136]Ibid.

evangelism, and social activity as a partner to evangelism.[137] Figure 5 adds to this nomenclature by placing the positions along a continuum moving from a uniquely spiritual focus on one side to a uniquely human on the other side. The spiritual only (S1) stands for "mere proclamation" or verbal evangelism. The human side (H1) stands for socio-economic and political transformation only. Four mediating positions are put forth: spiritual a priority, social a bridge (S2); spiritual equal to human with slight priority (SH1); spiritual and human equal (SH2); and human a priority with spiritual still included, usually as a moral basis for the human (H2).

The nascent tension between evangelism and social concern among evangelicals was evident in the Berlin 1966 conference. World evangelization being the major concern of the congress, "Evangelism and Social Concern" was discussed as a "Strategy for the Future" by Paul Rees, Vice President at Large for WVI, International,[138] and again by Bob Pierce, founder and president of WVI who spoke on "Commissioned to Communicate."[139] In the addresses of these men, the social responsibility of the church was forcefully brought before the congress.

Nevertheless, the Berlin 1966 Congress Statement addressed the relationship between evangelism and social responsibility somewhere between S1 and S2 in Figure 5. The conference stood strong on world evangelization: "Our goal is nothing short of the evangelization of the human race in this generation, by every means God has given to the mind and will of men."[140] The statement also left some breathing room for social responsibility, dealing with racism in a way reminiscent of Rauschenbusch.[141] While the bulk of the material in Berlin's "Closing Statement" dealt with non-evangelistic items, it was still in keeping with the

---

[137]John R. W. Stott, "Grand Rapids Report on Evangelism and Social Responsibility: An Evangelical Commitment," in *Making Christ Known: Historic Mission Documents from the Lausanne Movement, 1974-1989*, ed. John R. W. Stott (Grand Rapids: Eerdmans, 1996), 181-82.

[138]"We can be humbled before God and man because again and again we have failed to see—and to show—that if the *mission* of the Church is narrow, the *witness* of the believing community is broad" (Paul S. Rees, "Evangelism and Social Concern," in *One Race, One Gospel, One Task*, 1:308).

[139]"We must show people that we care not only about their eternal destiny but that we care about them in the here and now. Evangelism involves the whole man" (Bob Pierce, "Commissioned to Communicate," 2:21).

[140]"Closing Statement of the World Congress on Evangelism," in *One Race One Gospel, One Task*, 5.

[141]Rauschenbusch wrote of racism as the essence of all sin, "Every personal act, however isolated it may seem, is connected with racial sin" (Rauschenbusch, *A Theology for the Social Gospel*, 246).

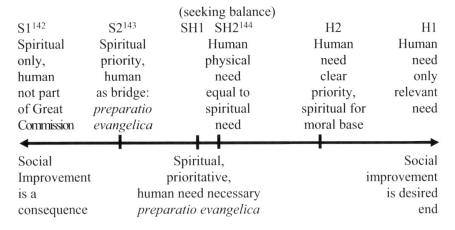

Fig. 5. Human and spiritual in evangelism continuum.

early Graham and lay somewhere between S1 and S2 on above figure.[145]

---

[142]S1 relates to "social activity is a *consequence* of evangelism" ("Grand Rapids Report on Evangelism and Social Responsibility," 181), as found in the Grand Rapids Report on Evangelism and Social Responsibility: An Evangelical Commitment.

[143]S2 relates to "social activity can be a *bridge* to evangelism" (ibid.)

[144]SH1 and SH2 relate to "social activity not only follows evangelism as its consequence and aim, and precedes it as its bridge, but also accompanies it as its *partner*" (ibid., 182).

[145]"We recognize the failure of many of us in the recent past to speak with sufficient clarity and force upon the biblical unity of the human race.

All men are one in the humanity created by God himself. All men are one in their common need of divine redemption, and all are offered salvation in Jesus Christ. All men stand under the same divine condemnation and all must find justification before God in the same way: by faith in Christ, Lord of all and Savior of all who put their trust in him. All who are "in Christ" henceforth can recognize no distinctions based on race or color and no limitations arising out of human pride or prejudice, whether in the fellowship of those who have come to faith in Christ or in the proclamation of the Good News of Jesus Christ to men everywhere.

We reject the notion that men are unequal because of distinction of race or color. In the name of Scripture and of Jesus Christ we condemn racialism wherever it appears. We ask forgiveness for our past sins in refusing to recognize the clear command of God to love our fellowmen with a love that transcends every human barrier and prejudice. We seek by God's grace to eradicate from our lives and from our witness whatever is displeasing to him in our relations with one another. We extend our hands to each other in love, and those same hands reach out to men everywhere with the prayer that the Prince of Peace may soon unite our sorely divided world" ("Closing Statement of the World Congress on Evangelism," 5).

Arthur Johnston considered that "Berlin gave little more than token theological consideration to the social pressures of the 60s."[146] The relationship of the two, according to Johnston, would receive greater elaboration in Lausanne 1974. Carl F. H. Henry was chair of the Berlin conference and Stanley Mooneyham, special assistant to Billy Graham, was its coordinating director. Yet, David Howard noted two conferences that opened "evangelicals" to the need for social responsibility.[147] Johnston also noted the importance of the time period between Berlin 1966 and Lausanne 1974 in which there were four regional conferences leading up to Lausanne: Singapore 1968, Minneapolis 1969, Bogota 1969, and Amsterdam 1971.[148] Each of these conferences, according to Johnston, paved the way for the "balanced" approach of the Lausanne Covenant landing somewhere between SH1 and SH2.[149] John Stott, chair of the International Congress on World Evangelization, held in Lausanne, Switzerland, July 16-25, 1974, gave the first plenary address of the congress:[150]

> The first plenary paper of John Stott, consequently, placed evangelism in the context of mission, and proceeded to unravel the new

---

[146]Arthur P. Johnston, *Battle for World Evangelism* (Wheaton, IL: Tyndale House, 1978), 221.

[147]"Before the decade of the 1970s it was highly suspect for evangelicals in general to become involved in "social action" activities. Such things seemed to smack of the "social gospel" from which fundamentalism had veered away in the earlier decades of the twentieth century. During the 1960s, however, there were a few glimmers of hope that evangelicals would begin again to recognize their responsibility to the physical and social needs of mankind. Examples of this were some parts of the Wheaton Declaration (a statement drawn up at the Congress on the Church's Worldwide Mission held in Wheaton, Illinois, in April, 1966) and some of the messages given at the Congress on Evangelism in Minneapolis in 1969. But in general it was a lonely voice among evangelicals that would speak out in favour of social action" (David M. Howard, *The Dream that Would Not Die: The Birth and Growth of the World Evangelical Fellowship 1846-1986* [Wheaton, IL: World Evangelical Fellowship, 1986, 2000], n.p.)

[148]Stott may have used these conferences to help finalize the slate of speakers he would recommend for Lausanne 1974.

[149]Arthur P. Johnston, *Battle for World Evangelism,* 238-73.

[150]Adrian Hastings asserted that Stott was to Graham as Oldham had been to Mott fifty years earlier during the founding of the IMCs and eventually the WCC: "Within the world Evangelical movement of the second half of the century he [Stott] played to Billy Graham a role not altogether unlike that which J. H. Oldham had played fifty years before to John R. Mott. In each case the less flamboyant but more intellectual Englishman was endeavouring to guide the movement into new, less simplistic vistas" (Adrian Hastings, *A History of English Christianity* 1920-1985 [London: Collins, 1986], 617; quoted in Iain Murray, *Evangelicalism Divided,* 49).

ecumenical knots in the historical evangelical vocabulary of evangelism.[151]

Thus it is not surprising that concepts from ecumenical mission were inserted into the Lausanne Covenant's definition of evangelism. Lausanne's definition of evangelism was titled "The Nature of Evangelism":

> To evangelize is to spread the good news that Jesus Christ died for our sins and was raised from the dead according to the Scriptures, and that as the reigning Lord he now offers the forgiveness of sins and the liberating gift of the Spirit to all who repent and believe. Our Christian presence in the world is indispensable to evangelism, and so is that kind of dialogue whose purpose is to listen sensitively in order to understand. But evangelism itself is the proclamation of the historical, biblical Christ as Savior and Lord, with a view to persuading people to come to him personally and so be reconciled to God. In issuing the Gospel invitation we have no liberty to conceal the cost of discipleship. Jesus still calls all who would follow him to deny themselves, take up their cross, and identify themselves with his new community. The results of evangelism include obedience to Christ, incorporation into his church and responsible service in the world.[152]

Two words are among the ecumenical concepts inserted into the historic biblical definition of evangelism: presence and dialogue. Bassham located the origin of the concept of "Christian presence" to the "worker-priest movement" in France from 1944-1945. This then led to the "Christian Presence Series" of M. A. C. Warren, used by the World Student Christian Federation in the 1960s.[153] "Presence" then appeared in Johannes Blauw's *The Missionary Nature of the Church*[154] and "became a central component

---

[151]Arthur P. Johnston, *Battle for World Evangelism*, 297.

[152]Stott, *Making Christ Known*, 20.

[153]Rodger C. Bassham, *Mission Theology: 1948-1975 Years of Worldwide Creative Tension Ecumenical, Evangelical, and Roman Catholic* (Pasadena: William Carey Library, 1979), 70. Bassham added, "Through its adoption of *The Church of Others*, the term [Christian presence] became practically a slogan for ecumenical mission strategy and was obvious in the preparatory documentation for the Fourth Assembly at Upsalla" (71).

[154]Johannes Blauw, *The Missionary Nature of the Church: A Survey of the Biblical Theology of Mission* (New York: McGraw-Hill, 1962; Grand Rapids: Eerdmans, 1974).

in later ecumenical mission theology."[155] Presence entered evangelical literature with Gabriel Fackre's *Do and Tell: Engagement Evangelism in the 70's*,[156] followed by C. B. Hogue's booklet titled *Lifestyle Evangelism*. Hogue continued the emphasis of Fackre adding, "The name of the game in lifestyle evangelism is 'Show and Tell.' This is what Jesus told the Gerasene demoniac to do after his conversion. It is *being* and *doing*."[157]

Bassham traced the concept of dialogue to the report on evangelism by D. T. Niles at the Second Assembly of the WCC in Evanston, Illinois, in 1954. He recommended a "new approach in our evangelizing task."[158] According to Bassham, dialogue was encouraged at the Third General Assembly of the WCC in New Delhi, 1961.[159] "Dialogue" was then picked up by Paul VI in his 1964 encyclical *"Ecclesiam Suam,"* where he introduced the concentric circles, encouraging dialogue with those in "the circle of Christianity."[160]

Both "Presence" and "Dialogue", which had a history of usage in ecumenical and Roman Catholic mission theology, were imported into the Lausanne 1974 definition of evangelism, as was also the "cost of discipleship," the "new community," and "responsible service." Each of these concepts served to blunt the cutting edge of the universal affirmative of the proclamation of the gospel as the only mission of the church.

In its fifth point, Lausanne 1974 included a statement on "Christian social responsibility."[161] This statement made it clear that

---

[155]Bassham, *Mission Theology.,* 72.

[156]Gabriel Fackre, *Do and Tell: Engagement Evangelism in the 70's* (Grand Rapids: Eerdmans, 1973).

[157]C. B. Hogue, *Lifestyle Evangelism* (Atlanta: Home Mission Board of the Southern Baptist Convention, 1973).

[158]Ibid., 84.

[159]Ibid.

[160]"But we must add that it is not in our power to compromise [in dialogue] with the integrity of the faith [Catholic doctrine] or the requirements of charity [the sacraments]" (Paul VI, *Ecclesiam Suam,* 6 August 1964, section 109). This encyclical came out four months prior to Vatican II's *Lumen Gentium,* 21 November 1964.

[161]"We affirm that God is both the Creator and the Judge of all men. We therefore should share his concern for justice and reconciliation throughout human society and for the liberation of men from every kind of oppression. Because mankind is made in the image of God, every person, regardless of race, religion, color, culture, class, sex or age, has an intrinsic dignity because of which he should be respected and served, not exploited. Here too we express penitence both for our neglect and for having sometimes regarded evangelism and social concern as mutually exclusive. Although

"evangelism and socio-political involvement are both part of our Christian duty."[162] This statement lowered evangelism from a mission to a "duty," and it raised socio-political involvement as a partner duty with evangelism. William Martin wrote that this balance was missing in evangelicalism since the "days of Charles Finney."[163] Thus evangelicalism reversed 120 years of mere proclamation and moved toward a mature balance of the human and the divine.[164] The sixth statement of Lausanne 1974, "The Church and Evangelism," noted the primacy of "sacrificial service" in evangelism. Thus Lausanne 1974 adopted a hesitant SH1 stance.

In 1982 a consultation was held in Grand Rapids resulting in a report, "The Grand Rapids Report on Evangelism and Social Responsibility: An Evangelical Commitment." John R. W. Stott was chairman of the drafting committee, as well as "responsible for the final editing."[165] This conference followed Lausanne in further elaborating the relationship of evangelism and social responsibility. Under the definition of evangelism, Stott seemed to promote his philosophy of evangelism by inserting the concepts of "personal encounter," "personal authenticity," "alienation," and

---

reconciliation with man is not reconciliation with God; nor is social action evangelism, nor is political liberation salvation, nevertheless we affirm that evangelism and socio-political involvement are both part of our Christian duty. For both are necessary expressions of our doctrines of God and man, our love for our neighbor and our obedience to Jesus Christ. The message of salvation implies also a message of judgment upon every form of alienation, oppression and discrimination, and we should not be afraid to denounce evil and injustice wherever they exist. When people receive Christ they are born again into his kingdom and must seek not only to exhibit but also to spread its righteousness in the midst of an unrighteous world. The salvation we claim should be transforming us in the totality of our personal and social responsibilities. Faith without works is dead" (Stott, *Making Christ Known,* 24).

[162]Ibid.

[163]"It [the Lausanne Covenant] was a cautious, even hedging sort of statement, and evangelism still held its position as the master motive, but the Lausanne Covenant furnished Evangelical Christianity with a rationale for social action that it lacked since the days of Charles Finney" (Martin, *Prophet with Honor*, 449).

[164]"In its extreme form this older view of mission as consisting exclusively of evangelism also concentrated on verbal proclamation. . . . At the opposite extreme of this unbiblical concept of mission as consisting of evangelism alone there is the standard ecumenical viewpoint. . . . the identification of the mission of God with social renewal" (Stott, *Christian Mission,* 15, 17, 18). Stott then explained that his view of mission had changed since Berlin 1966, "Today, however. I would express myself differently. . . . I now see more clearly that not only the consequences of the commission but the actual commission itself must be understood to include social as well as evangelistic responsibility, unless we are guilty of distorting the words of Jesus" (ibid., 23).

[165]Stott, *Making Christ Known,* 166.

"felt needs."[166] He seemed to be moving away from the legal emphasis (substitution) and spiritual bent of mere proclamation. Stott's call to social responsibility used emotionally-charged language, including terms such as "we are appalled" and "radical compassion."[167] The commitment then reaffirmed the definition of the Lausanne Covenant. In a next section, the commission examined the issue of the relationship between evangelism and social responsibility. Three relationships were proposed: "social activity is a *consequence* of evangelism," "social activity can be a bridge to evangelism," and "social activity not only follows evangelism as its consequence and aim, and precedes it as its bridge, but it also accompanies it as its partner."[168] Stott, however, was not satisfied to allow proposition one to stand on its own. He stated as part of proposition one, "Social responsibility is more than just a consequence of evangelism; it is also one of its principal aims. . . . Social responsibility, like evangelism, should therefore be included in the teaching ministry of the church."[169] Thus, Stott could not allow proposition one to stand on its own under its own definition without having to insert his rhetoric relating to position three, and then restating it in proposition three—begging the question.

Both International Conferences for Itinerant Evangelists (Amsterdam 1983 and 1987), the North American Conference for Itinerant Evangelists (NACIE 1994), and Amsterdam 2000 seemed to return to the position of a priority of evangelism, somewhere between S2 and SH1. For example, in his "prepared remarks" for Amsterdam 2000, Graham reverted to his disclaimer in dealing with the subject of the relationship of evangelism and social action.[170] Thus, Graham forcefully upheld the priority of evangelism, while leaving room for other purposes, duties, or responsibilities in the church. This begs the question: where has Graham fallen along the evangelism and social responsibility continuum throughout

---

[166]Ibid., 175-76.

[167]Ibid., 177.

[168]Ibid., 181-82.

[169]Ibid., 181.

[170]"Of course, winning the lost to a saving faith in Christ does not encompass everything the Church is called to do. We are called to make disciples (as Jesus said) by 'teaching them to obey everything I have commanded you' (Matthew 28:20). We are also called to worship and to prayer, and we are called to compassionate service in our world. We should be involved in many other social, educational and family ministries. However, in priority, evangelism comes first. It does not solve all problems, but it is still our priority. May this Conference be used of God to re-establish the priority of evangelism in our lives, and in our churches" (Billy Graham, "Why Amsterdam 2000? Prepared Remarks by Billy Graham" [Amsterdam 2000], 3).

his ministry?

Billy Graham

As we have seen, the conferences funded by Billy Graham left an unclear sound as concerns the relationship of evangelism and social responsibility. Our present concern is to note how Billy Graham viewed the Great Commission with regard to evangelism and social responsibility. It would seem, from analyzing his sermons and interviews, that Graham started out in the S1 camp, made an early move to the S2 position, and then settled down somewhere between SH1 and SH2, depending on his audience.

Starting Point. In 1950 Van Kampen Press published *Revival in Our Time* under the name of Billy Graham. In this book were included six of Graham's sermons. The first of these sermons was often the first topic that Graham would speak to when he opened an evangelistic campaign, "We Need Revival." In this sermon, Graham expressed an "inside-out" view to social change, "Finally, revival brings tremendous social implications."[171] He then went on to explain the fruits of revival in England and the United States. Thus, even early in his ministry, Graham saw a distinction between the "roots"—evangelism, and the "fruits"—social change. This was also his message in 1951:

> The basic difficulty in the world today is sin. Before we can solve the economic, philosophical and political problems of the world, pride, greed, lust and sin are first going to have to be erased.[172]

In 1953 Graham clearly believed that individual conversion led to social change in society. In "Three Minutes to Twelve," Graham said:

> It is not now time for further deliberation but for an all-out offensive by the church. The church, and the church alone, has the answer; therefore the church must go all out to get this message to the missions—their greatest need is not more money, food, or even medicine; it is Christ. It is Christ, and Christ alone, Who can change their hearts and make them new creatures. If we clean them up and educate them first, we would have millions of savages who would turn

---

[171]Billy Graham, "We Need Revival," in *Revival in Our Time*, 79.

[172]Billy Graham, "National Humility," in *America's Hour of Decision* (Wheaton, IL: Van Kampen, 1951), 130.

on their teachers. Give them the Gospel of love and grace first, and they will clean themselves up, educate themselves and better economic conditions.[173]

Graham's 1953 position of inside-out change was echoed by Graham's pastor, W. A. Criswell:

We must never forget that economic reform, political enlightenment, culture, and learning are by-products of the Christian faith. The main thing has always been and will always be the restoration of the soul, without which the rest is in vain.[174]

In 1955, however, Graham began to change. He spoke of doctrine, evangelism, and social concern in his sermon "The Sin of Omission":

In the parable of the last judgment the people were not asked questions of theology. As important as doctrine is, they were not asked about their doctrinal beliefs. Neither were they asked what sins they had committed. Theirs was chiefly and solely the neglect to do good and their sin was grave enough to send them into everlasting punishment. There must be a practical outworking of our faith here in this present world or it will never endure in the world to come. We need fewer words and more charitable works; less palaver and more pity; less creed and more compassion.[175]

Yet even so, in 1955 Reinhold Niebuhr believed that Graham had a lack of social concern.[176] Niebuhr continued his attack on Graham's

---

[173]Billy Graham, "Three Minutes to Twelve," *Hour of Decision Sermons*, no. 22 (Minneapolis: Billy Graham Evangelistic Association, 1953), 5-6.

[174]Criswell, *Criswell's Guidebook for Pastors,* 228.

[175]Billy Graham, "The Sin of Omission," *Hour of Decision Sermons,* no. 60 (Minneapolis: Billy Graham Evangelistic Association, 1955), 4-5.

[176]"There is, in short, a simple individualistic and moralistic version of the Christian faith which is quite irrelevant to the moral and spiritual perplexities of our age, partly because it does not know how to deal with the collective evils of civilizations and partly because it has too naïve conceptions of the 'good' that good men can do, being blind to the evil which we must risk in order to avoid a worse evil, for instance risking war in order to avoid war" (Reinhold Niebuhr, "Billy Graham's Christianity and the World Crisis," 3).

irrelevancy over the next several years.[177] Yet Graham continued in his "inside-out" approach to social ills, although his resolve seemed to be weakening. In 1955, before Niebuhr's sharp attacks against Graham prior to New York 1957, Graham spoke to the issue of a social application in his sermon "The Sin of Omission":

> My friends, if the Gospel we preach does not have a social application; if it will not work effectively in the work-a-day world, then it is not the Gospel of Jesus Christ.[178]

Thus, in 1955 Graham began to intertwine the fruit of evangelism in the work-a-day world with "a social application."

Stanley High. In 1956 we find another sign that Graham's understanding of social action was changing. Stanley High's biography of Graham translated his ministry for a less conservative audience.[179] High discussed the social gospel in his biography:

> There is, in those definitions, plenty of room for the preaching of what is described as the social Gospel. And that Gospel undoubtedly has an increasing place in Billy Graham's preaching. He himself has said, "The Gospel is both vertical and horizontal. The vertical signifies our relationship to God. The horizontal signifies the application of the principles of the teachings of Christ to our daily lives. At least a third of my preaching is spent encouraging and teaching people to apply the principles of Christianity in their personal and social lives. . . . I would like to say emphatically that any Gospel that preaches only vertical relationships is only a half-Gospel;

---

[177]For example, on another occasion Niebuhr wrote, "But I share . . . a certain uneasiness that his type of evangelism may seem to be irrelevant to the great moral issues of our day" (Reinhold Niebuhr, "Proposal to Billy Graham," *Christian Century,* 8 August 1956, 921).

[178]Billy Graham, "The Sin of Omission," 5.

[179]"That declaration—which I doubt Billy Graham would have made ten years ago—is evidence, I think, that the social implications of the Gospel will be increasingly emphasized in his preaching. Those implications, however, are still considerably short of central to his concern" (Stanley High, *Billy Graham: The Personal Story of the Man, His Message, and His Mission* [New York: McGraw-Hill Book Company, 1956], 62).

that a Gospel that preaches only horizontal relationships is only a half-Gospel. The message of evangelism must be for the whole man."[180]

Graham would come back to his contention that there are not two gospels but one in 1967 when he addressed the Kansas City School of Evangelism.

In 1957 Graham addressed the Conference on Evangelism of the Baptist General Convention of Texas. In this address he noted that social problems make men receptive to the gospel: "The social problems of the world have made men receptive to the Gospel."[181] Then Graham quoted Samuel Moffett:

> We do not go out as missionaries or evangelists because we want to help build the kingdom of God. That is not our first and primary motive. Our primary motive is not even to win souls. Our primary motive is because we are sent by Jesus Christ. 'Go into all the world and preach the gospel.' That is the command of Christ.[182]

Yet, Graham continued on his view that social change is an "inside-out" process. In 1958 Graham stated:

> If the United Nations would realize that the basic problem of the world is spiritual and moral, this would become the first step toward world peace. However, the United Nations is making the same mistake that all great deliberating bodies like it in the past have made. It deals with symptoms rather than causes. The cause is sin![183]

In 1959 Graham displayed the pressure that he was getting to release his grip on the universal imperative of the proclamation of the gospel and include social responsibility:

> Go ye into your world with the gospel! It is necessary for missionaries to be many things: doctors, farmers, counselors, technicians, and pilots, but always the main job is preaching the gospel. There is no substitute for that. We can give men skills, know-

---

[180]Ibid., 61.

[181]Billy Graham, "The World Need and Evangelism," 27-28.

[182]Ibid., 29.

[183]Billy Graham, "The Assurance of Salvation," *Hour of Decision Sermons,* no. 99 (Minneapolis: Billy Graham Evangelistic Association, 1958), 4. The version of the sermon that was revised in 1994 and 2000 changed the last sentence to read, "The cause of our problem is sin!"

how, and tools: but if we fail to give them the good news of salvation, we have left them without God and without hope. We have withheld the most precious gift that God has bestowed upon men.

Some will say back to me: "Oh, don't forget the social aspect of the gospel," and I will retort, "And don't you leave out the redemptive aspect of the gospel!"[184]

In 1965, Graham continued on the same theme of social change being a fruit of revival or transformed hearts—he taught inside-out change:

Often, however, a man preaching this message is labeled an obscurantist, "out of date." This is a day when a premium is placed on scholarship and objectivity. It is my humble opinion after having preached the gospel on every continent that this is absolutely the *only message* for our generation. No other message can change and transform. *We have to change men before we can change society.*

However, it is true that the evangelist must speak to the times. He must be contemporary in his outlook while remembering that his message is derived from the historic events, the death and resurrection of Christ. He must be contemporary and relevant. He must indeed express genuine social and ethical concern. However, his primary thrust is to proclaim the good news that God was in Christ reconciling the world unto himself.[185]

Up until 1965, it would seem that Graham stood strongly on social change as being a bi-product of evangelism.[186] He held to the universal affirmative of S1. Then a clear change seems to have occurred in Graham's commitment to the universal imperative.

Two responsibilities. While seeds of this change were found in Stanley High's biography, they were again expressed in 1960 when Graham explained "How My Mind Has Changed." The pressures on Graham as regards the so-called social implications of the gospel were evident in this article:

---

[184]Billy Graham, "The Gospel for the Whole World," 8.

[185]Billy Graham, "Evangelism Is Every Christian's Business," 72.

[186]"The changing of men is the primary mission of the church. The only way to change men is to get them converted to Jesus Christ. Then they will have the capacity to live up to the Christian command to 'Love thy neighbor.'" Billy Graham, *World Aflame* (Garden City, NY: Doubleday, 1965), 181.

A fifth change: my belief in the social implications of the gospel has deepened and broadened. I am convinced that faith without works is dead. I have never felt that the accusations against me of having no social concern were valid. . . . I have made the strongest possible statements on every social issue of our day. In addition, in our crusades we have tried to set an example. . . .

Yet I am more convinced than ever before that we must change men before we can change society.[187]

The change was evident in Graham's 1965 book *World Aflame:*

This sounds like a paradox, but it is not. We as Christians have two responsibilities. One, to proclaim the Gospel of Jesus Christ as the only answer to man's deepest needs. Two, to apply as best we can the principles of Christianity to the social conditions around us.[188]

Much like Lausanne 1974, Graham lowered the spiritual mandate of evangelism from its position of primacy, and raised alongside of the spiritual the social implications as a responsibility.

In 1967 Graham seems to have moved definitively to the SH1 position. In a sermon for the Kansas City Billy Graham School of Evangelism entitled "Communicating the Gospel," which he stated was in preparation for an article to be released in the *Ecumenical Review* entitled, "Conversion—A Personal Revolution,"[189] Graham moved away from the universal affirmative of evangelism alone, chiding evangelicals who focus on evangelism alone, "If evangelicals have forgotten their social responsibility it has been due to a perversion in their teaching and a reaction against the 'social gospel.'"[190] He expanded his concept of communicating the gospel using this transition statement, "Yet we live in a world of violence, revolution, hunger, difficulties and problems. How do we

---

[187]Billy Graham, "How My Mind Has Changed," in *How My Mind Has Changed,* ed. Harold E. Fey (Cleveland, OH: Meridian Books, The World Publishing Company, 1961), 65-66.

[188]Billy Graham, *World Aflame,* 187.

[189]Billy Graham, "Conversion—a Personal Revolution."

[190]Ibid., 282. At the end of this article, Graham called for three things, use of the Bible, a theology of evangelism, and "an awareness of the supernatural change brought about by the Holy Spirit" (ibid., 283). He closed with a challenge to personal evangelism: "I have no doubt that if every Christian in the world would suddenly begin proclaiming the kerygma and winning others to an encounter with Jesus Christ, we would have a different world over night. This is the revolution that the world needs!" (ibid., 284).

communicate to this world the Gospel of Christ?"[191] In answer to this question, Graham enumerated six main points:

> First I think we communicate the Gospel by the authoritative proclamation of the Gospel. . . .
> We communicate the Gospel by a holy life. . . .
> And then third, a big third, we communicate the Gospel by love.
> . . .
> And then fourth, we communicate the Gospel by a compassionate, social concern. . . .
> Big 5, we communicate the Gospel by our demonstration of unity in the spirit. . . .
> We communicate the Gospel by our contagious excitement about Christ.[192]

This expansion of his definition of "communicating the gospel" seemed to be new in the ministry of Graham. It was inclusive rather than exclusively proclamational as it had been in the past. In his next Kansas City School of Evangelism lecture, titled "Biblical Conversion," Graham continued to express a SH1 position:

> There is no doubt that the social gospel has directed its energies toward the release of many of the problems of suffering humanity. I

---

[191]Billy Graham, "Comunicating the Gospel," in *Lectures, Kansas City School of Evangelism, 1967*, 4.

[192]Billy Graham, "Communicating the Gospel," 4, 8, 10, 11, 15, and 16. It is interesting to compare Graham's six points with Bob Pierce's six points in his address to Berlin 1966 entitled "Commissioned to Communicate": "1. We are deluding ourselves if we think that most of the world is waiting eagerly for our Christian message. . . . 2. We are deluding ourselves if we think that evangelism is all talk. . . . 3. We are deluding ourselves if we think that Western missionaries and the Western cultural encrustations of the Christian Church will be accepted without question in the rest of the world. . . . 4. We are deluding ourselves if we think that our responsibility ends when our words of witness have been spoken, that it is then up to the other fellow to understand, appreciate and accept what we say. . . . 5. We are deluding ourselves if we think that the pressing issues of our day are best understood and described in an exclusively theological frame of reference. Our world has very little time for theological abstractions. . . . 6. We are deluding ourselves if we think that heroic missionary and evangelistic efforts of the past will stir the young people of today" (Bob Pierce, "Commissioned to Communicate," 2:21-22).

am for it! I believe it is biblical. However, I am convinced that we do not have a personal gospel and a social gospel."[193]

Graham then went to show that social change was a result of spiritual revival, quoting Timothy Smith.[194] Then Graham, in the parallel lecture edited for the *Ecumenical Review* added another quotation that chastised evangelicals:

> Kathleen Heasman, in her doctoral dissertation, wrote: "This personal approach which the evangelicals insisted upon coloured the forms which their social work took. It supplied the human touch that had been lacking in so much charity." If evangelicals have forgotten their social responsibility it has been due to a perversion in their teaching and a reaction against the "social gospel"; it is not because evangelism and the personal appropriation of Christ as Saviour and Lord does not involve the individual in the suffering of humanity.[195]

When stating this, Graham was chastising evangelicals who had perverted their teaching by reacting against the "social gospel." He was affirming the need to care for the "suffering of humanity." And he was taking a tactical position toward the worldwide readership of the *Ecumenical Review*. Graham seemed to ignore that Rauschenbusch's "social gospel" scoffed at the individualistic salvation that he preached. Or, if he did understand the antagonism of the "social gospel," then he sought to forge a new synthesis between the two. Thus he saw the pre-Rauschenbuschian "individual gospel" and the Rauschenbuschian "social gospel" working hand-in-hand— Graham did not see them as mutually exclusive and/or logically contradictory. He seemed to ignore that the theological constructs of the "social gospel" set themselves up *against* the personal gospel—even though his early liberal antagonists attacked him for that very reason.

Later in 1971, Graham possibly moved back to an S2 position, as can be noted in his message, "Challenge for Today's Church." [196] While

---

[193]Billy Graham, "Biblical Conversion," 10.

[194]"The revival idea that love to God and man was the chief fruit of Christian experience had equally significant consequences on social theory" (Timothy L. Smith, *Revivalism and Social Reform in the Mid-Nineteenth Century America* [New York: Abingdon, 1957], 158).

[195]Billy Graham, "Conversion—a Personal Revolution," *The Ecumenical Review* 19 (1967): 271-84, quoting Kathleen Heasman, *Evangelicals in Action* (London: Geoffrey Bles, 1962), n.p.

[196]"*Seventh,* I would call the church to a new relevancy. I would call the church to a proper perspective in coming to grips with the staggering social evils of our

allowing for social responsibility, Graham asserted that much of social responsibility is "sheer humanism." He also contended the "Inside-Out" notion that society will not be changed unless individuals are converted to Christ. Thus "man's greatest need is spiritual." Social change occurs through the instrument of the proclamation of the gospel which transforms

---

time. I would start, however, from a spiritual point of view. Only a healthy church can help a sick world. Much of our social action today is nothing but sheer humanism. I am convinced that we cannot save the world until we ourselves are first saved. We cannot change the world until we as members of the church have been transformed by the power of Christ. We cannot redeem society until we ourselves have first been redeemed by Christ.

In Great Britain today, where they have the welfare state, they are learning that man has far deeper problems than mere materialistic needs. Man has deep spiritual needs that have too long been neglected.

MAN'S GREATEST NEED

One of the leaders of the vast poverty program in this country recently told me that his experience in years of social work has led him to the conviction that man's greatest need is spiritual. This is precisely why Christ said, 'Ye must be born again' (John 3:7).

In the church though, there are those who hold that evangelism should be reinterpreted along the lines of social engineering, political pressure, and even violent revolution. We are told, 'That's the way to get things done.' We are witnessing today the greatest emphasis by ecclesiastical organizations on pronouncements, lobbying, picketing, demonstrating, and even now a call for violence to bring about social and political change in America. Certain church leaders feel that society must be compelled to submit to their ideas of social change. They say that this is the major part of the Christian mission.

We all agree that there is a sense in which the church is to advise, warn, and challenge society by proclaiming the principles of Scripture. But the church today is in danger of moving off the main track and getting lost on a siding. We have been trying to solve every ill of society as though society were made up of regenerate Christians to whom we had an obligation to speak with Christian advice.

We may try to legislate Christian behavior, but we soon find man himself remains unchanged. I believe that the changing of man's heart is the primary mission of the church. The only way to change men is to get them converted to Christ. Then they will have the capacity to live up to the Christian command to 'love thy neighbor as thyself' (Mark 12:31).

VITAL ACCOUNTABILITIES

We as Christians have two responsibilities: first, to proclaim the Gospel of Christ as the only answer to man's deepest needs; and, second, to apply as best we can the principles of Christ to the social conditions around us. The world may argue against a creed, but it cannot argue against changed lives. This is what the simple Gospel of Christ does when it is preached and proclaimed in the power and authority of the Holy Spirit.

I would call the church today back to its main task of proclaiming Christ and Him crucified, who can change lives and meet the deepest spiritual needs of mankind, as the only panacea for the problems that face the world" (Billy Graham, "Challenge for Today's Church," *Hour of Decision Sermons,* no.196 [Minneapolis: Billy Graham Evangelistic Association, 1971], 6-8).

individuals. Graham flatly said, "I believe that the changing of man's heart is the primary mission of the church. The only way to change men is to get them converted to Christ." Then, however, Graham again stated that the church has "two responsibilities," as he had in *World Aflame* in 1965.

> We as Christians have two responsibilities: first, to proclaim the Gospel of Christ as the only answer to man's deepest needs; and, second, to apply as best we can the principles of Christ to the social conditions around us.[197]

By placing the social responsibility side-by-side with the evangelistic responsibility, Graham showed his fluctuation between the S2 and SH1 approaches.[198] Yet if social service was a natural outflow of a changed life, it had no need to be mandated as a responsibility—it was the fruit of a changed life.

Drummond has argued that Graham has always held to the "two responsibilities" or "two obligations" position. In both of his books, each having a foreword by John R. W. Stott, chairman of the Lausanne Conference on World Evangelization and strong promoter of this "two responsibilities" position,[199] Drummond repeated a quote from T. B. Maston and a quote of Billy Graham from *World Aflame*.[200] He also explained that Graham held to two conversions, "Graham sees two types or aspects of conversion, the first being from the world to Christ, and the second from Christ back into the world."[201] Thus, it would seem that Drummond frames

---

[197]Ibid., 8.

[198]He repeated this same thought in Madison Square Garden in New York in 1969: "That's the flag I'm asking you to follow. That's what I'm asking you to believe. That's what I'm asking you to commit yourself to. We've seen these marvelous men and women of the Salvation Army here tonight, and we're honored to have General Coutts with us. These people have a cause; they take a cup of cold water in one hand; social activism of the highest order. They actually go out and help people in need, but in the other hand, they also carry the love of Christ. They carry the Gospel of the Lord Jesus Christ" (Billy Graham, "Man in Rebellion," in *The Challenge: Sermons from Madison Square Garden* [Garden City, NY: Doubleday, 1969], 49).

[199]See Stott, *Christian Mission*, and *Balanced Christianity* (Downers Grove, IL: InterVarsity, 1975).

[200]Drummond follows David Lockard's heavy reliance on T. B. Maston, *Christianity and World Issues* (New York: Macmillan, 1957) for his social construct.

[201]Drummond, *Canvas Cathedral: Billy Graham's Ministry Seen through the History of Evangelism* (Nashville: Thomas Nelson, 2003), 227. This important reference to "two conversions" was quoted from David Lockard, *The Unheard Billy*

the question to result in the position that Graham held to a "holistic" evangelism throughout his ministry.

Wolfhart Pannenberg, Professor of Systematic Theology on the Protestant Theological Faculty, University of Munich, admitted the positive impact of conservative evangelicals on secular culture in two articles.[202] While Pannenberg did not agree with Protestant evangelicals and fundamentalists, academic credibility led him to affirm that lasting social change did not come from emphasizing social change, but from lives transformed by the gospel.

World Emergency Fund, Lausanne, and LCWE. In 1973 Graham initiated the World Emergency Fund as an arm of the BGEA. This move, as he explained, happened gradually. First, Graham noted that the funding for the World Emergency Fund came from "a large part of our undesignated giving."[203] Its purpose was "to bring humanitarian aid to places facing natural disasters or other emergencies."[204] Graham's reasons for founding the World Emergency Fund as part of the BGEA were reminiscent of Bob Pierce's reasons for founding WVI:

Graham, 92, which quoted Graham in an article in the *Houston Chronicle* (6 December 1966).

[202]"Accommodation to secularity is in fact perceived as a sign of weakness, as a loss of Christian confidence. It has frequently been noted that the mainline and accommodating churches are in decline, while conservative churches continue to grow. Evangelicals and fundamentalists are not embarrassed to challenge the prevailing patterns of thought and behavior associated with secularity. This growth, however, does not come without paying a price. That price includes a loss of openness to the human situation in all of its maddening variety, and a quenching of the unprejudiced search for truth. *That said, the irony is that those churches that are dismissed as irrelevant by more "sophisticated" Christians often turn out to be most relevant to our secular societies*" (Pannenberg, "The Present and Future Church," 47 [emphasis mine]). "Protestant evangelicalism and the reassertion of the confessional tradition of Roman Catholicism are, in principles, more authentically Christian answers to the challenges of secularism than is the strategy of cultural adaptation and assimilation" (Wolfhart Pannenberg, "Christianity and the West: Ambiguous Past, Uncertain Future," *First Things,* December 1994, 23.).

[203]Billy Graham, *Just As I Am,* 437. Drummond wrote of Graham's giving to the World Emergency Fund, "In 1995, for example, the fund sent more than $335,000 to needy areas around the world. BGEA officials make it clear that every dollar contributed to the World Emergency Fund goes directly to relief projects. Nothing is siphoned off for administrative expenses" (Lewis A. Drummond, *The Evangelist* [Nashville: Word, 2001], 79).

[204]Billy Graham, *Just As I Am,* 437.

1. "Demonstrating our love through acts of compassion"
2. "Our responsibility to do whatever we can as individuals to help those in need"
3. "We had a larger responsibility [than just preach the gospel]"
4. "The stark reality of human suffering and with the fact that many millions of people live on the knife-edge of starvation or chronic illness or disaster"
5. "Compassionate help often opened the door to opportunities in evangelism, as people saw Christ's love in action."[205]

The founding of the World Emergency Fund concretized Graham's paradigm shift from S1 to SH1. However, Graham's paradigm shift did not impact his ministry to the extent that it did John R. Mott's and Bob Pierce's—as Graham continued to preach the gospel.

Meanwhile, the WCC, grandchild of the Edinburgh 1910 World Missionary Conference and child of the IMCs, works to bring churches together in the "Ecumenical Movement."[206] Today WVI, founded by Bob Pierce, has as sixth on their list of purposes, *"Witness to Jesus Christ,* by life, deed, word and sign."[207] This evident progression leads this author to the conclusion that the paradigm shift in Graham did not play itself out, as it did with Mott[208] and Pierce—that may still to be seen in the future of evangelicalism. Graham's shift may have been more practical and tactical, as suggested in the fifth reason above, "compassionate help often opened the door to opportunities in evangelism." In fact, acts of compassion may have opened doors for Graham to foreign countries, as well as to less evangelistically-oriented denominations.

It is interesting to note that the World Emergency Fund was founded five years after Sherwood Eliot Wirt, editor of *Decision Magazine,* wrote *The Social Conscience of the Evangelical.*[209] Leighton Ford, in his

---

[205]Ibid., 518.

[206]"Yet they [churches of the World Council] are all committed to close collaboration in Christian witness and service. At the same time, they are also striving together to realize the goal of visible Church unity" (William H. Lazareth and Nikos Nissiotis, "Preface," in *Baptism, Eucharist and Ministry,* Faith and Order Paper No. 111 [Geneva: World Council of Churches, 1982], vii).

[207]World Vision International, "Who Is World Vision?" [on-line].

[208]Mott took thirty-nine years before he shared his paradigm shift in writing!

[209]This book was the culmination of a study at a meeting in Chicago on the evangelical social conscience. Attendees of this session were "Dr. Ted W. Engstrom, Dr. James Forrester, Dr. Frank E. Gaebelein, Dr. Lars Granberg, Dr. Richard C. Halverson,

foreword to this book, stated that he was encouraged by the new emphasis on social responsibility.[210] Further, the World Emergency Fund was founded three years after Bob Pierce founded Samaritan's Purse in 1970—who currently state their mission in two ways[211]—, and one year before Lausanne 1974. The BGEA organization seems to have changed to adapt to the theology of the International Conference on World Evangelization held in Lausanne, Switzerland in 1974, before it ever happened. Then at a January 1975 meeting in Mexico City, Graham "conceded the validity of Stott's interpretation,"[212] though insisting, "evangelism is primary." However, Leighton Ford suggested that following Lausanne, Billy Graham's views were broader than those of his own organization:

> I think Lausanne represents Billy. I don't think it represents his organization, which is centered on actually doing evangelism. Billy's broad view of evangelism and social issues and theology and

---

Dr. David A. Hubbard, Dr. Harold J. Ockenga, Rev. Floyd W. Thatcher, and Dr. Curtis Vaughan" (Sherwood Eliot Wirt, *The Social Conscience of the Evangelical* [New York: Harper and Row, 1968], ix). The heart of Wirt's apologetic for social ministry was found in a lengthy quotation of the words of Horace L. Fenton, Jr. spoken at a "Congress on the Church's Worldwide Mission" in Wheaton, Illinois, in 1965 (ibid., 150-53). Wirt wrote of his Fenton quotation, "Dr. Fenton's statements summarize what can be called the burden of this book" (ibid., 153).

[210]"For a long time I have been waiting to read this book—or one like it. My friend and colleague, Sherwood Wirt, has given us an exciting evangelical perspective on social responsibility, and he has done it with candor, with courage, and with grace" (Leighton Ford, "Foreword," in *The Social Conscience of the Evangelical*, vii).

[211]On a Yahoo search for Samaritan's Purse came the tag line, "international nonprofit Christian mission organization with a single-minded commitment to evangelism through aid relief." On the Samaritan's Purse homepage is the mission, "Samaritan's Purse is a nondenominational evangelical Christian organization providing spiritual and physical aid to hurting people around the world" (Samaritan's Purse, "About Us," [on-line]; accessed 19 July 2001; available from http://www.samaritanspurse.org/ home.asp; Internet).

[212]Martin, *A Prophet with Honor*, 451. Stott's interpretation was captured in his *Balanced Christianity*, "In urging that we should avoid the rather naïve choice between evangelism and social action, I am not implying that every individual Christian must be equally involved in both" (John R. W. Stott, *Balanced Christianity*, 41). Later he wrote, "I do not know any better statement of our double Christian responsibility, social and evangelistic, than that made during the Fourth Assembly of the World Council of Churches at Uppsala in 1968 by W. A. Visser't Hooft, former WCC General Secretary" (42).

churchmanship are not represented as much in the organization as in Billy himself.[213]

The later Graham. In 1977 Graham's *Hour of Decision* sermon titled "Ambassadors" further expressed Graham's "balanced" view of mission. His first point on living under the authority of God was "in our personal lives." His second point was "in our social relationships":

> Second, we are under the authority of the Word of God in our social relationships as well. As Christians we're not isolated persons; we are part of society with all of its difficulties and problems and hopes. The Bible has much to say about social justice and social actions. Human society is affected by sin, and we know that any effort we make to improve society will always be incomplete and imperfect. We are not going to build a Utopia on earth. Why? Because of human nature. Sin keeps us from building a paradise on earth.
>
> *But we are to work for social justice—that is our command in Scripture—we're to do all we can so that we can live a peaceable and a free life, and a life of human dignity. . . .*
>
> Only Christ can change hearts, but that does not mean that we neglect social and political responsibilities. Christ is concerned about the whole person, including the society in which he or she lives. Many of the great social reforms of the 19th century in Great Britain and America were inspired by evangelical Christians. But the time came when many forgot that the Gospel was both vertical and horizontal. This has changed now. Evangelicals are once again proclaiming a balanced Gospel of personal salvation on the one hand and social responsibility on the other, bringing their social action and responsibility under the authority of the Scriptures.[214]

Graham's third point was service, and in this point he discussed sowing the seed and holding forth the light. Yet, it is clear from the above quote that in 1977 Graham was planted right in the middle of the evangelism and social responsibility continuum.

In 1981 the same unclear middle ground tension was evident in Graham. He began with the same old message:

---

[213]Martin, *A Prophet with Honor,* 454.

[214]Billy Graham, "Ambassadors," *Hour of Decision Sermons,* no. 213 (Minneapolis: Billy Graham Evangelistic Association, 1977, revised 1996), 2-3 (emphasis mine).

But till then, whatever hour that may be—a thousand years from now, or a hundred years from now or tomorrow—we ought to be about the business of witnessing to the whole world of the gospel of the Lord Jesus Christ.[215]

But moments later, he moved to the particular affirmative by including social service into his paradigm, "I believe that mission can be summed up in two words: proclamation and service."[216] Billy Graham repeated this same idea at Urbana 87:

Who will declare—by word and deed—the love of Christ to those who do not know him? . . . If you're not winning people to Christ here, if you're not serving Christ here, he can't use you there.[217]

Here Graham affirmed the same two concepts that he did in 1981: proclamation and service. Affirmation XIV of the Amsterdam Affirmations (1983) reads as follows:

We share Christ's deep concern for the personal and social sufferings of humanity, and we accept our responsibility as Christians and as evangelists to do our utmost to alleviate human need.[218]

Graham began his exposition of the relationship between evangelism and social action as follows:

Often I am asked about the relationship between social action and evangelism. While evangelism has priority, social action and evangelism go hand in hand. We must have a burden for the needs of people that goes beyond just "concern" and results in action.[219]

Graham then discussed social movements as the fruit of revival. He seemed to confound the distinction between roots and the fruits that he was so careful to maintain in his early ministry. Graham continued, "We must be

---

[215]Billy Graham, "Mission Impossible: Your Commitment to Christ," 120.

[216]Ibid., 121.

[217]Billy Graham, "Are You a Follower of Jesus Christ?" in *Urban Mission: God's Concern for the City,* ed. John E. Kyle (Downers Grove, IL: InterVarsity, 1988), 117.

[218]Billy Graham, *A Biblical Standard for Evangelists* (Minneapolis: World Wide Publications, 1984), 115.

[219]Ibid.

concerned with human suffering wherever it is found because God is concerned about it."[220] Yet in his attempt at a synthesis,[221] Graham emphasized the need for spiritual salvation:

> But we Christians should do what we can to help the poor, to heal the sick, and feed the hungry—although we must never forget that how or when man dies is less important than where he will spend eternity. If you feed all the hungry and care for all the poor and heal all the sick, yet fail to explain the way of salvation to them, you have not reached their deepest need.[222]

Although in his later balance, he began adding to the list of possible ministries in which the Christian could be involved:

> The Church of the Savior requires that each member be actively working in some sort of outreach project, whether it be evangelism through a Bible study; a retreat ministry; rebuilding houses or feeding the poor; caring for orphans, widows, and transients; being involved in the primary concerns of education; public housing; or environment.[223]

Graham continued expressing his "balanced" view into his later life. *Approaching Hoofbeats* was expanded and republished as *Storm Warning*. In this book Graham stated, "We are called to minister to human bodies and human spirits simultaneously."[224] One must note that now the "human bodies" were placed prior to the "human spirits." Much as "Christian Social Responsibility" was placed before "The Church and Evangelism" in the

---

[220]Ibid., 116.

[221]"The fourth and unnecessary polarization concerns our Christian evangelistic and social responsibilities. . . . In recent years, however, there have been welcome signs of change. . . . In urging that we should avoid naïve choice between evangelism and social action, I am not implying that every individual must be equally involved in both. This would be impossible [a stunning admonition indeed!] . . . . Let us place our feet confidently on both poles. Don't let us polarize!" (John R. W. Stott, *Balanced Christianity*, 37, 39, 41, 43). In *Balanced Christianity* and in *Christian Mission,* both published the same year, Stott promoted the definition of W. A. Visser t'Hooft, as brought before the Fourth General Assembly of the WCC in Upsalla, as showing a proper balance.

[222]Billy Graham, *A Biblical Standard for Evangelists*, 117.

[223]Billy Graham, *Storm Warning* (Waco, TX: Word, 1992), 161. The exact author of these words is unclear. Yet, Graham gave his name to them.

[224]Ibid., 259.

Lausanne Covenant. One is also reminded of the penitence of Lausanne as regards the neglect of social responsibility.[225]

In noting the pronouncements of Graham on the relationship between evangelism and social responsibility, a change has been noted. Has Graham himself acknowledged the change? An interview and Harvard speech reported by Frye Gaillard, provided a view of Graham's view of his mission. The setting was as follows: in 1982 Graham went to Moscow to speak on peace at the "World Conference of Religious Workers for Saving the Sacred Gift of Life from Nuclear Catastrophe;" one week after his Moscow address, Graham received the Templeton Foundation Prize for Progress in Religion in London, England. Prior to the Moscow trip, Graham spoke at Harvard, sharing about his spiritual pilgrimage:

> "I would like to say some things informally about my own pilgrimage and my own witness," he [Graham] said. "My basic commitment as a Christian has not changed, nor has my view of the Gospel. But I've come to see in deeper ways some of the implications of my faith and the messages I've been proclaiming."[226]

Gaillard continued, "There has been an epic change in the heart of Billy Graham."[227] Gaillard quoted Graham as saying, "'I plan to spend the rest of my life,' he [Billy Graham] says, 'doing two things—preaching the gospel and working for peace'"[228] Was this "epic change" a reversal of what Graham said in 1957, "I could say to the president to the leaders of all governments today that there can be no peace until Christ has come to the hearts of men and brought his peace"?[229] Or was Graham including working for peace as a tactical move? The introduction and other portions of his

---

[225]"Here too we express penitence both for our neglect and for having sometimes regarded evangelism and social concern as mutually exclusive. Although reconciliation with man is not reconciliation with God; nor is social action evangelism, nor is political liberation salvation, nevertheless we affirm that evangelism and socio-political involvement are both part of our Christian duty. For both are necessary expressions of our doctrines of God and man, our love for our neighbor and our obedience to Jesus Christ" (Stott, *Making Christ Known,* 24).

[226]Frye Gaillard, "The Conversion of Billy Graham: How a Presidents' Preacher Learned to Start Worrying and Loathe the Bomb," *The Progressive* 46 (August 1982): 26.

[227]Ibid., 30.

[228]Ibid.

[229]Billy Graham, "The Grace of God," *Hour of Decision Sermons,* no. 82 (Minneapolis: Billy Graham Evangelistic Association, 1957), 7.

autobiography seem to substantiate what the words actually said,[230] as did the inaugural address of Charles Malik on the occasion of the inauguration of the Billy Graham Center in Wheaton, Illinois[231] and as did the biography written by William Martin,[232] Graham had significantly changed his view of mission, as well as adjusting his own disclaimer of being called to the narrow task of preaching the gospel.

---

[230]Graham spoke of his meeting with The Great Leader Kim Il Sung in his introduction as a hallmark of his worldwide peacemaking ministry (Billy Graham, *Just As I Am,* xxii-xxiii). During this meeting Graham brought "token gifts," a copy of *Peace with God* and a Bible, and he brought messages from President Bush and Pope John Paul II (626). He explained about his peacemaking mission in other places also: "The other emphasis was my desire to build bridges of understanding between nations" (479). Graham's words upon arrival in North Korea were as follows, "The D. P. R. K. and the United States are not natural enemies. It is past time that the suspicion and enmity which have characterized our relations for the last half-century were replaced with trust and friendship" (622). Graham continued, "I found President Kim to be very alert, with a deep, gravely voice and strong, charismatic personality. . . . Then, pointing outside at the early signs of spring, he expressed the hope that a new springtime was coming to D.P.R.K./U.S. relations" (625-26).

[231]"But if Christians do not care for the intellectual health of their children and for the fate of their own civilization—a health and a fate so inextricably bound up with the state of the mind and spirit in universities—who is going to care? For it to be accomplished, people must be set on fire for it. It is not enough to be set on fire for evangelization alone.

Responsible Christians face two tasks—saving the soul and saving the mind" (Charles Malik, "The Other Side of Evangelism" *Christianity Today,* 7 November 1980, 39, 40).

[232]"No single event was responsible for what would be a notable shift in tone and emphasis, but several Graham associates observed that he seemed to regard issues of peace and disarmament in a new light after his early visits to Eastern Europe, particularly after his 1978 pilgrimage to Auschwitz, where the meaning of the Holocaust burned itself into his consciousness. In addition, said one man who had accompanied him on the tour of Poland, 'He saw that the commitment of [Eastern European] religious leaders for peace and reconciliation was serious.'

A few months after the Polish tour, when the World Council of Churches began to call for approval of the new SALT II accords, Graham added his voice to their chorus. 'The people of the U.S. want peace,' he observed, as do the people of China and the Soviet Union. 'Why can't we have peace?' He conceded that defenses were necessary 'to keep madmen from taking over the world and robbing the world of its liberties' but noted that he had begun to take a new view of nuclear weapons. Moreover, he observed, it seemed his fellow Evangelicals were beginning to share his concerns—the Southern Baptist Convention had passed resolutions calling for multilateral nuclear disarmament and support of SALT II. Perhaps they had reached the same conclusion he had: 'I didn't really give it the thought that I should have given it in my earlier years, but I have come to the conviction that this is the teaching of the Bible'" (Martin, *A Prophet with Honor,* 500).

How can the change that Billy Graham underwent in the area of evangelism and social action be described? Perhaps, going back to Figure 5, it was a shift from S1 to SH1. Graham's views on this subject were admittedly quite complex. Was it his ecclesial environment or the Bible that caused him to start out with the universal affirmative of S1? What did this change represent theologically? An expanded analysis of the possible impact of this shift will be saved for further analysis of Graham's theology.

With evangelism and social responsibility in mind, another issue affected evangelicalism in regards to parameters for evangelism. Lifestyle evangelism swept across the United States and the world in the early eighties. How did Graham respond to lifestyle evangelism?

Lifestyle Evangelism

Lifestyle evangelism was a relatively new movement in evangelicalism. While there is nothing new under the sun (Eccl 1:9), the promotion of lifestyle evangelism among evangelicals began in the 1970s. Before giving a brief history of the movement, some definition is necessary. Lifestyle evangelism is the belief that the lifestyle or service[233] of the Christian is a necessary *preparatio evangelica* prior to the sharing of the gospel with another individual.[234] In other words, the *a priori* of relationship adds lifestyle to the *ordo salutis* as a *preparatio evangelica*.[235] Furthermore, Lifestyle evangelism teaches that evangelism is more productive or enjoys

---

[233]Servant evangelism was a further development of Lifestyle Evangelism. Steve Sjogren in his *Conspiracy of Kindness* (Ann Arbor, MI: Servant Publications, 1993) was negative to expectant evangelism, reminiscent of Joseph Aldrich, calling it "high risk-low grace" and "Russian Front" evangelism (ibid., 61). Donald Atkinson and Charles Roesel in *Meeting Needs—Sharing Christ* (Nashville: Lifeway, 1995) built upon a similar concept of *gratia preparatur*, yet did not come out against expectant evangelism.

[234]The 1918 Archbishops' committee had the same view regarding the need for social ministry, "He who applies Christian faith and living to the common relationships of life is the best evangelist. The translation of our creed into action by social service rendered from Christian motives is a true *preparatio evangelica*, and a presentation of the Gospel which ignores the social obligations of Christianity will not receive serious attention from increasing numbers of people to-day" (*The Evangelistic Work of the Church: Being the Report of the Archbishops' Third Committee of Inquiry* [London: SPCK, 1918], 17).

[235]Adding human relationship to the *ordo salutis* is in keeping with parents bringing their children for baptism in Roman Catholicism, and does not have any Reformation theological tradition to back it up. The lifestyle of, relationship of, or incarnational ministry of the gospel proclaimer was completely unknown in Protestant scholasticism when *ordo salutis* was a matter of discussion.

greater positive response than traditional, initiative, expectant, or proclamational evangelism. In fact, it is sometimes felt that without the *preparatio evangelica* of relationship, evangelism can be actually counterproductive. There are a number of theological fallacies in lifestyle evangelism which will be addressed briefly following the historical introduction. Then, Graham's role and response to lifestyle evangelism will be noted.

History of Lifestyle Evangelism

Among evangelicals a significant paradigm shift took place in the 1970s and 1980s. Prior to this time Southern Baptists and evangelicals looked to the Bible for *both* doctrine and practice. However, in the pivotal period of the 1970s and 1980s, while holding on to the Bible for their doctrinal understanding of the gospel, many evangelicals began to look elsewhere to formulate their practice of the gospel. In fact, it is currently in vogue to denigrate expectant evangelism—the initiating of conversations to share the gospel of Jesus Christ. It may be that as evangelicals were becoming mainstream,[236] they needed a mainstream-type of evangelism.

Three clarifications must be noted up front. First, the lifestyle of the Christian is very important. The need for a loving demeanor is taught throughout the Bible (e.g., John 13:35), and positive lifestyle is taught in relation to evangelism, as in the case of the woman married to the unsaved husband (1 Pet 3:1-2) and in other passages (e.g., Matt 5:16; 1 Pet 2:12; 3:15). Second, those who teach lifestyle evangelism are good people. They have led others to Christ and encouraged Christians to share their faith. This portion is not an attack on any personality. Rather, it is quite possible that these authors did not understand the theological impact of their proposed change in the practice of evangelism. Third, relational evangelism is both valid and necessary. At issue is not the reality of human relationship, but the demand for lifestyle as a *preparatio evangelica* prior to sharing. Also at issue is the consistent denigrating or demeaning of expectant evangelism. It would seem that the ambiguous theological foundations of lifestyle evangelism have gone virtually unnoticed. Notable conservative theologians

---

[236]*Time Magazine* claimed 1976 as "The Year of the Evangelical." Alister McGrath wrote: "Evangelicalism, once considered marginal, has now become mainline, and it can no longer be considered as an insignificant sideshow, sectarian tendency or irrelevance. It has moved from the wings to center stage, displacing others once regarded as mainline, who consequently feel deeply threatened and alienated. Its commitment to evangelism has resulted in numerical growth, where some other variants of Christianity are suffering from severe contraction" (Alister E. McGrath, *Evangelicalism and the Future of Christianity* [Downers Grove, IL: InterVarsity, 1995], 17).

have not observed the theological impact of this movement. However, lifestyle evangelism not only blunts the practice of evangelism, but it represents a doctrinal shift in Christian theology.

It must be stated up front when looking at historical precedents that lifestyle evangelism was prominent among Roman Catholics following the sacramentalism initiated by Gregory the Great and grounded in the theology of Thomas Aquinas. A notable example of lifestyle evangelism, for example, is found among the contemplative [closed] monasteries of the Franciscans originally founded by Francis of Assisi. Lewis Drummond affirmed Francis of Assisi as a historical precedent for Graham's "holistic evangelism" in his book, *The Canvas Cathedral: Billy Graham's Ministry Seen through the History of Evangelism.*[237] To Franciscans evangelism includes to "follow Christ," "live for God," and "live the Gospel."[238] In the contemporary Roman Catholic Church, this lifestyle emphasis was explained in Paul VI's 1975 encyclical *Evangelii Nuntiandi.*[239] Paul VI spoke of a "silent witness" as being central to the evangelization. Surely this "silent witness" provides a salient precedent for those promoting lifestyle

---

[237]"In light of this truth [love for a brother], an evangelism that accepts the full revelation of God in Scripture must be holistic in nature. This means that human needs, whether they are spiritual, physical, cultural, or economic, must be addressed by God's people. . . . Moreover, no one saw this truth more clearly than the renowned medieval man of God, St. Francis of Assisi" (Lewis A. Drummond, *The Canvas Cathedral,* 211). "As we looked into the life and service of St. Francis of Assisi, we learned that the man of God was a fervent evangelist. Like Graham, he too longed to see people come to faith in Jesus Christ. But history also attests to the fact that Francis felt a deep burden for the physical and social needs of his fellowman" (Ibid., 223).

[238]Words spoken by a Franciscan monk from a "closed cloister" (i.e. no contact with the outside world) upon a monastery visit in New Orleans, Louisiana, on June 7, 2001.

[239]"69. Religious, for their part, find in their consecrated life a privileged means of effective evangelization. At the deepest level of their being they are caught Up in the dynamism of the Church's life, which is thirsty for the divine Absolute and called to holiness. It is to this holiness that they bear witness. They embody the Church in her desire to give herself completely to the radical demands of the beatitudes. By their lives they are a sign of total availability to God, the Church and the brethren.

As such they have a special importance in the context of the witness which, as we have said, is of prime importance in evangelization. At the same time as being a challenge to the world and to the Church herself, this silent witness of poverty and abnegation, of purity and sincerity, of self-sacrifice in obedience, can become an eloquent witness capable of touching also non-Christians who have good will and are sensitive to certain values" (Paul VI, *Evangelii Nuntiandi,* 8 December 1975, section 69).

evangelism among evangelicals today—for their arguments are the same.[240] However, this definition of evangelism cannot be equated with the Scriptural definition of verbal evangelism as found in Mark 16:15, "Go in to the world and preach the gospel to all creation."

In the early part of the twentieth century the fundamentalist movement agreed on several points. First, they agreed on the fundamentals of the faith.[241] Second, they agreed on the urgent task of world evangelism.[242] This urgency anchored the spirit of the missionary movement in the nineteenth century.[243] A shift took place among evangelicals in the 1950s, 1960s, and 1970s. Evangelism lost its place as the universal affirmative. It went from being the reason for the church and the preeminent purpose of the Christian and the church to being one of several tasks and an important purpose of the church. It is to the point where some prominent evangelicals almost seem to despise expectant evangelism.[244]

---

[240]It would seem that the recent interest in Mother Teresa parallels the lifestyle evangelism approach (see Mother Teresa, *Total Surrender,* rev. ed. [Ann Arbor, MI: Servant, 1995]).

[241]When considering the fundamentals, evangelical writers often note the series of tracts by that name edited by R. A. Torrey of Moody Bible Institute and others. Some Roman Catholics locate the five fundamentals to the 1895 Bible Conference in Niagara. The "five fundamentals are: inerrancy of Scripture, deity of Christ, the virgin birth, substitutionary atonement, and bodily resurrection at the second coming of Christ (Commission Biblique Pontificale, 48).

[242]"The Commission according to Mark, therefore, in one phrase from Matthew, tells us that witnessing is the main work of the whole church in the whole world throughout the whole age" (J. E. Conant, *Every Member Evangelism* [New York: Harper and Brothers, 1922], 7).

[243]A. T. Pierson, in a final word to the World Missionary Conference, London 1888, stated, "A positive aggressive Gospel is the Gospel that will win the day" (Arthur T. Pierson, "Final Word," in *Report of the Centennary Conference on the Protestant Missions of the World Held in Exeter Hall (June 9th-19th), London, 1888,* ed. James Johnston [New York: Revell, 1888], 487).

[244]"There are some people who feel evangelism works best when you push people to commit their life to Christ. They do not even shy away from manipulative methods to reach this goal. No wonder many of us feel a strange sensation in our stomach when we hear the word 'evangelism.'

But it can be shown that 'pushy' manipulative methods represent the exact opposite of the practice we learn from growing churches" (Christian A. Schwarz, *ABC's of Natural Church Development.* (Carol Stream, IL: ChurchSmart, n.d.), 16). Note his words "exact opposite"!

Before the 1950s a strong belief in the primacy of evangelism was characteristic of the evangelical movement.[245] In fact, the name evangelical was borrowed because of an emphasis on evangelism and personal conversion. This primacy of evangelism began to erode in gradual way. It was not a question of "good or bad." Rather it was a question of "good, better, or best." Founded in the early 1950s, WVI sought to balance social responsibility with evangelism as the purpose of the church. Conversion began to be interpreted in psychological terms (human) rather than in spiritual terms (divine).[246] In the 1960s discipleship began to rival expectant evangelism as the true fulfillment of the Great Commission. It was not long before the process of making disciples (sanctification) was wrongly transferred to view evangelism (justification) as a process. Leighton Ford's *The Christian Persuader* persuaded Christians that the temporary, "Not yet" overruled the "Go" in the Great Commission.[247] He placed fellowship and demonstration in the *ordo salutis*. Ford followed this statement in his chapter entitled. "By All Means Save Some," with three points.[248] Ford's move away from proclamational evangelism seemed to echo the sentiments of Joseph Bayly's *The Gospel Blimp* (1960) that seemed to mock both program-oriented evangelism, as well as expectant evangelism. This book struck a nerve among evangelicals and was soon released as a film.

In the 1970s, social responsibility was placed side-by-side with proclamation evangelism in the Lausanne Covenant—a powerful document used to define evangelism for evangelicals worldwide. Also in the 1970s, a desire for the unity began to rival the task of evangelism. It was not long before denominational distinctives were viewed with suspicion. The primacy of evangelism was gradually diminished by rival purposes. The

---

[245]Notice the synonymous understanding of witnessing, discipleship, and preaching the gospel in J. E. Conant: "The Commission according to Mark, therefore, in one phrase from Matthew, tells us that witnessing is the main work of the whole church in the whole world throughout the whole age" (J. E. Conant, *Every Member Evangelism* [New York: Harper & Brothers Publishers, 1922], 7).

[246]For example, see Robert O. Ferm, *The Psychology of Christian Conversion* (Westwood, NJ: Revell, 1959), and James H. Jauncey, *Psychology for Successful Evangelism,* foreword by Leighton Ford (Chicago: Moody, 1972).

[247]"Not until they could show the fellowship of truth and demonstrate the deeds of truth, were they ready to speak the words of truth" (Leighton Ford, *The Christian Persuader* ([New York: Harper and Row, 1966], 68).

[248]"We must evangelize by the reality of our fellowship. . . . We must evangelize, not only by the reality of our fellowship, but also by the compassion of our service. . . . Then most of all, we evangelize by the faithfulness of our proclamation." (ibid., 69, 74, and 78).

time was ripe for a new methodology—a paradigm shift, if you will. The first use of the term "lifestyle evangelism" came from a 1973 publication by that title of C. B. Hogue, Director of the Division of Evangelism of the Home Mission Board of the SBC. The purpose of this publication was to introduce Southern Baptists to the publications and state directors of evangelism of the SBC. Hogue opened the book with the following words: "Lifestyle evangelism is incarnational evangelism."[249] He then explained the need for "being and doing" in evangelism.[250] With a foundation in incarnational theology, coming from directly ecumenical theology,[251] Hogue coined the term "lifestyle evangelism" as an expression of incarnational evangelism.

From 1979 to 1981 three books provided a new emphasis in the Great Commission as evangelism among evangelicals. All three joined in downplayed expectant evangelism and agreed that "lifestyle evangelism" was the answer. In 1979 Rebecca Manly Pippert wrote *Out of the Saltshaker and into the World*. In her first chapter Pippert wrote these words: "To evangelize, it seemed, required insensitivity and an inclination to blurt out a memorized gospel outline, without inhaling, to every stranger you met."[252] Throughout her book Pippert continued her assault on expectant evangelism, framing her "relational" model as superior. The second book came the next year. Jim Petersen wrote *Evangelism as a Lifestyle*. To promote his brand of "lifestyle evangelism," Petersen denigrated crusade evangelism because it was not relational. Petersen then wrote, "Our Western society is becoming less receptive to approaches that were effective in the past."[253] In this way he discounted virtually all the examples of evangelism in the New Testament and in church history, opting for the "relational"

---

[249]C. B. Hogue, *Lifestyle Evangelism*, 1.

[250]"The name of the game in lifestyle evangelism is "Show and Tell." This is Jesus told the Gerasene demoniac to do after his conversion. It is *being* and *doing*. . . .

What a difference it would make in our lives together as the people of God and in our own personal lives if we could all appropriate the fact that the church is the body of Christ and that every individual believer incarnates Christ in his body so that we become 'His hands, feet, tongue, heart, eyes et cetera'" (ibid).

[251]Bosch, *Transforming Mission*, 512-13.

[252]Rebecca Manly Pippert, *Out of the Saltshaker and into the World: Evangelism as a Way of Life* (Downers Grove, IL: InterVarsity, 1979), 16.

[253]Jim Petersen, *Evangelism as a Lifestyle* (Colorado Springs, CO: NavPress, 1980), 12. Five years later Petersen wrote *Evangelism for Our Generation* (Colorado Springs, CO: NavPress, 1985). The two books were combined to form *Living Proof* (Colorado Springs, CO: NavPress, 1989). *Living Proof* was made into a video series and its methodology was adopted by churches and organizations, such as the Christian Businessmen's Association.

approach. It may be good to be reminded of those who taught and exemplified the "approaches that were effective in the past": Jonathan Edwards, John Wesley, George Whitefield, William Carey, J. Hudson Taylor, Charles Haddon Spurgeon, J. Wilbur Chapman, D. L. Moody, R. A. Torrey, J. E. Conant, L. R. Scarborough, W. B. Riley, Faris D. Whitesell, C. E. Autrey, and Billy Graham. This brief sentence by Petersen had immense theological ramifications to the evangelistic methodology of evangelicals.

The *coup de grâce* came from Joseph Aldrich in his book entitled *Life-Style Evangelism*. Aldrich effectively edged those practicing expectant evangelism to the fringes of the evangelical movement. The paradigm shift from expectant to lifestyle was masterfully communicated and widely accepted. The heart of Aldrich's argument was clarified in his fourth chapter entitled "Practicing the Presence in Evangelism," in which he made use of equivocation to make his point. On one hand, he wrote that the Confrontational/ Intrusional Model "is legitimate."[254] Of "Proclamational Evangelism" Aldrich wrote:

> Although the proclamational approach to evangelism will have validity until Jesus comes, it is not a means by which the majority of Christians will reach their own private world.[255]

He drew the following conclusion regarding confrontational/intrusional evangelism:[256]

---

[254]Joseph Aldrich, *Life-Style Evangelism: Crossing Traditional Boundaries to Reach the Unbelieving World* (Portland, OR: Multnomah Press, 1981), 79.

[255]Ibid., 78. Aldrich defined "proclamational evangelism" by using the example of the early church: "The early church was planted because of the strong proclamational ministries of the apostles. They preached on street corners, in synagogues, and in marketplaces" (ibid.).

[256]Aldrich defined "confrontational/intrusional evangelism" in this way: "The *confrontational/intrusional* model is probably the most common one. Generally the 'target audience' is a stranger" (ibid.). Thus any non-relationally-based one-on-one evangelism can fall into the category of "confrontational/intrusional." However, of the fifty-two personal evangelism conversations in the New Testament, thirty-seven were with complete strangers (understanding that no one was a stranger to Jesus), five were with previous acquaintances, and the prior relationship of ten is unclear from the text (see Thomas P. Johnston, "An Analytical Study of Personal Evangelism Conversations in the Gospels and the Book of Acts," Classroom lecture notes, *BIB/CHM 230X— Biblical Evangelism,* Spring 1995, photocopy], 7). Whitesell cited 35 examples of personal evangelism in the ministry of Jesus, another 15 examples of personal evangelism in the Book of Acts, for a total of 50 examples (Faris D. Whitesell, *Basic New Testament Evangelism* [Grand Rapids: Zondervan, 1949], 107-08, 112).

The vast majority do *not* become Christians by confrontational, stranger-to-stranger evangelism. Furthermore, many are being kept from making an effective decision because of bad experiences with a zealous but insensitive witness.[257]

While on one hand saying that expectant evangelism was legitimate, on the other hand Aldrich proclaimed that it was counter-productive, actually hindering "effective decision." In two pages of his *Lifestyle Evangelism* Aldrich came full circle:

1. Expectant evangelism is valid and legitimate.

2. Expectant evangelism is not practical.

3. Expectant evangelism hinders effective decisions.[258]

Following his attack of expectant evangelism, Aldrich explained the benefits of his Relational/Incarnational Model using Maslow's "Hierarchy of Needs" to make his point.

It must be noted that the Pippert/Petersen/Aldrich models were published in three successive years, 1979, 1980, and 1981, immediately following the 1978 International Consultation on 'Gospel and Culture,' Willowbank, Bermuda. "The Willowbank Report," among other things, encouraged a "more radical concept of indigenous church life," which was expressed in the paper by Charles Kraft titled "A Dynamic Equivalence Model."[259] Similarly, other books on evangelism written in that same time period included similar concepts.[260] It would seem that the *ethos* of

---

[257]Aldrich, *Life-Style Evangelism,* 79, italics his.

[258]To back up this point, Aldrich quoted James Jauncey, *Psychology for Successful Evangelism* (Chicago: Moody, 1972), 123: "Just buttonholing a stranger, witnessing to him and pressing for a decision will likely do more harm than good. Most responsible people react negatively and often quite violently to this kind of assault. *It shows a fundamental lack of respect for human dignity and personality*" (Aldrich, *Life-Style Evangelism*, 80).

[259]Stott, *Making Christ Known,* 99, 111. Thus, it would seem that Lifestyle Evangelism is the biproduct of "Dynamic Equivalence" theory being superimposed on biblical evangelism. The resulting cry is 'more culture' (Charles Arn, "A Response to Dr. Rainer," 75-78).

[260]For example: Leighton Ford, *Good News Is for Sharing: A Guide to Making Friends for Christ* (Elgin, IL: David C. Cook, 1977); Wayne McDill, *Making Friends for Christ—A Practical Approach to Relational Evangelism* (Nashville: Broadman, 1979); Arthur McPhee, *Friendship Evangelism: The Caring Way to Share*

evangelicalism was undergoing a paradigm shift. The new methodology took hold and impacted not only the United States, but also the entire world through conferences and the translations of books on lifestyle evangelism.

Theology of Lifestyle Evangelism

Most discomforting, however, was the amputation of theology from practice in lifestyle evangelism. Lifestyle evangelism looked to the Bible for its theology of the gospel, but failed to look at the Bible for the work of the gospel. This severing of theology from practice was not without impact. In fact, key doctrinal commitments of evangelical churches were compromised by this accommodation to practice.

Table 2 enumerates twenty points which represent some of the biblical and/or doctrinal shifts resulting from adherence to the emphases of lifestyle evangelism. Some of these shifts impact the sufficiency of Christ and of the Bible. (1) Lifestyle evangelism undermines the evangelical concept of instantaneous conversion, as exemplified in Acts 16:14, "The Lord opened her heart to respond to the things spoken by Paul," by adding relationship to the *ordo salutis*. Instantaneous conversion was a hallmark of the nineteenth century missionary movement,[261] and in the belief of Billy Graham.[262] (2) Lifestyle evangelism is the natural emanation of the

---

Your Faith (Grand Rapids: Zondervan, 1979); Joyce Neville, *How to Share Your Faith without Being Offensive* (New York: Seabury, 1981); and Matthew Prince, *Winning through Caring: Handbook on Friendship Evangelism* (Grand Rapids: Baker, 1981).

[261]"There is the plan of preaching the gospel and looking forward to the gradual enlightenment of the people, to their being saved as it were by a process of gradual instruction and preaching. And there is another method of preaching the gospel; believing it to be the power of God unto salvation; preaching it in the expectation that He who first brought light out of darkness can and will at once and instantaneously take the darkest heathen heart and create light within. That is the method that is successful. It has been my privilege to know many Christians—I am speaking within bounds when I say a hundred—who have accepted Jesus Christ as their Saviour the first time they ever heard of Him" (J. Hudson Taylor, "The Source of Power," in *Ecumenical Missionary Conference, New York, 1900: Report of the Ecumenical Conference on Foreign Missions* [New York: American Tract Society, 1900], 91).

[262]Instantaneous conversion is intimately linked with the concept of the new birth. The new birth is not a gradual enlightenment, it is a crisis experience. Graham said, "I want to ask you straight out today—have you been born again?" (Billy Graham, "Christianism Versus Communism, *Hour of Decision Sermons,* no. 2 [Minneapolis: Billy Graham Evangelistic Association, 1951], 9).

Later Graham explained the instantaneous and the gradual in conversion: "Conversion at such a moment can be as sudden and dramatic as the conversion of pagans who transfer their affection and faith from idols carved of stone and wood, to the person of Jesus Christ. However, not all conversions come as a sudden, brilliant flash of

reconciliation model of the atonement.[263] (3) Lifestyle evangelism requires faith to come through hearing *and* seeing, contra Romans 10:17. (4) In lifestyle evangelism, the word of God *must* be accompanied by the *preparatio evangelica* of needs-oriented relationship to be powerful unto salvation, contra 1 Peter 1:23.[264] (5) Lifestyle evangelism requires the proclaimer to preach himself and Christ, contra 2 Corinthians 2:2 and 4:5. (6) In lifestyle evangelism, the merits of Christ must be accompanied by human merits of the proclaimer to be efficient unto salvation, contra Titus 3:5. (7) In lifestyle evangelism, Christ's love as demonstrated on the cross is not enough to show the love of God to the unsaved (Rom 5:8). Rather Christians must earn the right to share the gospel. (8) In lifestyle evangelism, the life of the Christian opens the heart of the unsaved to the gospel, contra 1 Corinthians 7:16 and the Parable of the Sower.[265] (9) In

---

soul illumination that we call a crisis conversion. There are many others that are accomplished only after a long and difficult conflict with the inner motives of the person. With others, conversion comes as the climactic moment of a long period of gradual conviction of their need and revelation of the plan of salvation. This prolonged process results in conscious acceptance of Christ as personal savior and in the yielding of life to Him. We may say, therefore, that conversion can be an instantaneous event, a crisis in which the person receives a clear revelation of the love of God; or it can be a gradual unfoldment accompanied by a climactic moment at the time the line is crossed between darkness and light, between death and life everlasting" (Billy Graham, "What Is Conversion?" *Hour of Decision Sermons,* no. 38 [Minneapolis: Billy Graham Evangelistic Association, 1953], 5-6).

When speaking of the conversions of the Apostle Paul and John Wesley, Graham stated, "In both cases the experience produced an immediate change in life and attitude and a sense of release from sin and guilt" (Billy Graham, "Christian Conversion," *Hour of Decision Sermons,* no. 111 [Minneapolis: Billy Graham Evangelistic Association, 1969], 8). A theology of instantaneous conversion drove the revivalist methods of Billy Graham. Ferm explained, "However, instantaneous conversions cannot be produced simply because the speaker seeks to produce conversions. . . . It appears evident therefore, that there is a direct relationship between the message preached and the resulting type of conversion" (Robert O. Ferm, "The Theological Presuppositions of Billy Graham," unpublished manuscript [Wheaton, IL: Billy Graham Archives, n.d.], 12).

[263]The view of James Denney as found in *The Christian Doctrine of Reconciliation* (New York: George H. Doran, 1918) will be discussed in the next chapter.

[264]"I have used Maslow's Hierarchy of needs for years as a teaching tool. I find it helpful in determining what level of need a person is struggling to satisfy" (Aldrich, *Life-Style Evangelism,* 90).

[265]In fact, Bob Pierce seems to have made an overstatement to this effect: "This was the first time these lepers ever had anybody do anything for them. They were the most radiant bunch, and they all became Christians (but not because of any theology)" (Franklin Graham, *Bob Pierce,* 70).

TABLE 2

THEOLOGICAL COMPARISION OF
EXPECTANT AND LIFESTYLE EVANGELISM

	Expectant Evangelism	Theological Implications of Lifestyle Evangelism[266]
1.	Instantaneous conversion, Acts 16:14; Rom 10:13	Progressive conversion/gradual enlightenment
2.	Substitutionary atonement, 2 Cor 5:21	Reconciliation model of the atonement (to be discussed in Chapter 3).
3.	Faith comes by hearing, Rom 10:17	Faith comes by seeing and hearing
4.	The word of God is the instrument of salvation, Rom 1:17; 1 Pet. 1:23	Sharing the gospel must be preempted by relationship
5.	Preaching Christ, 2 Cor 4:5	Preaching ourselves and Christ
6.	Christ alone saves, Acts 4:12; Rom 5:8-10, et al.	Christ's work needs human merits to be effective
7.	Christ earned the right for the message to be shared, Rom 5:8; 1 Tim 1:15	Christians must earn the right to share the gospel with others
8.	The lifestyle and miracles of Christ did not lead to faith in all those who observed them, John 12:37	The lifestyle of the Christian will lead the lost to become open to the message of the gospel
9.	Harvest is ripe, Luke 10:2, John 4:35	Harvest is not ripe; it needs cultivation
10.	Must evangelize by faith, John 4:35	Must use natural relational rules
11.	Christians' lives should be consistent with the gospel; Christians should live holy lives, 1 Pet 1:14-16	Christians must practice "radical identification" and "eat meat" (à la 1 Cor 10:23 ff.) to relate to the lost.

---

[266]It is important to understand that, as within any movement, there are degrees of adherance to lifestyle evangelism. Various Scriptures are also cited by those adhering to lifestyle evangelism to affirm their position (e.g., see Aldrich, Joseph C. *Gentle Persuasion* [Portland, OR: Multnomah Press, 1988]).

12.	Christians will be hated by the world due to their association with Christ, John 15:18-21	Christians are hated only because they are not culturally sensitive and open to the needs of the unsaved
13.	The gospel is a reproach, Heb 11:26, e.g. 1 Cor 1:23; it will be avoided by evildoers, lest their deeds be exposed, John 3:20-21	The gospel need not be a reproach (i.e. a moral philosophy); natural man can and will accept Christianity's rational superiority with proper apologetics
14.	Satan has blinded the minds of unbelievers so that they cannot see Christ, John 3:20-21, 2 Cor 2:17, 4:3-4	Man's sin has not fully blinded his mind; he can discern certain spiritual truths if properly communicated
15.	Rejection of gospel is due to lack of comprehension and spiritual blindness, Matt 13:19, 2 Cor 4:3-4 – Christian only responsible to share, Ezek 3:18-19, with patience, 2 Tim 4:2, and gentleness, 1 Pet 3:15	Rejection of gospel is due to a lack of relational cultivation; guilt is placed on the rejected Christian for his lack of proper cultivation, leading to a further fear of sharing the gospel to the unsaved
16.	Persecution is promised, 2 Tim 3:12, and is a blessing, Matt 5:10-11, 1 Pet 4:12-14	Persecution is a sign that the method of evangelism is faulty, needing modification
17.	Evangelism weapons are spiritual, 2 Cor 10:3-5	Must use both spiritual and carnal weapons (e.g., marketing techniques)
18.	Evangelism is both urgent and the preeminent priority for the Christian: (1) Return of Christ, Matt 24:14 (2) Mankind is totally depraved, Rom 3:9-20 (3) Reality of hell, Matt 25:46 (4) Christians are accountable, Ezek 3:16-21, Acts 20:26	Evangelism is one of many important aspects of the Christian life: (1) Emphasis on here and now (2) Total depravity may be an overstatement (3) Some question the reality of a literal hell (4) Mentioning accountability is putting guilt trips on Christians
19.	The Bible is authoritative in both doctrine and practice (i.e., the work of evangelism), 2 Tim 3:16-17; 1 Cor 11:1	The Bible is authoritative primarily for doctrine—the practice of evangelism must glean truth from culture
20.	Expectant evangelism is absolutely necessary in the ministry of the local church:	Expectant evangelism is counter-productive, negative to the world's view of the church, cf. 1

		Cor. 4:10:	
(1)	Expectant evangelism is commanded, Mark 16:15, et al.	(1)	Reinterpret Great Commission as a gradual process, e.g., make disciples in Matt 28:19
(2)	Expectant evangelism is exemplified, Acts 4:19-20; 5:29; cf. 2 Tim 4:1-5	(2)	Adapt evangelism methodology to truths in anthropology, sociology, and psychology

lifestyle evangelism, the harvest is not ripe, as stated in Matthew 9:37, Luke 10:2, and John 4:35. Rather the harvest needs a time of cultivation, contra John 4:35. (10) Lifestyle evangelism encourages bringing someone to Christ using natural relational means, contra 2 Corinthians 10:3-5. It also confuses the spiritual nature of salvation. (11) Lifestyle evangelism encourages "radical identification" and "eating meat and evangelizing," indicating a *penchant* for worldliness or compromise in lifestyle, contra Titus 2:11-14.[267] (12) In lifestyle evangelism, it seems to be assumed that Christians are hated by the world because they lack cultural sensitivity, contra Matthew 5:10-12 and John 15:18. (13) In lifestyle evangelism, the gospel does not need to be a reproach, contra 1 Corinthians 1:23, especially if it is communicated as a positive moral philosophy (Christian worldview) or as persuasive apologetics. Natural man will see the rational superiority of the gospel and godly life. (14) In lifestyle evangelism the minds of unbelievers are not considered blinded to spiritual truth (contra 2 Cor 4:3-4), rather they just need to see spiritual truth at work in the life of a believer to be convinced (contra Luke 16:31). (15) In lifestyle evangelism guilt for the rejection of the gospel is placed on the Christian because he has not properly cultivated the relationship, contra Matthew 5:11-12. (16) In lifestyle evangelism persecution is the sign of a faulty method of sharing the gospel, contra 2 Timothy 2:12. (17) In servant evangelism (a cousin of lifestyle evangelism) the *required* addressing of "felt needs" (*preparatio evangelica*) necessitates the use of carnal weapons along with the spiritual, contra 2 Corinthians 10:3-5. (18) In lifestyle evangelism the proclamation of the gospel is not urgent nor is it the church's preeminent priority. Rather, in lifestyle evangelism, evangelism is *one of many* priorities in the Christian life. (19) In lifestyle evangelism the biblical examples of evangelism are not

---

[267]For example, see Little's chapter, "Worldliness: External or Internal" (Paul E. Little, *How to Give Away Your Faith* [Downers Grove, IL: InterVarsity, 1966, 1988], 146-62), Aldrich's chapter titled "Eating Meat and Evangelizing" (Aldrich, *Life-Style Evangelism*, 57-76), or Pippert's chapters on holiness and evangelizing (Pippert, *Out of the Salt Shaker*, 81-102).

trustworthy guides for evangelism, thus the authority of the Bible is undermined. (20) Finally, the verdict of lifestyle evangelism is that the practice of expectant evangelism is counter-productive to the image, growth, and proper ministry of the local church. Hence, lifestyle evangelism, not only blunts the evangelistic thrust of the mainstream evangelical church, but it also compromises many of its core doctrinal beliefs.

Table 2 summarizes these doctrinal and practical differences between expectant evangelism and lifestyle evangelism. When seen in this light, the differences between lifestyle evangelism and expectant evangelism are drastic and alarming. While a positive Christian lifestyle is necessary and important, lifestyle evangelism's negativity to expectant evangelism represented an important paradigm shift in the evangelical movement's doctrine and practice. Lifestyle evangelism's methodology undermined the examples of the Bible, the thrust of the First Great Awakening, and the Pietistic evangelism that characterized nineteenth-century Protestant missions. How did Billy Graham fare with regard to lifestyle evangelism?

Billy Graham

At the start of Graham's ministry, he was very strongly oriented to expectant evangelism. He shared his early methodology with Ben Haden in a 1961 interview:

> [Haden] "Do you feel there is a difference between evangelism and witnessing?"
> [Graham] "I think they go hand in hand. I used to think that when I met anybody I had to ask him if he were a Christian. I felt legally bound to hand everybody a tract. This became a 'legalism'. . . ."[268]

Graham spoke of an era when he preached outside of bars, condemning those inside who were drinking. During the late 1930s Graham traveled with T. W. Wilson and Walter Meloon in the latter's station wagon preaching from town to town in Florida, and sleeping in the automobile. Roy Gustafson wrote of the ministry of Graham while he was attending Trinity College:

> Billy took advantage of and created opportunities to preach the gospel. A street meeting in Sulphur Springs, a Sunday afternoon jail

---

[268]Ben Haden, ""Dr. Graham, Exactly What Is Evangelism?" *Presbyterian Survey* (March 1962): 10.

service at the Tampa stockade, or a tiny group in a Spanish mission, were as challenging to him as speaking to larger groups in other places.[269]

Byram H. Glaze, a fellow-student with Graham, recollected Graham's early ministry of evangelism:

> But on Saturday afternoon on the streets of Sulphur Springs, Billy would preach that sermon and many people would be saved. On Saturday nights in a Tampa Rescue Mission, many men would come weeping after his preaching. How I've wished that I'd had that kind of courage.[270]

Was this early Graham guided by "zeal without knowledge"? Was this the result of the urgent preaching of Mordecai Ham, the example of Bob Jones, Sr., or the encouragement of W. T. Watson? Could this early zeal be attributed to Trinity Bible College's social environment? Or was this zeal the product of the Bible's own words emblazed on Graham's heart by the Holy Spirit and lived out in obedience?[271] The question of source is the crucial question—for in it lies the key to all great revival preachers of the church.

Graham's early sermons also strongly urged support of aggressive evangelism:

> I beg of you this year, nineteen fifty-four, to invest your time and money in lives. Invest your money in the salvation of souls. Invest your money in evangelism. Invest your money in the church that is winning men to Jesus Christ. . . . We must invite men first to be believers, then disciples, then witnesses. We must reach this generation for Christ. . . .[272]

Yet, this emphasis on aggressive evangelism also underwent a gradual change. In 1952, Graham defined evangelism as including a non-verbal

---

[269]Roy W. Gustafson, letter to W. T. Watson, in *The Bible School Days of Billy Graham*, ed. W. T. Watson (Trinity College, n.d.), 11.

[270]Byram H. Glaze, letter to W. T. Watson, in *The Bible School Days of Billy Graham*, 16.

[271]Some would see an urgent call to expectant evangelism in 1 Cor 9:16-17, 22-23; Col 1:28-29; 2 Tim 4:2, 5, not to mention the Great Commission passages or the examples of evangelism in Matt 10, Luke 9 and 10, and the Book of Acts.

[272]Billy Graham, "The Urgency of Revival," *Hour of Decision Sermons*, no. 36 (Minneapolis: Billy Graham Evangelistic Association, 1953), 8.

element when he spoke at the Church House in Westminster.[273] He began by stating that evangelism is first practiced "through the worship of the Church." Then he stated:

> Secondly, there is evangelism *by consistent Christian living.* A. T. Morrison, the great Methodist preacher in America, got converted by a Methodist circuit preacher riding his horse two hundred yards away. The fragrance of the man spread two hundred yards to the farm boy, and A. T. Morrison was converted to Christ. Wouldn't it be great if there was something about your bearing and something about the way you walked that would compel men to say, "I want to be a Christian?"[274]

Graham's last point in defining evangelism was "preaching to crowds as a method of evangelism."[275] In his 1953 *Peace with God,* Graham continued in a similar vein. He wrote, "We witness in two ways: by life and by word—neither by itself is enough."[276] He then used a series of well known terms to express the need for an urgent witness, "God's purpose for you and me . . . is that we be witnesses of His saving grace and power. You are to be a commando for Christ. You are a minute-man for Him." He shared a few verses about the need for a verbal witness, and then continued, "Very little originality is permitted the Western Union messenger boy. . . . Our Great Commander has said, 'Go, and take this message to a dying world.'"[277] He then continued speaking about holding a light, blowing a trumpet, kindling a fire, striking a hammer, using a sword, bread for a spiritually hungry world, and water for a famishing people.[278] He concluded, "be a soul-winner."[279]

---

[273]C. E. Autrey wrote, "To say that proclamation is verbal and witnessing is non-verbal is not in keeping with the Scriptures" (C. E. Autrey, *The Theology of Evangelism* [Nashville: Broadman, 1966], 54).

[274]Billy Graham, "The Work of an Evangelist," in *Introducing Billy Graham: The Work of an Evangelist—An Address Given at the Assembly Hall of the Church House, Westminster, on 20th March, 1952,* Prologue and Epilogue by Frank Colquhoun (London: World's Evangelical Alliance, 1953), 15.

[275]Ibid., 17

[276]Billy Graham, *Peace with God* (Garden City, NY: Doubleday, 1953), 167.

[277]Ibid.

[278]Graham used these same metaphors in his sermon "Retreat, Stand, Advance" in 1947 (Billy Graham, "Retreat, Stand, Advance," 44-45).

[279]Ibid., 169.

Yet with all these biblical metaphors, he had already moved away from a verbal universal affirmative.[280]

In 1955 Graham's theological and tactical change of heart was apparent as he gave greater credence to works or lifestyle. In his sermon "The Sin of Omission" Graham stated, "We need fewer words and more charitable works; less palaver and more pity; less creed and more compassion."[281]

In a 1961 interview with Ben Haden quoted above, Graham was asked directly about the subject of evangelism, lifestyle, and the verbal proclamation of the gospel. Graham explained his change of heart:

> [Haden] "Do you feel there is a difference between evangelism and witnessing?"
>
> [Graham] "I think they go hand in hand. I used to think that when I met anybody I had to ask him if he were a Christian. I felt legally bound to hand everybody a tract. This became a "legalism" until I began to realize that a witness is a person who is filled with the Holy Spirit, abiding in Christ. And when he is living the life and in tune with God-asking God to direct and lead in his life each day, totally yielded—he becomes a radio station. He's sending out beams all around, and there is a person over here to whom God is speaking. God will bring that person across his path.
>
> "I could tell you story after story of these unique experiences that occurred after I had laid this matter day by day in God's hands. He brought a person across my path whom the Holy Spirit had prepared. We can't go out and win a person, I don't think, unless the Holy Spirit has prepared the way.
>
> "The preparations of the heart are of the Lord, the scripture says (Proverbs 16:1) It is God that does the whole work. He only uses us as instruments and channels. So that is witnessing. Every Christian who is living the life of a witness will be a soul winner."
>
> [Haden] "Do you feel that evangelism is simply verbal?"

---

[280]The lifestyle of the Christian is definitely an important part of following Christ. There are numerous commands in Scriptures which admonish a holy lifestyle (e.g., 1 Pet 1:16), having a good lifestyle toward outsiders (1 Tim 3:7), and so forth. The admonitions which state "Let your light shine before men in such a way that they may see your good works, and glorify your Father who is in heaven" (Matt 5:16) and "they may on account of your good deeds, as they observe *them,* glorify God in the day of visitation" (1 Pet 2:12) assume that when people see the good deeds of the Christian they do not glorify the Christian (works salvation), but rather God. There is in these verses an encouragement to share Christ to the unsaved lest they believe that works of the Christian emanate from them and not from God (cf. John 3:20-21; Eph 2:10).

[281]Billy Graham, "The Sin of Omission," 5.

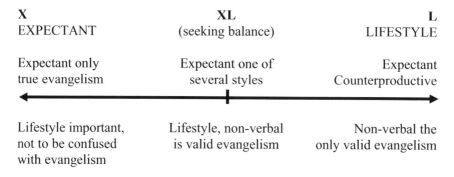

Fig. 6. Expectant compared to lifestyle evangelism.

[Graham] "In one sense, Yes. The scripture says, *Faith cometh by hearing.* In another sense, No. I think it was Henry Clay Morrison, president of Asbury College in Kentucky, who said he was converted out in a corn field, plowing in a field and watching the circuit rider (preacher) riding on a horse . . . and, he said, "There was just something about the way he sat on that horse, and the glow on his face, that caused me to be convicted and to get on my knees and receive Christ."

"I got a letter the other day from a man who said he was flying at night, over the stadium in Dallas, when the people were coming forward during a crusade meeting. He was in a commercial plane on his way to New York. He said the Holy Spirit spoke to him, and he was converted in that airliner. And yet he hadn't heard a thing." . . .

[Haden] "Do you believe a person can unconsciously evangelize?"

[Graham] "Yes, I do. I think of the story. I told a moment ago about the circuit rider: he probably never knew that Henry Clay Morrison was converted under him."[282]

A note about Graham's affirmation of a non-verbal element in evangelism: The examples Graham used for a non-verbal witness seem to indicate that a prior witness took place (cf., 1 Pet 3:1-2). It would seem to be completely against Graham's proclamational approach that faith was possible outside of special revelation of God through the Bible or a biblical gospel proclaimed, such as in Thomistic theology or natural theology.

Nevertheless, Haden's 1961 interview of Billy Graham provided a reliable pulse of Graham's changing view in relation to the concepts of

---

[282]Ben Haden, "Dr. Graham, Exactly What Is Evangelism?," 10.

lifestyle evangelism. Particularly interesting was Graham's acknowledgement that he did not always feel as he was then stating. In his early years as an evangelist, Graham shared, "I felt duty bound to hand everybody a tract." Thus, if Graham's early and latter approach to evangelism were placed on the Figure 6, what would be his progression? Graham in his early ministry was in the "Expectant Only" camp. He felt duty bound to hand out tracts, preach on the streets, and to literally proclaim the gospel to everyone he met. Then, he shifted to accepting that some are saved without an immediate verbal witness (1952)—although the implication was that they heard the gospel prior to the occasion of their conversion. By 1953 he had already affirmed that both word and deed are necessary. Therefore, Graham moved from the X position to the XL position. Clearly the verbal-only approach was a difficult doctrine for Graham to maintain.

In his 1955 sermon, "The Sin of Omission," Graham showed his openness to lifestyle evangelism:

> A true sacrament is not a mere creed or ordinance, or form, but it is a life of service to God and to man. The most eloquent prayer is the prayer through hands that heal and bless. The highest form of worship is the worship of unselfish Christian service. The greatest form of praise is the sound of consecrated feet seeking out the lost and helpless.
>
> In the parable of the last judgment the people were not asked questions of theology. As important as doctrine is, they were not asked about their doctrinal beliefs. Neither were they asked what sins they had committed. Theirs was chiefly and solely the neglect to do good and their sin was grave enough to send them into everlasting punishment. There must be a practical outworking of our faith here in this present world or it will never endure in the world to come. We need fewer words and more charitable works; less palaver and more pity; less creed and more compassion.[283]

These 1955 words of Billy Graham seemed to substantiate what became known as lifestyle evangelism. He emphasized "unselfish Christian service," as well as "less creed and more acts of compassion." This was a complete redefinition of the sins of omission which he explained in his 1950 sermon "How to Be Filled with the Spirit":

> Well there are sins of omission: the first one is ingratitude. . . .
> The second sin of omission is lack of love for God. . . .

---

[283]Billy Graham, "The Sin of Omission," 4-5.

The third sin of omission is neglect of the Word. . . .

The fourth sin is unbelief. . . .

The next sin is neglect of prayer. . . .

The sixth sin is failure to attend church services. . . .

Then we lack a passion for souls—a burning desire to lead unbelievers to Christ. Passion that is intense and deep. Do you feel that way about those afar from God?

Other sins of omission are the neglect of family duty—we forget family altar; our hospitality is cold; we refuse to deny ourselves; all these are sins.[284]

In the 1959 sermon "Three Dimensional Love of God," Graham stated, "The world waits in vain today for a demonstration of Christian love and forbearance. . . The church needs to rediscover the power of Christian love."[285] The sermon then gave an example of a soldier who came to Christ through the quiet love of a Christian fellow-soldier. In 1959 Graham began to speak to the need for lifestyle evangelism. In his 1965 book *World Aflame,* Graham posited a dual approach to mission: to proclaim the gospel and apply the principles of Christianity to social conditions around us.[286] This point was based on man's dual citizenship. Then he went from a social orientation to a lifestyle witness: "The lives of the early Christians was their invincible witness."[287]

The numerous definitions of evangelism Graham brought before the School of Evangelism in Kansas City in 1967 portrayed that Graham had broadened his approach to evangelism near the middle of Figure 5 and also near the middle of Figure 6. He explained that proclamation was one of six ways to communicate the gospel, including also a holy life (lifestyle), love, compassionate social concern, demonstration of unity in the spirit, and contagious excitement.[288] In Graham's list, however, he placed proclamation first, and he continued to practice proclamational evangelism in the revivalist style in his sixty-three years of evangelism ministry. Thus, there seemed to be a discord between Graham's theology, his practice, and his verbal definitions of evangelism. His biblical and revivalist theology necessitated an emphasis on verbal witness and instantaneous conversion.

---

[284]Billy Graham, "How to Be Filled with the Spirit," in *Revival in Our Time,* 110-12.

[285]Billy Graham, "Three Dimensional Love of God," *Hour of Decision Sermons,* no. 108 (Minneapolis: Billy Graham Evangelistic Association, 1959), 9.

[286]Billy Graham, *World Aflame,* 187.

[287]Ibid., 188.

[288]Billy Graham, "Communicating the Gospel," 4-16.

His practice followed this theology, but his definitions allowed for a more reconciliation-model approach to evangelism.

An interesting example of Graham's approach to teaching evangelism was found in the "Lifestyle Witnessing" material. In 1991 Tom Phillips put together a "Lifestyle Witnessing" course with Billy Graham's endorsement. A closer look at the course, however, reveals that it contained the same material that the BGEA had used for many years of training counselors for follow-up at crusades and for telephone ministry (the hand illustrations seem to come from Dawson Trotman's influence in early 1950s). The "Lifestyle Witnessing" material did not proffer the negativism to expectant evangelism that other books on lifestyle evangelism often did. Graham, however, saw the power of terminology, and thus it seemed that he sought to exploit new terms and phrases to further the cause of the gospel, rather than being trapped by them.[289]

What does this chapter teach about the parameters in Graham's definition of evangelism? First, it shows that Graham's view of evangelism did change during his years of ministry. Second, it explains that Graham went from being solely proclamational to becoming first more open to non-verbal witnessing (1952), to the importance of lifestyle evangelism (1961), and then open to social ministry (1967). In practice, Graham spent his life in proclamational ministry, not adding the World Emergency Fund (social responsibility) until 1973. From that time on he continued to seek to maintain the evangelistic and social in a balance, with the evangelism as the priority. Graham's sixty-four years of ministry practice remained similar to the tracks set in place when the BGEA was founded in 1950. Thus his practice continued in the revivalist traditions he ascribed to the Bible.

It would be interesting to see what his ministry would have been had he started out in 1937 believing that a definition of evangelism had six parts as expressed in 1967. While involving speculation, it would seem that Graham's street preaching in Sulphur Springs was born from a strong proclamational-approach to evangelism. Graham's revivalist crusade methodology and his invitation system bear witness to his view of instantaneous conversion as the work of the Holy Spirit directly, without mediation, upon the heart of man as a result of the transforming power of the word of God proclaimed in the power of the Holy Spirit. Because of this early theological and methodological foundation, it is the opinion of this author that Graham's ministry is best interpreted by his early theology and practice. His later approaches to the Great Commission, social responsibility, and lifestyle evangelism led to a level of discord between

---

[289]"They dressed this up with all kinds of legal pretences, but the true basis of their power was expressed by Hilaire Belloc in the words: We have the Maxim gun, And they have not" (A. J. P. Taylor, "Introduction," in *The Communist Manifesto* [New York: Penguin, 1967], 16).

Graham's theology and practice. Graham's theology of conversion will be a central element in the next chapter.

CHAPTER 4

MESSAGE

The same kerygma proclaimed through the lips of an interpreter in Spanish, Japanese, Tamil, or an African dialect will penetrate the darkened mind and flood it with the light of the Gospel. There seems to be no such thing as a language barrier when the Gospel is proclaimed. Even the voice of the interpreter does not hinder or limit its power. That is why we can go to any country, no matter what their language or their culture may be, and proclaim Christ crucified and risen, the only Savior from sin and the hope for the world, and they will respond.[1]

Billy Graham illustrated the heart of gospel proclamation as he spoke to pastors at one of the first schools of evangelism in Kansas City in 1967. He believed the *kerygma*, the simple message of the gospel, to have the power to penetrate the hearts, minds, and souls of people all over the world. And through the power of the Holy Spirit, according to Graham, those quickened would respond to the gospel message.

While seemingly a simple concept, the proclamation of the gospel and its corollary, responding to the gospel, became the focus of virtually every major doctrinal battle in church history. The Council of Nicea debated the Trinity, the Council of Chalcedon debated the person of Christ, and the Council of Orange debated soteriology. The Middle Ages experienced the continuing battles as sacramentalism and semi-Pelagianism gradually became the position of the Western Church. The Reformation era as exemplified in Martin Luther reaffirmed *sola scriptura, sola gratia,* and *sola fides.* Then in each of the streams of the Protestant Reformation the gospel and conversion became focal points of numerous controversies. Among Methodists, who grew at a very fast pace for their first 100 years, the Modernist-Fundamentalist Controversy over the authority and veracity of the Bible greatly effected evangelism and church growth. The sharpest decline in the Methodists can be pinpointed to the influx of Modernism into

---

[1]Billy Graham, "Biblical Conversion," *Kansas City School of Evangelism* (Kansas City, MO: Billy Graham Evangelistic Association, 1967), 11-12.

its pulpits.[2] Among Baptists, the gospel, conversion, and evangelism led to multiple controversies and schisms. The first major controversy centered on the extent of the atonement between the General Baptists and the Particular Baptists of the seventeenth century. Other Baptist controversies have included the Regulars and the Separatists, being for and against the First Great Awakening; the Primitive and Missionary Baptists, being against or for the use of means in missions, following the revival of missions in the early nineteenth century; the social gospel controversy of the early twentieth century; and battles for the Bible, particularly in the twentieth century.[3] If these disagreements did not focus directly on evangelism, such as the use of means in missions or the revival methodology, they focused on the extent of the atonement or the authority of the Bible. All of these controversies either directly or indirectly impacted evangelism. It would seem that church history is rife with theologies which dull the evangelistic edge of the church.

This chapter is entitled "Message." It seeks to focus on this important aspect of a theology of evangelism. Because of the breadth of the subject of this chapter, topics will be introduced with an analysis of Graham's views on the subject. The thesis of this chapter is that Billy Graham began by preaching the total depravity of man, the substitutionary atonement, and Pietistic Lutheran soteriology. He emphasized instantaneous conversion as a result of the ministry of God the Holy Spirit through His Word preached, followed by an immediate response through an invitation.

---

[2]The title "modernism" indicated a move away from "sectarianism." Finke and Stark borrowed the term "sectarian" from H. Richard Niebuhr (H. Richard Niebuhr, *The Social Sources of Denominationalism* [New York: Henry Holt and Company, 1929], 12-14) to describe the origin from which Methodism moved. Two distinctives of "sectarian" groups were biblical authority and evangelism. Following their shedding of these "sectarian" distinctives the Methodists had big losses in membership while Baptists continued to grow (Roger Finke and Rodney Stark, *The Churching of America 1776-1990: Winners and Losers in Our Religious Economy* [New Brunswick, NJ: Rutgers University Press, 1992, 1997], 145-48). Niebuhr, for his part, borrowed his concepts from Ernst Troelsch (Ernst Troelsch, *Die Soziallenhren der christlichen Kirchen und Gruppen* [1912]; *The Social Teaching of the Christian Churches,* 2 vols, trans. by Olive Wyon [London: George Allen & Unwin, 1931; New York: Macmillan, 1931]).

[3]This battle over the Bible was fought not long after the founding of the North Baptist Convention (NBC) in 1907, leading to the founding of several splinter groups: the Baptist Bible Union in 1922, the General Association of Regular Baptists in 1932, The North American Baptist General Conference (German-speaking) in 1940, the Baptist General Conference (Swedish-speaking) in 1944, and the Conservative Baptist Association in 1947. This loss of churches and support contributed to the renaming of the NBC as the American Baptist Churches (Donald Tinder, "Fundamentalist Baptist in the Northern and Western United States" [Ph.D. diss., Yale University, 1969], 362-442). While the battle for the Bible has also been waged among Southern Baptists on various occasions, the more recent battle led to the founding of a less-conservative offshoot in 1990, the Cooperative Baptist Fellowship.

Timo Pokki, who wrote *America's Preacher and His Message: Billy Graham's View of Conversion and Sanctification,* wrote that Graham's theology combined Augustinian anthropology,[4] experiential Puritanism,[5] Pietistic salvation,[6] and American revivalism. He summarized that Graham was in the "Democratic American and Arminian Tradition,"[7] and that he followed the views of the Southern Baptist Convention, "which have been classified as 'modified Calvinism' or 'modified Arminianism.'"[8] However, there is adequate proof that Graham did not maintain constant views throughout his ministry. Rather many of his views changed over the course of his sixty-three years of preaching. The challenge of this chapter will be to define Graham's views, as well as to note and chart possible changes.

This chapter will be divided into five sections, each providing a different angle on the message of Billy Graham. First, we will discuss the messenger of the gospel. Second, we will note the personal gospel. Third, we will study Graham's approach to sin. Fourth, we will discuss Graham on the atonement. And last, we will briefly look at Graham on judgment. While each of these is a weighty subject in and of itself, each subject will be briefly introduced, followed by looking directly at the sermons or writings of Graham on the topic. Secondary writings will be noted as they compliment or explain the writings of Graham.

The topic of conversion begins with a messenger of conversion. In the case of Billy Graham, he has been called an evangelist, preaching the message of the gospel and conversion. With this in mind, we begin by noting the messenger of the gospel.

The Evangelist

While nowhere in the Bible is the gift of evangelism mentioned, the evangelist is listed by the Apostle Paul in Ephesians 4:11 in the middle of a list of five leaders given to the church, "And He gave some as apostles, and some as prophets, and some as evangelists, and some as pastors and

---

[4]Timo Pokki, *America's Preacher and His Message: Billy Graham's View of Conversion and Sanctification* (doctoral diss., University of Helsinki, Finland, 1998; Lanham, MD: University Press of America, 1999), 74.

[5]Ibid., 27.

[6]"In Pietism the new birth was a deeply felt crisis event" (ibid., 35).

[7]Ibid., 44. Pokki concluded this section with the following, "If this is so, we can also state that American culture has had great influence on the way that Graham has preached the Gospel" (ibid., 46).

[8]Ibid., 253.

teachers." A discussion of conversion necessitates clarification of the messenger of the gospel, the evangelist. Two issues come to the fore in a discussion of the messenger of evangelism as related to Billy Graham: the role of the evangelist, and the general responsibility for all to evangelize.

The role of the evangelist is closely related to the concept of evangelism. Graham has repeated what I have called his "disclaimer" in the last chapter, that as an evangelist he is not called to do everything in the life of the church, but to preach the gospel.[9] Evangelicals, mainline Protestants, ecumenical theologians, and Orthodox, or Catholic leaders cannot ignore that Ephesians 4:11 includes the "evangelist" as a leader in the church. Hence, Graham seemed to appeal to this biblical title to explain and provide an apologetic for his ministry of preaching the gospel.

Yet, there has been some disagreement from the conservative side as to the role of the evangelist. On one hand, John MacArthur, while he affirmed that the gifts of apostle and prophet were "passed from the scene," believed that evangelists were "now in place in God's plan for the advancement of his church."[10] Meanwhile, the equally conservative Iain Murray did not agree with the need for the vocational or itinerant "evangelist" in his objection to revivalism.[11] Rather, for Murray, true revival and evangelism came from "the extraordinary blessing attending the normal means of grace," not from any unusual or protracted church meetings.[12] To this author's reading of Murray, there remains a question as

---

[9]"In the Bible, an evangelist is a person sent by God to announce the Gospel, the Good News; he or she has a spiritual gift that has never been withdrawn from the Church. Methods differ, but the central truth remains: an evangelist is a person who has been called and especially equipped by God to declare the Good News to those who have not yet accepted it, with the goal of challenging them to turn to Christ in repentance and faith and to follow Him in obedience to His will. The evangelist is not called to do *everything* in the church or in the world that God wants done. On the contrary, the calling of the evangelist is very specific" (Billy Graham, "Preface," *Just As I Am* [New York: Harper Collins, 1997], xv).

[10]John MacArthur, Jr., *Ephesians, The MacArthur New Testament Commentary* (Chicago: Moody, 1986), 142.

[11]Speaking of those who promoted Finney's "new measures," Murray writes, "This work was carried on by 'revival men', itinerant evangelists who moved from town to town. . ." (Iain Murray, *Revival and Revivalism: The Making and Marring of American Evangelicalism, 1750-1858* [Edinburgh: Banner of Truth, 1994], 287).

[12]Ibid., 129. He continued his argument, "There were no unusual evangelistic meetings, no special arrangements, no announcements of impending revivals. Pastors were simply continuing in the services they had conducted for many years when great change began" (ibid.). In a summarizing section of his book, Murray wrote, "The experience of all five men points to the same conclusion: revivals did not

to what Paul meant by "evangelist" in Ephesians 4:11. Thus, Murray took exception to Billy Graham's evangelism methodology,[13] as did Erroll Hulse and other high Calvinists.[14]

Nevertheless, Graham felt his calling was that of an evangelist and had a very narrow focus. Fred Moritz, a fundamentalist and antagonist of Billy Graham and New evangelicalism, refered to the role of the evangelist as that of a spiritual obstetrician.[15] Moritz' analogy is both interesting and fitting, the evangelist can be likened to a spiritual obstetrician, preaching the gospel and bringing the unsaved out of darkness to participate in the life of Christ (cf. Col 1:13-14). Murray, however, objected to this analogy stating that it confused the role of the evangelist with the role of the Holy Spirit in conversion.[16] However, as the obstetrician does not give life to the infant, neither does the evangelist bring salvation to the unsaved. Rather, the obstetrician participates in the miracle of birth, much as the evangelist marvels at the power of the gospel to bring about the new birth.

Although the Christian is commanded to evangelize through the universal imperative of the Great Commission, and although the pastor is told to "do the work of an evangelist," the evangelist has the God-given role as a church leader to proclaim the gospel. To him is entrusted the role of

---

occur in conjunction with any special efforts. They were not worked up, but were witnessed in the course of the ordinary services of the churches" (208).

[13]See also Iain Murray's, *The Invitation System* (Edinburgh: Banner of Truth, 1967), and idem, *Evangelicalism Divided: A Record of Crucial Change in the Years 1950-2000* (Edinburgh: Banner of Truth, 2000).

[14]See Erroll Hulse, *Billy Graham: The Pastor's Dilemma* (Hounslow, Middlesex, Great Britain: Maurice Allan, 1966, 1969), and idem, *The Great Invitation* (Welwyn: Evangelical Press, 1986). Thomas J. Nettles seems to argue against the public invitation in *By His Grace and for His Glory: A Historical, Theological, and Practical Study of the Doctrines of Grace in Baptist Life* (Grand Rapids: Baker, 1986), 423-24.

[15]"A doctor cannot perform a delivery without sterilization. The sterilized obstetrician who does not deliver the baby leaves the mother and her baby in need. He is like the separated, fundamentalist pastor who goes weeks without attempting to win people to Christ, and who, of course, does not lead his people to evangelize either. The unsterilized physician who delivers the baby will greatly heighten the risks to the mother and her newborn infant. So is the New Evangelical who evangelizes while honoring and working with unbelieving, apostate ministers" (Fred Moritz, *"Be Ye Holy"—The Call for Christian Separation* [Greenville, SC: Bob Jones University Press, 1994], 66).

[16]Iain Murray wrote against the evangelist as a spiritual obstetrician, "The invitation system misconceives the role of an evangelist. The gospel preacher is not a 'spiritual obstetrician' appointed to supervise the new birth of sinners; still less is he called to propose ways which, if complied with, will accomplish new birth" (Murray, *The Invitation System*, 29).

keeping evangelism central in the life of the church. Is the role of the evangelist in the church to be equated with the salesman in the business world? Graham was quoted as saying, "I am selling the greatest product in the world; why shouldn't it be promoted as well as soap."[17] The comparison of the evangelist and the salesman opens a complex issue beyond the scope of this paper. Two verses seem to speak to this issue: "My kingdom is not of this world" (John 18:36); and "The weapons of our warfare are not of the flesh" (2 Cor 10:4). Rather, the evangelist is called as a leader in the church, a dispenser of the gospel, and a protector of the work of conversion. The core message of the gospel Billy Graham called the "personal gospel."

The Personal Gospel

Graham, early in his ministry, noted the particular power when he proclaimed the personal gospel:

It was my privilege one year ago to be in Cambridge University. I spoke for a week. There are eight thousand students at Cambridge, and four thousand on the average came every single night. On the first two nights I gave them what I thought were intellectual dissertations, for I had prepared my messages with the help of a couple of Seminary professors, but when I had finished my message and had given the invitation, nothing happened. I threw those sermons away and got out John 3:16 and the Lord moved in and the Cambridge students began to come until six hundred had come forward publicly to give their lives to Jesus Christ.[18]

Graham learned the power of the personal gospel by experience as he preached to intellectuals and to illiterate peoples. Graham felt that the gospel and the gospel alone had the power to transform lives. In his sermon "Christ's Marching Orders," Graham explained the inadequacy of human efforts to improve man's lot. Graham affirmed that systems of government were not the answer.[19] He stated that education was not the answer.[20]

---

[17]Malcolm Boyd, "Crossroads in Mass Evangelism?" *Christian Century* (20 March 1957): 359.

[18]Billy Graham, "The World Need and Evangelism," in *The Doctrine of Evangelism,* ed. Clifford Wade Freeman (Nashville: Baptist General Conference of Texas, 1957), 28.

[19]"I believe that America has the greatest government in the world, but our government is certainly going to fall like a rope of sand if unsupported by the moral sentiments of our people. Our moral sentiment in this country comes from Christianity

Graham continued stating that science was not the answer.[21] Finally he explained that charity was not the answer.[22] Rather the only answer to man's spiritual need lay in the gospel.[23] He preached that the gospel "provides for man's physical being," "stimulates his intellect to the highest activity," "provides for man's sensibilities," "provides for man's will," "provides for man's moral nature," and "provides the only satisfaction in the universe for man's spiritual nature."[24] He continued, "You have to accept Christ. You have to become a Christian. You have to say yes to Christ."[25] And with this simple and forceful admonition, Graham left his *Hour of Decision* listeners. What was this gospel of which Graham was so confident?

This section of the chapter will seek to describe what Graham

---

accepted and practiced in everyday life. When this moral sentiment disappears the moral sentiment that shapes our nation's goal will disappear with it" (Billy Graham, "Christ's Marching Orders," *Hour of Decision Sermons*, no. 8 [Minneapolis, Billy Graham Evangelistic Association, 1951, 1955], 4).

[20]"It is not simply education in civilization that the world is wanting today, but civilization with enlightened conscience. . . . Would I drive out civilization you ask? No, I would reform it by regeneration. I would starve out graft and put in honesty; I would drive out prejudices and put in the Golden Rule. This can be done only through accepting Jesus Christ as personal Savior on the part of individuals who make up the society of the world" (ibid., 5-6).

[21]"We have educated thousands of men, their bodies are robust, their intellects keener than a sword, they can apply their forces without weariness or pain, but he has no moral motive. Turn that man loose upon the world, put him in your community with inexhaustible resources and with no power higher than his own, he is a monstrosity, he is but half-way educated and is more dangerous than though he were not educated at all" (ibid., 8)

[22]"Modern American philanthropy is weak inasmuch as it seeks a temporary relief and not a radical cure which comes through a personal knowledge of Jesus Christ" (ibid., 8-9).

[23]The gospel as man's only answer was an oft repeated theme in Graham's sermons, For example, "Revival Today," (*Hour of Decision Sermons*, no. 51 [Minneapolis: Billy Graham Evangelistic Association, 1955]) repeats the same items in a slightly different way: "First, the philosophy of rationalism has failed to satisfy the mind." "Second, modern political philosophies have failed to bring about the Utopia of which men have dreamed." "Third, materialism has failed to satisfy the soul." "Fourthly science has failed to bring peace to the world." "Fifthly, we are beginning to realize that human resourcefulness has come to the end of its tether." His sermon "The Rivers of Damascus" (*Hour of Decision Sermons*, no. 62 [Minneapolis: Billy Graham Evangelistic Association, 1956]) spoke of the false rivers of culture, self-respect, and pleasure. "Christ is the door (John 10:9) and there is no other entrance to eternal life" (10).

[24]Billy Graham, "Christ's Marching Orders," 9-10.

[25]Ibid., 11.

called the personal gospel[26] and what others call the "Simple Gospel."[27] It will briefly note the sources of this gospel, address a history of the four-point formulation, expound on the essence of the personal gospel, and address the question of its being too simplistic.

Source of the Personal Gospel

In conjunction with Graham's belief in an authoritative Bible, it follows naturally that the foundation of the personal gospel came from the Bible. Its biblical roots can be shown. The Bible included a number of short presentations, particularly in historical narratives. For example in Acts 2:37 the audience asked Peter and the Apostles, "Brethren, what shall we do?" Peter's simple answer was an abbreviated call to conversion:

> Repent, and let each one of you be baptized in the name of Jesus Christ for the forgiveness of your sins; and you shall receive the Holy Spirit. For the promise is for you and your children, and for all who arc far off, as many as the Lord shall call to Himself. (Acts 2:38-39)

Another abbreviated gospel call was given after the question of the Philippian jailer, "Sirs, what must I do to be saved?" Paul and Silas answered, "Believe in the Lord Jesus, and you shall be saved, you and your household" (Acts 16:31). A similar abbreviation is found in the words of Jesus to Nicodemus in John 3:16, "For God so loved the world that He gave His only begotten Son, that whoever believes in Him should not perish, but have eternal life."

Among these abbreviations of the gospel and calls to conversion as found in the historical narrative of the New Testament, there are also many teaching portions of the New Testament which outline the gospel presentation. Hence, one version of the personal gospel is called the "Roman Road."[28] In this gospel presentation, all the verses of the gospel are

---

[26]Billy Graham, "Biblical Conversion," 10.

[27]Arthur P. Johnston, "Definition of Evangelism," (classroom lecture notes, *ME 620—Theology of Missions and Evangelism,* Spring 1981, photocopy), 1.

[28]"(1) Need (Why?): God says that all are sinners, Rom 3:10, 23; God tells us the reason all are sinners, Rom 5:12; (2) Consequence (What?) God tells us the result of sin, Rom 6:23; (3) Remedy (How?) God tells us of His concern for sinners, Rom 5:8-9; (4) Condition (Who?) God's way of salvation is made plain, Rom 10:9-10, 13; (5) Results: God tells us the results of salvation, Rom 5:1, 8:1; (6) Assurance: God gives the saved sinner assurance, Rm. 8:16" ("Roman Road," [Chicago: Pacific Garden Mission, n.d.], 1-2).

taken from the book of the Apostle Paul to the Romans. The preaching of the gospel is said to be the main theme of the Book of Romans based on Romans 1:16: "For I am not ashamed of the gospel, for it is the power of God for salvation to every one who believes, to the Jew first and also to the Greek."[29]

Another source for the personal gospel is found in 1 Corinthians 15. The Apostle Paul in his letter to the Corinthian church prefaced his explanation of the essence of the gospel with these words:

> Now I make known to you, brethren, the gospel, which I preached to you, which also you received, in which also you stand, by which also you are saved, if you hold fast the word which I preached to you, unless you believed in vain. 1 Cor 15:1-2

In these two verses, Paul included five phrases modifying the term "gospel." Each phrase gave added weight to the verses that were to follow. Clearly, he was describing the simple gospel. In fact, after he explained that the gospel was of primary importance and he himself had received it, in the next six verses Paul delineated the simple gospel. The essence of the "Simple Gospel" was in fact Jesus Christ with four verbs, the last of which was repeated two times. Hence, the "Simple Gospel" was Jesus Christ, died, buried, raised, appeared, appeared, and appeared. Therefore, the simple gospel according to 1 Corinthians 15 revolves around the person of Jesus Christ, and particularly his work of atonement for personal sin. When this is combined with the gospel call of the examples of the book of Acts, one has the personal gospel as preached by Billy Graham. Yet the question still remains, how did the personal gospel evolve into four points and a prayer?

Origin and Early Formulation of the Personal Gospel

The four points and a prayer of the personal gospel plan of "Steps to Peace with God" developed over the years of church history. The early councils of the church defined the truth of the gospel and its antithesis,

---

[29]Cranfield wrote of Rom 1:16b-17, "These one and a half verses are at the same time both an integral part of Paul's expression of his readiness to preach the gospel in Rome and also the statement of the theological theme which is going to be worked out in the main body of the epistle. While it is no doubt formally tidier to treat them as part of the division which began with 1.8, the logical structure of the epistle stands out more boldly when they are presented as a separate main division" (C. E. B. Cranfield, *A Critical and Exegetical Commentary on the Epistle to the Romans* [Edinburgh: T. & T. Clark, 1975], 87).

heresy. For example, the Nicene Creed of AD 325 is still recited in churches across the world that adhere to its synopsis of the faith. However, it was not until the printing press and Protestant Reformation that printing became an important source for disseminating the gospel.

Paulus Scharpff in his *History of Evangelism* wrote of "evangelism through literature" during the early years of the Pietist movement in Germany:

> Without doubt it was Spener's *Pia Desideria* that gave the greatest impetus to German pietism. A significant number of lesser and greater writings that disseminated and promoted the movement followed. The Enlightenment had stimulated enthusiasm for the printed word, bringing a rash of newspapers, weekly and monthly magazines, periodicals and *belles lettres* of all kinds. This trend encouraged many pietists to record their experiences of faith.
>
> A. H. Francke was a pioneer in this literary activity with his Canstein Bible, the first edition of which appeared in 1712. Francke's various writings, including his theological papers and above all his sermons, came out in quick succession in pamphlet form. Between 1717 and 1723 alone more than a half-million pieces of his materials, including about 350,000 sermons, were distributed in addition to the *Predigtbuch (Book of Sermons)* and the Halle songbooks.[30]

Scharpff placed the printing and dissemination of gospel pamphlets back to the early eighteenth century. As regards a numbered outline of points, Philip Jacob Spener translated and quoted Abraham Calov's (1652) seven-step plan of reasons why students of theology should apply themselves to holiness of life:

> First, because Paul so instructs his Timothy (II Tim. 2:24; I Tim. 1:18-19,3:2, 4:7, 12; Tit. 2:7-8). Second, the Holy Spirit, who is the true and only schoolmaster, will not dwell in a heart subject to sin (John 16:12; I John 2:27). The world cannot receive the Spirit of truth (John 14:17). Third, a student of theology deals with divine wisdom, which is not carnal but spiritual and holy (James 3:15) and whose beginning is the fear of the Lord (Ps. 111:10; Prov. 1: 7; 9:10). Fourth, theology does not consist merely of knowledge but also of the feelings of the heart and of practice, as we have just heard from Justin Martyr. Fifth, blessed is the man who turns words into deeds, said the ancients. "If you know these things," said Christ, "blessed are you if

---

[30] Paulus Scharpff, *History of Evangelism: Three Hundred Years of Evangelism in Germany, Great Britain, and the United States of America* (Grand Rapids: Eerdmans, 1966), 52.

you do them" (John 13:17). So the disciples of Christ should search the Scriptures so as to put them into practice and do what they know. Sixth, wisdom will not enter into an evil soul and will not dwell in a body that is subject to sin (Wis. of Sol. 1:4). Whoever is addicted to sins, therefore, cannot become a dwelling place of the Holy Spirit. Seventh, as the Levites had to wash before they went into the tent of meeting (Exod. 30:18-21; I Kings 7:23-26; II Chron. 4:2-6), so those who wish to enter and leave the house of the Lord must also bestow pains on the sanctification and purification of their lives.[31]

The precedent for numbered outlines for instruction in godliness, with references of verses for each point, went back to as early as 1652. It is not surprising, therefore, that gospel presentations of the twentieth century often take numbered form and include Scripture references for each point.

At the forefront of the "Great Century of Missions,"[32] was the forming of numerous Bible societies and tract societies. For example, the London Tract Society was founded in 1799; the British and Foreign Bible Society was founded in 1804; the New York Tract Society was founded in 1812; the Baptist Board of Foreign Missions was founded in 1814; the American Bible Society was founded in 1816; and the Baptist General Tract Society was founded in 1824. In the case of the British and Foreign Bible Society, they could report in their Sixteenth Report (1820), "The Auxiliaries of the Society itself amount to 265, and the Branch Societies to 364; forming together a total as of last year, of 629."[33] What did the tract societies print? Often they printed gospel sermons and sometimes summaries of gospel sermons. Later in the century, for example, the Asher Publishing Company, affiliated with Union Gospel Mission of St. Paul, Minnesota, published a leaflet by Charles Haddon Spurgeon titled, "Salvation and Safety." In this booklet, Spurgeon described the blood atonement. Spurgeon wrote "O sinner" and "sinner" showing that his intended audience was non-Christian—it was a gospel tract. This tract, in

---

[31]Abraham Calov, *Paedia Theologica de Methodostudii Theologici* (Wittenberg, 1652), 57-58; quoted in Philip Jacob Spener, *Pia Desideria* (Minneapolis: Fortress, 1964), 105-06.

[32]Latourette explained, "As our story moves into the nineteenth century we come to the age of the most extensive geographic spread of Christianity" (Kenneth Scott Latourette, *A History of the Expansion of Christianity*, vol 4, *The Great Century: Europe and the United States, A.D. 1800 to A.D. 1914* [San Francisco: Harper and Row, 1941; Grand Rapids: Zondervan, 1970], 1).

[33]"British and Foreign Bible Society, Abstract of Sixteenth Report," *Christian Watchman and Baptist Register,* 27 January 1821, 1.

fact, even included a sinner's prayer:

> See the Savior hanging on the cross; turn your eye to Him, and say, "Lord I trust Thee; I have nothing else to trust to; sink or swim, my Savior, I trust in Thee." And surely, sinner, as thou canst put thy trust in Christ, thou art safe. . . . Trust in Jesus *now*, Jesus only.[34]

In 1935 Dawson Trotman, founder of The Navigators, began developing the *Topical Memory System*. It was through a French version of this system, used by my father in the early 1950s, that I first memorized a gospel plan. Betty Lee Skinner explained how the *Topical Memory System* was first developed:

> Starting with The Wheel, he [Dawson Trotman] chose the three best verses on the Word, prayer, living the life, and witnessing to be printed on twelve cards. To engineer the card size he borrowed a sailor's blue regulation jumper and measured the depth and width of the pocket often used for cigarettes, then tailored the cards so that a pack of them would fit neatly into that pocket. The reference was printed on the back of each card, the verse on the front.[35]

A gospel plan emerged with the following six points:

1. The fact of sin: Romans 3:23; 3:11, 12
2. The price of sin: Romans 6:23; 5:12; Gal 3:10
3. The price must be paid: Hebrews 9:27; Romans 2:12; Hebrews 2:2-3
4. The price has been paid by Christ: Romans 5:8; 1 Peter 3:18; Galatians 3:13
5. Salvation is a free gift: Ephesians 2:8-9; Romans 3:24; Titus 3:5
6. Salvation must be received: John 1:12; Revelation 3:20; Romans 10:9-10.[36]

---

[34]C. H. Spurgeon, "Salvation and Safety," *Royal Dainties*, no. 169 (Minneapolis: Asher Publishing Co., affiliated with The Union Gospel Mission, n.d.), 4.

[35]Betty Lee Skinner, *Daws: The Story of Dawson Trotman, Founder of the Navigators* (Grand Rapids: Zondervan, 1974), 103. The memory card method of memorizing Scripture was also taught by Oscar Lowry, "The Card System of Scripture Memorizing," *Scripture Memorizing for Successful Soul-Winning*, 6th ed. (Chicago: Moody Bible Institute, 1932; Grand Rapids: Zondervan, n.d.), 47-58.

[36]*Topical Memory System*, Guidebook 1 (Colorado Springs: NavPress, 1969), 19.

In 1948 Billy Graham came into contact with Dawson Trotman and in 1950 Graham asked him for assistance in follow-up. Although he was busy with his own worldwide organization, Trotman began helping Billy Graham at a crusade in Fort Worth, which was held February 24 to March 25, 1951.[37] He told his Navigator staff, "We've got to help Billy Graham."[38] Trotman worked with the Graham team to develop counselors before the meetings and network inquirers after the meeting.[39] Two Navigator staff members sent by Trotman then oversaw the Graham follow-up ministry, Lorne Sanny and Charlie Riggs. Trotman had a strong influence on Graham in the counselor training, which is the primary vehicle through which "Steps to Peace with God" was used. "Steps to Peace with God" provides a synopsis of Graham's personal gospel.

Essence of the Personal Gospel

The essence of Graham's personal gospel or "Simple Gospel" was captured in his pamphlet "Steps to Peace with God." This pamphlet was divided into four steps:

1. Step 1—God's purpose: peace and life. God loves you and wants you to experience peace and life.
2. Step 2—Our problem: separation. God created us in His own image to have abundant life. He did not make us as robots to automatically love and obey Him, but gave us a will and freedom of choice.

   We chose to disobey God and go our own willful way. We still make this choice today. This results in separation from God.
3. Step 3—God's remedy: the cross. Jesus Christ is the only answer to this problem. He died on the Cross and rose from the grave, paying the penalty for our sin and bridging the gap from God to man.
4. Step 4—Our response: receive Christ. We must trust Jesus Christ and

---

[37]"Select Chronology Listing of Events in the History of the Billy Graham Evangelistic Association" [on-line]; accessed 15 June 2000; available from http://www.wheaton.edu/bgc/archives/ bgeachro/bgeachron02.htm; Internet; henceforth referred to as "BGEA Chronology."

[38]Skinner, *Daws,* 322.

[39]Graham noted that Trotman was part of an advance team in London in 1954 (Billy Graham, *Just As I Am*, 214), and Dan Piatt, European director for The Navigators, trained 1,000 counselors for the June 22, 1954 Crusade in Amsterdam (ibid., 242).

receive Him by personal invitation.[40]

These four steps correspond to many other gospel pamphlets published by American evangelicals, including SBC's "Eternal Life" tract,[41] Campus Crusade for Christ's "The Four Spiritual Laws,"[42] and the Navigator's "Bridge to Life" tract.[43]

Other presentations of the personal gospel were developed specifically for memorizing. These also correspond to Graham's "Steps to Peace with God." Examples of these gospel presentations are FAITH,[44] the

---

[40]Billy Graham, "Steps to Peace with God" (Minneapolis: Billy Graham Evangelistic Association, n.d.), 2-10.

[41]"Introduction: God wants you to be sure, 1 John 5:13; You can know, John 3:16; (1) God's Purpose Is that We Have Eternal Life, Rom 6:23; John 10:10; (2) Our Need Is to Understand Our Problem, Rom 3:23; Eph 2:9; Rom 6:23; (3) God's Provision Is Jesus Christ, John 1:1, 14; 1 Pe 3:18; Rom 4:25; John 1:12; (4) Our Response Is to Receive Christ, Acts 3:19; 26:20; Eph 2:8; Jas 2:19; We Must Surrender to Jesus as Lord, Rom 10:9-10; Matt 7:21" (*Do You Know for Certain that You Have Eternal Life and that You Will Go to Heaven when You Die?* [Alpharetta, GA: North American Mission Board, n.d.], 2-12).

[42]"(1) God Loves You, and Offers a Wonderful Plan for Your Life, John 3:16; 10:10; (2) Man is Sinful and Separated from God. Therefore, He Cannot Know and Experience God's Love and Plan for His Life, Rom 3:23; 6:23; (3) Jesus Christ is God's Only Provision for Man's Sin. Through Him You Can Know and Experience God's Love and Plan for Your Life, Rom 5:8; 1 Cor 15:3-6; John 14:6; (4) We Must Individually Receive Jesus Christ as Savior and Lord; Then We Can Know and Experience God's Love and Plan for Our Lives: We must receive Christ, John 1:12; We receive Christ through faith, Eph 2:8-9; We receive Christ by personal invitation, Rev 3:20; You can receive Christ right now through prayer; and Do not depend on feelings: Fact—Faith—Feelings" (Bill Bright, *The Four Spiritual Laws* [San Bernardino, CA: Campus Crusade for Christ, 1965], 2-12).

[43]"(1) The Bible teaches that God loves all men and wants them to know him. But man is separated from God and His love, 1 Tim 2:5; (2) Because He has sinned against God, Isa 59:2; Rom 3:23; (3) This separation leads only to death and certain judgment, Heb 9:27; 2 Thess 1:8-9; (4) Jesus Christ, who died on the cross for our sins, is the way to God, 1 Tim 2:5-6; 1 Pet 3:18; (5) Yes. But only those who personally receive Jesus Christ into their lives, trusting Him to forgive their sins, can cross this bridge, John 1:12; (6) Everyone must decide individually whether to receive Christ, Rev 3:20; John 14:14" (*Bridge to Life* [Colorado Springs, CO: NavPress, 1969], 2-16).

[44]"F represents Forgiveness; A is for Available; I is for Impossible; T is for Turn; and H is for Heaven" (Charles E. Owens, "FAITH: Sunday School Evangelism Strategy" [Ph.D. colloquium paper, Billy Graham School of the Southern Baptist Theological Seminary, 1999], 8-9).

"Roman Road,"[45] the "ABC's for a Better Life,"[46] the Navigator's "Bridge Illustration,"[47] and Evangelism Explosion's "Gospel Presentation."[48] While there are many other good gospel presentations available, the previous list provides a sampling for the purposes of comparison and contrast. Commonalities of the gospel presentations are as follows:

1. Some type of introductory theme

2. The fact of sin and its consequences

3. The work of Christ on the cross

4. The need to believe in Christ for salvation.

Graham's "Steps to Peace with God" began with a positive affirmation of God's desire for mankind. This was reminiscent of Graham's desire to preach a positive gospel: "I am going to preach a gospel not of despair but of hope."[49] The verses he used in Step One were Romans 5:1; John 3:16; and John 10:10.

The listener or reader was then ready for the bad news, the problem of separation from God due to sin. Step Two of this personal gospel explained the problem of personal sin. The two verses used to teach

---

[45]"(A) Need (Why?): (1) God says that all are sinners, Rm. 3:10, 23; (2) God tells us the reason all are sinners, Rom. 5:12; (B) Consequence (What?) God tells us the result of sin, Rm. 6:23; (C) Remedy (How?) God tells us of His concern for sinners, Rm. 5:8-9; (D) Condition (Who?) God's way of salvation is made plain, Rm. 10:9-10, 13; (E) Results: God tells us the results of salvation, Rm. 5:1, 8:1; (F) Assurance: God gives the saved sinner assurance, Rm. 8:16" ("Roman Road," 1-2).

[46]"Introduction: John 10:10; Admit that you are a sinner, Rom 3:23; Believe on Christ, Acts 16:31; and Confess your faith, Rom 10:9" ("ABC's for a Better Life" [Chicago: Pacific Garden Mission, n.d.])

[47]"(1) God's Purpose: Abundant Life, John 10:10, and Eternal Life, John 3:16; (2) Our Problem: All Have Sinned, Rom 3:23 (Isa 53:6) and Sin's Penalty, Rom 6:23; Heb 9:27; (3) God's Remedy: Christ Paid the Penalty, Rom 5:8; 1 Pet 3:18, and Salvation Not by Works, Eph 2:8-9 (Tit. 3:5); and (4) Our Response: Must Receive Christ, John 1:12; Rom 10:9-10, and Assurance of Salvation, John 5:24 (1 John 5:13)" (*Bridge to Life*).

[48]For more details about Evangelism Explosion's "Gospel Presentation," please see D. James Kennedy, *Evangelism Explosion,* rev. ed. (Wheaton Il; Tyndale House Publishers, 1977), 16-44, or write Evangelism Explosion, International, P.O. Box 23820, Fort Lauderdale, FL 33308 U.S.A.

[49]Billy Graham, *Just As I Am,* 219.

about the personal sin of men were Romans 3:23 and Romans 6:23. The use of the language of separation from God corresponds to the "Bridge Illustration" which graphically portrayed the gospel throughout the pamphlet. Therefore, "Steps to Peace" used Proverbs 14:12 and Isaiah 59:2 to show that man's attempts to "Bridge the gap" outside of Christ were not sufficient.

With an understanding of personal sin, as well as personal accountability for sin, the way was prepared for the listener to hear about the work of Christ on the cross as the only remedy for forgiveness of sin. The text of Step Three read, "Jesus Christ is the only answer to this problem. He died on the Cross and rose from the grave, paying the penalty for our sin and bridging the gap from God to man."[50] This point taught the vicarious or substitutionary atonement, using three verses: 1 Timothy 2:5; 1 Peter 3:18; and Romans 5:8.

The final step in "Steps to Peace with God" involved the need for response, "We must trust Jesus Christ and receive Him by personal invitation."[51] At this point, the listener was encouraged to commit his life to Christ, using three verses to back this up, Revelation 3:20; John 1:12; and Romans 10:9. The "Bridge Illustration" graphically portrayed two sides of the bridge, and asked the question, "Are you here? . . . Or here?" Four steps were provided to summarize what was needed to receive Christ:

1. Admit your need (I am a sinner)
2. Be willing to turn from your sins (repent)
3. Believe that Jesus Christ died for you on the Cross and rose from the grave
4. Through prayer, invite Jesus Christ to come in and control your life through the Holy Spirit (Receive Him as Lord and Savior).[52]

"Steps to Peace with God" then included a sample "Sinner's Prayer":

Dear Lord Jesus,
I know that I am a sinner and need your forgiveness. I believe that You died for my sins. I want to turn from my sins. I now invite you to come into my heart and life. I want to trust and follow You as Lord and Savior. In Jesus' name. Amen.[53]

---

[50]Billy Graham, "Steps to Peace with God," 8.

[51]Ibid., 10.

[52]Ibid., 12.

[53]Ibid., 13.

The pamphlet included a place for signing and dating the commitment to Christ, affirming the concept of instantaneous conversion, as well as assurance of salvation.[54] Then on the remaining pages "Steps to Peace with God" offered three assurance verses and some information on how to mature in a relationship with Christ.

By way of quick analysis, when comparing "Steps to Peace with God" with other gospel plans, it is an excellent gospel plan. I have led dozens of persons to Christ, using this simple plan through Billy Graham Telephone Ministry. However, there may be several weaknesses. "Steps to Peace" does not emphasize personal accountability for sin, nor sin as disobedience of God's written word. It only spends two pages on Christ and His atoning work, which was so prominent to the Apostle Paul in 1 Corinthians 15. "Steps to Peace" makes no mention of the blood of Christ, a concept that was important in the early preaching of Billy Graham, nor does it mention of hell or judgment as the result of disbelief. [55] It does, however, mention "eternal life." The term for judgment used in "Steps to Peace with God" was "separation [from God]," a concept we will note is associated in the reconciliation model of the atonement. Thus, while "Steps to Peace" may soften some of the rough edges of the gospel, it follows in the line of simple formulations of the personal gospel.

Simplicity of Graham's Personal Gospel

One of the hallmarks of Graham's preaching was that he sought to keep the message simple. He told of his message to university students, "I

---

[54]Contra the advise of Schleiermacher: "The idea that every Christian must be able to point to the very time and place of his conversion is accordingly an arbitrary and presumptuous restriction of divine grace, and can only cause confusion" (Friedrich Schleiermacher, *The Christian Faith,* 2nd ed. [Edinburgh: Clark, 1960], 487).

[55]Ibid., 9. It must be stated that Billy Graham wanted to be sure that the term "hell" was used in the Amsterdam Affirmations and not "eternal conscious punishment," as that was perhaps too theological a term (cf. Billy Graham, *A Biblical Standard for Evangelists: A Commentary on the Fifteen Affirmations Made by Participants at the International Congress for Itinerant Evangelists in Amsterdam July 1983* [Minneapolis: World Wide, 1984], 41; and Arthur P. Johnston, telephone interview by author, February 16, 1999, handwritten notes). For example, Graham wrote, "Hell is not the most popular of preaching topics. I don't like to preach on it. But I must if I'm to preach the whole counsel of God. We must not avoid warning of it" (Billy Graham, *A Biblical Standard,* 45-46).

spoke just a simple gospel message."[56] He told pastors and church leaders at the 1967 Kansas City School of Evangelism, "I believe that preaching to be successful must be simple."[57] Even when the crowd was filled with the greatest leaders of the Anglican church, he spoke the simple gospel message.[58] Graham did not preach a simple message by choice, he felt compelled by the Holy Spirit that he could not depart from a simple message of the gospel. Graham wrote:

> Now, the evangelist's prime responsibility is to preach the "Word." We must tell people, simply and clearly, what God says about His Son Jesus Christ, what He has done for all, their eternal destiny and need of salvation, and the urgency of accepting and receiving Jesus as their personal Lord, Savior, and Master.[59]

Yet, some accuse Graham of being overly simplistic in his presentation of the gospel. These can be divided into two camps; the conservative camp that found Graham's preaching shallow, and the liberal camp that felt that Graham's understanding of individual or personal sin was too simplistic.

On the conservative side, Francis Schaeffer found that Graham emphasized the decision to the detriment of "history and reason," perhaps implying theology and doctrine. Harold O. J. Brown explained Schaeffer on Graham:

> Even more shocking was his failure to rejoice in what seemed to many the greatest triumphs of the modern evangelical movement as represented by Billy Graham and his mass evangelistic crusades, through which not a few of us had come to Christ. How could a Bible-believing Christian with a zeal for winning people to Christ criticize what was so evidently a good thing? If Barth's theology could not produce real converts (despite his personal faith) because he did not build on a sound foundation, Graham's approach, Schaeffer warned, produced a flock of pseudo-converts, because Graham (although he certainly *has* a sound foundation) did not start building there, or even at ground level, but in what Schaeffer called the "upper story"—that

---

[56]Billy Graham, "Communicating the Gospel," in *Lectures, Kansas City School of Evangelism, September, 1967* (Kansas City, MO: Billy Graham Evangelistic Association, 1967), 3.

[57]Ibid., 6.

[58]Billy Graham, *A Biblical Standard,* 40.

[59]Ibid., 35.

is, by calling for an emotional (or at best volitional) decision without giving an adequate warrant in history and reason.

Although Schaeffer's criticism of Graham's approach was not offered to a wide public, it soon became known. . . . Mass evangelism, for all its merits, is to some extent dependent on the media and on appearances. Schaeffer kept calling for solid foundations *as well as* good feelings.[60]

Thus, Schaeffer presumably did not approve of Graham's preaching because he felt it was shallow, perhaps emphasizing instantaneous conversion and cooperation so much that it did not provide the theological depth to warrant the decision for which Graham called.

On the liberal side, Reinhold Niebuhr, as has already been noted, felt that Graham was not grappling with the issues of the day. Because Graham's personal gospel was not a Rauschenbuschian "Solidaristic Gospel," Graham was woefully ignorant of the issues and out-of-touch with the real corporate sins of society. Rather he felt that Graham was Pietistic and legalistic.[61]

Thus, while there were some who questioned Graham's personal gospel, Graham's approach fit with his view of the power of Scripture, work of the Holy Spirit, and instantaneous conversion. Graham also wanted to preach the gospel simply so that all could understand.[62] The gospel is "the power of God for everyone who believes" (Romans 1:16). The real question then revolved around the central tenets of the gospel. Did Graham's preaching of the gospel warrant the decision for which he called? Was simplicity actually a mask for theological change? While answers will be left to the reader, Graham felt impressed that he needed to preach the cross if he was to successfully call for a decision. Graham's central focus on the cross was recorded in an interview with Ben Haden.[63] Thus to Graham, the

---

[60]Harold O. J. Brown, "Standing against the World," in *Francis A. Schaeffer: Portraits of the Man and His Work,* ed. Lane T. Dennis (Westchester, IL: Crossway, 1986), 21.

[61]Reinhold Niebuhr, "Editorial Notes," *Christianity and Crisis,* 5 March 1956, 18.

[62]Graham's explained his concern for the man on the street: "The Lord only knows we need something to shock the average man in the street out of his lethargy and get him talking about God again" (Billy Graham, "The Work of an Evangelist," *Introducing Billy Graham: The Work of an Evangelist. An Address Given in the Assembly Hall of the Church House, Westminster, on 20th March, 1952,* ed. Frank Colquhoun [London: World Evangelical Alliance, 1953], 25).

[63]"[Haden] Do you feel that the Holy Spirit—in your familiarity with the workings of the Holy Spirit—will bless certain messages and not bless other messages? I

cross, the death, burial, and resurrection of Jesus, as noted in 1 Corinthians 15:11-8, was the central theme which needed to be present in order for a decision to be called for. Graham felt that the preaching of the personal gospel was a necessity for him to call for a decision.

However, can a drift be discerned in Graham? The remainder of the chapter will address this question. Yet, by way of a summary answer— Yes, some drifting is discernible in Graham's sermons, similar to the drift noted in Graham's approach to the Great Commission, as noted in the previous chapter. Thus with this look at the personal gospel, we now begin to delve into topics which are typically a part of systematic theology. We begin analyzing the concept of instantaneous conversion as it relates to the ministry of Billy Graham.

Instantaneous Conversion

More than any other common point in all of Graham's sermons stands the common denominator of instantaneous conversion. In this point, Graham followed in the heritage of the Great Awakening: "The early Methodist preachers were called 'now preachers' because they offered salvation on the spot."[64] Graham's approach to instantaneous conversion also followed in the wake of nineteenth-century evangelicalism.[65] Yet,

---

recall specifically an article you wrote about an audience of 30,000 to 40,000 in Dallas where very few responded. Afterwards you went to your room and wept because someone told you that you had not preached "the Cross" that night.

[Graham] I think I have learned the Cross is to be central in our preaching. I don't preach a sermon now unless I bring the message of the Cross—not dragging it in, but making it central in the sermon. Whatever I'm talking on, the death and resurrection of Christ is the heart of the message-and the need for repentance and faith. This is used by the Holy Spirit to bring about conviction.

I do believe that the Lord does use certain scripture verses and certain thoughts to bring about interest, conviction, arousing the hearts of various individuals. He may use one sermon to bless one person or to touch one person. He may use another sermon to touch another. None of us can really know. And sometimes the sermon I thought was the biggest failure accomplished perhaps greater work" (Ben Haden, "Dr. Graham, Exactly What Is Evangelism?" *Presbyterian Survey,* March 1962, 11-12).

[64]Billy Graham, "The New Birth," in *Fundamentals of the Faith,* ed. Carl Ferdinand Howard Henry (Grand Rapids: Zondervan Publishing House, 1969), 193.

[65]"One other power is the gospel itself. The gospel itself is the power of God unto salvation to everyone that believeth. Now, there are different ways of preaching the gospel. There is the plan of preaching the gospel and looking forward to the gradual enlightenment of the people, to their being saved as it were by a process of gradual instruction and preaching. And there is another method of preaching the gospel; believing it to be the power of God unto salvation; preaching it in the expectation that He who first brought light out of darkness can and will at once and instantaneously take the darkest heathen heart and create light within. That is the method that is successful. It has

192

instantaneous conversion was more than a revivalistic methodology, it followed naturally from Graham's view of the substitutionary atonement. This is why it will be discussed as the first and perhaps most important theological concept of Billy Graham. In fact, virtually every one of his sermons ended with a call of commitment to Christ. Graham firmly held to the concept of instantaneous conversion both in his preaching and in his crusade methodology, while giving himself "wiggle room" for those that did not believe as such. Graham explained:

> We may say, therefore, that conversion can be an instantaneous event, a crisis in which the person receives a clear revelation of the love of God; or it can be a gradual unfoldment accompanied by a climactic moment at the time the line is crossed between darkness and light, between death and life everlasting.[66]

Several years later Graham continued to emphasize instantaneous conversion:

> Both of these conversions [the Apostle Paul and John Wesley] were sudden, though in both cases there had been a considerable period of restlessness beforehand. A sudden conversion does not preclude a good many preparatory incidents of one kind or another. Both were prompted by hearing the voice of the living God through a passage of Scripture. The Word of God had touched them. In both cases the experience produced an immediate change in life and attitude and a sense of release from sin and guilt.[67]

If Graham believed in instantaneous conversion, as seems consistent with his theology and with his methodology, his acceptance of the possibility of something other than instantaneous conversion moved

---

been my privilege to know many Christians—I am speaking within bounds when I say a hundred—who have accepted Jesus Christ as their Saviour the first time they ever heard of Him. The gospel itself is the power of God unto salvation" (J. Hudson Taylor, "The Source of Power," in *Ecumenical Missionary Conference, New York, 1900: Report of the Ecumenical Conference on Foreign Missions, Held in Carnegie Hall and Neighboring Churches, April 21 to May 1*, ed. James Johnston [New York: American Tract Society, 1900], 91).

[66]Billy Graham, "What Is Conversion?" *Hour of Decision Sermons*, no. 38 (Minneapolis: Billy Graham Evangelistic Association, 1957), 5-6.

[67]Billy Graham, "Christian Conversion," *Hour of Decision Sermons*, no. 111 (Minneapolis: Billy Graham Evangelistic Association, 1959), 8.

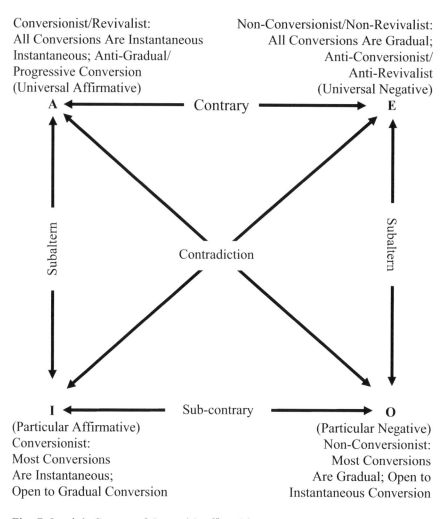

Conversionist/Revivalist:
All Conversions Are Instantaneous
Instantaneous; Anti-Gradual/
Progressive Conversion
(Universal Affirmative)

Non-Conversionist/Non-Revivalist:
All Conversions Are Gradual;
Anti-Conversionist/
Anti-Revivalist
(Universal Negative)

A — Contrary — E

Subaltern

Contradiction

Subaltern

I — Sub-contrary — O

(Particular Affirmative)
Conversionist:
Most Conversions
Are Instantaneous;
Open to Gradual Conversion

(Particular Negative)
Non-Conversionist:
Most Conversions
Are Gradual; Open to
Instantaneous Conversion

Fig. 7. Logic's Square of Opposition[68] and instantaneous conversion.

him from a universal affirmative to a particular affirmative, as shown Figure 7. Graham preached and practiced in keeping with instantaneous conversion. Yet, he was open to an instantaneous conversion working hand-in-hand with progressive conversion, even through the "nurture of grace" of

---

[68]Figure adapted from Brand Blanshard, "Logic."

the sacraments of the Church, as is exemplified in his *Ecumenical Review* article published in 1967.[69] Thus he was vacillating between a universal affirmative and a universal particular on this issue.

It must be noted that there is an antagonism built into the positions of the universal affirmative or in the universal negative in Figure 7. Those adhering to an instantaneous conversion cannot accept the validity of a gradual or progressive conversion, such as is found in the sacraments of the Roman Catholic church. On the other hand, those who adhere to a gradual conversion are likewise often antagonistic to those who are conversionistic. Many non-reconcilable differences exist between the soteriological systems characterizing each side of Figure 7, these are noted in Figure 8. There are several theological options in understanding the conversion of an individual. On the human side, conversion can be seen as a Buddhist-type quest for enlightenment, fully based on man's initiative and effort. Or on the divine side, conversion can be understood as fully wrought

---

[69]"The idea of conversion is often a difficult problem to those who hold a high view of sacramental grace. Many of the theologians and clergy cannot accept the idea of personal conversion on the part of those who were baptized in infancy. However, I have been agreeably surprised at the number of theologians and clergy who have successfully bridged this gap and successfully overcome this problem. Many Anglicans, Lutherans, Presbyterians, Orthodox and even Roman Catholic clergy have agreed that those within the Church need 'converting' even after baptism and confirmation. . . .

The question I want to raise is this: is the theology of adult conversion fundamentally different from that of a child who is cradled in the faith and nurtured in the arms of the Church? It is my opinion that we ought not to contrast the 'nurture of grace' and the 'grace of conversion' as many have tried to do. I am convinced that there are both, and happy is the man who by the nurture of grace is brought to the grace of conversion. Conversion can be an ultimate and proper fulfilment of all that baptism meant to the child, and perhaps later even in confirmation. Conversion must express itself in life as a change of mind, a radical break with the past, and a total commitment to Christ for the future. Whether conversion happens suddenly in adulthood or gradually through childhood is beside the point. The thing that counts is that it happens! As Dr. Paul Jewett says "If this does not happen in all its decisiveness, Christian education and even Christian preaching alike will produce nothing but 'culture Christians' who have, like John Wesley before Aldersgate, 'a rational conviction of all the truths of Christianity' yet are unable to say with Paul, 'I live, yet not I, but Christ lives in me' (Galatians 2. 20).

This is the greatest problem facing the Church today! The deep motivating spiritual power is almost non-existent! If confirmation as it is usually understood is followed to its logical conclusion it can and often does become conversion. . . . There are millions of professing Christians who have had just enough religion to inoculate themselves against a genuine relationship with Christ. The point I am trying to make is that in thousands of cases Biblical conversion is needed even after baptism and confirmation, to give meaning and reality to the earlier experience" (Billy Graham, "Conversion—a Personal Revolution," *The Ecumenical Review* 19 (1967): 277-78).

Instantaneous:	(Attempts to Balance)	Gradual
Emphasizing		Enlightenment:
God's part;		Emphasizing
Supernaturalistic		man's part; Naturalistic

$$\longleftarrow \quad\quad\quad | \quad\quad\quad \longrightarrow$$

Preaching the Cross	Educating the Mind
Dynamic of the Word of God	Providing Positive Environment
Work of the Holy Spirit	Result of a Good Example
Call to Commitment Necessary	Call to Commitment Negative
Point in Time Salvation	Salvation a Gradual Process

Fig. 8. Instantaneous versus gradual conversion continuum with associated methodologies.

in God, through His word, by grace, and through faith. The mediation of the conversion then becomes the important avenue for those desiring the conversion of others. Figure 8 seeks to place these concepts on a continuum.

While it is impossible to chart all the issues involved in a practical theology of conversion, the antithetical issues are evident (see Fig 8). Either conversion is instantaneous, and wrought by God alone, at a specific point in the time when:

1.   The will of man is bent to submit to the gospel preached, through repentance and belief (Mark 1:15; Acts 20:21);

2.   The heart is opened to respond to the gospel (Acts 16:14);

3.   God applies the atonement of Christ and imputes the repentant sinner with the righteousness of Christ (2 Cor 5:21);

4.   The truly converted is transferred from the domain of darkness to the kingdom of the beloved Son (Col 1:13-14);

5.   The old becomes new (2 Cor 5:17); and

6.   The forgiven sinner is raised up with Christ, and seated with Him in the heavenly places (Eph 2:6).

Or conversion has lost its divine meaning and becomes a progression of gradual enlightenment, a humanistic quest for self-fulfillment, and self-perfection. If Christ's atonement was truly substitutionary and if the converted is to believe in Him, then it necessarily follows that the substitution takes place at a point in time. There is no other option. The question then becomes, at what point in time and how? This point is where the debate rages.

Ordo Salutis and the Doctrines of Grace

As to the time of salvation, two theological concepts enter the equation. One is the "Order of Decrees," and the other is the *ordo salutis,* or the order of salvation. The two are linked, but distinct. As to the "Order of Decrees," Protestants read in their Bible that the Christian was chosen before the foundation of the world and predestined to adoption (Eph 1:4-5), and that the crucifixion of Christ was foreknown before the foundation of the world (1 Pet 1:20). If so, which came first, God's choosing of a people or God's preparing for the the death of Christ for sin? In answer to this question there arose three types of Calvinists: supralapsarians, believing that the decree to election came before the decree of the fall; infralapsarians, believing that the decree of the fall came before the decree for election and that the decree of election came before the decree of the atonement; and sublapsarians, who believe that the decree for election was the last decree. Millard Erickson footnoted Louis Berkhof[70] and Loraine Boettner[71] as describing these concepts noted in Table 3.

If God elected men prior to decreeing creation, permitting the fall, or providing for salvation (the supralapsarian position), then it seems to follow that in the *ordo salutis* regeneration precedes repentance. If, however, God permitted the fall prior to decreeing his election and providing salvation (infralapsarian), then regeneration still precedes repentance in the *ordo salutis,* but the call may be universal. Lastly, if God decreed His election of men last (sublapsarian, modified Calvinism, or "broadly Reformed tradition"), then not only can the call be universal, but redemption is "sufficient for all," and regeneration may take place after repentance in the *ordo salutis.*[72]

It is also important to place Calvinism in the context of other views of salvation. B. B. Warfield, in his book *The Plan of Salvation,* included not only these three views of Calvinists, but also other major ecclesial plans of salvation: The table provided by Warfield in this book has

---

[70]Louis Berkhof, *Systematic Theology* (Grand Rapids: Eerdmans, 1953), 118-25.

[71]Lorraine Boettner, "Predestination," in *Baker's Dictionary of Theology,* ed. Everett Harrison (Grand Rapids: Baker, 1960), 415-17.

[72]Bruce Demarest, *The Cross and Salvation: The Doctrine of Salvation* (Wheaton, IL: Crossway, 1997), 38-40.

TABLE 3

ADAPATION OF ERICKSON'S SUMMARY OF
LAPSARIAN VIEWS[73]

Supralapsarian	Infralapsarian	Sublapsarian
1. The decree to save (elect) some and reprobate others.	1. The decree to create human beings.	1. The decree to create human beings.
2. The decree to create both elect and reprobate.	2. The decree to permit the fall.	2. The decree to permit the fall.
3. The decree to permit the fall of both the elect and the reprobate.	3. The decree to elect some and reprobate others.	3. The decree to provide salvation sufficient for all.
4. The decree to provide salvation only for the elect.	4. The decree to provide salvation only for the elect.	4. The decree to save some and reprobate others

been adapted as Table 4 for this publication.[74] In the case of the non-Calvinistic systems of salvation the differences are perhaps more readily apparent than in the different lapsarian viewpoints. Warfield noted the tremendous difference between the Roman Catholic position on salvation, whereas the "Means of Grace" (i.e. the sacraments) are "the actual *quibus* of salvation,"[75] or as the Council of Trent explained it, *ex opere operato*,[76]

---

[73]Adapted from Millard Erickson, *Christian Theology* (Grand Rapids: Baker, 1985), 826 n. 2.

[74]Adapted from Benjamin B. Warfield, *The Plan of Salvation* (Philadelphia: Presbyterian and Reformed, 1918), 19.

[75]Warfield, *Plan of Salvation,* 19.

"from the work done."[77] The *Catechism of the Catholic Church* explained it this way: "By the action of Christ and the power of the Holy Spirit they [the sacraments] make present efficaciously the grace that they signify."[78] Some may feel that Vatican II changed the salvific theology of the Roman Catholic Church. To this charge John Paul II responded that the church is "still the same in its essence."[79] Therefore, since the Council of Trent, immediate or instantaneous conversion are not possible in the Catholic Church, as it does not conform with the Protestant concept of the soul being converted solely through God's work. Warfield explained the Protestant or evangelical view in this way:

> Over against this whole view [Roman Catholic] evangelicalism, seeking to conserve what it conceives to be only consistent supernaturalism, sweeps away every intermediary between the soul

---

[76]The Council of Trent, Session Seven (3 March 1547), "Concerning the Sacraments," Canon 8, stated, "If anyone says that by the sacraments of the New Law grace is not conferred *ex opere operato,* but that faith alone in the divine promise is sufficient to obtain grace, let him be anathema" (John H. Leith, ed., *Creeds of the Churches* [Atlanta: John Knox Press, 1982], 426).

[77]Erickson, *Christian Theology,* 1009. See also Bruce Demarest, *The Cross and Salvation,* 32.

[78]*Catechism of the Catholic Church* (Mahwah, NJ: Paulist Press, 1994), 282. "In the liturgy the Holy Spirit is teacher of the faith of the People of God and artisan of 'God's masterpieces,' the sacraments of the New Covenant. The desire and work of the Spirit in the heart of the Church is that we may live from the life of the risen Christ. When the Holy Spirit encounters in us the response of faith [in the liturgy] which he has aroused in us, he brings about genuine cooperation" (ibid., 283-84). "The Spirit and the Church [physical manifestation of the Roman Catholic hierarchy] cooperate to manifest Christ and his work of salvation in the liturgy" (ibid., 285). This portion of the *Catechism* footnotes the Vatican II document, *Sacrosanctum Concilium* (4 December 1963), which footnotes the Council of Trent, *Decree on the Holy Eucharist* and *Decree on the Holy Sacrifice of the Mass.* These historical precedents portray that salvation has not changed in Roman Catholicism since the Counter-Reformation Council of Trent (1545-1563), which confirmed much of Thomas Aquinas' *Summa Theologica* (1266-1272).

[79]"The Second Vatican Council wished to be, above all, a council on the Church. Take in your hands the documents of the Council, especially 'Lumen Gentium,' study them with loving attention, with the spirit of prayer, to discover what the Spirit wished to say about the Church. In this way you will be able to realize that there is not—as some people claim—a 'new church,' different or opposed to the 'old church,' but that the Council wished to reveal more clearly the one Church of Jesus Christ, with new aspects, but still the same in its essence" (John Paul II, "Mexico Ever Faithful," *Osservatore Romano,* 5 February 1979, 1).

TABLE 4

WARFIELD'S ORDER OF DECREES, EVANGELICAL VIEWS

PARTICULARISTIC			UNIVERSALISTIC		
Supralapsarian	Infralapsarian	Sublapsarian	Lutheran	Wesleyan	Pure Universalistic
Election of some to eternal life with God	Permission of Fall= guilt, corr., and total inability	Permission of Fall= guilt, corr., and moral inability	Permission of Fall= guilt, corr., and total inability	Permission of Fall= guilt, corr., and total inability	Permission of Fall
Permission of Fall= guilt, corr. and total inability	Election of some to life in Christ	Gift of Christ to render salv. possible to all	Gift of Christ to render satis. for sins of the world	Gift of Christ to render satis. for sins of the world	Predestination of all to life
Gift of Christ to red. the elect and ground offer to all	Gift of Christ to red. His elect and ground offer to all	Election of some for gift of moral ability	Gift of means of grace to comm. saving grace	Remission of orig. sin to all and gift to all of suff. grace	Gift of Christ to expiate the sin of all
Gift of the Holy Spirit to save the redeemed	Gift of the Holy Spirit to save the redeemed	Gift of the Holy Spirit to work moral ability in the elect	Pred. to life of those who do not resist the means of grace	Pred. to life of those who improve sufficient grace	Gift of the Spirit to apply the expiation of Christ to all
Sanctification of all redeemed and regenerated	Sanctification of all redeemed and regenerated	Sanctification by the Spirit	Sanctification through the means of grace	Sanctification of all who coop. with suff. grace	Salvation of all

TABLE 4—Continued

WARFIELD'S ORDER OF DECREES, NON-EVANGELICAL VIEWS

SACERDOTAL			NATURALISTIC	
Anglican	Roman	Orthodox Greek	Remonstrant	Pelagian
Permission of sin	Permission of Fall=loss of supernatural righteousness	Permission of Fall=loss of orig. right., inv. loss of know. of God & prone. to evil	Permission of Fall=(physical) deterioration (followed by moral)	Gift of free will by virtue of which each may do all required
Gift of Christ to make satisfaction for the sins of all men	Gift of Christ to offer satisfaction for all human sins	Gift of Christ to reconcile sinful mankind with God	Gift of Christ to render gift of sufficient grace possible	Gift of the law and gospel to illum. the way and persuade to walk in it
Establishment of Church as living agent for comm. God's sufficient grace	Institution of Church and the sacrament, to apply satis. of Christ	Establishment of Church for the continual supply of the benefits of the cross	Gift of sufficient (suasive) grace to all	Gift of Christ to (expiate past sin and to) set good example
Comm. of this grace through the sacr. as indispensable channels	Application of satis. of Christ through sacr., under oper. of second causes	Instruction, justification, and edification through the ord. of the Church	Salvation of all who freely cooperate with this grace	Acceptance of all who walk in right way
Salv. through sacrament of baptism impart. life; Eucharist nourishing it	Building up in holy life of all to whom the sacraments are continued	Building up in grace through the seven sacraments	Sanctification by cooperation with grace	Continuan-ce in right-doing by voluntary effort

and its God, and leaves the soul dependent for its salvation on God alone, operating upon it by his immediate grace. It is directly upon God and not the means of grace that the evangelical feels dependent for salvation; it is directly to God rather than to the means of grace that he looks for grace; and he proclaims the Holy Spirit therefore not only to act but actually operative where and when and how he will....

In thus describing evangelicalism, it will not escape notice that we are also describing Protestantism. . . . Evangelicalism . . . is the more consistently supernaturalistic, refusing any intermediaries between the soul and God, as the source of salvation. That only is true evangelicalism, therefore, in which sounds clearly the double confession that all the power exerted in saving the soul is from God, and that God in his saving operations acts directly on the soul.[80]

This unity of thought of historic Protestantism was perhaps what Graham appealed to when he stated in the 1953 *Hour of Decision* sermon "Labor, Christ and the Cross":

No man will ever be in heaven who did not by faith receive Christ as personal Savior. Every great denomination believes this truth. Every church has historically accepted this as the clear teaching of Scripture. If you are ever going to get to heaven, you must personally by faith receive Christ.[81]

However, if Graham included the Roman Catholic church in "every great denomination"—a term normally referring only to Protestants,[82] the

---

[80]Warfield, *The Plan of Salvation,* 19-20.

[81]Billy Graham, "Labor, Christ and the Cross," *Hour of Decision Sermons,* no. 30 (Minneapolis: Billy Graham Evangelistic Association, 1953), 8.

[82]H. Richard Niebuhr borrowed his antidenominational rhetoric from the sociologist Ernst Troesch's *Die Soziallenhren der christlichen Kirchen und Gruppen* (1912). Niebuhr wrote of North American Protestantism: "The orthodox interpretation of denominationalism in Christianity looks upon the official creeds of the churches as containing the explanation of the sources and of the character of the prevailing differences. . . . [schismatics] vary from each other on one or another point of doctrine, which, it is said, explains their division and accounts for their antagonism. . . .
. . . Yet it is no less evident that much opinion or belief is in fact mere rationalization and that the reasons advanced for pursuing a given course of action are often removed from inspiring motive. . . . Advancing and defending their positions on the basis of proof-texts drawn from the Scriptures, it has been possible for various sects to take antithetical views of the Christian or un-Christian character of these institutions (H. Richard Niebuhr, *The Social Sources of Denominationalism* [New York: Henry Holt, 1929], 12-14).

"historically" of Graham was referring back to before the Council of Trent, and even before the Thomistic takeover of the theology of salvation among Roman Catholics.[83]

The Arminian view of salvation placed the responsibility for a decision in the hands of the individual making the decision. In this view, God provided prevenient ("coming before") grace to all men. Thus, when they heard the gospel, they were able to make an informed judgment for or against it, thus exercising their freewill and calling upon themselves either eternal damnation or eternal bliss. Several questions emerge from this view. Is this salvific grace given to all men outside of the hearing of the gospel? If so, it can lead to a universalism. If this grace is given to all men upon the hearing of the gospel, why do some men not "see the light of the gospel of the glory of Christ, who is the image of God" (2 Cor 4:4)? Is Arminian prevenient grace not able to counteract the blinding influence of Satan? These are indeed mysteries. However, one truth that bound together Protestants was the power of the gospel to save the soul instantaneously without any human intermediaries.

As we have seen, the Protestant or evangelical belief in immediate or instantaneous conversion, supernaturally wrought through the intermediary of God alone, was defined in different ways by differing Protestant groups. Methodism, following John Wesley adhered to an Arminian view, which emphasized the freewill of man, and therefore limited the sovereignty of God and elevated man's natural ability or the prevenient grace of God. High Calvinists (supralapsarian), with their belief in election coming prior to the Fall, seem to place instantaneous conversion back in the decrees of God prior to the creation of the world. In this case, a human decision in this life was rendered almost superfluous.[84] Yet in both groups the central theme was the evangel—hence the term evangelical. For example, in the 1677 "Second London Confession" of the Particular (Calvinistic) Baptists, Chapter 20, "Of the Gospel, and of the extent of the Grace thereof," discussed issues in the centrality of the gospel and the work of the Holy Spirit:

---

[83]In his 1967 address to the "Kansas City School of Evangelism," Graham did include Catholics and Protestants in a similar context: "Second, there needs to be a clearly defined theology of evangelism. This is not so much a new theology but a special emphasis upon certain aspects of the theology that has been in the mainstream of the church throughout its history, both Catholic and Protestant" (Billy Graham, "Biblical Conversion," 15).

[84]"Closely allied to illumination and conviction is reformation of life. . . . On the personal level, the main point is that often people reform their way of life [indicating prior regeneration] considerably before they are converted" (Murray, *The Invitation System*, 16).

1. The Covenant of Works being broken by Sin, and made unprofitable unto Life; God was pleased to give forth the promise of *Christ,* the Seed of the Woman, as the means of calling the Elect, and begetting in them Faith and Repentance; in this Promise, the Gospel, as to the substance of it, was revealed, and therein Effectual, for the Conversion and Salvation of Sinners.

2. This Promise of *Christ,* and Salvation by him, is revealed only by the Word of God; neither do the Works of Creation, or Providence, with the light of Nature, make discovery of *Christ,* or of *Grace* by him; so much as in a general, or obscure way; much less that men destitute of the Revelation of him by the Promise, or Gospel; should be enabled thereby, to attain saving Faith, or Repentance.

3. The Revelation of the Gospel unto Sinners, made in divers times, and by sundry parts; with the addition of Promises, and Precepts for the Obedience required therein, as to the Nations, and Persons, to whom it is granted, is meerly [sic] of the Soveraign [sic] Will and good Pleasure of God; not being annexed by vertue [sic] of any Promise, to the due improvement of mens natural abilities, by vertue of Common light received without it; which none ever did make, or can so do: And therefore in all Ages the preaching of the Gospel hath been granted unto persons and Nations, as to the extent, or streightning [sic] of it, in great variety, according to the Councell [sic] of the Will of God.

4. Although the Gospel be the only outward means, of revealing *Christ,* and saving Grace; and is, as such, abundantly sufficient thereunto; yet that men who are dead in Trespasses, may be born again, Quickened or Regenerated; there is morover necessary, an effectual, insuperable work of the Holy *Spirit,* upon the whole Soul, for the producing in them a new spiritual Life; without which no other means will effect their Conversion unto God.[85]

Because the light of general revelation was not sufficient, because "salvation . . . is revealed only by the Word of God," and because "the Gospel be the only outward means" to effect conversion, it followed that the preaching of the gospel was the only means through which the unsaved had the hope of salvation. This belief in the centrality of the gospel was the common denominator for evangelicals[86] throughout the "Great Century of Missions."

---

[85]William L. Lumpkin, ed., *Baptist Confessions of Faith* (Valley Forge: Judson Press, 1969), 278-79.

[86]The publishers of the London-based *The Gospel Magazine or Spiritual Library, Designed to Promote Religion, Devotion, and Piety, from Evangelical*

A rational middle-of-the-road approach between Calvinism and Arminianism has proven difficult to explain. Charles Haddon Spurgeon spoke of the intricate nature of the two sides:

> The system of truth is not one straight line, but two. No man will ever get a right view of the gospel until he knows how to look at the two lines at once. Now, if I were to declare that man was so free to act, that there is no presidence of God over his actions, I should be driven very near to atheism; and if, on the other hand, I declare that God so overrules all things, as that man is not free to be responsible, I am driven at once to Antinomianism or fatalism.
>
> That God predestines, and that man is responsible, are two things that few can see. They are believed to be inconsistent and contradictory; but they are not. It is just the fault of our weak judgment. Two truths cannot be contradictory to each other. If, then, I find taught in one place that everything is fore-ordained, that is true; and if I find in another place that man is responsible for all his actions, that is true; and it is my folly that leads me to imagine that two truths can ever contradict each other. These two truths, I do not believe, can ever be welded into one upon any human anvil, but one they shall be in eternity: they are two lines that are so nearly parallel, that the mind that shall pursue them farthest, will never discover that they converge; but they do converge, and they will meet somewhere in eternity, close to the throne of God, whence all truth doth spring.[87]

Others have written on this mystery. J. I. Packer, in his *Evangelism and the Sovereignty of God,* called this an antinomy,[88] a mystery,[89] but not a paradox.[90] Erroll Hulse quoted Deuteronomy 29:29, "the secret things

---

Principles stated their purpose, ". . . to endeavor to instruct and improve our readers in the knowledge of the great truths of the gospel, and of those things related to their eternal salvation. . . . our aim being to lay before their families, the young ones especially, a plain account of the truths of the gospel, which contains the good news and glad tidings of salvation through Jesus Christ to lost sinners" ("The Design of the Gospel Magazine," *The Gospel Magazine,* January 1766, 3-4).

[87]Charles H. Spurgeon, "Sovereign Grace and Man's Responsibility," in *The New Park Street Pulpit* (London: Passmore and Alabaster, 1858), 4:336-37.

[88]J. I. Packer, *Evangelism and the Sovereignty of God* (Downers Grove, IL: InterVarsity, 1961), 18, 22, 23, 24.

[89]Ibid., 16, 19, 24.

[90]Ibid., 19.

belong to God," in his discussion of this issue,[91] basing himself on the work of John Owen, *The Death of Death in the Death of Christ,* in his discussion of the extent of the atonement.[92]

Graham accepted the two sides of Calvinism and Arminianism as irresolvable. He called them a paradox and a mystery:

> The Scripture teaches that God turns men to himself, but men are also exhorted to turn themselves to God. God is represented as the author of the new heart and the new spirit, yet men are commanded to make for themselves a new heart and a new spirit. It is the old paradox of Grace and free will.
>
> No one can be converted except by the Grace of God, for we are too weak to turn ourselves, unaided; and we turn only in response to some stimulus provided outside ourselves. But no one can be converted except with the consent of his own free will, because God does not override human choice. We may not be free to choose, because sin weakens our power of moral choice; but we are free to refuse. We can refuse to be chosen.
>
> Simon Peter could not become a disciple until Jesus called him and said, "Follow me." But others heard the same call and refused it or put it off. One said, "Lord, let me first go and bury my father." Another one said, "Let me first say farewell to those at my home." These men refused Christ's call.
>
> This combination of divine calling and the human responsibility of accepting or refusing God's Grace runs throughout the Bible and characterizes all God's dealings with men. The Bible confronts us with man's moral independence within himself and his spiritual dependence upon God. . . .
>
> The grace is God's; the faith is ours. But the free will with which we choose is God's gift, and the capacity to believe and trust is God's gift also. Therefore within every conversion there is a working of the divine and the human; but their relation to each other remains a mystery. It has been my privilege to see thousands converted to Christ, and I still do not understand the mystery of God's grace and man's faith. But I know that both are involved.[93]

Graham made several theological statements in this sermon. First, he spoke of man's being "weak." This was not the language of complete inability as

---

[91]Hulse, *The Great Invitation,* 71.

[92]Ibid., 69.

[93]Billy Graham, "Christian Conversion," 4-6.

noted in the Synod of Dort's "Total Depravity." Second, Graham explained, "We are free to refuse" or again, we have "the human responsibility of accepting or refusing God's Grace." This statement implied that, to Graham, the actual choice was in man's court. If rejection was man's part, then the contrary must also be true, man had the ability to not reject or accept. In fact, his use of rejection-language placed Graham under the Lutheran universalistic approach in Table 4 above, "Predestination to life of those who do not resist the means of grace."[94] Then Graham came back again by stating the ontological truth, "the free will with which we choose is God's gift, and the capacity to believe and trust is God's gift also." Graham's answer to the discussion of divine sovereignty with human freewill was, "The grace is God's; the faith is ours." Clearly, Graham placed both rejection and faith on the human side of the equation—rejection tending toward a Lutheran understanding and faith tending to a Wesleyan understanding.

In his sermon "What Is Conversion?" Graham used the same imperatives of Jesus in Mark 1:15: repent and believe:

> Actually, biblical conversion involves three steps—two of them active and one passive. In active conversion, repentance and faith are involved. Repentance is conversion viewed from its starting point, the turning from the former life. Faith indicates the objective point of conversion, the turning to God. The third, which is passive, we may call the new birth, or regeneration.[95]

Thus, in Graham's emphasis on the human decision, he emphasized the imperatives of Jesus, perhaps not considering which terminology would best suit which system of truth. And Graham sounded more Pietistic Lutheran or Modified Calvinist than anything.

Graham clarified his position on Calvinism in a 1962 interview with Ben Haden:

> [Haden] "Do you personally feel that a man prodded or prompted by the Holy Spirit to receive Christ has the actual ability or potential of resisting the Holy Spirit and refusing to accept Christ?"
>
> [Graham] "Yes, I most certainly do. This brings us into a theological realm of "irresistible grace"—which some Calvinists hold, but I don't. There is a mystery here that I don't understand. The relationship between "free will" (of man) and God's sovereignty is one that I don't think any of us will ever really be able to fathom

---

[94]Warfield, *The Plan of Salvation,* 33.

[95]Billy Graham, "What Is Conversion?" 6.

completely. But I do believe that men do have the ability to resist God. The scripture says, *Ye do always resist the Holy Spirit* (Acts 7:51). And I think this is possible. I have seen it many times in my own experience—men who deliberately resisted the Holy Spirit. . . ."

[Haden] "What urgency is involved in evangelism when the person doing the evangelizing believes that God has decided in advance those who are to be saved?"

[Graham] "I think his motive would be to obey the command of Christ—to go into all the world and preach the gospel. I know, for example, that Dr. Donald Grey Barnhouse held this view. Yet no man ever did any finer evangelism than he did. While I do not hold this view exactly as he did, I do know that there is a sovereignty of God involved in all of this. When I get up to preach, I pray, 'Lord, bring those whom Thou hast chosen to Christ tonight.'

"I know there is the choosing of God; and there is man's free will. I have never really been able to understand between them. I have to leave it in God's hands. I have heard the theologians debate. I have read what Wesley had to say on the one hand; and what Calvin had to say on the other hand. It seems to me that there is a meeting place here somewhere.

"One of the *motives* of my evangelism is to obey Christ . . . to go out and bring men to Christ. If free will is the total picture, or if the sovereignty of God is the total picture, it really is not altogether important to me as an evangelist. My job is to obey and to be faithful in the proclamation, and in trying to win people to Christ."

[Haden] "Well, do you believe that effective evangelism can bring a man to Jesus Christ who might otherwise be lost?"

[Graham] "Yes, I do. But some don't. . . . "

[Haden] "But you do?"

[Graham] "I do, yes."

[Haden] "Does this explain part of the urgency in your own message?"

[Graham] "I am sure it does. But if I held the other view, the command of Christ should give me just as much urgency."

[Haden] "As illustrated by Dr. Barnhouse?"

[Graham] "Yes."

[Haden] "Do you believe any man was predestined by God to go to hell?"

[Graham] "No, I don't. I most certainly don't! I think hell was created for the Devil and his angels—not for man. If man goes there, he goes because he rebels against God. He rejects God's offer of a pardon, and he goes there because of his own sins.

"We might bring this into the realm of foreknowledge and say that God foreknew (knew in advance), but did not predetermine (decide in advance) and destine people to go to hell. I don't hold that view at all that some of our ultra-Calvinists hold."[96]

From this 1962 interview, Graham distanced himself from irresistible grace, double-predestination, and ultra-Calvinism. Of irresistible grace, Graham said, "which some Calvinists hold, but I don't." Later of Barnhouse and his Calvinism Graham answered, "if I held the other view." Graham also leaned toward a view of foreknowledge when confronted with double predestination. However, in all this discussion Graham did not make strong statements against election or predestination as did his predecessor the evangelist John Wesley.[97]

Interestingly, Charles Dullea, a Roman Catholic theologian who studied Graham's theology in the late sixties and early seventies, stated that Graham remained in the Calvinistic tradition of Jonathan Edwards:

> [Erroll] Hulse reproves Graham for departing from the classic and original doctrine of the reformers by thus emphasizing free will. In his judgment of Graham's position, of course, Hulse is quite correct. Graham explicitly parts company with Calvinism by repudiating the concept of irresistible grace, and by implication the doctrines of predestination in the Calvinistic sense of limited atonement. In this he is following the traditional Revivalistic thought after the time of Calvinist Jonathan Edwards.[98]

Jonathan Edwards was noted for his emphasis on the religious affections. Dullea seemed comfortable placing Graham in the North American

---

[96]Haden, "Dr. Graham, Exactly What Is Evangelism?" 12-13.

[97]"This then is a plain proof that the doctrine of predestination is not a doctrine of God, because it makes void the ordinance of God [the preaching of the gospel]; and God is not divided against himself. . . . As directly does this doctrine [predestination] tend to destroy several particular branches of holiness. . . . This doctrine [predestination] tends to destroy the comfort of religion. . . . This uncomfortable doctrine [predestination] tends to destroy our zeal for good works. . . . [predestination] hath also a direct and manifest tendency to overthrow the whole Christian revelation. . . . it [predestination] does the same thing, by plain consequence, in making that revelation contradict itself. . . . For, seventhly, it [predestination] is a doctrine full of blasphemy. . . . This is the blasphemy clearly contained *in the horrible decree* of predestination. And here I fix my foot. On this I join issue with every asserter of it" (John Wesley, "Free Grace," sermon no. 128 [on-line], accessed 26 October 2001, available from http://gbgm-umc.org/ umhistory/wesley/sermons/serm-128.stm; Internet).

[98] Charles W. Dullea, *A Catholic Looks at Billy Graham* (New York: Paulist Press, 1973), 80. Dullea referred to Erroll Hulse's book *Billy Graham: The Pastor's Dilemma.*

revivalist tradition, while his discussion of the Doctrines of Grace were neither extensive nor well documented. However, Dullea may have been more accurate in his brief assessment had he placed Graham toward the freewill camp of Charles Finney.[99]

Throughout his ministry, it was clear that Graham placed a strong emphasis on persuading man to make a visible decision for Christ by an act of his will. In his "Invitation System" Graham could only look on the outward manifestation of man's will. The Bible says, "Man looks at the outward appearance, but God looks at the heart" (1 Sam 16:7). Thus, with his emphasis on the power of the gospel and with his corresponding emphasis on instantaneous conversion, Graham emphasized the need for a visible manifestation of a desire to come to Christ. Where does this place Graham in light of the Doctrines of Grace or the five points of Calvinism?[100]

1. Total Inability or Total Depravity: Graham stated, "No one can be converted except by the Grace of God, for we are too weak to turn ourselves, unaided; and we turn only in response to some stimulus provided outside ourselves. But no one can be converted except with the consent of his own free will, because God does not override human choice. We may not be free to choose, because sin weakens our power of moral choice; but we are free to refuse. We can refuse to be chosen."[101] Elsewhere he said, "Most thoughtful people recognize that man is a paradox. . . . From whence comes this strange mixture of good and evil? How did this paradox called man come to be the odd contradiction that he is?"[102]

2. Unconditional Election: Graham wrote, "Theologians have long debated exactly when regeneration takes place in a person's life. In spite of some disagreements, the central issue is clear: it is the Holy Spirit who regenerates us within."[103] "Graham does not explicitly support or deny the doctrine of predestination or election."[104]

---

[99]See Thomas J. Nettles, *By His Grace and For His Glory*, 418-20.

[100]Ibid.

[101]Billy Graham, "Christian Conversion," 4.

[102]Billy Graham, "Past, Present and Future," *Hour of Decision Sermons*, no. 100 (Minneapolis: Billy Graham Evangelistic Association, 1958), 1-2.

[103]Billy Graham, *The Holy Spirit: Activating God's Power in Your Life* (Waco, TX: Word, 1978), 79-80.

[104]Pokki, *America's Preacher*, 156.

TABLE 5

SUMMARY OF GRAHAM ON
THE FIVE POINTS OF CALVINISM[105]

1. Total Inability or Total Depravity	2. Unconditional Election	3. Particular Redemption or Limited Atonement	4. Efficacious Call of the Spirit or Irresistible Grace	5. Perseverance of the Saints
Man has a free will; man is a mixture of good and evil	It is the Holy Spirit who regenerates [no known direct statement on election]	Universal atonement	Man can resist the call of God	Discounts the possibility of the Holy Spirit leaving the person He has sealed

3. Particular Redemption or Limited Atonement: Graham stated, "It was not only universal sin which held Jesus to the cross—it was your sin."[106]

4. The Efficacious Call of the Spirit or Irresistible Grace: Graham wrote, "We do not passively sit back and wait for the Spirit to do His work before we come to Christ. . . . but we still have the responsibility to respond to the call and conviction of the Holy Spirit."[107] Graham stated, "But I do believe that men do have the ability to resist God."[108] Elsewhere he said, "Man, of his own free will, went away from God. He must, by deliberate choice, come back to God. God has done all the doing that needs to be done as far as the technical part of the

---

[105]Five points taken from David N. Steele and Curtis C. Thomas, *The Five Points of Calvinism: Defined, Defended, Documented*, ed. J. Marcellus Kik, "International Library of Philosophy and Theology: Biblical and Theological Study" (Philipsburg, NJ: Presbyterian and Reformed, 1963), 16-19.

[106]Billy Graham, "Labor, Christ and the Cross," 7.

[107]Billy Graham, *The Holy Spirit,* 80-81.

[108]Haden, "Dr. Graham, Exactly What Is Evangelism?" 12.

transaction is concerned, but there is one thing that He cannot touch . . . that is your will. He cannot force you to accept the life He holds out to you."[109]

5. Perseverance of the Saints: Graham wrote, "If the Spirit were to withdraw Himself from a believer He has sealed, would He not be denying the whole scheme of salvation?"[110]

The above points are not an attempt to paint Graham with one brush stroke. As it will be shown, there is some movement of Graham on the doctrine of sin and the atonement. However, his views of man's free will in salvation remained fairly consistent throughout his ministry. Thus, Graham, by his own words cannot be considered a Calvinist; but neither can he be considered Wesleyan or Methodist.[111] Rather, his theological conceptions may be described as Lutheran Pietist, without the sacramentalism of infant baptism and the Lord's Supper.[112] In Lutheran Pietism, one finds predestination, the universal atonement, and the ability to resist grace. Warfield explained the Lutheran view this way, "He cannot cooperate with God in producing it [regeneration through the sacrament]; but he can fatally resist."[113]

Warfield attacked the concept of Lutheran universal atonement as theologically inconsistent, when it does not correspondingly hold to universal salvation:

> The great problem to be faced by universalizing evangelicalism, therefore, of how it is God and God alone who saves the soul, and all that God does looking towards the saving of the soul he does to and for all men alike, and yet all are not saved.[114]

Graham's reply seems like it would be two-fold. First, It is a mystery that the mind cannot unravel. Second, from Scripture, Graham would state that

---

[109]Billy Graham, "The New Birth," *Hour of Decision Sermons,* no. 58 (Minneapolis: Billy Graham Evangelistic Association, 1955), 8.

[110]Billy Graham, *The Holy Spirit,* 189.

[111]Timo Pokki wrote, "Graham does not explicitly reveal his commitment to either the Calvinistic or the Arminian view" (Pokki, *America's Preacher,* 155).

[112]Some would say that Graham has rather inserted decisionism as a sacrament (e.g., Hulse, *The Great Invitation,* 100, 104-09; Hulse built on the work of Murray, *The Invitation System*).

[113]Warfield, *The Plan of Salvation,* 98.

[114]Ibid., 94.

God quickens and man can refuse salvation. Thus, there is no inconsistency. Rather Graham called it a mystery and a paradox.[115]

Defining Conversion

The mystery of conversion for Graham, however, had clarity when seeking to apply the Scriptures to conversion. This is why Graham developed clear practical steps in conversion. To Graham, conversion was the human part of the equation. In one place he said, "It [conversion] simply means 'stopping and turning.'"[116] Elsewhere he used many terms to describe conversion:

Actually the word conversion means "to turn around," "to change one's mind," "to turn back," or "to return." In the realm of religion it has been variously explained as "to repent," "to be regenerated," "to receive grace," "to experience religion," "to gain assurance."[117]

Therefore, to Graham the concept of conversion was associated primarily with the human side of the process, as we shall see, Graham called the divine side regeneration.

Almost a decade later, Graham continued to define conversion in human terms. He stated, "Conversion is the turning of the whole man to God; it is commitment to Christ as the first loyalty in life."[118] In a parallel article, Graham wrote, "There is no doubt that conversion and repentance are two ways of describing the same event."[119] The addition of repentance as a synonym to conversion, which lacks the faith element mentioned above, plays into the hand of more sacramental forms of conversion. This was expanded in his following statement:

These events demand a personal human response, repentance, turning to Christ as Lord and Saviour, and conversion (Acts 2.38; 3.19). In fact the only way to enter this Kingdom was by repentance and faith. This call to conversion is proclaimed both to Israel (Acts

---

[115]Billy Graham, "Christian Conversion," 5-6.

[116]Ibid., 4.

[117]Billy Graham, "What Is Conversion?" 4.

[118]Billy Graham, "Biblical Conversion," 3.

[119]Billy Graham, "Conversion—A Personal Revolution," 275.

2.22; 3.25) and to the Gentiles (Acts 17.30). It involves a personal response to the proclamation of the Good News of God's redemptive work in Jesus Christ and results in eternal life (Acts 11.18). Repentance is accompanied by faith! To believe in Christ (Acts 10.43) carried with it the idea of repentance. The whole response to the Gospel can be summed up as repentance toward God and faith in the Lord Jesus Christ (Acts 20.21). Faith in Jesus Christ means turning away from sin (Acts 3.26; 8.22) and turning to God (Acts 20.21; 26.20).[120]

Graham in this definition of evangelism written for a World Council of Churches' audience in *Ecumenical Review* may show several points:

1. Graham emphasized the need for personal conversion, as opposed to societal conversion and transformation

2. Graham seemed to be blending the concepts of conversion and repentance, perhaps appealing to more of a social understanding of the gospel

3. Graham was open to some type of *preparatio evangelica* or *gracia preparatur* coming through the sacramentalism of high churches as preceding a crisis conversion.[121]

Therefore, in spite of the pressure of a possibly antagonistic readership in the *Ecumenical Review*, Graham maintained a Mark 1:15 approach to defining conversion.

To Graham, throughout his ministry, conversion was closely tied to the new birth, or being "born again." Graham championed the need for the new birth and saw this as a focus of his ministry. He exclaimed his passion for others to be born again in the preface to his book *How to Be Born Again*:

---

[120]Ibid., 275-76.

[121]"The idea of conversion is often a difficult problem to those who hold a high view of sacramental grace. Many of the theologians and clergy cannot accept the idea of personal conversion on the part of those who were baptized in infancy. However, I have been agreeably surprised at the number of theologians and clergy who have successfully bridged this gap and successfully overcome this problem. Many Anglicans, Lutherans, Presbyterians, Orthodox and even Roman Catholic clergy have agreed that those within the Church need 'converting' even after baptism and confirmation" (ibid., 277-78).

My concern has been to make this book practical. Although we may not be able to say everything possible about the new birth, I have wanted to say everything that was necessary to help people who really want to know God. I want to help them come to have this life-changing experience. I want them—I want you—to be born again. I believe God wants you to be born again.[122]

To Graham, repentance, faith, and instantaneous conversion were all brought together in the concept of the new birth. Graham explained the new birth repeatedly by use of steps in conversion, often in his invitations to salvation.

Steps in Conversion

To Graham there were three steps in conversion. He explained these steps in his sermon, "What is Conversion?":

Actually, biblical conversion involves three steps—two of them active and one passive. In active conversion, repentance and faith are involved. Repentance is conversion viewed from its starting point, the turning from the former life. Faith indicates the objective point of conversion, the turning to God. The third, which is passive, we may call the new birth, or regeneration.[123]

As stated very clearly by Graham, the first two steps were repentance and faith, similar to the admonition of Jesus in Mark 1:15. These human steps were then followed by the divine step of regeneration. Several years later Graham added another point to the repentance step:

You say, "But, Billy, I would like to surrender my life to Christ but what do I have to do?" First, you have to acknowledge and confess that you have sinned against God. You have broken his commandments; you have failed to keep the teachings of the Sermon on the Mount. Secondly, you must renounce your sins, you must determine that you are not going to go back to your sins. And then thirdly, by faith you must receive Christ into your heart. Surrender

---

[122]Billy Graham, *How to Be Born Again* (Waco, TX: Word, 1977), 11.

[123]Billy Graham, "What Is Conversion?" 6.

your will and your total personality to Jesus Christ. He will come to live in your heart.[124]

In the invitation of this sermon, Graham was highlighting the human side of conversion. The repentance step Graham divided into confession and renouncement of sin. However, in this quote, one is left with the impression that a renouncement of sin is possible prior to regeneration. Nevertheless, this arrangement was changed slightly in Graham's 1956 sermon "Hope in Death," "But you say, 'What can I do?' You can renounce your sins, confess your sins, turn your back on your sins, receive Christ as your Savior now."[125] Three years later, Graham's steps in conversion had returned to his earlier emphases. He preached:

> Are you searching for an answer? The answer is simply this:
> First, you must recognize that you are a sinner. . . .
> Second, you must recognize that Christ died and rose for your sins. . . .
> Third, God requires that we receive His Son by faith. . .
> The moment you receive Christ by repentance and faith, then regeneration takes place and you become a new creature in Christ.[126]

To Graham, therefore, the steps to conversion were stated differently at different times. Yet, they remained similar throughout his ministry. Graham saw that man needed to repent and believe in response to the message and call of salvation, and he assured his listeners that God would hear them and regenerate their hearts.

The Invitation and Conversion

Graham's belief in instantaneous conversion, through the preaching of the gospel, accompanied by the power of the Holy Spirit, led him to emphasize an invitation in his crusade and radio preaching. Yet the invitation, to some Calvinists, gave too much preference to the human affections in the exercise of duty repentance and duty faith.

Therefore, Iain Murray did not appreciate the "Invitation System" which was a part of Graham's personal gospel. He felt that an

---

[124]Billy Graham, "Responsibilities of Parents," *Hour of Decision Sermons,* no. 57 (Minneapolis: Billy Graham Evangelistic Association, 1955), 11.

[125]Billy Graham, "Hope in Death," *Hour of Decision Sermons,* no. 71 (Minneapolis: Billy Graham Evangelistic Association, 1956), 8.

[126]Billy Graham, "Christian Conversion," 9-10.

invitation was too often confused with actual conversion, thus becoming a type of "sacrament." Murray accused Graham of emotionalism and shallow interpretation of Scripture. He even mentioned a jeering episode of David Hume, who attacked the preaching of George Whitefield, in defending his anti-emotionalism.[127] Murray also wrote against the notion of instantaneous conversion. Erroll Hulse, in his *The Great Invitation* expanded the theological portion of Murray's work. Rather than placing conversion in the space and time of a public prayer or confession, Hulse preferred to place conversion before profession of faith:

> Closely allied to illumination and conviction is reformation of life. . . . On the personal level, the main point is that often people reform their way of life considerably before they are converted.[128]

While Hulse noted a *gracia preparatur* of the Holy Spirit prior to bringing a sinner to salvation, on the other hand, he felt that emphasizing a public invitation unduly placed the time of conversion into the hands of the person making the decision, which, he felt, approached an Arminian view of conversion. However, both Murray and Hulse seem to ignore the power of the gospel and the supernatural character of the response to the preaching of the gospel. For example, Hulse sought to explain why the Philippian jailer (cf., Acts 16) was not saved instantaneously. He wrote, "All we can say is that there was some prior accumulation of knowledge and that the work proceeded with great speed."[129]

Thus, it would seem that Graham's invitation system caused a Calvinist like Erroll Hulse to espouse a type of progressive enlightenment approach to conversion in the lifetime of the elect.[130] This gradualism was a move away from Warfield's approach to the immediacy of conversion, as found in the New Testament conversions and teaching. And it was to the Scriptures to which Graham appealed for his methodology of instantaneous conversion. Yet to Murray and Hulse, Graham's approach to conversion was simplistic, as was his message.

Interestingly enough, John Owen, a strong believer in particular redemption, was also a strong biblicist as regards extending a general invitation:

---

[127]Murray, *The Invitation System*, 16.

[128]Hulse, *The Great Invitation*, 86-87.

[129]Ibid., 81.

[130]Ibid., 86-87.

The ministers of the gospel, who are stewards of the mysteries of Christ, and to whom the word of reconciliation has been committed, being acquainted only with revealed things . . . are bound to admonish all, and to warn all men to whom they are sent; giving the same commands, proposing the same promises, making tenders of Jesus Christ in the same manner, to all, that the elect, whom they do not know but by the event, may obtain, whist the rest be hardened.[131]

Elsewhere Owen wrote:

Secondly, That the Scripture sets forth the death of Christ, to all whom the gospel is preached [unto], as an all-sufficient means for the bringing of sinners unto God, so that as whosoever believe it and come in unto him shall certainly be saved. . . . And then it is by us fully granted, as making nothing at all for the universality of redemption, but only for the fullness and sufficiency of his satisfaction.[132]

Thus unlike Hulse and Murray, the issue of particularity for Owen did not hinder offers of grace. Rather the biblical examples of evangelism and its teaching overruled the need for supposed theological consistency.

From the centrality of instantaneous conversion in the preaching of Billy Graham, we now move to his doctrine of anthropology. It is in this context that Graham's theological progression becomes most evident.

Sin

To Graham, sin was a universal problem, so man's need for forgiveness was universal. To Graham acceptance of the gospel was the only way of salvation, so the proclamation of the gospel was a universal need. Therefore, Graham's understanding of sin was paramount not only to understanding his message, but also to understanding his tenacity in preaching the gospel for all the years of his ministry. Millard Erickson wrote of the importance of the doctrine of sin:

---

[131]John Owen, *The Death of Death in the Death of Christ* (Edinburgh: Banner of Truth, 1959; first published in 1684), 201.

[132]Ibid., 264. Owen explained the sufficiency of Christ's death for the sins of the world elsewhere: "Sufficient we say, then, was the sacrifice of Christ for the redemption of the whole world, and for the expiation of all sins of all and every man in the world" (183-84).

The doctrine of sin is both extremely important and much disputed. It is important because it affects and is also affected by many other areas of doctrine. . . . Our doctrine of salvation will be strongly influenced by our understanding of sin.[133]

Timo Pokki wrote, "Human sinfulness is the fundamental starting point of Graham's preaching."[134] In the same way, the redefinition of sin was the starting point of Rauschenbusch's theology of the social gospel.[135] And Graham's conception of sin was the starting point of Reinhold Niebuhr's contempt of Graham's message and methods.[136]

Niebuhr's criticism provide an understanding of Graham's early views of sin, and the critiques against him. However, were there any changes in Graham's understanding or communication about sin? The following answers this question in the affirmative by noting four stages in Graham's ministry: early-early, early, middle, and later.

The Early-Early Graham

The Early-Early Graham was clearly a biblicist as regards the fundamental truths of the faith. For example, in his sermon "A Midnight Tragedy," Graham used a litany of verses on the sinfulness of mankind:

Today God is weighing you by His own standard. As you are being weighed in the balance, God says:
1. "There is no man that sinneth not" (I Kings 8:46).

---

[133]Erickson, *Christian Theology,* 562.

[134]Pokki, *America's Preacher,* 77.

[135]Rauschenbusch took six chapters to redefine sin in democratic lines (Rauschenbusch, *A Theology for the Social Gospel* (New York: Macmillan, 1917; Nashville: Abingdon, 1990), 31-94), whereas he only spent one chapter debunking the cross and the substitutionary atonement (240-79).

[136]"He [Graham] will constantly present the 'Christian message' to an entire metropolitan center. The center is of course a Babylon, whose 'sins' invite the denunciations of any 'prophet.' But the question is whether the prophet is able to discern the real sins of such a Babylon, or to appreciate the virtues of such a vaste conglomerate community in which all peoples and racial stocks live in comparative brotherhood. . . . But the Graham revival will actually accentuate every prejudice which the modern 'enlightened,' but morally sensitive man may have against religion. . . . The task is made much more difficult by a literalistic interpretation of the Bible and by individualistic and pietistic versions of the Christian faith" (Reinhold Niebuhr, "Editorial Notes," *Christianity and Crisis,* 5 March 1956, 18).

2. "There is no man which sinneth not" (II Chron. 6:36).

3. "There is none good but one, that is, God" (Matt. 19:17).

4. "What then? are we better than they? No, in no wise: for we have before proved both Jews and Gentiles, that they are all under sin" (Rom. 3:9).

5. "There is none righteous, no, not one" (Rom. 3:10).

6. "There is none that doeth good, no, not one" (Rom. 3:12; Ps. 14:3).

7. "There is no difference: for all have sinned, and come short of the glory of God" (Rom. 3:22-23).

8. "If we say that we have no sin, we deceive ourselves, and the truth is not in us" (I John 1:8).

You are nervous and afraid. From the depths of your heart and soul you want these scales to balance. How can you balance them? Where can you turn?[137]

This sermon leaves us a clue that the Early-Early Graham, prior to his 1949 Los Angeles crusade, believed in total depravity. Three points can be made in reference to these verses and this sermon. First, when Graham quoted Romans 3:10 he left out "None seeks after God." Second, he did not appear to use this list of verses in any other published sermon after 1947. Third, it appears that Graham dropped the use of Daniel 5 as one of his primary sermons before 1949.[138] Thus, it would seem that this early description of sin seemed too restrictive for Graham to use after 1947.

During that same time period Graham also used the term "total depravity" when decrying the shallowness of preaching in some churches:

> Thousands of these men have denied that the Bible is the Word of God. Thousands of men standing behind the sacred desk today lied when they spoke their ordination vows. They deny the blood atonement; they deny the virgin birth; they deny the bodily resurrection of Christ; they deny the total depravity of man.[139]

Yet, as will be noted, he soon dropped the fundamentalist language, and seemed to opt for a more gentle approach to *La Condition Humaine*.

---

[137]Billy Graham, "A Midnight Tragedy," in *Calling Youth to Christ* (Grand Rapids: Zondervan, 1947), 59.

[138]"Billy Graham Sermon Series by Decade," research copy sent from Billy Graham Evangelistic Association, Minneapolis office, 16 March 2001.

[139]Billy Graham, "America's Hope," in *Calling Youth to Christ*, 23.

The Early Graham

Graham's early view of sin centered around individual and personal sin as an act of rebellion against God and His laws:

> He [God] hates the lust in your heart; He hates the wickedness in your heart; He hates the immorality in your heart; He hates the sin in your heart. The pride, the stubbornness, the rebellion of your soul as well—God hates it with a holy hatred; the Scripture teaches that.[140]

> The basic root of all sin is pride. The basic difficulty in the world today is sin. Before we can solve the economic, philosophical and political problems of the world, pride, greed, lust and sin are first going to have to be erased.[141]

> The third legitimate fear that the Bible speaks about is the fear that should come upon the wicked and the sinner when he realizes the terror, and the judgment of the Lord.[142]

In another 1951 sermon Graham expanded on the concept of sin:

> There are thousands of people today that think they are Christians because they belong to some church or they have been reared in a Christian home or they live a good moral life. But the Bible teaches that "All have sinned and come short of the glory of God." The Bible teaches, "Wherefore as by one man sin entered into the world and death by sin, so death passed upon all men, for that all have sinned." So every man is dead in trespasses and in sins and thereby alienated from the life of God. By his sin Adam had become a sinner and possessed a sinful nature. Then he had sons like him; they inherited his sinful nature and so has his posterity on down through the whole human family. Through Adam's one sin of disobedience all men have been constituted sinners in the sight of God. Therefore, Jesus said that before we can have a new social order the individual

---

[140]Billy Graham, "Will God Spare America?" in *America's Hour of Decision* (Wheaton, IL: Van Kampen, 1951), 120-21.

[141]Billy Graham, "National Humility," in *America's Hour of Decision*, 130.

[142]Billy Graham, "Fear," in *America's Hour of Decision*, 137.

must have a new birth. Jesus even went a step further and said that before a man could have eternal life, he must be born again.[143]

In his early ministry Graham viewed sin in individual terms, stating, "before we can have a new social order the individual must have a new birth."[144] Graham discussed the issue of sin from an individual point of view in his messages. This emphasis provided the setting for repentance and faith to be planted into the heart of listeners. The early Graham, however, while he used concepts logically related to total depravity, did seemed to avoid use of the term "total."[145] Thus he taught the depravity of all of mankind, due to the original sin of Adam, as federal head of the human race:[146]

> Man and woman being tempted of the Devil, ate of the tree. God's word had to be kept. God was not a liar. God had said in the day you eat, you will die. Therefore, Adam, the federal head, died spiritually. They were separated from God. Since that day man has been separated from God. Adam had acted as federal head of the human race.[147]

Because of man's state of sin in Adam, as well as because of man's individual sin, man was considered by nature spiritually dead. Thus, sin affected man's relationship with God. In his 1951 sermon "Grace Versus Wrath," Graham stated:

---

[143]Billy Graham, "Christianism Versus Communism," *Hour of Decision Sermons*, no. 2 (Minneapolis: Billy Graham Evangelistic Association, 1951), 8-9.

[144]Ibid., 9.

[145]It would seem that Graham, or the editor of *World Aflame,* did use the term "totally depraved," as will be noted in the Middle Graham.

[146]The terminology of "federal headship" was Calvinistic (see Erickson, *Christian Theology,* 635).

[147]Billy Graham, "Christianity Versus a Bloodless Religion," *Hour of Decision Sermons*, no. 6 (Minneapolis: Billy Graham Evangelistic Association, 1951), 7. In his sermon "Position Versus Penalty," Graham said the same thing: "Then came the *fall.* Adam being the federal head of the human race failed, and in that failure, by that fall, he became sinful" (Billy Graham, "Position Versus Penalty," 4). In "Peace Versus Chaos," Graham said, "Depravity has filled our jails. . . . We've tried to clean up the old depraved nature of man, but sin has not changed" (Billy Graham, "Peace Versus Chaos," *Hour of Decision Sermons,* no. 3 [Minneapolis: Billy Graham Evangelistic Association, 1951], 5-7).

There can be no question that the Scriptures teach that the devil is the "god of this Age," the present evil world system—that the carnal mind is enmity against God—that they that are in the flesh cannot please God, and that God in Christ was despised and rejected of men. . . .
It is the nature of man to run from God. . . .

Two thousand years ago they rejected God, "The Son," and today the same spirit of depravity is causing men to reject the call of God through the "Holy Spirit."[148]

Graham continued by pressing the depravity of mankind, "Judgment—the wrath of God against a depraved, doomed, debauched and a damned, sinful race—has hovered over the world for twenty centuries."[149]

To Graham, sin pointed directly to the cross:

It was not only universal sin which held Jesus to the cross—it was YOUR sin. If your sins are not responsible for Calvary, then Calvary has no responsibility for your sins. God, knowing the hearts of all men, and that they were only evil continually [Genesis 6:5], offered His Son to die for all men: those living and those yet unborn. Calvary is the place of decision. It is the eternal sword, erected to divide men into two classes, the saved and the lost. Embrace its truth and be saved. Reject it and be lost.[150]

As noted in his quote of Genesis 6:5 in the above portion, the early Graham discussed sin leaning very close to the doctrine of total depravity, although, because of his distancing himself from fundamentalism, his view must be considered moral depravity.

While the Early Graham came close to total depravity, and Timo Pokki proffered that total depravity was his view,[151] after 1947 Graham did

---

[148]Billy Graham, "Grace Versus Wrath," *Hour of Decision Sermons,* no. 7 (Minneapolis: Billy Graham Evangelistic Association, 1951), 2, 4-5.

[149]Ibid., 8.

[150]Billy Graham, "Labor, Christ and the Cross," 7.

[151]Pokki wrote, "Even if 'total depravity' is a very important concept for Graham, he maintains that man was created for freedom and something of this original freedom is still left in man because intellect and will are the things which constitute the *imagio Dei*" (Pokki, *America's Preacher,* 79).

not fully express the concept of total depravity.[152] Apel assumed Graham's view of man's depravity had a manipulative bent to it:

> For example, what we usually fail to recognize in Graham's denouncement of depraved man is the polemical nature of Graham's preaching. He does not degrade man because he believes man to be totally depraved; rather he shames man in order to convict him as a sinner who is in need of salvation. In other words, Graham does not preach a low anthropology   primarily as a theological conviction. Instead, his low anthropology is used as a homiletical technique to bring sinners to ask how they might be saved.
>
> After all, if Billy Graham were truly convinced of man's total depravity, he could not hold to the possibility of each man's personal salvation.[153]

Pokki sought to deduce Graham's view of depravity by working back from his view of salvation. This approach, however, failed to take into account that both Wesley, an Arminian, and Whitefield, a Calvinist, believed in total inability. One of the differences between the two was Wesley's concept of a universal prevenient grace, by which all men had the ability to respond to the gospel outside of the concept of predestination.

Graham, somewhat like Wesley, had a strong view of man's free will. In an early sermon, Graham stated, "You are a free moral agent! God did not create you as a machine to be compelled to love Him! You have the power of free choice."[154] Graham held this view simultaneously to his holding total depravity. However, some theologians objected to Graham's view of depravity by stating that it adhered to a practical belief that the will was untainted by sin, since he called individuals to repent and believe. However, outside of the prior work of the Holy Spirit, the "Early-Early Graham" believed that man was incapable of either repenting or believing.

---

[152]When Pokki used the term "Total Depravity" he did not have the Calvinistic concept in his mind. He explained as follows: "As regards the interpretation of *total depravity* Graham comes close to John Wesley, whose doctrine of total depravity differed from Lutheran and Calvinist diagnoses of the human condition on at least two points. The twofold clue here is in (1) Wesley's essentially catholic view of sin as a malignant *disease* rather than an obliteration of the *imago Dei* in fallen human nature, and (2) in his displacement of the doctrine of 'election' with the notion of 'prevenient grace', which creates new possibilities for human existence" (ibid).

[153]William Dale Apel, "The Understanding of Salvation in the Evangelistic Message of Billy Graham: A Historical-Theological Evaluation" (Ph.D. diss., Northwestern University, 1975), 48.

[154]Billy Graham, "Hell," in *Calling Youth to Christ*, 129. This language is similar to that found in "Steps to Peace with God."

He sounded more Lutheran when he preached, "You can only be converted when the Spirit of God is moving and speaking and convicting your soul, and He's doing that tonight."[155] The "Later Graham" continued to maintain God's role in salvation when he wrote:

> We need and desire to be filled and controlled by the Holy Spirit as we bear witness to the Gospel of Jesus Christ, because God alone can turn sinners from their sin and bring them to everlasting life.[156]

As has been noted, Graham's emphasis on free will was constant throughout his ministry. Pokki called Graham's conception of sin a paradox or *complexio oppositorum*, because Graham called people to repentance. Pokki noted that Calvinists believe that "man is completely alienated from God," and Arminians believe that "every human being as the image of God still has some kind of capability to obey God's law and be obedient to Him with the aid of some kind of prevenient grace."[157] Pokki saw that Graham held these contradictory views in a balance. However, Graham's view of total depravity and freewill were perhaps not as contradictory as Pokki believed.

Therefore the Early Graham never fully accepted that man's will was totally depraved, thus not adhering to total depravity. The Early Graham was in contrast to the Early-Early Graham that spoke out for total depravity, had his litany of verses on sin, and preached on sin from Daniel 5. The Early Graham, however, continued to preach sin as an individual transgression of the law of God. Is there evidence that Graham moved from these positions? There is evidence that later in his ministry he moved on both of these points. We now discuss the "Middle Graham," noting his *Hour of Decision Sermons,* and particularly his 1955 sermon, "The Love of God."

The Middle Graham

Prior to noting the progress of individual sermons and concepts in Graham, it is necessary to introduce his *Hour of Decision Sermons.* By the time sermon 100 rolled off of the presses in Minneapolis, some of the important Graham sermons were repeated two times in the *Hour of Decision* sermon series.[158] For example, Graham's sermon on revival was perhaps the

---

[155]Billy Graham, "Will God Spare America?" 125.

[156]Billy Graham, *A Biblical Standard for Evangelists*, 65.

[157]Pokki, *America's Preacher,* 76-77.

[158]Lois Ferm, archivist for Billy Graham and wife of Robert Ferm, research assistant for Billy Graham from 1959-1984, when speaking of the 321 *Hour of*

most repetitious. The sermon "We Need Revival" was published in the 1950 *Revival in Our Time*. Graham's *Hour of Decision* sermon number 15 was "Revival or Disintegration," sermon number 51, "Revival Today," sermon number 64, "The Revival We Need," and sermon number 92, "Revival or the Spirit of the Age." Revival continued to be a theme of Graham's into the late fifties when an associate of the Billy Graham team felt that the closest thing to genuine revival took place in Australia in 1959.[159] It would seem, however, that following Graham's 1957 crusade in New York the concept of revival began to diminish in Graham. Similarly, Graham's 1947 sermon on the blood was found in *Calling Youth to Christ,* sermon number 7, "A Scarlet Thread." A 1949 version was published titled "Atonement" in *Great Gospel Sermons,* volume 2, "Contemporary." Then a 1951 version was published as *Hour of Decision* sermon number 6, "Christianity and a Bloodless Religion." The same sermon was then repeated in the 1957 *Hour of Decision* sermon number 87, "The Suffering Savior on a Crimson Cross." From that time on his material on the blood was combined with his material on the cross, which we will note later. Another repeated sermon was found when Graham discussed persecution for the sake of Christ. *Hour of Decision* sermon number 17 is titled, "Branded." Then the same theme is picked up in *Hour of Decision* sermon number 55, "Scars of Battle." A study of Graham's *Hour of Decision* sermons shows both repetition and changes in Graham's use of illustrations and approach to theological issues. By sermon 100 many of his key published sermons had been revised at least once. The changes in these sermons provides an important source of information on changes in Graham's theology.

The love of God (1955). Another way of noting changes in Graham's theology, or in that of his editors, are to note the changes in the revisions of his *Hour of Decision* sermons that continue to be made available. For example, Graham's 1955 *Hour of Decision* sermon number 52, titled "The Love of God," went through two revisions, one at an unknown date, and another in 1995. The original sermon reported on his Scotland Crusade from March to May, 1955:

Decision Sermons, shared with me, "Graham only has thirty sermons" (interviews by author, Amsterdam, 31 July 2000 and 6 August 2000, notes). This insight led me to consider two types of research: (1) examine the same sermon over the fifty plus years of his ministry, and (2) note which sermons he ceased preaching and which ones he added to his repertoire.

[159]Lois Ferm told me that the Australia crusade in 1959 was the closest thing to revival that she had ever experienced. People were signing hymns in public transportation and speaking about Christ in public places (interviews by author, Amsterdam, 31 July 2000 and 6 August 2000, notes).

One of the truths we have been emphasizing over and over again is the love of God. More than any other Crusade that we have ever led, it seemed to be the dominant theme of song and word. Never before did we present so many messages with the theme of the love of God as in Scotland.[160]

"The Love of God" sermon was Graham's first *Hour of Decision* sermon fully devoted to the love of God, and from his own words, it seemed to indicate a change of emphasis in his preaching. It is interesting that the emphasis came at a time when Graham adjusted his view of sin, as will be noted in his 1955 *The Seven Deadly Sins*. By contrast, Graham's first *Hour of Decision* sermon is titled "Hate Vs. Love." Out of ten pages in this sermon two and a half pages are given over to love, the remainder addressed some kind of hatred. "The Love of God," however, was revised and republished twice. It was first revised at an unknown time when the introduction was changed; the voice in the remainder of the introduction was changed from second person plural, "they," to first person plural, "we;" two pages were added to the conclusion; and some other minor changes were made. Then it was revised in 1995. One change in this latter revision was to change "man" to "person" and "his" to "his or her." It is interesting that Graham preached an entire message on the love of God without mentioning Romans 5:8, which is often used in personal evangelism to show the extent of the love of God.

One passage in "The Love of God" typifies the changes made in this sermon, which may then provide insight into how other sermons have been updated through the years. In the original 1955 sermon, Graham spoke about the tree in the garden:

It was love, the love of God which was so concerned for man's welfare that He carefully marked the only danger spot in this exquisite garden of God. "Eat of every other tree," said God, "but not this one. There is death in this one."

Somehow in a way known only to God Himself, sin, that mysterious element of evil unleashed in the universe, had innoculated that particular tree and God in love warned His creature not to partake of it. It was love which moved God to seek out man after he had made that fatal blunder and against God's warning eaten of that tree. It was love which made God, perhaps in tones of stark

---

[160]Billy Graham, "The Love of God," *Hour of Decision Sermons,* no. 52 (Minneapolis: Billy Graham Evangelistic Association, 1955), 2.

disappointment, cry out, "Where art thou, Adam?" and then begin the long weary, planning in preparation for man to return to Himself.[161]

The 1955 revised reads as follows:

> It was love, the love of God, which was so concerned for man's welfare that He carefully marked the only danger spot in this exquisite garden of God. "Eat of every other tree," said God, "but not of this one. There is death in this one."
>
> It was love which moved God to seek out man after he had made that fatal blunder and had, in spite of God's warning, eaten of that tree.
>
> It was love which made God call out, "Where art thou, Adam?" It was love which initiated God's preparation for man to return to Himself.[162]

Finally, the following is the reading of the text in the 1995 revision:

> It was love, the love of God, which was so concerned for men and women's welfare that He carefully marked the only danger spot in this exquisite garden of God. "Eat of every other tree," said God, "but not of this one. There is death in this one."
>
> It was love which moved God to seek out the man and the woman after they made that fatal blunder and had, in spite of God's warning, eaten of that tree.
>
> It was love which made God call out, "Where art thou, Adam?" It was love which initiated God's preparation for us to return to Himself.[163]

Graham calling the Fall a "fatal blunder" dated from 1955. That terminology was never edited, yet it seems to approach Horace Bushnell's view of sin as a disease,[164] and James Denney's reconciliation model of the atonement. Graham also proferred an interesting view of the Tree of the Knowledge of

---

[161]Ibid., 5; emphasis mine.

[162]Billy Graham, "The Love of God," rev. ed. (Minneapolis: Billy Graham Evangelistic Association, n.d.), 4.

[163]Billy Graham, "The Love of God," 2nd rev. (Minneapolis: Billy Graham Evangelistic Association, 1995), 4.

[164]"Disease goes with sin, Healing with salvation" (Horace Bushnell, *The Vicarious Sacrifice Grounded in Principles of Universal Obligation* [New York: Scribner, 1866; Hicksville, NY: Regina Press, 1975], 134).

Good and Evil. He said, "That mysterious element of evil unleashed in the universe, had innoculated that particular tree." Somehow he felt that the locus of sin was not in disobedience of the command, but a "mysterious element of evil" in the tree. He may have been quoting some non-evangelical theologians on this point, as he did on "worldliness" in *Peace with God*.[165] Graham followed this up logically with a quote from Scripture adapted from 2 Kings 4:40, "O man of God, there is death in the pot," applying it to the Tree of the Knowledge of Good and Evil, "There is death in this one." Graham actually altered the words of God in Genesis 2:17 in this sermon! For the pot of stew in 2 Kings had nothing to do with man's sinful nature. Elisha purified the pot and the sons of the prophets ate. But in the case of the tree in the middle of the Garden of Eden, Adam and Eve were commanded not to eat from it. The commentators C. F. Keil and Franz Delitzsch discount the possibility of any material wrong in the fruit, but rather attribute it as a test of man's obedience to God's law, which would then give man true knowledge of good and evil.[166] Graham's original 1955

---

[165]He quoted Griffith Thomas' *The Catholic Faith: A Manual of Instruction for Members of the Church of England* (London: Hodder and Stoughton, 1905, 1908), in *Peace with God* (Garden City, NY: Doubleday, 1953), 165.

[166]"Are we to regard the tree as poisonous, and suppose that some fatal property resided in the fruit? A supposition which so completely ignores the ethical nature of sin is neither warranted by the antithesis, nor by what is said in chap. iii. 22 of the tree of life, nor by the fact that the eating of the forbidden fruit was actually the cause of death. Even in the case of the tree of life, the power is not to be sought in the physical character of the fruit. No earthly fruit possesses the power to give immortality to the life which it helps to sustain. Life is not rooted in man's corporeal nature; it was in his spiritual nature that it had its origin, and from this it derives its stability and permanence also. . . . The power which transforms corporeality into immortality is spiritual in its nature, and could only be imparted to the earthly tree or its fruit through the word of God, through a special operation of the Spirit of God, an operation which we can only picture to ourselves as sacramental in its character, rendering earthly elements the receptacles and vehicles of celestial powers. God had given such a sacramental nature and significance to the two trees in the midst of the garden, that their fruit could and would produce supersensual, mental, and spiritual effects upon the nature of the first human pair. The tree of life was to impart the power of transformation into eternal life. The tree of knowledge was to lead man to the knowledge of good and evil; and, according to the divine intention, this was to be attained through his not eating of its fruit. This end was to be accomplished, not only by his discerning in the limit imposed by the prohibition the difference between that which accorded with the will of God and that which opposed it, but also by his coming eventually, through obedience to the prohibition, to recognise the fact that all that is opposed to the will of God is an evil to be avoided, and, through voluntary resistance to such evil, to the full development of the freedom of choice originally imparted to him into the actual freedom of a deliberate and self-conscious choice of good. . . . But as he failed to keep this divinely appointed way, and ate the forbidden fruit in opposition to the command of God, the power imparted by

section seeking to explain the evil in the tree was removed in the two later additions (see emphasized text). Did Graham's 1955 sermon "The Love of God" indicate a change in his view of the Fall of man? Graham seemed to be explaining the Tree of the Knowledge of Good and Evil outside of the disobedience to the direct prohibition of God, as he was approaching the prohibition from the central-interpretive-motif of love rather than from the standpoint of *heilgeschichte*. Genesis actually says, "You shall surely die." God picked up on the importance of this language in Ezekiel 3:18, "When I say to the wicked, 'You shall surely die,' and you give him no warning. . . ." "The Love of God" manifested the change of heart to which Graham's original 1955 introduction may have attested. Superimposing the *a priori* of the love of God over the prohibition in the Garden of Eden led to an unusual interpretation of the Fall of man.

Whereas the early Graham seemed to have used "Total Depravity" once in 1947, he did speak of Adam as "Federal Head." This 1955 sermon, however, marks a change in Graham that is found in other places as well. Elsewhere Graham described man's sinful condition, "living under the burden of his own wretchedness."[167] Yet Graham's view of Adam's role in sin had several interesting nuances. First, Adam's sin did not make man by nature a sinner, rather each individual's sin made him a sinner. William Dale Apel explained:

Here his reference to Adam's sin, however, does not imply that Adam's descendants are accountable for Adam's sin. He admits that we are all affected by the "universal consequence" of Adam's sin, but we are held responsible only for our own sin. According to Graham, "God doesn't hold you responsible for Adam's sin—he holds you responsible for your own. Every day a million Edenic scenes are reinacted."[168]

God to the fruit was manifested in a different way. He learned the difference between good and evil from his own guilty experience, and by receiving the evil into his own soul, fell a victim to the threatened death. Thus through his own fault the tree, which should have helped him to attain true freedom, brought nothing but the sham liberty of sin, and with it death, and that without any demoniacal [sic] power of destruction being conjured into the tree itself, or any fatal poison being hidden in its fruit" (C. F. Keil and Franz Delitzsch, *The First Book of Moses* [Grand Rapids: William B. Eerdmans, 1986], 85-56.

[167]Billy Graham, "The Love of God" (1955), 3.

[168]Apel, "The Understanding of Salvation," 51. Apel quoted Graham's sermon "Made, Marred and Mended," *Hour of Decision Sermons*, no. 77 (Minneapolis: Billy Graham Evangelistic Association, 1956), 7.

This view is called the "Natural Headship" of Adam, rather than the "Early" Graham's view of "Federal Headship."[169]

Graham still preached that individual sin was a direct offense against God, "The Bible tells us that sin is more than overt acts that cause difficulties and troubles in this life. The Bible teaches that sin is an offense to God."[170] Although, as we will note, he added a social dimension to sin that was not found in the "Early Graham." This can be noted in his book, *Freedom from the Seven Deadly Sins.*

***Freedom from the Seven Deadly Sins* (1955).** Graham's 1955 book, *Freedom from the Seven Deadly Sins,* seemed to be a combination of marketing to a Roman Catholic audience, as well as a redefinition of the concept of sin. The seven sins were traditionally called cardinal or "capital" sins by the Roman Catholic Church.[171] Graham acknowledged that their origin came from "Pope," Gregory the Great (590-604),[172] who was most likely the first Bishop or Patriarch of Rome that could be considered a "Pope," as he gathered the Latin-speaking church under his care.[173] Graham also acknowledged that the sins were not listed together in any one place.[174] However, when taken as a whole, the cardinal sins may be understood as a reinterpretation of the doctrine of sin and that of the atonement on the part

---

[169]Natural headship was the view of James Denney (Denney, *The Christian Doctrine of Reconciliation* [New York: George H. Doran, 1918], 198-99).

[170]Billy Graham, "Great Sin! Greater Salvation!" *Hour of Decision Sermons*, no. 137 (Minneapolis: Billy Graham Evangelistic Association, 1961), 5.

[171]"Vices can be classified according to the virtues they oppose, or also be linked to the *capital sins* which Christian experience has distinguished, following St. John Cassian and St. Gregory the Great. They are called 'capital' because they engender other sins, other vices. They are pride, avarice, envy, wrath, lust, gluttony, and sloth or acedia" (*Catechism of the Catholic Church*, paragraph 1866, 457; the passage footnoted St. Gregory the Great, *Moralia in Job,* 31, 45: PL 76, 621A). Sir Henry Howorth argued that Gregory the Great's allegorical interpretation of Job, *Moralia in Job,* a book that he devoted a great deal of time and attention to, "would not be considered adequate by modern standards, because Gregory did not know either Hebrew or Greek and showed little acquaintance with Eastern history or culture even though he lived in Constantinople for several years" (Sir Henry H. Howorth, *Gregory the Great* [London: John Murray, 1912], 108).

[172]Billy Graham, *Freedom from the Seven Deadly Sins* (Grand Rapids: Zondervan, 1955, 1960), 9.

[173]Greg Likoudis, "Pope St. Gregory the Great Upheld Papal Supremacy," *Christ to the World* 34, no. 2 (March-April 1994): 160-62.

[174]Billy Graham, *Freedom from the Seven Deadly Sins*, 10.

of Gregory the Great.[175] This redefinition of salvation was confirmed by the fact that Gregory the Great was the first Roman Catholic leader to posit the addition of purgatory to salvation.[176] The pertinent question, however, for this section regards Billy Graham. Did *Freedom from the Seven Deadly Sins* give indications that Graham was broadening his view of sin, perhaps to include social sin? In fact, in *Freedom from the Seven Deadly Sins* Graham did communicate new concepts in his theology.

In the first of the cardinal sins, Graham addressed the sin of pride. Graham's first point regarded self-righteousness. In this point Graham attacked "those who think they have a corner on the Gospel."[177] He continued, "There are also others who think themselves to be pure and all others impure. They have forgotten that there is no such thing as a completely pure church."[178] Graham then addressed intellectual pride, pride in material things, and lastly social pride. Graham expanded on this point:

---

[175]The Cardinal Sins seem to be the antithesis of the Cardinal Virtues. With a philosophical understanding of salvation, the goal of the Christian life is to grow in the Cardinal Virtues, and hence diminish the Cardinal Sins. The four Cardinal Virtues are said to be: "The four principal virtues upon which the rest of the moral virtues turn or are hinged. . . . The origin of the fourfold system is traceable to Greek philosophy; other sources are earlier, but the Socratic source is most definite. . . . Plato wrote in 'The Laws' (Bk. I, 631), 'Wisdom is the chief and leader: next follows temperance; and from the union of these two with courage springs justice. These four virtues take precedence in the class of divine goods'" ("Cardinal Virtues," Catholic Encyclopedia; accessed 4 February 2003; available at: http://www.newadvent.org/cathen/03343a.ht; Internet).

[176]Howorth explained Gregory the Great's addition of penance into the process of forgiveness and restitution with God: "Christ did not satisfy the conditions of pardon and salvation unless and until sin itself had been purged, and this purging involved 'a system of compensations by which the good works are balanced against sins, and eternal punishment is remitted in consideration of adequate suffering'" (Howorth, *Gregory the Great*, 264).

[177]Billy Graham, "Pride," in *Freedom from the Seven Deadly Sins*, 18.

[178]Ibid. In these statements Graham distanced himself from fundamentalists. This was typical language for Graham repeated in many sermons after his dismal crusade in Altoona, Pennsylvania in 1949. Also, perhaps without knowing it, Graham was siding with Augustine who wrote *Contra Donatisten*. Gregory the Great, for his part, used administrative prowess to squelch the Donatists in North Africa by limiting their ability to become bishops. The following is a portion of a letter that he sent to the Tetrarch of Numidia, "And we, indeed, according to the tenour of your representation, allow your custom (so long as it clearly makes no claim to the prejudice of the catholic faith) to remain undisturbed, whether as to constituting primates or as to other points; save that with respect to those who attain to the episcopate from among the Donatists, we by all means forbid them to be advanced to the dignity of primacy, even though their standing should denote them for that position. But let it suffice them to take care of the

Then there is social pride. This manifests itself in class, racial and caste arrogance. . . .

There are few people today who really believe in the super race. The idea of a super race is unBiblical, unScriptural and unChristian. . . .

How many people have social pride that is sinful?[179]

It is interesting to the point of social pride is the only point for which Graham did not give Scriptural support. Did this constitute a change of approach in Graham?

In his second sermon on the cardinal sin of anger, Graham spoke of anger as revealing an animal trait in man, "Anger is a heinous sin because it reveals the animal nature of man."[180] He seemed to turn from the anti-evolutionary rhetoric of his early ministry.[181]

In sermon five on gluttony, Graham quoted from Amos 6:4, and then he said:

Three-fifths of the world live in squalor, misery and hunger. Too long have the privileged few exploited and ignored the underprivileged millions of the world. Our selfishness is at long last catching up with us. Unless we begin to act, to share, and to do something about this great army of starving humanity, God will judge us.

Communism, with its multiplied millions of adherents, promises to help the helpless. Unless Christians break with their selfishness and begin to help these millions of starving people out of their misery, they will turn to the only other alternative—Communism.

Even though this is an era of prosperity there is shocking evidence of selfishness and greed on every hand. Who knows but what God has permitted this prosperity to come that we may share it with the suffering and needy, and thus lure them away from

---

people committed to them, without aiming at the topmost place of the primacy in preference to those prelates whom the Catholic faith hath both taught and engendered in the bosom of the Church" (Gregory I, Pope, *Epistle LXXVII*, "To All the Bishops of Numibia"; accessed 3 February 2001; available at: ccel.wheaton.edu/Gregory/Register/E24.htm; Internet).

[179]Billy Graham, "Pride," 23.

[180]Billy Graham, "Anger," in *Freedom from the Deadly Seven Sins* (Grand Rapids: Zondervan, 1955, 1960), 29.

[181]In his early ministry he spoke plainly about the dangers of Darwinism: "Evolutionists deny direct creation as taught in the Bible. They deny a personal, creating God" (discussed in six paragraphs in Graham, "America's Hope," 21).

Communism by our love and compassion! I John 3:17 speaks for itself—"Whoso hath this world's good, and seeth his brother have need, and shutteth up his bowels of compassion from him, how dwelleth the love of God in him?"

We are not only to witness for Christ with our lips, but with our hands—hands laden with food for the hungry, clothes for the naked; and water for the thirsty.[182]

In this sermon, Graham described the sin of gluttony in a societal sense. In fact, later in the sermon he stated that the sin of gluttony, "as one of the worst of all sins."[183] When he added gluttony as a societal sin, his view of mission immediately responded to this theological change. He moved from the universal imperative of preaching the gospel to stating, "Unless we begin to act, to share, and to do something about this great army of starving humanity, God will judge us."[184] "We are not only to witness for Christ with our lips, but with our hands."[185] The inclusion of "witness . . . with our hands" with "witness . . . with our lips" portrayed that Graham was placing the humanitarian alongside the spiritual. This was a seismic statement for Graham to make in 1955.[186] Thus, a socializing shift in Graham's approach to sin was noticeable by 1955.

Stanley High on Graham. In 1956 Stanley High, in his biography of Graham, added momentum to the viewpoint that the "Middle" Graham's view of sin was broadening. High wrote and included quotes from Graham in his text:

---

[182]Billy Graham, "Gluttony," in *Freedom from the Deadly Seven Sins* (Grand Rapids: Zondervan, 1955, 1960), 78-79.

[183]"Yet the Bible is very specific in stating that gluttony is one of the worst of all sins, and the church has said that it is one of the seven deadly sins" (ibid., 83).

[184]Ibid., 78.

[185]Ibid., 79.

[186]The Roman Catholic Church also follows the social precedent of Gregory the Great. For example, Paul VI in his encyclical *Evangelii Nuntiandi* explained the human aspect of the evangelization mandate of the Roman Church: "But evangelization would not be complete if it did not take account of the unceasing interplay of the Gospel and of man's concrete life, both personal and social. . . . Hence, when preaching liberation and associating herself with those who are working and suffering for it, the Church is certainly not willing to restrict her mission only to the religious field and dissociate herself from man's temporal problems. . . . The Church links human liberation and salvation in Jesus Christ. . ." (Paul VI, *Evangelii Nuntiandi,* 8 December 1975, sections 29, 34, 35).

Sin is "anything which separates man from God." It is "transgression of the law of God." Or it is "iniquity—evil that springs from our inner motivations, those hidden things we so often try to keep from the eyes of men and God." Or it is "missing the mark—falling short of God's expectations for us and from our lives." Or it is "trespassing—the intrusion of self-will into the sphere of God's authority, the centering of affection in one's own being instead of reaching out, with all one's heart and mind and soul, to love God and to love our neighbor as ourself."

All men are sinners: "The Bible teaches 'all have sinned and come short.'" There is a real Hell, "an eternal judgment" toward which, aided by a real Satan, unrepentant man is headed. "Essentially, Hell is separation from God."

There is, in those definitions, plenty of room for the preaching of what is described as the social Gospel. And that Gospel undoubtedly has an increasing place in Billy Graham's preaching. He himself has said, "The Gospel is both vertical and horizontal. The vertical signifies our relationship to God. The horizontal signifies the application of the principles of the teachings of Christ to our daily lives. At least a third of my preaching is spent encouraging and teaching people to apply the principles of Christianity in their personal and social lives. . . . I would like to say emphatically that any Gospel that preaches only vertical relationships is only a half-Gospel; that a Gospel that preaches only horizontal relationships is only a half-Gospel. The message of evangelism must be for the whole man."

That declaration—which I doubt Billy Graham would have made ten years ago—is evidence, I think, that the social implications of the Gospel will be increasingly emphasized in his preaching. Those implications, however, are still considerably short of central to his concern. The righteousness he calls for with such authority in his preaching is still very largely a one-part matter of man's personally righteous relationship to his God, and not yet very insistently a two-part matter having, as its second part, man's socially righteous relationship to his fellows. His concept of sin is still very largely a Ten-Commandment concept which includes, it seems to me, too little of the beyond-the-Ten-Commandments sins which Amos, Hosea, and Micah—and Jesus most of all—cried out against. His idea of the Christian's social obligations is still too much limited to the charitable "cup of cold water"—a phrase he often uses—and extends too seldom to the Christian in his corporate, and communal, relationships.

"Every message that I preach," says Billy Graham, "carries with it social implications and social responsibilities." Inadequate and obscure though that emphasis may sometimes seem to be, no one can hear or read many of his sermons without being aware that it is on the increase.[187]

Stanley High seemed motivated to note that Graham's social emphasis was "on the increase." Several years later Donald Bloesch said the same thing about Graham:

> Graham has shown that he will listen to constructive criticism, however, and it is hope that he will move to challenge the deeper levels of cultural and national idolatry of our time just as did the Old Testament prophets in their time.[188]

The question before us at this time is this: how much did Graham listen to his "constructive criticism" from the socially-minded theologians who were attacking him in his early ministry? Apparently Graham did listen. Graham's 1960 sermon, "Needed! Strong Men," gave a hint that he had read both Stanley High and Donald Bloesch.[189]

---

[187]Stanley High, *Billy Graham: The Personal Story of the Man, His Message, and His Mission* (New York: McGraw-Hill, 1956), 61-62.

[188]Donald Bloesch, "Billy Graham: A Theological Appraisal," *Theology and Life* 3 (May 1960): 141.

[189]"The second enemy that America faces is inflation caused by greed and selfishness. If we go on spending ourselves deeper in debt, it will only be a matter of time until the American dollar will lose its stability and the confidence of the world. This is already beginning to happen as millions of dollars worth of gold flow out of this country every month. Few people realize that this is one of the objectives of the Communists—to get us to spend more and more on ourselves until we are financially bankrupt. President Eisenhower has seen this danger and has done his best to support the American dollar and to stop inflation that threatens the very structure of this country.

The Bible warns of getting a higher standard of living while our neighbors are living in poverty. To a people seeking only for ease and wealth, the Prophet Amos once cried,

'Ye that put far away the evil day, and cause the seat of violence to come near;

That lie upon beds of ivory, and stretch themselves upon their couches, and eat the lambs out of the flock, and the calves out of the midst of the stall;

That chant to the sound of the viol, and invent to themselves instruments of music, like David;

That drink wine in bowls, and anoint themselves with the chief ointments: but they are not grieved for the affliction of Joseph' (Amos 6:3-6)" (Billy Graham, "Needed! Strong Men," *Hour of Decision Sermons*, no. 130 [Minneapolis: Billy Graham Evangelistic Association, 1960], 7-8).

Man as basically wrong. However, while moving from the uniquely "inside-out" point of view, that social sin was the cumulative composite of numerous individuals living in sin, to acknowledging a level of societal sin, Graham never let go of two things: individual sin and individual salvation. Graham's insistence on individual sin and moral depravity was noted in the 1958 sermon "The Cross and Its Power." In this sermon, Graham noted first that the cross is "the clearest evidence of the world's guilt."[190] He continued:

> At the cross of Christ sin reached its climax. Its most terrible display took place at Calvary. It was never blacker nor more hideous. We see the human heart laid bare and its corruption fully exposed. The Scripture teaches that man's heart is desperately wicked.
>
> Many people have said that man has improved through the centuries and. that if Christ came back today, He would not be crucified but would be given a grand and glorious reception.
>
> Christ does come to us every day—in the form of Bibles that we do not read, in the form of churches that we do not attend, in the form of human need that we pass by. I am convinced that if Christ came back today, He would be crucified even quicker than He was 2,000 years ago. Sin never improves any more than a cancerous condition improves. . . .
>
> The answer is found deep in the human heart. Human nature has not changed, and as we stand and gaze at the cross, we see a clear evidence that man is basically wrong, and we hear the thunderous verdict of God Himself when He says, "All have sinned and come short of the glory of God."
>
> Secondly: In the cross we find the strongest proof of God's hatred of sin. God has stated over and over that "the soul that sinneth shall die." He also revealed the fact that "the wages of sin is death."
>
> . . . The tendency today is to feel that such a position on God's part is too severe. So we find ourselves manufacturing another gospel. Only those take this position whose understanding as to the true nature of sin is darkened. We may say that sin is not so bad—but God said it is very bad, so bad that He demands the death penalty.[191]

Graham stated that man is "desperately wicked" and ". . . God said it [sin] is very bad." Graham also touched on the societal impact of sin, stating that "if Christ came back today, He would be crucified even quicker than He was

---

[190]Billy Graham, "The Cross and Its Power," *Hour of Decision Sermons,* no. 103 (Minneapolis: Billy Graham Evangelistic Association, 1958), 4.

[191]Ibid., 4-6.

2,000 years ago." Yet he also said, "Man is basically wrong," a change from his statement that the cross reveals "the depth of man's depravity," in a 1957 sermon "The Suffering Savior on the Crimson Cross."[192] Thus, while thundering the power of the cross to show the full extent of man's evil, and affirming the corresponding enmity of society to the Cross and Christ, Graham shifted in the use of the term depravity for sin. The omission of the Romans 3:11 statement that "none seek after God" in his litany on sin in his 1947 sermon, "A Midnight Strategy," may have been indicative of a hesitancy on this point.[193] But the change is confirmed by 1959 in his sermon titled "Christian Conversion," when Graham stated, "we are too weak to turn ourselves."[194]

In his 1958 sermon titled, "The Assurance of Salvation," Graham again gave indications that his view of sin had changed. He used words such as "all of us are sinners," then he spoke of "the complex problems of the human heart."[195] Later he said, "You have offended God by your sin and found that there is no strength to live this kind of life you know you should live."[196] While seeming to address sin rightly, he did not use language of transgressing the law of God or of willful rebellion against a holy God.[197] These thoughts were concepts that represented the early Graham. In 1960 in a message where Graham quoted a litany of verses on the sinfulness of man (a different litany than found in "A Midnight Tragedy"), including Genesis 6:5, he stated:

> Confronted with evidences of spiritual and moral decay on every hand, we now find ourselves more frequently looking for relief

---

[192]Billy Graham, "The Suffering Saviour on a Crimson Cross," *Hour of Decision Sermons,* no. 87 (Minneapolis: Billy Graham Evangelistic Association, 1957), 4.

[193]Billy Graham, "A Midnight Tragedy," 59.

[194]Billy Graham, "Christian Conversion," 4.

[195]Billy Graham, "The Assurance of Salvation," *Hour of Decision Sermons,* no. 99 (Minneapolis: Billy Graham Evangelistic Association, 1958), 4.

[196]Ibid.

[197]Erickson posited the following definition of sin, "Sin is any lack of conformity, active or passive, to the moral law of God. This may be a matter of act, of thought, or of inner disposition or state" (Erickson, *Christian Theology,* 578).

from the consequences of our waywardness rather than the cause and cure of the desperate situation in which we find ourselves.[198]

Rather than use the term "depravity," here Graham used "waywardness," and later in this sermon "degradation."[199] Did this new terminology for sin impact Graham's view of free will? It was similar to that which he had expressed earlier. In his sermon, "Made, Marred, Mended," later included in a compendium of published sermons, the "Middle Graham" explained the free will of man:

> But the will of man remains intact. The first man used his will to choose death. You must use your will to choose life! Every provision has been made. Every promise is yours, but it will not be forced upon you. You must use this God-given power of choice for "every man decideth the way his soul shall go."
>
> God invites, but you must come. The Bible says, "The Spirit and the bride say come, And let him that heareth say, Come. And let him that is athirst come. And whosoever will, let him take of the water of life freely" (Rev. 22:17).[200]

David Lockard on Graham and *World Aflame*. One commentator on Graham quoted his book *World Aflame* to show that Graham believed in Total Depravity. David Lockard wroted *The Unheard Billy Graham* in 1971.[201] There are two reasons this book is important. First, Lewis Drummond relied upon it heavily, especially to show that Graham has always believed in a holistic evangelism. Second, It is a book written during the transition time in Graham's approach to social responsibility.

Lockard relied on T. B. Maston to explain an imperative balance in the doctrine of man: man's grandeur and man's misery. Lockard then painted Graham into Maston's anthropology, "Graham's doctrine of man, as will be shown, fulfills the theological balance which Maston regarded as

---

[198]Billy Graham, "Christ: The Ark of Safety," *Hour of Decision Sermons,* no. 126 (Minneapolis: Billy Graham Evangelistic Association, 1960), 2.

[199]Ibid., 4.

[200]Billy Graham, "Made, Marred and Mended," *Hour of Decision Sermons,* no. 77 (Minneapolis: Billy Graham Evangelistic Association, 1956), 10. This sermon was also published in a compendium of sermons (Billy Graham, "Made, Marred, Mended," in *Great Preaching: Evangelical Messages by Contemporary Christians,* ed. Sherwood Eliot Wirt and Viola Blake [Waco, TX: Word Books, 1970; London: Word Books, 1970]).

[201]David Locakrd, *The Unheard Billy Graham* (Waco, TX: Word, 1971).

imperative."[202] After discussing the grandeur of man, Lockard then discussed three aspects of sin in Graham's preaching: (1) "Rebellion against God;" (2) "Sin as Lawlessness;" and (3) "Sin as Bondage." In this last section, Lockard quoted Graham's *World Aflame*:

> . . . man is described as being totally depraved. This does not mean that man is totally sinful, hopelessly and irreparably bad, without any goodness at all. It means that sin has infected the totality of man's life, darkening his intellect, enfeebling his will, and corrupting his emotions. He is alienated from God and in need of restoration. His natural, instinctive inclinations are away from God and toward sin.[203]

The title of this chapter in Graham was "Man's Fatal Disease." The first sentence of the paragraph from which Lockard quoted was, "The totality of this infection is reflected in every part of Scriptures." Thus, rather than affirming that Graham believed in a Calvinistic total depravity, this quote confirms that the hinge between the middle Graham taught the outward locus of sin, as expressed in his 1955 sermon "The Love of God."

Graham's view of the free will of man remained constant throughout his ministry. However, the "Middle Graham" abandoned the conception of the Early-Early Graham's total depravity. In his sermons, he became dissatisfied with his earlier use of depravity. He finally settled down to using terminology of degradation and that sin was a sickness. Hence Graham's terminology approximated the reconciliation model of the atonement, as will be noted later.

The Later Graham

It seems that in his later ministry, after Lausanne 1974 and Mexico 1975 (a small gathering of theologians to discuss evangelism and social responsibility), Graham affirmed an individualistic view of sin, while he maintained his dual paradigm of ministry: evangelism and social

---

[202]Lockard quoted the following picture of man from Maston: "Men everywhere need to see man as one a little lower than God himself; one whose feet are planted upon the good earth, but whose soul reaches up to the throne of God. He should be seen as a human person, with all the limitations and weaknesses of the fleshly carnal nature, but at the same time as one with the divinely given potential, a potential beyond the imagination of the most discerning minds and the most creative souls" (T. B. Maston, *Christianity and World Issues* [New York: Macmillan, 1957], 59; quoted in Lockard, *The Unheard Billy Graham*, 39).

[203]Billy Graham, *World Aflame*, 73; quoted in Lockard, 44.

responsibility. Yet, while Graham became more strongly open to working with Roman Catholics in this later period, he did not continue down the road of social sin to social salvation, a complete acceptance of the social gospel, and a rejection of an individual gospel.

Graham continued throughout his ministry to address the concepts of individual sin and individual salvation. They were clearly communicated in his 1977 book *How to Be Born Again.* In his chapter on sin, Graham described sin as starting with Satan and moving to all people. He then addressed the nature of sin:

> You may be saying, "You make everyone out to be so rotten, and that isn't really true." Of course it isn't. A person may be a very moral individual and yet lack the love for God which is the fundamental requirement of the law.[204]

Sin to Graham was not a depravity of man's nature, but a wrong attitude toward God, an alienated relationship with God. Simultaneously, sin became primarily an antithetical, a lack of love for God. It is interesting to note that Drummond in *The Evangelist* takes three of the five quotes on the sinfulness of man from *How to Be Born Again* (1977), written after this shift in Graham's doctrine of sin.[205] Again Graham affirmed the fact of individual sin in his book *Storm Warning* (1992):

> The problem in the world today is that people do not do what they know to be right. They seek after their own wills, contrary to the will of God, and in the words of the prophet Hosea, "They sow the wind and reap the whirlwind" (Hosea 8:7). Paul wrote in his letter to the Romans, "For all have sinned and fall short of the glory of God" (Romans 3:23). The other half of this equation, Paul says, is that "the wages of sin is death" (Romans 6:23). The cause is our willfulness; the price is separation from God for all eternity.[206]

In this quote, one of the strongest statements on sin in *Storm Warning,* Graham highlighted sin as man ignoring his conscience—Augustinian *privatio boni.* The result of sin was separation from God. Sin as alienation and judgment as separation are biblical. Yet Graham's terminology was akin to Denney's reconciliation model of the atonement. However, throughout his ministry Graham upheld the concept of personal and individual sin,

---

[204]Billy Graham, *How to Be Born Again,* 71.

[205]Drummond, *The Evangelist,* 49.

[206]Billy Graham, *Storm Warning* (Waco, TX: Word, 1992), 134.

along with the need for personal and individual redemption. The concept of sin was to be found in virtually all of his sermons, as it was closely related to his emphasis on individual conversion.

In 1992 as he was slowing down the pace of his ministry, Graham emphasized individual sin, and the cross as the answer to sin:

> As this book has been researched, written, and revised, we have become even more aware of the dangerous storms sweeping through modern society. I have been confronted more directly than ever by the sinister implications of the dangerous social and political theories that have passed for truth in recent years. . . .
>
> Despite my concern, I have also become fully convinced of the Christian's responsibility to proclaim the truth of God's Word. We have a mandate to speak out against "the sin that so easily entangles" (Hebrews 12:1): for though we are not of the world, we are still in it, and we are expected to do whatever we can to preserve it.[207]

Interestingly, in this late book, Graham emphasized "speaking out against" sin and preserving the world—two concepts that may find their place more comfortably among those with a social orientation to sin.

In *How to Be Born Again*, Graham clearly stated that sin affects the mind, will, and conscience of a person: "Sin not only affects the mind and the will, but also the conscience."[208] Thus, while accepting some of the concepts of the social gospel later in his ministry, his concept of man's sinfulness remained steadfast. It would seem that one of the great divides between conservative and liberal Christian thought regards the nature of sin. Conservative theologians agree with Romans 3:23 and other verses that man is evil in his very nature. Liberal theologians prefer to think of man as essentially good with a propensity to do evil things given certain behavioral or environmental factors. Graham leaned toward the conservative side of this issue all throughout his ministry.

Sin as alienation from God. While Graham maintained his view on individual sin, there may have been a change in Graham's view of sin from a moral infraction of God's Laws—individual sins against God's laws, to alienation from God stemming from the individual pride of man.[209]

---

[207]Ibid., 30-31.

[208]Billy Graham, *How To Be Born Again*, 85.

[209]James Denney wrote, "The need of reconciliation is given in the fact of alienation or estrangement. Man requires to be put right with God because, as a matter of fact, he is not right with him" (Denney, *The Christian Doctrine of Reconciliation,* 187).

It is a move away from man being sinful by nature to man being sinful by action. James Guy Newbill's 1960 Master of Arts thesis noted this change in Graham:

> There is only one sin that cannot be pardoned, says Graham, and that is blasphemy of the Holy Spirit. The continuing until death without receiving Christ is to commit the unpardonable sin. This definition of the unforgivable sin is slightly more palatable than the one he had written a few months earlier, which said that this sin was a disposition or the heart and soul whereby we cannot believe. His most recent definition makes it possible to add the following: "I know of no living persons who can be said to have been guilty or this sin."[210]

In another passage on the unpardonable sin, Graham repeated his latter emphasis:

> In the work of evangelism, you seldom mention this because the "unpardonable sin," as it is called, is not characteristic of most people in an audience. In fact, the number who have thus sealed their doom is probably extremely small. But it does warn all of us to guard against any trifling with God's Spirit.[211]

While this change seems minor and innocent, it may mark a change in Graham's anthropology. What does he mean by "the number who have thus sealed their doom is probably extremely small"? Perhaps it refers to a broadened anthropology? If this approach was truly a change in Graham, as indicated by Newbill, then it may have impacted his message in two ways: (1) lessen Graham's emphasis on man being by sinful by nature; and (2) potentially move Graham down the theories of the atonement from substitutionary atonement toward the reconciliation model, which may be more acceptable to some mainstream denominations. Yet Graham continued preaching of the gospel. His persistence in issuing an invitation may have led conservative evangelicals to overlook these statements on sin as out of character for Graham. However, if we can discern that Graham's soteriology was in fact changing, the result may have resulted in a movement away from Luther's *sola Scriptura* toward a *sola invitatio* or even a *sola evangelium*.

---

[210]James Guy Newbill, "The Theology of Billy Graham" (M.A. thesis, University of Washington, 1960), 35; Newbill cited Billy Graham, "My Answer," May 14, 1954.

[211]Billy Graham, "The Unpardonable Sin," in *Billy Graham: Blow Wind of God*, ed. Donald E. Demaray (Grand Rapids: Baker Book House, 1975; Signet Book ed.), 8-9; citing Billy Graham, "My Answer: The Unpardonable Sin," (Chicago-Tribune-New York News Syndicate, 1974).

For example, let us see how "Steps to Peace with God" addressed sin. The second point of "Steps to Peace with God" stated:

> Our problem: separation. God created us in His own image to have abundant life. He did not make us as robots to automatically love and obey Him, but gave us a will and freedom of choice.
> We chose to disobey God and go our own willful way. We still make this choice today. This results in separation from God.[212]

Did Graham choose to avoid using the term "sin" as a moral infraction of God's laws in his explanation of "Step Two"? Although the pamphlet used the common verses for sin as found in the "Roman Road," Romans 3:23 and 6:23, in the infraction in "Steps to Peace" sin was separation or alienation from God. Similarly, hell was primarily viewed as "separation from God."[213] God then provided the way for fellowship with Him through the gospel.[214] This seems to be a change from the early Graham and his emphasis on sin as a moral infraction of God's written Law. Thus, not only did Graham give credence to social or solidaristic sin, he also seemed to avoid some of the rough edges of attacking sin as a moral infraction against the law of God.

In *How to Be Born Again* (1977) Graham treated sin in chapter five. He discussed sin as beginning with Satan's pride. This pride led to man's rebellion against God, based on man's freewill. This led to all of creation being in rebellion:

> Nature became cursed and the poison of sin infected the entire human family. The whole creation was thrown into disharmony and the earth was now a planet in rebellion![215]

Graham continued by discussing sin as "missing the mark." The use of poison reaffirmed his 1955 statement that sin was a poison coming from the fruit, "There is death in this one." Hence, the outside locus of sin. Man was understood as guilty by choice:

---

[212]Billy Graham, "Steps to Peace with God," 4.

[213]"Essentially, Hell is separation from God" (High, *Billy Graham*, 62).

[214]One can already see a movement in Graham as inferred by "Steps to Peace with God." In the case of sin being a moral infraction against God, salvation requires a substitutionary atonement. When sin is conceived as alienating man from God, salvation may only require a ransom to restore fellowship. The issue of sin and the atonement will be discussed later in this section.

[215]Billy Graham, *How to Be Born Again*, 70.

We are all sinners by choice. When we reach the age of accountability and face the choice between good and evil, we will slip. We may choose to get angry, to lie, or to act selfishly. We will gossip or slander someone's character.[216]

Sin was no longer a matter of nature, but rather of choice. Graham again affirmed Adam as natural head. Then Graham laid out the Ten Commandments as an example of the mark that was being missed by people who live in sin. He later wrote that sin carries the death penalty.[217]

The two faces of man. Up to this point Graham seemed to be gently emphasizing individual moral sin. However, in his later ministry there seemed to be a movement away from the moral depravity of his early ministry. Graham's 1958 sermon "Past, Present and Future" (1958) gave expression for the first time in Graham of what Graham later called "Two Faces of Man":

> Most thoughtful people recognize that man is a paradox. He is both dust of earth and breath of God. He is a contradiction of discord and harmony, hatred and love, pride and humility, tolerance and intolerance, and peace and turmoil. The depths to which he sinks only dramatizes the heights which by God's grace he is capable of rising. His very misery is in an indication of his potential greatness. His deep yearnings are an echo of what he might be.
>
> This man, this "horns and halo" personality, is capable of killing or curing, hurting or healing, maiming or mending and bludgeoning or blessing. From his lips flow both lies and truth. His hands are equally skilled at cracking safes or setting bones. His feet have scaled the highest mountains, but they also have taken him to the lowest depths of depravity. His imaginations have soared to the heavens, as in the case of Handel's "Messiah" or Milton's "Paradise Regained," or they have scraped the pits of the nether world in arts which appeal to the sensual and salacious.
>
> From whence comes this strange mixture of good and evil? How did this paradox called man come to be the odd contradiction that he is? To find the answer to that question we must go back to the beginning and trace his history. To find out why he is like he is, we must discover what he once was.

---

[216]Ibid., 71.

[217]Ibid., 87.

FIRST; man's dignity or what man was in the beginning. Man was not created a paradox—he was created in the image of God. . . .

Man is made in the image of God. . . We see it in his respect for good and his contempt for evil. . . .[218]

In Graham's description of man as "horns and halo" he was not referring to salvation, but to the state of natural man. This was a departure from depravity and a tactical move toward a more positive view of man. Therefore, this new terminology in *Hour of Decision* sermon 100 provides another clear marker between the early Graham and the middle Graham.

Again, in the 1977 *How to Be Born Again*, Graham included a section titled the "Two Faces of Man." Here he again explained the two natures of man, a good nature and an evil nature:

Man has two faces. One shows his ingenuity, his capacity to create, to be kind, to honor truth. The other face reveals him using his ingenuity maliciously. We see him doing kind acts in a shrewd manner in order to forward a private desire. We see one side of him enjoying a sunset, but at the same time working in a job that fills the atmosphere with waste products that nearly obscure the sunset. His search for truth often degenerates into a rat race to discover a scientific fact so the credit will be his.

Man is both dignified and degraded.

The need for spiritual rebirth is evident to the most casual observer of human nature. Man is fallen and lost, alienated from God. From the very beginning, all attempts to recover man from his lostness have revealed one or the other of two ways.[219]

Graham's later approach to sin seemed to say that natural man had a good side; he could honor truth and be kind.[220] Graham also described the fall by environmental abuse—"working in a job that fills the atmosphere with waste products that nearly obscure the sunset." Natural man, to the Later Graham, seemed to have enough light in him to search for truth. Graham

---

[218]Billy Graham, "Past, Present and Future," 1-3. Note how this language corresponds to James Denney's terminology, "The universe is a system of things in which good can be planted and in which it will bear fruit; it is also a system of things in which there is a ceaseless and unrelating reaction against evil. This view of nature is vital both to the doctrine of sin and to that of reconciliation" (Denney, *The Christian Doctrine of Reconciliation*, 202).

[219]Billy Graham, *How to Be Born Again*, 91.

[220]Again affirming the dual-nature position of T. B. Maston, *Christianity and World Issues*, 59, as quoted by David Lockard, *The Unheard Billy Graham*, 39.

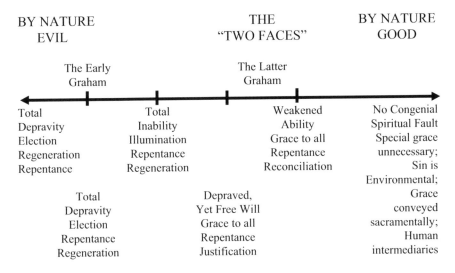

BY NATURE EVIL		THE "TWO FACES"	BY NATURE GOOD
The Early Graham		The Latter Graham	
Total Depravity Election Regeneration Repentance	Total Inability Illumination Repentance Regeneration	Weakened Ability Grace to all Repentance Reconciliation	No Congenial Spiritual Fault Special grace unnecessary; Sin is Environmental;
Total Depravity Election Repentance Regeneration	Depraved, Yet Free Will Grace to all Repentance Justification		Grace conveyed sacramentally; Human intermediaries

Fig. 9. Graham's approach to the doctrine of sin, with the addition of the order of salvation.

then used the word "degraded" in a context in which the word "depraved" would fit naturally—making sin a matter of degree rather than of nature. On the next page, Graham called sin "a fatal disease,"[221] also a move away from a depraved nature.[222] Graham beganto use the concept of restoring man's dignity in a number of places.[223] It must be noted that this terminology

---

[221]Graham said, "The Bible teaches that the human race is morally sick. This disease has affected every phase of our life in society. The Bible calls this disease by an ugly, three-letter word: sin. Dr. Karl Menninger, the noted psychiatrist, has startled some of his friends by a book he has written, entitled 'Whatever Became of Sin?'" (Billy Graham, "The Cradle, the Cross and the Crown," *Hour of Decision Sermons*, no. 206 [Minneapolis: Billy Graham Evangelistic Association, 1974], 7). James Guy Newbill in his 1960 dissertation on Billy Graham's theology finds this definition of sin in Graham's *Peace with God* (James Guy Newbill, "The Theology of Billy Graham," 29). *Peace with God* stated, "Consequently Cain and Abel were infected with the death-dealing disease, which they inherited from their parents and has been passed on to every generation since. We are all sinners by inheritance, and try as we will, we cannot escape this birthright" (Billy Graham, *Peace with God,* revised and expanded [Minneapolis: Grason, 1984], 47).

[222]Billy Graham, *How to Be Born Again,* 92.

[223]Billy Graham, "Past, Present and Future," 2, 7. Similarly, Augustine viewed in as the absence of moral righteousness according to Charles Hodge, "In the true Augustinian sense, therefore, sin is negation only as it is privation of moral good,—the *privatio boni,* or as it was afterwards generally expressed, a want of conformity to the

appears related to Charles Hodge's interpretation of Semi-Pelagianism,[224] as well as to Horace Bushnell's view of the atonement.[225]

The "two faces of man" theology appeared again in Graham's anthropology in 1974, simultaneous to his acceptance of a 'two faces to the Great Commission' approach as noted in the previous chapter. In a sermon preached at the White House on December 16, 1973, Graham spoke about man's sinfulness in much the same way as was found in *How to Be Born Again*:

> You see, man is actually a paradox. On the one hand there's futility and sin, on the other there's *goodness and kindness and gentleness and love*. On the one hand he's a moral failure, and on the other hand he has the capacities that would relate him to Almighty God. No wonder the apostle Paul called this moral failure, "the mystery of iniquity."[226]

Graham's approach to the sin of man on the basis of the previous considerations may be charted as in Figure 9. Graham walked an interesting tight-rope in his later ministry—he continued to maintain sin as an individualistic phenomenon and continued to affirm the need for an individualistic salvation; yet, he moved away from a position of moral depravity, and his view of sin added some social twists.[227] It would be natural, then, that Graham's view of the atonement would need to change to

---

law or standard of good" (Charles Hodge, *Systematic Theology* [New York: Scribner, Armstrong, and Co., 1873], 2:159).

[224]"He [Faustus of Rheguim] admitted that men could not save themselves; but held that they were not spiritually dead; they were sick; and constantly in need of the Great Physician" (Charles Hodge, *Systematic Theology,* 2:166-67).

[225]"Disease goes with sin, Healing with salvation" (Bushnell, *The Vicarious Sacrifice,* 134).

[226]Billy Graham, "The Cradle, the Cross and the Crown," 6. Italics mine.

[227]An interesting example of the tightrope that Graham walked is found in his peacemaking mission to North Korea. In Graham's formal greeting upon arriving in North Korea in 1992, Graham made a statement which assumes anthropological presuppositions and contains anthropological consequences. Graham told a delegation of Christians representing the Protestant Federation and Catholic Church: "The D. P. R. K. and the United States are not natural enemies. It is past time that the suspicion and enmity which have characterized our relations for the last half-century were replaced with trust and friendship" (Billy Graham, *Just As I Am,* 622). Graham was assuming that the nature of secular man was not to be in hostility with one another. Perhaps this was the tactical Graham, as opposed to the theological Graham, seeking to broker peace between two peoples. However, it is hard to differentiate between his tactical and theological sides.

adapt to this change in anthropology. Graham's soteriology will be our next area of investigation.

Central, however, in Graham's understanding of sin was its universality as part of fallen man's nature. Thus universal sin required a salvation that should be made available universally. Since he believed Christ as proclaimed in the personal gospel to be the only hope of salvation, and in light of the Great Commission mandate, it was incumbent upon Graham to seek to share that message to sinners across the world.

Salvation

The message of the atonement is no small part of the Christianity. It is the heart of the Christian message.[228] Thus, it can be safely assumed that, along with other major doctrines of Christianity, it has been a battleground of debate. For example, the substitutionary atonement was the very thing that Rauschenbusch discounted in his *The Theology of the Social Gospel*,[229] thus exemplifying that there was and is a theological dissonance between the social gospel and the personal gospel.[230] The atoning work of Christ on the cross was the cornerstone to Graham's evangelistic preaching, as he explained to evangelists at Amsterdam 83, "The message of the cross must be central in our preaching."[231] Yet, what were Graham's views of the atonement, especially in light of his approach to sin? To answer this question the concept of the atonement and mission will be introduced, followed by Graham's approach to this important subject.

---

[228] Erickson wrote of the atonement, "In the atonement, we come to the crucial point of Christian faith. It is, of course, essential that our understanding of God the Father and of his Son be correct, and that our conception of the nature of man and his spiritual condition be accurate. But the doctrine of the atonement is the most critical for us, because it is the point of transition, as it were, from the objective to the subjective aspects of Christian theology. Here we shift our focus from the nature of Christ to his active work in our behalf; here systematic theology has direct application to our lives. The atonement has made our salvation possible. It is also the foundation of major doctrines which await our study: the doctrine of the church deals with the collective aspects of salvation, the doctrine of the last things with its future aspects" (Erickson, *Christian Theology*, 781-82).

[229] Rauschenbusch, *A Theology for the Social Gospel*, 242-43.

[230] In chapter three, there are two quotes that show that Graham did not seem to understand that the two were mutually exclusive (see High, *Billy Graham*, 61; Billy Graham, "Biblical Conversion," 10).

[231] Billy Graham, *A Biblical Standard for Evangelists*, 51.

The Atonement and Mission

John Driver wrote *Understanding the Atonement for the Mission of the Church* to link the concepts of the atonement and mission.[232] Basing himself on Gustav Aulén's *Christus Victor,* he described the two basic views of the atonement as objective and subjective, with "Christus Victor" as being the third and classic view of the atonement. Franklin Johnson in his essay published in *The Fundamentals* also juxtaposed the substitution and moral-influence theories of the atonement.[233] Before delving into Aulén's views of the atonement, it was made clear by John Driver that the three categories of views of the atonement directly impacted the mission of the church. Therefore they are important in developing a theology of evangelism.

Gustav Aulén began by stating that "the traditional account of the history of the idea of the Atonement is in need of thorough revision."[234] He then described the same three views of the atonement using the following nomenclature: the Anselmic, objective, or Latin view; the *Christus Victor* or classic view; and the humanistic or subjective view. It was hoped that Aulén's classic view would provide grounds for the reunion of Christendom,[235] published eleven years after Archbishop Soderblom of Sweden envisioned the reunion of Christendom.[236] Aulén generalized the

---

[232]John Driver, *Understanding the Atonement for the Mission of the Church* (Kitchener, Ontario: Herald Press, 1986).

[233]Franklin Johnson strongly argued for the substitutionary atonement and stated: "These are the reasons which lead the Christian world as a whole to reject 'the moral-influence theory' of the atonement as inadequate" (Franklin Johnson, "The Atonement," in *The Fundamentals: A Testimony of Truth,* eds. R. A. Torrey and others [1917; reprint, Grand Rapids: Baker, 1998], 3:72).

[234]Gustav Aulén, *Christus Victor: An Historical Study of the Three Main Types of the Idea of the Atonement,* trans. A. G. Hebert (1930; New York: Macmillan, 1969), 1.

[235]"In our day the great hope of Reunion has come; but the Reunion movement is confronted by the immense difficulty of reconciling the Catholic and the Protestant conceptions of faith and order. But Dr. Aulén's interpretation of the history of the idea of the atonement throws real light on the situation. . . . Here, then, is a true hope of Reunion; not in the victory of 'Catholic' over 'Protestant,' or of 'Protestant' over 'Catholic,' but the return of both to the rock whence they were hewn" (A. G. Herbert, "Translator's Preface," in Gustav Aulén, *Christus Victor,* xxxvi).

[236] "In the same year (1919) in the distant city of Uppsala, Sweden, and apparently quite independently of the Patriarch of Constantinople, Archbishop Nathan Söderblom spoke in similar terms, advocating the formation of a common or ecumenical council whereby the evangelical catholicity and unity of the religious community of Christians might be more fully realized and expressed" (Jude D. Weisenbeck, S.D.S., 250

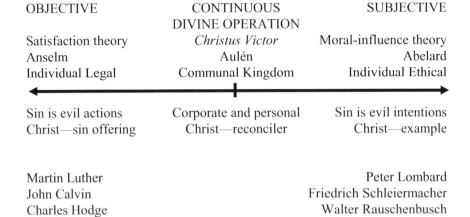

OBJECTIVE	CONTINUOUS DIVINE OPERATION	SUBJECTIVE
Satisfaction theory	*Christus Victor*	Moral-influence theory
Anselm	Aulén	Abelard
Individual Legal	Communal Kingdom	Individual Ethical

| Sin is evil actions | Corporate and personal | Sin is evil intentions |
| Christ—sin offering | Christ—reconciler | Christ—example |

Martin Luther		Peter Lombard
John Calvin		Friedrich Schleiermacher
Charles Hodge		Walter Rauschenbusch

Fig. 10. Gustav Aulén's three main theories of the atonement,[237] adapted from John Driver and including Driver's listed proponents.[238]

three views as follows. To Aulén the Anselmic or Latin view is juridicial, "The Atonement is worked out according to the strict requirements of justice."[239] Hence, in Anselm's view, God was the object of reconciliation and Jesus Christ was the subject. This view was called objective by Driver. The *Christus Victor* approach, which Aulén ascribed to the majority of early church theologians and the New Testament, did not acknowledge the total depravity of man, being by nature sinful. Rather, Aulén described sin "an objective power behind men" and redemption as a divine drama which changed God's and man's level of relationship.[240] Elsewhere Aulén expanded on this thought: "It is not only that the world now stands in a new relation to God, but also that God now stands in a new relation to the

---

S.T.L., "Conciliar Fellowship and the Unity of the Church" [Ph.D. diss., Rome, Pontifica Studiorum Universitas, A S. Thoma Aq. in Urbe, 1986], 108).

[237]Adapted from Aulén, *Christus Victor*, 1-16.

[238]Driver, *Understanding the Atonement*, 37-67.

[239]Aulén, *Christus Victor*, 90.

[240]On sin: "We next take the idea of sin. Here the classic type regards sin as an objective power standing behind men, and the Atonement as the triumph of God over sin, death, and the devil." (ibid., 147). On redemption: "A certain double-sidedness is an essential feature of the classic idea of the Atonement. On the one hand, the drama of Redemption has a dualistic background; God in Christ combats and prevails over the 'tyrants' which hold mankind in bondage. On the other hand, God thereby becomes the reconciled with the world, the enmity is taken away, and a new relation between God and mankind is established" (ibid., 55).

world."[241] In another place Aulén compared justification and the atonement, stating that they were the same.[242] The subjective view described by Aulén he calls the subjective or humanistic concept, of which Abelard was considered "the father."[243] Sin "was regarded as a state of imperfection," and "punishment could only be ameliorative."[244] This latter view Aulén described as subjective. Thus, at the end of his book the reader is left with three views, the Latin judicial view emphasizing satisfaction, the humanistic view in which Christ's example was exalted as primary in the atonement, and *Christus Victor* which interpreted the atonement as a divine drama where reconciliation was accomplished between God and man. *Christus Victor* was the mediating position, which leads to the Figure 10, as expanded from the text of John Driver in his *Understanding the Atonement for the Mission of the Church*. Driver pointed out that Abelard's subjective theory of the atonement gained prominence in nineteenth century theological liberalism:

> Abelard was the principal medieval exponent of this theory which has come to be called the moral-influence view. . . . In the modern period, especially since the rise of theological liberalism in the nineteenth century, the subjective view has enjoyed rather widespread popularity. This is seen in the thought of such exponents as the nineteenth century German theologian Friedrich Schleiermacher and the twentieth century American "social gospel" theologian Walter Rauschenbusch.[245]

In fact, Walter Rauschenbusch provided an excellent example of reinterpreting the atonement from the objective to the subjective view. Coming from the conservative background of an American Baptist and teaching under the presidency of A. H. Strong, Rauschenbusch mocked

---

[241] Ibid., 59-60. Note the relational language of reconciliation.

[242] "Therefore Justification and the Atonement are really one and the same thing; Justification is simply the Atonement brought into the present, so that here and now the Blessing of God prevails over the Curse" (ibid., 150).

[243] Ibid., 97.

[244] Aulén, *Christus Victor,* 134. Note that sin is not by nature, but more like a sickness.

[245] Ibid., 46.

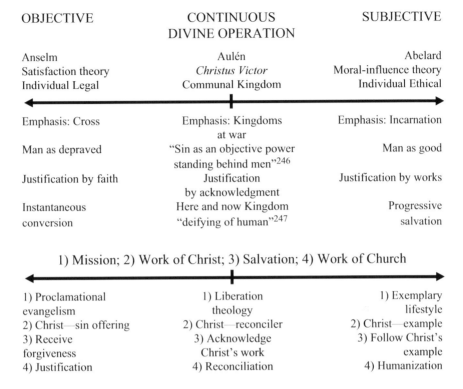

OBJECTIVE	CONTINUOUS DIVINE OPERATION	SUBJECTIVE
Anselm	Aulén	Abelard
Satisfaction theory	*Christus Victor*	Moral-influence theory
Individual Legal	Communal Kingdom	Individual Ethical

Emphasis: Cross	Emphasis: Kingdoms at war	Emphasis: Incarnation
Man as depraved	"Sin as an objective power standing behind men"[246]	Man as good
Justification by faith	Justification by acknowledgment	Justification by works
Instantaneous conversion	Here and now Kingdom "deifying of human"[247]	Progressive salvation

1) Mission; 2) Work of Christ; 3) Salvation; 4) Work of Church

1) Proclamational evangelism	1) Liberation theology	1) Exemplary lifestyle
2) Christ—sin offering	2) Christ—reconciler	2) Christ—example
3) Receive forgiveness	3) Acknowledge Christ's work	3) Follow Christ's example
4) Justification	4) Reconciliation	4) Humanization

Fig. 11. Gustav Aulén's theories of the atonement,[248] adapted by John Driver,[249] with the addition of mission, main work of Christ, salvation, and the work of the church.

earlier Christians for their "post-biblical ideas" of the atonement.[250] Rauschenbusch's incarnational approach to the atonement allowed him to emphasize Christ as an example to follow:[251]

---

[246]Aulén, *Christus Victor,* 147.

[247]Ibid., 149.

[248]Adapted from Aulén, *Christus Victor,* 1-16.

[249]Derived from John Driver, *Understanding the Atonement,* 37-67.

[250]"The Reformation made no essential change in this doctrine. Lutherans and Calvinists on the whole taught the same outline of atonement. God, in mercy toward fallen humanity, sent his Son, who shared both the divine and human nature, in order to redeem and reconcile. The justice of God demands the condemnation of all. God can

The fundamental first step in the salvation of mankind was the achievement of the personality of Jesus. Within him the Kingdom of God got its first foothold in humanity. It was by virtue of his personality that he became the initiator of the Kingdom.[252]

Thus, in order to accommodate his social gospel *a priori*, Rauschenbusch moved from one side to the other, as noted in Figure 10, first by redefining sin, redefining salvation, redefining the Christ's mission, and finally redefining the atonement. He moved from one extreme and went to the opposite extreme.[253] His example shows the dangers of an *a priori* imposed upon theology, especially to the detriment of expectant evangelism, as noted in Figure 11.

Figure 11 shows that atonement and mission are inseparable. Each of the three views of the atonement in Figure 11 lead to a distinct view of mission. In fact, the reflexive property (if A=B, then B=A) functions in this case where each distinct view of mission also presupposes a view of the atonement. Perhaps this is why the vicarious atonement was one of the five fundamentals of the faith in the 1895 Niagara Bible Conference.[254] When the sinful nature of man is changed, the atonement changes. When the

---

exercise mercy only if vicarious satisfaction is rendered. The infinite worth of the divine nature in Christ makes his suffering an equivalent for the infinite sins of mankind. Christ experienced the wrath of God in his suffering, and that wrath is now satisfied, so that God can forgive.

These traditional theological explanations of the death of Christ have less biblical authority than we are accustomed to suppose. The fundamental terms and ideas—'satisfaction,' 'substitution,' 'imputation,' 'merit'—are post-biblical ideas, and are alien from the spirit of the gospel" (Rauschenbusch, *A Theology for the Social Gospel*, 242-43).

[251]A. A. Hodge explained, "The modern theories of Jowett, Maurice, Bushnell, Young, &c., differ from that of Socinus only in being rhetorical where he is logical, confused when he is clear, and narrow and partial where he is comprehensive. . . . As to the entire essence of the doctrine, Anselm then stood precisely where the whole Church of Christ in all its branches has ever since stood; and the infamous Abelard taught in every essential respect the doctrine maintained by Socinus, and by Maurice, Bushnell, and Young, in our day" (A. A. Hodge, *The Atonement* [1867; Grand Rapids: Eerdmans, 1953], 316-17).

[252]Rauschenbusch, *A Theology for the Social Gospel*, 151.

[253]Rauschenbusch's *A Theology of the Social Gospel* did not address the issue of the divinity of Christ, which admittedly would be the final step in the movement from "one extreme to the other." Although he did admit that Unitarians could accept his theology of the social gospel (ibid., 148).

[254]Commission Biblique Pontificale, *L'Interprétation de la Bible dans L'Eglise* (Montreal: Fides, 1994), 48.

atonement changes, salvation changes. When salvation changes, the gospel message changes. When the gospel message changes, the mission of the church changes. When the mission of the church changes, the method of evangelism changes. Lewis Sperry Chafer also saw the importance of the substitutionary atonement,[255] as did J. E. Conant.[256]

There is a direct link between the objective view of the atonement and evangelism. In historic Protestant confessions, the objective view of the atonement led to belief in supernatural conversion outside of any human intermediaries.[257] The means of the supernatural conversion was the proclamation of the gospel.[258] Then following the proclamation there were those who received the message of the gospel by faith. Philip Jacob Spener, the father of German Pietism, wrote in 1675:

> We also gladly acknowledge the power of the Word of God when it is preached, since it is the power of God unto salvation to everyone who has faith (Rom 1:16). We are bound diligently to hear

---

[255]"This is an atonement based on substitution. . . . To reject this repeated and only revelation of the purpose of God in the cross is to set sail upon a sea of uncertainty, to abandon the only cure for sin the world can ever know, and to forsake the one and only foundation, according to God's revelation to man, upon which every hope for humanity is made to rest" (Lewis Sperry Chafer, *True Evangelism or Winning Souls by Prayer* [Wheaton, IL: Van Kampen, 1919], 32).

[256]J. E. Conant, *No Salvation without Substitution* (Grand Rapids: Eerdmans, 1941).

[257]"As all organized Christianity is clear and emphatic in its confession of a pure supernaturalism, so all organized Protestantism is equally clear and emphatic in its confession of evangelicalism. . . . Evangelicalism does not cease to be fundamentally antinaturalistic, however, in becoming antisacerdotal: its primary protest continues to be against naturalism, and in opposing sacerdotalism also it only is the more consistently supernaturalistic, refusing any intermediaries between the soul and God, as the sole source of salvation. That only is true evangelicalism, therefore, in which sounds clearly the double confession that all the power exerted in saving the soul is from God, and that God in his saving operations acts directly upon the soul" (B. B. Warfield, *The Plan of Salvation* [Philadelphia: Presbyterian Board of Publications, 1918], 20).

[258]John Owen wrote, "Secondly, That the Scripture sets forth the death of Christ, to all whom the gospel is preached [unto], as an all-sufficient means for bringing sinners unto God, so as that whosoever believe it and come in to him shall certainly be saved" (Owen, *The Death of Death*, 264). Thus, Owen called the preaching of the gospel "the only ordinary way" (Ibid., 85; cf. 295). Interestingly, however, Charles Hodge did not want to limit himself to the preaching of the Word only, but rather left the converting of the soul as an act of God's omnipotence (Charles Hodge, *Systematic Theology*, 3:31). Similarly, Warfield avoided the preaching of the gospel as the sole means of grace for the elect, a concept he placed in the Lutheran camp (Warfield, *The Plan of Salvation*, 104).

the Word of God not only because we are commanded to do so but also because it is the divine hand which offers and presents grace to the believer, whom the Word itself awakens through the Holy Spirit.[259]

John Owen, the Puritan divine, explained this same view of conversion in 1684:

> Also, what this condition is they give in, in sundry terms; some call it a *not resisting* of this redemption offered to them; some *a yielding* to the invitation of the gospel; some, in plain terms, *faith*. Now, be it so that Christ purchaseth all things for us, to be bestowed on this condition, that we do believe it. . . .[260]

Instantaneous conversion wrought by the supernatural work of God flows naturally from the substitutionary atonement. And hand-in-hand with instantaneous conversion precedes the only means (Pietistic)[261] or the normal means (Puritan) which is the preaching of the Word of God (Pietistic) or of the gospel (Puritan). Interestingly, the Word of God as the only means of salvation was what Luther meant by *sola Scriptura*.[262]

---

[259]Philip Jacob Spener, *Pia Desideria*, 63.

[260]Owen, *The Death of Death*, 122.

[261]Martin Luther wrote: "As we have said, God never has dealt, and never does deal, with mankind at any time otherwise than by the word of promise. Neither can we, on our part, ever have to do with God otherwise than through faith in his word and promise. . . .

For anyone readily understands that these two, promise and faith, are necessarily yoked together" (Martin Luther, "Pagan Servitude of the Church," in John Dillenberger, *Martin Luther: Selections from His Writings Edited and with Introduction* [Garden City, NY: Doubleday, 1961], 277).

[262]Charles Hodge quoted the Smalcald Articles on the agency of the Holy Spirit acting solely by means of the Word of God (ibid.). An English expansion of what Hodge quoted in Latin is as follows: "And in those things which concern the spoken, outward Word, we must firmly hold that God grants His Spirit or grace to no one, except through or with the preceding outward Word, in order that we may [thus] be protected against the enthusiasts, i.e., spirits who boast that they have the Spirit without and before the Word, and accordingly judge Scripture or the spoken Word, and explain and stretch it at their pleasure, as Muenzer did, and many still do at the present day, who wish to be acute judges between the Spirit and the letter, and yet know not what they say or declare. For [indeed] the Papacy also is nothing but sheer enthusiasm, by which the Pope boasts that all rights exist in the shrine of his heart, and whatever he decides and commands with [in] his church is spirit and right, even though it is above and contrary to Scripture

Driver, the atonement, and mission. John Driver, however, provides an example of a Mennonite (evangelical) missions theologian who did not accept the substitutionary atonement as the universal affirmative declaration of the atonement. Rather he attacked Anselm's substitutionary atonement with the same vigor as Rauschenbusch did seventy years before:

> It certainly is understandable that Anselm would want to articulate the meaning of the work of Christ in the categories of his time. However, the intrusion of all these extra-biblical ideas from the arena of contemporary medieval social, legal, and religious practices has served to vatiate fatally Anselm's satisfaction theory.[263]

Driver then continued by pointing out the flaws of the satisfaction theory as it related to philosophy of mission, "A fourth set of objections to Anselm's theory comes from the practical area of the Christian vocation to discipleship and mission." Driver then explained three shortcomings of the satisfaction theory in ethics, discipleship, and universalism. The remainder of his book, then, was given over to the "plurality of images" of the atonement.[264] In this way he sought to combined the vicarious satisfaction, the supreme expression of God's love, and the cosmic conflict of the classical view to buttress the various views of mission to which he ascribed. Driver blended the three views of the atonement as co-equal, and thus undermined the universal affirmative of the substitutionary atonement. He explained the illogic of his position: "These three apparently incompatible approaches to the work of Christ are actually complementary. The questions they pose are all important."[265] Then, departing from his introductory material, Driver expanded ten views of the atonement and discussed their missiological implications. Thus, pluriform views of the atonement led Driver to express pluriform missions of the church.[266]

---

and the spoken Word. . . . Without the outward Word, however, they were not holy, much less would the Holy Ghost have moved them to speak when they still were unholy [or profane]; for they were holy, says he, since the Holy Ghost spake through them" (Martin Luther, "Of Confession," Smalcald Articles, Part 3, Section 8 [on-line], accessed 11 October 2001, available from http://www.frii.com/ ~gosplow/ smalcald.html#smc-03h; Internet). Hodge also quoted Luther's Larger Catechism, "*In summa, quicquid Deus in nobis facit et operatur, tantum externis istius modi rebus et constitutionibus operati dignatur*" (Charles Hodge, *Systematic Theology*, 3:480).

[263]Driver, *Understanding the Atonement*, 62.

[264]Ibid., 67.

[265]Ibid.

[266]Compare this with David Bosch's view in *Transforming Mission:* "Instead of trying to formulate one uniform view of mission we should rather attempt to

Because the link between the atonement and mission is vital in a theology of evangelism, the ten views mentioned by Driver will be cited with quotations in the footnotes. Driver provides a vivid example of the link between the atonement and mission, as well as the result of antagonism to the substitutionary atonement and its impact on mission:[267]

1.   Conflict-Victory-Liberation view of the atonement[268]

2.   Vicarious suffering view of the atonement[269]

3.   Archetypal images of the atonement[270]

---

chart the contours of 'a pluriverse of missiology in a universe of mission'" (David Bosch, *Transforming Mission*, 8; Bosch quoted G. M. Soares-Prabhu, S.J., "Missiology or Missiologies?" *Mission Studies* 6 [May 1969]: 87).

[267]The views of the atonement expressed by Driver bear a striking similarity to the views expressed by Shailer Mathews, formerly Dean of the Divinity School of the University of Chicago, in his book *The Atonement and Social Process* (New York: Macmillan, 1930). Mathews' chapters are as follows: (1) "The Social Origin of Christian Doctrines"; (2) "Christian Doctrines as Social Patterns"; (3) "The Death of Christ interpreted in the messianic pattern"; (4) "The Death of Christ in the pattern of sacrifice"; (5) "The Death of Christ in the Pattern of Acquittal"; (6) "The Death of Christ Interpreted in the Pattern of Sonship"; (7) "The Rise of the Imperial Pattern in Western Christianity"; (8) "The Death of Christ in the Pattern of Feudalism"; (9) "The Death of Christ in the Pattern of Monarchy"; (10) "Modifications of the Political Pattern"; (11) "The Functional Value of the Doctrines of the Atonement"; (12) "The Death of Christ in the Pattern of Process."

[268]"However, when the church takes with New Testament seriousness the motifs of vicarious suffering and conflict-victory images for understanding the work of Christ, then all the forms of wholeness—physical as well as spiritual, social, and personal—will be greeted with joy as signs which anticipate the full realization of God's reign" (Driver, *Understanding the Atonement*, 86).

[269]"This view of servanthood, the true path to God's justice and salvation in which God's people are restored to wholeness, inspired by Jesus' messianic mission" (ibid., 94). "The offering of the lamb is a Paschal sacrifice rather than a temple sacrifice. Rather than being viewed as an expiatory sacrifice, it is perceived as a communal meal. . . . those who participated in the first Passover received strength to follow the Lord in the Exodus" (98).

[270]"In Christ's death he is representative of fallen humanity. In his resurrection Christ is representative of the new humanity" (ibid., 107). "Jesus' death was the death of the old humanity, and his resurrection is the beginning of a new humanity" (109). "So as perfecter of our faith Jesus is the once-for-all actualization of God's love in salvation history and the source of his community's faithful obedience to the point of suffering ([Heb] 12:3-4). According to these passages, the saving work of Christ can be understood in terms of his role as *archegos*. . ." (110).

4.   Martyr motif in the atonement[271]

5.   Sacrifice motif in the atonement[272]

6.   Expiation motif and the wrath of God[273]

7.   Redemption-purchase motif in the atonement[274]

8.   Reconciliation[275]

---

[271]"Traditionally, the martyr motif has occupied a relatively minor role in the Christian church's understanding of the work of Christ" (ibid., 127). "So here we are in the presence of an important image which the New Testament community used to understand the meaning of the saving work of Christ—that of witness-martyr" (116-17). "However, the character of their witness moves beyond the strictly literal sense of the term as attestation of externally demonstrable fact. Rather than being used in a strictly legal sense of law-court witness, the term here carries the meaning of confession, of the mission of God's witnessing community in the midst of the nations. Just as Israel's witness is clearly not limited to verbal attestation of externally demonstrable facts about Yahweh, neither is its confession limited to a strictly verbal declaration of Yahweh's uniqueness" (118).

[272]"Sacrifice, including the death of Christ, effectively serves to interrupt the spiral of human violence in all its spiritual and social dimensions" (ibid., 132). "Christian sacrifices are spiritualized in a way which makes them primarily ethical rather than ritual" (143).

[273]"About three-fourths of the occurrences of *kipper* in the Old Testament are in connection with specific sacrifices, so expiation was cultic" (ibid., 148). "Rather than attempting to force all of the Old Testament material into a rational theory of the atonement, we would do well to recognize the variety of ideas and motifs in the provision for making expiation and forgiveness concrete in the experience of God's people" (149). "So in these texts we find no warrant to link *hilarmos* exclusively with the death of Jesus. It is rather related to the total person and work of Jesus, of which his death is an indissoluble and climactic part" (153).

[274]"According to the context of this passage, Jesus' life of obedience and service, even unto death, functions as a model for his followers. . . . He is the prototype of what we should be" (ibid., 173-74).

[275]"Reconciliation is not a mere projection of faith, but the social reality of a community in which love for one another is motivated by the love of God. The new reality (the reconciled community) is both basically and continuously brought about by God's action toward humankind" (ibid., 180). "Without denying the personal dimensions of reconciliation, we should recognize that the reconciliation of Jew and Gentile in the new community is first of all a community event which cannot happen to an individual alone. The reconciling work of Christ draws the estranged and the hostile into the new community of salvation characterized by holiness and blamelessness (Col 1:21-22).

9.   Justification[276]

10.   Adoption-family image of the atonement[277]

Most of these motifs of the atonement were used by Driver to delegitimatize the judicial sense of the substitutionary atonement, and thus evangelism as the sole mission of the church. Rather, Driver placed the substitutionary atonement as a social construct of the medieval period,[278] much like Shailer Mathews.[279] Thus, while he gave periodic assent to the necessity of the substitutionary atonement—after all, he admitted that it became a test for orthodoxy[280]—he then went on to attack it from all sides.[281] Interestingly for our context, it is not so much a matter of adding to the biblical atonement as it is subtracting the legal sense of the atonement.

In his final chapter Driver addressed specific mission issues relating to the atonement. In a section called "Methodological implications of atonement" Driver posited seven missiological points related to his pluriform approach to the atonement:

Rather than being merely individual attributes, this is more properly a description of the church (Eph 1:4; 5:25b-27). Reconciliation includes the cessation of hostilities and the incorporation into the new community of God's Messiah" (185-86).

[276]"God's righteousness is not merely the declaration which pardons the individual, but that power which establishes as whole new world, the force that brought the kingdom of God into being. . . . This vindicates God in the face of human doubt and rebellion" (ibid., 203).

[277]"God's people are *shalom*-makers just as their Father is" (ibid., 207). "It was a relationship proclaimed and lived out by Jesus in the midst of his community. But now it is a relationship achieved through his messianic work and actualized by the presence of his spirit in his community (Rom. 8:23; Gal. 4:5)" (209).

[278]"The exegetical and theological criticisms of the Anselmic view are further underscored when we see that a number of the underlying presuppositions of the Anselmic theory really find their rootage in the Constantinian Christendom of the period rather than in the world of thought of the New Testament" (ibid., 59).

[279]"Contemporary feudalism of Anselm's time completes his theory as to the way in which the sinner can gain the forgiveness which the suffering God-man makes God free to give. Here again the social practice becomes the unquestioned pattern of thought" (Mathews, *The Atonement and the Social Process,* 107).

[280]"Protestantism has not only tended to reaffirm the satisfaction view but has made it more dominant and more nearly a test of faith than had been the case in the Middle Ages" (ibid., 50). "But in the church, while the doctrine of justification has been made a test of orthodoxy, other images have fallen into disuse" (Driver, *Understanding the Atonement,* 191).

[281]"According to this view, justification is a legal fiction, i.e., it exists only in abstract formulation—it is not concretely real" (ibid.).

1. Divine-human communion is God's intention from creation. . . .
2. The gospel may be addressed to the entire range of expressions of the human predicament. . . .
3. Peace and justice are rooted in the atoning work of Christ. . . .
4. The full-orbed New Testament vision for the work of Christ leads to the integration of justification and sanctification, of evangelism and nurture. . . .
5. The dynamic role of the Holy Spirit in effectual justification, as well as in the creation and sustenance of the new humanity, can be recognized as absolutely essential to the work of Christ. . . .
6. The fact that cosmic renewal in the New Testament is anchored in the death and resurrection of Christ calls us to make this dimension of God's saving intention seriously. ...
7. To evangelize is to become a martyr in the New Testament sense of this term, a faithful witness according to the likeness of our pioneer—the original Faithful Witness.[282]

For Driver to buttress his redefined view of world evangelism, he went at the taproot of New Testament theology—the atonement. He first eliminated the uniqueness of the objective and subjective views of the atonement. He followed Aulén by adding the *Christus Victor* notion as an acceptable balance. Then Driver went on to uncover a pluriform view of the atonement with one common thread: an antagonism to the penal substitutionary approach. This led Driver to accept the mission of the church as anything but the verbal proclamation of the gospel of Jesus Christ. Are atonement and mission linked? Yes, they definitely are!

Ron Sider, the atonement, and mission. Similarly to Driver and Rauschenbusch, Ron Sider underwent the same transformation of mission. When Rauschenbusch embraced a social gospel *a priori*, he emphasized the incarnation. Ron Sider likewise emphasized the incarnational ministry of Jesus in his book *Rich Christians in an Age of Hunger*.[283] In fact, Sider did not mention the death of Christ or the need for individual salvation outside of his solidaristic emphasis on the new community in Christ. Like Rauschenbusch, Sider's emphasis was on the incarnation of Christ. He even emulated Rauschenbusch's disdain for an emphasis on individual or personal sin:

---

[282]Ibid., 247-53.

[283]Sider, *Rich Christians in an Age of Hunger* (Downers Grove, IL: InterVarsity, 1977), 65-69.

The Bible and Structural Evil. Neglect of the biblical teaching of structural injustice and institutionalized evil is one of the most deadly omissions in evangelicalism today. . . .

Christians frequently restrict the scope of ethics to a narrow class of 'personal' sins. . . .

. . . In the twentieth century, as opposed to the nineteenth, evangelicals have been more concerned with individual sinful acts than with their participation in evil social structures.[284]

Thus while promoting himself as an evangelical, Sider seemed to be actually anti-evangelical as he rejected the universal affirmative of the proclamation of the gospel. The example of Sider's approach bears witness to the complexities of issues as regards the atonement, the emphasis of Christ's work, the state of man, and emphasis in ministry—they are all interrelated and cannot be separated. Sider promoted his incarnational view in the midst of Graham's ministry, at the time when Graham was preaching the "Two Faces of Man."

Introducing Graham on the atonement. How has Graham fared with his emphasis on the atonement in his sixty-three years of ministry? Has his view of the atonement showed any perceptible movement? In his 1957 sermon, "The Mystery of Righteousness," Graham explained "three aspects of this wonderful righteousness which God bestows upon us."[285] His three points were as follows:

1. First, the mystery of imputed righteousness
2. Secondly, we have the mystery of indwelling righteousness
3. And lastly, we have the mystery of completed righteousness.[286]

Point one of this sermon taught the substitutionary or vicarious atonement:

To impute means "to attribute something to another." Immediately our minds leap to Calvary where we see the sins of a helpless, hopeless race placed upon the guiltless shoulders of the Son of God. And we hear the words of Scripture saying, "For He hath

---

[284]Ibid., 133.

[285]Billy Graham, "The Mystery of Righteousness," *Hour of Decision Sermons*, no. 75 (Minneapolis: Billy Graham Evangelistic Association, 1956), 4.

[286]Ibid., 4-7.

made Him to be sin for us, who knew no sin; that we might be made the righteousness of God in Him" (II Corinthians 5:21).[287]

In the 1977 *How to Be Born Again* Graham continued to expound the substitutionary atonement:

> As a holy God, He hates sin and can have no fellowship with sin. Because the Bible tells us that the soul that sins must surely die, we can see that separation from God is a result of sin. However, because God is also mercy, He longs to save the guilty sinner and must then provide a substitute which will satisfy His divine justice. He provided that substitute in Jesus Christ.[288]

While Graham taught the vicarious atonement, as well as Christ as an example, throughout his ministry, the question before us is as follows: did his adjustments in his anthropology impact his approach to the atonement? Did Graham ever slowly emphasize something other than the theory of the vicarious atonement, such as a reconciliation model? Did he shift from emphasizing the cross to focusing on the incarnation? Did he ever become negative to the substitutionary atonement?

To answer these questions, we will analyze Graham's treatment of themes related to the atonement. In his ministry three concepts were important to Graham's preaching on the atonement as it relates to salvation: the blood, the cross, and judgment. By analyzing these concepts in the "Early," "Middle," and "Later" Graham's preaching, it may be possible to note changes in Graham's communication of and theology of the atonement.

The Blood

Early in his ministry, a sermon on the blood was part of his regular repertoire. Yet Graham acknowledged that some did not like to hear about the blood of Christ:

> Some months ago after I had given a message at a large Southern resort on "The Meaning of the Cross," a former professor at Cornell University came to me and said, "Young man, I enjoyed your message, but if you want to be a successful preacher you will have to

---

[287]Ibid., 4.

[288]Billy Graham, *How to Be Born Again,* 102.

leave out that 'blood stuff.' It is out of date. No enlightened man of the twentieth century will swallow that."[289]

In 1957 Graham stated, "Some might say that blood is somewhat revolting, but blood given is a blessing."[290] And again, "To many people the mention of the blood of Christ is distasteful."[291] Yet how did Graham react to this distaste throughout his ministry years? In order to ascertain Graham's approach to the blood, we will compare four sermons on the blood: 1947, 1949, 1951, and 1957.

In *Calling Youth to Christ* (1947) we find the first of Graham's published sermons on the blood. The 1947 sermon began with a graphic description of Aztec human sacrifice. In his first point Graham dealt with biblical atonement looking at the Old Testament concept of blood atonement. Second, he asked the question, "Why Does God Demand blood?"[292] In this point he detailed the substitutionary atonement. Thirdly, Graham discussed the results of the blood atonement. He concluded with this statement:

> Yes, the blood of Jesus Christ, the Son of God, can cleanse from the vilest sin and make you whole this very moment. Believe it! Receive it! Accept it! Sprinkle it by faith! Plunge in the fountain![293]

This third point of the 1947 sermon was expanded and repeated several times in his early ministry. So significant was Graham's sermon on the blood that it was included in a 1949 compilation of sermons. It his 1949 sermon, "Atonement," Graham dropped three illustrations from his 1947 sermon: the Aztec human sacrifice illustration as his introduction, a D. L. Moody illustration in point three of the results of the atonement, and a lengthy Oswald J. Smith illustration on Barabbas as his closing illustration. Then two years later, the same sermon was published as *Hour of Decision* sermon number six, "Christianity versus a Bloodless Religion." In this 1951 sermon, Graham expanded his opening illustrations to speak about the importance of blood in medical science. His nine pages on "Its Biblical Implications" in the prior sermons were abbreviated to two pages. Of the Old Testament sacrificial system he said:

---

[289]Billy Graham, "Atonement," in *Great Gospel Sermons* 2, "Contemporary" (London: Fleming H. Revell, 1949), 44.

[290]Billy Graham, *Peace with God,* 101.

[291]Billy Graham, "The Suffering Saviour on a Crimson Cross," 3.

[292]Billy Graham, "A Scarlet Thread," in *Calling Youth to Christ,* 106.

[293]Ibid., 115.

The Bible teaches that the blood of bulls and goats does not and never has saved from sin. But the blood of bulls and goats foreshadowed the slaying of the Lamb of God upon the cross of Calvary.[294]

Then, rather than getting into the five results of the atonement, he moved right into salvation:

Christ is the universal donor. Man has four major blood types. Type four is known as universal, for it has properties that the other blood types do not have. Christ's blood has no limitation, for we read, 'The blood of Jesus Christ, God's Son, cleanses us from all sins.'

It is not simply moral rearmament that we must have. We must individually and collectively accept the spiritual blood transfusion that only Christ can give. We must accept Christ's death as our substitute. There is no other way of salvation.[295]

Interestingly, there was less theology in his 1951 sermon than there was in his 1947 or 1949 sermon on the blood.

In 1957, when his sermon on the blood was published under the title, "The Suffering Savior on a Crimson Cross," he almost completely omitted any biblical theology of the blood, as he had done in 1947 and 1949. Rather than becoming more theological, it seemed that Graham was becoming less theological!

Early in the 1957 sermon Graham expounded his main theme, "I pray that we might grasp the full significance of the precious blood of Jesus."[296] The theme text for this sermon was Hebrews 9:22. Graham said:

Slowly we have drifted away from the old truth, without the shedding of blood there is no remission of sins [Heb 9:22]. Modern man would like to make of the cross a thing of sentiment. A trinket to be worn around the neck. An ornament on a church steeple or an emblem stamped in gold ink on our Bibles. Around the cross a certain romantic interest is gathered, but the cross and the blood of Christ symbolized man's utter helplessness to save himself. It reveals two basic facts that cannot be denied, the depth of man's depravity and the intensity of God's love. I cannot comprehend the chemistry and the efficacy of the blood of Christ. There is an element of mystery that

---

[294]Billy Graham, "Christianity Versus a Bloodless Religion," 8.

[295]Ibid., 9-10.

[296]Billy Graham, "The Suffering Saviour on a Crimson Cross," 3.

cannot be understood with our natural minds. But I do know that all who by faith test its power discover that it can wonderfully change their lives and lift them to a higher plane of living.[297]

Graham noted that "the cross reveals two basic facts that cannot be denied, the depth of man's depravity and the intensity of God's love." He then highlighted the results of the blood atonement, similarly to the third point in his 1947 and 1949 sermons. However, two additions lead to some questions. Was it possible to "test its [the blood's] power"? Was it possible for true saving faith to be tested? Was that not asking with a double heart (cf. Jas 1:6)? Was testing not holding onto the past, which Paul spoke against (cf. Phil 3:7)? And second, did saving faith "lift them to a higher plane of living"? The plain meaning of "higher plane" did not sit right with Paul's view of the life of faith,[298] or of the life of the nameless heroes of the faith.[299] Thus, some changes were taking place in Graham's approach to salvation and to the Christian life.

In his book *Freedom from the Seven Deadly Sins* (1955), Graham addressed the sin of impurity, dealing with the concept of sexual impurity from the Bible. When speaking of the hope for those who have committed this sin, he quoted the first verse of "There Is a Fountain Filled with Blood," by William Cowper (1731-1800), and said, "There is a crimson cure for the scarlet sin."[300] He then went on and discussed the woman caught in adultery from John 8. In this case, as in virtually all other cases of his discussion of the blood, Graham linked the blood of Christ with forgiveness of sins and justification by faith.

In 1977 Graham published *How to Be Born Again*. While we noted some changes in Graham's view of sin from this book, he still maintained the need for the blood atonement:

God chose blood as the means of our redemption. . . .

---

[297]Ibid., 3-4.

[298]"To this present hour we are both hungry and thirsty, and are poorly clothed, and a roughly treated, and are homeless. . . we have become as the scum of the world, the dregs of all things, even until now" (1 Cor 4:11, 13). "I have been in labor and hardship, through many sleepless nights, in hunger and thirst, often without food, in cold and exposure" (2 Cor 11:27).

[299]"They were stoned, they were sawn in two, they were tempted, they were put to death with the sword; they went about in sheepskins, in goatskins, being destitute, afflicted, ill-treated (men of whom the world was not worthy), wandering in deserts and mountains and caves and holes in the ground" (Heb 11:37-38).

[300]Billy Graham, "Impurity," in *Freedom from the Seven Deadly Sins*, 65.

When Jesus Christ, the perfect God-man, shed His blood on the cross, He was surrendering His pure and spotless life to death as an eternal sacrifice for man's sin. Once and for all, God made complete provision for the cure of man's sins. Without the blood of Christ, it is a fatal disease.[301]

The 1980 *Hour of Decision* sermon number 233 was taken from an August 1980 *Decision Magazine* article. Its title was "Why the Cross Is an Offense?"[302] This article included points from Graham's earlier sermons on the blood, as did the 1965 sermon "The Offense of the Cross."[303]

In 1984 the cover article for *Decision Magazine* was called "The Blood of Christ." This article was also published as *Hour of Decision* sermon number 244 in the same year. The 1984 article used theological terminology: redemption, remission, justification, cleansing, and peace. In his conclusion Graham wrote, "The blood of Christ accomplishes three things. It satisfies God, it saves sinners and it silences the devil."[304]

In *Storm Warning* (1992), an expansion of *Approaching Hoofbeats* (1983), Graham still held to the blood of Christ as the only way of salvation:

When sin and failure come in our lives, as they most certainly will, we still have the wonderful promise that "the blood of Jesus, his Son, purifies us from all sin" (1 John 1:7). That promise was written to believers. And the word used here, *purifies* (or, in the King James Version *cleanseth),* means "continuous cleansing."[305]

Therefore, throughout his ministry, Graham believed in the blood sacrifice of Christ on the cross as the only hope of forgiveness. Thus, while Graham mentioned the blood in his later sermons and maintained it as an essential part of the atonement, it seems that the blood was not one of his core messages in his crusades,[306] as it presumably was in his early years.[307]

---

[301]Billy Graham, *How to Be Born Again,* 91-92.

[302]Billy Graham, "Why Is the Cross an Offense?" *Hour of Decision Sermons,* no. 233 (Minneapolis: Billy Graham Evangelistic Association, 1980).

[303]Billy Graham, "The Offense of the Cross," in *Great Sermons on the Death of Christ by Celebrated Preachers; with Biographical Sketches and Bibliographies,* ed. Wilbur Moorehead Smith (Natwick, MA: W. A. Wilde Company, 1965), 89-96.

[304]Billy Graham, "The Blood of Christ," *Decision Magazine,* May 1984, 2.

[305]Billy Graham, *Storm Warning,* 157.

[306]"Billy Graham Sermon Series by Decade."

It is also interesting that Graham's explanation of the theology of the blood became less theological. The question follows from this analysis: how does Graham's decreasing use of his sermon on the blood impact his view of the atonement? A look at the cross may answer this question.

The Cross

Important to Graham's view of conversion was the cross. The cross was central to the entire Christian message. It spoke of man's sin. The cross showed the failure of man's way of salvation. It manifested God's love. The cross was God's greatest work in the world. According to Graham, the cross was foolishness and an offense to the world. Everything in Christianity and in history focused on the cross.

However, in his preaching, there were some emphases of the cross that show signs of change. Therefore, this section will divide Graham's approach to the cross by way of his early years, being up to 1955, his middle years, from 1955 to 1965, and his later years, from 1965 to the present time. We begin by noting the early Graham and his view of the cross.[308]

The early Graham. To Graham the cross of Christ was the central element in the Christianity and the defining purpose for the Incarnation of Jesus Christ. He believed that the entire life of Jesus centered around the cross. Graham spelled out the centrality of the cross in 1953 in a message entitled "Labor, Christ and the Cross":

---

[307]This was exemplified in the fact that this message was the only sermon of Graham listed in the 1949 compendium of sermons, *Great Gospel Sermons.* In his 1949 sermon series, Graham presumably spoke on the substitutionary atonement in his sermon on Tuesday, November 1, 1949, "John the Baptist," on Gen 22:1-5 and John 1:29, and on "Justification" on Wednesday, November 2, from Job 9:2 and Rom 5:9, "having been justified by his blood." However, as can be noted in "Billy Graham Sermon Series by Decade," Graham no longer used these sermons, and Graham's sermon on Heb 9:22, "Without the shedding of blood there is no remission of sins" (as quoted in the above text) is not found, nor is a sermon on 2 Cor 5:21.

[308]This author has not had access to sermonic material on Graham from 1937 to 1946, only one book of eight sermons published in 1947 (in *Calling Youth to Christ*), one sermon from 1949, and six sermons published in 1950 (in *Revival in Our Time*), and four sermons published in 1951 (*America's Hour of Decision*). The *Hour of Decision Sermons* upon which this study is largely based began their publication in 1951. Thus, it must be admitted that a formal study of the early-early Graham was not possible for this study, due to meager sources.

What, then, was His greatest work? His great work was culminated in those three dark hours on Calvary. There He entered a labor that no other person in all the universe has ever known. We see Him hanging on the cross for our sins. . . .

But Jesus, unperturbed by these existing prejudices, with Calvary His ultimate and determined goal, declared, "To this end was I born, and for this cause came I into the world." . . .

Jesus lived in the shadow of the cross. As a boy he spoke of His Father's business and referred to His sacrificial work upon the cross. His utterances were filled with allusions to His death on the cross. His whole ministry pointed like an arrow to Golgotha and the fulfillment of the divine purpose for His life. He said, "And as Moses lifted up the serpent in the wilderness, even so must the Son of Man be lifted up." . . .

Yes, we need as a nation to turn to the Christ of Calvary, who gave us a classic example of loyalty to a divine purpose. . . .

The principle of vicarious sacrifice is woven into the whole fabric of life. . . .

Christ's greatest work was the crucifixion. His primary purpose was to die, to shed His blood as a substitute in your place and my place. We must accept Christ's death as our substitute. There is no other way of salvation.[309]

The focus of Christ's ministry according to Graham resided in the cross, and the focus of the cross resided in the substitutionary atonement.[310] Graham also believed that the cross was central as it freed men from the power of sin, "Christ was so intolerant of sin that He died on the cross to free men from its power."[311] The cross was "the divine cancellation mark for sin."[312]

The cross was a central element in Graham's preaching. He told Ben Haden in an interview:

---

[309]Billy Graham, "Labor, Christ and the Cross," 2, 3, 4, 5, 6, 8.

[310]"But this we do know that Christ gave the uttermost farthing. He poured out the last ounce of blood to redeem us. He spared not Himself. He took heaven's best to redeem earth's worst. Here was the Son of God dying on a Cross which was made for the vilest of sinners. Here was the law of substitution raised to the highest degree. Here was the lamb of God who had come to take away the sin of the world. Here was the blood of God poured out in selfless love for a dying, hopeless, doomed world" (Billy Graham, "Suffering Savior on a Crimson Cross," 2).

[311]Billy Graham, "The Sin of Tolerance," *Hour of Decision Sermons,* no. 73 (Minneapolis: Billy Graham Evangelistic Association, 1956), 9.

[312]Billy Graham, "The Mystery of the Incarnation," *Hour of Decision Sermons,* no. 76 (Minneapolis: Billy Graham Evangelistic Association, 1956), 1.

I think I have learned the Cross is to be central in our preaching. I don't preach a sermon now unless I bring the message of the Cross—not dragging it in, but making it central in the sermon. Whatever I'm talking on, the death and resurrection of Christ is the heart of the message—and the need for repentance and faith. This is used by the Holy Spirit to bring about conviction.[313]

The centrality of the cross in the preaching of Graham was exemplified from Graham's early ministry. One of the main reasons for this focus on the cross was his concern for the salvation of those listening. He believed that there was no salvation outside the cross, "Christ made the way back to God by His death on the cross."[314] And again, "Christ dying on the cross was an act of the love of God for sinful men and only through the finished work of Christ will any man get to heaven."[315]

Early in his ministry Graham noted that some were seeking to remove the reproach of the cross from Christianity. In a very non-conformist way, Graham stated:

I am afraid that we in the church are making a great mistake by trying to make Christianity popular and pleasant. We have taken the cross away and substituted cushions; but Christ said that the world hated Him, and He predicted that it would hate us.[316]

Graham stated that men tried to circumvent the cross by focusing on man's righteousness or man's reason. Paul, he stated, focused on the cross:

A gospel that appeals to man's reason or man's righteousness, will always be popular, for man likes to feel that he can circumvent the cross of Christ. If Paul had gone to Corinth with the excellency of speech which he was capable of, all Corinth would have gone after him. But, knowing that man must be reminded that his righteousness

---

[313]Haden, "Dr. Graham, Exactly What Is Evangelism?" 11.

[314]Billy Graham, "What Is Conversion?" 1.

[315]Billy Graham, "Escape," *Hour of Decision Sermons,* no. 46 (Minneapolis: Billy Graham Evangelistic Association, 1955), 10. This sermon was also published in a compendium of sermons by Russell Victor DeLong (*Evangelistic Sermons by Great Evangelists* [Grand Rapids: Zondervan Publishing House, 1956]).

[316]Billy Graham, "Branded," *Hour of Decision Sermons,* no. 17 (Minneapolis: Billy Graham Evangelistic Association, 1952), 5.

and his reason are both rejected by God, he preached nothing but Christ and Him crucified.[317]

Graham also stated:

> Slowly we have drifted away from the old truth, "without the shedding of blood there is no remission of sins" [Heb 9:22]. Modern man would like to make the cross a thing of sentiment. . . . but the cross symbolizes man's utter helplessness to save himself.[318]

To the early Graham, however, the cross signified man's hatred of God:

> The hatred of man for God and God's love toward man, were both seen at the cross. It was at Calvary where man turned all his hate upon God; it was at Calvary where the Creator; it was at Calvary where God laid bare His heart and gave His only begotten Son as a sacrifice for the sins of mankind. It was at Calvary where God was in Christ, reconciling the world unto Himself, and where Christ, the Redeemer, died that man, the rebel, might live. Strange that God should love those that hate Him. Yet He did, and He does—God loved us; not because Christ died for us, but Christ died for us because God loved us. Yes, God loves the Communist, God loves the Atheist, He loves all sinners and He loves you.[319]

Graham felt that man would crucify Christ again if he had the chance,[320] only this time even faster![321]

Thus, to the early Graham, the only hope for man was to humbly bow at the foot of the cross to receive grace:

---

[317]Billy Graham, "Made, Marred and Mended," 9.

[318]Billy Graham, "The Suffering Saviour on a Crimson Cross," 3.

[319]Billy Graham, "Grace Versus Wrath," 2-3.

[320]"Two thousand years ago they rejected God, 'The Son,' and today the same spirit of depravity is causing men to reject the call of God. . ." (Billy Graham, "Grace Versus Wrath," 4-5). Also: "The cross still casts its shadow across the world, and the cry of 'Crucify Him,' still lurks in the throats of crucify Him rather than own Him as king" (Billy Graham, "Labor, Christ and the Cross," 7).

[321]"I am convinced that if Christ came back today, He would be crucified even quicker than He was 2,000 years ago" (Billy Graham, "The Cross and Its Power," 4).

> Only as we bow in contrition, confession and repentance at the foot of the Cross, can we find forgiveness. There, is the grace of God! We don't deserve it! A man said sometime ago, "When I get to the judgment of God all that I ask for is justice." My beloved friend, if you get justice, then you will go to Hell. You don't want justice. What you want is mercy. The mercy of God, the grace of God as it was in Christ Jesus who died and rose again.[322]

Thus, Graham in his early years understood the cross as signifying the substitutionary atonement, being the only way of salvation and pointing to the depravity of man's sin.

Graham in his middle years. While it is hard to pinpoint a change in Graham's view of the cross, as we have seen from Graham's 1955 *Seven Deadly Sins,* a theological change did begin to take place in Graham's anthropology. Also in 1955, we will note that Graham identified his sermon "The Love of God" as a new emphasis in his preaching. Graham's shift in anthropology became evident in the "Two Faces of Man" in his 1958 sermon "Past, Present and Future." The question is not one of if Graham changed, but rather when and how he changed, and how did his shift in anthropology impact his view of soteriology? Graham's change in the church's mission to include evangelism and social concern can be traced to 1965 in *World Aflame.*[323] The communication of a change in the church's mission, therefore, marks his entering of the stage of the "Later Graham."

By 1958 Graham had already been preaching "revivals" for twenty-one years, and he was now in his fortieth year. He had met with the President of the United States on several occasions, as well as had preached to the Queen of England. He had received a number of awards (see Appendix 4). Graham was well into completing his first worldwide conquest which would take him to every continent of the world by 1962. He was nurturing a close relationship with Anglicans since 1952 and seeking to nurture close relations with the Lutheran World Federation since 1954. Therefore, it would seem possible that there may be some movement in theology to facilitate these relationships.

---

[322]Billy Graham, "The Grace of God," *Hour of Decision Sermons,* no. 82 (Minneapolis: Billy Graham Evangelistic Association, 1957), 8.

[323]Billy Graham, *World Aflame* (Garden City, NY: Doubleday, 1965), 187.

The love of God. Graham in his 1955 sermon, "The Love of God," attributed God's love as the motive for His giving of the Ten Commandments. Graham preached:

> It was love which caused God to engrave these statutes upon the hearts of all people at all times and make them the basis of all civil, statutory and moral law. It was love seeing through the centuries that men were incapable of being what they ought to be without the help of God which promised a Redeemer, our Savior, who should save His people from their sins. It was love, the love of God, which put such words in the mouths and hearts of the prophets as they which said: "All we like sheep have gone astray. We have turned everyone to his own way. The Lord has laid on Him the iniquity of us all."[324]

Graham continued his litany on the love of God, moving into soteriology:

> It was love, the unerring love of God which brought these prophecies into precise fulfillment and on a specific day marked on earth's calendar and in a specific place marked on earth's map, the Son of God made His advent on this planet. It was love which prompted the Son of God to reflect the same affection for the world as did God, the Father, and to show a selfless compassion to the sick, the distressed and the sin-burdened. It was love which enabled Jesus Christ to become poor that we through His poverty might be made rich. It was love, divine love which made Him endure the cross despising its shame and made Him endure the contradictions of sinners against Himself lest we be weary and faint in our minds.[325]

Graham went into a paragraph in which he quoted John 3:16, and then went into his invitation:

> Now as in Eden disobedience has its consequences. Now as in the early era God's love brooks no spurning. Now as in the first dawn of creation He beckons you to fellowship with Him, and His great heart yearns for companionship with those for whom His Son died. . .
> .

---

[324]Billy Graham, "The Love of God" (1955), 6.

[325]Ibid., 6-7.

... Respond to the love of God and receive Jesus Christ as your personal Savior and be transformed by surrendering your will to Him.[326]

It is interesting to note that in this 1955 sermon, Graham seemed to avoid the issue of sin as a moral transgression of the law of God, although he had the opportunity to when he brought in verses that spoke of sin. In fact, his invitation was one of restoration of fellowship with God. This was in keeping with a later sermon on "The Incarnation."[327] It would seem that Graham was beginning to become selective in his description of the atonement. As Henry C. Sheldon pointed out, there are dangers in ignoring certain elements in the atonement, as well as dangers in "exaggerating some phase of Christ's work of atonement."[328] Two concerns may be considered at this point. Overemphasizing the love of God while at the same time avoiding terminology which specifically related to the blood atonement may have shown a movement *toward* a theology like that of Horace Bushnell.[329]

---

[326]Ibid., 8-9.

[327]"His incarnation—His being born in human flesh—was for the record. He came to the world, once and for all, that man might forever know that He had an absorbing interest in the way we live, the way we believe and the way we die. He came to demonstrate to us that God and man belong together. He came to man to mend the gap and fill the gulf that separated the creature from his Creator. And all this He did. Every time He fed a hungry man, He was saying, 'I am the bread of life.' Every time He healed a suffering person, He was saying, 'It hurts Me to see you hurt.' Every time He lifted a burden of sin, He was saying, 'Your God is grieved when you remove yourself from His grace.' Every move He made, every miracle He performed, every word He spoke, had been blueprinted in heaven and was for the purpose of reconciling a lost world to a loving, compassionate God. 'God was in Christ, reconciling the world' (II Corinthians 5:19)" (Billy Graham, "The Incarnation," *Hour of Decision Sermons*, no. 76 [Minneapolis: Billy Graham Evangelistic Association, 1956], 5-6.).

[328]Henry C. Shelton, *System of Christian Doctrine* (Cincinnati: Jennings and Graham, 1903), 393.

[329]"For a good being is not simply one who gives bounties and favors, but one who is in the principle of love; and it is the very nature of love, universally, to insert itself into the miseries, and take upon its feeling the burden of others. Love does not consider the ill desert of the subject; he may be a cruel and relentless enemy. It does not consider the expense of toil, and sacrifice, and suffering the intervention may cost. It stops at nothing but the known impossibility of relief, or benefit; asks for nothing as inducement, but the opportunity of success. Love is a principle essentially vicarious in its own nature, identifying the subject with others, so as to suffer their adversaries, their pains, and taking on itself the burden of their evils" (Horace Bushnell, *The Vicarious Sacrifice*, 41-42). Bushnell was said to have "devoted his life to constructive mediation between the older tradition and the demands of modernity" (Sydney E. Ahlstrom,
274

A second concern lay in the move from the satisfaction theory of the atonement toward the reconciliation model. The foundation for this move was viewing sin as alienation. Hence, James Denney in his 1917 Cunningham Lectures stated, "The need of reconciliation is given in the fact of alienation or estrangement. Man requires to be put right with God because, as a matter of fact, he is not right with him."[330] Later Denney expanded:

> Man is somehow wrong with God, and the task of reconciliation is to put him right again.
>
> The consciousness of being wrong with God—in other words the sense of sin—emerges in connection with some definite act, for which responsibility attaches to the actor.[331]

Denney then stated that speculation on the origin of evil or the primitive state of man are not necessary. He then began to move on the individual and social impacts of sin as alienation:

> But to limit our view thus—to speak as if God on one hand, and the soul estranged from Him by deliberate and isolated act on the other, were the only realities we had to consider—gives us a quite inadequate view of what is needed when we speak of the need for reconciliation. . . . All men are members of a society in which they live and move and have their being morally, and all that they do, of right or wrong, they both affect and are affected by the body to which they belong.[332]

Thus, to Denney, sin was not a matter of the nature of man, but of specific actions. To Denney, total depravity was unnecessary speculation.[333] The result of man's sin was alienation from God and moral paralysis: "It is a

---

"Introduction to the Reprinted Edition," in *The Vicarious Sacrifice,* by Horace Bushnell, 3d).

[330]Denney, *The Christian Doctrine of Reconciliation,* 187.

[331]Ibid., 189.

[332]Ibid., 191.

[333]Denney wrote, "On the other hand, there may be a doctrine of human depravity, not only seriously expressing serious facts, but so exaggerated and uncompromising as to exclude the very possibility of redemption" (ibid., 199). Again, "We cannot say that man's nature is sinful. . ." (201).

fundamental truth with which we have to deal, that a bad conscience, or a sense of sin, induces moral paralysis."[334]

What then of salvation for Denney's theory of reconciliation? Denney wrote, "God has not left Himself without a witness in the sinful heart, and His witness is being heard. The way to reconciliation is not closed."[335] Then what of the death of Christ? Denney stated:

> The work of Christ is not designed to impress men *simpliciter.* It is designed to impress them to a certain intent, to a certain issue; it is designed to produce in them through penitence God's mind about sin. It cannot do this simply as the exhibition of unconditioned love. It can only do it as an exhibition or demonstration of a love which is itself ethical in character and looks to ethical issues. But the only love of this description is love which owns the reality of sin by submitting humbly and without rebellion to the divine reaction against it; it is love doing homage to the divine ethical necessities which pervade the nature of things and the whole order in which men live. These divine ethical necessities are in the strictest sense objective.[336]

Denney continued on the subject of the atonement:

> It was commonplace of Christian teaching a generation ago to contrast Christ as our atonement and reconciliation with Christ as a 'mere' example; the latter was the Socinian, the former the evangelical view. But Christ, as the evangelical view sometimes led its adherents to forget, after all *is* an example; and it is at least possible that to be insensible to the inspiration of His example is to lie outside of His reconciling power.[337]

Elsewhere Denney added:

> He bore our sins. In every sense and to every extent to which love could do so, He made them His own. . . . He numbered Himself

---

[334]Ibid., 190.

[335]Ibid., 219. Notice Denney's openness to natural revelation implied in this statement.

[336]Ibid., 234-35.

[337]Ibid., 245-46.

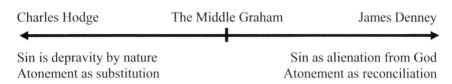

PENAL-SUBSTITUTIONARY
THEORY

RECONCILIATION
MODEL

Charles Hodge   The Middle Graham   James Denney

Sin is depravity by nature   Sin as alienation from God
Atonement as substitution   Atonement as reconciliation

Fig. 12. Penal-substitution and reconciliation compared.[338]

with transgressors, and made them His very own.[339]

Denney's theology no longer shouted about heaven or hell. The benefits of the atonement were in this life. Denney's positive gospel no longer hurled angry shouts about the holiness of God and man's *total* depravity. Rather it spoke of God's love as He experienced man's plight caught in the clutches of sin. God was sensitive and sent His Son to free mankind from the power of sin and to restore the broken relationship between God and man. Denney's reconciliation theory encouraged a lifestyle evangelism, not of words but of ethical social behavior. Graham, in his sermon "The Love of God," (preached in Scotland) seemed to move from a unique adherence to the substitutionary atonement *toward* preaching the reconciliation model of the atonement, similar to that espoused by the Scottish theologian James Denney.[340]

Graham seemed to nudge toward the middle of Figure 12. He seemed to maintain the penal-substitutionary theory in practice, but his

---

[338]Derived from Denney, *The Christian Doctrine of Reconciliation,* 185-232.

[339]Ibid., 251-52. Denney then showed his appreciation for two prior authors: "We have two books in our language by men of original spiritual insight and intellectual power which makes a noble contribution to this study. One is Bushnell's *The Vicarious Atonement,* the other is McLeod Campbell's *The Nature of the Atonement*" (ibid., 255).

[340]Graham said of Denney, "James Denney, the great Scottish theologian said, 'If you shoot over the heads of your hearers you won't prove anything, except you don't know how to shoot" (Billy Graham, "Communicating the Gospel," 6). Clearly, this quote doesn't prove any reliance on Denney's theology. Rather, the link being made between Graham and Denney regards the existence of a reconciliation model as a downgrade of the substitutionary atonement, and the circumstantial evidence that Graham's first *HOD* sermon where he admitted this theological adjustment was from his 1955 Scotland crusade.

language showed influence from the reconciliation model of mainstream denominations.[341] Simultaneously during this time, however, Graham continued to maintain a strong view of the cross and of the sufficiency of Christ:

> When Martin Luther saw the great truth that justification was by grace, that justification was by faith, that justification was by the blood of the Cross, he cried delightedly, "Calvary seems as though it were only yesterday." How true.[342]

Thus Graham seemed to be seeking a synergism between the satisfaction and reconciliation models of the atonement.[343] This assertion may become more evident as we take other snapshots of Graham's theology.

Three books. Another approach to ascertain the movement in Graham's theology of the cross, particularly in his "middle years," is to study his approach to the cross in three books: *Peace with God* (1953), *World Aflame* (1965), and *How to Be Born Again* (1977). Each one of these has almost identical sections on the cross, and each one was published in a different era of his theological maturation.[344]

In chapter 8 of *Peace with God* (1953), titled "Why Jesus Came," Billy Graham explained the cross in four sections: "Defeating the Devil," "Sinner or Substitute," "Three Things in the Cross," and "Five

---

[341]Note the terminology of the Thailand Statement (1980), "This is not to deny that evangelism and social action are integrally related, but rather to acknowledge that of all the tragic needs of human beings none is greater than their alienation from their Creator and the terrible reality of eternal death for those who refuse to repent and believe" (John R. W. Stott, *Making Christ Known: Historic Mission Documents from the Lausanne Movement, 1974-1989* [Grand Rapids: Eerdmans, 1996], 159).

[342]Billy Graham, "What Is the Gospel?" 6.

[343]It was noted above that Graham preached less on the blood of Christ, especially after 1957. However, he did continue to preach on the Prodigal Son, a passage that symbolizes the atonement as reconciliation and that makes more sense theologically to denominations which practice infant baptism. For example, according to "Billy Graham Sermon Series by Decade" which began with all his sermons in Los Angeles 1949 concluding with San Jose, California 1997, Graham first preached on the Prodigal Son in London on May 1, 1954. He preached Luke 15 on June 12, 1957. And Luke 15:11-32 was one of his ten sermons in the Denver crusade, preached on July 23, 1987 ("Billy Graham Sermon Series by Decade").

[344]It must be noted that *Peace with God,* written after sixteen years of Graham's revival ministry, is not an example of the early-early Graham. Rather it seems to be Graham's first concerted attempt to posit a broader theology.

Things the Blood Brings."[345] In the section on the blood the five points were identical to five points in his sermon "A Scarlet Thread" in the 1947 *Calling Youth to Christ*.[346] Under his section dealing with the cross, Graham's three points were as follows:

> In the cross of Christ I see three things: First, a description of the depth of *man's sin*. . . .
> Second, in the cross I see the overwhelming *love of God*. If ever you should doubt the love of God, take a long, deep look at the cross, for in the cross you find the expression of God's love.
> Third, in the cross is the only *way of salvation*.[347]

World Aflame (1965) had a chapter entitled "God's Foolishness." In this chapter Graham addressed the Fall of man, then he had two main sections: "Atonement" and "The Cross of Christ." Under the atonement Graham dealt with the Jewish sacrificial system and with Christ's atonement in a little more than two pages. However, Graham's "Five Things the Blood Brings" were not mentioned. Under the cross, Graham stated:

> Christ's dying on the cross was more than the death of a martyr. It was more than His setting a good example by offering His life for His fellow man. His was the sacrifice that God had appointed and ordained to be the one and only sacrifice for sin. The Scripture says: "The Lord hath laid on him the iniquity of us all . . . it pleased the Lord to bruise him; he hath put him to grief" (Isa. 53:6, 10). Because God Himself has set forth Christ to be the covering for human guilt, then God cannot possibly reject the sinner who accepts Jesus Christ as Saviour. "Whom God hath set forth to be a propitiation through faith in his blood" (Rom. 3: 25). . . .
> Christ's atonement is sufficient because God said it is.[348]

Then Graham continued by reworking the three points he had placed under the cross and making it into the following four points:

---

[345]The five points on the blood were "it first of all redeems," "it brings us nigh," "it makes peace," "it justifies," and "it cleanses" (Billy Graham, *Peace with God*, 101-02).

[346]Billy Graham, "A Scarlet Thread," 110-12. These points were "It redeems," "It brings us nigh," "It makes peace," "It justifies," and "It cleanses."

[347]Billy Graham, *Peace with God*, 99.

[348]Billy Graham, *World Aflame*, 119.

> As we look at the cross we see several things. *First, here is the clearest evidence of the world's guilt. . . .*
>
> *Second, in the cross we find the strongest proof of God's hatred of sin. . . .*
>
> *Third, as we stand at the cross we see a glorious exhibition of God's love. . . .*
>
> *Fourth, as we stand at the cross, we see in it a basis of true world brotherhood.*[349]

In the evolution of Graham's communication of the cross, when comparing *Peace with God* to *World Aflame*, he expanded point one, "man's sin" to include "the world's guilt" and "God's hatred of sin." Was this a move toward a less individualistic emphasis? Point two on the love of God remained identical. And point three was restated from "the only way of salvation" to "basis for true world brotherhood."[350] This last change also had an inclusivist sound to it, though Graham tactifully disclaimed a false concept of "the brotherhood of man":

> But the world seems to be blinded to the fact that for men to know God spiritually as Father they must take Christ in personal salvation. Only thus are we brought into the family of God. His spiritual Fatherhood belongs only to those who trust in Him.[351]

How to Be Born Again (1977) addressed the cross in a section similar to the previous mentioned books. This time the title of the chapter was "The King's Courtroom." Graham included a simple illustration in the early part of this chapter with the essence of sin being a privation of love for God and man:

> GOD: John (or) Mary, have you loved Me with all your heart?
> JOHN/MARY: No, Your Honor.
> GOD: Have you loved others as you have loved yourself?
> JOHN/MARY: No, Your Honor.
> GOD: Do you believe you are a sinner and that Jesus Christ died for your sins?

---

[349]Ibid., 121-23. These points are identical to Graham's 1958 sermon, "The Cross and Its Power," 4-7, thus showing that his adjustment in communicating on the cross was made long before it was published in a book.

[350]Graham also discussed "brotherhood" in "The Cross and Its Power." His fifth point was, "As we stand at the cross we see here the basis of true brotherhood" (Billy Graham, "The Cross and Its Power," 9).

[351]Billy Graham, *World Aflame*, 123.

JOHN/MARY: Yes, Your Honor.

GOD: Then your penalty has been paid by Jesus Christ on the cross and you are pardoned.[352]

He then added:

GOD: Because Christ is righteous, and you believe in Christ, I now declare you legally righteous.[353]

Graham, in this illustration, seemed to avoid the concepts of sin as a violation of God's written Word and moral commands and repentance. Rather, he seemed to be approaching sin from the Greatest Commandment and the second (cf. Matt 22:37-39), a lack of love, further redefining the atonement as he did in *Hour of Decision* sermon no. 52, "The Love of God." While sin being a lack of love is technically correct, this portion was the strongest language on sin that Graham provided his readers as he prepared them for the preaching of the cross. Graham seemed to have moved from a substitutionary concept of sin and the gospel *toward* a reconciliation-model of sin and the gospel.[354]

Following several pages discussing the substitutionary atonement, Graham provided some conclusions based on the death of Christ:

There are some vital conclusions we can draw from the death of Christ. First, at the cross we see the strongest evidence of the guilt of the world. . . .

The second conclusion we see at the cross is that God hates sin and loves righteousness. . . .

What other conclusion can we reach from the testimony of the cross? We see the greatest demonstration of God's love. . . .

The fourth conclusion that we can reach from the testimony of the cross is that it is a basis for true world brotherhood.[355]

When Graham's approach to brotherhood, although it did assume the need for a basic belief in Christ, was combined with the "Two Faces of Man"

---

[352]Billy Graham, *How to Be Born Again,* 118.

[353]Ibid., 119.

[354]"When Satan with his clever promises separated man from God in the Garden of Eden, he was more than a deceiver of Adam and Eve. . . . Through the cross, God not only overpowered Satan but brought Himself and man together" (ibid., 111).

[355]Ibid., 121-24.

approach to good and evil in anthropology,[356] it seemed to lead toward a man-centered approach, sin as a lack of love, a more simplistic view of the gospel, and a decision-oriented appeal to man's will.

Also the "Middle" Graham's move toward a type of decisionism seemed evident in his 1958 sermon, "Past, Present and Future," where he explained the "horns and halo" as referring to the state of natural man's will. He continued on point one, "God gives us a mind with which to think and a will to make a choice. If we choose unwisely then we must suffer the consequences of making a poor decision."[357] Graham was stating a position of free will, rather than the moral depravity of his early years.[358] Graham then moved into the topic of salvation, "Let us turn from this dark picture painted against the background of man's evil history and let us think hopefully, thirdly, of man's destiny through the Cross."[359] Then Graham used the verb "change" to describe the impact of salvation:

> Because the first Adam sinned, all those who followed his ways experienced the change for the worst. "In Adam all die, but in Christ shall all be made alive again," because Christ who is the second Adam was sinless. All who follow Him experience a change for the better.[360]

Graham seemed to downgrade the concept of conversion in two ways. First he used the word "change" making conversion a matter of degree rather than the complete transformation of man's nature (cf., 2 Cor 5:17; Eph 2:5; Col 1:13-14). Second, he did not speak of believing in Christ (*sola fides*), but of following Christ—which is unclear terminology. His next topics were propitiation, justification, and reconciliation. Propitiation showed that "The cross removes sin's defilement."[361] Again he approached salvation as a response to the natural headship of Adam and sin as a sickness. Justification

---

[356]Billy Graham, "Past, Present and Future," *Hour of Decision Sermons,* no. 100 (Minneapolis: Billy Graham Evangelistic Association, 1958), 1-3.

[357]Ibid., 3. Note how this follows James Denney's reconciliation approach: "The consciousness of being wrong with God—in other words the sense of sin—emerges in connection with some definite act, for which responsibility attaches to the actor" (Denney, *The Christian Doctrine of Reconciliation,* 189).

[358]The ontological responsibility for the decision was placed in man's purview.

[359]Billy Graham, "Past, Present and Future," 6.

[360]Ibid.

[361]Ibid., 7.

showed that "There is removal of sin."[362] Interestingly, he did not mention that Christ bore our sin, but emphasized that of sins being changed from blood red to "white as snow."[363] Reconciliation showed "This means removal of sins [sic] alienation."[364] Graham mentioned justification again and reconciliation, mentioning the bridge illustration. He ended the message with this invitation:

> Yes, God cares. He loves you. He gave His Son to die for you. Yes, you count so much that a cross was erected on a lonely hill two thousand years ago for the purpose of bringing you life abundantly. You count so much that God through the Spirit is trying to communicate His love to men even through your failures and defeats. You count so much that the central thought in God's scheme of things is to redeem the human race and reconcile them to Himself. Yes, you count. Use your God-given mind to grasp this glorious truth. Bring your will into play to accept it as a real fact. Take Jesus Christ as your personal Savior today "whom to know is life eternal."[365]

Among other things, Graham seemed to express that the natural mind can understand the truth of the gospel (contra 1 Cor 2:14 and 2 Cor 4:3-4). In fact, Graham's invitation corresponded with his other changes in terminology with regard to anthropology and soteriology.

It must be noted that while the "Middle Graham" began to include some nuanced language as regards the cross and salvation, even as he began broadening his anthropology, he still preached his early material on the cross. Hence in his sermon "The Offense of the Cross" (1965), Graham included many of the points of his early sermons on the blood. Graham said:

> There are four reasons that the cross is an offense:
> First, the cross of Christ condemns the world. . . .
> Second, the cross of Christ is an offense because blood was shed there. . . .
> Third, the cross of Christ is an offense because it sets forth an imperative ideal life. . . .

---

[362]Ibid.

[363]Ibid.

[364]Ibid., 8.

[365]Ibid., 9.

Fourth, the cross of Christ is an offense because it claims to be the power and salvation of God. . . .[366]

In his last point, Graham omitted his earlier language of the cross as "the only way of salvation."[367] Whereas later in his point he clearly stated, "The cross condemns every other way of salvation."[368] Yet, one senses a tension in the "Middle Graham" as regards making strong statements that would offend a less conservative audience.

Therefore, while continuing his emphasis upon preaching the cross, Graham began to omit several "negative" points that he preached in his earlier years: the cross shows man's hatred of God; the cross shows the depth (depravity) of man's sin; and the cross points to the only way of salvation. Additionally, Graham added several "positive" concepts to his preaching of the cross: sin as a lack of love, God's love for [man's?] righteousness, the concept of world's brotherhood, as well as the restoration of the dignity of man.

The later Graham. When did Graham move from the "Middle Graham" to the "Later Graham"? As noted above, the "Middle Graham" was the time period beginning with a change in anthropology (1955), moving to a change in soteriology (1957), and finally concluding in a change in the mission of the church (1965). It took Graham ten years for his view of mission to catch up to his change in anthropology. Then in the "Later Graham" stage, Graham adapted his organization to include a social arm, as well as his crusades to include a "Love in Action" committee. But Graham continued to use the revivalistic methods of his early years of ministry. Graham did not pull out of crusade evangelism, as Charles Templeton did, when his theology did not fully match his method. Graham continued preaching crusades. During this last portion of his life, Graham showed uncanny administrative prowess by walking the impossible middle that we have been describing in the last two chapters of this manuscript. A study of cooperation, as noted in the next chapter, highlights Graham's view and methodology of cooperation, perhaps providing a context for his synergism.

While further study of Graham's communication of the atonement would be of interest, space concerns make it impossible. However, the final section of this chapter on Graham's message asks three

---

[366]Billy Graham, "The Offense of the Cross," 91-95.

[367]Billy Graham, *Peace with God,* 99.

[368]Billy Graham, "The Offense of the Cross," 96.

questions. Did Graham show signs of moving toward a simplistic gospel during this final stage of his ministry? If Graham moved toward a simplistic gospel did his invitation system move toward a decisionism? And lastly, did Graham's simplistic gospel, if it became that, show signs of inclusivism? The answer of these questions will influence what parts of Graham's ministry are worthy of emulation, and which parts of his ministry may lead to consternation. It must be said that these conclusions are only true if Graham's *Hour of Decision* sermons and his books accurately communicate his thoughts and emphases in ministry. If these resources do not accurately convey his theology, then a study of Graham's theology is virtually impossible.

When Graham adjusted the evangelistic mandate of the church to a duty alongside of social responsibility in 1965, it presupposed a move away from the substitutionary atonement. Graham began to include the reconciliation model of the atonement more and more in his messages. In this respect, his theological adjustments were very consistent. Because of his desire to appeal to all churches, he began shedding fundamentalist terminology in the early 1950s. Rather, he quoted neo-orthodox theologians, and may have fallen prey to their question framing—as terminology shapes the question. Graham's gospel seemed to become gradually more simplistic, and less doctrinal and theological. He sought a "positive" gospel,[369] without speaking out against any theological heresy.[370] Graham was left with decrying individual and societal sin, but he could not define the gospel both in positive and negative terms as far as theological heresy—"it means this; it does not mean this." He was left to decrying cultural and individual sin, but would not attack any church doctrine, and even seemed to have avoided certain controversial issues. However, Graham still held to his revivalistic heritage of the invitation system—that was his trademark and kept most evangelicals assuming that his theology had not changed.[371] In his later

---

[369]"To gain a clear understanding of God's attitude toward sin we only have to consider the purpose of Christ's death. The Scripture says, 'Without the shedding of blood there is no forgiveness of sin.' Here is a positive statement that there can be no forgiveness of sin unless our debt has been paid" (Billy Graham, "The Cross and Its Power," 5).

[370]For example, Robert L. Kennedy documented the intense efforts of Graham to gain the acceptance of the Lutheran World Federation in his "Best Intentions: Contacts Between German Pietists and Anglo-American Evangelicals, 1945-1954" (Ph.D. diss., University of Aberdeen, 1990).

[371]An exception to this warm reception were evangelicals on the British Isles. It seems that British evangelicals recognized that Graham at Harringay, London, 1954 was different than the Graham of Earls Court, London, 1966. William Martin, quoting Maurice Rowlandson, explained that Graham did not return to the British Isles again until 1984 (William Martin, *A Prophet with Honor* [New York: Morrow, 1991],

years, Graham's preaching possibly approached a simplistic gospel, a decisionism, and perhaps even inclusivism. These issues will be noted in this section.

A Simplistic Gospel?[372] *Hour of Decision* sermon number 101 was titled "America at the Crossroads" from the "Middle" Graham. Early in the sermon Graham quoted Joshua 7:10-11. He discussed the treachery of Achan and related it to the United States in a principalized way. He stated, "He [Achan] had yielded to the secular rather than the religious. He had declared his love for gold over the love of God, and by that act of greed had jeopardized the safety of the whole nation of Israel."[373] From this statement, Graham then moved to a quote of Charles Malik, president of the United Nations. Graham came back to the issue of materialism, "We have given place to the accursed thing of materialism."[374] Then the bulk of the sermon was an exposition of Edward Gibbon's 1787 *The Decline and Fall of the Roman Empire.* Graham stated, "He gave five reasons why Rome fell, and I would like to give them to you today because these same five reasons are apparent in American life at this time."[375] He then preached the following five points he ascribed to Gibbon:

> First: the rapid increase of divorce. . . .
> Secondly: Gibbon said that Rome fell because of higher and higher taxes, and the spending of public monies for free bread and circuses for the populace. . . .
> Thirdly: Gibbon listed the mad craze for pleasure. . . .
> Fourthly: Gibbon listed the building of gigantic armaments as a contribution to the fall of Rome. . . .
> Lastly: Gibbon listed the decay of religion. . . .[376]

---

325). Iain Murray included a portion of the [British] Evangelical Alliance's 1968 statement which responded negatively to Graham's Earls Court, London, 1966 crusade: "the crusade did not make a lasting effect on the outsider" (Iain Murray, *Evangelicalism Divided,* 57).

[372]This author also considered the use of minimalistic gospel with a question mark as the title for this section.

[373]Billy Graham, "America at the Crossroads," *Hour of Decision Sermons,* no. 101 (Minneapolis: Billy Graham Evangelistic Association, 1958), 3.

[374]Ibid., 5.

[375]Ibid.

[376]Ibid., 6-9.

There was no Scripture mentioned for any of these points. His only biblical reference in these points was a mention of the morals of Sodom and Gomorrah under point one. Thus, using the "decay of religion" in Rome as an illustration Graham went directly from the political situation to a call to commitment. The following quotes the last five paragraphs in this sermon:

> I am convinced that America stands at the crossroads of her national destiny. One road leads to destruction, and the other leads to prosperity and security. At the moment, we are going down the broad road that leads to destruction. We are going the way of Rome rather than the way of the cross.
>
> Many of you will blame the Republicans or the Democrats. It is not the politicians that should take the blame. It is the American people as individuals. We backslide as individuals before we begin to decay as a nation. Fortunately, there is time to repair the breach. We are still on this side of judgment, though time is quickly passing by. God is sounding the warning. "Today, if you will hear His voice, harden not your heart." "Today is the day of salvation." "The Spirit and the Bride say, Come."
>
> Rome's fate need not be ours if we repent and turn to God.
>
> How shall we escape if we neglect so great a salvation?
>
> Thus today the greatest contribution you can make to your nation is to give your life and your heart to Jesus Christ because when you make your decision for Christ, it is America through you making its decision for Christ and trust in God.[377]

The final paragraph of this sermon asked listeners to give their hearts to Christ, yet they had never heard even one gospel verse. Was the gospel in the sermon originally, but edited out? Was it assumed that listeners had heard the gospel through other *Hour of Decision* broadcasts? Or, did Graham feel that the sociological principles of Gibbon on the fall of Rome carried the same weight as Romans 3:23 or some other verse on sin? Perhaps this sermon was an *Hour of Decision* sermon, but it was not typical of the crusade sermons of Billy Graham. Whatever the case, "America at the Crossroads" was an example of a simplistic gospel. And because Graham called for a decision without preaching Christ, it is also an example of decisionism.

The issues brought up in this sermon can be charted as illustrated in Figure 13. Early in Graham's preaching he seemed to know the importance of finding links with culture in his preaching. His early sermons were packed with illustrative material, yet he reminded his listeners that

---

[377]Ibid., 10.

secular truth was not the answer.[378] However, it would seem that "America at a Crossroads" is an example of "Finding truth in culture"—Graham basically preached Edward Gibbon's *The Decline and Fall of the Roman Empire*. In this case the bulk of the truth Graham related in his message was not the supernatural revelation as found in Scripture (which leads to conversion), but the sociological interpretation of Gibbon as to why Rome fell as a secular power (which leads to self-reformation). Perhaps this was an example of Graham's lacking to emphasize the gospel, thus leading to a minimal response.[379] Yet if this was the case, why was this sermon published, as only seven *Hour of Decision* sermons were published in 1958 and the radio program was aired weekly? Thus it seems that Graham felt that the logic of Gibbon in "America at a Crossroads" was powerful enough to call for a decision. Thus sociological analysis usurped the Bible content.

Another way that Graham may have practiced a simplistic gospel is through avoiding speaking out against heretical teaching. William Martin discussed this issue in his biography of Graham:

> Graham's ever-widening acceptance of others who professed to be Christians manifested itself not only in his continued association with the World Council of Churches—he attended its general assembly in New Delhi in 1961 at the council's invitation—but also in an improved relationship with Catholics, especially after John XXIII assumed the papal chair. Following John Kennedy's election, he scrupulously avoided any statements that could be construed as anti-Catholic, a relaxation of wariness that bothered some of Graham's colleagues.[380]

As regards a simplistic gospel, Martin alleged that Graham "scrupulously avoided" negative statements even seemingly in the theological arena if this meant alienating potential listeners. Back in 1947, when discussing annihilationism, Graham listed some who held to this view of final states: "Russellism, Millennial Dawnism, Jehovah's Witnesses, the Watch Tower and Tract Society."[381] When discussing sin Graham warned against idolatry,

---

[378]"Man in his pride, stumbling and fumbling, thinks that somehow he will pull himself out, and that by his own wisdom he can save himself. God warns that this perverted wisdom of man will lead only to destruction and judgment" (Billy Graham, "How Wise Is Man?" *Hour of Decision Sermons*, no. 125 [Minneapolis: Billy Graham Evangelistic Association, 1960], 10).

[379]Haden, "Dr. Graham, Exactly What Is Evangelism," 11.

[380]William Martin, *A Prophet with Honor*, 294.

[381]Billy Graham, "Hell" (1947), 120.

"To bow and worship before a saint of any kind is idolatry, whether that idol be a picture of Christ or an image of the Virgin Mary or a crucifix or the likeness of a saint."[382] He shared that a minister of the gospel must warn of heresy:

> A minister who is true to his calling must warn people against the danger of heresy and false doctrine. Many times he is tempted to soft-pedal because people may misunderstand and he may make enemies.[383]

Thus, avoiding negative statements about false teaching was a notable change in Graham's approach.

Could it be that Graham had given in to some compromise in his preaching of the gospel? How did this impact his preaching of the cross? Was Graham still preaching the "full counsel of God" (cf. Acts 20:27)? Figure 14 seeks to explain a continuum involved in the preaching of the gospel. Truth has two sides. The positive side is a belief in something. The negative side follows necessarily—fundamentalists believed the gospel, and likewise they did not believe contrary doctrine. However, Graham accused strict fundamentalists of emphasizing what they did not believe so greatly, that the gospel was barely perceptible.[384] However, it would seem that when Graham refused to make theological comments which would offend "liberal" Protestants and Roman Catholics, he was moving toward compromise.

The concern of Graham not to offend also impacted his use of illustrations. William Martin discussed Graham's avoidance of speaking against the White House appointment of an ambassador to the Vatican. Martin quoted a personal letter of Graham to President Truman, "I have refused to make any comment on the Vatican appointment because I didn't

---

[382]Billy Graham, "A Midnight Tragedy," 57.

[383]Billy Graham, "Retreat! Stand! Advance!" in *Calling Youth to Christ*, 33.

[384]For example, see Billy Graham, "Hate vs. Love," *Hour of Decision Sermons*, no. 1 (Minneapolis: Billy Graham Evangelistic Association, 1951, 1955), 4-7; "Peace vs. Chaos," *Hour of Decision Sermons*, no. 3 (Minneapolis: Billy Graham Evangelistic Association, 1951), 3-5; ". . .And Have Not Love," *Hour of Decision Sermons*, no. 9 (Minneapolis: Billy Graham Evangelistic Association, 1951), 2, 4; and "The Sins of the Tongue," *Hour of Decision Sermons*, no. 16 (Minneapolis: Billy Graham Evangelistic Association, 1952), 5-6.

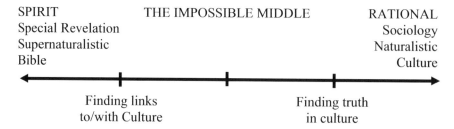

SPIRIT   THE IMPOSSIBLE MIDDLE   RATIONAL

Special Revelation   Sociology

Supernaturalistic   Naturalistic

Bible   Culture

Finding links   Finding truth

to/with Culture   in culture

Fig. 13. Bible and culture continuum: the Spirit and the rational in preaching.

want to be put into a position of opposing you."[385] According to Martin, Graham wanted to encourage Truman to join him on the platform at the Washington, D.C. crusade in early 1952. Thus, not using illustrations was another way that Graham may have simplified his gospel, thus possibly minimizing its impact.

Yet, with his avoiding antagonizing certain groups and his avoiding antagonizing important individuals, and even with his theological adjustments, Graham asserted that his message did not change regardless of the audience:

> My own position was that we should be willing to work with all who were willing to work with us. Our message was clear, and if someone with a radically different theological view somehow decided to join with us in a Crusade that proclaimed Christ as the way of salvation, he or she was the one who was compromising personal convictions, not we.[386]

Robert Ferm, Graham's research assistant, confirmed this with even greater clarity:

> It has been pointed out that the preaching of Mr. Graham has not come under the criticism of the fundamentalists. Most of those who criticize him on the above points [cooperation issues] concede that he has, soundly and faithfully, preached the Word of God, and

---

[385]Martin, *A Prophet with Honor*, 144.

[386]Billy Graham, *Just As I Am*, 303-04.

Fig. 14. The grace-truth continuum: balancing the gospel message.

has called men to salvation as set forth in the Scripture.[387]

Notice that Ferm appealed to the invitation as a proof of orthodoxy—*sola invitation*. Ferm continued elsewhere:

> What about compromise? It has been agreed by both his supporters and opponents that Billy Graham has never trimmed or diluted the message of the Bible. His pronouncements on every fundamental doctrine have been unqualified.[388]

Yet the total depravity of man is certainly a "fundamental doctrine" on which Graham changed before 1957. Also, as was noted by the above, Graham sought to avoid offending potential listeners. Thus, Graham may have adapted his message, and headed down a road which led him toward a simplistic gospel.

The result of Graham's theological openness was a clear change in anthropology, a change of emphasis in soteriology, and a change in the church's mission. The impact of his changes may very well have cost him his authority in the pulpit. A. Skevington Wood wrote on the necessity of preaching the whole counsel of God:

> We cannot deal solely with the surface trivialities of our belief. We must declare the whole counsel of God, and that will involve theological discipline. "You cannot drop the big themes," declared J. H. Jowett, "and create great saints." It is sadly true that, as an

---

[387]Robert Ferm, *Cooperative Evangelism* (Grand Rapids: Zondervan, 1958), 19. Iain Murray stated the same thing of Graham over forty years later, "From this it is clear that, while Graham has professed no change in his doctrinal beliefs, he had come to share the primary idea of ecumenism that there is shared experience of salvation in Christ [with Roman Catholics] which makes all differences of belief a very secondary matter" (Murray, *Evangelicalism Divided*, 69).

[388]Ferm, *Cooperative Evangelism*, 23.

American writer [R. G. Lee] has trenchantly expressed it, "sermonettes only produce Christiannettes."[389]

Returning back to the early years of Graham, one is reminded of his early power in the pulpit. The publishers of *Great Gospel Sermons* wrote these words of Graham in 1949:

> That is a long, long road he has traveled since the little mission service in the South, and he has done well along that road. Done well, because, walking with God, he has spoken, as another has said, 'as one having authority.'[390]

Graham, however, with his moving away from fundamentalist terminology, his hesitancy to speak negatively, his use of modernist theological definitions and terminology, his preaching less theological truth in his sermons, and even sometimes preaching topical sermons related to the Bible or the gospel only by principle, moved towards a more simplistic gospel in the late fifties and early sixties. Can it be noted that the "Later Graham" advocated a decisionism?

Decisionism? When is the invitation system theologically removed from the power of the gospel? When does its appeal become a form of godliness without any power? Graham's early theology advocated the preaching of the substitutionary atonement, not on the basis of Christian principles, but on the basis of the power of the Word of God proclaimed. If it can be shown that Graham moved from his Pietistic view of biblical authority in the gospel proclaimed to a preaching of Christian principles, still assuming the work of the Holy Spirit through these principles, and still calling for an invitation, then it would seem that Graham moved from an urgent invitation to a decisionism. In this latter case, Graham would have a Great Awakening method without the obligatory Great Awakening message.

In our last point we noted that Graham fell prey to a decisionism in his sermon "America at the Crossroads." He had not preached the cross, he had not preached the gospel, he barely referred to the Word of God, and yet he gave an invitation. Perhaps this is one example of what Graham said to Ben Haden:

---

[389]A. Skevington Wood, *Evangelism: Its Theology and Practice* (Grand Rapids: Zondervan, 1966), 24.

[390]Billy Graham, "Atonement" (1949), 40.

I think I have learned the Cross is to be central in our preaching. I don't preach a sermon now unless I bring the message of the Cross—not dragging it in, but making it central in the sermon. Whatever I'm talking on, the death and resurrection of Christ is the heart of the message-and the need for repentance and faith. This is used by the Holy Spirit to bring about conviction.[391]

The emphasis in this quote is on the experiential "I have learned." Perhaps "America at the Crossroads" was an exception to Graham's common style, and it did seem to be the case. However, when Graham's hesitancy to speak against "liberal" Protestants and Roman Catholics is combined with his desire to avoid opposition in his use of illustrations, as well as his desire to preach a positive gospel, the result can very easily lead to a simplistic gospel. It was clear from his sermon on the blood that Graham's movement was not toward theological or biblical depth, but rather to theological and biblical simplicity. It must be noted that simplicity and depth are not mutually exclusive, as can be noted by the simplicity and depth of the Gospel of John.

In the 1957 crusade in New York, Graham made a point to show that conversion was psychologically helpful and spiritually needful. Robert Ferm published *The Psychology of Christian Conversion.* (Westwood, NJ: Revell, 1959). James Jauncey more than a decade later wrote *Psychology for Successful Evangelism* (Chicago: Moody, 1972). Graham opened his sermon on conversion with a description of the psychological necessity of conversion.[392] Graham was doing one of two things in these examples. First, he may have been seeking a link with the audience that would see "conversion" around them every day. Or second, he was seeking to provide a natural or psychological basis for his emphasis on making a decision or the invitation. In this case, it is quite likely that both were involved.[393]

My conclusion is that although Graham softened his view of man, used terminology of the reconciliation model of the atonement, and adapted his view of mission, he did not fall prey to a complete decisionism. Rather, Graham regularly quoted Scripture and emphasized Christ and the cross. Thus, while Graham's message showed signs of being simplistic, and though he showed signs of viewing conversion in psychological terms, he

---

[391]Haden, "Dr. Graham, Exactly What Is Evangelism," 11.

[392]See Billy Graham, "Christian Conversion," 1-3.

[393]Thus Graham originally titled his article for the *Ecumenical Review* as follows, "Biblical Conversion and Why I Give a Public Invitation and Upon What Biblical and Psychological Basis Do We Base the Idea of Conversion" (Billy Graham, "Communicating the Gospel," 1).

likely did not fall prey to decisionism. However, lastly, did Graham succumb to inclusivism?

Inclusivism? Graham made some statements in several interviews which sounded very inclusive. In a 1978 *McCall's* interview, Graham reportedly told James Michael Beam:

> "I used to play God," he acknowledged, "but I can't do that any more. I used to believe that pagans in far-off countries were lost—were going to hell—if they did not have the Gospel of Jesus Christ preached to them. I no longer believe that."[394]

A 1978 *Christianity Today* article clarified Graham's position on salvation outside of the direct hearing of the gospel:

> Explaining the reference to "other ways of recognizing the existence of God," Graham pointed out that the Bible "says all men have some light given by God, both in creation and in human conscience. Whoever sees the footsteps of the Creator in nature can ask for help, and I believe God—in ways we may not fully understand—will give that person further light and bring him to a knowledge of the truth that is in Jesus Christ so that he will be saved. He may use our preaching or he may use any other way he chooses, but ultimately it is God . . . who saves men."[395]

Thus, while Graham maintained that Christ was the only way of salvation, by 1978 he had moved from the universal affirmative that the preaching of the gospel was the only way, to the sub-contrary negative that God could use any way he chose to save men.[396] His presumed openness to salvation

---

[394]James Michael Beam, "I Can't Play God Any More," *McCall's,* January 1978, 156, 158.

[395]"Graham's Beliefs: Still Intact," *Christianity Today,* 13 January 1978, 49.

[396]As an example of the movement of some mainstream churches towards an inclusivism, the 1982 WCC Committee on World Mission and Evangelism, started with the need for the "proclamation of the Gospel" (Michael Kinnamon and Brian E. Cope, eds., *The Ecumenical Movement: An Anthology of Key Texts and Voices* [Geneva: WCC; Grand Rapids: Eerdmans, 1997], 372). Then among a number of other subjects they discussed Witness among People of Living Faiths: "The Spirit of God is constantly at work in ways that pass human understanding and in places that to us are least expected. In entering into a relationship of dialogue with others [of 'Living Faiths'],

outside of the preaching of the gospel *as the only means of salvation* marked a clear change in the theology of Graham. Earlier in his ministry Graham was a vocal exclusivist.[397] Yet his response to the *McCall's* article was a move away from historic evangelicalism, and a change which may logically follow the other theological changes noted up to this point in this book.

Yet after 1978 Graham has continued to preach the gospel and call individuals to repentance and faith. Yes, he no longer spoke of total depravity. Yes, he omitted some of his best sermons on sin and the blood. And yes, his gospel became more inclined to the reconciliation model of the atonement. But he still preached Christ!

Then in 1997 Graham was interviewed by Robert Schuller, and made another inclusive statement:

> [Robert Schuller] "Tell me, what do you think is the future of Christianity?"
>
> [Billy Graham] ". . . And that's what God is doing today, He's calling people out of the world for His name, whether they come from the Muslim world, or the Body of Christ because they've been called by God. They may not even know the name of Jesus but they know in their hearts that they need something that they don't have, and they turn to the only light that they have, and I think that they are saved, and that they are going to be with us in heaven."
>
> [Schuller] "What, what I hear you saying that it's possible for Jesus Christ to come into human hearts and soul and life, even if they've been born in darkness and have never had exposure to the Bible. Is that a correct interpretation of what you're saying?"
>
> [Graham] "Yes, it is, because I believe that. I've met people in various parts of the world in tribal situations, that they have never seen a Bible or heard about the Bible, and never heard of Jesus, but they've believed in their hearts that there was a God, and they've tried to live a life that was quite apart from the surrounding community in which they live."

---

therefore, Christians seek to discern the unsearchable riches of God's and the way he deals with humanity" (ibid., 382).

[397]"It is Christ, and Christ alone, Who can change their hearts and make them new creatures. . . . If the entire world rejects the message of Christ, then all is lost and there is no hope" (Billy Graham, "Ten Minutes to Twelve," *Hour of Decision Sermons,* no. 22 (Minneapolis: Billy Graham Evangelistic Association, 1953), 6, 8). "If you are saved from sin at all, you are saved through personal faith in the gospel of Christ as defined in the Scriptures. Though it may at first seem dogmatic and narrow to you, the fact remains that there is no other way. . . . The Bible says that we are saved when our faith is in this objective fact. The work of Christ is a fact, His cross is a fact, His tomb is a fact, and His resurrection is a fact" (Billy Graham, *Peace with God,* 145-46).

[Schuller] "I'm so thrilled to hear you say this. There's a wideness in God's mercy."

[Graham] "There is. There definitely is"[398]

Graham again affirmed an inclusivism. How can we understand these seemingly inclusivist statements of Graham? One argument against Graham adhering to inclusivity was the fact that he continued to preach crusades after 1978, and that he continued to call people for decision, using his invitation system. Yet this argument may break down if it can be shown that his theology broadened past his financial support-base at some point in time during his sixty years of ministry, leading him to maintain his crusade ministry even though his theology may not have warranted it. A second argument put forward as to why Graham spoke out of place was because of the effects of his Parkinson's disease.[399] This argument may break down as Graham stated the same thing in 1978. However, it is the contention of this author that Graham remained an exclusivist throughout his ministry, even though he made several contrary statements. Although his theology was gradually broadening, Graham's sixty-three plus years of crusade ministry and gospel preaching provide poignant existential proof to his exclusivity.

Early in his ministry Graham was clearly exclusivistic as to salvation in Jesus Christ alone. For example, Graham's sermon, "Three Dimensional Christianity," from the "Middle Graham" period, was clear on exclusivity of salvation, "Nowhere in the Bible does it say that Christ is a way! It says, 'He is the way'—the one and only way."[400] Yet in the final pages of *Just As I Am,* Graham remained tactfully conservative on the issue of inclusiveness and exclusiveness. He began, "What is the message?"[401] Graham went on to begin with God and His love. He shared about the death of Christ on the cross to take away our sins, and about the resurrection. Graham's gospel presentation implied an exclusivism, but did not directly disclaim an inclusivism. One must note Graham's words in three paragraphs of his autobiography to read of his exclusiveness:

---

[398]Robert E. Kofahl, "Billy Graham's Gospel" [on-line]; accessed 27 October 2001; available from http://www.cet.com/~voice/discern/graham.htm#king; Internet.

[399]Billy Graham Evangelistic Association, "Response to the Schuller Show Statement of Billy Graham," unpublished statement, August 25, 1997.

[400]Billy Graham, "Three Dimensional Christianity," *Hour of Decision Sermons,* no. 53 (Minneapolis: Billy Graham Evangelistic Association, 1955), 7.

[401]Billy Graham, *Just As I Am,* 727.

Moreover, God has done everything possible to reconcile us to Himself. He did this in a way that staggers our imagination. In God's plan, by His death on the Cross, Jesus Christ paid the penalty for our sins, taking the judgment of God that we deserve upon Himself when He died on the Cross. Now, by His resurrection from the dead, Christ has broken the bonds of death and opened the way to eternal life for us.

The resurrection also confirms for all time that Jesus was in fact who He said He was: the unique Son of God, sent from Heaven to save us from our sins. Now God freely offers us the gift of forgiveness and eternal life.

Finally, this message is about our response. Like any other gift, God's gift of salvation does not become ours until we accept it and make it our own. God has done everything possible to provide salvation. But we must reach out in faith and accept it.[402]

Thus Graham wrote with an exclusive bent: Christ was the "unique Son of God;" He took the judgment we deserve; He died on the cross; and by His resurrection Christ opened the way for eternal life to those who will receive it.

Therefore it is the conclusion of this researcher that Graham held to an exclusive salvation by faith in Christ alone. Given Graham's tenacity in preaching the gospel and calling for a decision, and given his desire to avoid offending his audience, it would seem possible that Graham would state an opinion not in line with his theology or practice. In fact, his words are in keeping with an exclusive approach to salvation. The remarkable fact about Billy Graham is the length of time that he has been in the limelight and speaking all across the world, and only a few questionable concepts ever came out of his mouth from a theological point-of-view—remarkable! Moving from the issue of salvation, we now move to Graham on the final states.

Judgment

While Graham's October 16, 1949 sermon in Los Angeles was titled "Hellfire and Brimstone,"[403] he later told his audience in 1956 about the turmoil of speaking on hell:

---

[402]Ibid., 728.

[403]"Billy Graham Sermon Series by Decade."

The most unpopular subject a minister can choose is the subject of "Hell." However, I feel that the Spirit of God would have me to deal with this subject and I cannot avoid speaking frankly about it.[404]

Graham spoke similar words in his 1947 sermon on the same subject and by the same title. In fact, Graham in his 1947 sermon gave this warning:

Among those Christians to whom hell means little, Calvary means less. There is less emphasis on redemption by the blood of Christ. There is less teaching about sin, and very little warning of judgment.[405]

In this statement Graham made a link between the doctrine of judgment and the atonement. In fact, as noted by Graham, a change in one's doctrine of the "the blood of Christ," or the substitutionary atonement was associated to a change in the doctrine of eternal conscious punishment. The same links were also noted as we considered the sinfulness of man and the atonement. As noted earlier in this chapter, it seemed that Graham was moving toward a reconciliation model of the atonement. If this were truly the case, then his shift in anthropology and soteriology would also be evident in his doctrine of the final states.

In order to make an assessment of Graham's view of hell, we will consult the following documents: "Hell" (1947); *Peace with God* (pub. 1953); "A Religion of Fire" (1953); "Hell" (1957); "Heaven and Hell" (1969); and *A Biblical Standard for Evangelists* (1984). From these documents, we will seek to establish a historical theology of Graham's doctrine of hell.

In the 1947 sermon titled, "Hell," Graham preached hell as eternal, conscious punishment.[406] The outline of Graham's 1947 sermon consisted of the following format—as included with the text of the sermon:

I.   Objections:
    A.   Universalism
    B.   Annihilation
    C.   Future Probation

---

[404]Billy Graham, "Hell," *Hour of Decision Sermons,* no. 66 (Minneapolis: Billy Graham Evangelistic Association, 1957), 1. This sermon was published in 1956 and copyrighted in 1957.

[405]Billy Graham, "Hell" (1947), 128.

[406]Three years later, in 1950, Graham said, "Fire and Brimstones fell on Sodom and Gomorrah, and Sodom and Gomorrah were destroyed by the judgment hand of God" (Billy Graham, "Will God Spare America?" 122).

II.   The Certainty of Punishment:
    A.   The Bible says so
    B.   All peoples have believed it
    C.   Human experiences teaches it
III.   What Is the Nature of Hell?
IV.   Who Is Going There?[407]

This 1947 sermon included a list of eleven verses under "The Bible says so."[408] In fact, these verses were repeated in exactly the same order in Graham's 1953 *Peace with God*,[409] with the exception of dropping Mark 9:43-44, "Where the worm does not die and the fire is not quenched." By the time Graham preached this sermon on 1957, he included only three verses on hell, two from the list of eleven, Matthew 5:22 ("hell fire") and 25:41 ("everlasting fire"), and a new verse which uses the word "destroys," Matthew 10:28.[410]

    The 1953 version also introduced a new point in Graham's outline, "Hell on Earth." In this section, Graham discussed the difficulty of life on earth that some call "hell," a concept he developed in greater detail in his 1957 sermon. The concept of "hell on earth" coincides with Bushnell's doctrine of the retributive causes of nature or "natural retribution."[411] Following this excursus, Graham discussed four words for "hell" in the Bible—*hades, sheol, tartarus,* and *gehenna*. These four words were discussed in all three of his sermons. Then the 1947 Graham continued his Bible exposition, whereas these sections were not found in either *Peace with God* or in the 1957 sermon. As noted in his sermon "A Scarlet Thread," there was almost double the Bible exposition in his 1947 sermons as in his 1956-1957 parallel sermons. His 1947 sermon on hell continued, "Let's find out how God's Holy Word describes this awful place . . . ."[412] Graham then

---

[407]Billy Graham, "Hell" (1947), 119-25.

[408]Following are the eleven Scripture portions quoted on hell: Luke 16:24; Matt 5:22; 13:41-42, 49-50; 25:41; Mark 9:43-44; Matt 3:12; 2 Thes 1:8; Rev 14:10-11; 20:14-15; 21:8 (Ibid., 121-23).

[409]Billy Graham, *Peace with God,* 78-79.

[410]"And do not fear those who kill the body, but are unable to kill the soul; but rather fear Him who is able to destroy both body and soul in hell" (Matt 10:28).

[411]"But the judgment of the world under Christianity is made necessary, by the fact that, in a mixed experience under law and grace, where the penal order of nature is restricted, tempered, mitigated, by the supernatural interactions of grace, no punishment takes place in the exact manner and degree that it would under natural retribution, pure and simple" (Bushnell, *The Vicarious Sacrifice,* 353-54).

[412]Billy Graham, "Hell" (1947), 128.

listed twenty additional verses which gave biblical descriptions of hell.[413] These verses were also missing in the subsequent sermons and documents in question.

Other than the differences already mentioned, two striking points differentiate the 1947 and the 1957 sermons. The 1957 sermon spoke primarily of hell as separation from God:

> Eternal death means eternal separation from God, which Jesus termed hell. . . .
>
> Essentially and basically, hell is separation from God. . . .
>
> However, the Bible indicates that after death, there is also an appointment with God on the judgment day and that men who have deliberately ignored God during their lifetime will be banished from His presence. . . .
>
> Hell, whatever else it means, is death and separation from God. If you are out of Christ and away from God now, in many ways you are in hell; for hell is separation from God.[414]

Hell as separation from God coincides with sin as alienation from God, leading to the astonishing statement, "you are in hell; for hell is separation from God." Graham's view played into the reconciliation model of the atonement—broken relationships that need to be mended by the Incarnation and crucifixion. Hell as separation also coincides with the teaching of the Roman Catholic church on hell.[415] By defining of hell as separation from

---

[413]The twenty verses and their corresponding description of hell were: "1. Rev. 20:15—The lake of fire; 2. Ps. 11:6—A horrible tempest; 3. Ps. 18:5—A place of sorrows; 4. Matt. 13:42—A place of wailing; 5. Matt. 8:12—A place of weeping; 6. Matt. 13:41-42—A furnace of fire; 7. Luke 16:23—A place of torment; 8. Rev. 20:11-12—A place of filthiness; 9. Rev. 16:11—A place of cursing; 10. Matt. 8:12—A place of outer darkness; 11. Rev. 14:11—A place of unrest; 12. Luke 16:27—A place where people pray; 13. Luke 16:24—A place where people scream for mercy; 14. Matt. 25:46—A place of everlasting punishment; 15. Matt. 25:41—A place prepared for the devil and his angels; 16. Luke 16:24—A place where one begs for a drop of water; 17. Isa. 33:11—A place where one's breath is a living flame; 18. Luke 16:24—A place where one is tormented with fire; 19. Rev. 21:8—A place where one is tormented with brimstone; 20. Luke 16: 25—A place of memory; We need not add to or take away from this description" (Ibid.).

[414]Billy Graham, "Hell" (1957), 7, 9, 10, 10.

[415]"To die in mortal sin without repenting and accepting God's merciful love means remaining separated from him for ever by our own free choice. This state of definitive self-exclusion from communion with God and the blessed is called "hell." . . . The chief punishment of hell is separation from God. . . ." (*Catechism of the Catholic Church,* paragraphs 1033 and 1035, 269-70).

God, Graham adjusted his early approach to this difficult topic. Graham ended a series of questions with his main transition question: "why should we shun it [hell]?" His four points were:

> First, we should shun hell because of God's warnings concerning it. . . .
> Secondly, we should shun hell because of Christ's estimate of it.
> . . .
> Thirdly, we should shun hell because of what it cost God to save men from it. . . .
> Finally, we should shun hell because God did not create man for it.[416]

Graham's 1957 sermon emphasized a human decision to "shun hell," as it was not a good place to be. Gone was the litany of verses on fire and brimstone, and weeping and gnashing of teeth. Hell, at this point in Graham's theology, was best understood as separation from God. The differences between Graham's 1947 and 1957 sermons are amazing, and they point to the same change that was noted in Graham's view of man's sin and the issue of salvation.

Graham's 1953 sermon "A Religion of Fire" spoke of the property of fire as three active rays: the actinic ray, the chloric ray, and the luminiferous ray. In this sermon Graham never mentioned the concept of judgment as fire. In fact, in his point on the actinic ray, or heat property of light, Graham mentioned heat as bringing warmth to a cold world[417] and the warmth of God's love.[418] Hence, it would seem that Graham's communicated theology of judgment changed between 1947 and 1953. His theology moved from the substitutionary *toward* the reconciliation model of the atonement.

In his 1969 sermon, "Heaven and Hell," preached at Madison Square Gardens, Graham began with Psalm 23:6, ". . . I will dwell in the house of the Lord for ever." Then he read from Matthew 7:13-14, "Enter ye by the straight gate. . . ." His thematic sentence was followed by a brief introduction:

---

[416]Billy Graham, "Hell" (1957), 6-8.

[417]"This warmth—this heat—without which there would be no life, is but a material manifestation of the spiritual warmth which God bestows upon a cold, dark, frigid world" (Billy Graham, "A Religion of Fire," *Hour of Decision Sermons,* no. 29 [Minneapolis: Billy Graham Evangelistic Association, 1953], 2).

[418]"Jesus emphasized that God is love and warmth. In Christ we see the true picture of God's love and grace" (ibid.). Later he added, "This unquestionably referred to spiritual warmth, rather than the fire of judgment" (ibid., 3).

Jesus Christ taught that there are two roads of life. He taught there are two masters. You are either mastered by self or you are mastered by God, and He said you cannot serve both at the same time. And He said that there are two destinies, heaven and hell.[419]

Graham then defined hell for his audience:

Now what does that mean? What do all of those passages mean? Whatever Hell may be, and there are many mysteries, and I don't intend to solve them all—whatever Hell may mean, it is separation from God.[420]

Graham then continued with his list of words that describe hell: fire, darkness, and death. These words were quite a revision of his 1947 list of twenty descriptors.[421] Fire he described with a question:

Could it be that the fire Jesus talked about is an eternal search for God that is never quenched? Is that what it means? That, indeed, would be hell. To be away from God forever, separate from his presence.[422]

Graham's second descriptor of hell was darkness. He explained darkness as follows, "What does it mean? There again, the darkness is separation from

---

[419]Billy Graham, "Heaven and Hell," in *The Challenge: Sermons from Madison Square Gardens* (Garden City, NY: Doubleday, 1969), 71.

[420]Ibid., 74.

[421]"Let's find out how God's Holy Word describes this awful place: 1. Rev. 20:15—The lake of fire; 2. Ps. 11:6—A horrible tempest; 3. Ps. 18:5—A place of sorrows; 4. Matt. 13:42—A place of wailing; 5. Matt. 8:12—A place of weeping; 6. Matt. 13:41-42—A furnace of fire; 7. Luke 16:23—A place of torment; 8. Rev. 20:11-12—A place of filthiness; 9. Rev. 16:11—A place of cursing; 10. Matt. 8:12—A place of outer darkness; 11. Rev. 14:11—A place of unrest; 12. Luke 16:27—A place where people pray; 13. Luke 16:24—A place where people scream for mercy; 14. Matt. 25:46—A place of everlasting punishment; 15. Matt. 25:41—A place prepared for the devil and his angels; 16. Luke 16:24—A place where one begs for a drop of water; 17. Isa. 33:11—A place where one's breath is a living flame; 18. Luke 16:24—A place where one is tormented with fire; 19. Rev. 21:8—A place where one is tormented with brimstone; 20. Luke 16: 25—A place of memory. We need not add to or take away from this description" (Billy Graham, "Hell" [1947], 128).

[422]Billy Graham, "Heaven and Hell," 75.

God, God is light. Separation from light is darkness."[423] Graham's third and last descriptive word for hell was "death." Graham stated:

> God is life. Hell is death to the spirit, death to the soul, separation from God, "Death and hell were cast into the lake of fire." This is the second death, says the Scripture.[424]

Graham then exhorted his audience that God does not take delight in sending people to hell. He continued emphasizing the free will of man:

> If you are lost, and if you go to hell, it will be by your own deliberate choice, because God never meant that you go there. It is your decision. Now that is a terrifying thought, and it should disturb all of us.[425]

Graham's 1969 sermon, "Heaven and Hell," exemplified that he continued preaching hell as separation from God, the position that he had advanced in his 1957 sermon, "Hell."

In his 1984 exposition of the "Amsterdam Affirmations," Graham expanded on Affirmation IV, "God loves every human being, who, apart from faith in Christ, is under God's judgment and destined for hell."[426] In providing a context for his exposition on hell, he provided an interesting theological paragraph:

> Sin, like an infectious disease, has spread throughout the human race (Romans 5:12). Its root has been variously expressed as rebellion, selfishness, pride, egotism, and unbelief. The consequences or the "wages of sin" is death, both spiritual and physical (Romans 6:23). And yet God, in infinite grace and mercy, still loves us enough to provide a way for our salvation and the satisfaction of His justice (Romans 3:16-22).[427]

This paragraph set the theological context for Graham's explanation of hell. Graham spoke of sin as an "infectious disease," and he described that

---

[423]Ibid.

[424]Ibid.

[425]Ibid., 75-76. These statements sound like James Denney on the natural consequence of sin (Denney, 216).

[426]Billy Graham, *A Biblical Standard for Evangelists*, 41.

[427]Ibid., 44.

atonement as a "satisfaction of justice." Then Graham went into the doctrine of hell, beginning with a disclaimer:

> Hell is not the most popular of preaching topics. I don't like to preach on it. But I must if I am to proclaim the whole counsel of God. We must not avoid warning of it. The most outspoken messages on hell, and the most graphic references to it, came from Jesus Himself. He spoke of hell as "outer darkness" where there will be "weeping and gnashing of teeth" (Matthew 8:12; 24:51; 25:30). He contrasts "everlasting punishment" with "life eternal" (Matthew 25:46). He describes hell as a place of torment and agony and fire (Luke 16:23-24).
>
> Jesus used three words to describe hell. The first is "darkness." The Scripture teaches that God is light (1 John 1:5). Hell will be the opposite. Those who have rejected Christ will go into outer darkness (Matthew 8:12). The second word He used to describe hell is "death." God is life. Man is separated from the life of God and endures eternal or the second death. The third word that He used is "fire." Jesus used this symbol over and over. This could be literal fire, as many believe. Or it could be symbolic. God does have fires that do not burn. And also there is the figurative use of fire in the Bible. For example, in the epistle of James we read that the tongue "is set on fire of hell" (James 3:6). That doesn't mean that the tongue has literal combustion. I've often thought that this fire could possibly be a burning thirst for God that is never quenched. What a terrible fire that would be—never to find satisfaction, joy, or fulfillment! God takes no delight in people going to hell. He never meant that anyone would ever go to hell. He created it for the devil and his angels (Matthew 25:41). But those who persist in going the devil's way and obeying the devil instead of God are going to end up in hell.[428]

Several points may be made about Graham's 1984 definition of hell written and distributed to a worldwide audience of evangelists. First, he included the phrase "a place of torment and agony and fire"—harkening back to his 1947 description. Second, he used the same three words as found in his 1969 sermon, "Heaven and Hell," in a different order. Third, while leaving open the possibility of hell as literal fire, he expounded the view that the Bible's use of fire was probably figurative. Fourth, he stated, "God never meant that anyone would go to hell." This counters such passages that speak of people in hell by the description of their sins (e.g., Rev 21:8). Therefore, Graham's change of heart on hell, which primarily took place between 1953

---

[428]Ibid., 45-46.

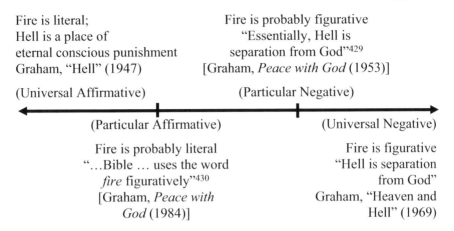

Fig. 15. Graham on hell.

and 1956, continued through 1984. Graham's thoughts on hell may by charted as shown in Figure 15. As has been shown and as he did on other conservative theological issues, Graham began to work his way around the square of opposition. Two points come to mind when observing these changes. First, they came in the early fifties. Second, his change began with the doctrine of hell (1953), moved to man's sin (1955), impacted the atonement (1957), and finally adjusted the mission of the church (1965).

Therefore, while Graham faithfully preached the gospel for over sixty years, there were some notable changes in his theology. His view of man's sin moved from total depravity to the "Two Faces of Man." His view of the atonement moved from the substitutionary theory *toward* the reconciliation model. And his view of judgment moved from eternal fire to

---

[429]"Others ask, 'Does the Bible teach literal fire in hell?' There is no doubt that the Bible many times uses the word *fire* figuratively. However, God does have a fire that burns and yet does not consume. . . . But whether it be literal or figurative does not effect its reality. If there is no fire then God is using symbolic language to indicate something that could be far worse" (Billy Graham, *Peace with God* [Garden City, NY: Doubleday, 1953], 77).

[430]"Others ask, 'Does the Bible teach literal fire in hell?' *If it is not literal fire, it is something worse. Jesus would not have exaggerated.* There is no doubt that the Bible many times uses the word *fire* figuratively. However, God does have a fire that burns and yet does not consume. . . . But whether it be literal or figurative does not effect its reality. If there is no fire, then God is using symbolic language to indicate something that could be far worse" (Billy Graham, *Peace with God,* rev. ed. [Garden City, NY: Doubleday, 1953, 1984], 81; the two italicized sentences were added in the 1984 revision).

eternal "separation" from God's presence. These changes early in his worldwide ministry are noted in humble acknowledgement of Graham's many years of obedience to the Great Commission through preaching the gospel to more people than anyone in the history of the church.

While keeping this theological analysis in mind, it is clear that some things did not change in the ministry of Graham. He continued to preach the deity of Christ. Graham continued to preach the cross of Christ. Graham continued to preach the atonement of Christ. Graham continued to preach against individual sin. Graham continued to preach heaven and hell. Graham continued to call people to salvation and invite them to get right with God. Graham continued to quote Scripture. Graham continued to unite churches for the purpose of evangelism. Graham continued to train church members in sharing their faith. And there is no doubt that because his faithfulness and tenacity in proclaiming the gospel there are multiple tens of thousands of individuals today who are Christians because they heard the gospel, and were called to repent and believe by Billy Graham. However, Graham made some significant theological moves in his ministry. Yet this author feels it important to offer a note of gratitude for the faithfulness with which Billy Graham discharged doing the work of an evangelist.

In conclusion, we will take a historical excursion and listen to the unusual urgency and unique sincerity of the young Graham as he preached in 1950 crowd:

> God's mercy is staying and holding His hand back for maybe one more year. We may have another year, maybe two years to work for Jesus Christ, and ladies and gentlemen, I believe it's all going to be over. Listen to me: I said a year ago that I believed we had five years. I said in Los Angeles one year ago that we had five years. People laughed; some sneered. I'd like to revise that statement and say that we may have two years. Two years, and it's all going to be over. *Either we shall have revival or judgment is going to fall upon this nation,* and the only thing which is keeping back the judgment hand of God, tonight, is the mercy of our God.[431]

Similarly, Graham exhorted the Los Angeles crowd in 1949:

> I don't believe there is a more wicked town in all the world than Los Angeles. One of these days the wrath of God is going to be poured out. Some of these people that laugh at prayer and revival meetings will change their minds. Brother, this old tent won't hold the people trying to get in. Those who now refuse Christ will come and

---

[431]Billy Graham, "Will God Spare America?" 119.

the houses of God will be filled. You won't have to advertise in the newspapers; you won't have to spend money on the radio to get people in; you won't have to have spot announcements; you won't have to have big signs. Brother, they will be coming in swarms and droves and there will be overflow services in the biggest buildings in town. People will be trying to get to God, but I'm afraid their praying will be too late![432]

And people responded to the message to pray for revival and give their lives to Christ.

Finally, Graham shared the mission and vision that fueled his sixty-three years of preaching the gospel at the evangelism conference of the 1957 Baptist General Convention of Texas:

We must aggressively, with fervor, energy, fire and vision, carry to them the authoritative message that Jesus Christ died to forgive sins, but He rose again and He is a living Christ who is coming back again someday.[433]

---

[432]Billy Graham, "The Resurrection of Jesus Christ," in *Revival in Our Time* (Wheaton, IL: Van Kampen Press, 1950), 141.

[433]Billy Graham, "The World Need and Evangelism," 27.

CHAPTER 5

COOPERATION

Do you know what prayer implies? Prayer implies that we must be in one accord. That means we can't have divisions among us. That means that if I am a Presbyterian or you are a Baptist, or if I am a Baptist or a Pentecostal, regardless of denomination, we have to forget our differences—forget any minor points of argument and join together around the cross of the Lord Jesus Christ. We must unite in prayer and supplication to the Lord, and God will send a revival. That means that we have to love one another, and our hearts must be bound together. When we love one another, there won't be any pride. When we love one another, there won't be any jealousy. When we love one another, there won't be any envy. When we love one another, there won't be any gossip. When we really love one another, there won't be any of these sins, because love binds us together and presents us to God in the purity of Christ.[1]

This call to prayer and unity was central to the success of Graham's 1949 "Christ for Greater Los Angeles" campaign. The audience resonated with the sincerity of the young Graham as he encouraged listeners, "we have to forget our differences—forget any minor points of argument and join together around the cross of the Lord Jesus Christ."[2] Months before Los Angeles, Graham had completed what he said was his worst ever crusade in Altoona, Pennsylvania—one in a saga of battles he faced because of strict fundamentalism. Then in Los Angeles, Graham insisted that "they were to try to broaden church support to include as many churches and denominations as possible."[3] He added, "The committee, I felt, represented too limited an evangelical constituency to make an

---

[1]Billy Graham, "We Need Revival," *Revival in Our Time: The Story of the Billy Graham Evangelistic Campaigns Including Six of His Sermons* (Wheaton, IL: Van Kampen, 1950), 77-78.

[2]Ibid, 77.

[3]Billy Graham, *Just As I Am* (New York: Harper Collins, 1997), 144.

impact."[4] Graham explained:

> "I stand upon the brink of absolute fear and trembling when I think we might come to Los Angeles with only a small handful of churches," I wrote in February 1949. "The city of Los Angeles will not be touched unless the majority of the churches are actively back of this campaign."
>
> My limited experience had already shown me that without the cooperation of the local churches and their pastors, not only would attendance suffer but so would the follow-up of new Christians.
>
> One of my objectives was to build the church in the community. I did not simply want the audience to come from the churches. I wanted to leave something behind in the very churches themselves.[5]

Thus forty-eight years later, Graham explained the view of cooperation which prompted him to ask for broader church support of the 1949 "Christ for Greater Los Angeles." Graham's vision was broader than the individual churches sponsoring him. His vision was for the city of Los Angeles. His objective was for citywide revival.

Could it be that nestled in his greatest asset was also Graham's greatest weakness—his flaw? Undoubtedly, Graham's vision was his greatest asset. His vision was larger than a local church, a city, or a nation—his vision was for a worldwide ministry perhaps as Torrey Johnson had communicated to him. His vision was for evangelicalism. His vision was for Protestantism. His vision was for world Christianity.

Also encapsulated in his vision was revival. As a sociology major, he spoke often in his early years of social transformation as a result of the salvation of individuals within a group or culture. He recalled to his hearers the benefits of revival being a list of social improvements. Thus, while maintaining a church-centered and church-oriented approach to crusades, Graham's view was larger than the churches themselves. His view of the lost in a city was broader than any local church. His view also included the social abuses of the city that needed to be rectified. In his opening sermon of the 1949 "Christ for Greater Los Angeles" campaign, Graham stated:

> Finally, a revival brings tremendous social implications. Do you know what came out of past revivals? The abolishment of slavery came out of revival. The abolishment of child labor came out of revival. When the Wesleys preached in England, people were working

---

[4]Ibid.

[5]Ibid., 145.

ninety hours a week! As a result of that revival, sixty working hours became standard, and our great trade unions were organized. Did you know that the Y.M.C.A., the Salvation Army, most of our charity organizations, many of our educational institutions, slum clearance programs, the Sunday School, Christian reform and Women's Suffrage are revival results?[6]

He recalled the same benefits of revival in his sermon at Westminster in 1952, along with a warning:

> Do you believe it can happen in Britain? Is there a need in Britain ? That is the first question. There is a need—we grant that. What is the message? It is the Word—the holy Word of God. That is the answer to our problem. There is no other answer. What is the method? You will have to get before God to find out the method. But I want to tell you this as a closing word: unless you have a spiritual awakening in Great Britain, you can say good-bye to the old Britain that you once knew. Communism is a spiritual force and it is moving with all of its dark and evil strength in every direction. The only thing that will stop it will be a spiritual force—the glorious light of the Gospel of Christ.[7]

Thus, armed with personal interest, the powerful words of a young preacher, and the corresponding belief in a gospel that can transform lives, Graham persuaded city after city that they needed revival that reached into the very social fabric of the people. Graham's tremendous vision for revival fueled his preaching, his ministry, and his rise to fame.

And it was not long after Los Angeles 1949 that Billy Graham became an icon among evangelicals. In 1947 Graham had assumed the presidency of the Northwestern Schools in Minneapolis, Minnesota, fulfilling the deathbed wish of its founding President W. B. Riley.[8] In 1949 Graham's sermon on the blood was included in *Great Gospel Sermons*.[9]

---

[6]Billy Graham, "We Need Revival," 79.

[7]Billy Graham, "The Work of an Evangelist," in *Introducing Billy Graham: The Work of an Evangelist. An Address Given in the Assembly Hall of the Church House, Westminster, on 20th March, 1952,* ed. Frank Colquhoun (London: World Evangelical Alliance, 1953), 30.

[8]See William Vance Trollinger, Jr., "God's Empire: William Bell Riley and Midwestern Fundamentalism" (Ph.D. diss., University of Wisconsin, Madison, 1990).

[9]Billy Graham, "Atonement," *Great Gospel Sermons,* Vol. II, "Contemporary" (London: Fleming H. Revell, 1949), 41-54.

And in 1950 he was already being compared with Billy Sunday.[10] His growing popularity was evident.

Yet Graham's greatest gift led him to make certain decisions in the early fifties that had ramifications for his entire ministry. Graham was to "tow the line" between grace and truth his entire ministry. While clearly seeking to maintain both, we have noted that Graham's theology adapted subtly to accommodate a broader constituency. Thus, when pushed to the limit, Graham seemed to emphasize "grace" over "truth," while never flagging in his crusade methodology. This movement toward including a broader constituency was both the first and the final major change in the ministry of Graham. It was a natural outflow of his early decision to preach a positive gospel and include as many churches as possible. Graham chose to avoid fighting "negative" battles for the truth and alienate potential cooperating churches and audiences. Then toward the end of his ministry, Paul VI noted that "popular religiosity [e.g. Graham] can be more and more for multitudes of our people a true encounter with God in Jesus Christ."[11]

The result of his early choice? On the positive side, Graham was able to preach the gospel to more people than anyone else in church history. He was able to gather theologians, evangelists, and Christian workers from more countries and languages than had ever been assembled in one place in the history of the world. And, quite likely, few individuals in church history have been privileged to lead more individuals to a saving knowledge of Jesus Christ.

Yet on the negative side, Graham increasingly seemed to move toward a simplistic gospel in order to maintain as wide a constituency as possible. He sometimes, though rarely, gave invitations when he had not presented a biblically-based gospel. And later in his ministry he even sounded inclusive in certain interviews. Richard Pierard wrote of this ecumenical trend in the ministry of Billy Graham:

> By insisting upon local-level ecumenical support for his various crusades, he broke out of a fundamentalist constriction and gradually

---

[10]"Not since the revival days of Billy Sunday has anything happened in Boston comparable to this" (Harld J. Ockenga, "Revival Visits Boston," *Revival in Our Time* [Wheaton, IL: Van Kampen Press, 1950], 6).

[11]Paul VI, *Evangelii Nuntiandi: On Evangelization in the Modern World,* 8 December 1975, section 48.

developed connections with a wide variety of expressions of Christianity.[12]

He continued: "He [Graham] went on to build bridges to the Jewish and Roman Catholic Communities."[13] Pierard gave two reasons for Graham's increasing openness to non-Protestant communities: greater travel and thereby association with persons of different theological persuasions, and a commitment to opening doors for the preaching of the gospel. Pierard summarized, "Thus, Graham is as fully committed as ever to his evangelistic mission and is willing to take whatever risks are necessary to gain new opportunities to preach. . . ."[14] An example of this growing inclusivism was found in Graham's words spoken to Robert Schuller in 1997. He told Schuller:

> I lost a very dear friend, and since that time, the whole relationship between me and my work, and you and your work, and the Roman Catholic Church has changed. They open their arms to welcome us and we have the support of the Catholic Church almost everywhere we go. And I think that we must come to the place where we keep our eyes on Jesus Christ, not on what denomination or what church or what group we belong to.[15]

In this quote, Graham stated the possibly nebulous, "keep our eyes on Christ," as a rallying point for inter-denominational work. What was meant by this statement? Clearly a study of cooperation requires definition as well as explanation. We will note that later in his ministry Graham opened the door to cooperation with Roman Catholic leaders.[16] This cooperation

---

[12]Richard V. Pierard, "From Evangelical Exclusivism to Ecumenical Openness: Billy Graham and Sociopolitical Issues," in *Journal of Ecumenical Studies* 20, no. 3 (1983): 427.

[13]Ibid.

[14]Ibid., 428.

[15]Robert E. Kofahl, "Billy Graham's Gospel" [on-line]; accessed 27 October 2001; available from http://www.cet.com/~voice/discern/graham.htm#king; Internet.

[16]Bishop Lawrence Welsh, "Catholics and a Billy Graham Crusade," *National Catholic Reporter,* 2 September 1982, 185-186. The arrangement between the crusade and the Catholic diocese was described in an editorial note prior to Bishop Lawrence Welsh's letter, "He [Bishop Welsh] said organizers of the crusade and officials of the diocese were developing plans for cooperation to follow-up people who ask during the crusade to be contacted by the Catholic Church. 'This follow-up—which is more

outside of evangelicalism and Protestantism was a major paradigm shift for Graham. But it is best understood as a succession of small changes. These changes will be the subject of this chapter.

In order to study the subject of cooperation, and specifically as it relates to the ministry of Billy Graham, we will divide our brief study into four headings. First, by way of introductory concerns, we will introduce the subject of cooperation, the complexity of cooperation, and some historical views of cooperation. Secondly, we will examine ecclesiology as it relates to crusade evangelism. Thirdly, we will note Graham's approach to separation and cooperation by way of several phases in his ministry.

Introductory Concerns

What level of cooperation should there be in the fulfillment of the Great Commission? The following quote from Norman Geisler and John MacKenzie portrayed the need for clear definition:

> Billy Graham has set the example for evangelical cooperation with Catholics in mass evangelism without compromising the basic gospel message. Despite ecclesiastical and doctrinal differences (see Part Two), there are some important things many Catholics and evangelicals hold in common not the least of which is the good news that Jesus died for our sins and rose again. Thus, there seems to be no good reason why there should not be increased ways of mutual encouragement in fulfilling our Lord's Great Commission (Matt. 28: 18-20). Catholics and evangelicals do not have to agree on everything in order to agree on some things—even something important. We do not need to agree on the authority of the church before we can cooperate in proclaiming the power of the uncompromising gospel (Rom. 1:16).[17]

What is meant by "fulfilling our Lord's Great Commission"? Are not follow-up, discipleship, and church planting part of fulfilling the Great Commission? Perhaps Geisler and Mackenzie defined "proclaiming the power of the uncompromising gospel" only in terms of cooperative crusade evangelism. However, when they wrote "fulfilling our Lord's Great Commission" the entire spectrum of the Great Commission was brought to

---

important than the crusade itself—often goes unnoticed and unpublicized as part of a Billy Graham crusade,' Welsh stated."

[17]Norman L. Geisler and Ralph E. MacKenzie, *Roman Catholics and Evangelicals: Agreements and Differences* (Grand Rapids, MI: Baker Book House, 1995), 428-29.

the table. In this light a question naturally follows: can a Baptist preacher partner to plant a church with a Jesuit priest? If so, what will the church be called? What will it teach about the sacraments and salvation? How will it reach its first converts, through personal evangelism or through getting a building permit? Will it look to Rome for an authoritative interpretation of Scripture and Tradition, or will it remain consistent with the Reformation's dictum—*sola Scriptura*? There are unending questions in this issue. This dilemma shows the need for clear definitions and parameters in the issues of cooperation, separation, and ecumenism.

The American church seems to have been strongly influenced in its unifying efforts by H. Richard Niebuhr. Niebuhr wrote, "Denominationalism in the Christian church is such an unacknowledged hypocrisy."[18] Building on the Liberal Niebuhr's understanding of ecclesiology, the evangelical Robert Webber continued this attack on sectarianism while also calling for unity:

> My conviction is that evangelicalism needs revitalizing. Her strong point is her grasp of the central message of the Christian faith and the zeal with which she proclaims it. Her weakness lies the lack of a truly historic substance of the Christian gospel. Therefore, the urgent necessity of evangelical Christianity is to become a more historic expression of the faith. It is my conviction that only through an understanding of the traditional shape of Christianity will evangelicals be able to provide a vision for the future which will bring all evangelicals together, and make Christianity a more powerful influence in the life of the world.[19]

Why was there a need to "bring all evangelicals together"? Was Webber not falling prey to Niebuhr's question-framing of fifty years earlier? Webber answered this question by quoting the Chicago Call's last point, "A Call to Church Unity":

> We deplore the scandalous isolation and separation of Christians from one another. We believe such division is contrary to Christ's explicit desire for unity among his people and impedes the witness of

---

[18]H. Richard Niebuhr, *The Social Sources of Denominationalism* (New York: Henry Holt and Company, 1929), 6.

[19]Webber, *Common Roots: A Call to Evangelical Maturity* (Grand Rapids: Zondervan, 1978), 34. Three points may be made with regard to this quote and missions. First, the urgency is no longer sharing the gospel, it is church unity. Second, the call is to a historic expression of the faith, rather than a New Testament expression of the faith. Third, the end is more influence in the world, rather than focusing on saving souls in the world to come.

the church in the world. Evangelicalism is too frequently characterized by an ahistorical, sectarian mentality. We fail to appropriate the catholicity of historic Christianity, as well as the breadth of the biblical revelation.[20]

Yes, Webber felt that denominationalism was "ahistorical" and "sectarian." Yet, was denominationalism truly "scandalous isolation"? Was it contrary to Christ's explicit desire? Or on the other hand, did denominationalism provide theological clarity, integrity, and cohesiveness? While brotherly love was certainly needed among biblically-based churches, did not denominationalism provide theological safeguards against heresy? Fortunately, there is a historical precedent for such discussions, and a historical reason that denominations were formed.

The need for denominational distinctives was discussed in the early eighteenth century by Count Ludwig Von Zinzendorf.[21] In 1831 an American writer by the penname of "Unity" discussed the need for unity and denominational distinctives:

For myself, I look forward, even in the most prosperous period of the Christian Church, to the total abolition of *party feeling* in religion. The respective fields of action, with the formal enclosures of each, among the friends of the Saviour, it is presumed, will ever remain. I cannot see that the charity and holiness of Millennial Days, will supercede the existing distinctions among believers. The fences which now divide their respective territories will continue to stand long after each shall have been brightened with a glorious harvest. . . . I am, therefore, not displeased, when I learn, as I often do, that

---

[20]Ibid., 256.

[21]"It has been thirty and several years that I began to receive through the preaching of the cross a deep impression of grace. The desire to bring souls to Christ seized my heart, that desired nothing but the Lamb. Thus to Halle, I searched for Him in unity; at Wittenberg, through ethics; in Dresden, by philosophy; later on also, since the happy founding of the Herrnhut community I approached Him through the simple doctrine of His sufferings and His death. . . . I have always acted solely in the love of Jesus and without looking back. . . . I plan to bring as many souls as I can to the knowledge of sin and of grace. . . . At last I also had the plan to reunite all the children of God who are now seperated one from another, and I pursued this without interuption from 1717 to 1739; but now I renounce this, for not only do I see that I am getting nowhere, but I am beginning to notice that there is in this a mystery of divine providence" (Ludwig Von Zinzendorf, "Letter written from Bâle in 1740," Cited by F. Bovet, *Zinzendorf* VI:31; taken from Jules-Marcel Nicole, *Précis d'Histoire de l'Eglise,* 3rd edition [Nogent-sur-Marne, France: Editions de l'institut Biblique, 1982], 211; translation mine).

Baptists, Presbyterians and Methodists can meet on common grounds of Christian co-operation, to help the Lord against the common foe.[22]

While "Unity" saw the place for co-operation among "friends of the Saviour" in areas of common ground, he also saw the need for the theological fences that denominations provide. Especially in the case of crusade evangelism, unity plays an important role. Yet how could this unity be nurtured while denominationalism is not maligned?

Two participants in the 1888 "World Missionary Conference" discussed the quandary of unity in their closing remarks. A. J. Gordon, of the American Baptist Missionary Union stated, "You shatter a mirror, and everyone of the fragments will reflect a full-orbed sun. Break the Church of God into a score of pieces, and yet we find that everyone of these fragments in this great Convention has mirrored a full-orbed Christ."[23] The words of

---

[22]"Unity, "On the Union of Different Denominations," *The Christian Index,* 23 July 1831, 1.

[23]Because of the importance of the context, a more lengthy quote is included as follows: "Well, first of all, we have found a Church divided in form, but united in spirit. I hope you will not make haste to quarrel with me, but rather wait for my explanation, when I say, that I believe that this is God's providential agency for making haste to evangelise the world. I have the profoundest sympathy with those Christian men who are uniting to pray and to labour for the re-union of Christendom. Yet I must remind you of this fact, which rests on good authority, that in those times and in those places in which the Church has manifested the most rigid outward uniformity there has been the least of Missionary zeal and aggressive evangelisation, while in this nineteenth century when, as you may say, the Church is unfortunately divided into many sects, we have seen the greatest Missionary movement that has occurred in any period of the Christian era. Now, I do not say that this is an ideal condition of things, but I do say that God is wonderfully overruling this state of things for His own glory. It has long been a motto with great generals, "Divide and conquer."

But you say, do not divide yourselves in order to conquer the enemy. Now, we know that God often turns Satan's methods to His own sublime use. Was not the Head of the Church Himself divided by Satan's art and malignity? His body went into the grave, and His spirit into the underworld; and was not that division, at the mention of which Simon Peter so stumbled, the means of reuniting us to God? "Except a corn of wheat fall into the ground and die, it abideth alone: but if it die, it bringeth forth much fruit." And so, when the Church of Jesus Christ, I doubt not by art and malignity, was broken into fragments, God took advantage of the fact that through these divers bodies He might the more rapidly carry the Gospel to the ends of the earth. Will you believe that if the Church had been one outwardly there would have been to-day thirty-three Missionary Societies in China, doing their work along various lines, with various methods, emulating each other in the swiftness, the zeal, and the eagerness, with which they press on to conquer that great empire? Do you believe that if the Church had been one outwardly there would have been more than thirty-five Missionary Societies on the dark continent to-day, coming in from every side like an investing army, that they may close up and conquer that Continent for Christ? Now, if you can prove to me that the

317

A. J. Gordon should not be ignored, as he saw the dangers of dropping denominational distinctives for the sake of unity. Rather, Gordon saw in the diversity of denominations God's sovereign hand, as did Count Ludwig Von Zinzendorf 140 years before. A. T. Pierson, pastor, author, and editor of *The Missionary Review of the World* from 1887-1900,[24] continued on the same line as Gordon when he spoke the final recorded words of the 1888 missionary conference:

We have spoken a great deal here in this Conference about the unity which has been expressed and experienced here. I want to say that, for myself, I find not the slightest ground for merit or credit in this unity. If in the presence of a gigantic foe that unites all its forces, and masses all its hosts against the kingdom of our Lord Jesus Christ, I did not forget that I was an American, and did not forget the denomination to which I belonged, I should consider myself a fossilised ecclesiastic, and not a disciple at all. When Herod and Pilate are made friends together to crush Christ and Christianity, it behoves all true disciples to gather shoulder to shoulder, and close about the Ark of God. The fact is that our unity is largely the involuntary and unconscious unity of those who, in the presence of gigantic and desperate foes, come together because they cannot help coming together in the realisation of a similar and common danger. I want to say, also, that I think the

---

Church being divided, we will say into a score of bodies, every one of those bodies has only a twentieth part of the power of the whole, or even less than that, then I shall concede much. But that is not the fact. You shatter a mirror, and everyone of the fragments will reflect a full-orbed sun. Break the Church of God into a score of pieces, and yet we find that everyone of these fragments in this great Convention has mirrored a full-orbed Christ.

But, you say, are we not to look for a reunion of the Church? I cannot dwell on this point long, but will simply say, "Yes, I beseech you, brethren, by the coming of our Lord Jesus Christ, and our gathering together unto Him." That will be the reunion of Christendom, a reunion in which will be included nothing that defileth, or worketh abomination, or maketh a lie.

We have a Bible that is one, but that has been translated into, according to your last report, at least three hundred languages. Now remember that the old Church that shed rivers of blood to prevent one Church of Jesus Christ being translated into various sects, also shed rivers of blood to prevent the Word of God being translated into various languages. That Church is just as oppose to a polyform Christianity as it is to a polyglot Bible. But we have both" (A. J. Gordon, "Closing Remarks," James Johnston, *Report of the Centenary Conference of the Protestant Missions of the World, Held in Exeter Hall [June 9th—19th], London, 1888,* Vol. 1 [New York: Fleming H. Revell, 1888], 439-40).

[24]"Meet Mr. Philadelphis [A. T. Pierson]" [on-line]; accessed 10 July 2002; available from http://www.whatsaiththescripture.com/Voice/Meet.Mr.Philadelphia.html, Internet.

methods adopted by these gigantic foes remind us that the only true policy of warfare, is a positive aggressive policy. Let us be done with all defensive methods of warfare. A positive aggressive Gospel is the Gospel that is going to win the day.[25]

Pierson's point was to continue aggressively preaching the gospel throughout the world, and not become complacent or be sidetracked by vain efforts at unity. The thoughts of Gordon and Pierson need to be remembered as unity is sought in cooperative evangelism. They seemed to anticipate Edinburgh 1910, the International Missionary Councils and the World Council of Churches that came out of this movement.

In 1958 Robert O. Ferm, author of *Cooperative Evangelism,* discussed the difficulty of developing principles of cooperation in evangelism:

> The problem [of fellowship and separation] becomes exceedingly complex when one's associations are with nominal Christians, especially when they manifest the Christian graces, yet cannot intellectually assent to every tenet of Fundamentalism. ...[26]

This difficulty stems from several theological aspects of evangelicalism and Protestant Christianity in general. As a starting point, Warfield defined evangelical soteriology as synonymous to Protestant soteriology.[27] Second, twentieth century evangelicalism was represented primarily by their adherents being "stepchildren of the Reformation."[28] Third, evangelicalism referred to a broad theological spectrum of denominations and groups.[29]

---

[25]A. T. Pierson, "Closing Remarks," James Johnston, *Report of the Centenary Conference of the Protestant Missions of the World, London, 1888,* 487.

[26]Robert Ferm, *Cooperative Evangelism* (Grand Rapids: Zondervan, 1958), 34.

[27]"It is in the interests of vital religion, therefore, that the Protestant spirit repudiates sacerdotalism. And it is this repudiation which constitutes the very essence of evangelicalism. Precisely what evangelical religion means is immediate dependence of the soul on God and God alone for salvation" (B. B. Warfield, *The Plan of Salvation: Five Lectures Delivered at the Princeton Summer School of Theology, June 1914.* [Philadelphia: Presbyterian Board of Publication, 1918], 82).

[28]See Leonard Verduin, *The Reformers and Their Stepchildren* (Grand Rapids: Eerdmans, 1964), 12-13.

[29]Robert Webber in *Common Roots* described the following "Subculture Evangelical Groups," their "Major Emphasis," and their "Symbols": "(1) Fundamentalist Evangelicalism; personal and ecclesiastical separationism, biblicism; Bob Jones University, American Council of Christian Churches, *Sword of the Lord;* (2)

Fourth, evangelical groups were historically decades or centuries away from persecution from state churches in Europe, as well as from theological splits from other denominational groups in the United States. Fifth, evangelical churches in their incipient stage were local church-centered, as opposed to denomination-centered. This led to a marked independence among them. Sixth, many nascent conservative denominations were anti-bishop rule, and were antagonistic to authority from the top down. If these six points are added to the fact that many groupings and sub-groupings were formed around linguistic lines, the number of revival movements in various linguistic groups multiplied the number of denominations. Yet, the social gospel had sapped the strength of mainline Protestant evangelism in the first decades of the twentieth century,[30] and in the decades that followed, the

---

Dispensational Evangelicalism; Dispensational hermeneutics, pretribulationalism and premillennarianism; Dallas Theological Seminary, Moody Bible Institute, *Moody Monthly;* Moody Press; (3). Conservative Evangelicalism; Cooperative evangelism, inclusive of all evangelical groups, broad theological base; Wheaton College, Trinity Seminary, Gordon-Conwell Seminary, *Christianity Today,* Billy Graham, The Zondervan Corp., National Association of Evangelicals; (4) Nondenominational Evangelicalism; Unity of the Church; restoration of N.T. Christianity; Milligan College; (5) Reformed Evangelicalism; Calvinism (some with a decidedly Puritan flavor), covenant theology and hermeneutics; Calvin College and Seminary, Westminster Seminary, Covenant Seminary, Reformed Seminary, Francis Schaeffer; (6) Anabaptist Evangelicalism; Discipleship, poverty, the Peace movement, pacifism; Goshen College, Reba Place Fellowship, John Howard Yoder; (7) Wesleyan Evangelicalism; Arminianism, sanctification; Asbury College and Seminary, Seattle Pacific College; (8) Holiness Evangelicalism; the second work of grace; Lee College, Nazarene Church; (9) Pentecostal Evangelicalism; gift of tongues; Church of God, Assembly of God; (10) Charismatic Evangelicalism; gifts of the Holy Spirit; Oral Roberts University, Melodyland School of Theology (11) Black Evangelicalism; Black consciousness; National Association of Black Evangelicals (12) Progressive Evangelicalism; Openness toward critical scholarship and ecumenical relations; Fuller Seminary; (13) Radical Evangelicalism; Moral, social, and political consciousness; *Sojourners; The Other Side; Wittenburg Door;* (14) Main-line Evangelicalism; Historic consciousness at least back to the Reformation; Movements in major denominations: Methodist, Lutheran, Presbyterian, Episcopal, Baptist" (32).

[30]In my study of mailine denominations, four characterstics emerged: 1) political clout; 2) wealth; 3) a social agenda; and 4) declining membership. To properly identify mainline denominations, five groupings emerged: 1) old European denominations; 2) old colonial denominations; 3) members of the Federal Council of Churches; 4) members of the National Council of Churches; and 5) members of the National Association of Evangelicals. This last grouping surprised me in my research. However, they fit the four characteristics of mainline as found above, with the possible exception of a current decline in growth, rather than decline in actual attendance (cf. Thomas P. Johnston, "Grappling for Institutional Survival—Postdenominationalism in Mainline Churches." Essay for Church Growth Seminar, The Southern Baptist Theological Seminary, 1999).

ecumenical movement, largely a mainline phenomenon, was also moving away from A. T. Pierson's "positive aggressive Gospel."

Into this mix came Billy Graham who sought to unite Christians for the purpose of evangelism. But where was Graham to draw the line? Graham's problem can be shown as a list of propositions:

1. The evangelist is called to preach the gospel

2. Preaching the gospel requires people to listen

3. Gathering people to listen requires accessibility to the people

4. Accessibility requires access to churches and money for publicity

5. Crusade evangelism requires a broad base of church support.

This chapter will address the "broad base of church support" to which Billy Graham appealed. It must be noted that Graham did not found a denomination, like his predecessor John Wesley, who was not welcome in Anglican churches because of his view of instantaneous conversion and his Revivalistic methodology. Graham, for his part, sought to gather a broad base of support. This approach was positive in that it allowed him greater opportunities to preach to larger audiences. But this approach was negative in that it seemed anti-denominational and implied a theological subjectivism—especially as the broad base of support was broadened to include non-conversionist churches.

Another dimension of cooperation regards the ends of cooperation in crusade evangelism. At least four ends are discernible for cooperation in evangelism:

1. Evangelizing the lost outside of churches

2. Evangelizing the lost within churches

3. Reinvigorating churches to the practice of evangelism

4. Unity as a witness to the world.

The first three ends of unity are discernible in Graham throughout his ministry. The last end, which often uses John 17:21 as a proof text, posits the concept that unity in and of itself can replace the preaching of the gospel. The complexities associated with defining the unity are noted in

Figure 16, "Levels of Ecumenism, Cooperation, and Separation"[31] These models, particularly on the unity side of the scale, portray a long history in a discussion of unity. Understanding this history will provide a framework to understand Billy Graham's view of unity, and in particular the "Ecumenical Movement."

History of Ecumenism

The historical roots of the Ecumenical Movement had its origin in the Pietistic missionary enterprise. The early missionary efforts of Pietists began among the Moravians of Halle and Herrnhutt. Johnston brought out a contrast between the Roman Catholic missionary efforts and those of the Moravians:

> Until the pietist missionary efforts from Halle and Herrnhutt, much of the Gospel was brought to other lands by those associated with the growing colonial empires, Spain and Portugal, for example. Mass conversions and baptisms contrast with the individualistic emphasis of pietism.[32]

Ziegenbald and Plütschau, pietist Germans from Halle, were sent by the King of Denmark to India in 1705.[33] They became the first non-Roman Catholic missionaries to leave Europe for India. They were then followed by Moravian missionaries who left for the West Indies and Greenland. However, it was not until William Carey penned his "An Enquiry into the Obligation of Christians to Use Means for the Conversion of the Heathens" in 1782 that Protestant missionary efforts began to mushroom. Not long after Carey's departure for India in 1793, numerous Protestant missionary efforts were initiated. Christianity made such great strides in the nineteenth Century that historian Latourette called it "The Great Century." Ruth Rouse summarizes the spirit of the evangelical awakening:

> But whatever its origins, its spirit and its underlying motives were always the same. Its passion was evangelism—evangelism at

---

[31]"Weisenbeck's Models of Unity" were taken from Jude D. Weisenbeck, S.D.S., S.T.L., "Conciliar Fellowship and the Unity of the Church" (Ph.D. Thesis, Rome, Pontifica Studiorum Universitas, A S. Thoma Aq. in Urbe, 1986), 62-104. The order of the nine models is Weisenbeck's; the summary comes from this author's understanding of the text defining each model.

[32]Johnston, *World Evangelism and the Word of God*, 35.

[33]Stephen Neill, *A History of Christian Missions* (Harmondsworth, Middlesex, England: Penguin Books, Ltd., 1964), 228.

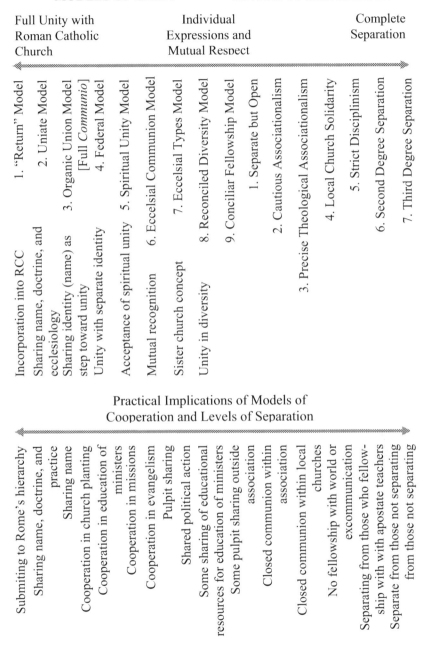

Fig. 16. Levels of Ecumenism, Cooperation, and Separation.

home and to the ends of the earth. One result of this passion was in evidence everywhere—the coming into being of societies, voluntary movements, or organizations, in which Christians of different Churches and different nations banded themselves together to win the world for Christ.[34]

The Great Century was marked by the founding of many Protestant missionary efforts. All five continents of the world were touched with the gospel. Comity agreements were made to most effectively reach unevangelized countries. Missionary councils were organized to share and advance missionary knowledge. Basic statements of faith were developed to guide the interdenominational missionary enterprise. These efforts were fueled with the pietistic zeal for individual conversion.

This pietistic emphasis led to three items of particular concern when viewing the nineteenth century to better understand the Ecumenical Movement: the role of revivalism, missionary conferences, and statements of faith. Revivalism was at the heart of the pietism movement. Spener saw the spiritual needs of Lutheran scholasticism in his day. Carey saw the needs among the Particular Baptists of his day. Wesley saw the same need among Anglicans in his day. However, revivalism received its greatest impetus when it was focused not inward toward the church, but outward toward a lost world. This outward look was the magic touch that Carey brought to the missionary movement—and that Wesley brought to evangelism. No longer bound by efforts of awakening the spiritually stagnant, the gospel went forth with power to the lost.

What was the reason that missionaries began to gather in the Word Missionary Conferences? William R. Hogg in his book *Ecumenical Foundations: A History of the International Missionary Council and Its Nineteenth Century Background* discussed William Carey's proposal for a decennial missionary conference:

> Carey wrote his friend Andrew Fuller, recommending a decennial conference that would meet at the Cape of Good Hope regularly from 1810, or at the latest 1812. It would be a "general association of all denominations of Christians from the four quarters of the world." . . . Carey was ahead of his time. . . . Two months later Carey outlined his idea to Henry Martyn who was very much pleased with the idea, "not

---

[34]Ruth Rouse, "Voluntary Movements and the Changing Ecumenical Climate," in Ruth Rouse and Stephen Charles Neill, eds, *A History of the Ecumenical Movement 1517-1948* (London: SPCK, 1954), 309.

on account of its practicality, but [because of] its grandeur." There it seems to have died.[35]

Several missionary conferences did gather during the nineteenth century. Some gatherings were on the mission fields of the world and others were from the sending nations. Missionaries gathered in Bombay in 1825, in North India in 1855,[36] 1857, and 1862; in South India in 1858, 1879, and 1893; and in Shanghai in 1877, 1890, and 1907.[37] They also gathered in various sending countries: at the World Missionary Conferences in New York in 1854, in Berlin in 1857, and in London in 1888.[38] These great missionary gatherings culminated at the Ecumenical Missionary Conference, New York (1900), and finally at the World Missionary Conference, Edinburgh (1910).[39] These were the missionary conferences of the nineteenth century.[40]

Four leaders are cited by Arthur Johnston to have been pivotal in the theology of New York (1900): Augustus H. Strong, Robert E. Speer, Hudson Taylor, and John R. Mott. Johnston noted that all these leaders

---

[35]William Richey Hogg, *Ecumenical Foundations: A History of the International Missionary Council and Its Nineteenth Century Background* (New York: Harper & Brothers, 1952), 17. Hogg provided three footnotes in the quoted portion.

[36]Hogg's date of 1855 (ibid., 18) conflicts with Johnston's date of 1854 (Johnston, *World Evangelism and the Word of God,* 56).

[37]Hogg, 18-21. These conferences are representative of many others that were taking place in India, Japan, and Africa.

[38]Johnston wrote: "It was at this latter conference [London 1888] that Gustav Warneck proposed a Standing Central International Committee with headquarters in London. Its representatives would be elected by the National Missionary Conferences of every land. This proposal became the blueprint for the IMC" (Johnston, *World Evangelism and the Word of God,* 57).

[39]At first Edinburgh 1910 was to be called the "Third Ecumenical Missionary Conference," this title was changed in 1908 (ibid., 93).

[40]In a interesting quote, Franklin H. Littell names the Evangelical Alliance as the starting point for religious pluralism: "The reality of religious pluralism was given institutional expression in America quite early, especially in the ecumenical beginnings such as the Evangelical Alliance during the nineteenth century" (Franklin H. Littell, "Making the Circles Larger," in Franklin H. Littell, ed. *The Growth of interreligious Dialogue, 1939-1989: Enlarging the Circle* [Toronto Studies in Theology, vol. 46. Lewiston, NY: The Edwin Mellen Press, 1989], 337). Historic "evangelicalism" has always had an openness to cooperation in the gospel (as was the case in the Evangelical Alliance), as noted by the 4,000 (1983) and then 7,000 (1987) evangelists gathered at the ICIE conferences sponsored by Billy Graham with more countries represented in one place than any time in world history. There was, however, a confessional basis for these alliances or conferences.

brought a pietistic orientation to New York (1900): A. H. Strong (1836-1921) brought the pietistic theology of an authoritative Bible and of the person and work of Christ; Speer, in his address "The Supreme and Determining Aim," brought evangelism clearly into focus;[41] Hudson Taylor, founding Secretary of the China Inland Mission brought a pietistic passion for reaching the lost;[42] and John R. Mott, General Secretary for the Student Volunteer Movement, brought the vigor of youthful zeal to New York (1900).

In New York (1900), Hudson Taylor, the great founder of the China Inland Mission, addressed the need for expectant evangelism:

> The gospel itself is the power of God unto salvation to every one that believeth. Now there are different ways of preaching the gospel. There is the plan of preaching the Gospel and looking forward to the gradual enlightenment of the people, to their being saved as it were by the process of gradual instruction and preaching. And there is another method of preaching the gospel; believing it to be the power of God unto salvation; preaching it in the expectation that He who first brought light out of the darkness can and will once and instantaneously take the darkest heathen heart and create light within. That is the method that is successful. It has been my privilege to know many Christians—I am speaking within bounds when I say a hundred—who have accepted Jesus Christ as their Saviour the first time they ever heard of Him.[43]

Taylor believed in expectant evangelism. In 1905 Hudson Taylor died. By 1899 D. L. Moody had died. These two men were great leaders of pietistic evangelism in the nineteenth century. Their passing marked the passing of an era in Christian missions. The leadership of the missionary movement then passed on to the next generation.

---

[41]Johnston included the entire address as his Appendix Five. One remarkable statement stands out, "Missions are powerful to transform the face of society, because they ignore the face of society and deal with it at its heart" (Johnston, *World Evangelism and the Word of God,* 271).

[42]"We have given too much attention to methods, and to machinery, and to resources, and too little to the Source of Power; the filling with the Holy Ghost" (J. Hudson Taylor, "The Source of Power," in *Ecumenical Missionary Conference, New York, 1900: Report of the Ecumenical Conference on Foreign Missions, Held in Carnegie Hall and Neighboring Churches, April 21 to May 1,* ed. James Johnston [New York: American Tract Society, 1900], 88).

[43]Ibid., 91. Expectant evangelism is derived from this quote. It may be defined as evangelism by faith that God will move in the hearts of the hearers to bring salvation, even upon the first hearing of the gospel.

The last World Missionary Conference was held in Edinburgh (1910). It marked the end of an era, and the beginning of a new era. Edinburgh (1910) was the hinge between evangelical cooperation and the beginnings of the Ecumenical Movement. It also marked the introduction of a social mandate alongside the evangelistic mandate of the missionary enterprise. In fact, Johnston showed that during the decade between 1900 and 1910 the missionary movement turned from its pietistic roots toward the liberalism of its day.[44]

The Ecumenical Movement, which started as Protestant World Missionary Conferences, fed its leadership and momentum into Edinburgh 1910, which then catalyzed the founding of the International Missionary Councils (IMCs). The IMCs were not organized until a strategy conference in Mohonk, NY in 1921. They gathered in Jerusalem (1928), Madras (1938), Whitby (1947), Willigen (1952), and Ghana (1958), and ultimately combined with the World Council of Churches (WCC) at their Third Assembly in Delhi in 1966. One of the leading points in the IMCs was the question of unity foreshadowed by the remarks of Pierson and Gordon quoted above at London 1888. The term "ecumenical" became a rallying point for all denominations of Protestant, later to be used positively and negatively of Graham's "ecumenical evangelism."

New York (1900) was called an "Ecumenical Missionary Conference." This was a change from the terminology "World Missionary Conference" used in the nineteenth century. While use of the term ecumenical for this conference may be striking when viewed from the end of the twentieth century, it must be understood that the term underwent significant change in meaning. The term was derived from the Greek οικουμενη, meaning "the inhabited earth, the world; world (in the sense of its inhabitants), humankind; the Roman empire; the whole world."[45] While this gives a start to understand the semantic range of the term, it does not focus on its precise historical-theological meaning. By the time, Stephen Neill, et al., published their *Concise Dictionary of the Christian World Mission,* the term ecumenical appeared in two articles, "Ecumenical Institutes" and "Ecumenical Mission."[46] In both of these articles the term was synonymous with the WCC. As ecumenical was used in New York

---

[44]Arthur Johnston, *World Evangelism and the Word of God,* 71-82. Johnston wrote, "The focus of the movement shifted from evangelization to the Christianization of society by the Church" (ibid., 80).

[45]Walter Bauer, *A Greek English Lexicon of the New Testament and Other Early Christian Literature,* A translated and adapted by William F. Arndt and F. Wilbur Gingrich, second edition(Chicago: University of Chicago Press, 1958), 561.

[46]Stephen Neill, Gerald H. Anderson, and John Goodwin, *Concise Dictionary of the Christian World Mission* (Nashville: Abingdon Press, 1971.), 179-80.

(1900), however, it did not have this worldwide structural church emphasis. Rather, it alluded to the voluntary universal representation of pietistic mission agencies. Later, ecumenical included the structural unity of non-Catholic churches. Then it moved to a gathering of all Christian churches, including the Roman Catholic Church (RCC). Finally it has come to imply the gathering of all religions (beginning with inclusion of Judaism,[47] then Islam, then other moralistic religions, and finally all religions).[48] This progression is evident when studying the IMCs, followed by the unity work of the WCC,[49] followed by that of the RCC.

New York (1900) was anything but all-inclusive. It upheld the historic theological formulations of the Evangelical Alliance. Its theology was based on an authoritative Bible, as found in the "five fundamentals"—

---

[47]"During the 1920s the circles were widened to include Roman Catholics and Jews where it could be managed" (Littell, 338). Pope Paul VI, in his encyclical *Ecclesiam Suam,* 6 August 1964 (Paul VI, *Ecclesiam Suam: On the Paths of the Church.* 6 August 1964 [on-line]; accessed 15 July 2001; available from http://www.ewtn.com/library/ENCYC/P6ECCLES.HTM; Internet), proposed "a series of concentric circles" (paragraph 96). He explained these circles as "all things human" (paragraph 97), "men who adore the one, supreme God whom we to adore" (paragraph 107), "the circle of Christianity" (paragraph 109), and "the children in the house of God, the one, holy, catholic and apostolic Church, of which this Roman Church is 'mother and head'" (paragraph 113). These same concentric circles were expanded upon in the *Catechism of the Catholic Church,* paragraphs 836-45.

[48]The book edited by Mott in 1924 (*Conferences of Christian Workers Among Moslems, 1924: A Brief Account of the Conferences Together with Their Findings and Lists of Members* [New York: International Missionary Council, 1924]), clearly differentiates Islam from Christianity, and stated, "The facts before us prove that the call to evangelize Moslems has taken on a new urgency" (17). Fifty-five years later, The WCC published guidelines on Interfaith dialogue (1979), which included accepting the legitimacy of other faiths, "Dialogue helps us not disfigure the image of our neighbours of different faiths and ideologies. It has been the experience of many Christians that this dialogue is indeed possible on the basis of mutual trust and a respect for the integrity of each participant's identity" (Michael Kinnamon and Brian E. Cope, eds., *The Ecumenical Movement: An Anthology of Key Texts and Voices* [Geneva: WCC Publications; Grand Rapids, MI: William B. Eerdmans Publishing Company, 1997], 407). Aram Keshishian (1990) was more cautious, "We need a new theology that is strong enough to be open to 'mutual witness,' at the same time resistant to any temptation to possible compromise" (ibid., 257).

[49]"After only three decades, however, it has already become a remarkable community of some three hundred members. These churches represent a rich diversity of cultural backgrounds and traditions, worship in dozens of languages, and live under every kind of political system. Yet they are all committed to close collaboration in Christian witness and service. At the same time, they are also striving together to realize the goal of visible Church unity" (*Baptism, Eucharist and Ministry* [Geneva: World Council of Churches, 1982], vii).

although this was changing too, necessitating the 1907-1010 series of tracts on the fundamentals to be discussed later. New York 1900 focused on conversion, as expressed by Hudson Taylor. It affirmed not a theology of consensus, but an evangelical confessional theology.

This common evangelical theology was not true of Edinburgh (1910). As the second generation of leaders of the missionary movement came into power, they emphasized a theology of consensus.[50] This emphasis continued until the IMC merged with the WCC in 1961. This consensus seemed to be forced because of the spectrum of denominations represented. So much so that it was quite an administrative task to keep everyone at the same table. But Mott and Oldham were effective leaders and able administrators in this regard.

The first move away from missions and towards ecumenism (as understood today) was the incorporation of church bodies with the mission agencies in Edinburgh (1910). In particular, the Anglican presence had an important effect upon the conference. However, William T. Gairdner following the conference pushed for more interdenominational representation:

> The communions whose absence at once strikes the observer are of course the great Greek and Roman Churches—the former with its notable Japan mission, the latter (Church of Xavier yesterday and Lavigerie to-day) with foreign missions all over the world. But who on this ridge of memories and of hopes, can say what the future may bring forth?[51]

Johnston noted that Oldham, Executive Secretary of Edinburgh (1910), acknowledged the importance of Gairdner's comments.

In 1919 two important leaders made predictions of a "League of Churches" much like the "League of Nations," which was to eliminate the possibility of another world war of the same magnitude as World War I. W. A. Visser 't Hooft in his book, *The Genesis and Formation of the World Council of Churches,* chooses the January 10, 1919 initiative of the Holy Synod of Constantinople as the first spark of the World Council of Churches. In this synod

> It was officially decided to take steps to issue an invitation to all Christian churches to form a 'league of churches'. Thus the Church of

---

[50]Johnston, *World Evangelism and the Word of God,* 94-95.

[51]William T. Gairdner, *Edinburgh 1910* (Edinburgh: Oliphant, Anderson and Ferrier, 1910), 50. Quoted by Johnston, 120, footnote 18.

Constantinople became the first church to plan for a permanent organ of fellowship and cooperation between the churches.[52]

Jude Weisenbeck, retired Director of Ecumenism for the Archdiocese of Louisville, in his dissertation entitled, *Conciliar Fellowship and the Unity of the Church,* also noted a statement of Archbishop Söderblom, of the Lutheran Rite, in the same year. Weisenbeck explained:

> In the same year (1919) in the distant city of Uppsala, Sweden, and apparently quite independently of the Patriarch of Constantinople, Archbishop Nathan Söderblom spoke in similar terms, advocating the formation of a common or ecumenical council whereby the evangelical catholicity and unity of the religious community of Christians might be more fully realized and expressed.[53]

Then, in 1920, J. H. Oldham predicted the gathering of Christians into a "league of churches."[54] From the critique of Gairdner, to the eventual Encyclical of the Archbishop of Constantinople (1920), to the call for unity of Söderblom, and finally to Oldham, first Secretary of the IMC,[55] the mission of the IMC changed its focus from the evangelization of the world (New York [1900]), to the gathering of all Christian churches into a "league of churches."

Madras (1938) was the last conference in which Mott had leadership. The movement was changing hands to a third generation of leadership. They were to build upon the foundation left them by Mott and Oldham. The cover to the report on the Madras (1938) IMC revealed its emphasis:

> The central theme of the meeting was The Church,—the universal Christian community, the faith by which it lives, the nature of its witness, the conditions of its life and extension, the relation it

---

[52]W. A. Visser 't Hooft, *The Genesis and Formation of the World Council of Churches* (Geneva: World Council of Churches, 1982), 1.

[53]Jude Weisenbeck, "Conciliar Fellowship and the Unity of the Church," 108.

[54]Ibid., 109.

[55]Kenneth Scott Latourette, "Ecumenical Bearings of the Missionary Movement and the International Missionary Council," in *A History of the Ecumenical Movement 1517-1948*, Ruth Rouse and Stephen Charles Neill, eds. (London: SPCK, 1954), 370.

must hold to its environment, and the increase of cooperation and unity within it. This theme was discussed in sixteen sections.[56]

It was clear from this paragraph on the cover that the focus had shifted dramatically. In 1900 the focus was how to reach the lost with the gospel. By the time of Madras, the focus was inward on the Church. The IMCs had moved from being missiocentric to becoming ecclesiocentric, and they were to become ecumenocentric.

Report XVI of Madras (1938) was titled, "Co-operation and Unity." The following are some segments from this report:

> Reports from all parts of the world show a truly remarkable development of co-operation within the Christian Church since the Edinburgh Conference of 1910. . . . This unity of spirit has made us realize more fully how gravely our outward divisions are hindering the extension of the Kingdom of God, and indeed are stultifying our message of the love of God as the great reconciling force in a world that desperately needs it. . . .
>
> We therefore urge the continuance and further extension of co-operation in fields and in types of work where it is imperfectly practiced. At present, co-operation in institutional work absorbs most of the men and money and time available for co-operative activities. Such institutions are outstanding examples of the indispensability of joint effort for effective working.[57]

Unity had become an end in itself, and missionary efforts prior to Edinburgh (1910) were apparently considered "stultifying" efforts.

From Madras (1938) to the Third Assembly of the World Council of Church in New Delhi (1961), it was a matter of time before the IMC would be absorbed into the WCC. In fact, Oldham, who was Executive Secretary of Edinburgh 1910, Secretary of the Continuation Committee, and the first Secretary of the IMC, was also chairman of the Preparatory Committee for the Life and Work Conference of 1937.[58] After merging with

---

[56]*The World Mission of the Church: Findings and Recommendations of the International Missionary Council, Tambaras, Madras, India, December 12th to 29th, 1938* (London: International Missionary Council, 1939), cover.

[57]Ibid., 128. Mott's *Cooperation and the World Mission* (New York: International Missionary Council, 1935) was footnoted in this report after the following sentence: "We have evidence that results have been achieved which humanly speaking could not have been secured by separate action" (ibid.).

[58]Latourette, 356.

the WCC in 1966, a division was formed to replace the role of the IMC, the "Commission for World Mission and Evangelization."

Graham and Ecumenism

Billy Graham attended the founding of the WCC at Amsterdam in 1948, and seemed to have an admiration for the ministry of John R. Mott,[59] whom Graham called an evangelist. Similarities between Graham and Mott were notable, as were differences. Both had worldwide ministries and worldwide impact. Mott gathered together world missionary bodies in voluntary conferences to discuss missions. Graham gathered together world evangelical theologians and evangelists in voluntary conferences to discuss evangelism. Mott used the Student Volunteer Movement and Protestant mission agencies as the vehicle through which he gained recognition all across the world. Graham networked with Youth for Christ contacts, the Evangelical Alliance, the Anglican Church, as well as evangelical mission agencies to gain access into many countries of the world for the purpose of crusade evangelism. In fact, crusade evangelism was a difference between Mott and Graham. Graham's purpose for entering countries appeared primarily to be to preach the gospel. However, Graham did not seem to succumb to Mott's "Larger Evangelism"[60] until perhaps 1965, 1973, or 1975. But it did not alter Graham's methodology significantly. Mott's change of heart took place in 1905, and the impact of that change was felt in Edinburgh 1910. It did not seem to hinder the cause of world evangelism until higher criticism and the social gospel took root in most mainline Protestant mission agencies.

At the beginning of Graham's ministry, he faced three major world bodies of Christianity: his own evangelicals and all their mission organizations who supported him wholeheartedly, the WCC, of which the Anglican Church and the Lutheran World Federation were a part, and the RCC. Graham's ministry impacted evangelicalism, made some inroads into many of the churches represented in the WCC, and also received the Pope's consent, as surmised in Pope Paul IV's encyclical *Evangelii Nuntiandi* (8 December 1975). In this important document, Paul VI addressed the Catholic charismatic movement, other regional churches, and "popular religiosity"—quite likely an indirect reference to the crusade efforts of Billy Graham, as well as to charismatic groups. The Pope's advice to "popular religiosity" was: "When it is well-oriented, this popular religiosity can be

---

[59]Lois Ferm, personal interview with author, 31 July 2000, Amsterdam, the Netherlands.

[60]See John R. Mott, *The Larger Evangelism: The Sam P. Jones Lectures at Emory University, 1944* (New York: Abingdon-Cokesbury Press, 1944).

more and more for multitudes of our people a true encounter with God in Jesus Christ."[61] And later Paul VI included an admonition to his Synod of Bishops:

> Moreover we make our own the desire of the Fathers of the Third General Assembly of the Synod of Bishops, for a collaboration marked by greater commitment with the Christian brethren with whom we are not yet united in perfect unity, taking as a basis the foundation of Baptism and the patrimony of faith which is common to us. By doing this we can already give a greater common witness to Christ before the world in the very work of evangelization. Christ's command urges us to do this; the duty of preaching and of giving witness to the Gospel requires this.[62]

The only catch, according to this encyclical, was that movements of "popular religiosity" not speak against the RCC:

> 16. There is thus a profound link between Christ, the Church and evangelization. During the period of the Church that we are living in, it is she who has the task of evangelizing. *This mandate is not accomplished without her, and still less against her.*[63]

Speaking against the RCC was something that Graham was careful not to do, as was noted by William Martin of the post-Kennedy election years.[64] Graham's approach to the RCC was quite different from A. J. Gordon of the American Baptist Missionary Union,[65] other evangelical

---

[61]Pau VI, *Evangelii Nuntiandi* (8 December 1975), paragraph 48.

[62]Ibid., paragraph 77.

[63]Ibid., paragraph 16. Italics mine.

[64]William Martin, *A Prophet with Honor: The Billy Graham Story* (New York: William Morrow, 1991), 294.

[65]"We have a Bible that is one, but that has been translated into, according to your last report, at least three hundred languages. Now remember that the old Church that shed rivers of blood to prevent one Church of Jesus Christ being translated into various sects, also shed rivers of blood to prevent the Word of God being translated into various languages. That Church is just as oppose to a polyform Christianity as it is to a polyglot Bible. But we have both" (A. J. Gordon, "Closing Remarks," *Report of the Centenary Conference of the Protestant Missions of the World, Held in Exeter Hall, London, 1888,* Vol. 1 (New York: Fleming H. Revell, 1888), 440.

missionaries of that era,[66] authors of pamphlets published in *The Fundamentals*,[67] and the cautious reminders of the historian Stephen Neill.[68]

---

[66]Principal D. H. MacVicar, Montreal, Canada, addressed the subject of Roman Catholic missions. A copy of his outline will suffice to note the emphases of his speech to *Centenary Conference of the Protestant Missions of the World.* "So much for the extent of Roman Catholic Missions. What of their character? They are distinguished:— 1. By unity and comprehensiveness of plan. . . . 2. Aggressive and persistent zeal in gathering all into the one fold. . . . 3. A third element in the character of these Missions is the use of coercive measures. . . . 4. A fourth factor in the character of these Missions is the dominancy of ecclesiastical authority. . . . 5. These missions are characterized by unworthy and unjustifiable methods of support. . . . 6. The sixth and worst feature of Romish Missions is the practical suppression of the Word of God" (D. H. MacVicar, "The Missions of the Roman Catholic Church to Heathen Lands, Their Character, Extent, Influence, and Lessons," *Report of the Centenary Conference of the Protestant Missions of the World,* 74-76). Following MacVicar was Dean Vahl of the Danish Evangelical Missionary Society, who said, "As to the Roman Catholic Church, I have not much sympathy with her, I cannot look upon her as a true branch of the Holy Catholic Church. . . . the more I see how old Mission-fields of the Roman Catholic church have, not all, but many of them, been totally neglected and new fields taken up, where Evangelical Missions have already begun, as it seems only, that they may be spoiled. . . . the Roman Catholic Missions have been rotten in themselves" (ibid., 78-79). Then the chairman spoke, "the object of our meeting to-day is not to discuss the Roman Catholic Church, about which we are all tolerably unanimous, if not wholly unanimous. . ." (ibid., 80). The next speakers all spoke likewise of the tone and character of Roman Catholic Missions: Rev. Henry Stout of Japan and Rev. G. E. Post of Syria, with discussion by Rev. J. A. B. Cook of Singapore, Rev. G. W. Clarke of China, Rev. H. Williams of Bengal, Rev. J. Murray Mitchell of India, Count van Limburg Stirum of Celebes, Rev. E. E. Jenkins regarding India, Rev. John Hesse of India, and Rev. N. Summerbell of the United States.

Twelve years later, though not listing Roman Catholic Missions as a category in the 1900 "Ecumenical Missionary Conference," missionaries from predominantly Roman Catholic lands made mention of their difficulties. Hence, among others, Senor F. de Castells, agent of the British and Foreign Bible Society in Costa Rica said, "We find there [South America] the lowest and most degraded form of Romanism that can be conceived" (Seno F. de Castells, "South America," *Ecumenical Missionary Conference, New York, 1900* [New York: American Tract Society, 1900], 477).

[67]For example among the tracts published in the series titled "The Fundamentals" were two titles which discussed the Roman Catholic Church. T. W. Medhurst of Glascow, Scotland, wrote "Is Romanism Christianity?" (R. A. Torrey, A.C. Dixon, et al., eds. *The Fundamentals,* [Grand Rapids: Baker, 1998], 3:288-300). Mehurst's first paragraph reads, "I am aware that, if I undertake to prove that *Romanism is not Christianity,* I must expect to be called 'bigoted, harsh, uncharitable.' Nevertheless I am not daunted; for I believe that on a right understanding of this subject depends the salvation of millions" (ibid., 288). J. M. Foster of Boston wrote the second tract on the topic of Roman Catholicism by the title, "Rome, The Antagonist of the Nation" (ibid., 301-314). He began his tract with the following, "The Roman Catholic Church, both in Scriptrues and in Christian history, figures as a politico-ecclesiastical system, the

It was obvious that Moody's tolerance and amicability with Roman Catholics, if not somewhat exaggerated, was not at all typical of most evangelicals of his day.[69] It was notable that the Berlin 1966 reports from predominantly Roman Catholic countries felt that Vatican II had somehow changed the theology of Catholicism.[70] There was also little negativism toward Roman Catholicism at Berlin '66, with the exception of several lines in several reports.[71] It would seem that the "Bravo Billy!" in the Archbishop

---

essential and deadly foe of civil and religious liberty, the hoary-headed antagonist of both Church and State" (ibid., 301).

[68]Stephen Neill, not given to a spirit of negativity, wrote of Roman Catholic mission work in general, "It was taken for granted by the majority of Roman Catholics that the Protestants were the enemy. This attitude was succinctly set forth in a directive alleged to have been issued from the early days of the Propaganda in the early days of the Congo missions: 'The heretics are to be followed up and their efforts harassed and destroyed'" (Stephen Neill, *A History of Christian Missions* (Middlesex: Penguin Books, 1964), 438). He also added about the methods of Roman Catholic missions in the South Pacific, "The Roman Catholics entered comparatively late, and inevitably, in a great many cases their work consisted not of preaching the Gospel to the heathen but of attempting to detached baptized Christians from the Churches to which they belonged" (ibid., 418).

[69]Dorsett wrote, "Although he [Moody] saw no virtue in abolishing denominational distinctives, he carried an abiding aversion to focusing on what he considered nonessentials. . . . Moody insisted that workers in his meetings drop all mention of Catholics who were entering into a deeper relationship with Christ" (Lyle W. Dorsett, *A Passion for Souls: The Life of D. L. Moody* [Chicago: Moody Press, 1997], 204). Later he added, "Obviously Moody's students in Massachusetts were not taught that nothing much worthwhile in Christianity existed between the time of Saint Augustine and the Protestant Reformation" (ibid., 289).

[70]"We must also mention the progressive influence of the Second Vatican Council which is penetrating the mentality of a number of Spanish Catholics; this is creating a climate of more respect, understanding and tolerance toward the 'separated brethren.' . . . Ecumenism and the newer thinking within Catholicism also affect the position of many sincere Catholics. Several years ago these persons may have felt dissatisfied with their faith and with the church, but now they are discovering new spiritual possibilities within post-Council Catholicism, enough to satisfy them without having to join another Christian group outside the Catholic church" (José M. Martinez, *"Spain," One Race, One Gospel, One Task: World Congress on Evangelism, Berlin, 1966, Official Reference Volumes: Papers and Reports*, eds. Carl F. H. Henry and W. Stanley Mooneyham [Minneapolis: World Wide, 1967], 1:242, 243).

[71]"French-speaking Europe has been sprinkled with the blood of martyrs for the Gospel; it still appears to be a mission field almost without fruit" (Jacques Blocher, "French-speaking Europe," in *One Race, One Gospel, One Task*, 1:250). "Another obstacle to evangelism is the religious oppression of many Roman Catholic priests and the individual influence of many Roman Catholics upon the political administration of the country. There are a few who sympathize with us. . . . we need a

soon-to-be Cardinal Cushing's diocesan paper made a marked influence on Billy Graham's view of Roman Catholicism, which may have followed him for the rest of his ministry![72]

What was the main danger with the ecumenical agenda, according to Pierson and Gordon, as noted above? They clarified three points: missionary zeal and aggressive evangelism would be lost in a quest for unity; true Christian reunion would take place in heaven; and Christian discipleship demanded that the focus be a positive aggressive gospel. Thus, they reminded future generations that the beginning or end of mission is not unity, but rather the fulfillment of the Great Commission.

With this preparatory discussion, we now look at ecclesiology and crusade evangelism. As may be expected, the issue of international cooperation in evangelism provides unique and major challenges.

Ecclesiology and Crusade Evangelism

Ecclesiology is a broad topic. It involves the church and its mandate. It is important to recognize three points when considering the church and the Great Commission, or crusade evangelism in particular: the question of absolutes, the need for parameters, and the complexities of international Christian ministry.

First, in a para-denominational setting, such as a Graham crusade, or even in an independent mission organization, questions are raised about denominationalism. If denominations can, do, and should work together, what is their purpose? More basic to this issue is a question of biblical interpretation: is there such a thing as a New Testament church in the Bible? Or again, does the Bible teach one way of doing church? Evangelicals and inerrantists have long answered "Yes" to these questions, and thus maintain the Bible as their rule of faith for ecclesiology. They have discussed ecclesiology, disagreed over ecclesiology, and separated over ecclesiology. This has led to the accusation of sectarianism.

However, when one is willing to drop the absolute teaching of

---

united program of social work in order to fight the poverty and miserable conditions of the people, (Here we could co-operate with the Roman Catholics.)" (Augusto A. Esperança, "Portugal," in *One Race, One Gospel, One Task,* 1:246).

[72]Graham spoke in Boston from December 31, 1949 to January 16, 1950. The "Bravo Billy!" article was written during the crusade. Graham wrote, "Heartening us also was the response of the Roman Catholic Church, especially in light of the fact that the landmark decisions on ecumenism of the Second Vatican Council were still years away" (Billy Graham, *Just As I Am,* 161). Interestingly enough, the progressive Pope Pius XII dropped hints, shortly after Cushing's wise approach in dealing with Graham, that he would become a Cardinal ("Abp. Cushing to Get Red Hat, Rome Hints," *Boston Evening Globe,* 14 January 1950, 1, 2).

the Bible, whatever that might be, in the area of ecclesiology, it moves into other areas also. Hence, other foundations are sought to replace *sola Scriptura,* such as typically Tradition, creedalism, pragmatism, or some other *a priori.* Today, for example, the RCC, Orthodox churches, and the Anglican church all use a historical precedent argument at some point to validate their ecclesiology. Several other non-absolutist para-denomination ecclesiologies have also entered American evangelicalism in the past twenty-five years. The "Seeker Church" movement, while having worthy ends, are not always noted for finding their ecclesiological concepts in the pages of the New Testament. Rather, especially for the secondary churches in this movement, they seem to be developing a theology of culture through "dynamic equivalence" with cultural anthropology.[73] Likewise, the Church Growth Movement, and its offshoot, Natural Church Development, may be considered pragmatically-driven. Thus, the latter would shed "'pushy' manipulative methods" of evangelism as it turns people off.[74] A radical change in the theology of the Great Commission became warranted because it was not pragmatic for growing churches.[75] This pragmatic view is indeed quite removed from the concept of a New Testament church and its corresponding "Primitivism" out of which most evangelical denominations were formed when the Bible was disseminated by the Bible societies. Thus, while one may appreciate ecclesial and cultural differences in various denominational bodies, that does not mean that the Holy Spirit, who inspired the Scriptures, is multiform on ecclesiology.

Yet, by its very nature, multi-church crusade evangelism must not dwell on denominational differences in order to unite various groups in the crusade. Ignoring these, however, can lead to a denominational and

---

[73]See Charles Arn, "A Response to Dr. Rainer: What Is the Key to Effective Evangelism?" *Journal of the American Society for Church Growth* 6 (1995): 75.

[74]"There are some people who feel evangelism works best when you push people to commit their life to Christ. They do not even shy away from manipulative methods to reach this goal. No wonder many of us feel a strange sensation in our stomach when we hear the word 'evangelism.'

But it can be shown that 'pushy' manipulative methods represent the exact opposite of the practice we learn from growing churches" (Christian Schwarz, *The ABC's of Natural Church Development* (Carol Stream, IL: ChurchSmart, 1998), 16).

[75]Thom Rainer noted that an anti-initiative view of evangelism did not correspond with his research of over 600 churches growing by conversion growth. Rather, he wrote, "We have heard from the leaders of nearly six hundred evangelistic churches. Over one-half (50.2 percent) of these leaders ranked weekly outreach [later called "the traditional method"] as one of the most effective evangelistic tools. Only four other methodologies fared better" (Thom Rainer, *Effective Evangelistic Churches Reveal What Works and What Doesn't* (Nashville: Broadman and Holman, 1996), 19).

theological minimalism—exactly what happened to the WCC as they were seeking to develop ecclesial views in *Baptism, Eucharist and Ministry*.[76] The issue of an absolute ecclesiology is very important in developing a consistent theology of evangelism.

Secondly, there is a need for ecclesial and theological parameters in a theology of evangelism. Although these parameters do not need to be "worn on one's sleeve," they are important. It would seem that in Graham's ministry there was a set of parameters, but there also seemed to be a lack of clarity, especially as personnel changes took place in the 1980s and following.

A dissertation by David Bruce exemplifies the lack of specificity. Bruce focused his work on the follow-up procedures following a Billy Graham crusade, using the 1982 Spokane, Washington crusade for his research. It discussed the questions asked by the counselor, or personal worker, during the invitation procedures:

> The inquirers are asked which church they regularly attend, and that church name is listed on the card. If they did not attend any church regularly, then another question is asked: "Who brought you to the Crusade tonight?" If the answer is a church, that church name is placed on the inquirer card. If no church name is given, that space is left blank for later referral work.[77]

Bruce continued explaining what happened to those who listed no church:

> The majority of people who come forward as inquirers will list a particular church as their preference. Provided the church is not a cult or an unacceptable church as deemed by the Crusade Follow-up Committee, that individual's name is referred directly to that particular church. If an individual inquirer does not have a church home, yet was brought by a church body, and the inquirer gives that church name, then that church and pastor are notified of the inquirer's commitment to Christ. Those who have no church background, who were not brought by church people, and have absolutely no affiliation with a local body of Christ, or who may have listed a cult or unacceptable church, are referred to the Designation Committee made of local pastors from the entire geographical area. This Designation

---

[76]*Baptism, Eucharist and Ministry,* Faith and Order Paper, no. 111 (Geneva: World Council of Churches, 1982).

[77]David Phillip Bruce, D.Min. essay: "A Program to Evaluate the Effectiveness of the Follow-up Activity of the Spokane, Washington, Billy Graham Crusade" (Louisville, KY: The Southern Baptist Theological Seminary, 1986), 57.

Committee designates or refers that inquirer to the closest participating church in Crusade work to that individual's zip code.[78]

It must be noted that Bruce never defined or described a "cult" or an "unacceptable group." This lack of explanation was especially noteworthy as the 1982 Spokane, Washington, crusade was the first time, to this researcher's knowledge, that the RCC was openly involved in follow-up efforts following a crusade. The *National Catholic Reporter* quoted Bishop Lawrence Welsh's letter in his diocesan newspaper, the *Inland Register*. A partial, but lengthy, quote is included in the footnote to provide a sense of the equivocal tone in the letter.[79] It is noteworthy that Bruce, "Executive

---

[78]Ibid., 58-59.

[79]"Dr. Billy Graham, the worldwide evangelist, will be conducting a crusade in Spokane at Joe Albi stadium Aug. 22-29. This crusade both poses some concern for us in the Catholic tradition and provides us with opportunities to reflect on the nature of evangelization and our relationship to Protestants who profess faith in Jesus Christ.

The Second Vatican Council's Decree on Ecumenism, reflecting on the Gospel, reminds us that despite historical and theological differences 'all who have been justified by faith in baptism are incorporated into Christ; they therefore have a right to be called Christians, and with good reason are accepted as brothers and sisters by the children of the Catholic Church' (no. 3). We cannot forget this basic principle of charity and faith when dealing with our Protestant brothers and sisters.

That spirit of charity and eagerness for the spread of the good news of Jesus Christ welcomes Dr. Graham to Spokane and eastern Washington. As members of that community and as Catholics, we also welcome Dr. Graham as he comes to share the Gospel with us. Those who have seen Dr. Graham in person or have watched his frequently televised crusades know of his enthusiasm for Christ and his personal conviction to preach the Gospel. Such virtues are laudable in an age which tends to treat faith and religious matters with apathy, if not disdain.

It is true that Dr. Graham's preaching style leaves some of us uncomfortable. For some his interpretation of holy scripture seems too literal and fundamentalistic; for others his themes are too simplistic and not sufficiently nuanced with an integrated theology. In varying degrees those responsible for leadership in the Christian community voice these criticisms of Dr. Graham's evangelistic style and content. Each of these concerns is in itself subject matter for ongoing discussion and examination.

Our Catholic tradition and teaching have clear positions regarding some of these concerns, but it would be unfair for Catholics to look with disdain on Dr. Graham and his effort. Taken in broad perspective the Gospel he preaches is the Gospel of Jesus Christ.

Because for all Christians Jesus is at the center of life, Dr. Graham always ends his sermons with what he terms an 'altar call,' an opportunity for personal commitment to Jesus Christ. This kind of activity is foreign to Catholic celebrations; the very vocabulary may leave us puzzled. Our theological perspective tells us that we are saved, that we belong to Christ because of what God has done for us in baptism. For the

Assistant to Mr. [Billy] Graham" at the time of this writing, did not seem to be aware of this landmark letter by a Roman Catholic bishop. This omission is especially unusual since Bruce's Doctor of Ministry essay was titled, "A Program to Evaluate the Effectiveness of the Follow-up Activity of the Spokane, Washington [1982], Billy Graham Crusade." Was this omission unintentional or tactical?

The concern remains: what were the theological parameters by which the BGEA operated in their cooperation? While these parameters will be discussed later in this chapter, a parallel consideration involves the complexity of levels of cooperation. At least six distinct levels of cooperation can be considered as relates to crusade evangelism:

1. Who is part of the formal invitation, who sponsors the crusade, and who supports the crusade financially?[80]

---

believing Christian conversion is a life-long process of dying to self and rising in Christ, it does not depend upon peak moments such as those experienced at religious crusades.

By this observation I do not intend to belittle the validity of religious experiences enjoyed by numerous people at Dr. Graham's crusades (or in other circumstances). It is important to note, however, that our Catholic understanding of conversion places such experiences within a broader context. The Gospel calls all of us to rely on personal and living relationship with Christ, theology comes afterward.

For many people the Graham crusade will be a catalyst for evoking that rich awareness. Such an experience does not mark a participant as disloyal to the Catholic Church but it can be if not nourished by a community of faith. Without community support and sharing, faith experiences quickly fade. This is one of my chief concerns in relationship to Dr. Graham's crusade.

Dr. Graham and his organizers share that concern and have developed an elaborate follow-up system for those who seek a deeper walk with Christ as a result of the crusade. This follow-up—which is more important than the crusade itself—often goes unnoticed and unpublicized as part of a Billy Graham crusade.

Recently several priests and deacons met with me and with representatives of the crusade to discuss Catholic involvement with this follow-up program for Catholics who seek guidance and spiritual direction after their experiences at the crusade. Explicit steps are currently under way to assure that necessary support and guidance are provided.

. . . Catholics who attend the crusade are not acting against Catholic teaching; the church recognizes the power of events such as the Billy Graham crusade for the building of faith among Christians. Those who may choose to attend are invited to bring the graces of the crusade back to their home communities" (Bishop Lawrence Welsh, "Catholics and a Billy Graham Crusade," 185-86)

[80]Sterling Huston called this step one in his "Steps for Developing a Crusade Invitation for Billy Graham Crusades." Note the control of the BGEA in recommending the constituency of the "Invitation Committee": "Assessing initial interest. The first step is to assess the interest in a Billy Graham Crusade by key clergy and judicatory leadership from three major areas of the religious community: 1. Those traditionally supportive of Crusade evangelism; 2. Those from principal 'mainline'

2.   Who is on the executive committee and the other committees of the crusade?

3.   In what churches are the "Christian Life and Witness" classes held?

4.   What churches and individuals are involved in the follow-up during and after the crusade?

5.   Who welcomes the speaker and the crusade—often on the first night of the crusade?

6.   Who are the musicians, who translates for the speaker (if translation is needed), or who is up on the platform of the crusade?

Each of these questions raises possible levels of cooperation for a crusade. Conversely, each level of cooperation necessarily has its parallel antithetic, a level of separation. Thus, the focus could shift to who is excluded from sponsoring the crusade, sitting on the executive committee, etc. The issues are complex, and show the great need for theological discernment and administrative tact.

Other levels of involvement relate to pastoral training conferences, the hiring of personnel, and in particular the hiring of associate evangelists and executive staff who represent crusades and make decisions regarding the crusades. While theological parameters for these levels of involvement may have been defined by the BGEA, and may be found in writing somewhere, this author worked his way back by noting Graham's sermons and his crusade methodology as found in primarily in public

---

denominations; 3. Those from the major ethnic group(s). If there is sufficient interest after contacting key individuals representative of these groups, the next step should be the formation of a Temporary Committee.

Step 2: *Form Temporary Committee.* A small ad hoc group (ten to fifteen persons maximum), composed of key leadership from each of the above-listed three groupings, should be formed. Representation on the committee should reflect the religious structure of the Protestant community and should include both laity and clergy in approximately a 40 percent to 60 percent ratio, respectively. . . .

Note: Usually the Director of Crusades will meet with this ad hoc group, once formed, for an exploratory meeting. From that meeting the group will be offered additional guidance concerning future organizational steps. Future steps usually include the development of an Invitation Committee and the accumulation of letters of invitation.

Step 3: *Develop an Invitation Committee.* The purpose of an Invitation Committee is to reflect to the Billy Graham Team the broad representative Christian support for a Crusade in a community. It also permits every major segment of the Christian community to begin on the ground floor of a Crusade invitation" (Sterling Huston, *Crusade Evangelism and the Local Church* [Minneapolis: World Wide Press, 1984], 181-83).

documents. Much of this evaluation is *very sensitive* and therefore requires wisdom and discernment.

As noted above in Figure 16, discussion of unity and levels of cooperation have led to numerous "Models of Unity." The issues are so sensitive that Jeffrey Gros, Eamon McManus, and Ann Riggs in their *Introduction to Ecumenism* omitted perhaps the most important element of unity—what will it look like?[81] While stating abstractions that the Bible calls for unity, affirming the necessity of dialogue, and encouraging koinonia and "full communion," they did not explain the visible methodology for working together in church planting and evangelism or fulfilling the Great Commission. In fact, the RCC and the WCC are both against "proselytism" or the manipulating and coercing others.[82] Thus ecumenical unity puts a moratorium on biblical evangelism, much like the anti-sect law in France passed on May 30, 2001 which places a ban on mental manipulation![83]

---

[81]Jeffrey Gros, F. S. C., Eamon McManus, and Ann Riggs, *Introduction to Ecumenism* (Mahwah, NJ: Paulist Press, 1998).

[82]Gros et al. addressed proselytism as follows: "This study will concentrate upon two ecumenical principles that are fundamental for Catholic ecumenical relations: (A) The Declaration on Religious Liberty; (B) Aversion to all forms of proselytism" (ibid., 76). Then they quoted from a strongly anti-proselytism "Vatican-World Council" text, *The Challenge of Proselytism and the Calling to Common Witness* (1995), "Religious freedom involves the right to freely adopt or change one's religion and to 'manifest it in teaching, practice, worship and observance' without any coercion which would impair such freedom. We reject all violations of religious freedom and all forms of religious intolerance as well as every attempt to impose belief and practices on others or to manipulate or coerce others in the name of religion. (15)

Freedom of religion touches on 'one of the fundamental elements of the conception of life of the person' For these reasons, international instruments and the constitutions and laws of almost all nations recognize the right to religious freedom. Proselytism can violate or manipulate the right of the individual and can exacerbate tense and delicate relations between communities and thus destabilize societies. (16)

The responsibility of fostering religious freedom and the harmonious relations between religious communities is a primary concern of the churches. Where principles of religious freedom are not being respected and lived in church relations, we need, through dialogue in mutual respect, to encourage deeper considerations and appreciation of these principles and of their practical application for the churches. (17)" (ibid., 78-79).

[83]"Ce texte, adopté par le Sénat en deuxième lecture le 3 mai (*Le Monde* du 5 mai), permet la dissolution par le tribunal de grande instance des personnes morales ayant pour but *'d'exploiter la sujétion psychologique ou physique de personnes'*, et qui ont été condamnées définitivement à plusieurs reprises. Il étend la responsabilité pénale de personnes morales à certaines infractions graves. Il élargit le délit d'abus frauduleux de faiblesse à la situation de personnes *'en état de sujétion psychologique ou physique résultant de pressions graves et réitérées ou de techniques propres à altérer le*

The third ecclesiological point when addressing the particular issues of crusade evangelism relates to the complexities of international ministry. Churches that carry a name in one country often differ from churches of the same name in another country. Churches in each country are moving on a denominational life-cycle at a different pace as they deal with different cultural, theological, and ecclesial challenges. Hence, some Anglican Churches in Australia are far more evangelistic than Episcopal churches who ordain homosexuals in the United States. The Free Church in France is amillennial, whereas the Evangelical Free Church of America is premillennial. The RCC in the Midwestern United States is quite different from that in Haiti or Peru. In fact, I was privileged to be an assistant pastor of a church in Quebec-city between two Catholic parishes. The high-town parish was the ecumenical "St. Sacrément" parish and the low-town parish was the "Old Catholic" "St. Joseph" parish. In our work of door-to-door evangelism we noted the marked differences between parishioners of these two adjacent parishes.

According to Robert L. Kennedy, Graham never received the support of the Lutheran World Federation, based in Germany, even though he had multiple crusades in Germany in 1955, 1960, 1963, 1966, and 1970. The reason for the lack of support from German Lutherans was a desire to maintain good relations with American Lutherans:[84]

> Dannenhaus concluded that since Lilje was president of the Lutheran World Federation, any strong support of a Baptist would compromise his position. It was not even certain whether Lilje would be permitted to do anything of that sort [support Billy Graham] "in light of the American Lutherans."[85]

Graham's difficulties in soliciting the support of the Lutheran World Federation exemplifies the challenges of international cross-denominational crusade evangelism. The three main supporting bodies for Graham's international crusades were thus American evangelical missionaries, the Evangelical Alliance, and the Anglican church.

Therefore, a theology of cooperation in crusade evangelism needs to address the necessity for absolutes in ecclesiology, as well as in

---

jugement'" (Xavier Ternisien, "Adoption définitive par les députés de la loi anti-sectes," *Le Monde,* 31 May 2001; accessed 11 July 2002; available from http://membres.lycos.fr/tussier/rev0105.htm#3a; Internet).

[84]"The faith taught by Graham is, therefore, not the same faith as taught in the Confessions" (Wilhelm Stoll, *The Conversion Theology of Billy Graham in the Light of the Lutheran Confessions* [St. Louis: Concordia Student Journal, 1980], 64).

[85]Robert L. Kennedy, *Best Intentions,* 506.

soteriology. A theology of cooperation needs clear parameters for ministry. And a theology of cooperation must be flexible to work with the complexities of international Christian denominational nuances. With these introductory topics out in the open, we turn to discuss particular phases in Graham's approach to cooperation.

Graham on Cooperation

After nine years of preaching church revivals and pastoral ministry, Graham began to travel as an evangelist with United States-based ministry called Youth for Christ (YFC). YFC was a para-church ministry founded by Torrey Johnson which gathered youth from conservative churches in rallies and regular meetings following World War II. Graham was the first full-time evangelist and vice-president with YFC. YFC provided an umbrella organization to further the work of ministries like Jack Wyrtzen's Saturday evening gathering at New York's Time Square.

Through Graham's experiences with Christian and Missionary Alliance youth ministry in Florida, his opportunities to preach revivals in Southern Baptist churches, his brief experience at Bob Jones, his education at Florida Bible Institute and Wheaton College, his pastoral ministry, his radio ministry, and his YFC preaching, Graham knew that cooperation among Christians was needed for successful revival ministry. However, this cooperation needed and had boundaries. The remainder of this chapter will exemplify and explain Graham's approach to cooperation, noting periods when his approach to cooperation shifted and how it shifted.

The Early-Early Graham

Because little is available on Graham in the first twelve years of his ministry, little can be said about Graham's view of cooperation during this time period. There is one statement which Graham made in 1947 that portrays his attitude toward the local church and toward the fundamentals of the faith:

> Is there not now a decay of religion? Less than 5 per cent of the citizenry of our land frequented a place of worship last Sunday night. Is there not something wrong! The President of the Ministerial Association of the greatest churchgoing town in America told me some time ago that 85 per cent of the people in his city never darken the door of a church or attend Sunday school. Is there not something wrong when during the last ten years ten thousand churches have been forced to close their doors? Is there not something wrong when last year seven thousand churches reported not one convert? This means

that seven thousand ministers preached for an entire year without reaching one lost soul. Using a low average, suppose that they preached forty Sundays, not including extra meetings, which would mean that these seven thousand ministers preached five hundred and sixty thousand sermons in a year. Think of the labor and the money expended on salaries to make this possible, and yet five hundred and sixty thousand sermons preached by seven thousand ministers in seven thousand churches to thousands of hearers during the last twelve months failed to bring one soul to Christ! There is something radically wrong somewhere. There is either something wrong with these seven thousand ministers, or with their five hundred and sixty thousand sermons, or both!

John Wesley said, "The Church has nothing to do but to save souls; therefore spend and be spent in this work. It is not your business to speak so many times, but to save souls as you can; to bring as many sinners as you possibly can to repentance."

Thousands of these men have denied that the Bible is the Word of God. Thousands of men standing behind the sacred desk today lied when they spoke their ordination vows. They deny the blood atonement; they deny the virgin birth; they deny the bodily resurrection of Christ; they deny the total depravity of man. One segment of the Church has gone into apostasy, another segment has gone into a state of lethargy, indifference, passionless, cold, formal, orthodoxy. Another segment has gone to the extreme of so called "ultra-Fundamentalism" whose object is not to fight the world, the flesh and the devil, but to fight other Christians whose interpretation is not like theirs. Thus the Church has lost its power. Our beautiful sanctuaries have steeples that tower toward the sky, but the millions of dollars that are being spent every year are making less impact upon the nation today than at any other time in our history.

The Church should be setting the pace. The Church should be taking its proper place of leadership in the nation. But, alas, it has failed sadly, with the result that millions of the new generation never enter a church. They walk the streets without God, without Christ, without any religious instruction whatsoever. God help the Church to wake up![86]

Three important points on the early-early Graham can be demonstrated from this quote. First, Graham was critical of churches and pastors that did not win souls Sunday-by-Sunday. Second, Graham assumed that the church was under orders for the saving of souls. Third, he enumerated the fundamentals

---

[86]Billy Graham, "America's Hope" (1947), 22-24.

of the faith as being important for ministers: the Bible is the Word of God, the blood atonement, the virgin birth; the bodily resurrection of Christ, and the total depravity of man. Fourth, he included an evangelistically-driven cultural agenda for the church. Thus, the early-early Graham was clearly theologically aligned to the fundamentalist movement of the early twentieth century.

The Early Graham

The "Early Graham" was described in the last chapter as the period after Los Angeles 1949 to approximately New York 1957. During this time period Graham became more and more intolerant of those who championed denominational distinctives. For example, as a prerequisite to revival, Graham felt that unity was key:

> That means that if I am a Presbyterian or you are a Baptist, or if I am a Baptist or a Pentecostal, regardless of denomination, we have to forget our differences—forget any minor points of argument and join together around the cross of the Lord Jesus Christ. We must unite in prayer and supplication to the Lord, and God will send a revival.[87]

The significant statement as regards the Early Graham's view of cooperation was the prerequisite of dropping denominational distinctives, "regardless of denomination, we have to forget our differences." Of course the danger lies in which distinctives are deemed necessary and which are not. Yet in 1950 he still spoke out against desolate church-life, "The fires of the reformation have all but flickered out, leaving a great religious desolation of tombs and ashes and dead man's bones in many places."[88] But the Early Graham was increasingly being pushed to choose between fundamentalism and non-fundamentalism.

During his days as President of Northwestern, the Graham campaigns elicited some controversy in the area of cooperation, in particular including a non-fundamentalist on the campaign committee. Two quotes give examples of the early Graham on fundamentalism. The first was quoted by Brad Gsell:

> In a letter to a supporter dated May 29, 1951, Graham wrote: "I have never been, nor will I ever be, in favor of a Modernist being on

---

[87]Billy Graham, "We Need Revival," 77.

[88]Billy Graham, "Whither Bound?" *America's Hour of Decision,* 141.

the committee or in any way having any working fellowship in this meeting."[89]

The second quote had similar content regarding Graham's early view of cooperating with Modernists:

> Contrary to any rumours that are constantly floating about, we have never had a modernist on our Executive Committee, and we have never been sponsored by the Council of Churches in any city except Shreveport and Greensboro—both small towns where the majority of the ministers are evangelical.[90]

Whereas the source of these quotes may appear questionable to some, they illicit several questions. First, was the early Graham operating within fundamentalist circles? Secondly, Did the early Graham ascribe to fundamentalist theology? Thirdly, did Graham's views on cooperation move him beyond fundamentalist circles? It is the conclusion of this author that all the above questions can be answered with an "aye". However, something happened in the ministry of the early Graham to lead him to move beyond fundamentalist circles, and even to distance himself from strict fundamentalism.

Distancing Himself from Fundamentalists

From his autobiography, two experiences mark occasions that may have left in Graham a distaste for extreme fundamentalists. These experiences coupled with the fact that Graham "will go as far as he possibly can to get a hearing,"[91] led him to distance himself from legalistic fundamentalism.

The first experience was Graham's pastoral experience at

---

[89]Brad Gsell, *The Legacy of Billy Graham: The Accommodation of Truth to Error in the Evangelical Church* (Charlotte, NC: Fundamental Presbyterian Publications, 1998), 11.

[90]*The Sword of the Lord* (June 6, 1952), 9; quoted in J. A. Johnson, *Billy Graham—The Jehoshaphat of Our Generation?* (Bangalore, India: Berean Publications, n.d.), 11. This same quote, which is oft repeated to show the early Graham's attitude toward fundamentalism, is also found in Erroll Hulse, *The Pastor's Dilemna* (Houslow, Middlesex, England: Maurice Allan, 1966), 35 and Brad Gsell, *The Legacy of Billy Graham,* 11.

[91]Robert Evans, personal interview with author, July 2, 2001, handwritten notes in possession of the author.

Western Springs Baptist Church. When new believers came to Christ, the Grahams noticed that the church had "a judgmental attitude based on different lifestyles and associations."[92] Graham's second experience with fundamentalists was at a crusade in Altoona, Pennsylvania, which was just prior to his famous 1949 Los Angeles crusade. In Altoona, Graham noted:

> The community itself seemed apathetic, competing ministerial associations squabbled over trivia, and organization for the Campaign was poor. There were other problems that we had not encountered before to any extent. Altoona was a center of extreme fundamentalism (and also strong liberalism), and some people yelled out in the meetings, not out of enthusiasm but to condemn me for fellowshipping with Christians they considered too liberal (and for other perceived faults). . . .
>
> Not surprisingly, the attendance was small when compared to the turnout we had just had in Baltimore, and the results were insignificant by my own measurement.[93]

Altoona combined many points that were not helpful to a citywide crusade. First, there were theological debates. This difficulty included "separate inquiries from rival ministerial associations that were in each other's throats. . ."[94] Second, there was poor organization. Third, it is assumed that there was a small group of churches working together. Fourth, there was a small turnout to the meetings, which were held in the Jaffa Mosque Auditorium.[95] Fifth, there were disturbances at the meeting from disgruntled people and a disturbed woman in the choir. Sixth, there was no significant response to the gospel. Graham's conclusion regarding this crusade was, "But if ever I felt I conducted a Campaign that was a flop, *humanly* speaking, Altoona was it!"[96]

Right after Altoona was Los Angeles—almost the opposite in every way. One of the significant differences between the two was church sponsorship. Martin wrote that "The sponsoring committee enjoyed good support from approximately a quarter of Los Angeles-area churches."[97] Los Angeles had better publicity. And at Los Angeles, Graham was plugged into

---

[92]Billy Graham, *Just As I Am,* 89.

[93]Ibid., 134.

[94]William Martin, *A Prophet with Honor,* 108.

[95]*Altoona Mirror,* June 11, 1949, 1, 14.

[96]Billy Graham, *Just As I Am,* 134.

[97]William Martin, 113.

the "Hollywood Christian Group" through Henrietta Mears who taught a Sunday School class at First Presbyterian Church in Hollywood, California. The result of Graham's 1949 Los Angeles crusade propelled him into another fifty-plus years of crusade evangelism ministry.

A core difference between Altoona and Los Angeles was the sponsoring churches. One group was "extreme" fundamentalist and the other was a more open crowd of fundamentalists. Graham saw the dangers of extreme fundamentalism, and during the early fifties, he took pains to distance himself from extreme fundamentalism.

Ecclesiologically (churches with whom Graham chose to identify), Graham's early *Hour of Decision* sermons speak volumes as to his distancing himself from extreme or separating fundamentalism. For example, the first published pamphlet, *Hour of Decision* sermon number one was titled "Hate vs. Love." In this sermon Graham spent quite some time considering the problem of extreme fundamentalism.[98] He said:

---

[98]"Hate knows no bounds. It operates on the social level as well as the broader bases. 'Look Out for Number One,' has become the motto of scores of people. To make good they kick anyone who threatens their careers. Jealousy is a form of hatred.
. . .

It has been said by reliable commentators that one of the reasons for the lack of leadership all over the world has been because of this jealousy and hatred on the part of those already in power. We are told that promising leaders have been eased out of influence for fear they would usurp authority or were getting too popular. . . .

We are living in a world that hates. Even the Christian Church in America is being gripped by a certain form of hatred that is paralyzing evangelism and quenching revival. It is becoming almost impossible in certain cities to preach the Gospel and try to win souls without being attacked by extreme groups in the Church. Certain of these men are far more interested in controversy, in putting people in categories, trapping God's servants or trying to hang them on the horns of a dilemma, than they are in the souls of men. These men are the authors of confusion and have become modern day Pharisees whom Christ severely condemns. Unless these men change their ways, I am fearful of the judgment of God upon them in this hour when the people are crying, longing and praying for revival. The Scriptures clearly teach that Christians are to love one another. We're told in Deuteronomy 10:19 to love even strangers that we have never met. We are told in Scripture to love our neighbor as ourselves. We are told even to love our enemies. But the Scripture emphasizes and underscores from Genesis to Revelation that the believer is particularly to love other believers. The Scripture declares in Proverbs 10:12 'Hatred stirreth up strifes but love covereth all sins.' In Psalm 133:1 the Psalmist said 'Behold, how good and how pleasant it is for brethren to dwell together in unity! It is like precious ointment.' In the Song of Solomon, Chapter 8 and Verse 6, we read, 'Love is strong as death but jealousy is cruel as the grave.' How can Christian leaders fight and strive with one another when they read of their master washing the feet of even him that in a few hours would be denying Him? How can Christians be jealous of one another when Jesus said. 'This is My Commandment that ye love one another as I have loved you.' Church leaders across America need to get on their knees and read Romans 12:9

These men are the authors of confusion and have become modern day Pharisees whom Christ severely condemns. Unless these men change their ways, I am fearful of the judgment of God upon them in this hour when the people are crying, longing and praying for revival.[99]

In the *Hour of Decision* sermon number three Graham again discussed the issue of extreme fundamentalism:[100]

---

and 10. . . . Would to God the Christian leadership of America could be baptized with a baptism of love that would cause us to contend for the faith without being contentious; that would cause us to stand without compromise with love even for those who might be enemies of Christ. Senator Byrd is reported to have said this week that he is more fearful of the division that has gripped the American people than he is of the Communists and that this division and strife threatens to destroy us quicker than Communism. The same could be said of the Christian Church. Ladies and gentlemen, the Church needs a revival of love" (Billy Graham, "Hate vs. Love," *Hour of Decision Sermons,* no. 1 [Minneapolis: Billy Graham Evangelistic Association, 1951, 1955], 4-7).

[99]Ibid., 5-6.

[100]"Even the church is going through its convulsions and turmoil: extreme liberalism on one side that denies the deity of Christ and ultra-fundamentalism on the other side that is orthodox but knows nothing of the power of the Spirit of God nor the love of God for their own brethren.

Dr. Stephen Paine, president of Houghton College, has just written a book entitled 'Separation Is Separating Us.' I have not read it, but the title hits the nail on the head. These dissensions in the ranks of Evangelical Christians are a stench in the nostrils of God. If ever there was a time for Evangelical Christians to demonstrate unity and love, it is now.

Christians, this is all emergency—this is a war to the death with Satan and all his host—this is a time for prayer on the part of God's people, not dissension and strife. *Certainly* we are to be separated from the world. The Bible teaches that. But I find nowhere that we are to be separated from Bible-believing Christians. Because of all these discussions the average Christian has a tendency to become discouraged. The rank and file of Christians across the country are getting sick and tired of the fightings and bickerings among many of our leaders. I warn you, fighting and bickering leaders today, the people are going to rise against you—they long for revival and will not long tolerate this dissension among Christians.

I have determined that I shall not engage in these controversies, bikerings, and fightings that are partially responsible for keeping revival from the church at this hour. By God's grace I shall continue to preach the Gospel of Jesus Christ and not stoop to mud-slinging, name-calling, and petty little fights over non-essentials. If I did not know the Word of God promises final and complete victory to Christ, I, too, might be discouraged when I see these things taking place. If it were not for the confidence we have in the Eternal Promise of the Word of God, we would be alarmed as we see signs which indicate on every hand that we are going into apostasy on the one hand and extreme Phariseeism on the other" (Billy Graham, "Peace vs. Chaos," *Hour of Decision Sermons,* no. 3 [Minneapolis: Billy Graham Evangelistic Association, 1951], 3-5).

Even the church is going through its convulsions and turmoil: extreme liberalism on one side that denies the deity of Christ and ultra-fundamentalism on the other side that is orthodox but knows nothing of the power of the Spirit of God nor the love of God for their own brethren.[101]

Graham then toned down his attack on ultra-fundamentalism, taking a positive approach. In his sermon ". . .And Have Not Love." Graham said, "This is the hour for the church to show forth the love and grace of God."[102] Later in that sermon he gave application to I Corinthians 13:2:

> I could know the Bible from one end to the other; memorize thousands of verse of Scripture; I could be a great Bible teacher; I could even be a preacher from the pulpit—and have not love. I know men in this country who are conservative in their theology—men who would die contending for the inspiration of the Bible—and yet there is so little love. I might know the Bible from Genesis to Revelation but, if I had not love, it would mean absolutely nothing in the sight of God.[103]

It was clear that Graham was seeking to distance himself from extreme fundamentalists in these 1951 quotes, even while he was still the president of Northwestern Bible College, which was a fundamental school. He resigned his position as president of Northwestern Schools on February 25, 1952. Then after that time an *Hour of Decision* sermon delved on the subject of criticism and true worldliness:

> Another sin of the tongue that is prevalent among Christians is the sin of criticism—going around and trying to take a speck out of our brother's eye when we have a log in our own. Jesus said, "Judge not, that you be not judged. For with the judgment you pronounce you will be judged, and the measure you give will be the measure you get" (Matthew 7:2). And in the same chapter we read, "You hypocrite, first take the log out of your own eye, and then you will see clearly to take the speck out of your brother's eye" (Matthew 7:5). This advice from Christ does not mean that we should condone evil, but that we should deal with wrongdoing in our own lives first.

---

[101]Billy Graham, "Peace vs. Chaos," *Hour of Decision Sermons*, no. 3 (Minneapolis: Billy Graham Evangelistic Association, 1951), 3-5.

[102]Billy Graham, "...And Have Not Love," *Hour of Decision Sermons,* no. 9 (Minneapolis: Billy Graham Evangelistic Association, 1951), 2.

[103]Ibid., 4.

There are many Christians who would not dare do certain worldly things, and yet they are filled with pride, gossiping, malice and sins of the spirit that are far more worldly and evil in God's sight than some of these outward things. Worldliness is anything that comes between the Christian and God.[104]

While Graham was forthright in distancing himself from separatist fundamentalists, he seemed to have changed his tactic from direct attack on Pharisaical fundamentalists, to one of turning the other cheek. However, just as a vacuum left to the open air will be filled, Graham needed to replace certain fundamentalist tendencies with something else. His early theological moves were evident by 1953 in the only book he personally wrote, *Peace with God.*[105]

Peace with God (1953)

Presumably, Graham was laid up with an illness during his "Mid-century Campaign" in Hatford, Connecticut on April 24, 1950. William Martin explained:

When Graham fell ill in Hartford for several days (Jack Wyrtzen drove up from New York to fill in for him), Beavan stayed at his bedside and read to him from Bishop Fulton Sheen's *Peace of Soul* and Rabbi Joshua Loth Liebman's *Peace of Mind.* From that experience, Graham began to consider writing a book on the same theme. Published in 1953, it bore the title, *Peace with God.*[106]

Archbishop Fulton Sheen was a very popular Roman Catholic,[107] and his

---

[104]Billy Graham, "The Sins of the Tongue," *Hour of Decision Sermons,* no. 16 (Minneapolis: Billy Graham Evangelistic Association, 1952), 5-6.

[105]William Martin, personal words by author, June 24, 2001, Louisville, handwritten notes in author's possession.

[106]William Martin, *A Prophet with Honor,* 130.

[107]John Hohenberg wrote of Fulton John Sheen, S.T.B., Ph.D., D.D. (1895-1979), "Already noted as a lecturer, he was chosen to preach on 'The Catholic Hour' over NBC [television] (1952-1957) achieved great popularity with both Catholics and non-Catholics. . . . A striking appearance, first-rate intelligence, and magnificent voice, timing, and delivery combine to make Bishop Sheen internationally recognized as one of the most influential preachers of the twentieth century" (John Hohenberg, "Sheen, Fulton J[ohn]," *Collier's Encyclopedia* (New York: Crowell-Collier, 1961), 17:225).

Peace of Soul was quite popular.[108] Rabbi Joshua Roth Liebman's 1946 *Peace of Mind* was a bestseller.[109] Graham seemed to have patterned his book along the same themes of these renowned religious figures in American life.

Graham mulled over *Peace with God* for two years, and it was to become his only book to come exclusively from his pen. Originally Graham had presumably asked someone else, perhaps the son of Donald Grey Barnhouse, to compile *Peace with God* for him. However, he was unhappy with the results and took it upon himself to rewrite it. His intended readership may be noted by those listed in his preface as having read the manuscript and offered suggestions. This list included the following names or titles (in his order):

The Bishop of Barking, Church of England, Dr. Donald Grey Barnhouse, Dr. Robert O. Ferm, Mr. Mark Lee, Dr. Harold John Ockenga, Dr. Cecil Thompson, and Dr. John S. Wimbish.[110]

Those who read the manuscript and offered suggestions were as follows: Bishop of Barking, Church of England; Donald Grey Barnhouse, Presbyterian minister in Philadelphia; Robert Ferm, Graham's research Assistant and Dean of Houghton College; Mark Lee; Harold J. Ockenga, pastor of Park Street (Congregational) Church in Boston; Cecil Thompson; and John S. Wimbish. The influence of these readers and/or Graham's repositioning of his approach to his intended audience may have occasioned several nuances in *Peace with God*.

First, the issue of worldliness brought up in his 1952 *Hour of*

---

[108]"An enthralling preacher and lecturer with a theatrical style, he won a huge audience for his talks on radio, the Catholic Hour (1930-52), and his television series, Life is Worth Living (1952-65), and for books such as Peace of Soul (1949); he also recruited funds for the missions as national director of the Society for the Propagation of the Faith. After serving as an auxiliary bishop of New York, he was named bishop of Rochester, N.Y. (1966), retiring with the title of archbishop (1969)" ("Sheen, Fulton J (John)" (b. Peter Sheen" [on-line]; accessed 5 July 2001; available from http://www.biography.com/cgi-bin/biomain.cgi; Internet).

[109]"Joshua Loth Liebman (1907-1948): Rabbi, author; born in Hamilton, Ohio. He entered college at age 13, and graduated from the University of Cincinnati at 19. Following his ordination at Hebrew Union College in Cincinnati, he became a lecturer there in Greek philosophy. He was rabbi of Temple Israel in Boston from 1939 until his death. An active Zionist and public speaker, he preached on the radio and served on many national government and religious groups. His 1946 book, *Peace of Mind*, was a best-seller" ("Liebman, Joshua Loth" [on-line]; accessed 5 July 2001; available from http://www.biography.com/cgi-bin/ biomain.cgi; Internet).

[110]Billy Graham, *Peace with God* (1953), 8.

Decision sermon, "Sins of the Tongue," found its way in Graham's 1953 *Peace with God.* In the book, Graham seems to have redefined worldliness more along the lines of the Greek Golden Mean—"Moderation in all things." He used a lengthy quote from Griffin Thomas' *The Catholic Faith.*[111] Prior to the quote Graham wrote, "Worldliness, however, has been vastly misunderstood on the part of thousands of Christians. It needs a little clarification."[112] The quote of Thomas, which lacked reference information in *Peace with God,* included the following statements:

> Abuse literally means extreme use, and in many instances overuse of things lawful become sin. . . . Worldliness is thus not confined to any particular rank, walk, or circumstance of life so that we cannot separate this class from that and call one worldly and the other unworldly . . . One spiritual and the other unspiritual. Worldliness is a spirit, an atmosphere, an influence permeating the whole of life and human society, and it needs to be guarded against constantly and strenuously.[113]

This redefinition of worldliness using philosophical categories, and moving away from the *a priori* of worldliness as disobedience of God's word, seems a move away from Graham's fundamentalist roots.[114] For example, I John

---

[111]Griffin Thomas, *The Catholic Faith: A Manual of Instruction for Members of the Church of England* (London: Hodder and Stoughton, 1905, 1908). J. I. Packer wrote a foreword for the 1971 reprint of *The Catholic Faith.* Packer wrote, "Much that has been written on the Anglican faith and life in the last sixty-seven years has simply been Griffith Thomas spread thin, and nothing that could replace this manual has come out at all. . . . His teaching is consistently reliable, both Biblically and historically" (iii, iv).

[112]Billy Graham, *Peace with God* (1953), 156.

[113]Ibid., 156-57. A quote of Griffith Thomas, *The Catholic Faith,* 16.

[114]Graham in his 1947 sermon "Final Exam," after discussing I John 2:16, Graham defined worldliness as follows: "All of this is worldly. Don't make a mistake, however. Don't become the victim of the unscriptural teaching of separation which Stacy Woods calls 'legality in the guise of spirituality.' This modern legality has placed its taboo on certain practices, while sometimes ignoring more harmful ones. We call a person 'separated' if he does not attend certain places of amusement. This is one of Satan's lies and has become a great stumbling block to many young people.
What is worldliness actually? Mr. Woods describes it very aptly: 'It is the self-indulgent attitude of the heart and mind toward life. . .' It is not merely doing certain forbidden things or going to certain prescribed places. Worldliness is what we are not just what we do. It is in reality an inner attitude, for as a man 'thinketh in his heart, so is he.' Any Christian whose interest is directed toward himself is worldly" (Billy Graham, "Final Exam," *Calling Youth to Christ,* 70).

2:3-6 speaks of knowing God and keeping His commands, while I John 2:15-17 speaks of loving God, not the world. By 1953, Graham was beginning to communicate using categories that moved him from his "Bible-only" fundamental roots.

Secondly, in his chapter on "The Christian and the Church" Graham proffered seven purposes for the church. They were as follows:

> The purpose of this Christian society called the "church" is, First: to glorify God by our worship. . . . Second: the church is for fellowship. . . . Third: the church is for strengthening of faith. . . . Fourth: the church is a medium of service. . . . Fifth: the church should be a means of channeling your funds for Christian work. . . . Sixth: the church is for the spreading of the gospel. . . . Finally: it is through the church that our humanitarianism finds widest expression.[115]

By the time he wrote *Peace with God* it is clear that Graham was moving from his Southern Baptist *a priori*, the universal affirmative of saving souls, as confirmed by W. A. Criswell, former pastor of Graham's home church.[116] Graham showed his skill at walking along the fine line between two points of view in his affirmation of evangelism:

> The only feet that Christ has are your feet. The only hands that He has are your hands. The only tongue that He has is your tongue. Use every talent, facility, and method possible to win men to Christ. This is the great mission of the church. Our methods may vary. We may use visitation evangelism, educational evangelism, preaching missions, industrial evangelism, cell evangelism, radio-television

---

[115]Ibid., 178-183.

[116]"In the work of an evangelist, great effort is poured into organization devised for winning the lost. In the tremendous Philadelphia campaign of Billy Sunday, the organization reached down to the last city block. The entire city was touched by it and moved by it. As a result of the revival, more than six thousand souls were baptized into the churches of the metroplex. If the pastor is under authority to do the work of an evangelist, then he must do the same thing; namely, he must use his church organization to win the lost. To what better use could they be dedicated.And what a powerful instrument for witnessing the pastor has in the marching members of his many-faceted ministry through the church. The way the church is put together is inherently, intrinsically made for soul winning, for reaching lost people. It is the thing that comes naturally" (W. A. Criswell, *Criswell's Guidebook for Pastors* (Nashville: Broadman, 1980), 133).

evangelism, movie evangelism, or so-called mass evangelism. Whatever it may be, let us use it to win other people to Christ.[117]

Graham affirmed by his life and in his sixth point that his view of the purpose of the church was primarily the saving of souls. However, in placing evangelism sixth, he may have moved to a particular affirmative as a concession to his "wider" readership, most of whom would agree with Charles Templeton, as noted in chapter three. This is more than a question of the semantics between the words "purpose" and "mission." The two words are basically synonyms. If a differentiation would have been deemed necessary or important, Graham could have discussed it and placed evangelism as the first and primary purpose of the church. He chose not to do this. Perhaps this "one of six" idea was "the tactical Graham," to borrow the terminology of Robert Evans as we discussed Graham. Yet, as noted in chapter three, the particular affirmative became a part of Graham's "core belief" sometime between 1965 and when he acquiesced to John Stott in 1975—which may also have been tactical. Yet, this writer can only judge by the words of Graham in print. I cannot differentiate motives between tactical beliefs and true core beliefs.

Throughout his purpose of the church section, Graham was sending signals to socially-oriented mainline leaders that he is not far from their view. Graham discussed the church as a social institution. He continued by providing a relativistic view of worship and service in choosing a church,[118] apart from the preaching of the Word of God. In fact, in one point where he could have discussed the proclamation of the Word of God in church, point three, "strengthening in the faith," Graham wrote a disappointing paragraph explaining that he had already covered this point in the previous chapter.[119] When looking in the prior chapter for information, the only place it could have been mentioned was his fourth rule of the Christian life, "attend church regularly." This section lacked a clear definition of the concept "attend a Bible-believing church." Graham did

---

[117]Billy Graham, *Peace with God,* 183.

[118]"Some people find it easier to draw closer to God in magnificent buildings and with some form of ritual. Others find they can seek God only in stark simplicity. Some people find themselves in sympathy with one kind of service, others feel more at home in a different atmosphere. The important thing is not *how* we do it, but the sincerity and depth of purpose *with which* we do it, and we should each find and join the church in which as individuals we can best accomplish this" (ibid., 177).

[119]"Third: *the church is for the strengthening of faith.* Through joint prayers, testimonies, and the preaching and the teaching of the various organizations of the church, your faith will be strengthened. The church will build you up in the most holy faith by reemphasizing the points that we have already covered in 'The Rules for the Christian Life'" (ibid., 179).

include one phrase in four paragraphs when he mentioned the Word of God: "The church is Christ's organization upon earth. It is a place where we worship God, learn His Word, and fellowship with other Christians."[120] Yet he did not emphasize at all the absolute importance of a Bible-believing and Bible-preaching church. Rather, he wrote in the context of encouraging church attendance rather than listening to radio preaching:

> You do not go to church to hear a sermon. You go to church to worship God and to serve Him in the fellowship of other Christians. You cannot be a successful and happy Christian without being faithful in church. In the church you will find your place of service. We are saved to serve. The happy Christian is the busy Christian.[121]

Thus, Graham's ecclesiology had adjusted significantly by the time he wrote *Peace with God.* He seemed to be making allowances for his audience to take part in churches that were not necessarily Bible-believing or Bible-preaching.

The subject of ecclesiology brings one to discuss the role of the Holy Spirit in follow-up and the role of the church in follow-up. Bob Jones, Sr. was said to have been a powerful preacher of the Word of God. Many committed their lives to Christ through his ministry. Yet, he presumably did nothing for follow-up of the new believers, other than lead them in a prayer of salvation after the invitation.[122] It would seem that Jones used Philip, the evangelist, as his example, as he did not or could not follow-up the Ethiopian Eunuch. Yet, simultaneously Jones strongly believed in the necessity of membership in a Bible-believing church. Was his view of conversion and eternal security so strong that he believed that God would take care of his own? Graham may have had a similar view of conversion. While Graham worked hard at follow-up, he worked with mainline groups regularly from 1952 on. Could it be that he believed one of two points: 1) God would take care of His own, as to their nurture and spiritual growth, and would lead them to the right church, or 2) God may use the crusade to reawaken or revive the non-evangelistic churches to their mandate, thus they would be "forced" (as it were) to serve as good places for follow-up, making use of his materials. Yet Graham seems to have showed a tactical

---

[120]Ibid., 166.

[121]Ibid.

[122]Testimony of Samuel Faircloth, attested to without use of Jones' name in his *Church Planting for Reproduction,* "It is unscriptural as well as deplorably neglectful to leave new converts without adequate spiritual nurture and care" (*Church Planting for Reproduction* (Samuel D. Faircloth, Grand Rapids, MI; Baker Book House, 1991), 175).

belief in not stressing the need for a Bible-believing church in his *Peace with God.*

Thirdly, Graham spent a chapter, "Social Obligations of the Christian," noting the social implications of the Christian life. He used an inside-out approach to social problems, while highlighting that the Christian ought to be in the foray to solve the social problems of the day. The following was his thematic paragraph for the chapter:

> Many people have criticized the so-called "social gospel," but Jesus taught that we are to take regeneration in one hand and a cup of cold water in the other. Christians, above all others, should be concerned with social problems and social injustices. Down through the centuries the church has contributed more than any other single agency in lifting social standards to new heights. Child labor has been outlawed. Slavery has been abolished. The status of woman has been lifted to heights unparalleled in history, and many other reforms have taken place as a result of the influence of the teachings of Jesus Christ. The Christian is to take his place in society with moral courage to stand up for that which is right, just, and honorable.[123]

As he wrote the chapter, it would seem that Graham was trying to provide a synthesis between the fundamentalist and modernist views of the gospel and its social implications. This same effort was evident in his founding of *Christianity Today* three years later.

Christianity Today (1956)

Graham began to distance himself from extreme fundamentalists in 1951 and 1952. By the publishing of *Peace with God* Graham had held out an olive branch to modernists in their view of worldliness, their view of the church, and their view of the priority of social problems. By 1956, Graham was more clearly moving down the road of seeking to establish a new middle road.

Graham expressed this new middle road in his founding of *Christianity Today* four or five years later.

> By 1955, Graham was ready to move, and it was clear he had been thinking about the character of the publication. In a letter to Fuller professor Harold Lindsell, he elaborated on his plans. The magazine would, he wrote, "plant the evangelical flag in the middle of the road,

---

[123]Billy Graham, *Peace with God*, 190-91.

taking a conservative theological position but a definite liberal approach to social problems." It would be critical of both the National and World Council of Churches when that was appropriate but would also commend them for their good work rather than align itself in unvarying opposition, in the manner of Carl McIntire's journal, the *Christian Beacon.* It would, of course, promulgate a high view of biblical authority, but "its view of inspiration would be somewhat along the line of [*The Christian View of Science and Scripture* by] Bernard Ramm," an Evangelical scholar's book that challenged the belief that the Bible could be taken as authoritative on scientific matters and left open the possibility that a divinely guided form of evolution might have played a role in the origin of species and the development of humankind. Graham's positive assessment of Ramm's controversial book was significant in that despite his unshakable confidence in the trustworthiness of Scripture, he was wary of making stronger claims for the Bible than the Bible makes for itself and was opting for an approach sure to draw fire from many Fundamentalists.[124]

It seemed important to Graham, to distance himself from extreme fundamentalism, characterized by Carl McIntire in the above portion, and the "liberalism" of the National and World Council of Churches. Graham wanted the message of the fundamentalists and the social views of the modernists (both Anselm and Abelard!). In order to accomplish this, he encouraged the scientific view of Scripture as typified by the interpretive scheme of Bernard Ramm (faith—biblical authority and reason—empirical science). Graham's was the challenge of grasping the impossible middle.

E. Stanley Jones, Methodist evangelist, noted the same middle road approach of Billy Graham, relating it to Hegelian dialectics (in which the synthesis is related to the thesis and the antithesis). He wrote to the *Christian Century* during the 1957 New York crusade:

> The Graham crusade is a symptom of that emerging synthesis. Both groups want to share Christ in differing terminology and in differing methods, but both want to share Christ. The synthesis is emerging at a very important place—at the place of evangelism. There conservative and liberal could join in the only place they could get together—at the place of making Christ known to people inside and outside the churches who need conversion. That synthesis is a good one, the best possible one. For it is vital, not verbal. Hence the

---

[124]William Martin, 212.

conservative groups and the Protestant council of churches could come together on this basis in the New York crusade—and rightly.[125]

Hence, as will be discussed in the conclusion, Graham forged a new middle ground between fundamentalism and modernism. The first clear portrayal of steps toward that new middle ground lay in his revising his ecclesiology in *Peace with God.* And what happened personally as he held a pen in his hand became etched in the psyche of *Christianity Today.*

Adjusting the Gospel toward Modernism

Theologically, Graham's 1953 *Peace with God* began to pave the way toward a theological reductionism which became more apparent in 1957 and changed his view of mission in 1965, 1973, 1974, and 1975. Graham seemed to be framing the biblical gospel in such a way as to provide him an audience with modernistic leaders and their churches. His ends were worthy and his theological changes very slight at first. It was a matter of the omission of one or two concepts that would be distasteful to modernistic audiences, and adding one or two concepts to show that the modernistic audience did have legitimate concerns. However, it must be noted that Graham did not shed use of the word "sin" and "hell" as his contemporary Robert Schuller was alleged to have done. And Graham continued to preach the death of Christ for sin and the need for conversion. For Graham, however, his movement was in the direction of sin as alienation and hell as separation. Both of these beliefs with which Graham could find common ground with mainline churches.

Therefore, the Early Graham made the necessary practical and theological adjustments to make his gospel message palatable to a modernistic audience. Graham's use of the invitation system, and its corollary, instantaneous conversion, gave him continued credibility with his evangelical audience. By the Middle Graham, however, his distancing himself from the fundamentalists of his earlier years was now evident to the fundamentalists. They sensed that he had changed, noting only that it was in the area of separation from the world (and from apostate teachers) that he had changed. His theological adjustments were undetected by most evangelicals, as they accepted him in his theological reductionism.

---

[125]E. Stanley Jones, "*Higher* Synthesis?" *The Christian Century,* 14 August 1957, 970.

The Middle Graham

While Graham's approach to "ecumenical evangelism" brought him criticism early on—as was evidenced by his statements in the Northwestern *Pilot* and some letters that Graham wrote to John R. Rice, as noted above. During his 1957 crusade in New York, Graham faced intense pressure from both sides. The fundamentalists accused Graham of compromising his faith because of his relationship with the Federal Council of Churches. Whereas, using the medium of the *Christian Century* and *Christian and Society*, as well as other media, modernists attacked Graham as being irrelevant and actually negative to the Christian cause.

New York, 1957

Graham's 1957 crusade, using the same approach to cooperation he had used for several years, placed him under the nation's eye. And simultaneously, it brought him the most intense criticism of his ministry from fundamentalists. This crusade actually provided a clear division in the relationship between fundamentalists and evangelicals. It occasioned the writing of Robert Ferm's *Cooperative Evangelism,* and the criticism that followed. The following timeline of criticism provides a glimpse of some of the *ethos* of that time:

March 5, 1956: Reinhold Niebuhr decried the invitation of Graham, stating "We dread the prospect."[126]

May 23, 1956: Reinhold Niebuhr accused Graham of irrelevancy, stating, "Graham still thinks within the framework of pietistic moralism."[127]

August 8, 1956: Reinhold Niebuhr wrote an open letter to Billy Graham encouraging him to include the cause of social justice and love commandment into his revival message.[128]

---

[126]Reinhold Niebuhr, "Editorial Notes," *Christianity and Crisis*, 5 March 1956, 18.

[127]Reinhold Nieburh, "Literalism, Individualism and Billy Graham," *Christian Century*, 23 May 1956, 641.

[128]"There is more hope that Graham himself will see the weaknesses of a traditional evangelical perfectionism in an atomic age than his clerical and lay sponsors, with their enthusiasm for any kind of revival, will see it. For Graham is a world traveler

October 15, 1956: First issue of *Christianity Today*. L. Nelson Bell editor. Graham's article "Biblical Authority in Evangelism" included.[129]

March 6, 1957: Ferm received letter from Bob Jones, Sr. decrying the liberal sponsorship of the New York crusade.[130]

March 20, 1957: Malcolm Boyd discussed the use of means in mass evangelism, quoting Graham, who said, "I am selling the greatest product in the world; why shouldn't it be promoted as well as soap?"[131]

April 21, 1957: Stanley Rowland Jr. interview of Graham published in *New York Times*.[132]

May 4, 1957: Gustav Weigel, S.J., at the end of a cynical article hoped "that God may lead him [Graham] to the One Faith [Roman Catholic] that is worthy of all man's dedication."[133]

May 15, 1957: New York crusade began [134]

---

and a very perceptive observer of the world scene with its many collective problems. His instincts are genuine and his sense of justice well developed. He could embody the cause of justice—particularly where it is so closely and obviously related to the love commandment as on the race issue—into his revival message. The only thing that could prevent such a development is that it is contrary to the well established 'technique' of revivalism. That technique requires the oversimplification of moral issues and their individualization for the sake of inducing an emotional crisis. Collective sins are therefore not within the range of a revival. It may be that Graham is good enough to break from this tradition and obvious technique. In that case he would cease to be merely the last exponent of a frontier religious tradition and become a vital force in the nation's moral and spiritual life" (Reinhold Niebuhr, "Proposal to Billy Graham," *Christian Century,* 9 August 1956, 922).

[129]Billy Graham, "Biblical Authority in Evangelism," 5-7, 17.

[130]Letter from Bob Jones, Sr. to friend, dated March 6, 1957 (Wheaton, IL: Billy Graham Archives, Collection 19, Accession 88-16, Box 1, Item 3).

[131]Boyd, Malcolm, "Crossroads in Mass Evangelism," *The Christian Century,* 20 March 1957, 359-361.

[132]Stanley Rowland Jr., "As Graham Sees His Role," *New York Times Magazine,* 21 April 1957, 17-25.

[133]Gustav Weigel, S.J., "What to Think of Billy Graham," 164.

[134]Graham, *Just As I Am,* 299.

May 15, 1957: *Christian Century* ran cynical expose of the success that Graham would have through the pre-arranged crowds at his crusade.[135]

May 27, 1957: *Life Magazine* ran an article on Graham.[136]

May 29, 1957: An editorial in *Christian Century*, presumably by Martin Marty, decried Graham's emphasis on conversion, calling him rather to participate in Christian suffering.[137]

June 5, 1957: Avalanche of mail began arriving at *Christian Century* for and against Graham crusade.[138]

June 12, 1957: Martin Marty's cynical article acknowledged, "The rally is sufficiently popular to make dissent sound like 'sour grapes.'"[139]

June 19, 1957: *Christian Century* editorial highlighted the fundamentalist revival and how Graham's crusade fit into that shifting paradigm. Also accused Graham of preaching "without reference to the 'fundamentals.'"[140]

June 26, 1957: Cecil Northcott, who opposed Graham's crusade in London, wrote of the bleak response to that crusade.[141]

September 1, 1957: New York crusade ended.

September 4, 1957: Niebuhr wrote an article describing the mail that he had received to the *Christian Century* and seeking to

---

[135]"In the Garden," *Christian Century,* 15 May 1957, 614-15.

[136]"A Mighty City Hears Billy's Mighty Call," *Life,* 27 May 1957, 20-26.

[137]"Editorial: Mass Conversions," *Christian Century,* 29 May 1957, 677-79.

[138]"Correspondence," *The Christian Century,* 5 June 1957, 711-12.

[139]Martin Marty, "Editorial Correspondence: A Tale of Two Cities," *The Christian Century,* 12 June 1957, 727

[140]"Editorial: Fundamentalist Revival," *The Christian Century,* 19 June 1957, 750.

[141]Cecil Northcott, "Editorial Correspondence: Needed: Evangelism in Depth," *The Christian Century,* 26 June 1957, 782-83.

assuage "Christians who are worried about a new wave of fundamentalism and biblicism that threatens to undo the discriminations of a century and make the Christian faith unavailable. . . ."[142]

April 1958: Zondervan published Robert Ferm's *Cooperative Evangelism.*

May 10, 1958: Robert Ferm received a letter from Bob Jones Sr., asking him to explain who he was referring to on page 94 of *Cooperative Evangelism.*[143]

May 23, 1958: Bob Jones expanded on his prior letter asking for an answer to his May 10, 1958 letter.

May 24, 1958: Letter from student body president and vice-president at Bob Jones University decrying the fact that *Cooperative Evangelism* was sent to every student at Bob Jones, and asking to be removed from the mailing list. This letter included a petition by the student body decrying the above mentioned action.[144]

1958: Ferm received an unfavorable evaluation of the impact of the 1954 London crusade written by Cecil Northcott, "Four Years After," accompanied by a summary evaluation entitled "Cecil Northcott Sums It Up," published in the *British Weekly.*[145]

---

[142]Reinhold Niebuhr, "After Comment, the Deluge," *The Christian Century,* 4 September 1957, 1035.

[143]Letter from Bob Jones, Sr. to Robert O. Ferm, dated May 10, 1958 (Wheaton, IL: Billy Graham Archives, Collection 19, Accession 88-16, Box 1, Item 3). Ferm wrote on page 94, "One of the tragedies of contemporary Christendom is that some once-honored and used evangelists, men who once knew the power of God in their preaching and whose altars were once filled with repentant sinners, no longer preach the Gospel with power, much of their time being apparently spent with others of like mind in concerted attack on some of God's servants. By word of mouth and printed page there continues to pour forth a volume of criticism, abuse and even distortion which must bring great joy to the enemies of the Cross" (Robert Ferm, *Cooperative Evangelism* [Grand Rapids: Zondervan, 1958], 94).

[144]Letter from Charles Britt and Don Horton to Robert O. Ferm, dated May 24, 1958 (Wheaton, IL: Billy Graham Archives, Collection 19, Accession 88-16, Box 1, Item 3).

[145]Cecil Northcott, "Four Years after Graham" (Wheaton, IL: Billy Graham Archives, Collection 19, Accession 88-16, Box 1, Item 3).; Cecil Northcott,

1958: R.T. Ketcham, national representative of the General Association of Regular Baptist Churches and associate editor of *The Baptist Bulletin,* sent out "Special Informational Bulletin #8" in which he chastised Graham for not speaking out on believers baptism when he spoke at Colgate Rochester Divinity School and accused Harold Ockenga of speaking at a Unitarian church.[146]

June 30, 1958: Ferm received a seventeen-page letter from Rev. W. E. Abernathy, pastor of First Baptist Church, Newfield, New Jersey. This letter critiqued chapter three of *Cooperative Evangelism,* which dealt with the ministry of Christ, the Apostles, and the Apostle Paul.[147]

August 11, 1958: Bob Jones, Sr. wrote a harsh letter to Wayne Livesay. Livesay explained in a cover letter that he had invited two new Christians from Billy Graham's Bay Area crusade to attend a Bible Conference where Drs. John R. Rice and Bob Jones, Sr. were speakers. He was amazed to find that Jones spent all of his time criticizing Graham. Livesay sent Jones a letter to which Jones was responding.[148]

The preceding timeline outlines the *pathos* to which Graham was subjected because of the New York 1957 crusade. While it was clearly a mile-marker for Graham's ministry, it is difficult to judge the impact of New York 1957 on Graham's theology. Perhaps two comments from onlookers were perceptive from a theological standpoint. The E. Stanley Jones letter regarding Graham creating a synthesis between conservative and liberal was already noted above. However, the editorial titled "Fundamentalist Revival" did bring up theological points.

"Cecil Northcott Sums It Up" (Wheaton, IL: Billy Graham Archives, Collection 19, Accession 88-16, Box 1, Item 3).

[146]R. T. Ketcham, "Special Information Bulletin #8" (Wheaton, IL: Billy Graham Archives, Collection 19, Accession 88-16, Box 1, Item 3).

[147]Letter from William E. Abernathy to Robert O. Ferm, dated June 30, 1958 (Wheaton, IL: Billy Graham Archives, Collection 19, Accession 88-16, Box 1, Item 3). Gary Cohen took the same route as he critiqued Ferm in his *Biblical Separation Defended.* His arguments were one-sided and do not take in to account the possible validity of opposing arguments.

[148]Letter from Wayne Livesay to Billy Graham, dated August 14, 1958, enclosures (Wheaton, IL: Billy Graham Archives, Collection 19, Accession 88-16, Box 1, Item 3).

"Fundamentalist Revival"

Fifteen years after the founding of the National Association of Evangelicals (1942), ten years after the founding of Fuller Theological Seminary (1947), seven months after the founding of *Christianity Today* (1956), and one month into Graham's 1957 New York crusade, the editors of *The Christian Century* were considering the phenomenon of "New Evangelicalism," as it would be called.[149] Their concern was etched into two articles: one titled "Intruders in the Crowded Center" and the other titled "Fundamentalist Revival." While not dealing directly with the Graham crusade, "Intruders in the Crowded Center," by Martin Marty, reviewed a book edited by Carl F. H. Henry, *Contemporary Evangelical Thought.* Marty explained:

> Ten competent scholars of the self-styled neo-evangelical school have now, for one instance, published a symposium which seeks to establish their group at dead center in Christian theology.[150]

Among his sarcastic comments about neo-evangelicals, Marty did commend one chapter in the book, "Andrew Blackwood, in perhaps the best chapter in the book, lists Billy Graham first among the present proclaimers of 'evangelicalism.'"[151] The attempt of the book, it seems was to provide a mediating position between supernaturalism (inerrancy) and naturalism (use of the sciences in serious theological research). Marty continued:

> What unites this school is opposition to liberalism, a conservative ethos, a desire to occupy the center, and doctrinally, an attitude toward the Scriptures which excludes many who could be allies on the other three scores. Almost without exception the nearly-evangelical theologians listed in the book are dismissed because they do not view the Bible as "Inerrant"; classical doctrines of the trinity, Christology, the sacraments and so on are not the issue.[152]

---

[149]Marsden wrote of this term, "In a lengthy press release of December 1957, labeled in an Associated Press dispatch as from 'the originator of "The New Evangelicalism,"' Ockenga defined the term" (George M. Marsden, *Reforming Fundamentalism: Fuller Seminary and the New Evangelicalism* [Grand Rapids: Eerdmans, 1987], 167).

[150]Martin Marty, "Intruders in the Crowded Center: A Review Article," *The Christian Century* 3 July 1957, 820.

[151]Ibid.

[152]Ibid., 821.

Into this theological war-zone entered Billy Graham as the "first among the present proclaimers of 'evangelicalism.'" His was also a centrist position, but centrist in a different way. He shared the views of the authors in *Contemporary Evangelical Thought,* but rather than "coming out" as many of the authors were forced to do because of their theology, Graham sought to come alongside his liberal opponents. Graham's theological position was described in the editorial "Fundamentalist Revival."

The antagonism of the editorial was evident from the start:

> The narrow and divisive creed which the churches rejected a generation ago is staging a comeback. Through skillful manipulation of means and persons, including a well publicized association with the President of the United States, fundamentalistic forces are now in position aggressively to exploit the churches. If their effort succeeds it will make mincemeat of the ecumenical movement, will divide congregations and denominations, will set back Protestant Christianity a half-century.[153]

If Graham's New York 1957 crusade were to succeed, according to the editor of *The Christian Century,* Christianity would be set back fifty years.[154] It is interesting to note that nineteen years after Graham's 1957 crusade was called "The Year of the Evangelical" on the cover of *Time Magazine* (1976). Thirty-eight years later, Alister McGrath would write that evangelicalism was now "mainline":

> Evangelicalism, once considered marginal, has now become mainline, and it can no longer be considered as an insignificant sideshow, sectarian tendency or irrelevance. It has moved from the wings to center stage, displacing others once regarded as mainline, who consequently feel deeply threatened and alienated. Its commitment to

---

[153]"Editorial: Fundamentalist Revival," *The Christian Century,* 19 June 1957, 749.

[154]A fear of moving back is all too common. Note the words of Robert Andringa in *The Future of Christian Education*: "But we must shuck the remaining vestiges of the anti-intellectualism of Christian fundamentalism and move forward with full confidence that the highest scholarship is honoring to God and, indeed, expected of those who call themselves Christian. These capable authors help us move *forward* in our understanding of Christian scholarship" (Robert C. Andringa, "Foreword," David S. Dockery and David P. Gushee, eds, *The Future of Christian Higher Education* (Nashville: Broadman, 1999): xvii). Marsden also wrote of education, "As should be apparent by now, the prescription for American higher education is not a call to return to the past" (George Marsden, *The Soul of the American University* (New York: Oxford University Press, 1994), 439).

evangelism has resulted in numerical growth, where some other variants of Christianity are suffering from severe contraction.[155]

The fear of the editors of *The Christian Century* actually took place— liberalism was overtaken by neo-fundamentalism. Yet it was not without a theological price.

The editorial continued by defining the fundamentals of the faith:

> The five doctrines of the fundamentalist creed are all espoused by Billy Graham and by the organizations, associations and groupings with which he is identified. They are: (1) the virgin birth of Jesus ; (2) the infallible inerrancy of the Bible in every detail; (3) the resurrection of the physical body of Jesus and of the saints at the end of history ; (4) the substitutionary blood atonement; and (5) the imminent return of Christ in person to establish his kingdom. Fundamentalism makes these points the test of orthodoxy, the essence of the Christian faith.[156]

The editorial continued recounting that fundamentalism had failed in the earlier part of the century:

> Fundamentalism suffered an ignominious defeat a generation ago, when it failed to capture a single major denomination. This time it has reasons for anticipating a different outcome.
>
> The reasons include Billy Graham, an attractive and luminous national figure.[157]

The editorial attributed motives to the rising evangelical movement:

> It is instructive to note that increasingly fundamentalism seeks to press the good word "evangelical" into its service. Having by its dogmatism made a once favorable term obnoxious, it is trying to appropriate a designation which is in better repute. This strategy

---

[155]Alister E. McGrath, *Evangelicalism and the Future of Christianity* (Downers Grove, IL: InterVarsity Press, 1995), 17. McGrath identified contextualized evangelism as the glue which held a varied evangelicalism (ibid., 113-14).

[156]"Editorial: Fundamentalist Revival," 749.

[157]Ibid., 750.

cannot succeed for long, for the five points are still the core of the fundamentalist creed.[158]

With that note of doom pronounced on the incipient evangelical movement, the editorial continued its line of thinking by evaluating Billy Graham along the five points of fundamentalism:

> Members of his party regularly reassure suspicious fundamentalists that he is inflexibly faithful to the "fundamentals." His preaching at no point crosses the fundamentalist line, although he carefully omits any reference to its militant motivation. As an evangelist claiming sponsorship of a wide variety of denominations, however, he assumes that he can preach against sin, call men to faith as well as to repentance and offer the grace and forgiveness of God through Christ without reference to the "fundamentals" of the Christian faith, except as one is implied in his frequently repeated "the Bible says." There is a peculiar mental, if not ethical twist in this procedure. One might suppose that it is tolerated only because the evangelist knows that if he preaches what he holds to be the fundamentals his crusade would be disrupted overnight. Strange evangelistic relegation of "fundamentals," but if it helps the crusade get by, the fundamentalists will have no trouble proving, shortly thereafter, who has really moved in.[159]

The editorial then accused evangelical churches of exploiting fundamentalist churches, which, he prophecied, was going to lead to disastrous ends—the seeds of "confusion, division and paralyzing controversy" were being sown as a recipe for future disaster, "Certain pro-tem ecumenics may take the biggest fall yet out of long-term ecumenics."[160]

In this litany of doom, the editor did make an interesting comment regarding Graham's adherence to the five fundamentals. He wrote that Graham omitted direct reference to the fundamentals, with the exception of the implication of "the Bible says." The decision of Graham to redefine certain points as he wrote *Peace with God* with a mainline audience in mind seemed to intensify. The last chapter already noted the changes in Graham's communication of the concept of sin in 1955 and hell in 1957. It between 1957 and 1965 that Graham continued to give balance his fundamentalism with modernistic theology. His 1955 sermon on the love of

---

[158]Ibid.

[159]Ibid.

[160]Ibid., 751.

God[161] coincided with the beginning of his redefinition of sin as a moral sickness. In 1957 Graham preached hell as separation from God,[162] which is a place to be "shunned."[163] In 1958 he balanced man's essential goodness with his essential degradation.[164] All of these were adjustments to fundamental doctrines of the faith. The editor of *The Christian Century* may have rightly noted these during the 1957 crusade.

"Fellowship and Separation"

The August 1961 *Decision Magazine* carried an article by Graham titled "Fellowship and Separation." This article was reprinted as *Hour of Decision* sermon number 140. The article started as follows:

> What should a Christian do about his associations? Whom should he seek out and whom should he shun? As I study the subject of separation in the Old and New Testaments, I discover that the weight of Scripture lies in the direction of fellowship rather than separation.[165]

The sermon highlighted the fact that there was a revival taking place in virtually every denomination, "Even the unsympathetic are admitting that there is a renaissance of evangelicalism sweeping through our major denominations."[166] Later he said, "The harvest is ripe. We may be living at the last moment before the coming of the Lord Jesus Christ."[167] This repeated the optimism Graham expressed in his comments at the Church House, Westminster on March 20, 1952.[168]

---

[161]Billy Graham, "The Love of God" (1955), 6-7.

[162]Billy Graham, "Hell" (1957), 7, 9, 10.

[163]Ibid., 6-8.

[164]This was his addition in the "Two Faces of Man," to use his terminology (Billy Graham, "Past, Present and Future," 1-3).

[165]Billy Graham, "Fellowship and Separation," *Hour of Decision Sermons,* no. 140 (Minneapolis: Billy Graham Evangelistic Association, 1961), 1.

[166]Ibid., 6.

[167]Ibid., 9.

[168]"But I am delighted to report to you to-day that all that has changed. There is an entirely new outlook in America at the moment toward evangelism. At this moment every major denomination in the United States is putting nearly all its emphasis on evangelism" (Billy Graham, "The Work of an Evangelist," 12).

With the ripe harvest and the talk of evangelism among various denominations,[169] Graham also posited that Jesus Christ wanted visible unity, having quoted John 17:21:

> Jesus Christ clearly was speaking of visible unity such as can be seen by the world. . . There is a kind of unity in diversity, a unity compatible with variety, and it is this pattern which Christ lays down for the church.[170]

Then after explaining the need for maintaining harmony, Graham declared his theological basis for this unity:

> If I see a man who is teaching that salvation is other than by faith in Jesus Christ . . . or if I see a man who is not bearing the fruit of love, I am warned to avoid that man because he will eventually cause divisions among the people of the Lord. Thus the Scriptures teach that in order to preserve unity among believers, we are to be separated from those who deny the deity of our Lord Jesus Christ.[171]

Therefore, Graham posited two of his lowest common denominators to unity: belief in the deity of Christ (the concept of faith in Christ being mentioned only once) and love. Of the weight of the doctrine and love, Graham clarified:

> The New Testament seems to indicate that the real test is not only creeds but in deeds. . . . Our loyalty to the truth is not measured so much by our creedal orthodoxy as by the temper and quality of our lives, the purity of our motives and the love we show to our fellow Christians.[172]

In this statement, Graham added his third test for cooperation: moral integrity—"quality of our lives, [and] the purity of our motives." Simultaneously Graham downplayed doctrinal orthodoxy, which may result in his moving toward a doctrinal minimalism. Graham quoted 2 John 10, 11 and expanded on the deity of Christ as the doctrinal measure for unity or

---

[169]Later this interest in evangelism seemingly also included the RCC: Cardinal Cushing's "Bravo Billy!" (January 1950), Vatican II's *Lumen Gentium* (November 21, 1964), and Paul VI's *Evangelii Nuntiandi* (December 8, 1975).

[170]Billy Graham, "Fellowship and Separation," 1.

[171]Ibid., 5.

[172]Ibid., 4.

disunity. He wrote:

> Here we have the deity of our Lord Jesus Christ involved. If a man blatantly denies the deity of Christ or his coming in the flesh, we are not to 'greet' him in the sense of having spiritual fellowship with him.[173]

Thus Graham repeated his 1951 position that the deity of Christ should be the doctrinal measure of unity.[174] In fact, in "Fellowship and Separation" Graham eliminated any other theological measuring stick:

> In 2 Thessalonians 3:6, 14, 15 Paul advises Christians to separate from a brother because he is "walking disorderly," not because he is talking heretically. This brother may be perfectly sound as regards his faith, but his life is wrong. In some instances the warnings against false prophets (such as we find in Jude) are actually warnings against men of immoral life rather than men holding erroneous opinions.[175]

Graham felt that disunity should primarily be directed toward those who were living immoral lives, not those "talking heretically" or "holding of erroneous opinions." This viewpoint of the "Middle Graham" indicated a very broad view of Christian unity, as the deity of Christ was his only theological measuring stick. Graham seems to have felt that the doctrinal statement of the Evangelical Alliance (1846),[176] the five fundamentals

---

[173]Ibid., 5.

[174]"Even the church is going through its convulsions and turmoil: extreme liberalism on one side that denies the deity of Christ and ultra-fundamentalism on the other side that is orthodox but knows nothing of the power of the Spirit of God nor the love of God for their own brethren" (Billy Graham, "Peace vs. Chaos," 3)

[175]Ibid., 4.

[176]"1. The Divine inspiration, authority, and sufficiency of the Holy Scriptures. 2. The right and duty of private judgment in the interpretation of the Holy Scriptures. 3. The Unity of the Godhead, and the Trinity of Persons thereof. 4. The utter depravity of the human nature in consequence of the fall. 5. The incarnation of the Son of God, his work of atonement for sinners of mankind, and his mediatorial intercession and reign. 6. The justification of the sinner by faith alone. 7. The work of the Holy Spirit in the conversion and sanctification of the sinner. 8. The immortality of the soul, the resurrection of the body, the judgment of the world by our Lord Jesus Christ, with the eternal blessedness of the righteous, and the eternal punishment of the wicked. 9. The Divine institution of the Christian ministry, and the obligation and perpetuity of the ordinances of baptism and the Lord's Supper" (J. W. Massie, *The Evangelical Alliance: Its Origin and Development* (London: John Snow, 1847), 302-05).

(1895),[177] or the doctrines of the Baptist Faith and Message (1963)[178] were too narrow for practical use in cooperative evangelism. In fact, with the deity of Christ being the only theological determinant, one wonders if the only ones who could not participate in Graham crusades for doctrinal reasons were Unitarians (Socinians), Protestants in the "God is Dead" movement, and the cults—as described in Walter Martin's *The Kingdom of the Cults*.[179] Yet, Graham even seemed to be soft on the deity of Christ—he had Methodist bishop Gerald Kennedy as his 1963 Los Angeles crusade chairman of the general committee![180] Perhaps this theological minimalism is why Graham could write in his autobiography:

> My own position was that we should be willing to work with all who were willing to work with us. Our message was clear, and if someone with a radically different theological view somehow decided to join with us in a Crusade that proclaimed Christ as the way of salvation, he or she was the one who was compromising personal convictions, not we.[181]

Graham then restated the warning of *The Christian Century* that the "Fundamentalist Revival" would bring division,[182] writing as his fourth point to "Fellowship and Separation," "Fourth, we are to separate from

---

[177]Cardinal Joseph Ratzinger, Prefect of the Congregation for the Doctrine of the Faith, described the five fundamentals from the 1895 Niagara Bible Conference as inerrancy of Scripture, the deity of Christ, the virgin birth, vicarious expiation, and the bodily resurrection (Commission biblique pontificale, *L'interprétation de la Bible dans l'Église*, 18).

[178]*Baptist Faith and Message* (Nashville: The Sunday School Board of the Southern Baptist Convention, 1963). This document was slightly revised in 2000.

[179]Walter R. Martin, *The Kingdom of the Cults* (Minneapolis: Bethany Fellowship, 1965).

[180]"In Fundamentalist eyes, the Los Angeles campaign set another, less glorious record, when Graham acquiesced in the choice of Methodist bishop Gerald Kennedy as the chairman of the crusade's general committee. Though the position was largely honorary—most of the real oversight of the crusade was done by Graham's team and the local executive committee, which was usually dominated by Evangelicals—Kennedy was, in truth, a surprising choice. His theology was frankly liberal—he had once ventured that he doubted the deity of Christ and admitted he had never believed in the Virgin Birth" (William Martin, 293-94).

[181]Billy Graham, *Just As I Am*, 303-04.

[182]Editorial: Fundamentalist Revival," 749.

those who are deliberately causing divisions among the Lord's people."[183] Graham was concerned that petty differences would hinder the work of evangelism in the church. Yet in his quest for unity did Graham open the theological doors go too far?

In his deity-of-Christ-as-the-only-theological-measure, Graham agreed with John Stott, who affirmed Graham's view of cooperation in his *The Epistles of John: An Introduction and Commentary*. In his introductory comments to this commentary, Stott spoke of "the three cardinal tests" of Robert Law:[184]

> Robert Law called his studies in the First Epistle *The Tests of Life* (1885) because in it are given what he terms 'the three cardinal tests' by which we may judge whether we possess life eternal or not. The first is theological, whether we believe that Jesus is 'the Son of God' (iii. 23, v. 5, 10, 13), 'the Christ come in the flesh' (iv. 2; 2 Jan. 7). . . . The second test is moral, whether we are practising righteousness and keeping the commandment of God. . . . The third test is social, whether we love one another.[185]

Stott then organized his commentary on First John around these three tests of Robert Law, finding three applications of the three tests. For example, the first cycle of applications (2:3-27) was as follows: the moral test—beginning in 2:3-6, the social test—beginning in 2:7-11, and the theological test—beginning in 2:18-27. The second application was 2:28-4:6,[186] and the

---

[183]Billy Graham, "Fellowship and Separation," 6.

[184]"The great tests of Christianity, the enforcement of which constitutes its chief purpose,—the tests of practical Righteousness and Love, and of Belief in Jesus as God Incarnate,—are those which are of perennial validity and necessity; yet it was just by these that the wolf of Gnosticism could be most unmistakably revealed under its sheep's clothing, and they are presented in such fashion as to certify that this was the object immediately aimed at. . . . The three great falsehoods it [the Epislte of First John] combats are moral indifferentism, lovelessness, and denial of the reality of the Incarnation." (Robert Law, *The Tests of Life* (Edinburgh: T. & T. Clark, 1909) [on-line]; accessed 10 July 2001; available from http://www.dabar.org/NewTestament/Commentaries/1-John/Law/LC2.html; Internet). Without clarifying, Timothy George wrote, "Law's category has its problems" (Timothy George, "notes" [on-line]; accessed 10 July 2001; available from http://www.sbts.edu/news/sbjt/summer98/Sum98forum.html; Internet).

[185]John R. W. Stott, *The Epistles of John: An Introduction and Commentary* (Grand Rapids: Eerdmans, 1960, 1981), 53.

[186]Ibid., 115.

third application was 4:7-5:5.[187] Portions that did not follow the three tests organizational categories of Stott were referred to as "digressions."[188] The first test is the social test of love (4:13-16), the second involved a combination of the doctrinal and social tests (4:13-21), and the third involved a combination of all three tests (5:1-5). Thus, Stott's commentary on First John provided Graham with biblical and scholarly approval for his three tests for cooperation: the deity of Christ, moral rectitude, and love.[189] Of the three tests, the deity of Christ is the only theological test. The question naturally follows: does this reading of First John contain *all* the doctrinal or theological tests which characterize false teachers or false prophets? And correspondingly, did Robert Law assert that these were the only theological tests to which false teachers or false prophets be subjected? The last question necessitates further study of Robert Law and his teachings. To the first question, the book of Galatians would disagree. For Paul in the book of Galatians argues not for the deity or humanity of Christ, but for salvation by grace through faith alone. Thus Stott's possible prooftexting of cooperation on the basis of the theological test in First John opened the door for his own involvement in the WCC, his doctrinal minimalism in certain areas, and his strong influence upon Dr. Graham in this regard.

Likewise, Graham's deity-of-Christ-as-the-only-theological-measure viewpoint explains why he was open to working with leaders and churches such as non-evangelical Anglican Churches, the World Council of Churches, the Eastern Orthodox rites, and the RCC. Had the books of Romans or Galatians been his measuring stick, as it was for Martin Luther, Graham may not have been so generous in his associations. However, it seems that Graham felt that his influence would lead WCC and the historic churches back to a renewed emphasis on evangelism, thus leading them towards justification by faith, and thus causing them to return to their historic orthodoxy—however historically remote it was. Recent history

---

[187]Ibid., 159.

[188]For example, "d. A digression about the world (ii. 15-17)" (ibid., 98). In this portion, Stott wrestled with a concept that did not fit into his paradigm. He wrote in a section titled "the world and the Christian," "Though the world hates the Christian, the Christian must not hate the world. . . . What then is to be the Christian's attitude to the world? He is not to escape out of it; he is to remain in it. He is to be 'unworldly' without becoming 'otherworldly', living 'in' it without being 'of' it" (ibid., 102-03). Or another example of a digression, "c. A digression about assurance and the condemning heart (iii. 19, 20)" (ibid., 145).

[189]"It is important to note that John's three tests are not arbitrarily selected. . . . A fresh certainty about Christ and about eternal life, based upon the fresh grounds that John gives, can still lead Christian people into that boldness of approach to God and of testimony to men, which is sorely needed as it is sadly missing in the Church today" (Ibid., 53, 54).

proves that the churches in question have not moved to a conservative position. In fact, the WCC churches have continued to slip theologically and the RCC merely had a public relations "face lift" through Vatican II.[190] Thus, Graham's 1961 sermon "Fellowship and Separation" showed how much doctrine he was willing to give up for cooperative or ecumenical evangelism. With Graham's broad theological parameters for cooperation in mind, we will continue by noting the Middle Graham's cooperation with the WCC.

Graham and the World Council of Churches

Graham seems to have had a tactical affiliation with the World Council of Churches. Graham was invited as an observer by General Secretary Willem Visser t' Hooft to the 1948 meeting when the WCC was formed.[191] William Martin wrote:

> He was uncomfortable with the liberal theology dominating the WCC and the ecumenical movement it represented, but he remembered that two of the movement's most important spiritual ancestors had been D. L. Moody and one of Moody's close friends, John R. Mott, and he felt that evangelicals had been partly to blame for the direction it had taken, since they had pulled out to maintain separatist purity instead of remaining involved and trying to check the movement's drift to the left.[192]

If this statement correlates to Graham's true thoughts on the subject, he ignored the direction of Edinburgh 1910, as earlier decried by Secretary, Board of Foreign Missions, Presbyterian Church U. S. A,. Robert Speers' message to New York 1900, who quoted Behrends, "it is fatal."[193] Edinburgh 1910 took a fatal turn towards accepting a social gospel,

---

[190]Pope John Paul II stated, "The Second Vatican Council wished to be, above all, a council on the Church. Take in your hands the documents of the Council, especially 'Lumen Gentium', study them with loving attention, with the spirit of prayer, to discover what the Spirit wished to say about the Church. In this way you will be able to realize that there is not—as some people claim—a 'new church', different or opposed to the 'old church', but that the Council wished to reveal more clearly the one Church of Jesus Christ, with new aspects, but still the same in its essence" (John Paul II, "Mexico Ever Faithful," *Osservatore Romano,* 5 February 1979, 1).

[191]Billy Graham, *Just As I Am,* 125.

[192]William Martin, 103-04.

[193]Robert Speer, "The Supreme and Determining Aim," 1:75.

simultaneously turning away from the universal imperative of evangelism, and thus ended the "Great Century of Missions."

Graham, however, perhaps thinking that the revivals which were taking place in certain towns where he held crusades would turn modernistic churches back to a more fundamentalist view of the atonement and conversion, began to cooperate more and more with mainline churches (beginning in the 1948 Augusta, GA campaign),[194] and to require that the committees be broadened. Not only did these broad committees provide:

1. Greater entrée to churches,

2. A greater potential audience for the crusade,

3. Greater opportunities and contacts for publicity,

4. Greater number of personal workers trained,

5. Potentially greater numbers of first time decisions for Christ,

6. Greater numbers of churches for follow-up, and

7. A greater financial base,

8. But the churches or pastors may possibly be turned around theologically as they sat under the hearing of the Word and the example of Graham.

Thus, increasingly the "Middle Graham," now openly working with mainline churches by New York 1957, continued to broaden his contact base and adjust his theology and sense of the mission of the church, the latter two points changing more slowly, as discussed in Chapters 4 and 3 respectively.

Graham attended the WCC meetings at Evanston in 1954 and New Delhi in 1961, sending representatives to subsequent WCC assemblies.[195] The beginning of Graham's change in his view of the universal imperative of evangelism related a 1966-1967 interchange of Graham with the WCC. Martin explained:

---

[194]Billy Graham, *Just As I Am,* 125.

[195]My father, Arthur P. Johnston, was the official observer sent by Billy Graham to report on subsequent WCC assemblies.

On some issues, however, Graham was taking a more definite stand. At the Miami meeting of the NCC shortly after the Berlin Congress, he had criticized church leaders who "call for social service without also providing a solid spiritual basis for it." Less than a year later, however, he sent the central committee of the World Council a surprising paper in which he said, "There is no doubt that the Social Gospel has directed its energies toward the relief of many of the problems of suffering humanity. I am for it! I believe it is Biblical."[196]

These remarks were concomitant with 1967 Graham's statements at the *Kansas City School of Evangelism,*[197] as well as with his 1967 article published in the WCC's *Ecumenical Review.*[198] Therefore, while the Early Graham maintained a tactical relationship with the WCC, that relationship seems to have had an impact on his view of mission.

In conclusion, the following five points of fundamentalism display where Graham was willing to concede in his cooperative evangelism. The five fundamentals are taken from Cardinal Ratzinger and the Pontifical Commission on Biblical Interpretation:[199]

1. Inerrancy of Scripture: "its [*Christianity Today's*] view of inspiration would be somewhat along the line of [*The Christian View of Science and Scripture]* by Bernard Ramm"—a type of limited inerrancy. Ramm wrote when speaking interpreting the Bible through the eyes of science, "Exegesis and science are both developing and progressing."[200]

2. Deity of Christ: "If a man blatantly denies the deity of Christ or his coming in the flesh, we are not to 'greet' him in the sense of having spiritual fellowship with him."[201]

3. Virgin birth: Not discussed as an issue for cooperation or against separation.

---

[196]William Martin, 343.

[197]Billy Graham, "Biblical Conversion," 10.

[198]Billy Graham, "Conversion—a Personal Revolution," 281.

[199]Commission biblique pontificale, 18.

[200]Bernard Ramm, *Protestant Biblical Interpretation,* rev. ed. (Boston: W. A. Wilde, 1956), 194.

[201]Ibid., "Fellowship and Separation," 5.

TABLE 6

SUMMARY OF GRAHAM ON THE FIVE FUNDAMENTALS

FIVE FUNDAMENTALS		1. Inerrancy of Scripture	2. Deity of Christ	3. Virgin Birth	4. Vicarious Expiation	5. Bodily Resurrection
Early-Early Graham (pre-1949)	Preaches	Inerrancy	Deity of Christ	Virgin Birth	Substitutionary Atonement	Bodily Resurrection
	Cooperates with	Inerrancy	Deity of Christ	Virgin Birth	Substitutionary Atonement	Bodily Resurrection
Early Graham (1949-1955)	Preaches	Inerrancy	Deity of Christ	Virgin Birth	Substituttionary Atonement	Bodily Resurrection
	Cooperates with	Limited Inerrancy	Deity of Christ	Virgin Birth	Reconciliation Theory	Resurrection unto Life
Middle Graham (1955-1965)	Preaches	Limited Inerrancy	Deity of Christ	Virgin Birth	Moving Toward Reconciliation Theory	Bodily Resurrection
	Cooperates with	Inerrancy of Purpose	Deity of Christ?	Miraculous Birth	Reconciliation Theory	Resurrection unto Life
Late Graham (1965-pres.)	Preaches	Limited Inerrancy	Deity of Christ	Virgin Birth	Reconciliation Theory	Bodily Resurrection
	Cooperates with (extremes)	Accomodated Revelation	Veneration of Mary	Miraculous Birth	Moral-Influence Theory	Annihilationism

4.   Vicarious expiation: When discussing the "social gospel" Graham

wrote and said, "I am for it! I believe it is Biblical."[202] Rauschenbusch's social gospel denounced the vicarious atonement as post-biblical.[203] Thus he was willing to work with those who did not affirm the vicarious expiation.

5.   Bodily resurrection: Not discussed as an issue for cooperation or against separation.

Table 6 takes the five fundamentals and shows the movement in Graham's preaching as well as in his cooperative boundaries. Graham conceded on inerrancy, allowing for a limited inerrancy position, rather than an absolute or full inerrancy position. Obviously, when Graham worked with mainline churches he did not at all try to keep the doctrinal boundaries in the area of biblical authority. To his defense, it may have been nearly impossible to do so, unless he worked only with evangelical and fundamental churches. Graham proved tactical even on the deity of Christ as a basis for separation.[204] And as to the other three points, Graham mentioned in his sermon "Fellowship and Separation" that "The apostles were not given to quarrelling over secondary points of doctrine."[205] Perhaps the Virgin Birth, the Vicarious Atonement, and the bodily resurrection are peripheral doctrines that need not be the cause for division in cooperative evangelism.

Figure 17 considers a variety of "union" activities in which various churches may be engaged. These activities move from social endeavors to theological endeavors, and finally to mission endeavors. Some historic theological comments are placed at the bottom to portray several nineteenth evangelical parameters used for "union" activities. Graham's parameter of the deity of Christ is placed at the bottom to portray his theological basis for inter-church cooperative ventures. This table shows a continuum in church cooperation beginning with effecting social change to full communion. As is clearly evident, *a line needs to be drawn somewhere* to protect and affirm denominational distinctives for which many gave their lives, as in the case of Protestantism.

The impact of Graham's two fundamentals of cooperation, the deity of Christ and love for the brethren, was a strong theological shift from

---

202William Martin, 343. Also found in Billy Graham, "Biblical Conversion," 10, as well as Billy Graham, "Conversion—a Personal Revolution," 281.

203"The fundamental terms and ideas—'satisfaction,' 'substitution,' 'imputation,' 'merit'—are post-biblical ideas, and are alien from the spirit of the gospel" (Rauschenbusch, 243).

204William Martin, 293-94

205Billy Graham, "Fellowship and Separation," 1-2.

nineteenth century evangelical and Protestant missions endeavors. Likewise, Graham's broad policy of cooperation led to other evangelical emulators, such as Campus Crusade for Christ and Promise Keepers [and Luis Palau?]. Donald Sweeting explained:

> Why rehearse the changes that have taken place in Billy Graham's own thinking about Roman Catholics? First of all because the influence of Graham has been great, not only in the United States and the world, but within American Evangelicalism. . . .
>
> Secondly, the historic significance of Graham's actions in cooperative evangelism and ecumenical outreach have been duly noted. . . .
>
> Thirdly, Graham's example is now being held up as a model for the future. . . .
>
> Finally, not only has Graham's example been noted and commended, it has been followed by key Evangelical leaders and parachurch organizations.[206]

Thus, Graham's ecumenical policy of cooperative evangelism had a wider influence than just his crusade evangelism, as noted in the "Evangelicals and Catholics Together" statement, and it began to include theological agreement. Even conservative evangelical theologians, who saw the wide chasms of theological differences between Graham and Roman Catholics began to follow Graham's lead:

> Billy Graham has set the example for evangelical cooperation with Catholics in mass evangelism without compromising the basic gospel message. Despite ecclesiastical and doctrinal differences (see Part Two), there are some important things many Catholics and evangelicals hold in common not the least of which is the good news that Jesus died for our sins and rose again. Thus, there seems to be no good reason why there should not be increased ways of mutual encouragement in fulfilling our Lord's Great Commission (Matt. 28:18-20). Catholics and evangelicals do not have to agree on everything in order to agree on some things—even something important. We do not need to agree on the authority of the church

---

[206]Donald Sweeting, "From Conflict to Cooperation? Changing American Evangelical Attitudes toward Roman Catholics: 1960-1998" (Ph.D. diss., Trinity Evangelical Divinity School, 1998), 145-48.

Fig. 17. Union Work and Theological Parameters Continuum. [207]

---

[207]Each of the areas of cooperation, "Unity in Mission Endeavors," "Unity in Theological Endeavors," and "Unity in Social Endeavors," increase in cooperation as they go from left to right. As for the theological formulations, the greater need for theological commonality increases from left to right.

before we can cooperate in proclaiming the power of the uncompromising gospel (Rom. 1:16).[208]

The precedent set by Billy Graham in his views on cooperation dealt a firm theological blow to American evangelicalism.

Perhaps Graham's impact on other countries had even greater theological and ecclesial consequences. For example, Graham's 1954 London crusade began a rift among evangelicals in England. Iain Murray explained:

> For men who had long felt it necessary to remain apart from the prevailing denominational influences, and to stand only with other evangelicals when it came to evangelism, it had been a near-stunning sight to see the readiness of non-evangelical clergy and ministers to join in the crusade. Was it possible that the comparative isolation that British evangelicals had been experiencing, and the smallness of their influence (compared with the 38,000 who made decisions in the 1954 meetings), had been largely brought upon themselves? This disturbing possibility was the more credible as evangelical leaders became conscious that Graham was clearly able to strike up friendships with church figures with whom they had never known any such relationship. Among that number, for instance, was Mervyn Stockwood who at first had taken pains to distance himself from the evangelist's beliefs when his church had been used by the Cambridge Inter-Collegiate Christian Union in 1955. A decade later, when Stockwood, as Bishop of Southwark, was making his diocese the most *avant-garde* in the country, he would be found on the council supporting another BGEA crusade in London.
>
> No less surprising was the relationship which Graham was able to establish with Archbishop Michael Ramsey.[209]

This rift led to a ecclesiological show-down at the National Assembly of Evangelicals in 1966 between Martyn Lloyd-Jones and John R. W. Stott, in which Stott, who had WCC sympathies, won the upper hand.[210] Similarly, Graham's crusade in Hungary engineered by Haraszti marginalized and

---

[208] Norman L. Geisler and Ralph E. MacKenzie, *Roman Catholics and Evangelicals: Agreements and Differences* (Grand Rapids, MI: Baker Book House, 1995), 428-29.

[209] Iain Murray, *Evangelicalism Divided,* 40.

[210] Ibid, 44.

angered the Baptists who had first invited him.[211] While the short-term gain was greater acceptance and larger crowds in larger auditoriums, the long-term results on world-wide and American evangelical churches may follow the pattern of Edinburgh 1910 and the WCC. This potential long-term change is foreshadowed in the books of Lewis Drummond on Graham, particularly in *Canvas Cathedral,* where Graham's theology of evangelism is painted in a conciliatory light.

The Later Graham

Graham's cooperative openess was guarded by at least three important factors, a call to preach the cross, a general commitment to mainstream evangelicalism, and a need for continued financial support, which came predominantly (presumably) from evangelical Christians. Graham had built the BGEA on the platform of preaching crusades. To keep his financial momentum he needed to continue preaching crusades and inviting people for commitment to Christ—that was his signature, his market niche. We noted in chapter one that Graham held conferences and trained pastors during this last segment of his ministry. If the early Graham

---

[211]"As word spread that the Foreign Ministry, which far outranked the Ministry for Church Affairs, would welcome Graham warmly, the Lutheran and Reformed bishops, both of whom had been quite cool toward his coming, suddenly decided it would be marvelous if the evangelist would consent to preach in some of their churches as well as in the Evangelical churches that were his ostensible hosts. That, of course, pleased Billy Graham and Alexander Haraszti. It did not please Sandor Palotay and his colleagues in the Council of Free Churches.

Palotay had gotten state approval of the invitation by convincing Imre Miklos and other government officials that the meetings at which Graham would preach would be small and meaningless, heartening to Evangelical Christians but of no consequence to anyone else. . . . Would he be preaching in the Reformed church in Debrecen, the center of Calvinism in eastern Hungary? And were any plans being made for him to preach at the large Roman Catholic cathedral in pecs, in southern Hungary? And just one other thing: Had any provision been made for him to meet with Hungary's Jewish leaders?

Palotay was understandably livid when he learned of the cablegram. He had worked five years to arrange the invitation. Now, what he had regarded as a signal triumph the Foreign Ministry was calling a potential disaster, and Billy Graham was complaining about the itinerary. . . . When Haraszti and Walter Smyth returned to Hungary in late August to make final preparations for Graham's visit, the Council of Free Churches summoned him to what amounted to a kangaroo court, demanding that he give a full report of his activities following his receipt of the official invitation from Palotay. Haraszti, who relishes a battle of wits, expressed surprise that he was facing an inquiry, when what seemed appropriate was some expression of appreciation" (William Martin, 484-85).

was 1949 to 1957; and if the Middle Graham was 1957 to 1965; then the later Graham incorporated all the conferences supported by Graham including Lausanne 1974, Amsterdam 1983, Amsterdam 1987, Louisville 1994, and Amsterdam 2000, as well as numerous other conferences. Each of these conferences had a roster of speakers and involved Christian leaders from various lands. The cooperative web for Graham conferences was immense and may be confusing to unravel. It would be fascinating research beyond the scope of this study. Therefore, rather than deal with these gatherings, this final section will deal with two large segments of Christendom.

Wolfhart Pannenberg wrote that the church in the third millennium would consist of three groups:

> It is quite possible that in the early part of the third millennium only the Roman Catholic and Orthodox churches, on one hand, and evangelical Protestantism, on the other, will survive as ecclesial communities. What used to be called the Protestant mainline churches are in acute danger of disappearing.[212]

Graham's relationship to Roman Catholics greatly impacted "evangelical Protestantism." But one growing branch of this movement was relatively untouched by Graham, the charismatic movement. This movement was fulfilling Graham's early vision of reviving historic Protestant churches and even perhaps the RCC. And the evangelical/Pentecostal churches in South America were growing annually in the double digits.[213] With these factors in mind, in looking at the Later Graham on cooperation, the two groups we will address are the Charismatic movement and the RCC.

Graham and the Charismatic Movement

Graham's reason for reaching out to the Charismatic movement is uncertain. In the late sixties, Graham identified with the late sixties youth movement by accepting an unusual invitation to preach at the Miami Rock Festival in 1969[214] and by writing *The Jesus Generation* in 1971.[215] He

---

[212]Wolfhart Pannenberg, "Chritianity and the West: Ambiguous Past, Uncertain Future," 23.

[213]"The annual population growth in Latin America is 2.6 per cent while the growth of Protestantism is an encouraging 15 per cent! (as reported in the *Pentecostal Evangel* of August 8, 1965)" (Paul Finkenbinder, "Latin America," *One Race, One Gospel, One Task,* 1:280).

[214]Billy Graham, *Just As I Am,* 419-22.

published *How to Be Born Again* in 1977,[216] one year after the "Year of the Evangelical"[217] and Charles Colson published *Born Again*.[218] Whatever the historical precedent, Billy Graham published *The Holy Spirit* in 1978 in the midst of the "Third Wave" of the Pentecostal movement. The Catholic Charismatic movement was in full force,[219] being effectively checked by Paul VI's 1975 encyclical *Evangelii Nuntiandi*.[220] The Vineyard movement became a factor as John Wimber sought to "charismatize" evangelicals. He published *Power Evangelism* in 1986.[221] The Holy Spirit became a rallying point for Christians from all denominations. It was thought that true ecumenical unity would be found in relation to the charismatic movement. Sweeting explained:

> Long before anyone was talking about Evangelicals and Catholics coming together (ECT) there was talk about Pentecostals and Catholics coming together (PCT). During the course of our time period [1960-1998], there has been an amazing convergence of

---

[215]Billy Graham, *The Jesus Generation* (Grand Rapids: Zondervan, 1971).

[216]Billy Graham, *How to Be Born Again* (Waco, TX: Word, 1977).

[217]Cover, *Time Magazine*.

[218]Charles W. Colson, *Born Again* (Old Tappan, NJ: Revell, 1976).

[219]The Catholic charismatic movement started in Duquesne University in 1967. By 1974 "The National Directory currently lists hundreds of charismatic prayer communities" (Msgr. Vincent M. Walsh, *A Key to Charismatic Renewal in the Catholic Church* [Holland, PA: Key of David Publications, 1974], 7).

[220]"58. The last Synod devoted considerable attention to these "small communities," or *communautes de base*, because they are often talked about in the Church today. . . . In other regions, on the other hand, *communautes de base* come together in a spirit of bitter criticism of the Church, which they stigmatize as 'institutional' and to which they set themselves up as charismatic communities, free from structures and inspired only by the Gospel. Thus their obvious characteristic is an attitude of fault-finding and of rejection with regard to the Church's outward manifestations: her hierarchy, her signs. . . . they will be a hope to the universal Church to the extent: . . . that they avoid the ever present temptation of systematic protest and a hypercritical attitude, under the pretext of authenticity and a spirit of cooperation; . . . that they maintain a sincere communion with the pastors . . . and with the magisterium. . . . that they never look to themselves as the sole beneficiaries or sole agents of evangelization—or even the only depositories of the Gospel . . . . that they show themselves to be universal in all things and never sectarian. On these conditions . . . they will soon become proclaimers of the Gospel themselves" (Paul VI, *Evangelii Nuntiandi: On Evangelization in the Modern World* [8 December 1975], section 58).

[221]John Wimber, *Power Evangelism* (San Francisco: Harper and Row, 1986).

Pentecostals and Charismatics with Roman Catholics that began early in the 1960s and continues to this day.[222]

C. Peter Wagner added, "The movement crosses the boundaries of more ecclesiastical traditions than in any other time this side of the first century."[223]

Into this charismatically-charged world, Graham was seeking to unite churches for ecumenical or cooperative evangelism. However, Graham had never focused on the Holy Spirit in his ministry, as far as the gifts of the Spirit. It was at this time that Graham commissioned perhaps his most systematic theological book, *The Holy Spirit*. Graham explained numerous purposes for commissioning the writing of *The Holy Spirit*. Graham began by sharing that John XXIII said that the doctrine of the Holy Spirit needed reemphasis and Karl Barth thought that the next emphasis in theology should be the Holy Spirit. Then Graham acknowledged as a testimony, "Throughout my ministry as an evangelist I have had a growing understanding of the ministry of the Holy Spirit."[224] He then explained another purpose, "I became concerned over the misunderstanding and even the ignorance in some Christian circles concerning the Third Person of the Trinity."[225] Next he wrote of the ecumenical nature of his book, "I also pray that it will be a unifying book. The Holy Spirit did not come to divide Christians but, among other reasons, He came to unite us."[226] Graham added:

> My sole concern has been to see what the Bible has to say about the Holy Spirit. The Bible—which I believe the Holy Spirit inspired—is our only trustworthy source, and any reliable analysis of the person and work of the Holy Spirit must be biblically-based. As never before I have realized that there are some things we cannot know completely, and some issues are open to differences of interpretation by sincere

---

[222]Donald Sweeting, *From Conflict to Cooperation*, 155.

[223]C. Peter Wagner, *Your Spiritual Gifts Can Help Your Church Grow* (Ventura: Regal, 1979, 1994), 19.

[224]Billy Graham, *The Holy Spirit: Activating God's Power in Your Life* (New York: Warner Books, 1978), 10.

[225]Ibid.

[226]Ibid.

Christians. About areas where there are honest differences among Christians I have tried not to be dogmatic.[227]

Then, acknowledging the charismatic movement taking place, Graham concluded his introductory comments, "I am thankful the Holy Spirit is at work in our generation, both in awakening the Church and in evangelism. May God use this book to bring renewal and challenge to many."[228]

Was this book an olive branch to the charismatic movement, of which Graham was not a part? One of the stated reviewers of *The Holy Spirit* was Dr. Thomas Zimmerman, General Superintendent of the Assemblies of God, as was Canon Houghton, former chairman of the British Keswick. Did *The Holy Spirit* succeed in bringing Charismatics online with Graham crusades? The response is mixed. As chair of the College and Singles Committee for the 1996 Greater Twin Cities Billy Graham Crusade, this author attempted to contact a large independent charismatic church in Minneapolis to solicit the participation of their college group. They were not interested. They said, "We already have our evangelist." However, a large number of participants in Amsterdam 2000 from South America were charismatic. Therefore, Graham may have achieved an important goal through writing this book, gaining influence in South America, even though he had held few crusades in Central and South America (Brazil—1962, 1974, 1979, Mexico City—1981, Argentina—1991, and Puerto Rico—1995), and he held none in the following countries: Columbia, Chile, Venezuela, Peru, Bolivia, Ecuador, Guatemala, Honduras, Nicaragua, Costa Rica, and Panama.

In his book, Graham took the "open but cautious" view to the sign gifts, similar to the view of Robert L. Saucy in *Are the Miraculous Gifts for Today? Four Views*.[229] Graham wrote:

> To summarize there is no doubt in my mind that there is a gift of healing—that people are healed in answer to the prayer of faith—and that there are other healings, such as healings of relationships. There is also need for a word of caution. There are many frauds and charlatans in the field of medicine and faith healing. Again, one must have discernment.[230]

---

[227]Ibid., 10-11.

[228]Ibid., 11.

[229]Robert Saucey, "An Open but Cautious View," Wayne A. Grudem, gen. ed., *Are Miraculous Gifts for Today? Four Views* (Grand Rapids: Zondervan, 1996).

[230]Billy Graham, *The Holy Spirit,* 244.

He continued on this "open but cautious" viewpoint as he discussed miracles. On the gift of tongues, Graham asserted that "the gift of tongues is not necessarily a sign of the baptism of the believer by the Holy Spirit into the body of Christ."[231] Thus, Graham addressed the sign gifts, while trying to call his readers from an overemphasis on the phenomenal manifestations as an end in themselves. The charismatic movement impacted certain portions of the RCC for a time, and it may be that Billy Graham's "popular religiosity" also impacted the RCC's approach to church unity for a time.

Graham and the Roman Catholic Church

When Bishop Cushing published "Bravo Billy" in his diocesan paper during Graham's 1950 campaign in Boston, it sent tremors to the theological core of the irenic Graham. Cushing was seemingly rewarded by Pius XII for his ecclesial prowess with the title Cardinal. And he extended his influence on Graham to a forty-five minute television conversation in 1964. Martin explained:

> The forty-five televised conversation surely rivaled any of Graham's mutual admiration sessions with Lyndon Johnson. . . . He [Cushing] urged Catholic young people to attend the crusade service. . . [saying] ". . . I'm one hundred percent for Dr. Graham. . . ." Never one to be outcomplimented, Graham professed to regard his new friend as "the leading ecumenist in America," lavished further praise on Pope John XXIII and his recent successor, Paul VI, and heralded Vatican II as a major step in dissipating the clouds of resentment and mistrust that had separated Catholics and Protestants. As for himself, he announced that he felt "much closer to Roman Catholic traditions than to some of the more liberal Protestants."
> While most observers either praised or paid little attention to the conversation, some in both camps showed discomfort at its amicable spirit.[232]

This conversation, was in fact quite descriptive of the *modus operandi* of Billy Graham, as well as his open view of Roman Catholicism. Yet, in order to comprehend what was happening, a short history of recent Catholic ecumenism is necessary.

In 1896, in his encyclical *Apostolicae Curae* (September 13, 1896), the infallible Leo XIII wrote concerning the Anglican rite, "We

---

[231]Ibid., 258.

[232]William Martin, 309-10.

pronounce and declare that Ordinations carried out according to the Anglican rite have been and are absolutely null and entirely void."[233] This strong statement was made in the midst of the Lambeth Conferences on unity between the Anglican and Eastern Orthodox held in 1874-1875, 1884, 1920, and 1930. In contrast to Rome, Constantinople in 1922 declared the Anglican orders valid.[234] Thus, while Rome disowned the Anglican rite, Constantinople accepted it as valid. In this spiritual and territorial interchange, however, Rome continued its isolationist stance. In 1928 Pius XI, very much continuing in the legacy of his predecessor, as stated in his encyclical *Mortalium Animos*, "the Apostolic See cannot on any terms take part in their [ecumenical] assemblies, nor is it anyway lawful for Catholics either to support or to work for such enterprises."[235] Thus, Pius XI felt that the International Missionary Councils, the precursors to the WCC, were "a false Christianity." Then there was a change in strategy in Rome.

With Pius XII in the Apostolic See, Rome had an immense change of heart. So important was Pius XII that John Paul II discussed his role of Pius XII in his 1994 encyclical *Tertio Millennio Adviente*.[236] What

---

[233]*The Great Encyclical Letters of Pope Leo XIII*, translations from approved sources (New York: Benzinger Brothers, 1903), 405.

[234]"3. That the orthodox theologians who have scientifically examined the question have almost unanimously come to the same conclusions and have declared themselves as accepting the validity of Anglican Orders.

4. That the practice in the Church affords no indication that the Orthodox Church has ever officially treated the validity of Anglican Orders as in doubt, in such a way as would point to the re-ordination of the Anglican clergy being regarded as required in the case of the union of the two Churches" (Henry Bettenson, ed., *Documents of the Christian Church,* second ed. (London: Oxford University Press, 1967), 330).

[235]"Meanwhile they affirm that they would willingly treat with the Church of Rome, but on equal terms, that is as equals with an equal: but even if they could so act. it does not seem open to doubt that any pact into which they might enter would not compel them to turn from those opinions which are still the reason why they err and stray from the one fold of Christ.

8. This being so, it is clear that the Apostolic See cannot on any terms take part in their assemblies, nor is it anyway lawful for Catholics either to support or to work for such enterprises; for if they do so they will be giving countenance to a false Christianity, quite alien to the one Church of Christ" (Pius XI, *Mortalium Animos: On Religious Unity,* 6 January 1928 [on-line]; accessed 15 July 2001; available from http://www.ewtn.com/library/ENCYC/ P11MORTA.HTM; Internet, sections 7-8).

[236]"The Second Vatican Council is often considered as the beginning of a new era in the life of the church. This is true, but at the same time it is difficult to overlook the fact that the council drew much from the experiences and reflections of the immediate past, especially from the intellectual legacy left by Pius XII. In the history of the church, the 'old' and the 'new' are always closely interwoven. The 'new' grows out of the 'old,' and the 'old' finds a fuller expression in the 'new.' Thus it was for the
390

was it about Pius XII that quite likely eventuated John Paul II's equivocation on the "old" and the "new," especially as John Paul II clearly said that Vatican II *had not changed* the essence (doctrine or Traditions) of the RCC?[237] Pius XII changed two important points. First, Pius XII changed the anti-modernism hermeneutic of Leo XIII[238] in his 1943 encyclical *Divino Afflante Spiritu*,[239] moving from Leo XIII's inerrancy position,[240] to

---

Second Vatican Council and for the activity of the popes connected with the council, starting with John XXIII, continuing with Paul VI and John Paul I, up to the present pope" (John Paul II, *Tertio Millennio Adviente,* 14 November 1994, section 18).

[237]"The Second Vatican Council wished to be, above all, a council on the Church. Take in your hands the documents of the Council, especially 'Lumen Gentium', study them with loving attention, with the spirit of prayer, to discover what the Spirit wished to say about the Church. In this way you will be able to realize that there is not— as some people claim—a 'new church', different or opposed to the 'old church', but that the Council wished to reveal more clearly the one Church of Jesus Christ, with new aspects, but still the same in its essence" (John Paul II, "Mexico Ever Faithful," 1).

[238]"The main point to be attained is that Catholics should not admit the malignant principle of granting more than is due to the opinion of heterodox writers. . . . 'It is therefore not permitted to any one to interpret the Holy Scriptures in any way contrary to this sense, or even in any way contrary to the universal opinion of the Fathers'" (Leo XIII, *Vigilantiæ, The Great Encyclical Letters of Pope Leo XIII,* 539-540).

[239]"30. For thus at long last will be brought about the happy and fruitful union between the doctrine and spiritual sweetness of expression of the ancient authors and the greater erudition and maturer knowledge of the modern, having as its result new progress in the never fully explored and inexhaustible field of the Divine Letters. . . . Let the interpreter then, with all care and without neglecting any light derived from recent research, endeavor to determine the peculiar character and circumstances of the sacred writer, the age in which he lived, the sources written or oral to which he had recourse and the forms of expression he employed" (Pius XII, *Divino Afflante Spiritu,* 30 September 1943 [on-line]; accessed 15 July 2001; available from http://www.ewtn.com/library/ENCYC/ P12DIVIN.HTM; Internet, sections 30, 33).

[240]"For all the books which the Church receives as sacred and canonical are written wholly and entirely, with all their parts, at the dictation of the Holy Ghost; and in so far as possible that any error can co-exist with inspiration, that inspiration not only is essentially incompatible with error, but excludes and rejects it absolutely and necessarily as it is impossible that God Himself, the Supreme Truth, can utter that which is not true. . . . And the Church holds them as sacred and canonical not only because. . . they contain revelation without error, but because. . . they have God for their Author. . . . It follows that those who maintain that an error is possible in any genuine passage of the sacred writings either pervert the Catholic notion of inspiration or make God the author of error" (Leo XIII, *Provendissimus Deus,* 18 November 1893, in *The Great Encyclical Letters of Pope Leo XIII,* 296-97).

a limited inerrancy position on biblical authority.[241] And second, Pius XII lifted the ban on "pan-Christian" activities of Pius XI,[242] and formed the Unitas Ecumenical Center ("Associazione Unitas") in 1945,[243] building on the work of the Dominican Congar who wrote *Chrétiens désunis* in 1937, as well as the *Una Sancta* movement born in Germany in 1938.[244] Thus Pius XII set in motion the machinery by which the RCC shifted its educational and financial attention towards unity, both in the area of ecumenicity and in the area of biblical research. The Vatican II Council and the push for unity

---

[241]"When, subsequently, some Catholic writers, in spite of this solemn definition of Catholic doctrine, by which such divine authority is claimed for the 'entire books with all their parts' as to secure freedom from any error whatsoever, ventured to restrict the truth of Sacred Scripture solely to matters of faith and morals, and to regard other matters, whether in the domain of physical science or history, as 'obiter dicta' and—as they contended—in no wise connected with faith, Our Predecessor of immortal memory, Leo XIII in the Encyclical Letter *Providentissimus Deus*, published on November 18 in the year 1893, justly and rightly condemned these errors and safeguarded the studies of the Divine Books by most wise precepts and rules. . . . There is no one who cannot easily perceive that the conditions of biblical studies and their subsidiary sciences have greatly changed within the last fifty years. . . . Hence this special authority . . . is shown . . . to be free from any error whatsoever in matters of faith and morals" (Pius XII, *Divino Afflante Spiritu*, sections 1, 11, 21).

[242]"This being so, it is clear that the Apostolic See cannot on any terms take part in their assemblies, nor is it anyway lawful for Catholics either to support or to work for such enterprises; for if they do so they will be giving countenance to a false Christianity, quite alien to the one Church of Christ" (Pius XI, *Mortalium Animos: On Religious Unity,* 6 January 1928, section 8).

[243]"Associazione Unitas, Via del Corso, 306, I-00186 ROME, ITALY, Tel. (+39) 06 68 90 52, F[ounded]: 1945, A[gency]: Roman Catholic supported, P[eriodical]: *Unitas* [frequency] (4/yr)" ("Centro Pro Unione" [on-line]; accessed 10 July 2001; available from http://www.prounione.urbe.it/dir-dir/e_dir-list_ie.html; Internet).

[244]"Jusque-là les catholiques qui s'étaient consacrés à la construction de l'unité étaient des pionniers isolés, souvent suspectés, voire suspendus dans leur tâche. Ces initiatives personnelles permirent, toutefois, cette ouverture récente. Mentionnons les conversations de Malines (1920-1926), menées à l'initiative de l'abbé Portal et de Lord Halifax, sous la présidence du cardinal Mercier, qui entamèrent le dialogue avec l'Église anglicane. En 1925, Dom Lambert Beaudouin fonda l'abbaye de Chevetogne; en 1926, le dominicain C.J. Dumont créa «Istina». Ces deux institutions, officiellement vouées aux contacts œcuméniques avec l'Orient chrétien, ont joué un rôle important et élargi progressivement leur intérêt à l'ensemble des problèmes œcuméniques. En 1937, un autre dominicain, le père Congar, publia *Chrétiens désunis*, ouvrage qui a été pendant vingt ans la charte théologique de l'œcuménisme catholique. En 1939, se créa en Allemagne le mouvement *Una Sancta*. Mais, sauf quelques ouvertures en faveur de l'Orient, les autorités romaines restèrent le plus souvent en retrait sur ces initiatives" ("L'œcuménisme" [on-line]; accessed 10 July 2001; available from http://fr.encyclopedia.yahoo.com/ articles/ni/ni_1212_p0.html; Internet).

toward a common Eucharist in the year 2000 were a part of "the intellectual legacy left by Pius XII."

Rome, a well-funded research center with quite likely the best libraries and archives in the modern world, was certainly aware of Graham's early preaching career prior to Los Angeles 1949. However, Bishop Cushing's wise response to Graham in January 1950 fit perfectly into the "intellectual legacy" of the sitting Pope, Pius XII (1939-1958). Cushing became a Cardinal in 1950. In fact, the openness to non-Catholic Christians in Vatican II, its allowing the Mass in venacular, as well as its emphasis on the lay study of the Bible was likely directed to influence the WCC, Billy Graham (who was compared more than once to the Pope),[245] and the South American evangelicals.[246]

Billy Graham, for his part, seems to have begun his ministry with a typical fundamentalist view of Catholicism. However, this point is difficult to make as direct illustrations that are negative to the RCC are

---

[245]"The Religious News Service reported that its coverage matched that given to the Second Vatican Council, and Vatican Radio itself took sympathetic notice. A Religious News Service reporter, in fact, went so far as to compare Graham to Pope John XXIII" (William Martin, 335). Alexander Haraszti to Metropolitan Filaret: "I don't compare Dr. Graham with the patriarch or the pope," he told Filaret, "because Dr. Graham is not the head of a church. He is the head of all Christianity. He actually is the head of the Roman Catholics, the Orthodox, the Protestants—everybody—in a spiritual way, because the pope cannot preach to all the Protestants, but Billy Graham can preach to all the Roman Catholics. The patriarch cannot preach to all the Roman Catholics; they will not listen to him. But Billy Graham can preach to all the Orthodox, and they will listen to him, because he is above these religious strifes. He is a man of much higher stature than any of these people. I do not mean any offense to His Holiness, the patriarch, but Billy Graham deserves more than three metropolitans or three cardinals" (ibid., 496).

[246]"I have included a chart bearing the title: 'Growth of Protestants in Latin America, 1875-1966.' The information is based on statistical studies of Protestantism in Latin America undertaken by the Roman Catholic Church and reported by Prudencio Damboriena and Enrique Dussel in the book, *Protestantismo en Latino América,* 1962.

The graph tells the following story:

From 1875 to 1935—a period of sixty years—Protestantism won a million converts.

In 1935, the line representing Protestant growth suddenly shoots upward; by 1949, only fourteen years later, Protestant converts tripled to a total of 3,171,980.

Today, the three million figure has been more than tripled again, making the Protestant population in Latin America more than ten million" (Paul Finkenbinder, "Latin America," 280). And more recently, "Observers say that by 2005 Guatemala will have more Pentecostals than Roman Catholics. In the 30 years after that, Robeck says, half a dozen Latin American countries will have a Pentecostal majority" (Steve Rabey, "Ecumenical Dialogue: Conversation or Competition?" *Christianity Today,* 7 September 1998, 22).

difficult to find.[247] The only negative view of the RCC came from William Martin's material on Graham's letter to President Truman stating that he did not speak against the President's desire to appoint an ambassador to the Vatican.[248] A fear of Catholicism was also the noted in Graham's father-in-law, L. Nelson Bell, the first editor of *Christianity Today*.[249]

The Middle Graham said in the context of ecclesial fellowship said, "One of the things that grieves me today is to discover how prone some people are to believe the worst. They take half truths and build completely fabricated stories."[250] Thus, it is proposed that Graham made very few negative comments of Roman Catholics from 1950 on. In 1957, William Martin stated that Graham refrained from making negative comments about Roman Catholics.[251] Later, during and after the Kennedy years, Graham made a point not to mention anything negative about Roman Catholicism. William Martin explained:

> Following John Kennedy's election, he scrupulously avoided any statements that could be construed as anti-Catholic, a relaxation of wariness that bothered some of Graham's colleagues.[252]

It is uncertain why Graham was willing to overlook the tremendous theological, ecclesiological, and evangelistic differences between his message of instantaneous conversion and the Roman Catholic sacramental salvation, with purgatory, Mary, all the intermediaries, and its meritorious system. His silence was particularly perplexing to those from

---

[247]Other than a brief illustration in a 1947 sermon (Billy Graham, "A Midnight Tragedy," in *Calling Youth to Christ* [Grand Rapids: Zondervan, 1947],57).

[248]Martin, *A Prophet with Honor,* 144.

[249]L. Nelson Bell, *Protestant Distinctives and the American Crisis* (Weaverville, NC: Presbyterian Journal Book Room, 1960).

[250]Billy Graham, "Fellowship and Separation," 7.

[251]"Catholics also took critical aim at Graham's crusade, but with a blend of warmth and wariness that reflected a fascinating ambivalence toward him. Graham shared in a general Evangelical antipathy toward Catholicism, but Catholics benefited from his uncommon spirit of openness and conciliation toward those with whom he disagreed. Team members might speak of Catholics who had been 'won to Christ,' clearly implying they had moved from a lost to a saved state, but Billy himself had never engaged in the Catholic bashing to which many Fundamentalists were prone, and Catholics seemed to appreciate this" (William Martin, 229).

[252]William Martin, *A Prophet with Honor,* 294.

predominantly Roman Catholic lands.[253]

For example, in 1962, Graham explained his attitude toward the RCC when he traveled to Latin America:

> My goal, I was always clear, was not to preach against Catholic beliefs or to proselytize people who were already committed to Christ within the Catholic Church. Rather it was to proclaim the Gospel to all those who had never truly committed their lives to Christ.[254]

It must be granted *Just As I Am* was written thirty-two years after the fact, but the passive stance soon became a positive stance. Graham added that Ken Strachan, son of the founder of Latin America Mission, felt the same as him, "Ken held the same view I did: that there needed to be a coming together in some way and some form between Catholics and Protestants."[255] Anybody who has lived in and tried to win souls in a predominantly Roman Catholic country understands Graham's purported concern for "coming together" as completely incomprehensible.[256]

Yet he refused to say anything negative—and the conferences that he supported were careful to do the same. They did not follow the lead of the Missionary Conference in London, 1888.[257] The *aggiornamento* of Vatican II left evangelicals at Berlin 1966 uncertain as to how to respond. José Martinez, when he gave a report on evangelism in Spain, stated:

> We must also mention the progressive influence of the Second Vatican Council which is penetrating the mentality of a number of

---

[253]Wilson Ewin, late Baptist pastor in Quebec and former Catholic priest, wrote a section in his *The Assimilation of Evangelist Billy Graham into the Catholic Church* (Compton, QC: Quebec Baptist Missions, 1992) titled "Graham's Deafening Silence" (ibid., 9-10). While evidence of Graham's outright cooperation existed, Ewin had a point, Graham's silence may have spoken more loudly than his words.

[254]Billy Graham, *Just As I Am,* 357.

[255]Ibid.

[256]"Many evangelicals (not all) consider the institution, theology, and everyday practice of Latin American Catholicism as unbiblical. The commitment to evangelize those within that Church becomes for them a genuine duty" (M. Daniel Carroll R[odas], "The Evangelical-Roman Catholic Dialogue: Issues Revolving Around Evangelization—An Evangelical View from Latin America," *Trinity Journal* 21, no. 2 [Fall 2000] 200).

[257]See "The Missions of the Roman Catholic Church to Heathen Lands; Their Character, Extent, Influence, and Lessons," James Johnston, ed., *Report of the Centenary Conference on the Protestant Missions of the World, Held in Exeter Hall, London, 1888* (New York: Fleming H. Revell, 1888), 1:73-90.

Spanish Catholics; this is creating a climate of more respect, understanding and tolerance toward the "separated brethren."[258]

Martinez reported the uncertainty that was also evident among Catholics.[259] Benjamin Mores explained the same uncertainty among evangelicals in Brazil.[260] Even Graham's autobiography indicates the same uncertainty.[261]

In 1967, Donald Sweeting noted that Graham shared the platform with Orthodox and Catholic leaders. Sweeting explained, "This [Zagreb, Yugoslavia] appears to be the first time that Graham had Roman Catholics on the platform in his meetings."[262]

In 1971, Charles Dullea, S.J., a student at the Pontificiae Universitatis Gregorianae in Rome wrote his dissertation comparing salvation in Graham with the *Spiritual Exercises* of Ignatius Loyola, founder of the Jesuits.[263] He ended by indicating that the message of Graham was

---

[258]José Martinez, "Spain," Carl F. H. Henry and Stanley Mooneyham, eds., *One Race, One Gospel, One Task:World Congress on Evangelism—Berlin 1966, Official Reference Volume* (Minneapolis: World Wide, 1967), 1:242.

[259]"Ecumenism and the newer thinking within Catholicism also affect the position of many sincere Catholics. Several years ago these persons may have felt dissatisfied with their faith and with their church, but now they are discovering new spiritual possibilities within post-Council Catholicism, enough to satisfy them without having to join another Christian group outside the Catholic church.

"However, there are also a good many people who react favorably to the Gospel. Wherever the message of Christ is preached faithfully, there is usually very encouraging spiritual fruit" (ibid., 243).

[260]"For many years, Roman Catholic authorities forbade Catholics even to enter a Protestant church. Evangelism, in those days, was very aggressively opposed to Roman theology and the Roman hierarchy. After John XXIII and Vatican Council II, relations improved a great deal between Catholics and Protestants. Many priests now visit evangelical churches and Roman Catholics are replacing their former antagonistic attitude with a new friendly one. Instead of calling Protestants "heretics," they call them "separated brethren." This area of relationship is today the largest open door for evangelism in Brazil. Most evangelicals unfortunately do not recognize this opportunity and are wary , even fearful of this friendship by the Catholics" (Benjamin Moraes, "Brazil," *One Race, One Gospel, One Task,* 278).

[261]"Second, the city [Chicago] was a major Roman Catholic center; in those pre-Vatican II days, we had little open support from the Roman Catholic community, although a number of Catholics (including some priests) attended the meetings" (Billy Graham, *Just As I Am,* 369).

[262]Donald Sweeting, *From Conflict to Cooperation?* 126.

[263]Published with omissions as Carolo W. Dullea, S.J., "W. F. 'Billy' Graham's Decision for Christ": A Study in Conversion," (Dissertatione ad Lauream,

not to dissimilar from that of Loyola. This dissertation by a Jesuit comparing Graham with the founder of the Jesuits seemed to pave the way to an official sanctioning for Catholics to work with Graham.

Several years later, in 1975, Paul VI wrote an encyclical on evangelism titled *Evangelii Nuntiandi*. This encyclical made it clear that charismatic Catholics were not to speak against the Church, her traditions, or her hierarchy.[264] Negative speech was already something that Graham had shunned. The encyclical also allowed for "popular religiosity" as a "true encounter with God."[265] And ninety of its 135 footnotes referred to biblical texts. Surely there was perhaps a springtime of biblicism and evangelism in the RCC!

Several years later, when overseas, Graham began to urge the participation of the RCC, when it was an important percentage of the population. When planning the 1977 trip to Hungary, Martin wrote:

> Haraszti informed the Hungarian ambassador in Washington of the evangelist's concern over the modest agenda the Council of Free Churches had set for him. If at all possible, Graham wished to broaden the scope of the visit just a bit; specifically, to include preaching appointments at major Reformed and Catholic churches and a meeting with key leaders of the Jewish faith.[266]

The request was similar in planning the 1978 trip to Poland: "Graham wanted an invitation from the Catholic hierarchy but did not want the Church to control the visit."[267] During that trip, Graham just missed meeting Stefan Cardinal Wyszynski, as he was in Rome being elected John Paul II.[268] In 1981, John Paul II "welcomed him [Graham] to the Vatican for a half-hour visit, the first time any pope had received him."[269] Graham explained their discussion:

> Noting that they had talked of "inter-church relations, the emergence of Evangelicalism, evangelization, and Christian responsibility

---

Roma: Typis Pontificiae Universitatis Gregorianae, 1971); identical text published as Charles W. Dullea, S.J., *A Catholic Looks at Billy Graham* (New York: Paulist), 1973.

[264]Paul VI, *Evangelii Nuntiandi,* section 58.

[265]Ibid., section 48.

[266]Martin, 484.

[267]Martin, 489.

[268]Ibid., 490.

[269]Ibid., 491.

towards modern moral issues" (an indication it had been a full half-hour), Graham told a press conference that "we had a spiritual time. He is so down-to-earth and human, I almost forgot he was the pope."[270]

In 1982 Sterling Huston became the North American Crusade Director for the BGEA, and in the Spokane Crusade, Bishop Lawrence Welsh wrote the letter quoted above in his diocesan paper encouraging his people to attend the crusade, as they were "developing plans for cooperation to follow up with people who ask during the crusade to be contacted by the Catholic Church."[271] This letter seemed to mark the beginning of Graham's official involvement in cooperation with the RCC in the United States.

In 1987, John Paul II asked Graham to participate in a combined ecumenical worship service in Columbia, South Carolina. Both Tex Reardon and John Akers of the BGEA were assisting in arrangements. Graham, however, had to cancel the meeting due to a prior invitation to China.[272]

Later in 1992, Graham shared in his biography that he brought a message from the Pope to President Kim of Korea. He shared:

> Pope John Paul II had also asked me to convey a message—a rather detailed one—to the North Korean leader. President Kim listened carefully but had no response. Our contacts later indicated that the pope had presented too comprehensive a proposal for the North Koreans to accept at that stage, given the lack of previous contact between the Vatican and the D.P.R.K.[273]

This occasion was a real turning of the tables. The RCC has been sending bishops to influence kings since the sixth century. For example, the efforts of Bishop Leander influenced the Arian King Leogivild of Spain to convert from Arianism to Orthodoxy. In 579, it seems Leovigild's son, Hermenigild, married the daughter of the King of Austrasia, Ingunthis, who was devoutly orthodox, and he converted to orthodoxy, as did his father later.[274] In our case, Graham, a Southern Baptist preacher, was the messenger for the Pope to the Communist North Korean president. This arrangement was especially

---

[270]Ibid.

[271]Bishop Lawrence Walsh, "Catholics and a Billy Graham Crusade," 185.

[272]Billy Graham, *Just As I Am,* 599.

[273]Ibid., 740.

[274] Howorth, 131.

odd as Paul VI in his encyclical *Evangelii Nuntiandi* said that "an individual church [i.e. Southern Baptist Convention]" cut off "from the universal Church . . . finds itself all alone and a prey to the most varied forces of slavery and exploitation."[275] Paul VI continued:

> The more an individual church is attached to the universal Church by the solid bonds of communion. . . . The more will it also be truly evangelizing, that is to say, capable of drawing upon the universal patrimony in order to enable its own people to profit from it, and capable too of communicating to the universal Church the experience and the life of this people, for the benefit of all.[276]

Thus, the wide political sway of the RCC, its information systems, and its research tools would be made available to the "individual church" the more it was attached to Rome in charity. Given its worldwide influence, it is interesting to note that the Pope needed the messenger services of Billy Graham. Yet this occurrence fits with Graham's 1982 addition of "peacemaker" to his mission of evangelism.

There remained and remains one further problem between Catholics and evangelicals, that is proselytism. Stephen Neill explained the nineteenth century Protestant missionary spirit regarding proselytism in largely Roman Catholic lands:

> American Protestants, unlike most other Christians, have never had any hesitation over proselytizing work in nominally Roman Catholic countries, and treat such efforts as 'missions' without distinction from missions in non-Christian countries.[277]

Continuing in the heritage of nineteenth century Protestant missions, Berlin 1966 spoke out for proselytism.[278] However, the WCC and the Roman Catholics are agreed that they do not like proselytism:

---

[275]Paul VI, *Evangelii Nuntiandi*, section 64.

[276]Ibid.

[277]Stephen Neill, *A History of Christian Missions* (New York: Penguin, 1964), 389.

[278]For example, in the Pentecostal/Catholic dialogues, proselytism seemed to be the thorny issue. Steve Rabey reported, "proselytism is described as a 'disrespectful, insensitive, and uncharitable effort to transfer the allegiance of a Christian from one ecclesial body to another'" (Steve Rabey, 23).

25. Christian witness, to those who have not yet received or responded to the announcement of the Gospel or to those who are already Christians, should have certain qualities, in order to avoid being corrupted in its exercise and thus becoming proselytising. Furthermore, the ecumenical movement itself had made Christians more sensitive to the conditions proper to witness borne among themselves. This means that witness should be completely

—conformed to the spirit of the Gospel, especially by respecting the other's right to religious freedom, and

—concerned to do nothing which could compromise the progress of ecumenical, dialogue and action.[279]

The 1982 WCC Commission on World Mission and Evangelism called proselytism a sin.[280] Graham, in order to assuage doubts, assured countries and churches that his role was not to proselytize, but to preach the gospel.[281] Thus, Graham's practice of sending inquirers back to their church of choice gave credence to his non-proselytism. However, other evangelicals saw proselytism as necessary for obedience to the Great Commission. Jacques Blocher explained that the decline in Protestant church membership in France was partially due to a lack of proselytism.[282]

Lausanne 1974, never using the term proselytism, inserted two ecumenical concepts into the statement on evangelism, which soften the "proselytizing" impact: presence and dialogue.[283] In this way, it would seem, the Lausanne Statement sought to bridge the gap between the WCC's anti-proselytism and evangelical proselytism.

The discussion continues with expectant evangelism continuing to bring tension and strife, as some appreciate it and others do not. Thus in cooperative evangelism, some will be pleased and some will not. The evangelist needs to be mindful to Acts 20:28, "Be on guard for yourselves."[284] Graham, however, had the unusual abiblity of ridding the

---

[279]Joint Working Group between the Roman Catholic Church and the WCC, "Common Witness and Proselytism—a Study Document" (1970), Michael Kinnamon and Brian E. Cope, eds., *The Ecumenical Movement: An Anthology of Key Texts and Voices* (Grand Rapids: Eerdmans, 1977), 351.

[280]WCC Commission on World Mission and Evangelism, "Mission and Evangelism—An Ecumenical Affirmation" (1982), *The Ecumenical Movement,* 381.

[281]Billy Graham, *Just As I Am,* 357.

[282]Jacques Blocher, "France," *One Race, One Gospel, One Task,* 1:249.

[283]John Stott, ed., *Making Christ Known,* 20.

[284]The evangelist, as other Christian leaders, in his cooperative ventures may need to keep in mind the three weeds described by Jesus Christ in Mark 4:19: the

theological fence on many issues and staying on the good side of most people. Cardinal Lekai, Catholic Primate of Hungary told Billy Graham in 1985:

> "To be perfectly honest, Dr. Graham," he said, "and please don't be offended, but I call you one of the greatest actors on the human scene. Without all the resources that the President has, or the built-in influential factors that the pope has, you have built yourself up and gone further than either one."[285]

In conclusion, Graham's preaching ministry stretched from 1937 to the present, or over sixty-five years. During these years he underwent major changes as to those with whom he was willing to cooperate. He went from uniquely fundamentalist single-church revivals in Florida to cooperative youth meetings with Youth for Christ. He began city-wide campaigns in 1947, making his Augusta, Georgia campaign a pattern.[286] During these years his mention of the fundamentals relaxed, and his message focused more on reviving the churches and saving the lost. Los Angeles 1949 was his "Watershed" campaign, thrusting him to national prominence. It was not long until Graham distanced himself from fundamentalists, for example not allowing the fundamentalist Carl McIntyre to take part in the Berlin 1966 Congress,[287] because he failed the "social test" of love for the brethren.[288] Graham, with his deity-of-Christ-as-the-only-theological-test, became more and more inclusive in his cooperative

---

worries of the world, the deceitfulness of riches, and the desire for other things. As we have discussed cooperation, the three weeds that attack the seed that falls in the thorny group seem to attack the evangelist. First, the worries of the world can be the constant concern for reputation, public relations, and informational polls. None of these are bad in and of themselves, unless they snuff out the fruit. Second, the deceitfulness of riches attacks the evangelist at his pocketbook and family. When there is a lack of funds, when fundraising is at a low point, that is when shortcuts become palatable. Third, Jesus mentioned the desire for other things. Other things may be the desire for more church involvement, greater crowds, bigger facilities, or larger budgets. However, a trap is found behind each of these desires. No, God does not want mediocrity. But when it comes to cooperation, the example of Moses may be the high road for some evangelists, "By faith Moses, when he had grown up, refused to be called the son of Pharoah's daughter; choosing rather to endure ill-treatment with the people of God, than to enjoy the passing pleasures of sin; considering the reproach of Christ greater riches than the treasures of Egypt; for he was looking to the reward" (Hebrews 11:24-26).

[285]William Martin, 526.

[286]Billy Graham, *Just As I Am,* 125.

[287]William Martin, 334-35.

[288]See John Stott, *Commentary on First John,* 53.

evangelism. It became clear from New York 1957 that Graham did not hold dogmatically even to this unique theological test. Thus, the Graham crusades began to openly work with RCC leaders and churches in Eastern Europe and in the United States. By 1982, it became protocol for the Graham advance team to encourage a broad-base of church support which sought to include the Roman Catholic hierarchy.

This study shows that parameters for cooperation were needed, as well as accountability in safeguarding those parameters. Graham experienced some slippage in his parameters perhaps for the purpose of expediency. Graham was accountable to everyone and to no-one, to all of his supporters, and to none of his supporters. Graham maintained the financial support of those he influenced for the gospel throughout his ministry, his workers affirmed that he had not changed theologically, and he continued to call persons to faith through the invitation system. Yet his cooperative associations and actions were quite distant from his early view of instantaneous conversion. Yet Graham continued to preach Christ.

"Christ is proclaimed; and in this I rejoice, yes, I will rejoice" (Phil 1:18).

CHAPTER 6

CONCLUSION

oratio Basilii erat tonitru, quia vita ejus fulgur—
Basil's speech was like thunder because his life was like lightning[1]

The thundering voice of Graham, known for his "machine-gun" style of preaching, clearly flowed from a life that practiced what he preached. This one factor, maybe more than any other human factor, set him apart from many of his contemporaries. Yet, even a life of lightning cannot explain Graham's tremendous appeal and his tenacity over sixty-three years of preaching the gospel. The sovereignty of God and the work of the Holy Spirit through the ministry of Billy Graham remained factors upon which all Christians can agree. Graham's life and ministry is best explained in light of God's hand of blessing.

How best to conclude a manuscript on the evangelistic theology and methodology of Billy Graham? This conclusion will discuss three points. First, it will address Graham's move to the middle, as well as the philosophical, theological, and practical results of that move. Secondly, it will discuss the importance of words to convey meaning. Thirdly, it will provide specific conclusions based on the research.

The Impossible Middle

Graham often responded in a gracious way when quizzed theologically. Yet, he may have used his lack of education to exonerate himself when he was walking a middle path between two non-resolvable theological points. William Martin explained Graham's habit of taking a middle road in connection with the Lausanne 1974 conference:

---

[1]"Gregory Nazianzen declares in his panegyric on Basil that Basil's speech was like thunder because his life was like lightning (*oratio Basilii erat tonitru, quia vita ejus fulgur*)" (Philip Jacob Spener, *Pia Desideria* [1675]. trans. by Theosore G. Tappert [Minneapolis: Fortress, 1964], 104; quoting Gregory Nazianzen [329-389], *Carmina*, 119).

Billy Graham, as usual, paced back and forth across the middle line, insisting that 'our witness must be by both word and deed.' But wary lest undue attention to works sap the faith that produced them.[2]

This example was multiplied in many of Graham's theological dealings. Chapter four showed that Graham moved to the middle as regards his doctrine of hell in 1953. It showed that Graham moved to the middle on sin, moving to "The Two Faces of Man" in 1955. While it can be showed that Graham that held to a type of inerrancy in practice, he chose not to use the term in 1956.[3] As a Board Member, he seemed silent as Fuller Theological Seminary to move down the path to dynamic equivalence—a sociological approach to the impossible middle.[4] Chapter four also showed that by 1957

---

[2]William C. Martin, *A Prophet with Honor: The Billy Graham Story* (New York: William Morrow, 1991)*,* 448.

[3]Marsden explained, in the context of the founding of *Christianity Today*: "During campaigns in England in 1954 Graham received broader church support than his fundamentalist supporters would have allowed him in the United States. Such successes in culturally influential religious circles were leading Graham toward the conviction that he could make marvelous inroads into America's major denominations if he could only jettison the disastrous fundamentalist images of separatism, anti-intellectualism, and contentiousness. As his letter to Lindsell indicated, this would also involve at least distancing himself from some of the more restrictive shibboleths. He would not tie his ministry to a narrow view of the implications of the inerrancy of Scripture for modern science. He would not identify evangelical Christianity with only the most conservative politics. His recent stand for racially integrating his crusades exemplified this point. Nor would he totally condemn the ecumenical movement. Graham himself was ready to weather the storms that such moderate stances would surely bring. So in speculating to Lindsell about Carl Henry he asked: would he 'be ready to take a certain amount of criticism from typical fundamentalist leaders?' More basically, 'Would he be willing to recognize that fundamentalism is in need of an entirely new approach and that this magazine would be useless if it had the old fundamentalist stamp on it?'

"When the search turned explicitly to Carl Henry the next summer, Graham was still worried that Henry might be 'too well known as a fundamentalist' and even wondered if the magazine might not be edited under an assumed name for a year or two" (George M. Marsden, *Reforming Fundamentalism: Fuller Seminary and the New Evangelicalism* [Grand Rapids: Eerdmans, 1987], 159-60).

[4]Marsden explained, "The dominant leadership of the original new evangelicalism hoped through the influence of Billy Graham and *Christianity Today* to mobilize these diverse evangelicals into an effective coalition. Despite some openness, however, their emphasis on inerrancy kept them close to classic fundamentalism and limited their influence largely to those traditions that had shared these concerns. Fuller Seminary under Hubbard's leadership, on the other hand, took the principle of openness one more step and simply dropped the distinctly fundamentalist agenda. In doing so, they cut themselves off from the strict inerrantists. But at the same time they were opening

Graham had moved toward a middle road between the substitutionary theory and the reconciliation model of the atonement. Chapter three showed that by 1965 Graham had moved to the middle on evangelism and social responsibility, as expressed in the above quote. Thus Graham emphasized a theological "impossible middle" on some doctrines through most of his ministry.[5] Graham, however, when asked the following question in 1967, "Do you still believe in the same fundamental doctrines that you did when you began preaching?" answered, "Yes, but methods change."[6] This middle road calls for analysis in two ways. First, we will note some historical precedents for the middle road. Secondly, we will posit several consequences of the middle road.

Using philosophical or mathematical categories that A and B stand for two different and exclusive viewpoints, there are a limited number of ways to view the two. Only A and only B are the first two approaches. These Graham did not adhere to. Thirdly, if one holds to A=B, it leads to "madness and folly" (cf. Eccl. 1:17; 2:12). One is left with an irrationalism much like what is found in Buddhism. A fourth alternative is to posit some type of synthesis: A+B=C. Philosophically, the synthesis may parallel the concept of a Hegelian dialectic, where the synthesis is quite different from either of the thesis or antithesis. This synthesis may be called *scientia media,* as considered by posited by William Lane Craig.[7] Graham, however, seemed to adopt a view of eliminating from A (fundamental theology) what was most obstructive to B (modernist theology), while continuing to affirm the methods and some terminology of A (fundamental theology). The resultant theology was a hybrid of theologies. Theologically, both Bushnell[8]

---

themselves to forming other alliances within many-faceted American evangelicalism" (ibid., 230).

[5]Graham did preach the deity of Christ, the Virgin Birth, the veracity of Scripture, the supernatural nature of conversion, the fact of the second coming, and the existence of heaven and hell.

[6]O. Charles Horton, "An Analysis of Selected Published Sermons of Billy Graham" (Th.M. thesis, New Orleans Baptist Theological Seminary, 1967), 96.

[7]Building off the theory of *scientia media* put forth by the Spanish Jesuit Luis Molina (1535-1600), William Lane Craig posited "middle knowledge" with the ability to "avoid the Protestant error of denying genuine human freedom, yet without thereby sacrificing the sovereignty of God" (William L. Craig, "Middle Knowledge a Calvinist-Arminian Rapprochement?" in *The Grace of God and the Will of Man,* gen. ed. Clark Pinnock [Minneapolis: Bethany House, 1989], 141). Likely Craig, however, did not accept the purely sacramental view of salvation that emanated from a divine-human cooperation in ecclesiology and salvation as in Molinas and Aquinas.

[8]Sydney E. Ahlstrom, "Introduction to the Reprinted Edition," in *The Vicarious Sacrifice Grounded in Principles of Universal Obligation,* by Horace Bushnell (New York: Scribner, 1866; Hicksville, NY: Regina Press, 1975), 3d.

and Aulén[9] sought to forge a middle road in their theology of the atonement. Practically, this middle road may be somewhat similar to the "Bipolar Approach" proposed by Christian Schwarz in his *Paradigm Shift in the Church*.[10] Graham seemed to approximate the moves of Craig and Schwarz in his preaching of the gospel, while maintaining instantaneous conversion. Graham may have reduced his theology to *sola invitatio* (invitation alone) or *sola evangelium* (gospel alone). While the invitation system is helpful, and while the gospel is central to Christian theology, Luther posited *sola Scriptura* (Scriptures) as the first basis of his disenchantment with the soteriology of Roman Catholic theology.

Interestingly enough, E. Stanley Jones, in a 1957 letter to the editor of the *Christian Century* also noted in Graham a movement from the fundamentalist roots of his theology toward a synthesis with modernist theology. Surprisingly, Jones called this a "higher [Hegelian] synthesis."[11]

---

[9]A. G. Herbert, "Translator's Preface," in Gustav Aulén, *Christus Victor* (1930; New York: Macmillan, 1969), xxxvi.

[10]Christian Schwartz provided a theological justification for his "pibolar approach" in his *Paradigm Shift in the Church: How Natural Church Development Can Transform Theological Thinking* (Carol Stream, IL: ChurchSmart, 1999). In his *Natural Church Development,* he explained the two positions he was bridging: "This illustration shows us that the two positions are in one sense quite different: monism treats the two poles as one, dualism disconnects the two poles" (Christian Schwarz, *Natural Church Development: A Guide to Eight Essential Qualities of Healthy Churches,* 3rd ed. [Carol Stream, IL: ChurchSmart, 1998], 86). "Adopting the bipolar approach removes the need for this type of dialectic" (99). Then ultimately, "Natural church development is made up of principles God created and revealed to us. . . . The *research techniques* we used to empirically identify the principles are flawed—like any scientific method. . . . But all this does not change one basic fact: the *principles* that we have groppingly tried to search out and blunderingly tried to communicate find their source in God" (127).

[11]"SIR: If there is truth in Hegel's dictum, and I believe there is, that thought moves from thesis to antithesis to synthesis, then it seems to be applicable to the controversy regarding the Graham crusade going on in your pages. Hegel said that thesis produces its opposite antithesis and then out of a struggle of opposites a third something is born in which the truth in thesis and the truth in antithesis are gathered up into something larger than each, a synthesis.

The thesis in this controversy in its larger aspects is conservatism, and it has produced its opposite, liberalism. (Historically it may have been the other way around, but which produced which is irrelevant for the matter in hand. Incidentally, I use 'conservatism' and 'liberalism' instead of 'fundamentalism' and 'modernism,' for both of the latter have a bad odor.) Out of this struggle of thesis and antithesis there is emerging a something which seems to be gathering up the truth in each in a higher synthesis.

The Graham crusade is a symptom of that emerging synthesis. Both groups want to share Christ in differing terminology and in differing methods, but both want to share Christ. The synthesis is emerging at a very important place—at the place of

In 1957 Jones noted that Graham was forging a synthesis. Marsden affirmed the same thing.[12] It is no surprise that this synthesis effected some foundational doctrines of the Christian faith.

William G. McLoughlin, in his *Billy Graham: Revivalist in a Secular Age,* also affirmed that Graham represented a "middle ground." He wrote:

> Graham has become a spokesman for a newly consolidated and articulate pietistic movement which is challenging the old Protestant church system. Theologically this movement is an amalgamation of the mellowing fundamentalism of the 1920's and the maturing Pentecostalism of a much older date. Whether it is called the "new evangelicalism" or "neofundamentalism," this theology represents a middle ground between the fanatical or ultra-fundamentalist fringe groups (Carl McIntire, Holly Rollers, faith healers, snake handlers)

---

evangelism. There conservative and liberal could join in the only place they could get together—at the place of making Christ known to people inside and outside the churches who need conversion. That synthesis is a good one, the best possible one. For it is vital, not verbal. Hence the conservative groups and the Protestant council of churches could come together on this basis in the New York crusade—and rightly.

This coming together, as in all such cases, will be opposed by two groups: the radical conservatives and the radical liberals. Both of them will see in it compromise, not comprehension. This is happening in regard to Billy Graham. The ultra-conservatives are attacking him in their papers and the ultra-liberals are doing the same. But both of them are fringe movements. The rest of the main body of conservatives and liberals, tired of 'acrid fundamentalism' and 'arid liberalism,' see in this crusade a symptom of the possibility of working together to win men to Christ and have eagerly embraced it—and rightly. It is the open door out of the impasse, a door upward.

After talking personally with Billy Graham I am persuaded that he is more or less consciously one of the meeting places of this movement toward synthesis. And therefore the movement is to be welcomed. It is a movement of the Spirit. There are symptoms everywhere of a feeling toward something beyond thesis and beyond antithesis. A conservative journal discussed the question: 'Is Stanley Jones a modernist?' and came to the conclusion that 'he has a fundamental soul and a modern mind.' And the point is that, though conservative, they accepted that combination. More and more Christians are feeling after the synthesis.

Billy Graham's crusade, while having things here and there which may not be wholly acceptable, nevertheless is a very healthy meeting place for conservative and liberal, and in the contact each may gain something from the other and then something beyond each may emerge—the Christian" (E. Stanley Jones, "*Higher* Synthesis?" *The Christian Century,* 14 August 1957, 970).

[12]Marsden, *Reforming Fundamentalism*, 159-60.

and the liberalism or modernism that is associated with the major denominations.[13]

Similarly, Martin Marty wrote an article during Graham's 1957 New York Crusade called, "Intruders in the Crowded Center." The article was a book review of *Contemporary Evangelical Thought,* edited by Carl F. H. Henry. Marty wrote:

> Ten competent scholars or the self-styled neo-evangelical school have now, for one instance, published a symposium which seeks to establish their group at dead center in Christian theology.[14]

Marty then concluded his comments about Graham's walking a middle road:

> The man [Graham] in the Christian's center is, much like W. H. Auden's "Double Man," perched on the sharp arête where, if he does not move, he will fall; yet movement is heretical. The revolt of these immoderate moderates may yet tumble him, and we shall be diverted from the current ecumenical inquiries which would lead us all to be ever new in Christ. In such a diversion we would sow various seeds before we would—all of us—inherit the wind.[15]

According to Martin Marty, the 1957 Graham was perched in the impossible middle, without the opportunity to move one way or the other. Graham, however, survived another forty-four years as an evangelist straddling this middle road.

For a theologian, Graham relied on John R. W. Stott, chairman of Lausanne 1974, an Anglican evangelical who was President of the British Evangelical Alliance. John R. W. Stott, for his part, also posited a middle road approach to mission in his *Balanced Christianity* and in his *Christian Mission in the Modern World,* both published one year after Lausanne 1974. Adrian Hastings explained Stott's relationship to Billy Graham as follows:

> Within the world Evangelical movement of the second half of the century he [Stott] played to Billy Graham a role not altogether unlike that which J. H. Oldham had played fifty years before to John

---

[13]William G. McLoughlin, *Billy Graham: A Revivalist in a Secular Age* (New York: Ronald Press Company, 1960), 205; quoted in O. Charles Horton, "An Analysis of Selected Published Sermons of Billy Graham," 96.

[14]Martin Marty, "Intruders in a Crowded Center," *Christian Century,* 3 July 1957, 820.

[15]Ibid., 821.

R. Mott. In each case the less flamboyant but more intellectual Englishman was endeavouring to guide the movement into new, less simplistic vistas.[16]

Although there might be slight overstatement, Stott had a definite influence on Graham. Stott began his *Balanced Christianity* decrying the polarization that *The Christian Century* had predicted in 1957:[17]

> My concern is to draw attention to one of the great tragedies of contemporary Christendom, a tragedy which is especially apparent among those of us who are called (and indeed call ourselves) *evangelical* Christians. In a single word, this tragedy is *polarization,* but I shall need to spell out what I mean.[18]

Stott further stated the oft repeated quote which he attributed to Meldenius "and quoted by Richard Baxter: 'In essentials unity, In non-essentials liberty, In all things charity.'"[19] Stott then ascribed to Aristotle's Golden Mean at the end of his introductory chapter as a justification for his mature evangelical approach, a "balanced" approach.[20]

Simultaneously, Stott confused the issue by comparing his balanced approach with the need to balance between the extremes of Calvinism and Arminianism.[21] With this introduction, Stott then, as a skillful expositor, used "the ladder outline"[22] to work his way from the less controversial points to the most controversial point. His next chapters covered the following points: intellect and emotion, conservative and

---

[16]Adrian Hastings, *A History of English Christianity* 1920-1985 (London: Collins, 1986), 617; quoted by Iain Murray, *Evangelicalism Divided: A Record of Crucial Change in the Years 1950-2000* (Edinburgh: Banner of Truth, 2000), 49.

[17]"Fundamentalist Revival," editorial, *Christian Century,* 19 June 1957, 751.

[18]John R. W. Stott, *Balanced Christianity* (Downers Grove, IL: InterVarsity, 1975), 7.

[19]Ibid., 8.

[20]Ibid., 10. This same approach was used by Griffith Thomas in his redefinition or deconstruction of the concept of worldliness, as quoted by Graham (Griffith Thomas, *The Catholic Faith: A Manual of Instruction for Members of the Church of England* (London: Hodder and Stoughton, 1905, 1908); quoted in Graham, *Peace with God,* 156).

[21]Stott, *Balanced Christianity,* 10.

[22]John A. Broadus, *On the Preparation and Delivery of a Sermon,* 4th ed. (New York: Harper and Row, 1979), 68-69.

radical, form and freedom, and evangelism and social action. On his last point, Stott pointed out that evangelicals have polarized evangelism and socio-political action from one another, "despite the outstanding record of nineteenth century evangelicals."[23] With this false representation of means and ends, of evangelism and its results,[24] Stott used the example of the Jesus People as an example of removing themselves from society. Then Stott posited the World Council of Churches as the other extreme of the evangelical pole. Stott then stated that "evangelism-only" evangelicals were like the Jesus People—pulling themselves away from the world in which they live. He finally showed hope that evangelicals were learning and maturing in their balance:

> We are not likely to mistake justice for salvation, but we have often talked and behaved as if we thought our only Christian responsibility toward non-Christian society was evangelism, the proclamation of the good news of salvation. In recent years, however, there have been welcome signs of change. We have become disillusioned with the "cop-out" mentality, the tendency to opt out of social responsibility, the traditional fundamentalist obsession with "micro-ethics" (smoking, drinking and dancing) and the corresponding neglect of "macro-ethics" (race, violence, poverty, pollution, justice and freedom). There has also been among us a growing recognition of the

---

[23]Stott, *Balanced Christianity*, 37.

[24]"It will help us in defining it to remind ourselves, for one thing, that we must not confuse the aim of foreign missions with the results of foreign missions. . . . I read in a missionary paper a little while ago that the foreign mission that was to accomplish results of permanent value must aim at the total reorganization of the whole social fabric. This is a mischievous doctrine. We learn nothing from human history, from the experience of the Christian Church, from the example of our Lord and His apostles to justify it. They did not aim directly at such an end. They were content to aim at implanting the life of Christ *in* the hearts of men, and were willing to leave the consequences to the care of God. It is a dangerous thing to charge ourselves openly before the world with the aim of reorganizing States and reconstructing society. . . . It is misleading, also, as Dr. Behrends once declared, to confuse the ultimate issues with the immediate aims; and it is not only misleading, it is fatal. Some things can only be secured by those who do not seek them. Missions are powerful to transform the face of society, because they ignore the face of society and deal with it at its heart. They yield such powerful political and social results because they do not concern themselves with them" (Robert Speer, "The Supreme and Determining Aim," *Ecumenical Missionary Conference New York 1900, Report of the Ecumenical Conference on Foreign Missions Held in New York, April 1900* [New York: American Tract Society], 1:74-75).

biblical foundations, both theological and ethical, for Christian social action.[25]

Stott seemingly ignored the abiblical and atheological nature of Rauschenbusch's *Theology of the Social Gospel.* It is interesting to note that Stott wisely reminded Graham of his shift from "the traditional fundamentalist obsession with 'micro-ethics'" in *Peace with God,* and he also related Graham's stand on the race issue as co-equal with the WCC's view of seeking justice. Finally, Stott then made his point, ". . . we should avoid the rather naïve choice between evangelism and social action. . ."[26] He followed this statement up with the variety of gifts in the church as a sign that "God calls different people to different ministries. . ."[27] and then with a lengthy quote of Visser't Hooft, introduced in this way:

> I do not know of any better statement of our double Christian responsibility, social and evangelistic, than that made during the Fourth Assembly of the World Council of Churches at Uppsala in 1968 by W. A. Visser t' Hooft, former WCC General Secretary.[28]

In his quote, Visser t' Hooft differentiated between the vertical and horizontal aspects of God's saving action, indicating that both were needed. This dual mission was exactly the point of John Stott in his *Balanced Christianity.*[29] Not astonishingly, Stott's position as expressed in *Christian Mission in the Modern World* was quite similar. However, even more boldly, Stott used Hegelian terminology when he called for "a Biblical Synthesis,"[30] assuming that evangelism and socio-political action are like the Hegelian thesis and anti-thesis. The problem is that Hegel's synthesis resembles neither the thesis or the antithesis—so much for proclamational evangelism! Graham, in a similar fashion, more and more as his ministry progressed, existed on a series of tightropes between opposing theological,

---

[25]Ibid., 39.

[26]Ibid., 41.

[27]Ibid.

[28]Ibid., 42.

[29]It is important to note that this evangelism-only pole existed and exists in every century regardless of the continuous attack each century launched against it, theological, ecclesiological, or pragmatic. It would seem that the Holy Spirit working through the Scriptures alone has sufficed for the existence of a revivalism and a prioritative evangelism to exist in every century.

[30]John R. W. Stott, *Christian Mission in the Modern World* (Downers Grove, IL: InterVarsity, 1975), 20-22.

missiological, and even ecclesial poles in Christianity.

Graham's walking the tightrope between fundamentalism and modernism had some consequences. On the positive side, it opened unprecedented doors for Graham and the preaching of Christ. On the negative side, it may have moved the mainstream of evangelicalism away from *sola Scriptura*, toward lifestyle evangelism—and away from initiative evangelism, toward a theological pragmatism, and toward ecclesial unity without adequate theological consideration.

Yet the reason for Graham's success in the pulpit was his sincerity and ability as a wordsmith. He knew the power of words, and he used them to convey the gospel message in simple terms and to avoid alienating his hearers through secondary theological discussions. This great strength, however, also had its down side.

The Power of Words

Words are a powerful medium. The Bible says that they contain life and death. God chose to reveal Himself through words in a book. At the end of time human beings will be judged according to their words. Postmoderns and cultural anthropologists may emphasize the fluidity of words. They look to the social and cultural context of words. When taken to this extreme, the words in the Bible may become devoid of authoritative meaning. Yet the absence of words also conveys meaning about what is important and what is not. Words can also frame a question. The difference between anti-abortion and pro-life, although implying the same thing, resonates quite differently. Likewise, the use and non-use of theological terms frames the question, as does the use of various definitions of terms. Perhaps this was one of Graham's greatest influences to evangelicalism. He wanted to communicate to unreached constituencies. He reached out to various denominational and religious people. And in all the good he did, his silence on some theological issues may not have been as helpful.

In crusade evangelism and in united ministry among those interested in evangelism, what should be the lowest common denominator in the use of words? A suggestion comes from the speech of the Apostle Paul to the Ephesian elders. In Acts 20, Paul gave a warning to those gathered about the inevitability of false teachers and prophets. Then he wrote, "And now I commend you to God and to the word of His grace, which is able to build you up and give you an inheritance among all those who are sanctified" (Acts 20:32). The words of the Bible—the full counsel of God (Acts 20:27)—should be the lowest common denominator. The words of grace are God's, and they will protect. Therefore it is fitting that Graham should be known for his often used phrase, "The Bible says."

But how can the power of terminology be studied? The following are four separate scenarios. First, Graham used words A (fundamental) and anti-B (anti-modernist), because he believed theology A, which corresponded to practice A. Second, Graham avoided words anti-B, yet maintained theology A, along with practice A. Third, Graham used words non-A (non-fundamental) or B (modernist), yet maintained theology A, and practice A. Four, Graham used words B, maintained theology B, and followed practice A. In this case, the purpose was to better communicate the gospel to those who hold to non-A or B. After a time, dissonance can eventuate, especially in the third and fourth scenarios. The possible result in the long term was fallout in the theological legacy of A. The difficulties involved are that primary sources are sermons made out of words. If a person were to apply 1 Corinthians 9:20-22 to evangelism, it may impact not only the method used, but also the message. In an interview earlier this year, Robert Evans, founder of Greater Europe Mission and close associate of Graham in his European ministry, reminded me to consider the possible differences between the tactical Graham and the theological Graham.[31] These tensions are not easily resolved. However, what is the lowest common denominator in terminology for church life and evangelism? Is not the Bible a book of words? Because of Graham's repeated and regular use of Scripture, it grounded his message as the Word of God.

Graham chose in the early 1950s to distance himself from fundamentalist terminology and to begin to quote Modernists and use their terminology. Yet he maintained the revivalist methodology. The result was that he was able to walk the impossible middle. With this look at the basic theological approach of Graham, we now move to further conclusions based on this study. These conclusions seek to draw balanced and thoughtful points of application from this research.

Particular Conclusions

The following conclusion will emulate the final chapter of Jude Weisenbeck's dissertation, as found in his *Conciliar Fellowship and the Unity of the Church.*[32] It will move chapter by chapter providing insights that have been gleaned from this study.

---

[31]Robert Evans, telephone interview by author, 2 July 2001; handwritten notes in author's possession.

[32]In his second doctoral dissertation completed at the Pontifical University of St. Thomas in Rome, Weisenbeck explained, "The following sets of propositions, corresponding to the chapters, summarizes the principal findings of this study, including assessments and evaluation" (Jude Weisenbeck, *Conciliar Fellowship and the Unity of the Church,* [Ph.D. diss. Rome: Pontifica Studiorum Universitas, A S. Thoma Aq. in Urbe, 1986], 261).

Chapter One

1. Graham's pietistic lifestyle and holy caution kept him virtually above reproach from any criticism of a personal nature his entire ministry.

2. Graham's sincerity allowed him to maintain cordial relationships with persons of various theological and ecclesial groups throughout his ministry.

3. Graham combined vision and giftedness with humility and grace. He was more than a remarkable speaker, he was a keen administrator—he gathered talented and gracious individuals around him and united churches and people for the cause of gospel proclamation.

4. Graham's worldwide appeal affirmed the universal impact of the "Personal Gospel" and the Bible.

5. The urgency of evangelism as often noted in fundamental writings on evangelism seemed to drive Graham's vision to preach the gospel around the world.

Chapter Two

1. Graham's belief in Scripture provided him a uniting point for the gospel, salvation, and the invitation.

2. Graham's belief in the power of Scripture legitimated his worldwide preaching of the Personal Gospel.

3. A firm commitment to the authority of the Bible buttresses an evangelist's commitment to the need for instantaneous conversion and evangelism.

4. Although Graham kept a practical belief in inerrancy throughout his ministry, his use of infallibility and his avoidance of making inerrancy an issue did not prove beneficial to evangelicalism in the long run.

Chapter Three

1. While two of Graham's Youth for Christ colleagues drifted significantly from YFC's original vision and emphasis of gospel-oriented rallies, Graham did not significantly depart from this vision.

2. Graham maintained a consistent, though expanding, methodology of gospel proclamation throughout the sixty-three years of his ministry.

3. While Graham's methodology remained relatively constant throughout his ministry, his view of the church's mission adapted to include both lifestyle evangelism and social responsibility, whereas in his early years it focused uniquely on proclamational evangelism.

4. Affirming the universal affirmative of a biblically-oriented gospel proclamation, uniting churches in evangelism, and remaining winsome and gracious proves a difficult mix to maintain.

Chapter Four

1. The personal gospel was not new to Graham nor to North American Christianity, as is often supposed, having its roots in the Bible, as well as in German Pietism and British evangelicalism.

2. Systematic theology and evangelism (the mission of the church) are integrally related, each influencing the other:
   Views on anthropology and the atonement directly impact both the methods used in evangelism and the message shared in gospel proclamation

3. Graham focused on instantaneous conversion throughout his ministry:
   Graham's focus on instantaneous conversion and the invitation system seemed to protect him from the slowly smothering theological influences of ascribing to both evangelism and social responsibility.

4. Graham seems to have fallen prey to a downgrade on three challenging doctrines important to historic evangelicals: total depravity, the substitutionary-vicarious-blood atonement, and hell as everlasting conscious punishment.

5. Ability to ride the impossible middle:
   Graham seemed to avoid controversial conservative doctrine, while still maintaining a theology consistent with crusade evangelism and acceptable to his supporters.
   Most evangelicals viewed Graham through the eyes of *sola invitatio* or *sola evangelium,* and in conjunction with his sterling character, thus not taking notice of his theological movement.
   Graham seemed to gradually de-emphasize doctrinal preaching on topics that sounded too fundamental.

6.   Dealing with the changes in Graham's theology:

From 1950-1953, in conjunction with writing *Peace with God,* Graham seems to have made a calculated adjustment in his theology and methodology. The issue was one of emphasis. Would he include non-evangelicals in his crusade efforts, or would he work only through evangelical churches?

Because Graham chose to include non-evangelicals within his crusade methodology, he gradually adjusted his theology. This move had several repercussions. First, he gradually adapted his theology to be more acceptable to non-evangelical (non-conversionistic) participants (possibly accepting the reconciliation model of the atonement) while continuing to preach the cross and instantaneous conversion, and while continuing to use the invitation system.

Second, Graham's view of mission changed to adapt to his redefined anthropology, the "Two Faces of Man." Thus he included social responsibility as a unique and separate mission of the church, rather than as a natural biproduct of individual conversion as in his early years.

Third, Graham began to broaden his appeal to include Roman Catholics in his crusades. This gradual change in methodology moved his cooperative efforts toward the sacramental camp of salvation.

Is it possible to move from preaching the "full counsel of God," to a "higher" purpose of preaching the gospel to more people? Graham may have sought to preach a more positive gospel and thus may have adapted his theology to be more mainstream.

Chapter Five

1.   Does effective crusade evangelism or other multi-denominational efforts necessitate the minimalizing of theology? This question begs for and necessitates theological boundaries.

2.   The theological boundaries prescribed by the precedents of the 1846 Evangelical Alliance or the 1895 Niagara Bible Conference provided wise theological boundaries for inter-denominational cooperative evangelistic ministry.

3.   Take away theology from the historic churches, and one is left with ecclesial hierarchy. Take away the doctrinal distinctives emanating from an authoritative Bible from congregational churches, and one is left with nothing.

4. If an evangelist is preaching Christ, even if it is not fully as another person would want, it is a loosing proposition for such a person to be openly antagonistic to the evangelist.

While this book has noted changes and shifts in Graham's theology, much of his core theology remained constant. He held to the Virgin birth and the deity of Christ. He preached individual sin and the cross. Graham not only spoke of the veracity of Scripture, but quoted frequently from it. He maintained a belief in the need for individual conversion. Graham called sinners to repentance. These constants must be kept in mind when looking at some of his theological movement.

Graham accomplished an incredible feat: he was covered by the media for over fifty-three years—they scrutinized his life; he had ecclesial and theological antagonists—they scrutinized his life; and yet he maintained a sterling reputation. Though this researcher has sought to dissect Graham's ministry and preaching to better understand and communicate his theology of evangelism, it is hope that the same grace that Graham exemplified throughout his entire life has been in evidence. This author is grateful to have studied the ministry of Billy Graham. His example of tenacity in preaching the gospel provides an example for all Christians who follow him to "Do the Work of an Evangelist."

APPENDIX 1

CHRONOLOGICAL ARRANGEMENT OF
OFFICIAL AND UNOFFICIAL BOOKS BY BILLY GRAHAM

Calling Youth to Christ.[*][1] Intro. by Torrey M. Johnson. Grand Rapids: Zondervan, 1947; London: Marshall, Morgan and Scott, n.d.

Revival in Our Time: The Story of the Billy Graham Evangelistic Campaigns Including Six of His Sermons. Special ed. for Northwestern Schools. Wheaton, IL: Van Kampen, 1950; 2nd ed. Wheaton, IL: Van Kampen, 1950.

America's Hour of Decision:[*] *Featuring a Life Story of Billy Graham, and Stories of His Evangelistic Campaigns in Portland, Ore., Minneapolis, Atlanta, Fort Worth, Shreveport, La., Memphis, and the Rose Bowl, Pasadena, California, Includes Four of the Evangelist's Sermons.* Wheaton, IL: Van Kampen, 1951.

I Saw Your Sons at War:[*] *The Korean Diary of Billy Graham.* Minneapolis: Billy Graham Evangelistic Association, 1953.

Peace with God.[*][2] Garden City, NY: Doubleday, 1953; Kingswood, Surrey: for Billy Graham Evangelistic Association, 1966; Old Tappan, NJ: Revell Publishing Co., 1968; Garden City: Doubleday, 1968; rev. and expanded. Waco, TX: Word, 1984. Chapters published as *Guide for Christian Living.* Minneapolis: Billy Graham Evangelistic Association, 1953. Chapters published as *How to Find Peace with God.* Minneapolis: Billy Graham Evangelistic Association, n.d. Chapters published as *Rules for Christian Living.* Minneapolis: Billy Graham Evangelistic Association, n.d. Six chapters published as *How to Find God.* Minneapolis: Billy Graham Evangelistic Association, n.d.[3]

---

[1]Books with * were listed as official Billy Graham books in his *Just As I Am: The Autobiography of Billy Graham* (New York: HarperCollins Publishers, 1997), 741-42. Other books claim Billy Graham as their author, but may not have been authorized by Billy Graham or may have been reprints of portions of previously published works, as is the case of those published by the Billy Graham Evangelistic Association, World Wide Publications, or Grason. Books in this appendix have been limited to those published in the English language and include a select publishing history for historical and research purposes.

[2]Other than books of sermons, *Peace with God* was the only book written by Graham without the assistance of a ghostwriter. Originally a ghostwriter was used to assist him in writing *Peace with God.* Then Graham decided to rewrite the entire content of the book himself.

[3]*Peace with God* was translated and published in thirty-eight languages.

The Seven Deadly Sins. Minneapolis: Billy Graham Evangelistic Association, 1955; rev. as *Freedom from the Seven Deadly Sins.** Grand Rapids: Zondervan, 1955; London: Marshall, Morgan and Scott, 1956; rev. as *Find Freedom.* Grand Rapids: Zondervan, 1971.

*The Secret of Happiness: Jesus' Teaching on Happiness as Expressed in the Beatitudes.** Garden City, NY: Doubleday, 1955; Kingswood, Surrey: The World's Work, 1959; New York: Pocket Books, 1974; rev. and exp. Waco, TX: Word, 1985.

*Billy Graham Talks to Teen Agers.** Wheaton, IL: Miracle Books, 1958; Grand Rapids: Zondervan, 1958; New York: Pyramid, 1958, 1969; London: Oliphants, 1960; Grand Rapids: Zondervan, 1971; London: Marshall, Morgan and Scott, 1971.

*My Answer.** Garden City, NY: Doubleday, 1960; Westwood, NJ: Revell, 1967.

Billy Graham Answers Your Questions.[2] Minneapolis: World Wide, 1960.

*World Aflame.** Garden City, NY: Doubleday, 1965. Excerpts published as *The New Birth.* Washington, DC: Christianity Today, 1965.

Flint, Cort R., ed. *The Quotable Billy Graham.* Anderson, SC: Droke House, 1966.

Alder, Bill, ed. *The Wit and Wisdom of Billy Graham.* New York: Random House, 1967.

The Faith of Billy Graham. Anderson, SC: Droke House, 1968; New York: New American Library, 1970; New York: Wing Books, 1995.

Flint, Cort R., ed. *Billy Graham Speaks! The Quotable Billy Graham.* New York: Grosset and Dunlap, 1968.

*The Challenge: Sermons from Madison Square Garden.** Garden City, NY: Doubleday, 1969.

Lockard, David. *The Unheard Billy Graham.* Waco, TX: Word, 1971.

*The Jesus Generation.** Grand Rapids: Zondervan, 1971; Minneapolis: World Wide, 1971. *The Jesus Generation, by Billy Graham; True Spirituality, by Francis A. Schaeffer; and Brethren, Hang Loose, by Robert C. Girard: A Christianity Today Trilogy.* New York: Iverson-Norman Associates, 1972.

*Angels: God's Secret Agents.** New York: Doubleday Books, 1975; rev. and exp. Waco, TX: Word, 1985; pub. as *Angels.* Dallas: Word, 1994.

Demaray, Donald E., ed. *Blow Wind of God: Spirited Messages from the Writings of Billy Graham.* Grand Rapids: Baker, 1975; *Blow, Wind of God! Selected Writings of Billy Graham.* New York: Signet Books, New American Library, 1977; Old Tappan, NJ: Revell, 1977; London: Lakeland, 1975, 1978.

*How To Be Born Again.** Waco, TX: Word, 1977.

*The Holy Spirit: Activating God's Power in Your Life.** Waco, TX: Word, 1978; New York: Warner, 1980; Nashville: Word, 1988.

The Holy Spirit: Personal Bible Studies on the Holy Spirit—A Workbook. Waco, TX: Word, 1980.

*Till Armageddon: Trusting God in a Suffering World.** Waco, TX: Word, 1981.

Approaching Hoofbeats: The Four Horsemen of the Apocalypse.[3] Waco, TX: Word, 1983.

Billy Graham, TV Evangelism: Billy Graham Sees Dangers Ahead. Radnor, PA: Triangle Publications, 1983.

*A Biblical Standard for Evangelists:** A Commentary on the Fifteen Affirmations Made by Participants at the International Congress for Itinerant Evangelists in Amsterdam July 1983.* Minneapolis: World Wide, 1984.

*Unto the Hills.** Waco, TX: Word, 1986.

*Facing Death—and the Life After.** Waco, TX: Word, 1987; Garden City, NY: Doubleday Direct, 1999.

*Answers to Life's Problems: Guidance, Inspiration, and Hope for the Challenges of Today.** Waco, TX: Word, 1988.

The Early Billy Graham: Sermon and Revival Accounts [reprint of Van Kampen, *Calling Youth to Christ* and *Revival in Our Time*] New York: Garland Publications, 1988.

*Hope for the Troubled Heart.** Waco, TX: Word, 1991.

*Storm Warning.** Waco, TX: Word, 1992. Expansion of *Approaching Hoofbeats*. Waco, TX: Word, 1983.

The Collected Works of Billy Graham [*Angels; How to Be Born Again;* and *The Holy Spirit*]. New York: Inspirational Press, 1993; *His Greatest Works* [*Angels; How to Be Born Again;* and *The Holy Spirit*]. New York: Inspirational Press, 1995.

Griffin, William, and Ruth Graham Dienert, eds. *The Faithful Christian: an Anthology of Billy Graham.* Minneapolis: Grason, 1994.

*Just As I Am: The Autobiography of Billy Graham.** Carmel, NY: Guideposts, 1997; New York: HarperCollins Publishers, 1997.

Lowe, Janet, ed. *Billy Graham Speaks: Insight from the World's Greatest Preacher.* Thorndike, ME: G. K. Hall, 1999, 2000.

APPENDIX 2

HOUR OF DECISION SERMONS
AND SELECT PUBLISHED SERMONS

The following provides a listing of select published sermons of Graham in English. The dates vary somewhat due to the difference between the year preached, the year published, and the year copyrighting took place. Also, *Hour of Decision Sermon* (*HOD*) no. 140 was taken from a *Decision Magazine* article by the same name published the same year. Use of *Decision Magazine* articles as *Hour of Decision* sermons became more common after *Hour of Decision* sermon no. 215. This Appendix does not contain any *Decision Magazine* articles, which were often condensations of sermons, nor does it contain articles from Graham's syndicated column, "My Answer."

1947[1]		**1950**[3]	
CYC-1	America's Hope	RIOT-1	We Need Revival
CYC-2	Retreat! Stand! Advance!	RIOT-2	The Home God Honors
CYC-3	A Midnight Tragedy	RIOT-3	How to Be Filled with the Spirit
CYC-4	Final Exam	RIOT-4	Prepare to Meet Thy God
CYC-5	The Power of Secret Sin	RIOT-5	The Resurrection of Jesus Christ
CYC-6	Youth's Hero	RIOT-6	Judgment
CYC-7	A Scarlet Thread	VM-1	[no title][4]
CYC-8	Hell		
1949		**1951**	
GGS-1	Atonement[2]	AHD-1[1]	Will God Spare

[1] Sermons in Billy Graham *Calling Youth to Christ* (Grand Rapids: Zondervan, 1947).

[2] Billy Graham, "Atonement," in *Great Gospel Sermons* 2, "Contemporary" (New York: Revell, 1949), 2:41-54.

[3] Sermons in Billy Graham, *Revival in Our Time: The Story of the Billy Graham Evangelistic Campaigns Including Six of His Sermons* (Wheaton, IL: Van Kampen, 1950).

[4] In *Billy Graham's Message to the Texas Baptist Convention, Thursday, November 9, 1950, at Fort Worth, Texas* (Fort Worth: Baptist General Convention of Texas [mimeographed], 1950).

	America?
AHD-2	National Humility
AHD-3	Fear
AHD-4	Wither Bound?
HOD-1	Hate Versus Love[2]
HOD-2	Christianism Versus Communism
HOD-3	Peace Versus Chaos
HOD-4	What is God Like?
HOD-5	Position Versus Penalty
HOD-6	Christianity Versus a Bloodless Religion
HOD-7	Grace Versus Wrath
HOD-8	Christ's Marching Orders
HOD-9	". . . And Have Not Love"
HOD-10	Program for Peace
HOD-11	Our Bible
HOD-12	The Second Coming—A Glorious Truth

1952

HOD-13	Revival or the Spirit of the Age
HOD-14	The Life that Wins
HOD-15	Revival or Disintegration
HOD-16	Sins of the Tongue
HOD-17	Branded
HOD-18	Organized Labor and the Church
HOD-19	The Despair of Loneliness
HOD-20	Peace in our Time
HOD-21	Christmas in Korea

BG-1	The Christ-Centered Home[3]
WEA-1	The Work of an Evangelist[4]

1953

HOD-22	Three Minutes to Twelve
HOD-23	Teach Us to Pray
HOD-24	Why Christians Suffer
HOD-25	Victorious Christian Living
HOD-26	Mother's Day Message
HOD-27	Facts, Faith and Feeling
HOD-28	America's Decision
HOD-29	A Religion of Fire
HOD-30	Labor, Christ and the Cross
HOD-31	The Bible and Dr. Kinsey
HOD-32	Spiritual Inventory (1955)
HOD-33	The Answer to Teen-Age Delinquency
HOD-34	The Answer to Broken Homes
HOD-35	Satan's Religion
HOD-36	The Urgency of Revival
HOD-37	The Responsibilities of the Home
HOD-38	What is Conversion?
HOD-39	Our Spiritual Debt to

---

[1]AHD sermons in Billy Graham, *America's Hour of Decision* (Wheaton, IL: Van Kampen, 1951).

[2]*HOD* sermons are *Hour of Decision Sermons* (Minneapolis: Billy Graham Evangelistic Association). Date shown is date of first publication. Number refers to the particular sermon. Publishing history not provided.

[3]Billy Graham, "The Christ-Centered Home" (Minneapolis: Billy Graham Evangelistic Association, 1952).

[4]Billy Graham, "The Work of an Evangelist," in *Introducing Billy Graham: The Work of an Evangelist. An Address Given in the Assembly Hall of the Church House, Westminster, on 20th March, 1952,* ed. Frank Colquhoun (London: World Evangelical Alliance, 1953).

England

1954

HOD-40	Miracles in Britain
HOD-41	Juvenile Delinquency and Its Cure
HOD-42	Our Teen-Age Problem
HOD-43	America's Immorality
HOD-44	The Cure for Discouragement
HOD-45	Partner's With God
EJD-1	The Bible and Dr. Kinsey[1]

1955

HOD-46	Escape
HOD-47	Drunkenness
HOD-48	Christ is Coming
HOD-49	Heaven (1955)
HOD-50	Prayer
HOD-51	Revival Today
HOD-52	The Love of God
HOD-53	Three Dimensional Christianity
HOD-54	Things God Hates
HOD-55	Scars of Battle
HOD-56	Highway Safety. . . A Spiritual Problem
HOD-57	Responsibilities of Parents
HOD-58	The New Birth
HOD-59	That Day
HOD-60	The Sin of Omission
SDS-1	Pride[2]
SDS-2	Anger
SDS-3	Envy
SDS-4	Impurity
SDS-5	Gluttony

SDS-6	Slothfulness
SDS-7	Avarice
GPB-1	His Unchanging Word in an Changing World[3]

1956

HOD-61	Faith
HOD-62	The Rivers of Damascus
HOD-63	God and Crime
HOD-64	The Revival We Need
HOD-65	The Home
HOD-66	Hell
HOD-67	What God Can Do for You
HOD-68	Father
HOD-69	Americanism
HOD-70	The Cause and Cure for Uncertainty
HOD-71	Hope in Death
HOD-72	Emotion
HOD-73	The Sin of Tolerance
HOD-74	The Mystery of Iniquity
HOD-75	The Mystery of Righteousness
HOD-76	The Mystery of the Incarnation
HOD-77	Made, Marred and Mended
HOD-78	The Mystery of God's Will
HOD-79	God's D-Day
HOD-46x	Escape: God's Way— Man's Way[4]

---

[1]Billy Graham, "The Bible and Dr. Kinsey," in *I Accuse Kinsey,* ed. Elam J. Daniels (Orlando: Christ for the World Publishers, 1954).

[2]SDS sermons in Billy Graham, *Freedom from the Seven Deadly Sins* (Grand Rapids: Zondervan, 1955, 1960).

---

[3]Billy Graham, "His Unchanging Word in an Changing World," in *Best Sermons,* ed. George Paul Butler (New York: T. Y. Crowell Company, 1955), 292-98.

[4]Billy Graham, "Escape: God's Way—Man's Way," in *Evangelistic Sermons by Great Evangelists,* ed. Russell Victor DeLong (Grand Rapids: Zondervan, 1956), 47-56.

1957

HOD-80	The Signs of the Times
HOD-81	Immortality
HOD-82	The Grace of God
HOD-83	The Last Prayer Meeting
HOD-84	The Tyranny of Time and Space
HOD-85	Are You Getting What You Want?
HOD-86	The Cure for Anxiety
HOD-87	The Suffering Saviour on a Crimson Cross
HOD-88	Four Great Crises
HOD-89	The Ten Virgins
HOD-90	God's Warning
HOD-91	The Fruit of the Spirit
HOD-92	Revival or the Spirit of the Age
HOD-93	The Life that Wins
HOD-94	Be Prepared
HOD-95	Our Bible
HOD-96	Teen-Age Vandalism
BGCT-1	The World Need and Evangelism[1]
ROF-1	What Is Conversion?[2]
GAF-1	God's Answer to Sin, Sorrow, and Death[3]

1958

HOD-97	The Brevity of Life
HOD-98	The Ten Commandments
HOD-99	The Assurance of Salvation
HOD-100	Past, Present and Future
HOD-101	America at the Cross Roads
HOD-102	The Cross and Its Meaning Today
HOD-103	The Cross and Its Power
ROF-2	The Offense of the Cross[4]
WAB-1	Hope for Tomorrow[5]

1959

HOD-104	Nonconformity to the World
HOD-105	Moral Degeneration and Its Cure
HOD-106	The Most Wicked Man That Ever Lived
HOD-107	Spiritual Maturity
HOD-108	Dimensional Love of God
HOD-109	Youth Aflame
HOD-110	The Cure for Worry
HOD-111	Christian Conversion
HOD-112	The Gospel for the

---

[1] Billy Graham, "The World Need and Evangelism," in *The Doctrine of Evangelism,* ed. Clifford Wade Freeman (Nashville: Baptist General Conference of Texas, 1957), 25-36.

[2] Billy Graham, "What Is Conversion?" in *They Met God at the New York Crusade, Madison Square Garden* (Minneapolis: World Wide, 1957).

[3] Billy Graham, "God's Answer to Sin, Sorrow, and Death," in *The Upper Room Chapel Talks*, ed. Gustave A. Ferré (Nashville: The Upper Room, 1957), 65-71.

---

[4] Billy Graham, "The Offense of the Cross," in *Persuaded to Live: Conversion Stories from the Billy Graham Crusades,* ed. Robert Oscar Ferm (Westwood, NJ: Revell, 1958).

[5] Billy Graham, "Hope for Tomorrow," in *Mass Public Education: The Tool of the Dictator by Hubert Eaton, And Hope for Tomorrow by Billy Graham—Addresses given at the 10th Annual Writers Awards Banquet, Beverly Hills, CA, April 24, 1958*, ed. Hubert Eaton (Glendale, CA: Forest Lawn Memorial Park Association, 1958).

	Whole World
HOD-113	Christian Philosophy of Education
HOD-114	Alcoholism
HOD-115	The Old Book and the Old Faith
HOD-116	The Invitations of Christ
HOD-117	Youth of Today
HOD-118	This is the Victory
HOD-119	Moral Impurity
AWB-1	The Grace of God[1]

1960

HOD-120	How to Overcame Temptation
HOD-121	Be Ye Separate
HOD-122	Christian Discipline (1960)
HOD-123	Call to Commitment
HOD-124	Clouds
HOD-125	How Wise is Man?
HOD-126	Christ: The Ark of Safety (1960)
HOD-127	What is the Gospel? (by Roy Gustafson)
HOD-128	Manpower for the Master (by Howard Butt, Jr.)
HOD-129	What is Wrong?
HOD-130	Needed! Strong Men
HOD-131	Worldliness
BG-2	The Bible Says[2]
BG-3	The Challenging

	Church[3]
BWC-1	God So Loved the World[4]
MCT-1	Christ in the Believer[5]
PFG-1	The Responsibilities of the Christian Home[6]

1961

HOD-132	Delusion or Deliverance
HOD-133	It's Later Than You Think
HOD-134	Man-Made Religion
HOD-135	Youth in Rebellion
HOD-136	Are You Robbing God?
HOD-137	Great Sin! Greater Salvation!
HOD-138	Moral Degeneracy
HOD-139	Prepare for the Storm!
HOD-140	Fellowship and Separation
HOD-141	The Ultimate Weapon
HOD-142	There's a Great Day

[3]Billy Graham, "The Challenging Church: A Message by Billy Graham to American Ministers" (Minneapolis: Billy Graham Evangelistic Association, 1960).

[4]Billy Graham, "God So Loved the World," in *Tenth Baptist World Congress, Rio de Janeiro, Brazil, June 26-July 3, 1960,* ed. Arnold T. Ohrn (Nashville: Broadman for the Baptist World Alliance, 1961), 225-31.

[5]Billy Graham, "Christ in the Believer," in *The Word for This Century,* ed. Merrill Chapin Tenney (New York: Oxford University Press, 1960), 87-107.

[6]Billy Graham, "The Responsibility of the Christian Home," in *Great Sermons by Great Preachers,* ed. Peter F. Gunther (Chicago: Moody, 1960), 91-101.

[1]Billy Graham, "The Grace of God," in *Evangelical Sermons of our Day; Thirty-Seven Foremost Examples of Bible Preaching,* ed. Andrew Watterson Blackwood (New York: Harper, 1959).

[2]Billy Graham, "The Bible Says" (Minneapolis: Billy Graham Evangelistic Association, 1960).

	Coming		CLW-1	Happiness Through
HMC-1	How My Mind Has			Purity[5]

---

[1]Billy Graham, "How My Mind Has Changed," in *How My Mind Has Changed,* ed. Harold E. Fey (Cleveland: Meridian, 1961), 55-68.

[2]Billy Graham, "The Secret of Spiritual Maturity," in *Special-Day Sermons for Evangelicals: Thirty-Eight Representative Examples of Bible preaching on Red-Letter Days of the Christian Year and the Calendar Year,* ed. Andrew Watterson Blackwood (Great Neck, NY: Channel, 1961), 105-14.

[3]Billy Graham, "Evangelism in the Church Today" (Minneapolis: Billy Graham Evangelistic Association, 1962).

[4]Billy Graham, "In God Let Us Trust," in *And Our Defense Is Sure: Sermons and Addresses from the Pentagon Protestant Pulpit,* ed. Harmon D. Moore, Ernest A. Ham, and

Clarence E. Hobgood (New York: Abingdon, 1964), 151-55.

[5]Billy Graham, "Happiness through Purity," in *88 Evangelistic Sermons,* ed. Charles Langworthy Wallis (New York: Harper and Row, 1964).

[6]Billy Graham, "Youth of Today," in *Christian Youth and Morals* (Lincoln, NE: Back to the Bible, 1965).

[7]"Evangelism Is Every Christian's Business," in *Herald of the Evangel,* ed. Edwin T. Dahlberg (St. Louis: Bethany, 1965), 61-75.

[8]Billy Graham, "The Offence of the Cross (Galatians 5:11)," in *Great Sermons on the Death of Christ by Celebrated Preachers; with Biographical Sketches and Bibliographies,* ed. Wilbur Moorehead Smith (Natwick, MA: W.A. Wilde, 1965).

[9]Billy Graham, "Freedom Through Truth," in *Effective Evangelistic Preaching,* ed. Vernon Latrelle Stanfield (Grand Rapids: Baker, 1965), 41-47.

1966

HOD-158   It Is the Time to Seek the Lord
HOD-159   Gateway to Truth
HOD-160   Is God then Dead?
HOD-161   Let Christ Control Your Car
HOD-162   Today's Apostasy
HOD-163   Youth, Sex, and the Bible
HOD-164   Our God Is Marching On
HOD-165   Changing the Tide of History
BER-1   Opening Greetings[1]
BER-2   Why the Berlin Congress?
BER-3   Address at Kaiser Wilhelm Memorial Church
BER-4   Stains on the Altar
IGD-1   God Is Not "Dead"[2]
BWA-1   The New Morality[3]

1967

HOD-166   Social Injustice
HOD-167   The Transforming Power of Christ

---

[1]BER sermons in *One Race, One Gospel, One Task: World Congress on Evangelism, Berlin 1966,* ed. Carl F. H. Henry and W. Stanley Mooneyham (Minneapolis: World Wide, 1967).

[2]Billy Graham, "God Is Not 'Dead,'" in *Is God "Dead"?* (Grand Rapids: Zondervan, 1966), 59-81.

[3]Billy Graham, "The New Morality," in *The Truth that Makes Men Free: Official Report of the Eleventh Congress, Baptist World Alliance, Miami Beach, Florida, U.S.A., June 25-30, 1965,* ed. Josef Nordenhaug (Nashville: Broadman for the Baptist World Alliance, 1966), 54-65.

HOD-168   Is Christianity Out of Date?
HOD-169   Joy in Tribulation
HOD-170   The Church's Primary Responsibility (by Joe Blinco)
HOD-171   The Meaning of Repentance
HOD-172   Rebels for God
HOD-173   Rioting or Righteousness
HOD-174   The "Sick" Society
KCS-1   Communicating the Gospel[4]
KCS-2   Biblical Conversion
ER-1   Conversion—A Personal Revolution[5]

1968

HOD-175   In the World But Not of It
HOD-176   Did Christ Die for You?
HOD-177   The Young in Heart
HOD-178   God and Golf

1969

HOD-179   The Second Coming of Christ
HOD-180   This Is Progress (by Leighton Ford)
HOD-181   Do Whose Thing? (by Leighton Ford)
HOD-182   God's Universe (by Grady Wilson)
HOD-183   Join the Third Force

---

[4]KCS sermons in *Lectures, Kansas City School of Evangelism, September, 1967* (Kansas City, MO: Billy Graham Evangelistic Association, 1967).

[5]Billy Graham, "Conversion—a Personal Revolution," *The Ecumenical Review* 19 (1967): 271-84.

MSG-1	Come and Know God[1]
MSG-2	The Other Death
MSG-3	Man in Rebellion
MSG-4	The Prodigal Son
MSG-5	Heaven and Hell
MSG-6	Truth and Freedom
MSG-7	Let's Be Radical
MSG-8	Two Sets of Eyes
MSG-9	The Giants You Face
MSG-10	The Day to Come
BWA-2	Christ for the World[2]
MIN-1	Orientation and Welcome[3]
MIN-2	Commitment to Serve
MIN-3	The Message for Our Times
HLE-1	The Climax of History[4]
CFHH-1	The New Birth[5]

[1]MSG sermons found in Billy Graham, *The Challenge: Sermons from Madison Square Garden* (Garden City, NY: Doubleday, 1969).

[2]Billy Graham, "Christ for the World," in *One World, One Lord, One Witness: The Offical Report of the 7th Baptist Youth World Conference, Berne, Switzerland, July 22-28, 1968,* ed. Cyril E. Bryant (Waco, TX: Word for the Baptist World Alliance, 1969).

[3]MIN sermons in *Evangelism Now: U.S. Congress on Evangelism—Minneapolis, MN 1969: Official Reference Volume: Papers and Reports,* ed. George Wilson (Minneapolis: World Wide, 1969).

[4]Billy Graham, "The Climax of History," in *Last Things: A Symposium of Prophetic Messages,* ed. H. Leo Eddleman (Grand Rapids: Zondervan, 1969), 17-28.

[5]Billy Graham, "The New Birth," in *Fundamentals of the Faith,* ed. Carl F. H. Henry (Grand Rapids: Zondervan, 1969), 189-208.

430

WHS-1	[no title][6]
WHS-2	[no title]

1970

HOD-184	America Facing God's Judgment (by T. W. Wilson)
HOD-185	Short Cuts to Nowhere (by Leighton Ford)
HOD-186	The Drug Turn On (by Leighton Ford)
HOD-187	Perfect Justice
HOD-188	Play by the Rules! (by Lane Adams)
HOD-189	Honor America
HOD-190	Hope for the Future
HOD-191	God's Blueprint for Revival (by Grady Wilson)
HOD-192	Hell Is Real (by Grady Wilson)
HOD-193	The Great White Throne Judgment (by Roy Gustafson)
HOD-194	Twenty Years of Preaching the Gospel
SEW-1	Made, Marred, Mended[7]

1971

HOD-195	"21 Miles to Utopia" (by Leighton Ford)
HOD-196	Challenge for Today's Church
HOD-197	Student Power for Christ (by Leighton Ford)

[6]WHS sermons in *White House Sermons*, ed. Ben Hibbs (New York: Harper and Row, 1969).

[7]Billy Graham, "Made, Marred, Mended," in *Great Preaching: Evangelical Messages by Contemporary Christians,* eds. Sherwood Eliot Wirt and Viola Blake (Waco, TX: Word, 1970; London: Word, 1970).

HOD-198	Angels Innumerable
HOD-199	Something Is Happening in America
HOD-200	Pentecost Revisited (by Leighton Ford)
HOD-201	A Challenge to the Jesus People (by Leighton Ford)
HOD-202	Witches, Demons, and the Devil
20C-1	Saved or Lost?[1]
20C-2	Why God Allows Suffering and War
20C-3	The Fruit of the Spirit
20C-4	The Home
20C-5	Faith
20C-6	Are You Getting What You Want?
20C-7	Organized Labor and the Church

1972

HOD-203	The Generation Gap
HOD-204	The Sex Revolution, by Leighton Ford
HOD-205	Always Room for One More! (Master Plan for Marriage) (by Leighton Ford)
EXP-1	[no title][2]

1974

HOD-206	Cradle, Cross, and Crown
HOD-207	God's Exorcist (by Leighton Ford)
HOD-208	What Do You Do with a Burden? (by Leighton Ford)
BG-5	The Devil, Demons, and Exorcism[3]
BG-6	The National Crisis[4]
BG-7	Christmas Hope[5]
LAUS-1	Let the Earth Hear His Voice[6]
LAUS-2	Why Lausanne?
LAUS-3	Laustade Message
LAUS-4	The King Is Coming
JWW-1	Signs of Future Hope[7]

1975

HOD-209	The Economics of the Apocalypse
HOD-210	The Craziest Football Game Ever Played (by Leighton Ford)

1976

HOD-211	The Great King's City
BG-8	Can the Tide Be Turned?[8]

---

[1]20C sermons in *Twenty Centuries of Great Preaching*, 2 "Marshall to King" (Waco, TX: Word, 1971).

[2]In *Explo '72 Official Program: In Our Generation Taking God's Love to the World* (San Bernardino, CA: Campus Crusade for Christ, International, 1972).

[3]Billy Graham, "The Devil, Demons, and Exorcism" (Minneapolis: Billy Graham Evangelistic Association, 1974).

[4]Billy Graham, "The National Crisis" (Minneapolis: Billy Graham Evangelistic Association, 1974).

[5]Billy Graham, "Christmas Hope" (Minneapolis: Billy Graham Evangelistic Association, 1974).

[6]LAUS sermons in *Let the Earth Hear His Voice: International Congress on World Evangelization, Lausanne, Switzerland* (Minneapolis: World Wide, 1975).

[7]Billy Graham, "Signs of Future Hope," in *Future Hope,* ed. John Wesley White (Carol Stream, IL: Creation House, 1974).

[8]Billy Graham, "Can the Tide Be Turned?" (Minneapolis: Billy

BG-9	Keeping the Unity of the Spirit[1]
BG-10	Our Bicentennial: America at the Crossroads[2]

1977

HOD-212	The Abuse of Alcohol
HOD-213	Ambassadors
HOD-214	We Can Have Peace
BG-11	Certainties for 1977[3]
BG-12	Our Financial Commitment to You[4]
URB-1	Responding to God's Glory[5]

1978

HOD-215	We Want It Now
HOD-216	The Water of Life
HOD-217	God Loves Your Family

Graham Evangelistic Association, 1976).

[1]Billy Graham, "Keeping the Unity of the Spirit" (Minneapolis: Billy Graham Evangelistic Association, 1976).

[2]Billy Graham, "Our Bicentennial: America at the Crossroads" (Minneapolis: Billy Graham Evangelistic Association, 1976).

[3]Billy Graham, "Certainties for 1977" (Minneapolis: Billy Graham Evangelistic Association, 1977).

[4]Billy Graham, "Our Financial Commitment to You" (Minneapolis: Billy Graham Evangelistic Association, 1977).

[5]Billy Graham, "Responding to God's Glory," in *Declare His Glory among the Nations: Inter-Varsity Missionary Convention, 11th, Urbana, Ill., 1976,* ed. David M. Howard (Downers Grove, IL: InterVarsity, 1977), 141-53.

HOD-218	Do You Know Where You Are Going?
HOD-219	Where Are Your Roots?

1979

HOD-220	Jesus Will Keep His Promise
HOD-221	Reading the Signs
HOD-222	There's Hope—Christ Is Coming Back
HOD-223	We Can Know God
HOD-224	You Can Be Secure
HOD-225	Do You Want to Be Made Whole
HOD-226	Time
HOD-227	The University of Life

1980

HOD-228	Let Christ Take You Home
HOD-229	How Can You Be Sure?
HOD-230	Does God Have You?
HOD-231	Learn to Follow Jesus
HOD-232	You Have to Choose
HOD-233	Why Is the Cross an Offense?
HOD-234	What Is Your Obstacle?
HOD-235	"A Letter to Richard" (by Leighton Ford)
URB-2	That I Might Believe and Obey[6]

1981

HOD-236	Why Is Your Soul Valuable?
HOD-237	You Can Be Truly Free
HOD-238	The Battle to Win Your Mind

---

[6]Billy Graham, "That I Might Believe and Obey," in *Believing and Obeying Jesus Christ: The Urbana 79 Compendium,* ed. John W. Alexander (Downers Grove, IL: InterVarsity Press, 1980), 143-53.

HOD-239   A New Age Is Coming

1982

HOD-240   Youth, Sex, and the Bible

URB-3   Mission Impossible: Your Commitment to Christ[1]

SBTS-1   The Minister God Uses[2]

1984

HOD-241   The Magnificent Claims of Jesus, by Roy Gustafson

HOD-242   You Can Have Resurrection Life

HOD-243   Can God Forgive?

HOD-244   The Blood of Jesus Christ

HOD-245   The Last Summit

HOD-246   Satan Is Desperate

HOD-247   There Is a Real Hell

HOD-248   No Shortcuts to Heaven

HOD-249   Forgiveness: A New Beginning

AMS1-1   Are We Evangelists Acceptable to God?[3]

AMS1-2   Affirmation I, "We Confess Jesus Christ as God, Our Lord and Savior, who is revealed in the Bible, which is the infallible word of God."

AMS1-3   Peace in a Broken World

AMS1-4   The Evangelist in a Torn World: We Are Called by God

AMS1-5   The Evangelist's Appeal for Decision: We Plead on Christ's Behalf

1985

HOD-250   What Is Truth?

HOD-251   Jesus Is Who He said He Is

HOD-252   Does the Holy Spirit Shine through You?

HOD-253   How Shall We Escape?

HOD-254   Building Relationships

BG-13   A Nation Under God[4]

URB-4   Faithful in our commitment to Jesus Christ[5]

1986

HOD-255   You Cannot Be Neutral

HOD-256   When Will Jesus Come Again?

HOD-257   What Is the World Coming To?

HOD-258   [not used]

HOD-259   The Man Who Had It

---

[1]Billy Graham, "Mission Impossible: Your Commitment to Christ," in *Confessing Christ as Lord : The Urbana 81 Compendium,* ed. John W. Alexander (Downers Grove: InterVarsity, 1982), 119-31.

[2]Billy Graham, "The Minister God Uses," *The Southern Baptist Journal of Theology* 1, no. 4 (Winter 1997): 4-12.

[3]AMS1 sermons in *The Work of an Evangelist: International Conference for Itinerant Evangelists, Amsterdam, The Netherlands* (Minneapolis: World Wide, 1984).

[4]Billy Graham, "A Nation Under God" (Minneapolis: Billy Graham Evangelistic Association, 1985).

[5]Billy Graham, "Faithful in our commitment to Jesus Christ," in *Faithful Witness: The Urbana 84 Compendium,* ed. James McLeish (Downers Grove, IL: InterVarsity Press, 1985), .

All

1987

HOD-260	Needed: A Heaven Sent Revival
HOD-261	AIDS, Sex, and the Bible
HOD-262	The World, the Flesh, and the Devil
HOD-263	Suffering: Why Does God Allow It?
HOD-264	Trust God With Your Marriage and Home
HOD-265	Death the Enemy
HOD-266	The Event that Set Heaven Singing
HOD-267	Rushing Toward the End
HOD-268	We Reap What We Sow
HOD-269	What Does Christmas Mean to You?
HOD-270	The Real Meaning of the Cross
HOD-271	How to Face Temptation
HOD-272	We Cannot Escape God's Law
HOD-273	True Christian Character
HOD-274	Are You Far from Home?
HOD-275	Obeying Whatever the Cost
HOD-276	The Suffering Savior
HOD-277	Are You Saved?
AMS2-1	Approaching the End of the Age[1]
AMS2-2	Preaching the Word— Reaching the World
AMS2-3	The Evangelist's

	Appeal for Decision
AMS2-4	The Gift and Calling of the Evangelist

1988

HOD-278	Are You Lonely?
URB-5	Are You a Follower of Jesus Christ?[2]

1989

HOD-279	He Is Coming
HOD-280	Live Your Entire Lifetime for Christ
HOD-281	Faithful in Our Commitment

1990

HOD-282	A Cure for Heart Trouble
HOD-283	Not Drugs . . . Christ!
HOD-284	What Does Christmas Mean to You?

1991

HOD-285	Jesus Christ Is the Truth
HOD-286	Why Did Jesus Say, "I Am"?
HOD-287	The King Is Born

1992

HOD-288	All It Takes Is One
HOD-289	Certainty in an Uncertain World
HOD-290	Power When You Pray
HOD-291	The King Is Born
HOD-292	All It Takes Is One

1993

HOD-293	Christ Gives Hope
HOD-294	The Person and Work of the Holy Spirit
HOD-295	Ten Commandments for the Home
HOD-296	On Course to Heaven

[1]AMS2 sermons in *The Calling of an Evangelist: Second International Conference for Itinerant Evangelists, Amsterdam, The Netherlands* (Minneapolis: World Wide, 1987).

[2]Billy Graham, "Are You a Follower of Jesus Christ?" in *Urban Mission,* ed. John E. Kyle (Downers Grove, IL: InterVarsity, 1988).

HOD-297	A House in Order		HOD-317	America's Great Crises
HOD-298	Thank You, Lord		HOD-318	Labor, Christ and the Cross
HOD-299	The Game of Life		HOD-319	God's View of Sex

1994

HOD-300 Strength to Say "No"

HOD-301 Freedom through Truth

HOD-302 The Secret of Happiness

HOD-303 God Does Not Change

1995

HOD-304 You Can Be Sure of Your Salvation

HOD-305 My Moment of Decision

HOD-306 Are You Ready for the Last Days?

1996

HOD-307 The Sin of Tolerance

HOD-308 The Despair of Loneliness

HOD-309 The Greatest News Ever Heard

NACIE-1 The Evangelist in a Changing World: It's a New Day[1]

1997

HOD-310 Revival or Disintegration

HOD-311 [not used]

HOD-312 Peace Versus Chaos

HOD-313 Without Love I Am Nothing

HOD-314 Be Strong

1998

HOD-315 God's Heart-Warming Fire

HOD-316 God's "D-Day"

HOD-317 America's Great Crises

HOD-318 Labor, Christ and the Cross

HOD-319 God's View of Sex

HOD-320 [not used]

HOD-321 The Emotion of Love

HOD-322 Christmas, A Time of Renewed Hope

2000

BG-14 Why Amsterdam 2000?[2]

---

[1]Billy Graham, "The Evangelist in a Changing World: It's a New Day," in *NACIE 94: Equipping for Evangelism,* ed. Charles G. Ward (Minneapolis: World Wide, 1996), 15-25.

[2]Billy Graham, "Why Amsterdam 2000?" (Minneapolis: Billy Graham Evangelistic Association, 2000).

APPENDIX 3

CRUSADES OF BILLY GRAHAM AND FRANKLIN GRAHAM

The years 1937-1946 taken from "Select Chronology Listing of Events in the History of the Billy Graham Evangelistic Association" [on-line]; accessed 19 October 2001; available from http://www.wheaton.edu/bgc/archives/bgeachro/bgeachron02.htm; Internet. 1947-1997 taken from Billy Graham, *Just As I Am: The Autobiography of Billy Graham* (New York: HarperPaperbacks, HarperCollins Publishers, 1997), 866-69. 1997 to present taken from "Select Chronology."

Pre-Youth for Christ Evangelistic Meetings

1937
Palatka, Florida
Hope Mission, West Tampa, Florida

1938
Tampa, Florida Baptist Church, Capitola, Florida
Peniel Baptist Church, East Palatka, Florida
Florida State Young People's Rally of the C&MA, West Palm Beach, Florida
Tampa Gospel Tabernacle, Tampa, Florida
Pomona, Florida

1939
Young People's Services, Melrose, Florida
Florida State Young People's Rally of the Christian and Missionary Alliance (C&MA), Tampa,

Florida Young People's Revival Campaign, St. Petersburg, Florida

1940
C&MA Church, Robeson, North Carolina
Baptist Church, Level Grove, Georgia
York, Pennsylvania

1941
Moline, Michigan
Ottawa, Illinois
Gospel Tabernacle, St. Petersburg, Florida
Cornelia, Georgia

1942
Park Ridge Bible Church, Park Ridge, Illinois
Zion Evangelical Free Church, Zion, Illinois

1943
Fundamental Young People's Fellowship, Cicero, Illinois
Youth Conference, Fort Wayne Gospel, Temple, Indiana

1944
Roseland Evangelical Mission Church, Chicago, Illinois

Youth for Christ and Related Evangelistic Meetings

1944
Indianapolis, Indiana
Chicago, Illinois
Miami, Florida
Orlando, Florida

1945
Atlanta, Georgia
Peoria, Illinois
Minneapolis,
Minnesota
Elgin, Illinois
Asheville, North
Carolina
Memphis, Tennessee

1946
Detroit, Michigan
Manchester, England
Rennfield Street
Church, Aberdeen,
Scotland
Gilcomston Church,
Aberdeen, Scotland
Dundee, Scotland
Carruber's Close
Mission, Edinburgh,
Scotland
Templeton Hall,
Belfast, Ireland
Albert Hall, Belfast,
Ireland
Scot's Presbyterian
Church, Dublin,
Ireland
Birmingham, England
Dudley, England
Stockholm, Sweden
Copenhagen, Denmark
Brussels, Belgium
Kingsway Hall,
London, England
Tempest Anderson

Hall, York, England
Liverpool, England
Central Hall, Renshaw
Street, Liverpool,
England
Elgin, Illinois
Toronto, Ontario
San Antonio, Texas
Ocean City, New
Jersey
Salem, Oregon
Medicine Lake,
Minnesota
Gospel Temple,
Bristol, England
Free Church,
Gorseinon-
Caersalem, Wales
Penuel Chapel,
Ponlypridd, Wales
Bethany Baptist,
Cardiff, Wales
Houldsworth Hall,
Manchester, England
Hull, England
Brunswick Methodist
Church, Newcastle,
England
Stockton-on-Tees
York, England
Grange Road
Methodist Church,
Birkenhead, England
Liverpool, England
Birmingham, England

1947
Belfast, Ireland
Reading, England
Dublin, Ireland
Lewisham, London,
England
Chatham, England

Aberdeen, Scotland
Glasgow, Scotland
Oldham, England
Chicago, Illinois
Hollywood, California
Moline, Illinois
Grand Rapids,
Michigan
Charlotte, North
Carolina
Hattiesburg,
Mississippi

1948
Des Moines, Iowa
Cedar Rapids, Iowa
Baptist Church,
Bancroft, Iowa
Grand Rapids,
Michigan
Manchester, England
London, England
Winnipeg, Manitoba
Winona Lake, Indiana
Beatenburg,
Switzerland
Medecine Lake,
Minnesota
Nimes, France
Birmingham, England
Des Moines, Iowa
Detroit, Michigan
Powderhorn Park
Baptist Church,
Minneapolis,
Minnesota

1949
Des Moines, Iowa
Chicago, Illinois
Ocean City, New
Jersey

1950	1951	Orlando, Florida
Mound, Minnesota	St. Petersburg, Florida	
Rose Bowl, Pasadena,	Des Moines, Iowa	
California	Kansas City, Missouri	

Billy Graham City-Wide Evangelistic Meetings[1]

1947
Grand Rapids, Michigan
Charlotte, North Carolina

1948
Augusta, Georgia
Modesto, California

1949
Miami, Florida
Baltimore, Maryland
Altoona, Pennsylvania
Los Angeles, California

1950
Boston, Massachusetts
Columbia, South Carolina
Tour–New England States
Portland, Oregon
Minneapolis, Minnesota
Atlanta, Georgia

1951
Tour–Southern States
Fort Worth, Texas
Shreveport, Louisiana

Memphis, Tennessee
Seattle, Washington
Hollywood, California
Greensboro, North Carolina
Raleigh, North Carolina

1952
Washington, D.C.
Tour–American Cities
Houston, Texas
Jackson, Mississippi
Tour–American Cities
Pittsburgh, Pennsylvania
Albuquerque, New Mexico

1953
Tour–Florida Cities
Chattanooga, Tennessee
St. Louis, Missouri
Dallas, Texas
Tour–West Texas
Syracuse, New York
Detroit, Michigan
Asheville, North Carolina

1954
London, England
Europe Tour–
Amsterdam, Berlin, Copenhagen, Düsseldorf, Frankfurt, Helsinki, Paris, Stockholm
Nashville, Tennessee
New Orleans, Louisiana
Tour–West Coast

1955
Glascow, Scotland
Tour–Scotland Cities
London, England
Paris, France
Zurich, Switzerland
Geneva, Switzerland
Mannheim, West Germany
Stuttgart, West Germany
Nürnberg, West Germany
Dortmund, West Germany
Frankfurt, West Germany
U.S. Service Bases

---

[1]William Martin called the Manchester 1947 meeting Graham's "first true citywide campaign" (Martin, *A Prophet with Honor: The Billy Graham Story* [New York: William Morrow, 1991], 97). Though it is not listed as a 1947 crusade, Graham seems to have preached in Manchester, Birmingham, Belfast, and London in early 1947. The Billy Graham Evangelistic Association (BGEA) was founded September 17, 1950, following the Portland crusade.

Rotterdam, The
 Netherlands
Oslo, Norway
Gothenburg, Sweden
Aarhus, Denmark
Toronto, Ontario,
 Canada

1956
Tour–India and the Far
 East
Richmond, Virginia
Oklahoma City,
 Oklahoma
Louisville, Kentucky

1957
New York City, New
 York

1958
Caribbean Tour
San Francisco,
 California
Sacramento, California
Fresno, California
Santa Barbara,
 California
Los Angeles,
 California
San Diego, California
San Antonio, Texas
Charlotte, North
 Carolina

1959
Melbourne, Australia
Auckland, New
 Zealand
Sidney, Australia
Perth, Australia
Brisbane, Australia
Adelaide, Australia
Washington, New
 Zealand
Christchurch, New
 Zealand

Canberra, Lauceston
 and Hobart, Australia
Little Rock, Arkansas
Wheaton, Illinois
Indianapolis, Indiana

1960
Monrovia, Liberia
Accra, Ghana
Kumasi, Ghana
Lagos, Nigeria
Ibadan, Nigeria
Kaduna, Nigeria
Enugu, Nigeria
Jos, Nigeria
Bulawayo, South
 Rhodesia
Salisbury, Rhodesia
Kitwe, North Rhodesia
Moshi, Tanganyika
Kisumu, Kenya
Usumbara, Ruanda-
 Urundi
Nairobi, Kenya
Addis Ababa, Ethiopia
Cairo, Egypt
Tour–Middle East
Washington, D.C.
Rio de Janeiro, Brazil
Bern, Switzerland
Zurich, Switzerland
Basel, Switzerland
Lausanne, Switzerland
Essen, West Germany
Hamburg, West
 Germany
Berlin, West Germany
New York City, New
 York (Spanish)

1961
Jacksonville, Florida
Orlando, Florida
Clearwater, Florida
St. Petersburg, Florida
Tampa, Florida
Bradenton-Sarasota,

Florida
Tallahassee, Florida
Gainesville, Florida
Miami, Florida
Cape Canaveral,
 Florida
West Palm Beach,
 Florida
Vero Beach, Florida
Peace River Park,
 Florida (Sunrise
 Service)
Boca Raton, Florida
Fort Lauderdale,
 Florida
Manchester, England
Glascow, Scotland
Belfast, Ireland
Minneapolis,
 Minnesota
Philadelphia,
 Pennsylvania

1962
Tour–South America
Chicago, Illinois
Fresno, California
Redstone Arsenal,
 Alabama
Tour–South America
El Paso, Texas

1963
Paris, France
Lyon, France
Toulouse, France
Mulhouse, France
Nürnberg, West
 Germany
Stuttgart, West
 Germany
Los Angeles,
 California

1964
Birmingham, Alabama
Phoenix, Arizona

San Diego, California
Columbus, Ohio
Omaha, Nebraska
Boston, Massachusetts
Manchester, New
Hampshire
Portland, Oregon
Bangor, Maine
Providence, Rhode
Island
Louisville, Kentucky

1965
Hawaiian Islands:
Honolulu, Oahu,
Kahului, Maui, Hilo,
Hawaii, Lihue, Kauai
Dothan, Alabama
Tuscaloosa, Alabama,
University of
Alabama
Auburn, Alabama,
Auburn University
Tuskegee Institute,
Alabama
Montgomery, Alabama
Copenhagen, Denmark
Vancouver, British
Columbia, Canada
Seattle, Washington
Denver, Colorado
Houston, Texas

1966
Greenville, South
Carolina
London, England
Berlin, West Germany

1967
Ponce, Puerto Rico
San Juan, Puerto Rico
Winnipeg, Manitoba,
Canada
Great Britain
Turin, Italy
Yagreb, Yugoslavia

Toronto, Ontario,
Canada
Kansas City. Missouri
Tokyo, Japan

1968
Brisbane, Australia
Sydney, Australia
Portland, Oregon
San Antonio, Texas
Pittsburgh,
Pennsylvania

1969
Auckland, New
Zealand
Dunedin, New Zealand
Melbourne, Australia
New York City, New
York
Anaheim, California

1970
Dortmund, West
Germany
Knoxville, Tennessee
New York City, New
York
Baton Rouge,
Louisiana

1971
Lexington, Kentucky
Chicago, Illinois
Oakland, California
Dallas-Fort Worth,
Texas

1972
Charlotte, North
Carolina
Birmingham, Alabama
Cleveland, Ohio
Kohima, Nagaland,
India

1973
Durban, South Africa
Johannesburg, South
Africa
Seoul, Korea (South)
Atlanta, Georgia
Minneapolis-St. Paul,
Minnesota
Raleigh, North
Carolina
St. Louis, Missouri

1974
Phoenix, Arizona
Los Angeles,
California (25th
Anniversary
Celebration)
Rio de Janeiro, Brazil
Norfolk-Hampton,
Virginia

1975
Albuquerque, New
Mexico
Jackson, Mississippi
Brussels, Belgium
Lubbock, Texas
Taipei, Taiwan
Hong Kong

1976
Seattle, Washington
Williamsburg, Virginia
San Diego, California
Detroit, Michigan
Nairobi, Kenya

1977
Gothenburg, Sweden
Asheville, North
Carolina
South Bend, Indiana
Tour–Hungary
Cincinnati, Ohio
Manila, Philippines
Good News Festivals

in India

1978
Las Vegas, Nevada
Memphis, Tennessee
Toronto, Ontario,
　Canada
Kansas City, Missouri
Oslo, Norway
Stockholm, Sweden
Tour–Poland
Singapore

1979
São Paulo, Brazil
Tampa, Florida
Sydney, Australia
Nashville, Tennessee
Milwaukee, Wisconsin
Halifax, Nova Scotia,
　Canada

1980
Oxford, England
Cambridge, England
Indianapolis, Indiana
Edmonton, Alberta,
　Canada
Wheaton, Illinois
Okinawa, Japan
Osaka, Japan
Fukuoka, Japan
Tokyo, Japan
Reno, Nevada
Las Vegas, Nevada

1981
Mexico City, Mexico
Villahermosa, Mexico
Boca Raton, Florida
Baltimore, Maryland
Calgary, Alberta,
　Canada
San Jose, California
Houston, Texas

1982
Blackpool, England
Providence, Rhode
　Island
Burlington, Vermont
Portland, Maine
Springfield,
　Massachusetts
Manchester, New
　Hampshire
Hartford, Connecticut
New Haven,
　Connecticut
New England
　University and
　College Lecture
　Tour:
Boston,
　Massachusetts,
　Northeastern
　University
Amherst,
　Massachusetts,
　University of
　Massachusetts
New Haven,
　Connecticut, Yale
　University
Cambridge,
　Massachusetts,
　Harvard University
Newton,
　Massachusetts,
　Boston College
Cambridge,
　Massachusetts,
　Massachusetts
　Institute of
　Technology
South Hamilton,
　Massachusetts,
　Gordon-Conwell
　Seminary
Hanover, New
　Hampshire,
　Dartmouth College
Boston, Massachusetts

Boise, Idaho
Spokane, Washington
Chapel Hill, North
　Carolina
German Democratic
　Republic Tour:
　Wittenberg, Dresden
　(Saxony), Görlitz,
　Stendal, Stralsund,
　Berlin
Czechoslovakia Tour:
　Prague, Brno,
　Bratislava
Nassau, Bahamas

1983
Orlando, Florida
Tacoma, Washington
Sacramento, California
Oklahoma City,
　Oklahoma

1984
Anchorage, Alaska
Mission England:
　Bristol, Sunderland,
　Norwich,
　Birmingham,
　Liverpool, Ipswich
Seoul, Korea (South)
Union of Soviet
　Socialist Republics:
　Leningrad, Russia;
　Tallin, Estonia;
　Novosibirsk, Siberia;
　Moscow, Russia
Vancouver, British
　Columbia, Canada

1985
Fort Lauderdale,
　Florida
Hartford, Connecticut
Sheffield, England
Anaheim, California

Romania: Suceava,
Cluj-Napoca,
Oradea, Arad,
Timisoara, Sibiu,
Bucharest
Hungary: Pecs,
Budapest

1986
Washington, D.C.
Paris, France
Tallahassee, Florida

1987
Columbia, South
Carolina
Cheyenne, Wyoming
Fargo, North Dakota
Billings, Montana
Sioux Falls, South
Dakota
Denver, Colorado
Helsinki, Finland

1988
People's Republic of
China: Beijing,
Huaiyin, Nanjing,
Shanghai,
Guangzhou
Union of Soviet
Socialist Republics:
Zagorsk, Russia;
Moscow, Russia;
Kiev, Ukraine
Buffalo, New York
Rochester, New York
Hamilton, Ontario,
Canada

1989
Syracuse, New York
London, England

Budapest, Hungary
Little Rock, Arkansas

1990
Berlin, West Germany
Albany, New York
Long Island, New York
Hong Kong

1991
Seattle and Tacoma,
Washington
Scotland: Edinburgh,
Aberdeen, Glascow
East Rutherford, New
Jersey
New York, New York
(Central Park)
Buenos Aires,
Argentina

1992
Pyongyang, Korea
(North)
Philadelphia,
Pennsylvania
Portland, Oregon
Moscow, Russia

1993
Essen, Germany
Pittsburgh,
Pennsylvania
Columbus, Ohio

1994
Tokyo, Japan
Beijing, People's
Republic of China
Pyongyang, Korea
(North)
Cleveland, Ohio
Atlanta, Georgia

1995
San Juan, Puerto Rico
Toronto, Ontario,
Canada
Sacramento, California

1996
Minneapolis-St. Paul,
Minnesota
Charlotte, North
Carolina

1997
San Antonio, Texas
Bay Area, California

1998
Ottawa, Ontario,
Canada
Tampa, Florida

1999
Indianapolis, Indiana
St. Louis, Missouri

2000
Nashville, Tennessee
Jacksonville, Florida

2001
Louisville, Kentucky
Fresno, California

2002
Cincinnati, Ohio
Dallas-Fort Worth,
Texas

2003
San Diego, California
Oklahoma City,
Oklahoma

Franklin Graham Crusades[1]

North American crusades from 1990-1996 were often in cooperation with BGEA associate evangelist John Wesley White.

1990
Dayton, Ohio

1991
Shawnee, Oklahoma
Tucson and Yuma, Arizona
Brawley, California

1992
Nongstoin, West Khasi Hills, India
Crawfordsville, Indiana
Sunnyside, Washington
New London Connecticut
Arvado, Colorado
Fredericton and Moncton, New Brunswick, Canada

1993
Managua, Nicaragua
Santa Fe, Texas
Marquette, Michigan
Albion, New York
New Bedford, Massachusetts
Great Bend, Kansas
Sitka, Alaska

1994
Charleston, West Virginia
Lewisburg and Dubois, Pennsylvania
Newport News, Virginia (with Ralph Bell)

1995
San Jose, California
Ketchikan, Arkansas
Anchorage, Alaska
Wilmington, North Carolina
Bend, Oregon
Cranbrook, British Columbia
Bozeman and Helena, Montana
Sacramento, California

1996
Sydney, Cairns, and Townsville, Australia
Newnan, Georgia
Kitchner, Ontario
Columbus, Ohio
Farmington, New Mexico
Tegucigalpa, Honduras

1997
Tupelo, Mississippi
San Antonio, Texas (with Billy Graham and T.W. Wilson)
Viscalia, California
Capetown and Johannesburg, South Africa
Wichita, Kansas

1998
Adelaide and Perth, Australia
Lima, Peru
Charlottesville, Virginia
Alexandra, Louisiana
Albuquerque, New Mexico (with Billy Graham)
Greenville, North Carolina

1999
Buff Bay, Ocho Rios, Morant Bay, Brown's Town, Port Antonio, Savana-la-Mar, Mandeville, May Pen, Montego Bay, and Kingston, Jamaica
Tuscaloosa, Alabama
Perth, Scotland
Calgary, Alberta
Santa Cruz, Bolivia

2000
Managua, Nicaragua
Lubbock and Amarillo, Texas
Boone, North Carolina
Lexington, Kentucky

---

[1]Franklin Graham crusades or festivals are from *BGEA Chronology,* 166-99. Franklin began filling in as needed for his father's crusades after Billy Graham fell in Toronto, Canada, 1995.

2001

San Pedro Sula, Honduras

Santo Domingo, Dominican Republic

Tallahassee, Florida

Spartanburg, South Carolina

Recife, Brazil

2002

San Salvador, El Salvador

Gainesville, Florida

Bryan/College Station, Texas

Spokane, Washington

Mendoza. Argentina.

2003

Veracruz, Mexico

Roanoke, Virginia

Tulsa, Oklahoma

APPENDIX 4

CHRONOLOGICAL LISTING OF
SELECT HONORS AND AWARDS OF BILLY GRAHAM[1]

The two major sources for this information are Billy Graham's bio ("Biography: William (Billy) F. Graham," Minneapolis, MN: BGEA, May 2000) and the BGEA chronology ("Select Chronology Listing of Events in the History of the Billy Graham Evangelistic Association" [on-line]; accessed 17 July 2001; available from http://www.wheaton.edu/bgc/ archives/bgeachro/bgeachron02.htm; Internet). Items from Graham's bio will be followed by the letter "B." Items from the chronology will be followed by "C." Honors or awards from other sources will be footnoted as such.

Honorary Doctorates

Year
1948
   Honorary Doctor of Divinity, King's College, Newcastle, Delaware (C)
   Honorary Doctor of Humanities, Bob Jones University, Greenville, South
      Carolina (C)
1950
   Honorary Doctor of Laws, Houghton College, Houghton, New York (C)
1956
   Honorary Doctor of Letters, Wheaton College, Wheaton, Illinois (C)
1967
   Honorary Doctorate of Humane Letters, Belmont Abbey College,
      Belmont Abbey, North Carolina (C)
1973
   Honorary Doctorate of Humane Letters, Jacksonville University,
      Jacksonville, Florida (C)
1981
   Honorary Doctorate of Theology, Christian Theological Seminary,
      Warsaw, Poland (C)[2]

---

[1]Some dates may vary. Jon P. Alston, "Popularity of Billy Graham, 1963-1969: Review of the Polls," *Journal for the Scientific Study of Religion* 12 (June 1973): 227-230, included four tables showing the increase in popularity of Billy Graham over the years covered. The first table, based on Gallup Organization polls, asked "how they would vote if the presidential election were being held at the time of the interview and the candidates were Billy Graham (Republican) and John Kennedy (Democrat). . . . Tables 2, 3 and 4 document Billy Graham's increase in popularity between 1963 and 1969" (ibid., 227). Was Gallup seeking to influence Graham to enter politics by asking these questions?

[2]In his sermon "Mission Impossible: Your Commitment to Christ," 119, Graham stated, "One year ago I was in Poland, lecturing and speaking at the University

445

> Honorary Doctorate of Theology, Reformed Theological Academy, Debrecan, Hungary (C)

1985

> Honorary Doctor of Christianity, Dallas Baptist University, Dallas, Texas (C)

1996

> Honorary Doctor of Divinity, University of North Carolina at Chapel Hill, Chapel Hill, North Carolina (C)

Other Awards and Honors

Year

Repeated or Unconfirmed Dates

> Top Ten Most Admired Men in the World, Gallup Organization (39 appearances in 45 years, 32 consecutive appearances) (B)
>
> Most Admired Men Poll, Good Housekeeping (1993-1997, number one, 16th time in top ten) (B)
>
> Clergyman of the Year, National Pilgrim Society (B)
>
> Distinguished Persons Award, Freedoms Foundation (numerous years) (B)
>
> Distinguished Service Medal, Salvation Army (B)

1954

> Who's Who in America, first listing (B)

1955

> Annual Citation, Salvation Army Association (C)
>
> Number X, Most Admired Men in the World, Gallup Organization (B)

1956

> Admiral of the Fleet of the Navy of the State of Oklahoma, Oklahoma City, Oklahoma (C)
>
> Clergyman of the Year, Religious Heritage of America (C)

1957

> Gold Medal Award, National Institute of Social Science (B)

1959

> Honorary LLD, William Jewell College, Liberty, Missouri (C)

1960

> Good Citizen's Award, Citizens of America, Burbank, California (C)

1961

> Award, International Society of Christian Endeavor, Chicago, Illinois (C)
>
> Radio 720 Award, WSB Radio, Atlanta, Georgia (C)

1962

> Annual Guttenberg Award, Chicago Bible Society, Chicago, Illinois (B) (C)
>
> Certificate of Recognition, Interfaith Movement, New York, New York

---

in Warsaw. They were kind enough to give me an honorary doctor's degree" (Billy Graham, "Mission Impossible: Your Commitment to Christ," in *Confessing Christ as Lord: The Urbana 81 Compendium,* ed. John W. Alexander [Downers Grove: InterVarsity, 1982], 119-31).

(C)

1963

Honorary Colonel, State of Tennessee, Nashville, Tennessee (C)

1964

Distinguished Citizen Award for North Carolina, Raleigh, North Carolina (C)

Freedom Award, Spartanburg, North Carolina (C)

Gold Award, George Washington Carver Memorial Institute (B) (C)

Piedmont Sertoma Award, Spartanburg, North Carolina (C)

1965

Deputy Constable, Precinct no. 1, Houston, Texas (C)

Golden Plate Award, American Academy of Achievement (B)

Honorary Membership, Big Thicket Association, Houston, Texas (C)

Horatio Alger Award, America Schools and Colleges (B) (C)

National Citizenship Award, Military Chaplains Association of the U.S.A. (B) (C)

Principal Award, Freedom Foundation, Valley Forge, Pennsylvania (C)

Robins Award, University and College Students of America, Logan. Utah (C)

Service to Humanity Award, Northeast High School, Philadelphia, Pennsylvania (C)

Speaker of the Year Award, Delta Sigma Rho-Tau Kappa Alpha, University of Indiana (B, 1964) (C)

Wisdom Award of Honor, Wisdom Magazine and Wisdom Society (B) (C)

1966

Big Brother of the Year Award, White House, Washington, D.C. (B) (C)

Concurrent Resolution of Appreciation, South Carolina House of Representatives, Columbia, South Carolina (C)

1967

Silver Medallion Award, National Conference of Christians and Jews, Charlotte, North Carolina (C)

1968

Billy Graham Appreciation Day, September 20, 1968, Charlotte, North Carolina

Great American Award, WSB Radio, Atlanta, Georgia

Member, Hole in One Club, Sebring Shores Country Club, Sebring, Florida (C)

1969

Certificate of Appreciation, National Press Club, Washington D. C. (C)

Commendatory Resolution, Republican Central Committee of San Diego, San Diego, California (C)

Diamond Award, Youth for Christ, Winona Lake, Indiana (C)

George Washington Honor Medal, Freedom's Foundation of Valley Forge, Valley Forge, Pennsylvania (B) (C, 1968)

Golden Rule Award, St. George's Association, New York, New York (C)

Hall of Fame, Studio City Historical Museum, Studio City, California (C)

Honorary Member, Alfredian Order, Hull, England (C)

Morality in Media Award, Greater New York Committee for Morality in Media (B) (C)

Mr. Travel Award, Travel Magazine, New York, New York (C)

Torch of Liberty Award, Anti-Defamation League of B'Nai B'rith, Charlotte, North Carolina (B) (C)

Tuss McLaughry Award, American Football Coaches Association, Durham, North Carolina (C)

1970

Fifteen Best Dressed Men in America, Fashion Magazine (C)

Hall of Fame, North Carolina Broadcasters, Fayetteville, North Carolina (C)

Service to Mankind Award, Asheville Sertoma Club, Asheville, North Carolina (C)

Truth Award, Burlington Truth Telling Club, Burlington, Wisconsin (C)

1971

George Washington Honor Medal, Freedom's Foundation, Valley Forge, Pennsylvania (C)

Grand Marshall, Rose Bowl Parade, Los Angeles, California (C)

Grand Marshall, Salute to America Parade, WSB-TV, Atlanta, Georgia (C)

Honor Billy Graham Day, October 15, 1971, Charlotte, North Carolina (C)

International Brotherhood Award, National Conference of Christians and Jews, Cleveland, Ohio (B) (C)

National Vice President, National Police Officers Association, Venice, Florida (C)

Salute to America Award, WSB-TV, Atlanta, Georgia (C)

Sir Walter Award, North Carolina Order of Sir Walter, Chapel Hill, North Carolina (C)

1972

Billy Graham Parkway, Charlotte, North Carolina (C)

Celtic Cross Award, Catholic War Veterans, Clifton, New Jersey (C)

Distinguished Service Award, National Association of Broadcasters, Chicago, Illinois (B) (C)

Franciscan International Award, Prior Lake, Minnesota (B) (C)

Grand Marshall, Shenandoah Apple Festival, Winchester, Virginia (C)

Honorary Member, United Daughters of the Confederacy, Denver, Colorado (C)

Sarah Coventry "Man of the Year" Award, New York, New York (C)

Sylvanus Thayer Award, United States Military Academy Association of Graduates at West Point, West Point, New York (B) (C)

1973

Billy Graham Mountain, Xiango, Nigeria (C)

George Washington Honor Medal, Freedom's Foundation, Valley Forge, Pennsylvania (C)

Most Admired American Living Today Award, National Enquirer

Magazine (C)

Morality and Decency plaque, Americans United Against Obscenity, Union, New Jersey (C)

1974

George Washington Medal Award for Patriotism, Freedoms Foundation of Valley Forge, Pennsylvania (B)

Honorary Citizen, West Helena, Arkansas (C)

1975

America's Greatest American Award, Miss National Teenager Pageant, Atlanta, Georgia (C)

Great American for 1975 Award, Dixie Business Editors, Charlotte, North Carolina (C)

Liberty Bell Award, United Service Organizations, Philadelphia, Pennsylvania (C)

Man of the South Award, Dixie Business Editors, Charlotte, North Carolina (C)

Philip Award, Association of United Methodist Evangelists, Cherokee Village, Arkansas (B, 1976) (C)

Salesman of the Decade award, Direct Selling Association, Washington, D. C. (B) (C)

1976

Award for Contributions to Mankind, Civitan International, Charlotte, North Carolina (C)

Honorary Citizen of Los Angeles, Los Angeles, California (C)

Merit and Distinguished Service in the Sight of All Mankind Award, University Forum Academy, Shaker Heights, Ohio (C)

Valley Forge Honor Certificate Award, Freedom's Foundation, Valley Forge, Pennsylvania (C)

1977

Hall of Fame, Johnson Elementary School, Flint, Michigan (C)

Honorary Member, Reachout Iowa State Men's Reformatory, Anamosa, Iowa (C)

Medal of Honor, Daughters of the American Revolution, Norfolk, Virginia (C)

[First] National Interreligious Award, American Jewish Committee, Atlanta, Georgia (B, from United Jewish Committee) (C)

1978

Distinguished Communicator of 1977, Abe Lincoln Awards, Radio and Television Commission of the Southern Baptist Convention, Fort Worth, Texas (B, 1977) (C)

1979

Big A Award, Chamber of Commerce, Asheville, North Carolina (C)

1980

Evangelist of the Year, International Welcoming Committee of Indianapolis, Indianapolis, Indiana (C)

Jabotinsky Centennial Medal, the Jabotinsky Foundation (B)

Billy Graham Center dedicated at Wheaton College, Wheaton, Illinois, to house the Billy Graham Archives, Wheaton Graduate School, Graduate School Library, and other initiatives

1981

Honorary Member, 700 Club, Virginia Beach, Virginia (C)

President's Medal of Honor, North Carolina Wesleyan College, Rocky Mountain, North Carolina (C)

Religious Broadcasting Hall of Fame award (B)

1982

Prize for Progress in Religion award, Templeton Foundation, London, England (B) (C)

1983

Billy Graham Day, November 7, 1983, Los Angeles, California (C)

Medal of Honor, Daughters of the American Revolution, Orlando, Florida (C)

Order of the Basin and Trowel given to the BGEA, Christian College Coalition, Washington, D. C. (C)

Presidential Medal of Freedom, United States President, Washington, D. C. (B) (C)

1984

Angel Award, Religion in Media, Hollywood, California (C)

1985

Billy Graham Day, March 24, 1985, Dallas, Texas (C)

Silver Good Shepherd Award, Boy Scouts of America, Los Angeles, California (C)

1986

Award of Merit, National Religious Broadcasters, Morristown, New Jersey (B) (C)

North Carolina Award in Public Service (B)

1987

Billy Graham Day, July 26, 1987, Mayor of Denver, Denver, Colorado (C)

Billy Graham Week, July 17-26, Governor of Colorado (C)

Tribute to Dr. Billy Graham, Christmas Jubilee Concert, Charlotte, North Carolina (C)

1989

Star on Hollywood Walk of Fame, Hollywood, California (C)

1991

Lifetime Achievement in Publishing, Capital Cities/ABC, New York, New York (C)

1993

Number One Most Admired Men, Good Housekeeping (B)

Number Four, Top Ten Most Admired Men in the World, Gallup Organization[1]

---

[1] The Gallup Organization, "Most Admired Man and Woman" [on-line]; accessed 17 July 2001; available from http://www.gallup.com/poll/indicators/indadmired.asp; Internet.

1994

Number One Most Admired Men, Good Housekeeping (B)

Number Four, Top Ten Most Admired Men in the World, Gallup Organization

Billy Graham School of Missions, Evangelism, and Church Growth established at the Southern Baptist Theological Seminary in Louisville, Kentucky

1995

Honored for Fifty Years of Evangelism, Southern Baptist Convention, Atlanta, Georgia (C)

Number One Most Admired Men, Good Housekeeping (B)

Number Six, Top Ten Most Admired Men in the World, Gallup Organization

1996

Billy Graham Highway, Interstate 240, Buncome County, North Carolina (C)

Congressional Gold Medal, U.S. Congress, Washington, D. C. (B) (C)

Number One Most Admired Men, Good Housekeeping (B)

Number Six, Top Ten Most Admired Men in the World, Gallup Organization

1997

Number One Most Admired Men, Good Housekeeping (B)

Number Six, Top Ten Most Admired Men in the World, Gallup Organization

1998

Number Five, Top Ten Most Admired Men in the World, Gallup Organization

1999

Gospel Music Hall of Fame, Gospel Music Association (B)

Number Seven, Top Ten Most Admired Men in the World, Gallup Organization

2000

Freedom Award, Ronald Reagan Presidential Foundation (B)

Other awards and titles:[1]

Fellow, Royal Geographic Society

Member, Royal Literary Society

Ninth International Youth's Distinguished Service Citizen.

---

[1] Edwin T. Dahlberg, *Herald of the Evangel* (St. Louis, MO: Bethany Press, 1965), 60.

APPENDIX 5

BILLY GRAHAM EVANGELISTIC ASSOCIATION
MISSION AND STATEMENT OF FAITH[1]

Mission Statement

BGEA exists to support the evangelistic ministry and calling of Billy Graham to take the message of Christ to all we can by every prudent means available to us.

The Billy Graham Evangelistic Association believes

- The Bible to be the infallible Word of God, that it is His holy and inspired Word, and that it is of supreme and final authority.
- In one God, eternally existing in three persons--Father, Son, and Holy Spirit.
- Jesus Christ was conceived by the Holy Spirit, born of the Virgin Mary. He led a sinless life, took on Himself all our sins, died and rose again, and is seated at the right hand of the Father as our mediator and advocate.
- That all men everywhere are lost and face the judgment of God, and need to come to a saving knowledge of Jesus Christ through His shed blood on the cross.
- That Christ rose from the dead and is coming soon.
- In holy Christian living, and that we must have concern for the hurts and social needs of our fellowmen.
- We must dedicate ourselves anew to the service of our Lord and to His authority over our lives.
- In using every modern means of communication available to us to spread the Gospel of Jesus Christ throughout the world.

---

[1]Billy Graham Evangelistic Association, "About Us" [on-line]; accessed 15 February 2001; available from http://www.billygraham.org/about/ statementoffaith.asp; Internet.

SELECT BIBLIOGRAPHY

Articles with Billy Graham as author are limited to the English language editions, unless important for the purposes of this dissertation. While foreign materials are important, and their contexts unique, they are not included in this study. *Decision Magazine* includes four English-language monthly or bimonthly editions for almost forty years (United States—from November 1960, Canada—from January 1961, Austral-Asia—from May 1961, and United Kingdom—from November 1961), as well as editions in French (from 1963), German (from 1963), Spanish (from 1964). Some of the sources listed under "Other Primary Sources" were restricted. For example, Billy Graham's personal correspondence is closed until at least five years after his death. The Grady Wilson collection in the Billy Graham Archives in Wheaton, Illinois is restricted until 2052. These sources are listed as they may be available in the future.

The potential number of sources for a study on Billy Graham is quite extensive. Along with audio and video sources, Graham had a syndicated column, "My Answer," which began in 1952 and continued through 1990. Each crusade also generated dozens of news releases, as well as news conferences, media events, and special preaching opportunities for Billy Graham and others working for the crusade. Sources were diversified in numerous languages, and events were often covered in newspapers, magazines, and on television. Each of his books and the films generated reviews and summaries. Only articles important for this dissertation were included in this listing. Also, because of the extensiveness of the original bibliography, secondary books were removed from the dissertation's original bibliography.

Primary Sources not Listed in Appendixes

Articles, Essays, or Excerpts by or Reporting on Billy Graham

Clinton, Bill, Billy Graham, and Frank Keating. "Remarks by President, Governor and Rev. Billy Graham at Memorial Service." *New York Times,* 24 April 1995, A12.

Graham, Billy. "A Plea for a Christian Philosophy of Education," *The Presbyterian Journal,* 2 December 1959, 5-6.

_____. "A Time for Moral Courage." *Reader's Digest,* July 1964, 49-52.

_____. "Biblical Authority in Evangelism." *Christianity Today,* 15 October 1956, 5-7, 17.

_____. "Billy Graham." In Gammon, Roland, ed. *Faith is a Star.* New York: E. P. Dutton, 1963.

_____. "Billy Graham: A Change of Heart." *Sojourners Magazine,* August 1979, 12-14.

_____. "Billy Graham Answers His Critics." *A. D. Magazine,* March 1973, 47-51.

_____. "By the Foolishness of Preaching." *Preaching* 4 (January-February 1989): 23-25.

_____. "Clarification." *Christianity Today,* 19 January 1973, 36.

_____. "Conversion—a Personal Revolution." *The Ecumenical Review* 19 (1967): 271-84.

_____. "Does a Religious Crusade Do Any Good?" *U.S. News and World Report.* 27 September 1957, 72-78, 81.

_____. "Facing the Anti-God Colossus." *Christianity Today,* 21 December 1962, 6-

8.

_____. "False Prophets in the Church." *Christianity Today,* 19 January 1968, 3-5.

_____. "Foreword." In J. D. Douglas, ed. *The Work of an Evangelist: International Congress for Itinerant Evangelists, Amsterdam, The Netherlands.* Minneapolis: World Wide, 1984.

_____. "God Is Not Dead: Interview." *U. S. News and World Report,* 25 April 1966, 74-80.

_____. "God's Revolutionary Demand." *Christianity Today,* 21 July 1967, 3-5.

_____. "How to Live the Victorious Life." *Crusade* 1, no. 1 (1955): 13-15.

_____. "Interview with David Frost." *Decision,* 5 October 1964, 14-16.

_____. "Keswick's 100th Birthday." *Decision* (British ed.), November 1975, 1, 12.

_____. "Loneliness: How It Can Be Cured." *Reader's Digest,* October 1969, 135-38.

_____. "Man Needs New Birth." *Christianity Today,* 29 March 1968, 16-17.

_____. "Marks of the Jesus Movement." *Christianity Today,* 5 November 1971, 4-5.

_____. "My Greatest Concern for 1974." *Eternity,* January 1974, 15-16.

_____. "New Crusades in Europe: An Interview with Billy Graham." *U. S. News and World Report,* 27 August 1954, 82-90.

_____. "Opening Words." In J. D. Douglas, ed. *The Calling of an Evangelist: The Second International Congress for Itinerant Evangelists, Amsterdam, The Netherlands.* Minneapolis: World Wide, 1987.

_____. "Racism and the Evangelical Church." *Christianity Today,* 4 October 1993, 27.

_____. "Repentance Before Renewal." *Christianity Today,* 5 April 1993, 17.

_____. "Reply to J. W. Lawrence, p. 168, Autumn 1965." *Frontier* 8 (Winter 1965-1966): 250.

_____. "Richard Nixon and American Religion." *Christian Century,* 11 May 1994, 488-89.

_____. "Standing Firm, Moving Forward." *Christianity Today,* 16 September 1996, 14-15.

_____. "The Marks of a Christian." *Christianity Today,* 13 October 1958, 3-5.

_____. "The Minister God Uses." *The Southern Baptist Journal of Theology* 1, no. 4 (Winter 1997): 4-12.

_____. "The Needed Revolution." *Newsday,* 23 December 1967, n.p.

_____. "Three American Illusions." *Christianity Today,* 19 December 1969, 12-14.

_____. "Unfinished Dream." *Christianity Today,* 31 July 1970, 20-21.

_____. "Watergate Interview with Billy Graham." *Christianity Today,* 4 January 1974, 9-19.

_____. "What Ten Years Have Taught Me." From series "How I Changed My Mind." *Christian Century,* 17 February 1960, 186-89; Series published in Harold E. Fey, ed. *How My Mind Has Changed.* Cleveland: Meridian Books, The World Publishing Company, 1961.

_____. "What the Bible Says to Me." *Reader's Digest,* May 1969, 83-87.

_____. "Why Lausanne?" *Christianity Today,* 3 September 1974, 4-14.

_____. "Why the Berlin Congress?" *Christianity Today,* 11 November 1966, 3-7.

Graham, Billy, and C. E. Tucker. "The 1969 Protestant Inaugural Prayers." *Christianity Today,* 14 February 14, 1969, 27.

Haden, Ben. "Dr. Graham, Exactly What Is Evangelism?" *Presbyterian Survey,* March 1962, 9-17.

**Crusade Summaries and Conversion
Stories—Official and Unofficial**

Akers, John N., ed. *Billy Graham in Washington D.C.* Minneapolis: World Wide, 1986.
_____. *Billy Graham in Budapest.* Minneapolis: World Wide, 1989.
Allan, Thomas, ed. *Crusade in Scotland: Billy Graham.* London: Pickering and Inglis, 1955.
Asociación Billy Graham. *Billy Graham in Puerto Rico.* Santurce, Puerto Rico: Asociación Billy Graham, 1967.
Babbage, Stuart Barton, and Ian Siggins. *Light Beneath the Cross.* Garden City, NY: Doubleday, 1960; Kingswood and Melbourne: The World's Work, 1960.
Back, Phil. *Where Are They Now?: Churches Reflect on Mission England 1984.* Bromley, Kent, England: MARC Europe, 1988.
Barker, Dianne. *Billy Graham in Big Orange Country: The East Tennessee Crusade, 1970: Official Document.* Knoxville: East Tennessee Crusade, 1970.
Bennet, James E. *A Ministry of Disobedience: Christian Leaders Analyze the Billy Graham New York Crusade, May-September, 1957.* Collingswood, NJ: Christian Beacon Press, 1959.
Billy Graham in Bluegrass Country. 1 film reel; sd., bandw ; 16 mm. Minneapolis: World Wide Pictures, 1971.
Billy Graham in Romania. Minneapolis: World Wide Pictures, 1989.
Billy Graham Presents Man in the 5th Dimension. Pictorial Highlights of the TODD-AO and Technicolor Motion Picture Shown at the New York World's Fair, 1964-1965. Photographs by Russ Busby. Minneapolis: World Wide, 1964.
Bolton, John. *Report on Indian Mission of Billy Graham.* Bombay: N.p., 1956.
Brabham, Lewis F. *A New Song in the South: The Story of the Billy Graham Greenville, S.C. Crusade.* Grand Rapids: Zondervan, 1966.
Burnham, George. *Billy Graham: A Mission Accomplished.* Westwood, NJ: Revell, 1955; London: Marshall, Morgan and Scott, 1956.
_____. *Billy Graham and the New York Crusade.* Grand Rapids: Zondervan, 1957.
_____. *To the Far Corners: With Billy Graham in Asia.* Westwood, NJ: Revell, 1956; *With Billy Graham in Asia.* London: Marshall, Morgan, and Scott, 1956.
Burnham, George, and Lee Fisher. *Billy Graham: Man of God.* Westchester, IL: Christian Readers Club, 1950, 1959.
Cook, Charles Thomas. *London Hears Billy Graham: The Greater London Crusade.* London: Marshall, Morgan and Scott, 1954.
Colquhoun, Frank. *Harringay Story: The Official Record of the Billy Graham Greater London Crusade, 1954.* London: Hodder and Stoughton, 1955.
Douglas, J. D., Gill A. Stricklin, and Sherwood E. Wirt, eds. *A Lantern in Tokyo.* Minneapolis: World Wide, 1968.
Duncan, George B. *Bearings on Life.* London: The C.S.S.M., 1955.
Elworthy, John. *Billy Graham in Oxford and Cambridge.* London: Regal Books, 1980.
England, Edward Oliver. *Afterwards: A Journalist Sets out to Discover What Happened to Some of Those Who Made a Decision for Christ during the Billy Graham Crusades in Britain in 1954 and 1955.* London: Victory Press, 1957.
_____. *Hallowed Harringay.* London: Victory Press, 1955.
Ferm, Robert Oscar. *Billy Graham: Do Conversions Last?* Minneapolis: World Wide, 1988.
_____. *Persuaded to Live: Conversion Stories from the Billy Graham Crusades.* Including a message from Billy Graham. Intro. by Frank E. Gaebelein. Westwood, NJ: Revell, 1958.
_____. *They Met God at the New York Crusade, Madison Square Garden.* Foreword and message by Billy Graham. Minneapolis: World Wide, 1957.

_____. *World-Wide Witness: Conversion Experiences.* Intro. by Billy Graham. Minneapolis: Billy Graham Evangelistic Association, 1959.

Foster, Dave. *Billy Graham: A Vision Imparted. Amsterdam 83—International Conference for Itinerant Evangelists: A Pictorial Report.* Minneapolis: World Wide, 1974.

_____. *Billy Graham, Euro '70: Eight Days when the Miracle of Modern Technology Projected the Christian Message across Europe.* Minneapolis: World Wide, 1971; *Billy Graham, Euro '70: Acht Tage Verküdigung der Christlichen Botschaft mit den Mitteln Moderner Technik in Europa.* Frankfurt: World Wide, 1971.

_____. *Euro Fest 75: A Pictorial Review.* Minneapolis: World Wide, 1976.

Gillenson, Lewis W. *Billy Graham, and Seven Who Were Saved.* New York: Trident Press, 1967; New York: Pocket Books, 1968.

_____. *Billy Graham: The Man and His Message.* Greenwich, CT: Fawcett Publications, 1954.

Harrison, John K. *Le prêcheur des temps modernes Billy Graham.* Montréal: Edimag, 1990.

Hutchinson, Warner, and Cliff Wilson. *Let the People Rejoice: Billy Graham Crusade, An Amazing Week in New Zealand.* Wellington, New Zealand: Crusader Bookroom Society, 1959.

Keysor, Charles W. *Billy Graham: The Story of a 20th Century Ambassador for Christ.* Elgin, IL: David C. Cook, 1968.

Kiefel, Gerhard. *Fazit EURO 70 [siebzig]: die Billy-Graham-Evangelisation; eine Herausforderung an Verkindigung u. Seelsorge d. Kirche.* CITY: Schriftenmissions-Verlag, 1971.

Hosier, Helen Kooiman. *Transformed: Behind the Scenes with Billy Graham.* Wheaton, IL: Tyndale House, 1970.

LeTourneau College. *Founder's Week, October 12-18, 1971; Silver Anniversary [and] Billy Graham Crusade [and] Founder's week, October 23-27, 1972.* Longview, TX: LeTourneau College, 1972.

Life Link: Satellite TV, July 20-24, 1987: Rocky Mountain Billy Graham Crusade, Mile High Stadium, July 17-26, 1987. Minneapolis: Billy Graham Evangelistic Association, 1987.

London Crusade News. London: Greater London Billy Graham Crusade, 1953-1954. Vol. 1, Nos 1-7.

McMahan, T. *Safari for Souls: with Billy Graham in Africa.* Columbia, SC: State-Record Co., 1960.

Messages from Manila: Metro-Manila Billy Graham Crusade '77. Baquio City, Philippines: Seminary Press, Philippine Baptist Theological Seminary, 1979.

Mitchell, Curtis. *God in the Garden: the Story of the Billy Graham New York Crusade.* Garden City, NY: Doubleday, 1957.

_____. *The All Britain Crusade of 1967: A Pictorial Report Plus "Crusading in Italy and Yugoslavia."* Minneapolis: World Wide, 1968.

_____. *The Billy Graham London Crusade.* Vincent Hayhurst, official photographer. Minneapolis: World Wide, 1966.

_____. *Those Who Came Forward: Men and Women Who Responded to the Ministry of Billy Graham.* Preface by Billy Graham. Philadelphia: Chilton Books, 1966; *Those Who Came Forward: an Account of Those Whose Lives Were Changed by the Ministry of Billy Graham.* Kingswood, Tadworth, Surrey: World's Work, 1966.

Mondragón, Rafael. *Watergate, Vietnam, Billy Graham.* Mexico City: Ediciones de Cultura Popular, 1981.

Nichols, Allan, and Warwick Olson. *Crusading Down Under: The Story of the Billy

Graham Crusades in Australia and New Zealand. Minneapolis: World Wide, 1970.

North Korean Journey: Billy Graham in the Democratic People's Republic of Korea. Minneapolis: World Wide Pictures, 1993.

Plowman, Edward. *Billy Graham in China.* Minneapolis: Billy Graham Evangelistic Association, 1988.

Plowman, Edward E., and John Akers. *Billy Graham in Budapest.* Minneapolis: World Wide, 1989.

Pollock, John Charles. *Crusade '66: Britain hears Billy Graham.* London: Hodder and Stoughton, 1966.

Powell, Gordon. *Six Months after Billy Graham: An Address Delivered by the Rev. Gordon Powell at the University of Sydney, Australia.* Minneapolis: Billy Graham Evangelistic Association, 1960.

Pyne, Cliff, designer. *Billy Graham Crusade, 1966.* Leicester, England: J. C. Culpin for the East Midlands Billy Graham Television Relays, n.d.

Report of the Billy Graham Crusades in Australia and New Zealand, February 15-May 31, 1959. Sydney: Ambassador Press, 1959.

Rodgers-Melnick, Ann. *A Gathering at the Rivers.* Pittsburgh: Pittsburgh Post-Gazette, 1993.

Terrell, Bob. *Billy Graham in Hungary.* Minneapolis: World Wide, 1978; Hungarian translation: *Billy Graham Magyarországon: Szeptember 3-10, 1977.* Budapest, Hungary: Magyarországi Szabadegyházak Tanácsa, 1978.

_____. *Billy Graham in the Soviet Union.* Minneapolis: Billy Graham Evangelistic Association, 1985.

There Will Always Be an England . . . Billy Graham London Crusade. Minneapolis: Billy Graham Evangelistic Association, 1952.

Wells, Paul. *Billy Graham in Sheffield 1985: A Pictorial Report.* Minneapolis: Billy Graham Evangelistic Association, 1985.

Wellman, Sam. *Billy Graham the Great Evangelist.* Young Reader's Christian Library. Uhrichsville, OH: Barbour, 1997.

Williams, Derek. *Billy Graham in England 1984.* Moor Park, Northwood, Middlesex, England: Creative Publishing, 1984.

_____. *One in a Million: The Story of Billy Graham's Missions in England during 1984.* Berkhamsted: Word, 1984.

Wirt, Sherwood Eliot. *Crusade at the Golden Gate.* New York: Harper and Brothers, 1959.

Crusade Follow-Up Materials, Books, and Pamphlets

Follow-Up Department, Billy Graham Evangelistic Association. *Knowing Christ.* Minneapolis: Billy Graham Evangelistic Association, 1967.

Growing in Christ. Minneapolis: World Wide, n.d. [copyrighted 1968].

Graham, Billy. *Billy Graham Tells the Story of the Holy City, Jerusalem as Presented in the New World Wide Picture Film.* Minneapolis: Billy Graham Evangelistic Association, 1962.

_____. *Billy Graham with Cliff Barrows Presents: The Story of Naaman the Leper.* Minneapolis: Billy Graham Evangelistic Association, 1951.

_____. *The Bible Says: 540 Selected Verses on the Bible, Sin, Salvation, Christian Living, the Future.* Minneapolis: Billy Graham Evangelistic Association, 1960.

_____. *The Chance of a Lifetime: Helps for Servicemen by Billy Graham.* Grand Rapids: Zondervan, 1952.

_____. *The Church-Centered Crusade: How It Works.* Minneapolis: Billy Graham

Evangelistic Association, 1964.

Mitchell, John G. *Personal Workers Handbook.* Portland, OR: Greater Portland Gospel Crusade, 1950.

Riggs, Charles. *Learning to Walk with God: Twelve Steps to Christian Growth.* Minneapolis: World Wide, 1988.

_____. *Living in Christ.* Minneapolis: World Wide, 1980, 1990, revised 1993, 1996.

_____. *Practicing His Presence.* N.p. 1991, 1995.

_____. *Thirty Discipleship Exercises.* Minneapolis: Billy Graham Evangelistic Association, 1980, revised 1982, 1987, published with Tom Phillips, 1992.

"Scripture Memory 'Motivator': Start a Life-Changing Habit of Scripture Memory." *Roots Bible Studies Series.* Minneapolis: Billy Graham Evangelistic Association, 1972.

Ward, Charles G. *Preliminary Witness Training Sections I and II.* Audiocassette. Minneapolis: Billy Graham Evangelistic Association, 1990.

_____. *Preliminary Witness Training Sections III and IV.* Audiocassette. Minneapolis: Billy Graham Evangelistic Association, 1988.

Ward, Charles G., ed. *The Billy Graham Christian Worker's Handbook: A Layman's Guide for Soul Winning and Personal Counseling.* Compiled by the Christian Guidance Department of Billy Graham Evangelistic Association in conjunction with the Counseling and Follow-up Department. Minneapolis: World Wide, 1981, 1984, 1993, 1996; *The Billy Graham Christian Worker's Handbook: A Topical Guide with Biblical Answers to the Urgent Concerns of Our Day.* Minneapolis: World Wide, 1996.

Interviews

Corts, John. Personal interview by author, 29 January 2001, Minneapolis, MN. Handwritten notes in author's possession.

Evans, Robert. Telephone interview by author, 2 July 2001. Handwritten notes in author's possession.

Ferm, Lois. Telephone interview by author, 19 July 1999. Handwritten notes in author's possession.

_____. Three personal interviews by author, 31 July, 4 August, and 6 August 2000, Amsterdam, the Netherlands. Handwritten notes in author's possession.

Frost, David. *Billy Graham in Conversation.* Bath: Chivers, 2000.

_____. *Billy Graham: Personal Thoughts of a Public Man, Thirty Years of Conversations.* Colorado Springs: Chariot Victor Publishing, a division of Cook Communications, 1997.

_____. *Billy Graham Talks with David Frost.* Philadelphia: A.J. Holman Company, 1971; London: Hodder and Stoughton, 1972.

Johnston, Arthur P. Telephone interview by author, February 16, 1999. Handwritten notes in author's possession.

Lenning, Scott. Personal interview by author, August 4, 2000, Amsterdam, the Netherlands. Tape recording in author's possession.

Martin, William. Conversation with author. Louisville. June 24, 2001. Handwritten notes in author's possession.

Olford, Stephen. Telephone interview by author. June 26, 2001. Handwritten notes in author's possession.

Patterson, Vernon William. Personal interview by Robert Schuster, March 5, 1985. Wheaton, IL: Billy Graham Archives, Collection 5, Tape 4.

Rainer, Thom. Personal comments, September 19, 2001. Notes written on manuscript.

Schuller, Robert D. Interview by Billy Graham. United States Public Broadcasting System. Aired on June 8, 1997.

Weisenbeck, Jude, F.S.C. Personal discussion with author, handwritten notes, Louisville, November 16, 1998 and May 26, 1999.

Other Primary Sources

A Billy Graham Crusade 4 Complete Messages. Four sound disks (33 1/3 rpm). Minneapolis: Billy Graham Evangelistic Association, 1962.

Audio Tapes. 4,585 Audio Tapes. Collection Number 26, Billy Graham Center Archives, Wheaton College, 1950-1991.

Beavan, Jerry. "The Church and City-Wide Crusades." In Sherwood Eliot Wirt, ed. *Spiritual Awakening.* Los Angeles: Cowman Publications, 1958.

Bibliography: Billy Graham Magazine Articles. Minneapolis: Billy Graham Evangelistic Association, 1963.

Billy Graham and the Black Community. Minneapolis: World Wide, 1973.

Billy Graham Center Archives,. *Select Chronology Listing of Events in the History of Billy Graham Evangelistic Association* [on-line]. Accessed 15 July 2001. Available from http://www.wheaton.edu/bgc/archives/bgeachro/bgeachron02.htm; Internet.

Billy Graham Collection 1863, 1989 (Bulk 1949-1983). Wheaton, IL: Billy Graham Center Archives.

"Billy Graham Crusade Statistics." Minneapolis, MN: Billy Graham Evangelistic Association, December 1997.

Billy Graham Discusses the Role of the Evangelical Churches in a Starving World. One sound tape reel: 7.5 ips, mono.; 7 in, 1/4 in. tape. Broadcast on Merv Graham Show, 15 October 1974.

Billy Graham Evangelistic Association. *Church Leaders' Handbook.* Minneapolis: Billy Graham Evangelistic Association, 1982.

_____. "About Us" [on-line]. Accessed 15 February 2001. Available from http://www.billygraham.org/about/statementoffaith.asp; Internet.

_____. *Meet Billy Graham: A Pictorial Record of the Evangelist, His Family and His Team.* Pitkin Pictorials, 1966.

_____. "Response to the Schuller Show Statement of Billy Graham." Unpublished statement, August 25, 1997.

Billy Graham School of Evangelism. Audio Tapes. Minneapolis: World Wide, 1990.

Billy Graham School of Evangelism Program Guide, June 18-21, 1990. Billy Graham Center, Wheaton, IL. Minneapolis: Billy Graham Schools of Evangelism, 1990.

"Billy Graham Sermon Series by Decade." Research copy sent from Billy Graham Evangelistic Association, Minneapolis office, 16 March 2001.

"Billy Graham's News Conferences." Collection Number 24, Billy Graham Center Archives, Wheaton College, 1963-1977.

"Biography: William (Billy) F. Graham—Evangelist." Minneapolis: Billy Graham Evangelistic Association, May 2000.

Brookshire, Elsie. "Greater New York Billy Graham Crusade, Madison Square Garden, New York City, May 15—September 1, 1957." Unpublished resource.

Calendar [on-line]. Accessed 15 July 2001. Available from http://earth.com/ calendar; Internet.

"Christianity Today, Inc." Collection Number 8, Billy Graham Center Archives, Wheaton College, 1954-1977.

"Clipping File." 350 scrapbooks. Collection Number 360, Billy Graham Center Archives, Wheaton College, 1932, 1949-1989, n.d.

Coffan, Barbara. *Manual for the Local Deaf Committee of the Billy Graham Crusade.* Minneapolis: Billy Graham Evangelistic Association, 1987.

Conducting Effective Crusades: The Billy Graham Model. Two audiocassettes.

Alpharetta, GA: Home Mission Board, Southern Baptist Convention, 1995.

Congressional Gold Medal Award: May 2, 1996: Honoring Billy and Ruth Graham. Minneapolis: World Wide, 1996.

Decision Index: 1986-1995. Minneapolis: Billy Graham Evangelistic Association, 1996.

Decision Magazine Index: Billy Graham Sermons, 1996-October 2000. Minneapolis: Billy Graham Evangelistic Association, 2000.

Ferm, Robert O. *Index for Hour of Decision Sermons 1-130.* Collection Number 19, Billy Graham Center Archives, Wheaton College, n.d.

_____. "The Theological Presuppositions of Billy Graham." Unpublished manuscript. Collection Number 19, Billy Graham Center Archives, Wheaton College, n.d.

From the Archives of the Billy Graham Center. Billy Graham Center Archives, Wheaton College, September 1984 to September 1986 (?).

Hoglund, Kenneth G. *The Gospel in America: A History of Evangelism and Revival in America 1650-1950: An Exhibit Script from the Billy Graham Center Museum.* Wheaton, IL: Billy Graham Center Museum, 1988.

"Hour of Decision Audio Tapes." 2,300 Audio Tapes. Collection Number 191, Billy Graham Center Archives, Wheaton College, 1950-1980.

Hour of Decision Sermons. Sermons 1-130 in ten volumes. Billy Graham Archives, The Southern Baptist Theological Seminary, Louisville, 1949-1961.

"Hour of Decision Television Programs." Collection Number 54, Billy Graham Center Archives, Wheaton, IL, 1950.

Huston, Sterling W. *Crusade Evangelism and the Local Church.* Minneapolis: World Wide, 1984, 1991. Portions published early for Amsterdam 1983 as *The Billy Graham Crusade Handbook.* Minneapolis: World Wide, 1983.

Index: 1960-1985—Titles and Subjects Which Have Appeared in Decision *Magazine, November, 1960 through December, 1985.* Minneapolis: Billy Graham Evangelistic Association, 1986.

Lawson, Steven J. *Maximum Involvement: Your Church and the Billy Graham Crusade.* Minneapolis: World Wide, 1980, 1989.

Lifestyle Witnessing Seminar. Audio Tapes. Minneapolis: Billy Graham Evangelistic Association, n.d.

Lifestyle Witnessing Seminar. Notebook. Minneapolis: Billy Graham Evangelistic Association, 1991, 1992, 1993.

Morris, Leon Aubrey. *Billy Graham Greater Chicago Crusade Survey of Inquirers, 1963.* 1 box. Billy Graham Center Archives, Wheaton, IL.

North American Conference for Itinerant Evangelists. Audio Cassettes. Minneapolis: NACIE 94, 1994.

Northcott, Cecil. "Cecil Northcott Sums It Up." Wheaton, IL: Billy Graham Archives, Collection 19, Accession 88-16, Box 1, Item 3.

_____. "Four Years After Graham." Wheaton, IL: Billy Graham Archives, Collection 19, Accession 88-16, Box 1, Item 3.

Political Leaders Testify: "What Christ Means to Me." Minneapolis: Billy Graham Evangelistic Association, 1952.

Preparing for a Billy Graham Crusade: Eight Ministers from Various Cities Share Their Experiences to Help You in Preparing for a Billy Graham Crusade. Minneapolis: Billy Graham Evangelistic Association, n.d.

"Profile: William (Billy) F. Graham." Minneapolis: Billy Graham Evangelistic Association, November 2000.

Resource Notes. Billy Graham Center Library. Vol. 1, no. 1 (January 1, 1987)—Vol. 9, no. 1 (January 31, 1996). Completed.

Roberts, Richard Owen. *A Preliminary Checklist of Books and Pamphlets by and about Billy Graham and His Associates.* Wheaton, IL: Billy Graham Center Library,

1977.

_____. *Revival Literature: An Annotated Bibliography with Biographical and Historical Notices.* Wheaton, IL: Richard Owen Roberts, 1988.

Schuster, Robert D., James Stambaugh, and Ferne Weimer. *Researching Modern Evangelicalism: A Guide to the Holdings of the Billy Graham Center, With Information on Other Collections.* New York: Greenwood Press, 1990.

"Team Office: Crusade Books." Collection Number 16, Billy Graham Center Archives, Wheaton College, 1957-1981.

"Team Office: Crusade Organization and Team Activities." Collection Number 17, Billy Graham Center Archives, Wheaton College, 1949-1979, n.d.

Twenty Years in Review. Minneapolis: Billy Graham Evangelistic Association, 1967.

"Statistics [Billy Graham Crusade]: Alphabetical by Continent." Minneapolis: Billy Graham Evangelistic Association, December, 2000.

"Statistics [Billy Graham Crusade]: Alphabetical (City)." Minneapolis: Billy Graham Evangelistic Association, December, 2000.

"Statistics [Billy Graham Crusade]: Chronological." Minneapolis: Billy Graham Evangelistic Association, December, 2000.

Spiritual Counseling Department of Billy Graham Evangelistic Association. "TV Phone Ministry: Informational Folder." Minneapolis: Billy Graham Evangelistic Association, 1996.

United States. *An Act to Award a Congressional Gold Medal to Ruth and Billy Graham, 1996.* U.S. G.P.O.: Supt. of Docs., U.S. G.P.O., distributor, 1996.

"Untitled Personal Scrapbook." Collection Number 15, Billy Graham Center Archives, Wheaton College, 1938-1945.

Wirt, Sherwood Eliot, and Mavis R. Sanders, eds. *Great Reading from Decision: Selections from the First Ten Years of Publication.* Minneapolis: World Wide, 1970.

Wirt, Sherwood Eliot, ed. *Spiritual Awakening.* Los Angeles: Cowman Publications, 1958.

Secondary Sources

Books on or about Billy Graham—
Official and Unofficial

Aaseng, Nathan. *Billy Graham.* Grand Rapids: Zondervan, 1993.

Alder, Bill, ed. *The Wit and Wisdom of Billy Graham.* New York: Random House, 1967.

Ashman, Chuck. *The Gospel According to Billy Graham.* Secaucus, NJ: Lyle Stuart, 1977.

Beavan, Jerry. *This Is Billy Graham: Over 100 Pictures of Billy Graham's Life and Work.* Philadelphia: Walfred Pub., 1957.

Barnhart, Joe E. *The Billy Graham Religion.* Philadelphia: Pilgrim Press Book from United Church Press, 1972; London: Mowbray, 1974; *Die Billy Graham Story; Seine Botschaft und ihre Wirkung in Politik und Gesellschaft.* Munich: Claudius Verlag, 1973.

Billy Graham, TV Evangelism: Billy Graham Sees Dangers Ahead. Radnor, PA: Triangle Publications, 1983.

Billy Graham Evangelistic Association, Spiritual Counseling Department. *Helping Others Find Christ.* Chicago: Moody, 1955.

Billy Graham Evangelistic Association. *Tenth Anniversary Book of Remembrance.* Minneapolis: Billy Graham Evangelistic Association, 1960.

The Billy Graham Story as Told in America's Leading Magazines. Minneapolis: Billy

Graham Evangelistic Association, 1951.

Bishop, Mary. *Billy Graham, the Man and His Ministry*. New York: Grosset and Dunlap, 1978.

Blewett, Lois, and Bob Blewett. *Twenty Years Under God: Proclaiming the Gospel of Jesus Christ to the World*. Edited by George Wilson. Minneapolis: World Wide, 1970.

Brauer, Wilhelm, herausgegeben. *Billy Graham: ein Evangelist der Neuen Welt*. Geleitwort von Karl Heim. Giessen: Brunnen-Verlag, 1955.

Brown, Joan Winmill, ed. *Day by Day with Billy Graham: A Devotional Book*. Minneapolis: World Wide, 1976.

Bundy, E. G. *Billy Graham: Performer? Politician? Preacher? Prophet? A Chronological Record Compiled from Public Sources by the Church League of America, 1951 through 1978*. Wheaton, IL: The Church League of America, 1978, 1979, 1982; *Billy Graham: Performer? Preacher? Prophet?* Wheaton, IL: The Church League of America, 1982.

Busby, Russ. *Billy Graham, God's Ambassador: A Lifelong Mission of Giving Hope to the World*. New York: Time-Life Books, 1999.

Chapple, Arthur H. *Billy Graham*. Grand Rapids: Zondervan, 1950; London: Marshall, Morgan and Scott, 1954.

Colquhoun, Frank, ed. *Introducing Billy Graham: The Work of an Evangelist. An Address Given in the Assembly Hall of the Church House, Westminster, on 20th March, 1952*. London: World Evangelical Alliance, 1953.

Cook, Charles T. *The Billy Graham Story: "One Thing I Do."* Wheaton, IL: Van Kampen, 1954.

Cooper, Richard. *Billy Graham, Preacher to the World*. Raleigh, NC: Creative Productions, 1985.

Daniels, Glenn. *The Inspiring Life and Thoughts of Billy Graham: The Man Who Walks with God*. New York: Paperback Library, 1961.

Deckard, Bill, ed. *Breakfast with Billy Graham: 120 Daily Readings*. Ann Arbor, MI: Vine Books, 1996; New York: Walker and Company, 1997.

Decorvet, Boris. *Billy Graham: evangéliste du XXe siècle*. Vevey, Switzerland: Éditions des Groupes missionnaires, 1960.

Dinneen, Joseph Francis. *The Sawdust Trail: The Life Story of Billy Graham*. Boston: E. S. Dangel, 1950.

Drummond, Lewis A. *The Canvas Cathedral: Billy Graham's Ministry Seen Through the History of Evangelism*. Nashville: Thomas Nelson, 2003.

_____. *The Evangelist: The Worldwide Impact of Billy Graham*. Nashville: Word, 2001.

Elwood, Roger, ed. *To God Be the Glory: The Words of Billy Graham and Corrie Ten Boom*. New York: Phoenix Press, 1977.

Emert, Charles. *Billy Graham's 23 Years of Theological Change—Why Bible Believing Fundamentalist Christians Cannot Take Part in His Evangelistic Crusades*. ed. D. A. Waite.Colingswood, NJ: Bible for Today, 1971.

Enlow, David R. *Men Aflame: The Story of the Christian Business Men's Committee International*. Grand Rapids: Zondervan, 1962.

Evangelism: Strategy for the '80s: Essays Presented to Dr. Billy Graham. New York: Ward Books, 1978; London: Pickering and Inglis, 1980.

Ewin, Wilson. *The Assimilation of Evangelist Billy Graham into the Roman Catholic Church*. Compton, Québec: Québec Baptist Missions, 1992.

Ferm, Robert O. *Cooperative Evangelism: Is Billy Graham Right or Wrong? Are His Policies Supported by Scripture and the Great Evangelists of History?* Grand Rapids: Zondervan, 1958.

Fisher, Lee. *A Funny Thing Happened on the Way to the Crusade.* Carol Stream, IL: Creation House, 1974.

Flint, Cort R., ed. *Billy Graham Speaks! The Quotable Billy Graham.* New York: Grosset and Dunlap, 1968.

_____. *The Quotable Billy Graham.* Anderson, SC: Droke House Publishers, 1966.

Frady, Marshall. *Billy Graham: A Parable of American Righteousness.* Boston: Little, Brown, 1979.

French, John with Charles Goodman. *My Fight with Billy Graham.* Memphis: C. Goodman Publisher, 1959; Golden, CO: Castle Books, 1959.

Garland Publications. *The Early Billy Graham: Sermon and Revival Accounts* [reprint of Van Kampen, *Calling Youth to Christ* and *Revival in Our Time.*] New York: Garland Publications, 1988.

Gsell, Brad K. *The Legacy of Billy Graham: The Accommodation of Truth to Error in the Evangelical Church.* Rev. ed. Charlotte, NC: Fundamental Presbyterian Publications, 1998.

Hallmark Cards. *Billy Graham, The Miracle of Christmas.* Kansas City, MO: Hallmark Cards, 1972.

Ham, Edward Everett. *The Story of an All-Day Prayer Meeting and Revival when Billy Graham Found Christ.* Murfreesboro, TN: Sword of the Lord, 1955.

High, Stanley. *Billy Graham: The Personal Story of the Man, His Message, and His Mission.* New York: McGraw-Hill Book Company, 1956; Kingswood, Surrey: The World's Work, 1957, 1959.

Hulse, Erroll. *Billy Graham: The Pastor's Dilemma.* Hounslow, Middlesex, Great Britain: Maurice Allan (Publishers), 1966, 1969.

Inspirational Press. *The Collected Works of Billy Graham* [*Angels; How to Be Born Again;* and *The Holy Spirit*]. New York: Inspirational Press, 1993; *His Greatest Works* [*Angels; How to Be Born Again;* and *The Holy Spirit*]. New York: Inspirational Press, 1995.

Jefferson, Bill. *Billy Graham, Footprints of Conscience.* Minneapolis: World Wide, 1991.

Jensen, Richard K. *The Billy Pulpits: Chronicles of Billy Graham and Billy Sunday— Biographies of Both Men Are Common, and* The Billy Pulpits *Does Not Attempt to Reinvent Those Wheels; This Book Examines How the Careers of the Two Billys Are Alike and Dissimilar.* Collierville, TN: First Foundations, 1996.

Johnson, J. A. *Billy Graham, the Jehoshaphat of Our Generation?* Bangalore, India: Berean [Biblical] Publications, 1968, 1983.

Kerr, Grahame. *Martin Luther, We Have Not Forgotten You: An Assessment of the Billy Graham Movement.* 4th ed. Lithgow, N.S.W.: Covenanter Press, 1995.

Kilgore, James E. *Billy Graham, The Preacher.* New York: Exposition Press, 1968.

Levy, Alan. *God Bless You Real Good: My Crusade with Billy Graham.* New York: Essandess Special Editions, 1967, 1969.

Lockard, David. *The Unheard Billy Graham.* Waco, TX: Word, 1971.

Lowe, Janet, ed. *Billy Graham Speaks: Insight from the World's Greatest Preacher.* Thorndike, ME: G. K. Hall, 1999, 2000.

Lutzweiler, James. *The "Chronic Negro Mourner" and the Conversion of Billy Graham: To which is appended 174 newspaper clippings from* The Charlotte Observer *that chronicle Mordecai Ham's Charlotte, North Carolina, revival between 30 August 1934 and 26 November 1934.* Copy 13 of 100. Boyce Library, The Southern Baptist Theological Seminary library, 1998.

Malik, Charles Habib. *The Two Tasks.* Westchester, IL: Cornerstone Books, 1980.

Marshall, Frady. *Billy Graham, a Parable of American Righteousness.* Boston: Little, Brown, 1979.

Martin, William C. *A Prophet with Honor: The Billy Graham Story.* New York: William

Morrow, 1991; *The Billy Graham Story.* London: Hutchinson, 1992.

McLoughlin, William Gerald, Jr. *Billy Graham: Revivalist in a Secular Age.* New York: Ronald Press Company, 1960.

Mitchell, Curtis. *Billy Graham: Saint or Sinner?* Old Tappan, NJ: Revell, 1979.

_____. *Billy Graham: The Making of a Crusader.* Foreword by George M. Wilson. Philadelphia: Chilton Books, 1966.

Paisley, Ian R. K. *Billy Graham and the Church of Rome.* Belfast, Ireland: Martyrs Memorial Free Presbyterian Church, 1970; Greenville, SC: Bob Jones University Press, 1972.

Paul, Ronald C. *Billy Graham—Prophet of Hope.* New York: Balantine Books, 1978.

Peterson, F. Bredahl. *Billy Graham Som Han Er: Med en Tal af Billy Graham.* Copenhagen: J. Frimodts Forlag, 1954.

Peterson, F. Paul. *The Other Side of Billy Graham and Watergate.* Fort Wayne, IN: American Liberty Press, 1974.

_____. *The Truth about Billy Graham and a Documentary on the Vatican Appointment.* N.p.: F. P. Peterson, 1986.

Poling, David. *Why Billy Graham?* Grand Rapids: Zondervan, 1977.

Pollock, John Charles. *Billy Graham: The Authorized Biography.* New York: McGraw-Hill Book Company, 1966; Grand Rapids: Zondervan Publishing Company, 1967; Minneapolis: World Wide, 1969; *Crusades: 20 Years with Billy Graham.* Special Billy Graham Crusade ed., Minneapolis: World Wide, 1969; *Billy Graham: The Authorized Biography,* London: Hodder and Stoughton, 1966, 1967; trans. into Spanish as *Billy Graham: la biografía autorizada.* Casa Bautista de Publicaciones, 1968.

_____. *To All Nations: The Billy Graham Story.* San Francisco: Harper and Row, 1985; trans. into French as *A toutes les nations: biographie de Billy Graham.* Cachan, France: Décision, 1986.

_____. *Billy Graham: Evangelist to the World, an Authorized Biography of the Decisive Years* [1969-1978]. San Francisco: Harper and Row, 1979; Crusade ed. Minneapolis: World Wide, 1979.

_____. *Billy Graham: Highlights of the Story.* Basingstoke, United Kingdom: Marshall, Morgan and Scott, 1984.

_____. *Billy Graham: Man of Decision: The Authorized Biography (1960-1966).* Unpublished manuscript. Billy Graham Center Archives, Wheaton, IL.

Rasmussen, Roland. *Back Billy Graham? California Baptist Pastor Says No.* Morriston, Swansea: D. Roberts, 1960.

Rice, John R. *Dr. Graham's Daring: Both Ways at Once!* Morriston, Swansea: D. Roberts, 1962.

Rowlandson, Maurice. *Life with Billy: An Autobiography.* London: Hodder and Stoughton, 1992.

Salvation Army. *Celebrate! A Salute to Dr. Billy Graham: The Salvation Army proudly presents a salute to Dr. Billy Graham: Celebrating 40 years of international crusades: Thursday, October 12, 1989, The Beverly Hilton, Beverly Hill, California.* Alexandria, VA: Salvation Army, 1989.

Sellers, James Earl. *The Outsider and the Word of God: A Study in Christian Communication.* Nashville: Abingdon, 1961.

Settel, T. S., ed. *The Faith of Billy Graham.* Intro. by Cort R. Flint. Anderson, SC: Droke House, Publishers, 1968; New York: New American Library, 1970.

Smart, William James. *Six Mighty Men* [George Muller, Dwight L. Moody, Hudson Taylor, Samuel Chadwick, Hugh Redwood, Billy Graham]. New York: Macmillan, 1956, 1957.

Spillman, Sandy. *Billy Graham: A Photobiography.* Houston: Epps-Praxis Publishers, 1976.

Stoll, Wilhelm. *The Conversion Theology of Billy Graham in the Light of the Lutheran Confessions.* St. Louis: Concordia Student Journal, 1980.

Streiker, Lowell, and Gerald S. Strober. *Religion and the New Majority: Billy Graham, Middle America, and the Politics of the 70's.* New York: Association Press, 1972.

Strober, Gerald S. *Billy Graham, His Life and Faith: A Biography of the World-Famous Evangelist Who Has Advised Presidents and Kings.* Waco, TX: Word, 1977, 1978; New York: Pocket Books, 1977.

_____. *Graham: A Day in Billy's Life.* Garden City, NY: Doubleday, 1976; New York: Dell Publishing, 1977; Old Tappan, NJ: Revell, 1977; Boston: G. K. Hall, 1977; London: Hodder and Stoughton, 1977; *Ein Tag in Billy Graham Leben.* Stuttgart: Hänssler, 1978.

Stucki, Alfred. *Billy Graham und Charles Fuller: Amerikas grosse Evangelisten.* Basel: H. Majer, 1955.

Svärd, Arvid. *Billy Graham, Tänd av Gud, Sänd av Gud: Några Drag i Bilden av de Moderna Miljonstädernas Apostel.* Stockholm: Westerbergs, 1954.

Target. G. W. *Evangelism Inc.* London: Allen Lane, Penguin Press, 1968.

Thomson, David Patrick. *Dr. Billy Graham and the Pattern of Modern Evangelism.* Crieff, Scotland: Book Department, St. Ninian's, 1966.

Tuck, J., ed. *This Is Their Life: Thrilling Stories of Men and Women Who Have Given Their Time and Their Talents to God for the Spreading of the Gospel.* Worthing, England: Walter, 1966.

Van Houten, T. B. *Billy Graham: Een Evangelist van Onze Tijd.* Den Haag, J. N. Voorhoeve, 1954.

Waite, Donald Allen. *4 Billy Graham Reports.* Colingswood, NJ: Bible for Today, 1971.

Walker, Jay. *Billy Graham: A Life in Word and Deed.* New York: Avon Books, 1998.

Wellington, S. Simbi. *With the Big Three: Dr. Billy Graham, Rev. H.O. Jones and Dr. M.I. Okpara; Religious and Economic States of Nigeria in 1960.* Aba, Nigeria, 1960.

Wellman, Sam. *Billy Graham.* Uhrichsville, OH: Barbour, 1997.

_____. *Billy Graham the Great Evangelist.* Philadelphia: Chelsea House, 1999.

Westman, Paul. *Billy Graham: Reaching Out to the World.* Minneapolis: Dillon, 1981.

Whitney, Harold. *Tell Australia.* Brisbane, Australia: W. R. Smith and Patterson Pty, 1958.

Wilson, George M., ed. Lois Blewett and Bob Blewett, joint authors. *Twenty Years under God—a Proclaiming the Gospel of Jesus Christ to the World: A Pictorial Review of the Billy Graham Ministries.* Minneapolis: World Wide, 1970.

Wilson, Grady. *Billy Graham as a Teen-Ager.* Grand Rapids: Zondervan, 1957.

Wilson, Jean Verseput. *Crusader for Christ: The Story of Billy Graham.* Fort Washington, PA: Christian Literature Crusade, 1966, 1973.

Wirt, Sherwood Eliot. *Billy: A Personal Look at Billy Graham, the World's Best-Loved Evangelist.* Wheaton, IL: Crossway, a Division of Good News, 1997.

_____, ed. *Evangelism: The Next Ten Years: Essays Presented to Dr. Billy Graham.* Waco, TX: Word, 1978.

Wooten, Sara McIntosh. *Billy Graham: World-Famous Evangelist.* Berkeley Heights, NJ: Enslow Publishers, 2001.

Periodicals

Alston, Jon P. "Popularity of Billy Graham, 1963-1969: Review of the Polls." *Journal for the Scientific Study of Religion* 12 (1973): 227-30.

Arn, Charles. "A Response to Dr. Rainer: What Is the Key to Effective Evangelism?" *Journal of the American Society for Church Growth* 6 (1995): 75.

Arnold, Bob. "Billy Graham, Superstar." *Southern Exposure* 4, no. 3 (Fall 1976): 76-82.

Beam, James Michael. "I Can't Play God Any More." *McCall's,* January 1978, 100-58.

Beaven, J. "The Billy Graham I Know." *The Christian Herald,* August and September 1966.

Berg, Thomas C. "'Proclaiming Together'? Convergence and Divergence in Mainline and Evangelical Evangelism, 1945-1967." *Religion and American Culture* 5 (Winter 1995): 49-76.

"Billy Graham's Son Named Successor." *Christian Century,* 22 November 1995, 1107.

"Billy Won't Run for President." *Christian Century,* 12 February 1964, 197.

Bloesch, Donald G. "Billy Graham: A Theological Appraisal." *Theology and Life,* 3 (May 1960): 136-43.

Bloom, Harold. "Billy Graham." *Time,* 14 June 1999, 194-95.

"Book News—Harper Signs Billy Graham Autobiography 'Commonplace Book' from Uncommon Rep Book Bytes." *Publishers Weekly* 243, no. 40 (1996): 26-31.

"Born Again!" *Newsweek,* 25 October 1976, 76.

Boyd, Malcolm. "Crossroads in Mass Evangelism?" *The Christian Century,* 20 March 1957, 359-61.

Brantly, W. T. "The Common Odium." *The Christian Index,* 31 March 1832, 1.

Carnell, Edward J. "Can Billy Graham Slay the Giant?" *Christianity Today,* 13 May 1957, 3-5.

Carpenter, Joel A. Review of *A Prophet With Honor: The Billy Graham Story*, by William Martin. *Theology Today* 50, no. 3, (1993): 464.

Carroll R[odas], M. Daniel. "The Evangelical-Roman Catholic Dialogue: Issues Revolving Around Evangelization—An Evangelical View from Latin America." *Trinity Journal* 21, no. 2 (Fall 2000): 189-207.

"Case Dismissed." *Christianity Today, 27* April 1973, 37.

"A Case of Mistaken Identity." *Christian Century,* 23 March 1966, 358.

Clelland, Donald A., Thomas C. Hood, C. M. Lipsey, and Ronald Wimberley. "In the Company of the Converted: Characteristics of a Billy Graham Crusade Audience." *Sociological Analysis* 35 (Spring 1974): 45-56.

Coleman, Calmetta Y. "Luis Palau: The Next Billy Graham of Everywhere?" *Wall Street Journal*, 16 November 1995, sec. B, pp. 1, 9.

Cooke, Phil. "Star Tech: What Was Required to Produce Global Mission With Billy Graham, the World's Largest Point-to-Point Relay?" *Religious Broadcasting* 27, no. 6 (June 1995): 20.

Cornwell, Patricia. "The Romance of Ruth Bell and Billy Graham." *Good Housekeeping,* September 1997, 199-202.

Craston, Richard Colin. "Crusade Evangelism." *Churchman* 85 (Winter 1971): 263-73.

"The Design of the Gospel Magazine." *The Gospel Magazine* 1 (January 1766): 3-4.

Douglas, J. D. "Graham Alters Altar Call." *Christianity Today,* 24 June 1966, 43.

_____. "Graham's Rousing Red Welcome." *Christianity Today,* 18 August 1967, 45.

Drucker, Peter F. "The New Pluralism." *Leader to Leader* (Fall 1999): 18-23.

Drummond, Lewis A. "The Use of Scriptures in the Evangelistic Preaching of Billy Graham." *Preaching* 7 (January-February, 1992):35-39.

Duin, Julia. "Religion: Evangelist Billy Graham received the Congressional Gold Medal—After Criticizing President Clinton for His Abortion Policy." *Insight* 12, no. 21 (3 June 1996): 38.

"Edict of Nantes Revoked by Louis XIV." *The Gospel Magazine* 1 (1766): 549-50.

Escobar, Samuel. Review of *A Prophet with Honor: The Billy Graham Story*, by William Martin. *Missiology* 22 (1994): 254-55.

Eskridge, Larry. "'One Way': Billy Graham, the Jesus Generation, and the Idea of an Evangelical Youth Culture." *Church History* 67 (1998): 83-107.

"Face to Face: He has preached the Gospel to millions and has had the ear of every

President since Harry Truman. Now Billy Graham speaks candidly about his own remarkable life--and looks ahead to the hereafter." *Life*, November 1994, 104.

"Fundamentalist Revival." Editorial. *Christian Century,* 19 June 1957, 749-51.

Gaillard, Frye. "The Conversion of Billy Graham: How a Presidents' Preacher Learned to Start Worrying and Loathe the Bomb." *The Progressive* 46 (August 1982), 26-30.

Garfield, Ken. "The Last (Hometown) Crusade: Billy Graham Preaches to Record Crowd in Charlotte." *Christianity Today,* 28 October 1996, 82-83.

Gibbs, Nancy, and Richard N. Ostling. "God's Billy Pulpit: At 75, Billy Graham is America's perennial deus ex machina, sweeping in the lift up those befuddled by modernity. But what will happen to evangelism when he passes from the scene?" *Time Magazine,* 15 November 1993, 70-78.

Gilbreath, Edward. "The Lord's Crusader." *New Man,* March-April 1997, 28-31.

Gilling, Bryan D. "'Back to the Simplicities of Religion': The 1959 Billy Graham Crusade in New Zealand an its Precursors." *The Journal of Religious History* 17, no. 2 (December 1992): 222.

"Graham and King as Ghetto Mates." Editorial. *Christian Century,* 10 August 1966, 976-77.

"Graham Memo." *Christianity Today,* 26 April 1974, 50-51.

"Graham on the SBC." *Christian Century,* 20 May 1992, 536.

"Graham on the U.S." *Christian Century,* 22 April 1992, 423-24.

"Graham Regrets Remarks on AIDS." *Christian Century,* 27 October 1993, 1043.

"Graham Sets Off on Largest Crusade Ever." *Christian Century,* 22 March 1995, 322.

"Graham Wins Friends but Alienates Moslems." *Christian Century,* 17 February 1960, 180-81.

"Graham's Beliefs: Still Intact." *Christianity Today,* 13 January 1978, 49-50.

"Graham's Gospel Goes Global." *Christianity Today,* 6 March 1995, 57.

"Graham's Inaugural Role Opposed." *Christian Century,* 20 January 1993, 48-49.

"Graham's Son Subs for Dad Down Under." *Christianity Today,* 29 April 1996, 55.

"Graham's View from Japan." *Christianity Today,* 7 February 1994, 47.

Gray, James. "Expounding Scripture." *The Columbian Star,* 9 November 1822, 161.

Greene, Mark. "The Billy Graham Global Mission Sermons: The Power of Belief." *Vox Evangelica* 26 (1996): 43-46.

Gros, Jeffrey, F.S.C. "Baptism, Eucharist and Ministry." *One World* (March 1985): 11-14.

"Guardian Angel." *U. S. News and World Report,* 5 May 1997, 56-70.

H., J. "The Bible, an Affecting and Remarkable Fact." *Christian Watchman and Baptist Register,* 1 April 1820, 1.

Harrell, David Edwin, Jr. "Martin, William, A Prophet with Honor: The Billy Graham Story." *A Journal of Church and State* 35, no. 1 (Winter 1993): 170.

Hatch, Nathan, and Michael S. Hamilton. "Can Evangelicalism Survive It's Success?" *Christianity Today,* 5 October 1992, 20-31.

Hattori, Yoshiaki. "Evangelism—The Bible's Primary Message." *Evangelical Review of Theology* 12, no. 1-B (January 1998): 5.

Hayford, Jack. "Let's Learn From Billy Graham. What Is This Man's Secret? Billy Graham's Ministry Values Are Worth Studying." *Ministries Today* 13, no. 2 (March 1995): 24.

Henry, Carl F. H. "Billy Graham's Impact on New York." *Christianity Today,* 16 September 1957): 3-5.

Herendeen, Dale. "Graham Preaches Peace in Viet Nam." *Christianity Today,* 20 January 1967, 36-37.

Hirshberg, Charles. "The Eternal Crusader." *Life,* November 1994, 104-16.

Holmes, Urban T., III. "Revivals Are Un-American: A Recalling of America to Its

Pilgrimage." *Anglican Theological Review Supplemental* (1973): 58-75.

Horton, Michael S. "Evangelicals and Catholics Together: The Christian Mission and the Third Millenium—A Critical Review." *Modern Reformation,* January 1994, 22-33.

"House Endorses Honor for Grahams." *Christian Century,* 6 March 1996, 256.

Howard, Thomas. "Witness for the Faith: What Catholics Can Learn from Billy Graham." *Crisis,* April 1991, 38-41.

Howse, Christopher. "One Man's Mission." *The Tablet,* 4 August 1984, 747-48.

Hunse, Henrietta. "Mail from Mali: Billy Graham Comes to Mali." *The Banner,* 22 May 1995, 30.

"Interview: The Preacher and Politics: Billy Graham talks about his friendship with Presidents, scandals in the television ministries and how Satan tempts God's people." *Time,* 28 May 1990, 12.

Johnston, Arthur P. "Lausanne II and Missions Today and Tomorrow—A Forum." *Trinity World Forum* (Winter 1990): 1-4.

_____. "Unity and the New 'Socialized Gospel.'" *Trinity World Forum* (Winter 1995): 6-8.

Jones, E. Stanley. *"Higher* Synthesis?" *The Christian Century,* 14 August 1957, 970.

Jones, Jim. "Latino Catholics Boost Graham Crusade Attendance." *Christianity Today* 19 May 1997, 51.

Jongeneel, Jan A. B. "Open Letter [to Billy Graham] Gulf War, World Mission, and Evangelism." *Mission Studies* 8 (1991): 113-15.

Jorstad, Erling. "Two on the Right: A Comparative Look at Fundamentalism and the New Evangelicalism." *Lutheran Quarterly* 23 (May 1971): 107-17.

Kennedy, John W. "Graham Leaves His Imprint: Faithful Learn at the Cove Bible-Training Center." *Christianity Today,* 25 October 1993, 89.

_____. "Innovation Remains Billy Graham's Specialty: Indoor-outdoor event the most 'technologically complex.'" *Christianity Today,* 11 December 1995, 62.

King, Randall E. "When Worlds Collide: Politics, Religion, and Media at the 1970 East Tennessee Billy Graham Crusade." *A Journal of Church and State* 39, no. 2 (1997): 273-77.

Kirkpatrick, Melanie. "North Korea's Unlikely Messenger." *Wall Street Journal,* 7 February 1994, sec. A, p. 14.

Kuchasky, David E. "Billy Graham and Civil Religion." *Christianity Today,* 6 November 1970, 56-58.

Labarraque, Guy. "Les Soires de Louange et d'évangélisation: Quelques Points d'Analyse et de Critique." *Revue de Théologie et de Philosophy* 128 (1996): 127-48.

Lee, Helen. "Not Your Typical Graham Crusade: Toronto crowd sets record despite evangelists ailment." *Christianity Today,* 17 July 1995, 58-59.

Levy, Deborah. "God'll fix it: Deborah Levy Reviews the Transcendental Showbiz of Billy Graham." *New Statesman Society,* 24 March 24, 1995, 20.

Likoudis, Greg. "Pope St. Gregory the Great Upheld Papal Supremacy." *Christ to the World* 34 (March-April 1994): 160-62.

"Luther to Melancthon, Letter Number 1." *The Columbian Star,* 18 June 1825, 97; 25 June 1825, 101.

Lyles, Jean Caffey. "Common Ground Seen for USA Evangelicals, 'Ecumenicals.'" *Ecumenical Press Service* (March 1985): 39.

Macleod, Donald. Review of *A Prophet with Honor: The Billy Graham Story,* by William Martin. *The Princeton Seminary Bulletin* 14 (1993): 203.

Malik, Charles. "The Other Side of Evangelism." *Christianity Today,* 7 November 1980, 38-40.

"Mangling the Bible." *Latter Day Luminary* 3 (September 1822): 265-67.

Manly, Basil, Sr. "To the editor of the Wesleyan Journal." Insert. *The Columbian Star*, 5 September 1826.

Martin, William. "A Workman that Needeth Not Be Ashamed." *Christianity Today*, 13 November 1995, 18.

Marty, Martin E. "Fundamentalism as a Social Phenomenon." *Review and Expositor* 79 (1982): 19-29.

_____. "Intruders in a Crowded Center: A Review Article." *Christian Century*, 3 July 1957, 820-21.

_____. "Watergate Year as Watershed Year." *Christian Century*, 26 December 26, 1973, 1272-75.

Martyn, Henry, "Infidelity Refuted." *Christian Watchman and Baptist Register*, 22 February 1823, 44.

"Martyrs in Spain." *The Columbian Star*, 27 March 1824, 76.

McAllister, James L. "Evangelical Faith and Billy Graham." *Social Action*, 19, no. 5 (March 1953): 3-36.

"A Mighty City Hears Billy's Mighty Call." *Life*, 27 May 1957, 20-27.

M'ilvaine, C. P., "Address to American Bible Society," *The Columbian Star*, 25 June 1825, 101.

Morgan, Timothy C. "From One City to the World: Billy Graham's Most Ambitious Crusade Transcends Racial, Cultural, and Class Barriers, as well as Time Zones." *Christianity Today*, 24 April 1995, 41-43.

Morris, Lee. "Projecting Pastoral Care in Revival Preaching: Billy Graham." *Pastoral Psychology* 19 (June 1968): 33-41.

Myra, Harold. "What Billy Graham Needs." *Christianity Today*, 9 November 1992, 13.

Neff, David. "'Personal Evangelism on a Mass Scale': Europeans to participate electronically in [Germany] crusade." *Christianity Today*, 8 March 1993, 64, 66.

_____. "ProChrist '93 Unifies European Evangelism." *Christianity Today*, 26 April 1993, 48, 58.

Neff, David, ed. "Fifty Years with Billy Graham." *Christianity Today*, 13 November 1995, 18-34.

Niebuhr, Gustav. "Choice of Billy Graham's Son as Successor May Signal Both Continuity and Change: Bringing an informal style to an organization built on formalities." *New York Times*, 26 November 1995, sec. I, p. 14.

_____. "Following Father's Path, on a Wing and a Prayer: Billy Graham's son has recently turned to preaching too." *New York Times*, 12 October 1994, sec. B, p. 6.

_____. "Graham Plans to Tell a Billion about Jesus." *New York Times*, 11 March 1995, 15.

_____. "Instilling Unity When a Leader is Absent." *New York Times*, 24 June 1995, 25.

_____. "New Voices for Jesus in Stadium Crusades: Is Billy Graham too Hard an Act to Follow?" *New York Times*, 7 August 1994, 10.

Niebuhr, Reinhold. "After Comment, the Deluge." *Christian Century*, 4 November 1957, 1034-35.

_____. "Billy Graham's Christianity and the World Crisis." *Christian and Society* (Spring 1955): 3-4.

_____. "Literalism, Individualism, and Billy Graham." *Christian Century*, 23 May 1956, 641-42.

_____. "Proposal to Billy Graham." *Christian Century*, 8 August 1956, 921-22.

Northcott, Cecil. "The Graham Crusade: Abdication of Evangelism." *Christian Century*, 25 May 1966, 673-75.

Olson, Ted. "Lutheran, Catholic, and Black Churches Join Crusade Effort: Crusade's Final Event Draws 95,000." *Christianity Today*, 15 July 1996, 67.

"Opposition to the Scriptures." *The Columbian Star*, 17 September 1825, 151.

Pannenberg, Wolfhart. "Christianity and the West: Ambiguous Past, Uncertain Future." *First Things,* December 1994, 18-23.

_____. "The Present and Future Church." *First Things,* November 1991, 48-51.

Perry, James M. "Can't Get Enough of a Book? Buy a CD-ROM." *Wall Street Journal,* 23 May 23, 1994, sec. B, pp. 1, 6.

Pierard, Richard V. "From Evangelical Exclusivism to Ecumenical Openness: Billy Graham and Sociopolitical Issues," *Journal of Ecumenical Studies* 20, no. 3 (Summer, 1983): 425-46.

_____. Review of *Religion and the New Majority,* by L. D. Streiker and G. S. Strober. *Fides and Historia* 5 (Fall-Spring 1972-1973): 127-31.

"A Plea for More Coverage of Religion: The Rev. Billy Graham complains to the American Society of Newspaper Editors that religion news is 'relegated' to a few columns Saturdays." *Editor and Publisher* 127, no. 18 (30 April 1994): 22.

Plowman, Edward E. "Relations Improve Between Church and State in Hungary: Evangelistic Services," *Christianity Today,* 22 November 1985, 64-66.

Pollock, John. "One Man's Furrow." *Christianity Today,* 13 September 1974, 14-21.

Rabey, Steve. "Ecumenical Dialogue: Conversation or Competition?" *Christianity Today,* 7 September 1998, 22.

Randall, Ian M. "Conservative Constructionist: The Early Influence of Billy Graham in Britain." *The Evangelical Quarterly* 67 (October 1995): 309-33.

Read, David H. C. "The Real Billy Graham." *The Atlantic,* September 1957, 42-45.

"The Return and Rise of the Prodigal Son—Franklin Graham was born to be born again—and to inherit the Evangelical kingdom of his father Billy. It was an overwhelming fate for the Grahams' first-born son and he rebelled against it." *Time* 13 May 1996, 66-76.

"Reverend Billy Graham and Ruth Bell—Crusade after Crusade, He Always Returned to Her Waiting Arms." *People Weekly,* 12 February 1996, 155.

Rice, Chris. "Billy Graham and Martin King: The Road Not Traveled." *Sojourners,* 1 January 1998, 13.

Rosell, Garth M. "Grace Under Fire." *Christianity Today,* 13 November 1995, 30.

Rowland, Stanley. "As Billy Graham Sees His Role: Bringing His Crusade to New York." *The New York Times Magazine,* 21 April 1957, 17-25.

Runia, Klaas. "When Is Separation a Christian Duty?" Part I. *Christianity Today,* 23 June 1967, 3-5.

_____. "When Is Separation a Christian Duty?" Part II. *Christianity Today,* 7 July 1967, 6-8.

"Silencing Graham's Daughter Regretted." *Christian Century,* 24 February 1993, 201-02.

Smart, Judith. "The Evangelist as Star: The Billy Graham Crusade in Australia, 1959." *Journal of Popular Culture* 33 (1999): 165-77.

Smith, C. Ralston. "Billy Graham's Evangelistic Thrust: The Crusaders in Changing Times." *Christianity Today,* 10 November 1961, 3-7.

Smylie, James Hutchinson. "On understanding Billy: Frady's Graham and Graham's friends." *Presbyterian Outlook,* 9 June 1980, 7-8.

Soares-Prabhu, G. M., SJ. "Missiology or Missiologies?" *Mission Studies,* 6 (May 1969): 85-87.

"Soft Sell and Satellites Deliver Biggest Audience." *Christianity Today,* 18 August 1989, 48-49.

Speers, Archer, "Billy Graham's 'Invasion,' His Mission, 'Save New York.'" *Newsweek,* 20 May 1957, 66-70.

Stackhouse, John G., Jr. "Billy Graham and the Nature of Conversion: A Paradigm Case." *Studies in Religion/Sciences Religieuses* 21 (1992): 337-50.

_____. "The Compleat Billy Graham." *Christianity Today,* 10 February 1992, 70-73.

Ternisien, Xavier. "Adoption définitive par les députés de la loi anti-sectes." *Le Monde,* 31 May 2001. Accessed 11 July 2002. Available from http://membres.lycos.fr/tussier/rev0105.htm#3a. Internet.

Terry, John Mark. "Billy Graham's Contribution to World Evangelism." *Baptist History and Heritage* 30 (January 1995): 5-13.

Thorkelson, Willmar. "Billy Graham advised Reagan on Vatican ties." *National Catholic Reporter,* 16 March 1984, 4.

Unity. "On the Union of Different Denominations." *The Christian Index* (23 July 1831): 1.

Van Biema, David. "In the Name of the Father." *Time,* 13 May 1996, 66-75.

Wacker, Grant. "'Charles Atlas with a Halo': America's Billy Graham." *The Christian Century,* 1 April 1992, 336-41.

Wark, Andrew. "Graham Visits President Kim." *Christianity Today,* 7 March 1994, 55.

Waterman. "Bible Society," and "American Tract Society." *The Columbian Star,* 2 July 1825, 105.

Weigel, G., S.J. "What to Think of Billy Graham." *America,* 4 May 1957, 161-64.

Welsh, Bishop Lawrence. "Catholics and a Billy Graham Crusade." *National Catholic Reporter,* 2 September 1982, 185-86.

Wooding, Dan. "Now! Global Mission With Billy Graham Was Seen by 1 Billion People. Discover the Human Factor in This Worldwide Evangelistic Effort." *Religious Broadcasting* 27, no. 6 (June 1995): 14.

"A Word for the Bible." *The Columbian Star,* 29 April 1826, 65-66.

Wörle, Wilhelm. "Billy Graham in Deutschland." *Der Gärtner,* 11 July 1954, 434.

Yoder, Bill, and Wolfgang Polzer. "Graham Preaches at Berlin Wall." *Christianity Today,* 9 April 1990, 59.

Young, Pete. "Trading Absolution for Support." *Christianity and Crisis,* 9 June 1969, 162-66.

Zoba, Wendy Murray. "Billy's Rib." *Christianity Today,* 13 November 1995, 28.

Published Monographs

Ahlstrom, Sydney E. "Introduction to the Reprinted Edition." In *The Vicarious Sacrifice Grounded in Principles of Universal Obligation,* by Horace Bushnell. Hicksville, NY: Regina Press, 1975.

Bonnell, John Sutherland. "Billy Graham." In *Thirteen for Christ,* ed. Melville Harcourt. New York: Sheed and Ward, 1963.

Campbell, Will D., and J. Y. Holloway. "An open letter to Billy Graham." In *The Failure and the Hope; Essays of Southern Churchmen,* ed. Will D. Campbell. Grand Rapids, Eerdmans, 1972.

Carson, Donald A. "Evangelicals, Ecumenism and the Church." In *Evangelical Affirmations*, ed. Kenneth S. Kantzer and Carl F. H. Henry. Grand Rapids: Zondervan, 1990.

Cooper, William. "Preface." In *The Distinguishing Marks of a Work of the Spirit of God,* by Jonathan Edwards. Edinburgh: Banner of Truth, 1999.

Demaray, Donald E. "Billy Graham, Authoritative Preacher." In *Pulpit Giants; What Made Them Great,* ed. Donald E. Demaray. Chicago: Moody, 1973.

Fishwick, Marshall. "The Blessing of Billy." In *The God Pumpers: Religion in the Electronic Age,* ed. Marshall Fishwick and Ray B. Browne. Bowling Green, OH: Bowling Green State University Popular Press, 1987.

Harrell, David Edwin, Jr. "American Revivalism from Graham to Robertson." In *Modern Christian Revivals*, ed. Edith L. Blumhofer and Randall Balmer. Urbana, IL: University of Illinois Press, 1993.

Latourette, Kenneth Scott. "Ecumenical Bearings of the Missionary Movement and the

International Missionary Council." In *A History of the Ecumenical Movement 1517-1948*, ed. Ruth Rouse and Stephen Charles Neill. London: SPCK, 1954.

Linder, Robert D. "The Resurgence of Evangelical Social Concern (1925-1975)." In *The Evangelicals: What They Believe, Who They Are, Where They Are Going*, ed. David F. Wells and John D. Woodbridge. Grand Rapids: Zondervan, 1977.

Lippy, Charles H. "Billy Graham." In *Twentieth Century Shapers of American Popular Religion*, ed. Charles H. Lippy. New York: Greenwood Press, 1989.

_____. "Southern Revivalism and Billy Graham." In *Bibliography of Religion in the South*. Macon, GA: Mercer University Press, 1986 (1985).

Luther, Martin. "Pagan Servitude of the Church," In *Martin Luther: Selections from His Writings*, ed. John Dillenberger. Garden City, NY: Doubleday, 1961.

Marsden, George M. "Unity in Diversity in Evangelical Resurgence." In *Altered Landscapes: Christianity in America, 1935-1985*, ed. David W. Lotz. Grand Rapids: Eerdmans, 1989.

Martin, William. "Billy Graham." In *Varieties of Southern Evangelicalism*, ed. David E. Harrell, Jr. Macon, GA: Mercer University Press, 1981.

Niebuhr, Reinhold. "Explore God's Word." In *1966 Annual of the North American Baptist General Conference*. Chicago: North American Baptist General Conference, 1966.

Silk, Mark. "The Rise of the 'New Evangelicalism': Shock and Adjustment." In *Between the Times: The Travail of the Protestant Establishment in America, 1900-1960*, ed. William R. Hutchison. Cambridge, England: University Press, 1989.

Spurgeon, Charles H. "Soul-Saving Our One Business." In *The Soul-Winner*, by Charles H. Spurgeon. Grand Rapids: Eerdmans, 1963.

Venable, James Wayne. "Billygrahamism and America." In *Church and State Relations: Christian Ethics 97D*. Louisville: Southern Baptist Theological Seminary, 1974.

Williams, George H., and Rodney L. Petersen. "The Evangelicals: Society, the State, the Nation (1925-1975)." In *The Evangelicals: What They Believe, Who They Are, Where They Are Going*, ed. David F. Wells and John D. Woodbridge. Grand Rapids: Zondervan, 1977.

**Creeds, Decrees, Conference Papers,
and Ecclesiatical Items**

Amsterdam '83, International Conference for Itinerant Evangelists: Program Notebook. Minneapolis: World Wide, 1983.

Amsterdam 2000, Conference for Preaching Evangelists: Program Notebook. Minneapolis: Billy Graham Evangelistic Association, 2000.

An Exposition from the Faculty of the Southern Baptist Theological Seminary on the Baptist Faith and Message 2000. Louisville: The Southern Baptist Theological Seminary, 2000.

Baptism, Eucharist and Ministry. Faith and Order Paper, no. 111. Geneva: World Council of Churches, 1982.

Baptist Faith and Message: A Statement Adopted by the Southern Baptist Convention. Nashville: The Sunday School Board of the Southern Baptist Convention, 1963, 2000.

Bettenson, Henry, ed. *Documents of the Christian Church*. 2nd ed. London: Oxford University Press, 1963.

The Bible: Its Authority and Interpretation in the Ecumenical Movement. Faith and Order Paper, no. 99. Geneva: WCC, 1980.

Catechism of the Catholic Church. Mahwah, NJ: Paulist, 1994.

Commission Biblique Pontificale. *L'Interprétation de la Bible dans l'Eglise*. Montréal: Fides, 1994.

Conciliorum Oecumenicorum Decreta. Bologna, Italy: Instituto per le Scienze Religiose, 1973.

Dominus Iesus: Declaration on the Unicity and Salvific Universality of Jesus Christ and the Church. Rome: Vatican, 2000.

Douglas, J. D., ed. *Let the Earth Hear His Voice: International Congress on World Evangelization, Lausanne, Switzerland, Official Reference Volume.* Foreword by Billy Graham. Minneapolis: World Wide, 1975.

_____. *Proclaim Christ Until He Comes: Calling the Whole Church to Take the Whole Gospel to the Whole World, Lausanne II in Manila, International Congress on World Evangelization.* Minneapolis: World Wide, 1990.

_____. *The Calling of an Evangelist: The Second International Congress for Itinerant Evangelists, Amsterdam, The Netherlands.* Minneapolis: World Wide, 1987.

_____. *The Work of an Evangelist: International Congress for Itinerant Evangelists, Amsterdam, The Netherlands.* Minneapolis: World Wide, 1984.

Drummond, Lewis A., gen. ed. *Biblical Affirmations for Evangelism: NACIE 94, North American Conference for Itinerant Evangelists.* Minneapolis: World Wide, 1996.

Ecumenical Missionary Conference—New York, 1900: Report of the Ecumenical Conference on Foreign Missions, Held in Carnegie Hall and Neighboring Churches, April 21 to May 1. Vol. 1. New York: American Tract Society, 1900.

Escobar, Samuel. "The Social Responsibility of the Church." In CLADE (Latin American Congress on Evangelism) paper. Bogota, 1969. reproduced.

The Evangelistic Work of the Church: Being the Report of the Archbishop's Third Committee of Inquiry. London: SPCK, 1918.

Henry, Carl F. H., and W. Stanley Mooneyham, eds. *One Race, One Gospel, One Task: World Congress on Evangelism, Berlin, 1966, Official Reference Volumes: Papers and Reports.* 2 vols. Minneapolis: World Wide, 1967.

John Paul II. *Apostolic Letter Tertio Millenio Adveniente of His Holiness Pope John Paul II, to the Bishops, Clergy, and the Lay Faithful on Preparation for the Jubilee of the Year 2000.* Vatican City: Libreria Editrice Vaticana, 1994.

_____. *Celebrate 2000! Reflections on Jesus, the Holy Spirit, and the Father—A Three-Year Reader.* Ann Arbor, MI: Servant Publications, 1996.

_____. "Mexico Ever Faithful." *Osservatore Romano,* 5 February 1979, 1.

_____. *Redemptoris Mater: Encyclical on the Blessed Virgin Mary in the Life of the Pilgrim Church, March 25, 1987* [on-line]. Accessed 15 June 2000. Available from http://www.knight.org/advent/docs/ jp02rm.htm; Internet.

Johnston, James. *Report on the Centenary Conference on Protestant Missions of the World Held in Exeter Hall (June 9-19), London, 1888.* Vol. 1. London: James Nisbet, 1888; New York: Revell, 1888.

Joint Declaration on the Doctrine of Justification: The Lutheran World Federation and the Roman Catholic Church. English Language ed. Grand Rapids: Eerdmans, 2000.

Kinnamon, Michael, and Brian E. Cope, eds. *The Ecumenical Movement: An Anthology of Key Texts and Voices.* Geneva: WCC; Grand Rapids: Eerdmans, 1997.

Kirby, Gilbert W., ed. *Evangelism Alert: Official Reference Volume, European Congress on Evangelism, Amsterdam, 1971.* London: World Wide, 1972.

Leith, John H., ed. *Creeds of the Churches: A Reader in Christian Doctrine from the Bible to the Present.* 3rd ed. Atlanta: John Knox Press, 1982.

Leo XIII. *Apostolicae Curae: On the Anglican Orders,* 13 September 1896. *The Great Encyclical Letters of Pope Leo XIII.* New York: Benzinger Brothers, 1903.

_____. *Provendissimus Deus: On the Study of Holy Scripture.* 18 November 1893. *The Great Encyclical Letters of Pope Leo XIII.* New York: Benzinger Brothers, 1903.

Lumen Gentium. Decrees of Vatican II. Rome, 1965.

Lumpkin, William L. *Baptist Confessions of Faith.* Rev. ed. Valley Forge: Judson Press, 1969.

Luther, Martin. *Martin Luther's Larger Catechism* [on-line]. Accessed 19 October 2001. Available from http://www.iclnet.org/pub/resources/ text/wittenberg/wittenberg-luther.html#sw-lc.

_____. *Smalcald Articles* [on-line]. Accessed 11 October 2001. Available from http://www.frii.com/~gosplow/smalcald.html#smc-03h.

[Madras] Tambaram Series. 7 vols. London: Oxford University Press, 1939.

Message, Messenger, Methods: Program Notebook for NACIE 94. Minneapolis: NACIE 94, 1994.

Messages and Findings of the Fifth Annual Conference, Evangelical Literature Overseas, Lincoln, Nebraska, December 10-13, 1956. Wheaton, IL: Evangelical Literature Overseas, 1956.

Mooneyham, W. Stanley, ed. *Christ Seeks Asia: Official Reference Volume, Asia-Pacific Congress on Evangelism, Singapore 1968.* Hong Kong: The Rock House, 1969.

Norgren, W., ed. *The Meanings and Practices of Conversion: Papers from the National Faith and Order Colloquium.* Indianapolis: Council on Christian Unity, 1969.

Orchard, Ronald K. *The Ghana Assembly of the International Missionary Council, December 28, 1957 to January 8, 1958.* London: Edinburgh House, 1958.

Paul VI. *Ecclesiam Suam: On the Paths of the Church.* 6 August 1964 [on-line]. Accessed 15 July 2001. Available from http://www.ewtn.com/ library/ENCYC/ P6ECCLES.HTM; Internet.

_____. *Evangelii Nuntiandi: On Evangelization in the Modern World,* 8 December 1975 [on-line]. Accessed 16 July 2001. Available from http://listserv.american.edu/catholic/church/papal/paul.vi/p6evang.txt; Internet.

Pius XI. *Mortalium Animos: On Religious Unity.* 6 January 1928 [on-line]. Accessed 15 July 2001. Available from http://www.ewtn.com/library/ ENCYC/ P11MORTA.HTM; Internet.

Pius XII. *Divino Afflante Spiritu: On Promoting Biblical Studies.* 30 September 1943 [on-line]. Accessed 15 July 2001. Available from http://www.ewtn.com/library/ ENCYC/P12DIVIN.HTM; Internet.

Ranson, C. W., ed. *Renewal and Advance: Christian Witness in a Revolutionary World* [Whitby 1947 Messages and Findings]. London: Edinburgh House, 1948.

Report of the Jerusalem Meeting of the I. M. C. [International Missionary Council], March 24th-April 8th, 1928. London: Oxford University Press, 1928.

Schaff, Philip. *Creeds of Christendom with a History and Critical Notes.* 3 vols. 4th rev. ed. New York: Harper and Brothers, 1877, 1905, 1919.

"Secularization and Conversion." *Study Encounter,* Vol. 1, No. 2. Geneva: WCC, 1965.

Stott, John R. W., ed. *Making Christ Known: Historic Mission Documents from the Lausanne Movement, 1974-1989.* Grand Rapids: Eerdmans, 1996.

Ward, Charles G., ed. *Equipping for Evangelism, NACIE 94, North American Conference for Itinerant Evangelists.* Minneapolis: World Wide, 1996.

Wilson, George M., ed. *Evangelism Now: U.S. Congress on Evangelism, Minneapolis, 1969, Official Reference Volume: Papers and Reports.* Minneapolis: World Wide, 1970.

World Congress on Evangelism. "Study Papers: World Congress on Evangelism, 26 October-4 November 1966." 2 vols. Berlin: mimeographed.

World Missionary Conference, Edinbugh, 1910. Vols 1-4. Edinburgh: Oliphant, Anderson and Ferrier, 1910; New York: Revell, 1910.

Published Speeches, Sermons,
and Scholarly Papers

Caillouet, Larry Martin. "A Digest of Findings in the Media Survey for the Northern Alberta Billy Graham Crusade." Presented at the sixty-ninth annual meeting of the Speech Communication Association. Washington, DC: Speech Communication Association, 1983.

Caneday, Ardel B. "The Role of Billy Graham's Cooperative Evangelism in the Division of Evangelicals in the 1950s." Paper presented at the Midwestern Regional meeting of the Evangelical Theological Society, St. Paul, MN, March 16-18, 1995.

Davis, Jimmy Thomas. "John Clark, Billy Graham and Baptist Trends toward Cultural Legitimacy." Paper presented at the Annual Meeting of the Speech Communication Association, Boston, MA, November 5-8, 1987.

Foster, J. M. "Rome, the Antagonist of the Nation." In In *The Fundamentals,* eds. R. A. Torrey, A.C. Dixon, et al. Grand Rapids: Baker, 1998, 3:301-314.

Herbert, A. G. "Translator's Preface." In *Christus Victor: An Historical Study of the Three Main Types of the Idea of the Atonement,* by Gustav Aulén. 1930; New York: Macmillan, 1969.

Johnson, Franklin. "The Atonement." In *The Fundamentals: A Testimony of Truth,* ed. R. A. Torrey and others. 1917; reprint Grand Rapids: Baker, 1998.

MacDonald, Gordon. *Billy Graham, 1982: Prospects for New England.* Boston, MA: Sturbridge Continuation Committee, Evangelistic Association of New England, 1981.

Medhurst, T. W. "Is Romanism Christianity?" In *The Fundamentals,* eds. R. A. Torrey, A.C. Dixon, et al. Grand Rapids: Baker, 1998, 3:288-300.

Overstreet, R. Larry. "Billy Graham's Sermonic Reasoning: A Critique." Paper Presented at the Midwest Meeting of the Evangelical Theological Society on March 22-23, 1991. Evangelical Theological Society papers, ETS-0215.

Pierce, Bob. "Commissioned to Communicate." In *One Race, One Gospel, One Task,* ed. Carl F. H. Henry and Stanley Mooneyham. Minneapolis: World Wide Publications, 1967.

Rees, Paul S. "Evangelism and Social Concern." In *One Race, One Gospel, One Task,* ed. Carl F. H. Henry and Stanley Mooneyham. Minneapolis: World Wide Publications, 1967.

Speer, Robert E. "The Supreme and Determining Aim." In *Ecumenical Missionary Conference New York 1900, Report of the Ecumenical Conference on Foreign Missions Held in New York, April 1900.* Vol. 1. New York: American Tract Society, 1900.

Taylor, A. J. P. "Introduction." In *The Communist Manifesto.* New York: Penguin, 1967.

Taylor, J. Hudson, "The Source of Power." In *Ecumenical Missionary Conference New York 1900, Report of the Ecumenical Conference on Foreign Missions Held in New York, April 1900.* Vol. 1. New York: American Tract Society, 1900.

Visser 't Hooft, W. A. "Our Ecumenical Task in the Light of History." Inaugural Address of the John Knox House Lectureship. Geneva: John Knox House, 1955.

_____. "The Task of the World Council of Churches." Report Presented on Behalf of the Provisional Committee, The First Assembly of the World Council of Churches, Amsterdam, August 22-September 4, 1948.

Wesley, John. "Free Grace." Sermon no 128 [on-line]. Accessed 26 October 2001. Available at http://gbgm-umc.org/umhistory/wesley/ sermons/serm-128.stm; Internet.

Dissertations, Theses, and Doctoral Essays

Adams, John Marion. "The Making of a Neo-Evangelical Statesman: The Case of Harold John Ockenga." Ph.D. diss., Baylor University, 1994.

Adkerson, Sonya Jeanne. "A Comparative Analysis of Selected Sermons of Jonathan Edwards and Billy Graham." M.A. thesis, Southern Illinois University, Dept. of Speech, 1964.

Apel, William Dale. "The Understanding of Salvation in the Evangelistic Message of Billy Graham: A Historical-Theological Evaluation." Ph.D. diss., Northwestern University, 1975.

Appenzeller, Karl. "Das problem der Bodenständigkeit von Christentum und Kirche auf dem Missionsfeld in den Verhandlungen der Weltmissionskonferenz zu Edinburgh (1910)." Inaugural-Dissertation zur Erlangung des Doktorgrades einer Hohen Evangelisch-Theologischen Fakultät der Eberhard-Karls-Universität zu Tübingen, 1940.

Auchmuty, James Adair. "The Concept of Revelation in the Thought of Five Contemporary Southern Baptists: Billy Graham, Roland Q. Leavell, R. G. Lee, Carlyle Marney, and Eric C. Rust." Th.M. essay, Southeastern Baptist Theological Seminary, 1961.

Baird, John Edward. "The Preaching of William Franklin Graham." Ph.D. thesis, Columbia University, 1959.

Baker, Rodney. "The Impact of Prayer on the Ministries of D. L. Moody, C. H. Spurgeon, and Billy Graham: A Descriptive Study." D.Min. thesis, Liberty Baptist Theological Seminary, 1999.

Barrett, Daniel Arthur. "A Rhetorical Analysis of a Series of Sermons by Dr. William Franklin (Billy) Graham." M.A. thesis, University of Hawaii (Honolulu), 1961.

Bettermann, James A. "The Preaching of Billy Graham: A Lutheran Theological Analysis." M.Div. thesis, Concordia Theological Seminary, Ft. Wayne, 1983.

Bond, Wayne Stanley. "The Rhetoric of Billy Graham: A Description, Analysis, and Evaluation." Ph.D. diss. Southern Illinois University at Carbondale, 1973.

Bowers, G. "An Evaluation of the Billy Graham Greater Louisville Evangelistic Crusade." M.A. thesis, The Southern Baptist Theological Seminary, 1958.

Boyce, Rudolph Harding. "Four Speeches of Billy Graham Delivered in Detroit, 1953." M.A. thesis, Wayne University, 1954.

Breznen, Michael A. "Eschatology and the Preacher: A Comparison of the Doctrine of Eschatology in the Preaching of Bultmann and Graham." B.D. thesis, Concordia Theological Seminary, Springfield, IL, 1969.

Brown, Darlene Novakovich. "Audience and Speaker Perceptions of the Arizona Billy Graham Crusade." M.A. thesis, Arizona State University, 1976.

Bruce, David Phillips. "A Program to Evaluate the Effectiveness of the Follow-up Activity of the Spokane, Washington, Billy Graham Crusade." D.Min. essay, Louisville: The Southern Baptist Theological Seminary, 1986.

Burkhead, Howell Walker. "The Development of the Concept of Sin in the Preaching of Billy Graham." Ph.D. diss., Southwestern Baptist Theological Seminary, 1998.

Butler, Farley Porter, Jr. "Billy Graham and the End of Evangelical Unity." Ph.D. diss., University of Florida, 1976.

Butterfield, Ronald Paul. "An Evaluation for Churches of Christ of the Evangelistic Methods of Billy Graham." M.A. thesis, Harding College Graduate School of Religion, 1966.

Caldwell, Carole. "Coverage of Billy Graham in the Charlotte Observer and the New York Times." M.A. thesis, University of North Carolina at Chapel Hill, 1992.

Carpenter, Jean Leroy. "Billy Graham—A Good Man Speaking Well; an Analysis of the Persuasive Style of the Twentieth Century's Leading Evangelist." M.A. thesis,

Chico State College, 1969.

Carpenter, Joel Allan. "The Renewal of American Fundamentalism, 1930-1945." Ph.D. diss., The John's Hopkins University, 1984.

Cheeley, Michael C. "A Rhetorical Analysis of Two Sermons Delivered by Billy Graham in the 1961 Upper Midwest Crusade." M.S. thesis, St. Cloud State College, 1970.

Coleman, Hubert H. "A Comparative Rhetorical Analysis of Speeches of Stokely Carmichael and Billy Graham." M.A. thesis, Bowling Green State University, 1970.

Crim, Louie Alvah. "A Rhetorical Analysis of the Preaching of Billy Graham in the Indianapolis, Indiana crusade, October 6 through November 1, 1959." A.M. thesis, Indiana University, 1961.

Cruz, Ernesto Montalbo. "An Evaluation of Decisions Made at the All-Philippines Billy Graham Crusade Held March 10 to 17, 1963 in Manila, Philippines." M.R.E. thesis, Conservative Baptist Theological Seminary, 1965.

Dalhouse, Mark Taylor. "Bob Jones University and the Shaping of Twentieth Century Separatism, 1926-1991." Ph.D. diss., Miami University, 1991.

Davis, Larry Joe. "Interpretation of Scripture in the Evangelistic Preaching of William Franklin 'Billy' Graham." Ph.D. diss., Louisville: The Southern Baptist Theological Seminary, 1986.

Day, Danny R. "The Political Billy Graham: Graham and Politics from the Presidency of Harry S. Truman through the Presidency of Lyndon Baines Johnson." M.A. thesis, Wheaton College, 1996.

Day, John Daniel. "Comparison of the Understandings of Guilt in Biblical Thought and in Representative Contemporary American Protestant Proclamation." Th.D. diss., Southwestern Baptist Theological Seminary, 1973.

Delnay, Robert George. "A History of Baptist Bible Union." Th.D. essay, Dallas Theological Seminary, 1963; Winston-Salem, NC: Piedmont Bible College Press, 1974.

De Sousa, Walter. "Billy Graham, the Controversy over Cooperative Evangelism." M.A. thesis, Trinity Evangelical Divinity School, 1979.

Dickinson, Cyril Loren. "The Billy Graham Crusades: An Analysis of Crusade Organization." Ph.D. diss., University of Denver, 1968.

Dirkens, A. "The New Testament Concept of Metanoia." S.T.D. diss., Catholic University of America, 1932.

Drum, Starla Banta. "The Anti-Communist Rhetoric of Billy Graham in the Early 1950's." M.A. thesis, University of Oregon, 1970.

Dullea, Carolo W., S.J. "'W. F. "Billy" Graham's Decision for Christ': A Study in Conversion." Dissertatione ad Lauream, Pontificiae Universitatis Gregorianae, 1971; published as Charles W. Dullea, S.J. *A Catholic Looks at Billy Graham.* New York: Paulist, 1973.

Earl, Elizabeth Noel. "A Comparison of Billy Graham and Jerry Falwell: Ministers and their Presidents." Ph.D. diss., Ohio University, 1991.

French, James Wilford. "Billy Graham's Role in the Civil Rights Movement." M.A. thesis, California State University, Fullerton, 1975.

Garvin, Karen Jeannine. "A Rhetorical Study of Selected Crusade Speeches of William Graham." M.S. thesis, Mankato State College, 1975 [?].

_____. "Billy Graham in 1967: A Further Study of Adaptation to Audiences." Ph.D. diss., University of Minnesota, 1972.

Girtman, Harry Spruiell. "The Preaching of William Frank 'Billy' Graham." M.A. thesis, The Southern Baptist Theological Seminary, 1955.

Grist, Walter R. "Evangelism in India: Comparison of Evangelism Related to the People Movements before 1947 and Campaign Evangelism Related to Billy Graham Evangelistic Association from 1967-1977." D.Min. thesis, Bethel Theological

Seminary, 1979.

Gyi, Maung. "A Comparative Study of the Principles of Suggestion and Techniques of Persuasion Employed by Evangelist Billy Graham during His Crusades." M.A. thesis, University of Maryland, 1965.

Haas, Frederick William. "A Case Study of the Speech Situation Factors Involved in the Radio Preaching on the Hour of Decision Broadcast." Ph.D. diss., University of Wisconsin, 1964.

Hamilton, John Robert. "An Historical Study of Bob Pierce and World Vision's Development of the Evangelical Social Action Film." Ph.D. diss., University of Southern California, 1980.

Hangin, Tona J. "Redeeming the Dial: Evangelical Radio and Religious Culture, 1920-1960." Ph.D. diss., Brandeis University, 1999.

Hankins, Barry. "Billy Graham and American Nationalism." M.A. thesis, Baylor University, 1983.

Hedstrom, James Alden. "Evangelical Program in the United States, 1945-1980: The Morphology of Establishment, Progressive, and Radical Platforms." Ph.D. diss., Vanderbilt University, 1982.

Hempy, Robert W. "A Comparative Study of Selected Revivals in America." B.D. thesis, Western Evangelical Seminary, 1960.

Hill, Jonathan Yates. "World Wide Pictures Putting the Gospel on the Big Screen." M.A. thesis, University of North Carolina at Greensboro, 1991.

Hopkins, Jerry Berl. "Billy Graham and the Race Problem, 1949-1969." Ph.D. diss., University of Kentucky, 1986.

Horton, O. Charles. "An Analysis of Selected Sermons of Billy Graham." Th.M. essay, New Orleans Baptist Theological Seminary, 1967.

Hulse, Cy. "The Shaping of a Fundamentalist: A Case Study of Charles Blanchard." M.A. thesis, Trinity Evangelical Divinity School, 1977.

Hurst, Gayle A. "An Analog Criticism of Dwight Moody and Billy Graham." M.A. thesis, University of Kansas, Speech and Drama, 1971.

Jessee, Virginia Lee. "Some Elements of Drama in the Evangelistic Crusades of Dr. Billy Graham." M.S. thesis, East Texas State University, 1969.

Kennedy, Robert L. "Best Intentions: Contacts Between German Pietists and Anglo-American Evangelicals, 1945-1954." Ph.D. diss., University of Aberdeen, 1990.

Knippers, Michael Allen. "A Rhetorical Analysis of Selected Billy Graham Sermons." M.S. thesis, University of Southern Mississippi, 1967.

Kvam, Roger A. "Evaluating Mass Evangelism: A Case Study of the 1982 Billy Graham Crusade in Boston, Massachusetts." D.Min. project report. Boston University, 1984.

Lacour, Lawrence Leland. "A Study of the Revival Methods in America: 1920-1955, with Special Reference to Billy Sunday, Aimee Semple McPherson and Billy Graham." Ph.D. diss., Northwestern University, 1956.

Larson, Richard Earl. "The Billy Graham Upper Midwest Crusade; A Study of Mass Religious Persuasion." M.A. thesis, University of Minnesota, 1967.

Lawson, Steven J. "Billy Graham and Crusade Follow Up." D.Min. thesis, Reformed Theological Seminary, 1990.

Lee, Young Han. "The Matter of the Past Great Awakenings in America and Future Awakening: Renewed Preacher and Renewed Preaching." D.Min. thesis, Columbia Theological Seminary, 1995.

Lockard, William David. "The Place of Ethics in the Evangelistic Ministry of Billy Graham." Ph.D. diss., Southwestern Baptist Theological Seminary, 1968.

Loucks, Clarence Melvin. "Mass Evangelistic Methodology: Charles Grandison Finney and William Franklin Graham." Th.M. thesis, Fuller Theological Seminary, 1973.

Lucas, Willis. "The Relevancy of Billy Graham's Evangelistic Ministry to Our Age."

B.D. thesis, Northern Baptist Theological Seminary, 1962.

Martin, Carey Lee. "An Examination of the Rhetorical Messages of Rev. Billy Graham and Rev. Jerry Falwell, as Manifested in Public Speaking and Television." Ph.D. diss., The Florida State University, 1997.

McCready, William P. "Struggles: Three Studies in Twentieth Century American Religious History." B.A. thesis, Linfield College, 1989.

Miller, Nicole H. "The Political-Religious Discourse of Billy Graham at the Presidential Prayer Breakfasts of the 1960s." M.A. thesis, Colorado State University, 1998.

Moore, Edward Lee. "Billy Graham and Martin Luther King, Jr.: An Inquiry into White and Black Revivalistic Traditions." Ph.D. diss., Vanderbilt University, 1979.

Moore, Howard Edgar. "The Emergence of Moderate Fundamentalism: John R. Rice and 'The Sword of the Lord.'" Ph.D. diss., The George Washington University, 1990.

Morris, Aubrey Leon. "A Study of the Psychological Factors in the Evangelistic Preaching of Billy Graham." Th.D. diss., The Southern Baptist Theological Seminary, 1966.

Newbill, James Guy. "The Theology of Billy Graham, Its Practical Applications, and Its Relative Position in the Contemporary Religious Scene." M.A. thesis, University of Washington, 1960.

Nickerson, Melvin Roy. "An Analytical Study of Selected Sermons of Billy Graham from the San Francisco Crusade of 1958 with Reference to Techniques of Persuasion: a Thesis." M.A. thesis, University of the Pacific, 1960.

Oats, Larry Russell. "The Relationship of Ecclesiology to the Doctrine of Ecclesiastical Separation Evidenced in the New Evangelical and Fundamentalist Movements of the Middle Twentieth Century." Ph.D. diss., Trinity Evangelical Divinity School, 1999.

O'Brien, J. "The Architecture of Conversion: Faith and Grace in the Theology of Jonathan Edwards." Excerpta ex dissertatione, Pontificiae Universitatis Gregorianae, 1967.

O'Neal, Glenn Franklin. "An Analytical Study of Certain Rhetorical Factors Used by Billy Graham in the 1949 Los Angeles Meetings." Ph.D. diss., University of Southern California, 1957.

Owles, R. Joseph. "Making the Good News Good Again: A Theology of Evangelism." Th.M. thesis, Louisville Presbyterian Theological Seminary, 1999.

Paddon, Eric John. "Modern Mordecai: Billy Graham in the Political Arena, 1948-1980." Ph.D. diss., Ohio University, 1999.

Phillips, Thomas Kent. "An Evaluation of the Ministry of Billy Graham Evangelistic Association with Special Reference to the Memphis Mid-South Billy Graham Crusade." D.Min. essay, The Southern Baptist Theological Seminary, 1979.

Pokki, Timo. *America's Preacher and His Message: Billy Graham's View of Conversion and Sanctification.* Doctoral diss., University of Helsinki, Finland, 1998; Lanham, MD: University Press of America, 1999.

Ripley, David L. "Developing an Outreach to International Students through a Billy Graham Crusade." D.Min. essay, Denver Conservative Baptist Seminary, 1989.

Schlick, Carol Wilder. "A Comparative Rhetorical Analysis of Sermons by Jonathan Edwards and William Franklin Graham." M.A. thesis, Miami University, 1966.

Sidwell, Mark Edward. "The History of the Winona Lake Bible Conference." Ph.D. thesis, Bob Jones University, 1988.

Simmons, Thomas W. "A Comparative Analysis of the Logical Modes of Persuasion Used by Billy Graham and Billy Sunday in Selected Sermons of Their New York Crusades." M.S. thesis, Kansas State University, 1968.

Simonsson, Bengt Karl David. "The Protestant Religious Press and the Billy Graham Revivals: a Study in Coverage and in Editorial Attitudes." M.A. thesis, Syracuse University, 1960.

Spicer, Thomas Otis. "Revival of Argumentation in the Preaching of Billy Graham." Th.M. thesis, Southwestern Baptist Theological Seminary, 1971.

Stanford, Alan Duke. "An Examination of the Sociological Theory of Charisma for Understanding Effective Christian Leadership as Illustrated by the Ministries of Robert Harold Schuller and William Franklin Graham." Ph.D. diss., Southwestern Baptist Theological Seminary, 1988.

Stansbury, George William, Jr. "The Music of the Billy Graham Crusades 1947-1970: An Analysis and Evaluation." D.M.A. thesis, The Southern Baptist Theological Seminary, 1971.

Strachan, Jill Penelope. "Richard Nixon: Representative Religious American." Ph.D. thesis, Syracuse University, 1981.

Streett, Richard Allen. "The Public Invitation: Its Nature, Biblical Validity and Practicability." Ph.D. thesis, California Graduate School of Theology, 1982.

Stricklin, Charles Ray. "The Public Relations Behind Billy Graham." M.A. thesis, University of Missouri, Columbia, 1971.

Sweeting, Donald W. "From Conflict to Cooperation? Changing American Evangelical Attitudes towards Roman Catholics: 1960-1998." Ph.D. diss., Trinity Evangelical Divinity School, 1998.

Taipale, Susanna. "Thou Shalt not Kill: Graham, Nixon, and the Anti-Vietnam War Demonstrators at the University of Tennessee, May 1970." Thesis (Pro Gradu), University of Tampere, Finland, 1990.

Tankersley, Nola Maxine Garner. "Billy Graham: A Descriptive Study Based on Biographical Information and Analyses of Eighteen Sermons." M.A. thesis, Stephen F. Austin State College, 1965.

Thomas, William. "An Assessment of Mass Meetings as a Method of Evangelism—Case Study of Eurofest '75 and the Billy Graham Crusade in Brussels." Thesis, Vrije Universiteit, Amsterdam, 1977; Amsterdam: Rodopi, 1977.

Thompson, William Oscar. "The Public Invitation as a Method of Evangelism: Its Origin and Development." Ph.D. diss., Southwestern Baptist Theological Seminary, 1979.

Tilden, Philip Nelson. "Classical Elements of Persuasion Used by Billy Graham during the San Francisco Bay Area Crusade." Th.M. thesis, Golden Gate Baptist Theological Seminary, 1961.

Tinder, Donald. "Fundamentalist Baptists in the Northern and Western United States, 1920-1950." Ph.D. diss., Yale University, 1969.

Tucker, Donald. "Billy Graham." M.A. thesis, California State University, Fresno, 1983.

Trollinger, William Vance, Jr. "God's Empire: William Bell Riley and Midwestern Fundamentalism." Ph.D. diss., University of Wisconsin, Madison, 1990.

Vaughn, Billy Edward. "Billy Graham: A Rhetorical Study in Adaptation." Ph.D. diss., University of Kansas, 1972.

_____. "A Burkeian Analysis of the Billy Graham New York Crusade of 1957." M.A. thesis, University of Kansas, 1964.

Waite, Donald Allen. "The Evangelistic Speaking of Billy Graham, 1949-1959." Ph.D. diss., Purdue University, 1961.

Walling, James David. "Study of the Characteristics of the Evangelistic Preaching of D. L. Moody and Billy Graham." M.A. thesis, Columbia Bible College, Columbia, SC, 1971.

Watt, David Harrington. "A Transforming Faith: Essays on the History of American Evangelicalism in the Middle Decades of the Twentieth Century." Ph.D. diss., Harvard University, 1987. Published as *A Transforming Faith: Explorations of Twentieth-Century American Evangelicalism.* New Brunswick, NJ: Rutgers University Press, 1991.

Weisenbeck, Jude D., S.D.S., S.T.L. "Conciliar Fellowship and the Unity of the Church." Ph.D. diss., Pontifica Studiorum Universitas, A S. Thoma Aq. in Urbe, 1986.

Wenger, Robert E. "Social Thought in American Fundamentalism." Ph.D. diss., University of Nebraska, 1973.

Whitam, Frederick L. "Adolescence and Mass Persuasion: A Study of Teen-Age Decision-Making at a Billy Graham Crusade." Ph.D. diss., Indiana University, 1965.

White, John Wesley. "The Influence of North American Evangelism in Great Britain between 1830 and 1914 on the Origin and Development of the World Council of Churches." Ph.D. diss., Mansfield College, Oxford University, 1963.

Williams, Larry Don. "The Changing Attitude and Involvement of Billy Graham in the Negro Race Problem in America." M.A. thesis, Ouachita Baptist University, 1966.

Winter, Terry Walter Royne. "Effective Mass Evangelism: A study of Jonathan Edwards, George Whitefield, Charles Finney, Dwight L. Moody, and Billy Graham." Doctor of Pastoral Theology thesis, Fuller Theological Seminary, 1968.

Wood, Clara. "A Study in Contemporary Evangelism: An Inquiry into the Results in Churches and the Thinking and Religious Experience of Individuals Making Decisions in the 1958 Graham Crusade in San Francisco." Th.D. thesis, Pacific School of Religion, 1959.

Zaremba, Wayne E. "To What Extent Has Billy Graham, a Nationally Known Individual in America, Who Claims a Religious Vocation, Had a Certain Influence on Society, Economics, and Religion in the Twentieth Century?" M.S.Ed. thesis, Chicago State University, 1998.

Zietlow, Paul H. "A Rhetorical Analysis of the Sermons of Billy Graham." M.A. thesis, Ohio State University, 1980.

Pamphlets

Almanac Publications. *This Is Billy Graham.* Philadelphia: Walfred Publishing, 1957.

Augsburger, Bryce B. *Shall We Cooperate with the Graham Campaign?* N.p., 1962.

Bell, L. Nelson. *Protestant Distinctives and the American Crisis.* Weaverville, NC: Presbyterian Journal Book Room, 1960.

Beougher, Timothy. *Overcoming Walls to Witnessing.* Minneapolis: Billy Graham Evangelistic Association, 1993.

Bridge to Life. Colorado Springs, CO: Navpress, 1969.

Bright, Bill. *Four Spiritual Laws.* San Bernardino, CA: Campus Crusade for Christ, 1965.

Do You Know for Certain that You Have Eternal Life and that You Will Go to Heaven when You Die? Alpharetta, GA: North American Mission Board, n.d.

Dunzweiler, Robert. *Billy Graham: A Critique.* Elkins Park, PA: Faith Theological Seminary, 1961.

Ehrhard, Jim. *The Dangers of the Invitation System.* Kansas City, MO: Christian Communicators Worldwide, 1999.

Ferré, Nels. *The Atonement and Mission,* Essay on Mission, no. 2. London: London Missionary Society, 1960.

Goforth, Jonathan. *When the Spirit's Fire Swept Korea.* Grand Rapids: Zondervan, 1943.

Griffith, Gordon David. *Anglicans and Billy Graham.* Sydney, Australia: Anglican Truth Society, 1959.

Guinness, Windham Howard. *I Object . . . to Billy Graham.* Drawings by Benier. Sydney: Ambassador Press, n.d.

Hogue, C. B. *Lifestyle Evangelism.* Atlanta: Home Mission Board of the Southern Baptist Convention, 1973.

Johnston, Thomas P. *Steadfast Truths in Evangelism.* Deerfield, IL: Evangelism

Unlimited, 1989.

Jones, Bob, Jr. *Scriptural Separation: First and Second Degree.* Greenville, SC: Bob Jones University Press, 1971.

Lee, Robert G. *Calvary.* Grand Rapids: Zondervan, 1940.

Mott, John R., ed. *The College Young Men's Christian Association: A Collection of Pamphlets Relating to its History, Methods, Purpose, and Achievements.* New York: The International Committee of Young Men's Christian Associations, 1895.

NAE publicity pamphlet. Summer 1943. Wheaton, IL: Billy Graham Archives, collection 20, box 65, folder 20.

Pickering, Ernest D. *Should Fundamentalists Support the Billy Graham Crusades?* Chicago: Independent Fundamental Churches of America, 1950, 1959.

Rapp, Robert S. *Campus Crusade and Explo '74 in Seoul, Korea.* N.p., 1974.

Riggs, Charles. *Steps to Peace with God.* Minneapolis: World Wide, n.d.; "Steps to Peace with God." *Ultimate Multimedia Bible Reference Suite.* Oconomowoc, WI: Rhinosoft Interactive, 1999.

Rooy, Sidney. *The Graham Crusades—Shall We Participate?* Grand Rapids: Eerdmans, 1958.

Schwarz, Christian A. *ABC's of Natural Church Development.* Carol Stream, IL: ChurchSmart, n.d.

Sukhia, Douglas. *Why We Are not Participating in the Billy Graham Crusade.* Orchard Park, NY: Bible Presbyterian Church, 1988.

Ward, Harry. *Why We Do not Support Billy Graham.* Greenville, SC: N.p., 1975.

Watson, W. T. *The Bible School Days of Billy Graham.* Dunedin, FL: Trinity College, n.d.

Whitney, Harold. *Will Australia Welcome Billy Graham?* Brisbane, Kemp Place, Valley, Australia: W. R. Smith and Paterson Pty., (1958).

Correspondence

Abernathy, William E., to Robert O. Ferm. June 30, 1958. Wheaton, IL: Billy Graham Archives, Collection 19, Accession 88-16, Box 1, Item 3.

Britt, Charles, and Don Horton to Robert O. Ferm. May 24, 1958. Wheaton, IL: Billy Graham Archives, Collection 19, Accession 88-16, Box 1, Item 3.

Bruce, David P., to Thomas P. Johnston. January 4, 1998. In the author's possession.

Carey, William, to Andrew Fuller. Quoted in William R. Hogg. *Ecumenical Foundations: A History of the International Missionary Council and Its Nineteenth Century Background.* New York: Harper and Brothers, 1952, 17.

Cousins, Jack, to Robert O. Ferm. May 14, 1958. Wheaton, IL: Billy Graham Archives, Collection 19, Accession 88-16, Box 1, Item 3.

Hostetter, Henry N., to Zondervan Publishing Company. July 14, 1958. Wheaton, IL: Billy Graham Archives, Collection 19, Accession 88-16, Box 1, Item 3.

Graham, Billy, to Harold Lindsell. 25 January 1955. Quoted in *Reforming Fundamentalism: Fuller Seminary and the New Evangelicalism,* by George Marsden. Grand Rapids: Eerdmans, 1987, 158.

Jones, Bob, Sr., to friend. March 6, 1957. Wheaton, IL: Billy Graham Archives, Collection 19, Accession 88-16, Box 1, Item 3.

_____, to Robert O. Ferm. May 10, 1958. Wheaton, IL: Billy Graham Archives, Collection 19, Accession 88-16, Box 1, Item 3.

Ketcham, R. T. "Special Information Bulletin, no. 8." Wheaton, IL: Billy Graham Archives, Collection 19, Accession 88-16, Box 1, Item 3.

King, Louis L., to Peter de Visser. September 10, 1958. Wheaton, IL: Billy Graham Archives, Collection 19, Accession 88-16, Box 1, Item 3.

Livesay, Wayne, to Billy Graham. August 14, 1958. Enclosures. Wheaton, IL: Billy Graham Archives, Collection 19, Accession 88-16, Box 1, Item 3.

Oldham, J. H., to Robert Speer. December 5, 1932. Geneva: WCC archives, I.M.C., Box 5. Quoted in *World Evangelism and the Word of God*, by Arthur P. Johnston. Minneapolis: Bethany Fellowship, 1974, 132.

Rice, John R., to Robert Ferm. April 2, 1962. Wheaton, IL: Billy Graham Archives, Collection 19, Accession 88-16, Box 1, Item 3.

Tenney, Merrill C., to Robert O. Ferm. November 10, 1958. Wheaton, IL: Billy Graham Archives, Collection 19, Accession 88-16, Box 1, Item 3.

Warnhuis, A. L., to R. E. Diffendorfer. June 24, 1930. Geneva: WCC Archives. Quoted in Arthur P. Johnston. *World Evangelism and the Word of God*. Minneapolis: Bethany Fellowship, 1974, 198, footnote 41.

Wither, Eugene R., to Zondervan. July 21, 1958. Wheaton, IL: Billy Graham Archives, Collection 19, Accession 88-16, Box 1, Item 3.

Other Material

"ABC's for a Better Life." Chicago: Pacific Garden Mission, n.d.

"About CBF [Cooperative Baptist Fellowship]" [on-line]. Accessed 3 December 2000. Available from http://www.cbfonline.org/about/ mission.cfm; Internet.

Ashbrook, John. "Billy Graham, the Compromising Prophet." One sound cassette; analog, 1 7/8 ips, mono. Pensacola, FL: AJX; Chapel Library, n.d.

Association of Evangelical Relief and Development Organizations. "About" [on-line]. Accessed 2 May 2001. Available from http://www.aerdo.org/about_aerdo.htm; Internet.

Bauder, Kevin T. "Bibliography on Fundamentalism, Evangelicalism, and Neoevangelicalism." St. Paul, MN: Central Baptist Bible College, n.d. [1997].

_____. "Documents of the New Evangelicalism Compiled for Use with Class Notes." St. Paul, MN: Central Baptist Bible College, n.d. [1995].

Beougher, Timothy K. "Overview of American Church History." Classroom lecture notes, *88700—Methods and Influence of North American Evangelists*. Spring 1998. Photocopy.

"Centro Pro Unione" [on-line]. Accessed 10 July 2001. Available from http://www.prounione.urbe.it/dir-dir/e_dir-list_ie.html; Internet.

Church of the Nazarene. "Church of the Nazarene: The Church" [on-line]. Accessed 2 May 2001. Available from http://www.nazarene.org/ hoo/articlesfaith.html; Internet.

Cloud, David C. "No Title" [on-line]. Accessed 15 June 2000. Available from www.whidbey.net/~dcloud/otimothy/otim000e.htm; Internet.

"A Concrete Curtain: The Life and Death of the Berlin Wall, 6—What is Left of the Wall" [on-line]. Accessed 10 August 2000. Available at http://www.wall-berlin.org/gb/ trace.htm; Internet.

Costella, Dennis. "Lausanne II." *Foundation* (May-June 1989) [on-line]. Accessed 15 June 2000. Available from http://www.tcsn.net/ fbchurch/fbcluss2.htm; Internet.

Evangelical Theological Society. "Doctrinal basis" [on-line]. Accessed 15 February 2001. Available from http://www.etsjets.org/; Internet.

Flirting with Rome: Evangelical Entanglement with Roman Catholicism. Oak Harbor, WA: Way of Life Literature, n.d.

The Gallup Organization. "Most Admired Man and Woman" [on-line]. Accessed 17 July 2001. Available from http://www.gallup.com/ poll/indicators/indadmired.asp; Internet.

George, Timothy. "Notes" [on-line]. Accessed 10 July 2001. Available from http://www.sbts.edu/news/sbjt/summer98/Sum98forum.html; Internet.

Gray, Wallace. "Billy Graham and Nels Ferré Discuss Evangelism: An Imaginary Dialogue." Unpublished manuscript. Collection Number 19, Billy Graham Center Archives, Wheaton College, n.d.

Harvey, Paul. *Billy Graham the Inside Story.* One videocassette. Minneapolis: World Wide Pictures, 1970, 1979.

Johnston, Arthur P. "Definition of Evangelism." Classroom lecture notes, *ME 620— Theology of Missions and Evangelism,* Spring 1981. Photocopy.

_____. "Pietism and Halle," Unpublished monograph, 1996.

Johnston, James A. "National Association of Evangelicals." Unpublished research for Th.M. thesis, Trinity Evangelical Divinity School, 1992.

Johnston, Thomas P. "An Analytical Study of Personal Evangelism Conversations in the Gospels and the Book of Acts." Classroom lecture notes. *BIB/CHM 230X— Biblical Evangelism.* Spring 1995. Photocopy.

_____. "Are You Ready for the Year 2000?—The Role of the International Missionary Councils in the Ecumenical Movement." Essay for History of Missions Seminar, The Southern Baptist Theological Seminary, 1998.

_____. "Evangelism and Discipleship: A Student Handbook." Deerfield, IL: Evangelism Unlimited, 1996.

_____. "Grappling for Institutional Survival—Postdenominationalism in Mainline Churches." Essay for Church Growth Seminar, The Southern Baptist Theological Seminary, 1999.

_____. "'I Am Going to Preach a Gospel Not of Despair But of Hope'—The Ministry and Methods of Billy Graham." Essay for Methods and Influence of North American Evangelists Seminar, The Southern Baptist Theological Seminary, 1998.

_____. "The Mindset of Eternity—A Biblical Introduction to Evangelism." 22nd rev. Deerfield, IL: Evangelism Unlimited, 1994.

_____. "Organizing for Outreach—A Historical and Theological Look at Organizational Development Among Baptists with a Particular Emphasis on the Early Nineteenth Century." Essay for Nineteenth Century Baptist Distinctives Seminar, The Southern Baptist Theological Seminary, 1999.

_____. "'The Salvation of Souls Was, Is and Always Will Be My Number One Task'—The Evangelistic Theology of Billy Graham." Essay for Theology of Evangelism Seminar, The Southern Baptist Theological Seminary, 1999.

_____. "Strategies for World Evangelization: The Approach of Gregory the Great." Essay for Methods of World Evangelization Seminar, The Southern Baptist Theological Seminary, 1997.

_____. "A Theology of Missions—Through the Lens of the Book of Acts." Essay for Theology of Missions Seminar, The Southern Baptist Theological Seminary, 1999.

Kofahl, Robert E. "Billy Graham's Gospel" [on-line]. Accessed 27 October 2001. Available at http://www.cet.com/~voice/discern/ graham.htm#king; Internet.

_____. "Graham Believes Men Can Be Saved Apart from Name of Christ" [on-line]. Accessed 27 October 2001. Available at http://www.cet.com/~voice/discern/ graham.htm#king; Internet.

Kuzmič, Peter. "Theology of Powers: Socio-Politial Realities as Challenge(s) to World Evangelization." Handout for presentation at the Theological Task Force, Amsterdam 2000, August 4, 2000.

"Liebman, Joshua Loth" [on-line]. Accessed 5 July 2001. Available from http://www.biography.com/cgi-bin/biomain.cgi; Internet.

"L'œcuménisme" [on-line]. Accessed 10 July 2001. Available from http://fr.encyclopedia.yahoo.com/articles/ni/ni_1212_p0.html; Internet

Mathews, Ed. "Mass Evangelism: Problems and Potentials" [on-line]. Accessed 1

December 2001. Available from http://www.ovc.edu/ missions/jam/massive1.htm; Internet.

"Meet Mr. Philadelphis [A. T. Pierson]" [on-line]. Accessed 10 July 2002. Available from http://www.whatsaiththescripture.com/Voice/ Meet.Mr.Philadelphia.html; Internet.

Merritt, James. "A Word from SBC President James Merritt" [on-line]. Accessed 3 December 2000. Available from http://www.sbc.net/default.asp; Internet.

"More than a Million Souls Hit the Sawdust Trail." In Basic Church Evangelism. ed. Jack Stanton. Kansas City, MO: Midwestern Baptist Theological Seminary, n.d.

National Association of Evangelicals, "Statement of Faith" [on-line]. Accessed 15 February 2001. Available from http://www.nae.net/ about-mission.html; Internet.

"Neo-Evangelicalism - Characteristics and Positions." [on-line]. Accessed 15 June 2000. Available from www.rapidnet.com/~jbeard/bdm/ Psychology/neoe.htm; Internet.

Owens, Charles E. "FAITH: Sunday School Evangelism Strategy." Ph.D. colloquium paper, Billy Graham School of the Southern Baptist Theological Seminary, 1999.

Patterson, Paige. "Anatomy of a Reformation—The Southern Baptist Convention 1978-1994." Paper presented at the Evangelical Theological Society, Chicago, 17 November 1994.

"Public Separation—II Corinthians 6:16-17—Study the Bible with Pastor Gregory" [on-line]. Accessed 15 May 2000. Available from www.byronbible.org/study/ separation4.htm; Internet.

"Roman Road." Chicago: Pacific Garden Mission, n.d.

Samaritan's Purse, "About Us" [on-line]. Accessed 19 July 2001. Available from http://www.samaritanspurse.org/home.asp; Internet.

"SBC President's Page" [on-line]. Accessed 19 July 2002. Available from http://www.sbc.net/presidentspage/default.asp; Internet.

"Seven Concluding Remarks" [on-line]. Accessed 15 May 2000. Available from www.swrb.ab.ca/newslett/actualnls/7_shipwr.htm; Internet.

"Sheen, Fulton J (John) (b. Peter Sheen" [on-line]. Accessed 5 July 2001. Available from http://www.biography.com/cgi-bin/biomain.cgi; Internet.

Spurgeon, Charles Haddon. "Salvation and Safety." Royal Dainties, no. 169. Minneapolis: Asher Publishing Co., affiliated with The Union Gospel Mission, n.d.

Sunday School Board of the Southern Baptist Convention. Baptist Faith and Message. Nashville: Sunday School Board, 2000 [on-line]. "SBC Faith and Facts." Accessed 15 June 2001; available from http://www.sbc.net/default.asp; Internet

Tarkowski, Ed. "Foundations for Apostasy: 1950-1985" [on-line]. Accessed 15 May 2000. Available from www.ncinter.net/~ejt/founda1.htm; Internet.

World Vision, International. "Word Vision Homepage" [on-line]. Accessed 15 June 2000. Available from http://www.worldvision.org/ worldvision/master.nsf; Internet.

_____. "Who Is World Vision?" [on-line]. Accessed 2 May 2001. Available from http://www.wvi.org/pages/news/who.htm; Internet.

**Select U.S. Archives and Other Sources
of Unpublished Information**

Archives. Bob Jones University. Greenville, SC.

Archives. Textile Hall Corporation. Greenville, SC.

Archives. The Church League of America. Wheaton, IL.

Billy Graham Archives. Asbury Theological Seminary. Wilmore, KY.

Billy Graham Archives. Billy Graham Center, Wheaton College. Wheaton, IL.
Billy Graham Archives. Southern Baptist Theological Seminary, Louisville, KY.
Billy Graham Archives. Trinity College of Florida. New Port Richey, FL.
Billy Graham Evangelistic Association, Headquarters. Minneapolis.
Billy Graham Evangelistic Association, Montreat Office. Montreat, NC
Billy Graham Training Center at the Cove. Asheville, NC.
Harry S. Dent Papers. Special Collections, Clemson University Libraries. Clemson, SC.
Richard Owen Roberts Library. Wheaton, IL.